To Rosemary

William S. Burroughs

A Life

~

BARRY MILES

Weidenfeld & Nicolson

LONDON

First published in Great Britain in 2014
by Weidenfeld & Nicolson

1 3 5 7 9 10 8 6 4 2

A CIP catalogue record for this book is available from the British Library.

ISBN: 978 0 297 86725 8

Printed in Great Britain by CPI Group (UK) Ltd, Croydon, CR0 4YY

The Orion Publishing Group's policy is to use papers that are natural, renewable
and recyclable and made from wood grown in sustainable forests. The logging and
manufacturing processes are expected to conform to environmental regulations of
the country of origin.

Weidenfeld & Nicolson
Orion Publishing Group Ltd
Orion House
5 Upper Saint Martin's Lane
London WC2H 9EA

An Hachette UK Company

www.orionbooks.co.uk

William S. Burroughs

Also by Barry Miles

A Descriptive Catalogue of the William S. Burroughs Archive (1973)

(With Joe Maynard) *William S. Burroughs: A Bibliography, 1953–73* (1979)

Ginsberg: A Biography (1989)

William Burroughs: El Hombre Invisible; A Portrait (1993)

Paul McCartney: Many Years from Now (1997)

Kerouac: King of the Beats; A Portrait (2001)

The Beat Hotel: Ginsberg, Burroughs, and Corso in Paris, 1958–1963 (2001)

In the Sixties (2003)

Hippie (2004)

Zappa: A Biography (2005)

Charles Bukowski (2005)

The Beat Collection (2005, compiler)

Peace: 50 Years of Protest, 1958–2008 (2008)

The British Invasion: The Music, the Times, the Era (2009)

London Calling: A Countercultural History of London Since 1945 (2010)

In the Seventies: Adventures in the Counterculture (2011)

Contents

Contents

Contents

BOOK FOUR
The Classic Stations of the Earth

Contents

BOOK FIVE
The City of Light

BOOK SIX
London Town

Contents

BOOK SEVEN
Burlington Billy

Contents

BOOK EIGHT
The Prodigal Son Returns

BOOK NINE
Return to Roots

Contents

Acknowledgments

My relationship with Burroughs began in 1965 when I published one of his three-column texts in an anthology called *Darazt*. I already knew his boyfriend, Ian Sommerville, and through Ian I became the UK distributor of Burroughs's first spoken-word album, *Call Me Burroughs*, that Ian had recorded. In October 1966, I cofounded *International Times*, known as *IT*, and Burroughs was closely involved from the very beginning. He gave us the script for *Towers Open Fire* for our second issue and published a number of articles in *IT* over the years. He liked the immediacy of being able to give us a text and see it in print a few days later. He ran an article on tape recorder experiments in the third issue. His interest in tape recorder experiments began in 1960 and extended for about a decade, as part of his extension of the use of cut-ups from written texts into tapes, and from there to photographic collages, films, and scrapbook layouts. Many years later, in 2007, I produced a three-CD set of his tape cut-ups called *Real English Tea Made Here.*[1]

Burroughs often visited when Ian Sommerville was installing the lighting and power circuits at Indica, the bookshop/art gallery I co-owned with John Dunbar and Peter Asher, in 1965, and when we moved the bookshop to a different address, he used the shop's bulletin board to advertise his availability as a Scientology auditor. In 1972 I spent about five months—spread over a seven-month period—cataloging his archives. This was when we became good friends, because in addition to working with him each day, we almost always had drinks and dinner together afterward. In the course of cataloging his papers, I was able to assemble what was then the only known copy of *Queer*, which was scattered throughout his folders and tied-up bundles of manuscript. It made sense to follow up on the catalog of the archives with a bibliography of his work, using the information I had uncovered. This was eventually coauthored with Joe Maynard (who did the books) and published by the Bibliographical

Acknowledgments

Society of the University of Virginia in 1978. James Grauerholz and I coedited the restored text edition of *Naked Lunch*, published in 2001.

In 1984, while researching a biography of Allen Ginsberg at the Butler Library of Columbia University, I ordered up a letter from Burroughs to Lawrence Ferlinghetti in order to see what the cryptic "enclosure" was. It turned out to be the complete manuscript of *Interzone*. I had it photocopied and gave it to my agent, Andrew Wylie, who also represented Burroughs. *Interzone*, along with *Queer*, was to form the backbone of a multibook publishing deal with Viking. In 1992, I published a "portrait" called *William Burroughs: El Hombre Invisible*, which began as part of the Virgin Modern Idols series, and finished up as a half biography, half introduction to his work. Over the years I visited Burroughs in London, New York, Boulder, and Lawrence, Kansas, and consequently met and got to know many of the characters in this book, beginning with Allen Ginsberg, who first stayed with me in London in 1965 and became a great friend. I also got to know Antony Balch, Robert Fraser, Herbert Huncke, Carl Solomon, Lucien Carr, Brion Gysin, Alan Ansen, Ian Sommerville, Mikey Portman, Gregory Corso, Panna Grady, John Giorno, Timothy Leary, Victor Bockris, Stewart Meyer, and of course James Grauerholz and his Lawrence, Kansas, circle. Many of them became friends, and over the years, as a result of countless hours of conversation, I accumulated a huge store of Burroughs lore.

Without James Grauerholz this book would simply not have been possible. James was William Burroughs's friend, companion, and manager from the time of his return to the United States, aged sixty, in 1974 until his death in 1997. James was commissioned to write a full-length biography in 1999 and did an enormous amount of research, but a combination of family matters and medical problems eventually caused him in 2010 to propose that I take over the project. I have drawn heavily on James's research into Burroughs's childhood and family history, particularly the story of Uncle Horace; his research into Burroughs's time at Harvard; his period in Chicago (in fact, we found the site of Mrs. Murphy's Rooming House and A. J. Cohen Exterminators together); his psychiatric history—Grauerholz had obtained many of Burroughs's psychoanalytic records—and the results of his trawl through Austrian paperwork to find traces of Burroughs's stay in Vienna, where he studied medicine, and Dubrovnik, where he met his first wife, Ilse Herzfeld Klapper, in 1937. I am deeply indebted to James for his book-length paper *The Death of Joan Vollmer Burroughs: What Really Happened?*, which is available online. He has uncovered literally thousands of new facts about Burroughs and corrected many hundreds more. I cannot thank him enough for sharing his discoveries with me. In addition I thank him for his friendship, for sharing his archives, for giving his time, and for his kind hospitality in Lawrence over the years. James is the master of all things Burrovian.

For the section on Burroughs in South Texas I have relied heavily on Rob Johnson's thorough study of the subject, *The Lost Years of William S. Burroughs*, and for Burroughs's late career years in New York I have drawn upon the unpublished journals of Stewart Meyer, and on Victor Bockris's *With William Burroughs: A Report from the Bunker*. I am enormously indebted to Simon Johnson, who shared with me his extensive research into Burroughs's family background and has corrected numerous errors. I am most grateful. Tribute must be paid to Ted Morgan, author of the groundbreaking *Literary Outlaw: The Life and Times of William S. Burroughs*. I have purposely not reread Morgan's book but I have used some of his research. On completion of his book, he sold his interview tapes, notes, and papers to the Rare Book Library of Arizona State University in Tempe, where they are all available for study and use by scholars. In the course of researching the restored text edition of *Naked Lunch* at Tempe, James Grauerholz and I made copies of Morgan's taped interviews with Burroughs, which I then transcribed, originally for another project, since abandoned. All quotes from these tapes in this book come from my own transcripts of Burroughs's words. I have drawn heavily on this archive of tapes, which is a treasure house for present and future Burroughs scholars.

In addition I must thank Christopher Gibbs for his kindness and hospitality in Tangier and assistance in seeking out traces of Burroughs's residency in that city. To John Howe, Christopher Gibbs, Genesis Breyer P-Orridge, Tom Peschio (TP), Jim McCrary, James Grauerholz, and Udo Breger for granting me interviews, and to Ed Sanders, Lawrence Ferlinghetti, Jean-Jacques Lebel, the late Allen Ginsberg, the late Lucien Carr, and the late Eugene Brooks for interviews given for a previous project, portions of which are used here. To Victor Bockris for transcripts of his interviews with Burroughs and for his hospitality, friendship, and conversation over the decades; to Stewart Meyer for granting me access to his Bunker journals; to Theo Miles for his translations from the French. To Andrew Sclanders at Beatbooks.com for photocopies and CDs of manuscripts and interview material. I'd like to thank my agent, James Macdonald Lockhart, at Antony Harwood, and Cary Goldstein, Deb Futter, my editor, Sean Desmond, and my copy editor Roland Ottewell at Twelve, and most of all, Rosemary Bailey, who has lived with all stages of the book, providing encouragement, editing skills, valuable suggestions, and love, as always.

Acknowledgments

Research on this book took me from London to Paris several times, to Vienna, to Tangier, New York, and to Kansas. For useful conversations, photocopies, CDs and DVDs, and helpful assistance on my travels I'd like to thank Patricia Allmer; Eric Anderson, Sophie Andrieu at the Musée d'art et d'histoire du Judaïsme in Paris; the late J. G. Ballard; Hervé Binet; James Birch; Jed Birmingham at Reality Studio; Charlotte Black; Jonathan Blumb; Udo Breger; Roger James Elsgood; Colin Fallows at Liverpool John Moores University; Neal Fox; Raymond Foye; Professor Hannah Gay at Imperial College London; Synne Genzmer at the Vienna Kunsthalle; Joseph Geraci; Hilary Gerrard; Isaac Gewirtz, curator of the Berg Collection at New York Public Library; Jeff Goldberg; Kathelin Gray at the October Gallery; Theo Green; Fran Greenwood of Harrogate Festival of the Arts; Peter Guest at Image; Hammond Guthrie; Peter Hale at the Allen Ginsberg Estate; Oliver Harris; Chili Hawes at the October Gallery; Axel Heil at ZKM/Zentrum für Kunst und Medientechnologie, Karlsruhe; Kurt Hemmer; Stellan Holm; John Hopkins (photographer); John Hopkins (writer); Michael Horovitz; John Howe; Rob Johnson; Elisabeth Kamenicek in Vienna; Catheryn Kilgarriff; Tom King at the WSB Estate, Kansas; the late José Ferez Kuri; Elisabeth Lalouschek at the October Gallery; George Lawson; Jean-Jacques Lebel; Liliane Lijn; Ed Maggs at Maggs Bros.; Alexandra Mattholie at BBC Arena; Ian MacFadyen; Paul McCartney; Jim McCrary; Sophie Parkin; Jim Pennington; Jim Perrizo; Tom Peschio at the WSB Estate, Kansas; Dick Pountain; Wayne Propst; Marcia Resnick; Frank Rynne; Jon Savage; John Sears; Keith Seward at Reality Studio; Bernard Sigaud; Ira Silverberg; Iain Sinclair; Martin Stone; Tony Sutcliffe; Anthony Wall, Series Editor BBC *Arena*; Ken Weaver; Maxine Weaver; Peter Weibel at ZKM/Zentrum für Kunst und Medientechnologie, Karlsruhe; Sylvia Beach Whitman at Shakespeare and Co., Paris; Carl Williams at Maggs Bros.; Andrew Wilson at Tate Britain; Shawn C. Wilson at the Kinsey Institute for Research in Sex, Gender and Reproduction; Terry Wilson; Peter Wollen; Eddie Woods; and Yuri Zupancic at the WSB Estate.

Proper names in Burroughs's books and letters, particularly of places in Central and South America, have been silently changed to their correct or current spellings. "Kasbah" is used except when in quoted letters from Burroughs or Kerouac, as that is the street name spelling in Morocco. "Story" in describing buildings uses American usage: i.e., "second story" is the European "first story." *The Naked Lunch* refers to the first (Paris) edition; *Naked Lunch* is the later U.S. edition and the restored text edition.

Introduction

The sweat lodge utilizes all powers of the universe: earth, and things
that grow from the earth; water; fire; and air.

— BLACK ELK

The sweat lodge ceremony had to be performed in darkness. Deep in the two-foot firepit the stones glowed, tended by the firekeeper, whose tasks were to heat and replenish the stones, guard the lodge, and make the food. Over the pit, the roof of the lodge was shaped like an igloo, carefully constructed from interlaced twigs and branches, covered with black plastic. The shaman himself was Melvin Betsellie, a Diné elder Navajo from the Four Corners area of New Mexico. He was young, round-faced, heavily built, his hair center-parted in the traditional manner like Geronimo in the old black-and-white photographs. Betsellie's calm, placid expression inspired confidence. He was a highly regarded shaman—the *Oinkiga*, purification ceremony, must be performed by an initiate who has had at least four years' apprenticeship, including the vision quest and four years of the sun dance, climaxing in the ceremony of being painted. Only then do the shamans have the right to pour the water of life (*mini wic'oni*) on the stone people (*inyan oyate*)—the hot rocks—to create *Inikag'a*, the purification ceremony.

Betsellie had been invited to Lawrence, Kansas, by Bill Lyon, an anthropologist who specialized in shamanism. Lyon had spent twelve years with Wallace Black Elk, a Sioux medicine man, and wrote *Black Elk: The Sacred Ways of a Lakota*, in which he explained how Black Elk called up animal spirits of all kinds. Lyon was a friend of William Burroughs's and they had a number of conversations about the efficacy of shamans in expelling evil spirits from the body. Burroughs had spent most of his life trying to exorcise what he called "the Ugly Spirit" and wondered if a Navajo shaman might finally succeed. Lyon arranged for a ceremony for the purification of Bill's spirit in March 1992, to take place on the grounds of his house.[1]

In the sweat lodge, all had stripped in preparation for the smoke and

1

heat and had towels wrapped around their waists. Burroughs wore just his shorts, the scar from his recent triple-bypass operation showing as a brown line on his wrinkled chest. Though stooped and soft-muscled, his skull bony, at seventy-eight years he was still vigorous. His old friend Allen Ginsberg was completely naked except for his glasses, as was his wont. The author of "Howl" was now sixty-five years old, his trimmed beard and mustache threaded with gray, potbellied with scrawny legs, slightly stooped. Also present were Burroughs's old friend James Grauerholz, Grauerholz's twenty-five-year-old boyfriend Michael Emerton, Burroughs's assistant Steven Lowe, and Bill Lyon.

Burroughs had warned the shaman of the challenge before the cere-mony: He "had to face the whole of American capitalism, Rockefeller, the CIA...all of those, particularly Hearst." Afterward he told Ginsberg, "It's very much related to the American Tycoon. To William Randolph Hearst, Vanderbilt, Rockefeller, that whole stratum of American acquisi-tive evil. Monopolistic, acquisitive evil. Ugly evil. The ugly American. The ugly American at his ugly worst. That's exactly what it is." William Burroughs believed in spirits, in the occult, in demons, curses, and magic. "I do believe in the magical universe, where nothing happens unless one wills it to happen, and what we see is not one god but many gods in power and in conflict."[2] He felt himself possessed, and had spent much of his life trying to isolate and exorcise this demon. Asked how he would describe his religious position, Burroughs replied, "An Ismailian and Gnostic, or a Manichean. [...] The Manichean believe in an actual struggle between good and evil, which is not an eternal struggle since one of them will win in this particular area, sooner or later."[3] Throughout his life Burroughs felt engaged in this struggle against the Ugly Spirit. This time he was determined to win.

Burroughs had first identified the Ugly Spirit very early on, back in St. Louis: "When I was a young child, a feeling of attack and danger. I remember when I was five years old, I was sitting with my brother in the house that we had on Pershing, and I got such a feeling of hopelessness that I began crying. And my brother said, 'What's the matter with you?' and I couldn't tell him. It was just a feeling of being completely at a hopeless disadvantage. It was a ghost of some sort, a spirit. A spirit that was inimi-cal, completely inimical. After that there were many times the condition persisted and that's what made me think that I needed analysis to find out what was wrong. [...] It's just I have a little bit, a much more clear insight than most people have, that's all. No problem like that is peculiar to one person."[4] He knew already that he had been invaded by the Ugly Spirit. It took him a lifetime to expel it.

Burroughs believed the Ugly Spirit was responsible for the key act that had determined his life since September 6, 1951. That day he had been walking in the street in Mexico City when he found that his face was wet. Tears were streaming from his eyes for no logical reason. He felt a deep-seated depression and when he got home he began throwing down drinks very quickly. It was then, later that day, that Bill killed his wife, Joan Vollmer, fatally wounding her while attempting to shoot a glass from her head in a game of William Tell at a drinks party. Burroughs never really understood what happened that day, except to recognize that what he did was madness. Near the end of his life he said, "My accidental shooting of my wife in 1951 has been a heavy, painful burden to me for 41 years. It was a horrible thing and it still hurts to realise that some people think it was somehow deliberate. I've been honest about the circumstances—we were both very drunk and reckless, she dared me to shoot a glass off her head, and for God knows what reason, I took the dare. All my life I have regretted that day."[5] It was not until 1959 that the malevolent entity was given a name. Burroughs and his friend Brion Gysin were conducting psychic experiments at the Beat Hotel in Paris when Gysin, in a semitrance state, wrote on a piece of paper, "Ugly Spirit killed Joan because..."

In the much-quoted introduction to *Queer*, Burroughs explained how writing became his main weapon against possession by the evil spirit: "I am forced to the appalling conclusion that I would never have become a writer but for Joan's death, and to a realization of the extent to which this event has motivated and formulated my writing. I live with the constant threat of possession, and a constant need to escape from possession, from Control. So the death of Joan brought me in contact with the invader, the Ugly Spirit, and maneuvered me into a lifelong struggle, in which I have had no choice except to write my way out."

The shaman was making his way around the lodge. He thanked each one of them, starting with Burroughs, for inviting him to share the traditional medicine of his grandfathers and giving him the opportunity to use his healing medicine to drive the bad spirit from Bill's body and out of his life. He turned to each of the four directions and prayed to the grandfathers, the water, the earth, the rocks, and the red-hot coals in the firepit, thanking them all and asking them to use their power to help Bill. He took a feather and wafted smoke toward each of the people there, and repeated the action with his hands. Then he threw water onto the hot stones, which exploded in great clouds of smoke and steam, filling the enclosed space, making it unbearably hot like a sauna. All anyone could see was the glow of the fire in the pit, and the vague shadowy outlines of their neighbors in the darkness, through the swirling, suffocating smoke. Their eyes ran with burning tears and the sweat began to pour off them. The ceremony was now under way. Chips of cedar wood thrown onto the stones gave off a powerful fragrance, mixed with the steam.

There were four long prayers, and after each prayer the shaman sprinkled more water on the hot rocks, which were replenished by the fire-keeper, to create more steam and heat. First he thanked the spirits, the grandfather spirit and the spirit that made Bill. He prayed to make Bill's passage easier when the time came for him to return to his creator. They were all asked to focus their attention on Bill and send him their healing thoughts. A heavy, long-stemmed pipe with a carved stone bowl filled with sweet, mild tobacco was passed around and each puffed three or four times, cradling it with one hand beneath the bowl and the other clasping the shaft. There were more rounds of tobacco and more prayers. Then, after the fourth round of steam heat, the shaman sprinkled water several times on each of them with his feathered fan. He took some of the hot coals in his hand and put them in his mouth, several times swallowing the coal that now contained the bad spirit and then retching it up. Michael Emerton and Steven Lowe were both stunned by the sight of the coals in his mouth, lighting up his throat. "It looked quite terrifying, the mask of his face openmouthed, the inside of his mouth lit up, you could see down to his throat in the red coal light," Lowe recalled.

Then the shaman approached Bill and touched him with a red-hot coal. Afterward Burroughs told Ginsberg, "I thought, my God, it's great that he touched me with the coal and I didn't feel any burns or anything. I was very impressed." Bill couldn't understand how the hot coal was circulating in the smoky darkness; it seemed to be flying through the air, circling around Bill and the fire, and then back again. But it was a long ceremony and the smoke and steam made Burroughs very uncomfortable. He felt weak and desperately needed to breath cool air, so he crawled nearer to the entrance. Afterward he told Allen Ginsberg, "I needed air, I needed to get out. I finally lay down near the door and then I felt better...and... I had to stick it out and stay there, I couldn't break the spell. As soon as he began using the coals, I immediately felt better."

Ginsberg wrote, "The spirit was caught, jiggled in the shrill flute and blown into the fire. Put the spirit into the rocky fire-pit still glowing, steaming with cedar-fragrant smoke in our eyes." Now the Ugly Spirit was in the firepit and Betsellie concentrated on sending it back to whoever, or whatever, put it in Bill in the first place: an animal, possibly, or more likely a malevolent person. Once more he wafted smoke at each of them separately and prayed. Burroughs was moved by the ceremony and kept repeating, "Yes, yes. Of course, thank you, I'm grateful," maintaining his customary good manners, until at the very end the heat and smoke were too much for him, and he begged, "Please. Please—open the door, I need to go out." But this was not the end of it.

At Lyon's house Betsellie had set up an altar with medicine bottles and skins, the bone flute, sand from a sacred power mountain, and a white bald eagle feather placed on top of feather fans all laid out before the big fireplace. The objects were all gifts from his grandfather and teachers. They were tended by a Winnebago Sioux woman. Here the ceremony carried on for another hour and a half before the altar with the shaman on his knees asking for help to preserve old medicines and old ways, to stay in touch with the grandfathers, sky, wood, rock, nature. He thanked his grandfathers and his parents who had died six years before and cried for his mother. At first Burroughs was given a blanket and a pillow to sit on the floor, then he was seated in a chair, facing the altar brazier, holding a sprig of green leaves. Then came the climax of the long ceremony. Betsellie dropped to his knees and chanted several very long prayers in his melodic native Navajo tongue while waving smoke at each of them separately. He prayed to the bear spirit, the four-legged people, the two-legged people, the crawling people, the insects, the families, the brothers and sisters there and everywhere, the relatives and their own brothers and sisters or relatives. "Family, all one family, no matter what race we come from. All relatives together in a room." He asked them all to help the old man on his way with a strong heart and clear head; to give him a long happy life, a peaceful life from now on, the bad spirit, the Ugly Spirit, having gone back to where it came from, and whoever it came from.

Finally the ceremony ended. The fire attendant had prepared a homely pot roast and gratin potatoes with salad followed by coffee and homemade iced cake. Afterward Ginsberg questioned Burroughs about his reaction to the exorcism ceremony, and how he felt about the waves of love and affection shown to him by the participants. "I feel it very deeply," he said. "I like the shaman very much... The way he was crying. Deeply sad, deeply... That was something..."

Afterward Burroughs and Melvin Betsellie sat together and discussed the evil spirit. The next day Bill explained to Allen, "He was suffering, he was hurt by this spirit. And he says he hadn't realized the power of this entity, the full, evil power. It was almost too much for him." The shaman had said it was the toughest case he'd ever handled and for a moment he thought he was going to lose. He wasn't expecting the strength and weight and evil intensity of this spirit, or "entity," as he called it. "The same way the priest in an exorcism has to take on the spirit," said Bill.

"Some of them are not strong enough. Some are killed." In the opinion of Bill Lyon, who had arranged the ceremony, "It scared Betsellie on a deep shamanic level. He entered into the purification of Bill's spirit in an incautious, overconfident manner. Yes, he'd got the bad spirit. He knew he'd got him, but it hit him harder than he anticipated."

Burroughs asked Betsellie what the spirit looked like. He said it had a white skull face but had no eyes, and there were some sort of wings. Discussing it the next day, Allen asked Bill if he recognized the image. Bill said that he had identified it many times in his paintings. He had shown some of them to Betsellie, who had immediately recognized the spirit in the swirls of abstract brushwork, pointing to it saying, "There it is, right there."

When Ginsberg asked him, "Did you get anything from the shaman's sweat lodge ceremony?" Burroughs replied, "That was much better than anything psychoanalysts have come up with. [...] Something definite there was being touched upon. [...] This you see is the same notion, Catholic exorcism, psychotherapy, shamanistic practices—getting to the moment when whatever it was gained access. And also to the name of the spirit. Just to know that it's the Ugly Spirit. That's a great step. Because the spirit doesn't want its name to be known."

This is the story of William Burroughs's battle with the Ugly Spirit.

BOOK ONE

⁓

An Education

Chapter One

As a child I had been a great dreamer, bordering on hallucinations which often involved animals. After years of trying to discover who and what I was, I suddenly awoke one morning and realized I didn't care. I didn't want insight. I wanted to escape and forget.[1]

1. St. Louis Toodle-oo

"It is self-evident that St. Louis affected me more deeply than any other environment has ever done. I feel that there is something in having passed one's childhood beside the big river, which is incommunicable to those people who have not. I consider myself fortunate to have been born here, rather than in Boston, or New York, or London."[2] So wrote T. S. Eliot, who grew up not far from Burroughs's house in St. Louis. Indeed Bill's mother had waltzed with Tommy Eliot at dance class.

St. Louis was founded by Pierre Laclède Liguest in 1764 on the west bank of the Mississippi as a fur trading post. When Burroughs was born there in 1914, St. Louis was the sixth largest city in the United States, with a population of about three-quarters of a million. The 1904 St. Louis World's Fair, to celebrate the centennial of the Louisiana Purchase, had given the city an enormous boost. It was the greatest event in the city's history, spread over 1,272 acres of the western half of Forest Park, attracting twenty million visitors. It focused attention on St. Louis's central location and triggered increased construction of hotels, office buildings, houses, and manufacturing industries. St. Louis in 1914 was prosperous. Safe drinking water had recently been installed and electric trolley cars connected all parts of the city. After the fair, Forest Park was laid out, using many of the World's Fair buildings: the zoo used the fair's giant aviary as its nucleus, and the Art Palace became the St. Louis Art Museum.

However, St. Louis was one of the most polluted cities in the United States, the result of burning soft bituminous coal for heat and a lack of proper zoning that allowed factories to be built next to residential neighborhoods. The town was always seen through a smoky haze, like

9

something out of a Sherlock Holmes story, the globe lampshades haloed through the fog. Burroughs could still remember the old nineteenth-century Riverfront area, the site of the original village, before the whole forty-block section was torn down in the thirties. There was a high level of corruption, particularly surrounding major civic projects. In "When Did I Stop Wanting to Be President?" Burroughs jested that his childhood ambition was to be appointed commissioner of sewers for the City of St. Louis, so that he could wallow in graft and corruption with the fat cats. St. Louis was infamously the site of the worst race riots in the United States, when from June 30 to July 2, 1917, in East St. Louis, across the river in Illinois, whites rioted, burned, and murdered blacks on the streets; many were stoned to death or torn apart by the mob. The *St. Louis Republic* for July 3 ran the headline, "100 Slain, 500 Hurt in Race Riot. 6 E St. Louis Blocks Burned by Mob to Wipe Out Blacks." The police and National Guard, rather than attempt to stop the violence, joined in.

Laura and Mortimer Burroughs lived on Berlin Avenue, a private gated street in the wealthy Central West End. The streets had night watchmen and guardhouses; one of them, the huge stone gatehouse guarding Portland Place, the extension of Berlin Avenue, is remembered in *The Place of Dead Roads*.[3] The Burroughs house at 4664 Berlin Avenue was built by Mortimer Burroughs in 1912 to his own design. The name of the street was changed to Pershing Avenue,[4] after General Pershing, a Missouri man, commander of U.S. forces during World War I. It was a large, comfortable five-bedroom house with a fifty-foot lawn in front sloping down to the street and a large garden behind with a fish pond surrounded by rocks. The backyards were separated by high wooden fences twined with roses and morning glory. At the bottom of each yard was an ash pit; the houses on the private roads were not connected to the main sewer, and from his bedroom window young Billy could sometimes see rats scurrying about. At the end of the garden the garage opened onto Carriage Lane behind.

The front door, with its yellow and blue stained glass panels, was reached by five stone steps. The door led to a large mahogany-paneled hall, set forward from the main house. A wide arch to the right led to the main reception room with more mahogany paneling, built-in bookcases and a fireplace, a high ceiling, and leaded windows looking out over the front lawn. Another wide arch led to the staircase, a large dining room, a study, and a big kitchen. Upstairs the master bedroom looked out over the lawn and was filled with light from an enormous window. There was a dressing room and bathroom, and a room at the back, facing south, where Bill and his older brother, Mort, slept. Mortimer, named after his father, was born on February 16, 1911. Mortimer senior was always called Mote to distinguish him from his son, known as Mort. The boys' floor had a further guest bedroom and a clapboard sleeping porch jettied out over the back garden. The top floor consisted of two large rooms and a nanny's bedroom overlooking the back. Despite the wooden paneling, the whole house was light and airy.

Mote was a keen gardener. The flower beds were filled with roses, peonies, irises. In an oft-repeated memory, Burroughs recalled, "The stars are coming out. There's the Big Dipper. His father points to Betelgeuse in the night sky over St. Louis...smell of flowers in the garden."[5] Laura enjoyed flower arranging—later, in 1940–42, she wrote three books on the subject for the Coca-Cola Company—so the house was always filled with the scent of fresh blooms. There was a permanent yard man, an African American gardener named Otto Belue. Otto played with Billy and let him help out; they got on well. Sometimes Otto brought his son to work and the boys played together. Burroughs always remembered "Otto's son, who played the violin." When Mote and Laura moved to Florida, they gave Otto enough money for him and his wife, Gertrude, to buy a house. When Laura died, Burroughs continued the family tradition of sending Otto twenty-five or fifty dollars every Christmas.

The family had three servants in the house. Burroughs remembered, "We usually had a black couple, one that did the cooking, and the man was sort of a butler."[6] He also recalled having an Irish cook. There was a maid who did the housework and served table, and Mary Evans, a Welsh nurse (or nanny or governess; Burroughs used all three terms), who lived in.

William Seward Burroughs II was delivered by a midwife in the master bedroom of 4664 Berlin Avenue on Thursday, February 5, 1914, a healthy full-term, nine-pound baby.[7] He was named after his grandfather, the inventor of the adding machine. The only family member not delighted to see him was Mort, his elder brother, then three years old and who no doubt deeply resented this intrusive stranger. Bill's mother, Laura Hammond Lee Burroughs, was then twenty-six. Bill's father, Mortimer Perry Burroughs, was twenty-nine. They had married five years before in November 1908. Although Bill was a wanted child, in 1940 Laura told a psychiatrist at the Payne Whitney Clinic in New York (where Bill was under care after a psychotic incident) that she thought she had really wanted a girl. Little Billy grew up surrounded by his extended family.

Laura's parents came from a religious background. Her father, James Wideman Lee, was born in Rockbridge, Georgia, in 1849 to parents who were only eighteen. He realized that the church was his "calling" at the age of sixteen and became a circuit-riding Methodist minister. He worked hard as a preacher, a fund-raiser, an author, and a church builder: he had built three new churches in Georgia by 1893. He transferred to the fashionable parish of St. John in St. Louis when he was forty-four. In 1903 he built the new St. John's, which still stands at "Holy Corners" at McPherson and Washington on Kingshighway.

When he was twenty-six, he married Eufaula Ledbetter, aged thirteen, then a marriageable age in the South. She was the daughter and granddaughter of Georgia preachers, which helps explain her attraction to James at such a young age. She had her first child at the age of fifteen. Of her twelve children, only six survived past infancy: Alice "Darly" May, Ivy Ledbetter, Kate Carter, James Wideman, Laura Hammond, and Lewis Hughes Lee, the youngest.

The Lees had a large, comfortable house and the family gathered there each year for reunions, Christmas, and Thanksgiving. It was something they had to do. The family patriarch also required the children to attend Sunday school at St. John's. Lee wrote more than a dozen books, including *The Romance of Palestine* (1897), *The Illustrated History of Methodism* (1900), and *The New Self Interpreting Bible* (1909) in four volumes, as well as coauthoring a eulogy to his friend Joel Chandler Harris, author of *Uncle Remus*. Harris wrote for the *Atlanta Constitution* and Lee was a close friend of both its publisher, Evan Howell, and its editor, Henry W. Grady, also the subject of one of Lee's biographies.[8] Bill was only five when James Wideman Lee died from complications from a broken hip, but remembered him as a fine-looking old man with a thin face and white mustache. He was said to have been a great charmer. Mote had insisted that Bill and Mort attend Sunday school, but when their grandfather died they were no longer required to do so. Mote and Laura were not religious and their sons were not brought up as believers, though, rather hypocritically, Mote once spanked Mort for fighting on a Sunday.

Laura, born in Atlanta in 1888, was the fifth of the six surviving Lee children. Her older brother, Ivy Ledbetter Lee, born 1877, was the success of the family, becoming a world-famous PR man. He is considered to be the founder of modern public relations, and his company, Parker and Lee, apparently issued the world's first press release, reporting news of the 1906 Atlantic City train wreck before journalists could get the facts elsewhere. In 1914 he worked for John D. Rockefeller Jr.—"to burnish the family image"—and to represent Rockefeller's Standard Oil Company. He was dubbed "Poison Ivy" by Upton Sinclair after the Ludlow Massacre when the Colorado National Guard and Rockefeller's camp guards fired on a tent city of twelve hundred striking miners, killing between nineteen and twenty-five people. Ivy Lee declared that the dead were victims of an overturned stove, when in fact they had been shot in cold blood by the Rockefeller-paid Colorado militia. He started Ivy Lee & Associates in 1919 and worked for Bethlehem Steel, George Westinghouse, Charles Lindbergh, and Walter Chrysler. He specialized in devising propaganda for clients despised by the public for their antiunion and strike-breaking activities. When he died in November 1934 the U.S. Congress was investigating him for his work in advising Joseph Goebbels on public relations techniques for the Nazi Party, and for his work for the IG Farben company, which manufactured the Zyklon B gas used in the Nazi death camps. He met with Hitler many times and told Bill, "The last time I saw him Hitler told me, 'I have nothing against the Jews.' He said, 'This is all exaggerated.'" Ivy Lee was so famous there was even a song that ran, "Even Rumania has Ivy Lee mania. Gosh how the money rolls in."

Burroughs disliked his uncle. "He was very pompous, you didn't talk to him, you listened. There was never any feeling at all between us. The last time that I saw him we'd been out to his house for dinner in Long Island, and he was sort of fuzzy. Fuzzy the way people get when they've got something wrong."[9] He died suddenly of a brain tumor during a board meeting, leaving his family destitute with huge bills to settle all around the world, including unpaid accounts at the Ritz hotels in Paris and Rome. He had been supporting his mother in style but she now fell back on the family. Burroughs remembered, "All the relatives were going around, 'Oh yes, sure, we'll take care of grandmother,' but when it came to a crunch it was my father."[10]

Laura's sister Kate became a real estate agent and married a St. Louis architect named Wilbur Trueblood. Alice married a businessman named Hoxie who died of cirrhosis of the liver despite never having taken a drink in his life. They lived close to the Burroughs household and Bill saw their three children, Prynne, Robert, and Jim, all the time. Robert became a bond salesman and died young of a brain tumor. Prynne died in a car crash, severing his jugular on a broken windshield when he was eighteen years old and a freshman at Princeton. Alice moved out west when her husband died and became very involved with spirit mediums to try and contact Robert and Prynne. Of the other children, James Wideman Lee Jr. joined his brother Ivy's firm in New York, and Lewis Hughes accepted help from Ivy to set up a brokerage firm in New York, so they only visited St. Louis for family reunions. Uncle Lewis was a heavy drinker and died of cirrhosis of the liver. Wideman Lee also went into advertising; he was a member of all the fashionable New York clubs and knew everyone. He married a wealthy woman and had an estate on Long Island with horses and hunting dogs, but he was hard hit by the Depression and had to move to a small apartment on Madison Avenue. It was through Uncle Wideman that Burroughs later joined the University Club in New York. All the St. Louis relatives were around all the time, grumbling about the servants, discussing the scandals of the day, and they formed a significant part of the social milieu that Burroughs was later to reject so completely.

The first William Seward Burroughs was the son of Edmund Burroughs and Ellen Julia Whipple. William was born in Rochester, New York, in 1857, the third of four children. By 1860, the Burroughs family had moved to live near William's paternal grandparents in Lowell, Michigan, and later settled in Auburn, New York, during the 1870s. Edmund was something of an inventor and apparently filed patents for a railroad jack and a paper guillotine. He was such a fervent admirer of William Henry Seward, the great abolitionist and two-term governor of New York, also a resident of Auburn, that he named his son after him. When he was eighteen William joined the Cayuga County National Bank in Auburn as a clerk and worked there for five years, during which time he contemplated the possibility of creating a mechanical adding machine to do his job. While still a resident of Auburn, William married Ida Selover from the nearby village of Moravia. They were married at Groton in Tompkins County, New York, on July 30, 1879.

William's father, Edmund, was living at St. Louis by 1880, where he was working as a model and pattern maker for castings. He set up a workshop at 114 North 7th Street, and lived close by at 703 Chestnut. The Gould's Directory for 1881 has a listing for "E. Burroughs & Son, model maker; steam gauge testing apparatus, models in wood and metal, forty years experience." Edmund's wife, Ellen, remained in the family home at Auburn with her daughter, Anna, a music teacher, and her youngest son, James, a printer. William and Ida, recently married, either moved to St. Louis with Edmund or followed him there shortly afterward. Simon Johnson proposes that Edmund's temporary separation from his wife and family in Auburn suggests that he moved to St. Louis to assist his son William in establishing himself there.

Before 1885, Edmund Burroughs returned to live with his family in Auburn, where he died in 1892, aged sixty-six years. By then William had established himself in St. Louis with his young family and was working for the Boyer Machine Company, owned by Joseph Boyer, a Canadian inventor who was of Edmund Burroughs's generation. At Boyer, William developed an adding machine prototype, and in 1886 he founded the American Arithmometer Company with three other men—Thomas Metcalfe, R. M. Scruggs, and W. C. Metcalfe—to manufacture and sell the machine. It was the company's only product and cost $475. Unfortunately, William was the only one who could operate the machines to get an accurate answer. They were all recalled until William invented a corrective hydraulic mechanism, a cylinder filled with oil with escape apertures that ensured that no matter how much pressure was exerted on the handle, the piston moved up and down the cylinder at the same rate each time. William was granted a patent for it in 1888. They were in business.

Meanwhile in 1880, William and Ida had their first child, Jennie. She was followed by Horace in 1882, Mortimer (Mote) in 1885, and Helen in 1892. Mote later told his son that his grandfather was a remote, cold man who would not allow his children to bother him when he was working. He worked long hours and had a reputation for eccentricity; he drank alcohol "to keep his energy up" and once became so frustrated with his work that he threw open his window and tossed out all his faulty machines to smash to pieces on the ground. He behaved like the classic absentminded inventor, with Ida having to remind him to change his clothes and to eat. She said she had five children: two boys, two girls, and a husband.

William had suffered all his life from chronic health problems, and in 1896 he and Ida moved to a hotel in the hot-springs spa of Citronelle, Alabama, where they hoped to regain their strength. Ida died first, in May 1896. William bought a twenty-square-foot burial plot in the old Bellefontaine Cemetery in St. Louis, which was to become the Burroughs family mausoleum. William remarried in St. Louis less than a month after Ida's death, to his children's nurse, Nina Keltner. But he did not long survive Ida, and on September 14, 1898, only two years after her, he died of tuberculosis at Citronelle, leaving young children: Jennie, eighteen; Horace, sixteen; Mortimer, thirteen; and Helen, six. William himself was only forty-one years old. He was buried next to Ida at Bellefontaine. After William's death, his widow, Nina, was initially appointed guardian of the children and was made executor of his estate. Nina married Clarence White in 1900 and they raised Helen, William's youngest child, as their own daughter, initially in St. Louis and later in Seattle.

In 1902, his supporter and backer Joseph Boyer became president of the American Arithmometer Company. Two years later Boyer moved the company to Detroit, taking with him all his employees on a special train. In 1904 the company's name was changed to the Burroughs Adding Machine Company. Over the next fifty years it grew to become the largest adding machine company in the United States. When their father died, the four children had each received a block of shares in the American Arithmometer Company, with the Mississippi Valley Trust Company appointed as financial advisers.

William Burroughs, the subject of this book, always thought that the Burroughs Company swindled the children out of their shares by buying them back at less than they were worth. We don't know when this was, but there is no evidence of chicanery. The Mississippi Valley Trust probably felt quite sincerely that it made better financial sense to cash in and diversify their investments, rather than have all their wealth concentrated in one new unproven company. There was no way of knowing then how important the company was to be. As it was, according to Burroughs they sold their shareholdings for an enormous sum: $100,000 each, equal to $2.8 million in purchasing power in 2012.[11] Burroughs also said that his mother, Laura, had persuaded Mote to hold back some of his shares, which is unlikely as his parents did not marry until November 1908, ten years after William Sr. died. For whatever reason, however, Mote did hold back some of his shares and benefited considerably in the rise in value of the corporation under its new management. The sale likely went through when the company was restructured and renamed in 1904. That same year, Burroughs's partner Joseph Boyer erected a mausoleum to mark the burial plot at Bellefontaine of his old friend. In Citronelle a stained glass window was installed in the local church with the words "Sacred to the memory of William S. Burroughs."

Of the four children, only Mote and Helen made a success of their lives. Helen is said to have suffered with tuberculosis. She married an insurance agent named Arthur Mercer in Detroit in 1913. They had a son, born in the same year as Bill, who later became a schoolteacher. Though the family home remained in Detroit, Helen spent some time living in Colorado Springs during the 1920s, presumably for her health. Bill met her in about 1920, and again briefly when he and his mother saw her on their way to Valley Ranch in New Mexico in 1925. Laura said Helen was "very intelligent." It seems that she and her husband lived a comfortable life in Detroit, and later in New Mexico, California, and Arizona. Prior to her death in 1972, Helen set up the Helen Burroughs Mercer Trust, which bequeathed $137,274 to the University of Arizona College of Medicine. This was used to recruit outstanding faculty members for the medical college.

Bill's mother had the opposite opinion of Jennie, whom she described as "just a little bit smarter than a moron." In 1902 Jennie married Sheldon Edler in Chicago and had four children: Charles in 1902, Kenneth in January 1905, and two daughters born in 1909 and 1910, the second of whom appears to have died in infancy. They moved back to Jennie's native St. Louis and in the July heat Jennie was preparing little Kenny for his bath in front of the open window when he fell naked through the mosquito screen, three floors to his death. Only two weeks before, Jennie had narrowly averted a similar fall by both children, but apparently learned nothing from the experience. Kenny was the third family member to be interred in the Bellefontaine mausoleum. Shattered by Kenny's death, Jennie became an alcoholic. She and Sheldon separated and she turned to her brother to help her. Mote would get telephone calls from the desk sergeant at the police station, "Mr. Burroughs, Jennie's here again," and he would have to go and get her. Mote never spoke about Jennie, or their uncle Horace, to the children. The last time Jennie made an appearance in St. Louis was when Bill was about eight years old. Bill's father gave her a one-way ticket to Seattle, where her son Charles was living, and they never heard of her again.

Bill's favorite uncle was Horace, the drug addict, but he never met him. Horace and Bill's father used to share a house at 4620 McPherson Avenue in 1904 when they were both still teenagers, but whereas Mote used his inheritance to enroll at MIT, Horace was the black sheep of the family. He used his money to live an extravagant lifestyle, carousing around St. Louis in a coach and four wearing a cape, drinking and leading a dissolute life. He married, divorced, and it was said that he lived for some time in Los Angeles and "made and lost several fortunes there." Horace sustained a shotgun injury to his arm and wrist while hunting and took morphine for the pain. It was legal then and could be bought over the counter in any pharmacy. He quickly became heavily addicted. On graduation Bill's father had moved to Detroit to work as a salesman for the Burroughs Adding Machine Company. Now Horace also moved to Detroit and Mote was continually having to extricate him from difficult situations. Still in his twenties, Horace had lost all of his teeth and looked like a tramp. Laura Burroughs described him as "just a derelict." He eventually went to pieces completely. The president of Burroughs, Joseph Boyer, sent him to a sanatorium to cure him of his habit, not for the first time and to no avail.

The Harrison Narcotics Tax Act of 1914 entered law on March 1, 1915, depriving morphine addicts of their drug supply. On March 4, Horace collapsed outside Harper Hospital and was released the next morning. Later that day police discovered him unconscious on the sidewalk on Park Boulevard and kept him overnight. He was released early on March 7. He rented a room at 208½ Michigan Avenue, telling the landlord, "I want to take a long sleep." He locked the door and braced it with a chair against the knob. He smashed the glass chimney of the oil lamp and cut the veins in the wrist and elbow of his left arm. Later that morning, the landlord was alerted to terrible groans coming from his room. Horace was still living when the police broke down the door, but he died that afternoon, one of the first victims of American antidrug hysteria. Dr. Eugene Smith told the *Detroit Free Press*, "It must have been a horrible death. Deprivation of morphine will drive a man temporarily insane with pain."[12] Horace was buried in Bellefontaine next to his father. Bill could never get his father to talk about him and could only glean snippets of information from his mother. Uncle Horace the morphine addict became a legendary, forbidden figure and his fate undoubtedly contributed to Burroughs's long campaign against American antidrug legislation.

Mote met Laura Hammond Lee on one of his frequent visits back to St. Louis to see the family. During their engagement Mote remained in Detroit and Laura in St. Louis. They were married by her father at the Holy Trinity Methodist Church in Atlanta in November 1908. Laura clearly had a lot of girlfriends, because the twenty-two-year-old had ten parties and receptions given in her honor in the three days before her wedding, which were all reported in the society columns of the local press. For their honeymoon they went to the spa town of French Lick, Indiana, to take the waters at the Pluto Spring. Afterward they continued to Detroit, to their new home, where the family firm, the Burroughs Adding Machine Company, presented them with a solid silver dinner service as a wedding gift.

Their first child, Mortimer Jr., was born in Detroit in 1911. Mote transferred to the St. Louis branch office of the Burroughs Company so that Laura could be close to her family with her new child. In 1912 he bought a plot of land on Berlin Avenue and built a house to his own design. On February 5, 1914, William Seward Burroughs II was born there. Mote did not stay with Burroughs for much longer. In 1916 he took a job at the Thatcher-Kerwin Glass Company, then in 1928 he used the remainder of his money from the original sale of Burroughs shares to start his own Burroughs Glass Company at 305 Arsenal Road, St. Louis, with Laura as vice president. This he owned and operated for many years. He was successful, employing several hundred people, and one year made $80,000. During the Great War, Mote was enrolled in the artillery, but was still in training at Jefferson Barracks when the war ended. He told his sons that during roll call in 1918, soldiers would simply keel over onto the parade ground as the global Spanish influenza pandemic took its toll.

In 1929 Mote sold for $276,000 (worth $3,642,425 in 2012) the remaining shares in the Burroughs Adding Machine Company that he had retained, just three months before the 1929 stock market crash. He continued to operate the Burroughs Glass Company until 1932, when he decided to retire. He sold the company, retaining a block of shares. Retirement did not suit Mote, so he started up as a landscape gardener, combining business with his love of gardening. But it didn't work out—he would execute a commission, then the client would say they didn't like the results and refuse to pay—so he and Laura started a garden and gift shop called Cobble Stone Gardens, located at 10036 Conway Road in Clayton. They sold garden furniture, antiques, barbecue sets, bric-a-brac, porcelain birds, upmarket gift items, and finally phased out the landscape gardening altogether.

It was through the art and antiques side of the business that Bill's parents encountered the homosexual world. They became friends with a gay couple who ran an antique shop, and by having direct contact and friendship with homosexuals they became far more tolerant than most people of their class and background. Burroughs commented, "When they were in the gift and art business they said my father was the only straight man in the industry. They went to the Gifts and Art show in Chicago, so she knew every fag in the industry. She knew all of these people were queer, she was no fool. My mother knew all these queers who loved her. She was well on the way to being a sort of fag hag!"[13] Laura thought of herself as something of an intellectual; she read Aldous Huxley in the 1920s but was shocked by the homosexuality portrayed in Thomas Mann's *Death in Venice*. She explained it all to her mother, Eufaula, who was equally shocked, even though she didn't actually read the book. "Things that you didn't know existed!" Grandmother said. It all helped prepare Laura for her youngest son's deviation from the society norm.

Chapter Two

Opening bars of East St. Louis Toodleoo . . . at times loud and clear then faint and intermittent like music down a windy street.[1]

1. The Green Reindeer

Burroughs grew up surrounded by family: his grandmother, two aunts, two uncles, and five cousins. After her husband died, Eufaula Lee traveled all over the world, visiting India and Europe, always bringing back souvenirs. Every Sunday they went to lunch with Grandmother and, as Burroughs put it, she would disinter her dead brother, killed fifty years before dragging his shotgun through a fence and blowing his lungs out. "So every Sunday at lunch there was the boy lying by the wood fence and blood on the frozen red Georgia clay seeping into the winter stubble."[2] There were frequent family reunions and she would lecture them on leading a spiritual life. "Faula" was a member of the Woman's Christian Temperance Union, so there was no alcohol in her house except that which Uncle Robert and Bill's cousin Fred would bring in their hip flasks. They would disappear into the bathroom and come back reeking of liquor, but Grandma never noticed. She always said she would rather see a son of hers come home dead than drunk; meanwhile the men would sit there dead drunk saying, "Aw, Grandmaw! Grandmaw!"

The Lees had been slave owners. Faula found a diary written by her own grandmother in which she said she felt responsible for the spiritual welfare of every slave on the property in Georgia. Eufaula lived to be eighty-nine, and died in October 1951, a month after hearing that her grandson had accidentally killed his wife in Mexico City. Another grandson described her as being livid with anger at the news.[3]

Burroughs described his father as reticent, remote, rather difficult to talk to, although he must have been animated enough to discuss adding machines, as he worked as a salesman for so many years. He was not a ladies' man and Burroughs thought that Laura was probably the only woman in his life, ever. Bill's parents were in the Social Register and knew all the doctors and lawyers, bankers and businessmen of the community, but Bill's father was not gregarious and didn't like parties. Mote drank very little when he was young and not at all later. They had few people around to the house other than family. One of their few regular guests was the famous newspaperman Oliver Kirby Bovard along with his wife, Suzanne. For thirty years O. K. Bovard was the managing editor of the *St. Louis Post-Dispatch* until he resigned in 1938 after the paper's owner, Joseph Pulitzer, objected to what he saw as Bovard's emerging socialist views. The staff were about to walk out in protest, but Bovard persuaded them to stay at work. He was renowned for his pioneering journalism in exposing corruption and graft. In order to remain objective, he did not mix with the St. Louis social set, which is probably why he chose Mote as his best friend.

Mote had a duck club, and from the age of eight, when Burroughs first began using guns, he would take his two sons along on the shoot: "I used to go out duck shooting with the old man and the president of the First National City Bank and the editor of the *St. Louis Post-Dispatch*. You have to get up real early, six o'clock, to catch the ducks. All in hiding in this marshy ground and we would put out decoys, and then as the ducks came in, all these fat old businessmen would stand up and blast away at them. We had retriever dogs to collect the ducks. I used to really enjoy it!"[4] Mote's other great interests were fishing and tinkering about in his workshop. Bill was welcome on the former but banned from the latter; he was too young to touch his father's tools, something that always rankled. Mort, however, being three years older, was encouraged to learn. Mote had a fully equipped workshop with a long workbench and power tools. He made a pirate chest for the boys that appears in *Cities of the Red Night*: "I open a rusty padlock into my father's workshop. We strip and straddle a pirate chest, facing each other."[5]

Bill's mother was clearly a profound influence on his life. It was a relationship out of Proust, who wrote, "I used to receive, in a kiss, my mother's heart, whole and entire, without qualm or reservation, without the smallest residue of an intention that was not for me alone."[6] William was his mother's favorite; she adored him and he could do no wrong. James Grauerholz reports that Margaret "Miggie" Vieths, who married Mort in 1934, never really liked or got along with her mother-in-law. "Laura was forever talking about how wonderful Billy was, how bright and clever and interesting."[7] When Laura was interviewed by psychiatrists at Payne Whitney in

New York in 1940, they noted that she was "intelligent, but emotional; inclined to be unable to see shortcomings in patient, and to stress what she regards as his successes." When Bill was an adult, she told him, "I worship the ground you walk on." Mote was prepared to go along with his wife's adoration of her younger son, to the extent that he continually bailed him out of trouble and paid him an allowance until he was fifty years old. This does not appear to have caused tension, certainly nothing that Burroughs ever saw. "My parents apparently got along just perfectly. There was never a quarrel. I never saw any signs of friction. Never. Not only were there no fights but there was never a raised voice. Nothing like that. It's amazing when you come to think of it. They saw each other all the time. All the time."[8]

Billy was a sensitive child and prone to visions. Much of the connection with his mother came from Burroughs's belief in magic and the world of the occult. He had intermittent fevers and saw "animals in the wall" of his bedroom. "I've always been a believer in spirits, the supernatural, like my mother. It was a weird family." When he was four years old he and Mort were playing in Forest Park. Mort had his BB gun and had gone on ahead when Billy saw a delicate little green reindeer, about the size of a cat, standing in a grove of trees, "clear and precise in the late afternoon sunlight as if seen through a telescope."[9] Billy called to Mort to come and look, but Mort refused. Mort said that Billy talked too much; Billy talked all the time, and Mort probably ignored most of what he said. "He wouldn't believe me. I can see it quite clearly now, the reindeer. Oh yes. It was very delicate, very thin legs, in a sort of green shade. So I was subject to those sort of things. To visions, hallucinations, whatever you want to call them."[10]

One morning, aged four, he woke up early in his and Mort's bedroom, where he had built a little house of building blocks on the floor. "I see little gray men playing in my block house. They move very fast, like a 1920 speed-up film...whisk...they are gone. Just the empty block house in gray dawn light. I am motionless in this sequence, a silent witness."[11] From an early age Burroughs was in contact with the magical medium. "So many people have had at least one of such experiences as a child." Laura was extremely interested in psychic phenomena, and Burroughs often spoke of her as having clairvoyant powers. Billy had a dream, accompanied by a smell of coal gas, that he was standing in front of his mother, leaning over her like a dinosaur and eating her back.[12] "Now Mother comes screaming into the room: 'I had a terrible dream that you were eating my back.' I have a long neck that reaches up and over her head. My face in the dream is wooden with horror."[13] This dream recurred throughout his life and was described in a number of his books. He and Laura seemed to be psychically connected. His childhood memories were almost all of his mother. "I remembered a long time ago when I lay in bed beside my mother, watching lights from the street move across the ceiling and down the walls. I felt the sharp nostalgia of train whistles, piano music down a city street, burning leaves."[14]

Burroughs was also exposed to the superstitious talk and ideas of the servants. Bill's only memory of the old Irish cook was that she taught him how to call toads. She must have been from the Dingle peninsula where the natterjack toad is found, the only species of toad native to Ireland. Bill had a toad that lived under a rock by the pool in the backyard. The call was a subtle cooing sound, not much like the toad's mating call, but it worked. Billy would call and his toad would come hopping out. Years later, in the seventies, Burroughs was visiting Ian Sommerville in Bath, in the west of England, and Ian informed him that there were toads in the garden. Bill's powers had not deserted him and soon one came hopping out. The cook also taught him the rhyme for bringing on the blinding worm curse: "Needle in thread, needle in bread. Eye in needle, needle in eye, and bury the bread deep in a sty." You took some rotten bread and threaded a needle with catgut and sewed it through the bread in a certain way and then buried it under a fencepost in a pigsty. And that would bring the blinding worm that gets in the eye and blinds the person. It is an old Irish curse. The counterspell was, "Cut the bread and cut the thread and send the needle back on red." Little Billy listened, fascinated, to these old Irish tales.

But it was Billy's Welsh nanny, Mary Evans, Mort's nanny before Billy was born, who remained uppermost in his memory because of a traumatic incident that occurred when Burroughs was four years old. Little Billy was very close to his nanny, so much so that when she had her Thursday off he would throw hysterical tantrums, screaming, "All I want is Nursy!" In the haut-bourgeois atmosphere of upper-class St. Louis, the children probably saw far more of their nurse than they did of their parents and so related to Nursy like a mother. Burroughs later assumed that his need for her must indicate that she fellated him to calm him and send him to sleep, but he also told one of his analysts that Nursy was "severe" and said that when she caught him masturbating she threatened to cut off his penis; hardly compatible with fellation. It was Nursy who took Billy and Mort the three blocks to Forest Park each day. At first he was taken in a perambulator, leather-padded with metal-spoked wheels, then, when he was capable of walking the distance and back, they went on "shanks pony," as Nursy called it[15]—on foot—unless the weather was inclement, often the case in the depths of the St. Louis winter. Like the Irish cook, Mary

Evans imparted her native folklore to the boys, old Welsh rhymes: "Slip and stumble, trip and fall. Down the stairs and hit the wall." It stayed in his memory, and his protagonist Kim used it in *The Place of Dead Roads* to make sex magic against Judge Farris.[16] Billy thought Nursy had unusual powers. The fireplace had a surround rail, covered with padded satin that you could sit on. Billy sat there with Nursy, who had just laid the fire. "We should light the fire," Billy said. She told him, "The fire will light," and sure enough, the coals began to burn. She had laid the fire on top of hot coals that she knew would ignite the kindling. It seemed like magic.

When he was old enough Bill shared a room with his brother. The three-year age difference was insurmountable for the first few years, but Burroughs claimed they got on very well. Bill looked to his older brother for guidance. One of his earliest memories was at age three telling his brother that people saw through their mouths. Mort told him, "Close your eyes." Bill realized that Mort was right. There were the usual fights, a memorable occasion being when Bill was four and asked Mort to play tenpin bowling and Mort refused. Bill threw a bowling pin at him, hitting him on the head. Mote spanked him, the only time Burroughs remembered his father doing so. There may have been more traumatic sibling incidents. In 1959, when Burroughs and the artist Brion Gysin were conducting psychic experiments in the Beat Hotel using a crystal ball and other devices, Gysin asked him, "What about your brother and your relationship with him?" Burroughs burst into tears. He later thought it must have related to "some awful thing with regards [to] my brother. This obviously means that there was something there, something that I probably did, that's all."[17]

Nursy was nevertheless responsible for a major trauma that occurred when Burroughs was four years old, something so extreme and shocking that despite ten years of psychoanalysis he was never able to properly retrieve it. Different analysts proposed various explanations, and Burroughs himself eventually identified some elements of the event. One Thursday in the late summer or autumn of 1918, possibly because of little Bill's hysterical tantrums, Mary Evans took him along with her on her day off. Mary Evans had a girlfriend whose boyfriend was a veterinarian who worked from his home on the outskirts of St. Louis. They went there for a picnic. It seems that Burroughs had been there before, because he also had a dim memory of seeing the vet deliver a foal, though he felt that this might be a "screen" memory. The general consensus among his analysts was that Mary had encouraged Billy to fellate the vet and that, scared, Billy had bitten the man's penis, causing him to smack Billy on the head. Bill also theorized that he had witnessed Mary and her girlfriend having sex, giving rise to an infantile idea that women had penises, but why would Mary have risked allowing Billy to watch, unless this was part of the same scenario involving the vet? Whatever happened, it disturbed Billy greatly and he told his brother. Bill later remembered Mort saying, "Should we tell on Nursy?" But they didn't. Afterward Billy had dreams in which Mary Evans threatened him if he should ever tell what happened. He told another psychiatrist that he wished Nursy and her girlfriend dead, and felt deeply guilty for feeling this.

Both Alan Ansen and James Grauerholz have identified a passage in "WORD," written in 1957–58 in Tangier at a time when Burroughs was off drugs and alcohol and conducting in-depth self-analysis, as being about this traumatic event:

> We are prepared to divulge all and to state that on a Thursday in the month of September 1917, we did, in the garage of the latter, at his solicitations and connivance, endeavor to suck the cock of one George Brune Brubeck, the Bear's Ass, which act disgust me like I try to bite it off and he slap me and curse and blaspheme. [...] The blame for this atrociously incomplete act rest solidly on the basement of Brubeck, my own innocence of any but the most pure reflex move of self-defense and—respect to eliminate this strange serpent thrust so into my face [...] so I [...] had recourse to nature's little white soldiers—our brave defenders by land—and bite his ugly old cock.[18]

Grauerholz wrote, "Searching the Gould's Directory for 1919 we find listings for eight or nine veterinary surgeons, and no 'Browbeck...but there *is* an Edward H. *Brune*, at 1623 Hodiamont, with his surgical practice at the same address—which would indeed have been exactly at the city limits in 1918. 'Brune'...B–R–U–N–E...'the Bear's Ass'...bruin... this name, although unearthed from a work of fiction, seems well established in Burroughs' mind. With all due respect to the late Dr. Brune's descendants, we cannot convict him on this slender evidence, but it certainly points in an interesting direction." Mary Evans returned to Britain abruptly in 1919, after a receiving a letter from England, which suggests a death in the family. When his mother told him, little Billy took it very calmly. Clearly the hysterical attachment had been broken. After she left, Billy wrote to her, dictating his letters to his mother. Mary Evans later ran a pub in Wales, and Mort and his future wife, Miggie, visited her there in 1934 when Mort was studying architecture in Paris. She was very hospitable toward them. There is very little cock-sucking in Burroughs's sex writing.

2. *The Autobiography of a Wolf*

In 1919, at age five, Billy was sent to the Community School, founded in 1914 by a group of young mothers living in Clayton who were influenced by John Dewey's *The School and Social Progress* (1899) and wanted a progressive school for their children. Laura was involved in fund-raising for the school. Billy and Mort were usually driven there, a five- or ten-minute drive, but would often come back on the Clayton trolley along with Jane Mathews, the girl next door, and other local children. "All the haut bourgeois went to the Community School."[19]

Bill was slow to begin reading, then suddenly it came quite easy. Before that, Mote read aloud to him: *Treasure Island*, *Kidnapped*, *Moby-Dick*, Victor Hugo's *Toilers of the Sea*. He was taught to write short stories and produced several westerns and "spooky things" that he read to the class. At an early age, Burroughs began to take refuge in fiction and to see himself as a fictional character. At the Community School he read a pirate book and wanted to become the coldest and nastiest of the pirates. He assigned a lesser role to his friend Eugene Angert, who wanted to be cold too. "Blundit was my name. I picked some old rat gambler up off the floor by his hair and ran a cutlass through his neck. The crew was chilled by the cold brutality of the act and they rushed me."[20]

The school practiced Pearlman Writing, a technique in which the child was not permitted to move the hand or wrist but used the entire arm from the elbow. It was supposed to produce a beautiful slanting hand, but none of the children mastered it. Billy was useless at addition and division, and never learned to spell properly. His eccentric spellings often remained in his books because editors thought he intended them that way. The children expressed themselves in modeling clay, by beating out copper ashtrays in a mold, making stone axes, and acting out the everyday life of Neanderthal man by draping blankets over the tables to make caves. Billy sat in his cave in his baggy green plus-fours, his long socks pulled high,

> my stone axe there and a pot made by a quiet, gloomy girl who solaced herself with Edna St. Vincent Millay and Sara Teasdale. "Read this and you will know!" she would say, fiercely thrusting a book of poems on one.
>
> So me and Sara Teasdale under the table go into our "Mr. and Mrs. Average Cave Man" act.
>
> "Did you kill a bison today my mate?"
>
> "Yes, we were lucky in the hunt. There will be no hunger in the cave tonight. My companion is bringing in the kill."
>
> And Vincent Price[21] who was in school at the time lugs in an old stuffed badger.

Bill wrote his first book at the Community School when he was eight years old. It was about ten pages long and was called *The Autobiography of a Wolf*, clearly inspired by Ernest Thompson Seton's *The Biography of a Grizzly*, in which an old grizzly, saddened by the death of his mate, slinks off to a canyon containing poisonous fumes to die. Billy didn't know the difference between biography and autobiography. "People said, 'Oh you mean a biography!' 'No,' I said, 'I mean an autobiography,' because I felt myself to be the wolf. I was Jerry the red-haired wolf. Grizzlies don't eat wolves, particularly such a scrawny wolf as that. Really funny. Hunters killed his mate. [...] Me and the wolf were one, Jerry the red-haired wolf and all the wolf boys, the wild boys, and so on. It goes back to that, *The Autobiography of a Wolf*."[22] The bear was called the Grey Ghost. "The Grey Ghost met his death at the hands of a grizzly bear after seven pages, no doubt in revenge for plagiarism."[23] Then there was a tale called *Carl Cranbury in Egypt*, which was abandoned. "Carl Cranbury frozen back there on yellow lined paper, his hand an inch from his blue steel automatic."[24] Bill also wrote ghost stories, westerns, and gangster stories. He already knew that he wanted to be a writer.

Billy got to know the neighbors through their children. Next door at 4662 lived an old Jewish doctor whose wife held mystical salons and had entertained such celebrities as the poet Witter Bynner and Gregory Zilboorg, the psychoanalyst and psychiatric historian. Next to them, at 4660, lived the Mathews family. Old Rive Skinker Matthews was a prosperous hardware dealer, with white hair, a high starched collar, and black tie. He was chauffeured home in a whitewalled Packard limousine. He was an old St. Louis resident, and Skinker Boulevard, which once marked the city's western limits, was named after his grandfather. Bill used to play with his son, Rives. Burroughs remembered, "The older sister Jane told chilling ghost stories on the front porch at twilight fireflies over the lawn. [...] Ghosts are gentle creatures need gas light slate roofs a blue mist."[25] One of the stories ended with the postscript, "I have leprosy and I cannot live."[26]

On the other side was Dr. Blair, and then came the Francis family. They were rather grand because their grandfather, David Francis, had been the state governor from 1889 until 1893. Mr. and Mrs. Tom Francis had two daughters, Sis and Jane. Sis was Billy's age and they sometimes played together. "Sis was a terrific person, sort of a Tallulah Bankhead, kind of a forthright hard-drinking girl. She said about me when I hadn't seen her for years, 'Who would have thought that ratty little kid could grow into something quite attractive.'" Bill stayed in touch and went to her wedding in St. Louis when she married Lancing Ray, the heir to the *Globe-Democrat*. Bill's mother said of Mrs. Francis, "She's the coldest woman I've ever seen." Burroughs clearly used Mrs. Francis as one of his models for a particular type of American woman that signified everything he hated most about his upbringing. "I remember going over there once and he's drunk and grabbing the children and patting them on the head and she's just sitting there like a block of ice with the most obvious complete contempt for him."[27] Oddly enough, one of Bill's classmates at his next school felt the same way about Laura Burroughs. Ann Russe Prewitt said, "I never felt that Mrs Burroughs had any warmth. Mr. Burroughs, on the other hand, spent considerable time with Bill. [...] Someone told me that Mr. Burroughs would have Bill pick out five new words each day and then put them into several sentences until they were solidly in his vocabulary."[28]

Bill's best friend was his first cousin Prynne Hoxie, Aunt Alice's boy, who lived nearby on Hirshman Avenue and went to the Community School. Prynne was the same age and his constant companion.[29] They had a secret cry with which to identify themselves: "Woo woo whoop!" They would often go to Forest Park and fish in the pond and liked to walk along the slippery grassy banks of the River des Peres to watch for the turds to drop into the brackish yellow water from the numerous sewer pipes that lined its banks. When one shot out they would yell, "Hey looky! Someone just did it!" The River des Peres was then little more than an open sewer. Burroughs wrote, "During the summer months the smell of shit and coal gas permeated the city, bubbling up from the river's murky depths to cover the oily iridescent surface with miasmal mists. I liked the smell myself."[30]

The River des Peres flooded in August 1915, killing eleven people, destroying a thousand homes, and sweeping away three bridges. The Jefferson Memorial Building became an island in a sea of bobbing sewage. In 1919, in a scene straight out of Burroughs, during the second week of the municipal opera's maiden season, the River des Peres again overflowed its banks, and a surging wave of fetid effluent swept into the outdoor theater, damaging the stage and routing the audience and cast of Michael William Balfe's *The Bohemian Girl*. The audience scrambled for the exits screaming and shouting. A bond issue was finally passed in 1923, and over the next few years the river was buried in a twenty-nine-foot-wide, twenty-three-foot-high cement sewer pipe.

In 1919 Bill's father bought forty acres of land on the south side of the Missouri River two miles south of the small hamlet of St. Albans, about thirty miles due west of the Central West End. He built a holiday cabin there for the family. A single-line railroad connected St. Albans with

St. Louis, with a stop at Kingshighway and Audubon, a short walk from Pershing Avenue, so their country place was within easy commuting distance. In a few short miles the urban sprawl and pollution of St. Louis gave way to trees. The train approached St. Albans through thick woodland, sometimes skirting the Missouri, then passed over Tavern Creek on a high trestle before reaching the hamlet. Many of their neighbors had places there. James Grauerholz reports that Mortimer Burroughs may also have had a cabin in St. Albans itself, "for William's memories of these summers vividly recreate the town."[31] It is St. Albans that Burroughs is remembering in *The Western Lands*: "In the 1920s, everyone had a farm where they would spend the weekends. I remember the Coleman lanterns that made a roaring noise, and the smell of the chemical toilets."[32]

Large sections of *The Place of Dead Roads* are set in St. Albans,[33] and the book features a map of the town, based on Burroughs's childhood memory of the place.[34] In the novel, Tavern Creek becomes "Dead Boy Creek," and Head's Store at the corner of St. Albans and Ridgeview Roads, in the same family since 1915, becomes "Uncle Kes's Saloon and General Store," the scene of a lovingly described shootout. The small town of Defiance, about four miles north of St. Albans, across the Missouri River, comes in for some rough treatment. Burroughs renames it "Jehovah": "Their horrid church absolutely spoiled his sunsets, with its gilded spire sticking up like an unwanted erection, and Kim vowed he would see it levelled."[35] Kim laid waste the town by distributing smallpox-laced illustrated Bibles. The town and its church previously came in for opprobrium in *Cities of the Red Night*: " 'When the fog lifts you can see their fucking church sticking up.' The boy spits."[36] Clearly the church irritated Burroughs enormously when he was a child.[37]

St. Albans was probably used mostly as a weekend retreat from St. Louis, but for their annual vacation the Burroughs family had a comfortable summer house in Harbor Beach, Michigan, on the western shore of Lake Huron, due north of Detroit. It was a small town of local residents and summer people. Bill's parents knew people with houses on the lake. They took a train from St. Louis to Port Huron and continued to Harbor Beach by ferry. Burroughs remembered an incident on the ferry at the age of four or five when he picked up a water glass, bit a piece out of it, and spat it out. His mother later told him how astonished everyone was that he did not cut himself. Later he seemed to attract jokes involving broken glass, as David Kammerer, Lucien Carr, Dennis Evans, and Burroughs himself all had broken glass acts. Bill performed another swallowing act, as he recalled in his journals. "Now when I was four or five years old I had a little gold knife and I used to suck it for the steel taste. Folded of course the puckering steely taste. Ended up swallowing the knife but let that pass as it did three days later."[38]

Bill learned to swim at an early age at Harbor Beach in the breakwater at Bathing Beach Park. It was at Harbor Beach that Mote moored his boat, a large, four-berth cabin cruiser, about fifty feet in length, with sails and an auxiliary motor. They would go out beyond the breakwater and chug along at five or six miles per hour across the lake. Mote loved to fish—it was his favorite occupation—and he passed the skill on to Bill. Harbor Beach is remembered with affection in the "From the lake, From the hill" section of *Port of Saints*: "The hills are very green in summer, surrounded by meadows and fields and streams with stone bridges, and further inland woods of oak and pine and birch."[39] The entire section could have come straight from a Denton Welch novel.

Though Harbor Beach was in no way a holiday camp, there was communal eating. A bell rang to tell residents to dress for dinner, and fifteen minutes later they would assemble in the dining hall. A typical Sunday menu consisted of plain mashed potatoes, fricasseed chicken, and rice. One resident got drunk and claimed that his flapjacks were soggy and slid them across the floor like curling stones. He was barred from the dining hall. Ringing the bell at the wrong time was a favorite prank of the summer children.

Bill used to go out to the end of the pier and catch a string of small rock bass and yellow perch using worms or minnows as bait. "I remember a yellow perch flapping on the pier, the stagnant water inside the breakwater where the carp lived."[40] He would ask the chef to cook them. Sometimes the family would fry the day's catch in the cottage on a kerosene stove. Burroughs adored fresh fish, and when he eventually retired to Kansas, he bought a fishing lodge and small boat on Lone Star Lake near Lawrence.

Burroughs's use of the word "nostalgia" in a memoir suggests that even in 1925, when he was eleven, he already had a premonition that these carefree days were limited. "The pure pleasure of cold Whistle on a hot summer afternoon of my childhood. [...] Sitting on the back steps drinking Whistle at twilight on a summer evening, hearing the streetcars clang past on Euclid Avenue, I felt the excitement and nostalgia of the twenties tingling in my groin."[41] In 1925, the year that the Burroughs family moved to the suburbs, a carbonated orange soda called Whistle had been introduced by the Vess soda company of St. Louis. These were poignant moments for Burroughs: sitting on the stoop, watching the lamplighter make his rounds through the veil of smoky brown mist at dusk on the tree-lined private roads of the Central West End. Burroughs was not the only one to feel nostalgia for those days. T. S. Eliot recalled "the yellow smoke that rubs its muzzle on the window-panes,"[42] and "the burnt-out ends of smoky days. / And now a gusty shower wraps / The grimy scraps / Of withered leaves about your feet / And newspapers from vacant lots."[43] However, the impact of the smog on people's health and on the environment was disastrous, but such was the corruption and political chicanery in St. Louis that nothing was done to alleviate the situation until 1940, long after Burroughs had left home. In 1906 the Public Library had to spend $10,000 to repair smoke damage to its collection, and "sulphuric gases from smoke" were killing the trees in Forest Park, one block away. By the 1920s the botanical gardens considered moving out of town because so many plants were dying. The Burroughs family made the same decision.

Bill spent part of the summer of 1924, when he was ten, at a dude ranch in New Mexico with his mother. Valley Ranch was owned by Mr. Miller, a matchstick figure in a dark gray suit. Billy was assigned a gentle old strawberry roan named Grant. If he got lost he was told to just let Grant have his head, and he did and Grant did. The food was terrible, but occasionally Bill caught a fish and added it to the meager fare. He also caught a large centipede that he preserved in alcohol. Bill spent several summers there.

Bill first went to Los Alamos Ranch School when he was eleven. He and Mort attended summer camp there for three years running, from 1925 to 1927. Bill joined the school itself in 1929 and stayed for three years. The idea that Bill's chronic sinus infection, no doubt caused by the filthy polluted air of St. Louis, would be improved by a summer in the West came from Dr. Eugene Senseney, who lived down the street at Pershing and Walton, and who was the doctor responsible for a botched job on Bill's tonsils. "I came near bleeding to death from his bungling hands."[44]

The family summer holiday in 1925 was, as usual, at Harbor Beach. That Christmas they spent in New York City. Bill's Uncle Ivy had invited all his siblings to bring their families for a family reunion in his eighteen-room mansion at East 66th Street and Fifth Avenue. There were twenty-six family members at the Christmas dinner, including Bill, resentful at being dragged to New York away from his friends and who particularly disliked being ordered around by Uncle Ivy. "He was very domineering. He put us all up in this huge apartment and he would organize sightseeing." The family were taken to see the sights, including FAO Schwarz's famous toy shop on West 23rd Street and the Woolworth Building on Broadway, then the tallest building in the world.[45] Burroughs told an interviewer, "Ivy Lee hated me on sight. He was part of that whole class of people that I was brought up with in St. Louis. And they all took one look at me and said, NO!"[46]

Chapter Three

A boy's will is the wind's will,
And the thoughts of youth are long, long thoughts.
—HENRY WADSWORTH LONGFELLOW, "MY LOST YOUTH"

1. Kells Elvins

The air pollution in St. Louis precipitated a flight to the suburbs by anyone who could afford it. On December 23, 1926, the *St. Louis Post-Dispatch* headline cracked, "Presumably the sun rose, but whether it did nobody knows." That year Mortimer Burroughs bought five acres of land at 700 South Price Road and hired Wilbur Trueblood's architectural firm, Trueblood and Graf, to design and build a house. Wilbur was married to Laura's sister Kate. Bill's natal house on what was now called Pershing Avenue was sold, but unfortunately the new house was not yet ready and the family had to spend a month living at the Fairmont Hotel, on nearby Maryland Plaza. Bill had with him his pet guinea pig, which "screamed and hollered, and the cage stunk something awful."[1]

The new house at 700 South Price Road was large, with steep gray sloping roofs, double-window dormers, and three chimneys, shielded from the road by a curve in the driveway and surrounded by trees. The front door opened into the usual hall with a dining room to the left. Behind that was the kitchen and the servant quarters. To the right of the front door was the living room and above that the master bedroom with its own bathroom and a balcony opening onto the garden. The boys lived and slept at the back in a large comfortable room with windows on three sides, two beds, and two closets. On the same floor was a bathroom and a guestroom.

With five acres of garden, Bill was able to get more pets. At Pershing Avenue he had had an Irish terrier, as well as his guinea pig. Now he added a raccoon and an angora goat, which lived in a special enclosure. It was pregnant and gave birth. Bill loved the kid; he would put his hand up in a fist and the kid would butt at it.

Most of the children from the Community School continued either to the boys-only Country Day or to the coeducational John Burroughs School, named after the great naturalist, no relation. Mort went to Country Day as the John Burroughs School was only founded in 1923, the year he went to high school. The big high school football games were between John Burroughs and Country Day. Bill went to John Burroughs in the seventh grade, and Laura and Mote clearly liked the way the school was run, because they moved Mort there to join Billy, a move that was no doubt resisted by Mort, as he had always told Bill, "Call yours the Sissy School so I'll know what you mean." Like the Community School, it was private and progressive, with friendly teachers and no bullying. It had the added advantage of being less than half a block from where they lived, so they could walk across to it along the leafy suburban lane. Burroughs particularly remembered his Latin teachers: Mr. Baker, a supporter of the Russian experiment in communism who could be very sarcastic, and Mrs. Grossman, whom Burroughs "had some difficulties with." Bill was sent to see the principal, Mr. Aitken, a few times but was never in serious trouble.

Burroughs has remarked on how utterly different life was in the twenties from the postwar life most of his readers knew. "If you want to get idea of what it's like read Fitzgerald. He was born in St. Paul, Minnesota, and I think the midwestern towns, places like St. Paul, Kansas City, Cincinnati, and St. Louis, were pretty much similar."[2] It was the time before mass entertainment: when he was twelve or thirteen, Bill was sent for piano lessons with a Mrs. Stowe, where he just about learned to play the "Marseillaise," "Frère Jacques," and "The Last Rose of Summer." He learned to waltz, foxtrot, tango, and to do the Charleston from a fat little man named Mr. Trimp and his plump little wife. Mechanically recorded sound was just being introduced into the home. Both cylinders and discs were available to play on your wind-up phonograph—the needle had to be changed for each playing. The movies were still silent: the first feature film with sound was *The Jazz Singer*, released in October 1927, but it was some time before Hollywood switched to "talkies"; Bill loved the movies and grew up with Rin Tin Tin the wonder dog, which played its first starring role in *Where the North Begins* in 1923. He loved the weekly serials. Other memorable films included Josef von Sternberg's silent crime thriller *Underworld* with George Bancroft (1927), and Richard Barthelmess in *Weary River* (1929). In 1925 Bill saw Rupert Julian's silent gothic *The Phantom of the Opera*: "How I loved the movies. 'Phantom of the Opera.' The scene where she comes up behind him while he's playing the organ and pulls his mask off, 'Feast your Eyes! Glut your soul on my accursed ugliness!'"[3] In the 1920s there were still stage shows between the films.

Bill disliked these because they went on and on and he just wanted to see the movies:

> I remember now an occasion, I was with my father, a big rawboned performer got up and sang:
> Sailing on
> Sailing on
> I am sailing on...
> That was sixty-odd years ago. Where was he sailing to? I can't remember the film but I can see him quite clearly from here. Not a young man, early to mid-forties, tall, angular, awkward, thick red wrists his sleeves too short, worn blue serge suit...
> What did my father say after the show? "Big raw boned fellow..."
> The full misery of the human condition hits me when I think about that long ago singer.[4]

St. Louis had its first radio station in 1921, and the Burroughs family had a crystal set, stringing the antenna between the trees and the house. Electric street lighting was being introduced. Horse-drawn vehicles and trolley cars filled the streets, but new forms of transport were making an appearance. One of Bill's aunts drove an electric car; they had a single lever and went at about twenty miles per hour, but they were heavy and the battery had to be recharged at frequent intervals. In the teens, several family members had steam cars, which had the advantage over gasoline cars of being faster; they could reach sixty miles per hour. The downside was they took some time to build up a head of steam, but in the days of servants that was not a problem. Bill rode around in his aunt's Stanley Steamer. "There was the Stanley Steamer and the White Steamer, but they were immediately knocked out by the gas car because you could just go out and start it when you wanted to whereas your steam car, you had to go out and light it and then wait about half an hour, have breakfast."[5] They stopped making steamers in the early twenties. Male members of the family drove Stutz Bearcats: "Stutz Bearcats outside, it's the 1920s."[6] When he was old enough to drive, Mort received a Model A Duesenberg, one of the grandest, most beautiful, and expensive American cars ever built: "firefly evenings at the Bellerive Country Club [...] Forest Park, my brother's silver 'Daisy' glinting in a distant sun."[7] Bill and Mort often visited the Forest Park Highlands, a huge funfair complete with roller coaster, shooting arcades, and the penny-arcade peep shows that appear in many of Burroughs's later cut-ups. "By the way, B.J. what ever happened to Forest Park Highlands?" "It burned down, boss—hot peep shows in the penny arcade."[8]

It was at the Community School that Bill met Richard Kammerer and his older brother David, but he didn't really get to know them until they were all at John Burroughs School. Richard was the same age as Burroughs, but Bill found him rather surly. He got on better with David, who was born in 1911 and was three years older. Kammerer came from the same wealthy St. Louis background as Bill: his father was a partner in the consulting engineers Von Schrenk and Kammerer. But the real friendship began later when they admitted to each other that they were gay. David enjoyed a drink, and he was energetic, charming, and the life of any party. For years they were best friends, and later they were neighbors, first in Chicago and then in New York, where David was to meet his end. Kammerer appears to have recognized a sensitivity, a vulnerability, in the younger boy that he could relate to. Although Burroughs said that he knew he was homosexual by the time he was thirteen, his early crushes and experiments were fraught with anxiety and difficulty. "At that time I was felt by the other boys to be not quite right. You're a character, just the wrong kind."[9] He was a very insecure twelve-year-old, hovering on the brink of adolescence: "I think it was always there, at the same time being afraid of the others and apart from them, I always felt a necessity to play it cool and conceal myself. I don't know how or at what age that it occurred to me that I was of another species. It would have occurred to me of course no matter where I lived, sooner or later. I felt inferior to other people at the same time I'd feel different from them, I'd feel better than them. It was a confused feeling. I was terribly afraid of any physical conflict."[10]

Other friends met at John Burroughs included Rex Weisenberger, whose father was president of the National Association of Manufacturers. Bill often visited his home and knew his father. "He was a big fat man and successful and worked hard and right on cue dropped dead of a heart attack at fifty-five leaving his widow with the money." Bill and Rex did a trip to Europe and North Africa in 1933 and were close friends. It was at the John Burroughs School that Burroughs met his lifelong friend and the first love of his life, albeit unconsummated—Kells Elvins. Kells lived down the road from Bill on the corner of Price and Ladue Roads. "I just fell in love with him and everyone around school said, 'Well, you're his slave!'" Kells was a beautiful boy, very strong though not too athletic, with curly hair and brown eyes, "Just a beautiful kid with a terrific amount of élan. [...] I was terribly obviously, in retrospect, attracted to him. He would take me on his lap and strum me like a banjo and I'd always get a hard-on."[11] Kells was entirely heterosexual but was prepared to tolerate Bill's signs of affection, such as walking to school with his arm draped over his shoulder. Burroughs was fascinated by Kells's parents, Lorrie "Lee" and Politte Elvins, because his father, who was an attorney, was clearly suffering from Tourette's syndrome. Bill and Kells were greatly amused by Politte's verbal incontinence, his rudeness and outrageous remarks. He was manic all the time, yelling and screaming. He once dumped a scrambled egg on the head of a waitress, claiming he'd ordered it fried. He was a tiny wreck of a man yet drove everywhere at ninety miles an hour. In Burroughs's words, he was "a very crooked nasty lawyer, an anti-Semite. He said, 'You know what I like about this place is the view,' and the view was of the Jewish cemetery. He says, 'I like to see it fill up!'"[12] Elvins and Burroughs roomed together as postgraduates at Harvard. Later they went into business together as farmers in Texas, were neighbors in Mexico City, toured Morocco together, and Bill visited him in Denmark when Elvins was married to a Danish actress.

"It was Lee Elvins who said I had the look of someone who would snap or take flight," said Burroughs. "It was Lee Elvins who said, 'That kid looks like a sheep-killin' dog. He's got an evasive, mean look.'"[13] This phrase was taken up and run with by Burroughs, who used it in a number of texts. Burroughs remembered many of these cutting remarks for the rest of his life, and modified and repeated them until they were drained of venom by constant use. They made very good performance pieces. Another unkind remark, endlessly reworked by Burroughs, was made by Mrs. Senseney, the wife of the doctor who botched Bill's tonsils, when Bill was thirteen. "She was a St. Louis matron, very poised and smug, very nasty. I was thin, she said to Dave Kammerer, 'Well listen, if you want to get ahead socially, get rid of him, it's a walking corpse!' 'It's a walking corpse!' she said. I said, when I heard of her death, 'It isn't every corpse than can walk. Her's can't.' Old bitch."[14]

2. Meet the Johnson Family

A whole beguiling new world was opened up for Burroughs when he read *You Can't Win* by Jack Black, the autobiography of a former burglar, drug addict, and railroad hobo published in 1926. He had not known that such a life existed and was immediately intrigued. It had such a lasting impact upon him that he was able to quote passages verbatim fifty years later. It was set in that forgotten era between the days of the Wild West and the development of the big metropolitan cities, between the death of Jesse James and the rise of Al Capone. "It fascinated me and I thought it would be great to be a burglar. I saw all these furtive seedy rooming houses. I got so much from that book, Salt Chunk Mary was one of his characters.

The whole idea of the Johnson Family comes from there."[15] He read and reread it, indulging in an adolescent *nostalgie de la boue*, longing for this other world of cheap hotels, smoky bars, pool halls, whorehouses, and opium dens, of cat burglars and hobo jungles. He wanted to be one of the Johnson Family, the good bums and thieves with a code of honorable conduct in direct contrast to the venal, corrupt, hypocritical behavior of people like Uncle Ivy or the parents of most of his friends. He became fascinated by gangsters and romanticized them. In a naïve attempt to emulate them Bill, Kells Elvins, and a friend, Richard Cameron, broke into an abandoned factory and smashed all the windows. They were caught and the man who owned the factory made a claim for damages amounting to about fifty dollars apiece. Bill's father paid up, and Cameron's father paid, but Politte contested the amount, insisting that the factory was already in decrepit condition, getting Kells to photograph the damage, and was so obdurate that the factory owner gave up.

Bill continued to write stories, mostly lurid adventure tales of derring-do, gothic horror, or westerns that were read aloud in class. Sometimes he wrote more philosophical essays, such as his first published work, "Personal Magnetism," which appeared in the February 1929 issue of the *John Burroughs Review*, about sending two dollars for instructions on "how to control others at a glance." His interest in control systems appeared early on.

The 1927 St. Louis tornado made a big impression on him. On September 29, the sky turned black and green and Bill was standing in the entrance to the boys' locker room when he saw a bolt of lightning strike the cornice of the school, knocking off bricks. The children ran through the corridors, screaming hysterically. Then the phone calls from concerned parents began, but no one in the school was hurt. In St. Louis itself the scene was very different; seventy-nine people were killed and over 550 injured. The fronts were torn off whole rows of buildings, leaving their interiors exposed, cars were flipped over, trees uprooted, telephone poles became javelins as the tornado cut a swath through the West End. It was left looking like a scene from a Great War battlefront, with houses reduced to rubble and tram lines twisted into bizarre sculptures. James Grauerholz points out that tornadoes appear throughout Burroughs's later work, "usually with a frisson of sexual excitement."[16]

That year Bill attended summer camp at Los Alamos with Mort, and they all made a family trip to France, staying in Paris, then spending two weeks in Cannes on the Riviera. Bill enjoyed himself immensely. It was his first trip abroad. The next year they remained in the States, with a family holiday in a rented house on the beach near La Jolla, California, and an extended period at the family summer cabin in St. Albans. As well as fishing, Bill was also keen on hunting for food: shooting quail or duck that he was going to eat was not a problem for him. Burroughs loved his food, and his books are filled with descriptions of meals and feasts: the fish he caught in Lake Huron; the preparation of a dish; how Virginia ham comes from hogs fed on peanuts; caviar. He became something of a gourmet.

Bill and all of his friends had chemistry sets, wooden boxes with little compartments filled with chemicals. He would pour ammonia over iodide crystals to make ammonium iodide. This compound, when it dries, is so sensitive that a fly will explode it. "I remember how I used to while away the long 1920's afternoons with sugar sprinkled around little heaps of ammonium iodide waiting for the flies to explode in little puffs of purple vapor."[17] Bill and his friends all made black powder, which they would put in boxes and throw, causing a loud explosion. When he was fourteen, he was at work in the basement of Price Road and had carefully packed a mixture of potassium chlorate and red phosphorus into a box. He was putting the top on when the friction caused the chemicals to explode, shredding his left hand. His father, who was working with his tools in the next room, rushed in, quickly wrapped his hand in a cloth, and drove him straight to the nearest hospital emergency room in University City. He was operated on by Dr. Masters, who spent two hours carefully removing the wooden splinters from his damaged hand. The injury was so serious that Bill remained in hospital for six weeks with his hands bandaged; in the days before penicillin there was a terrible danger of infection, which could have resulted in gangrene and amputation. Changing the dressings was terribly painful. Bill's father came to see him every day. It was a bad injury, and Bill was exempt from gym and athletics for a year. Dr. Masters told Bill's parents that he had given him "nearly an adult dose of morphine," something that stuck in Bill's mind.

The explosion and hospitalization transformed Bill from being a very talkative boy to a very reserved one; a profound character change. This change suggests that six weeks of enforced idleness and boredom brought about a sudden self-awareness; most people have an adolescent epiphany, a conscious moment when they realize they are the person looking through their eyes at the world, that they are on a small planet revolving in the middle of infinity. Being alone in hospital appears to have undermined Bill's unconditional acceptance of the all-encompassing bourgeois value system he grew up with. Suddenly finding himself outside it showed it was fallible and not permanent, fixed. He was alone with his thoughts, his experience of the green reindeer and his visions. He became afraid of the dark and kept a pair of brass knuckle dusters beneath his pillow at night. He always had sinus trouble and when he had a fever often saw animals in the wall; Laura thought nothing of this because she also had fever visions. In Burroughs's own cosmology, the damage to his hand would have provided an entry port for the Ugly Spirit. Self-awareness came with recognition of the Ugly Spirit. It was, incidentally, the same hand that he later mutilated by cutting off part of his finger in a psychotic episode.

The family had enjoyed themselves so much on their 1927 visit to France that in 1929 they did it again, in greater style. After staying in a luxury hotel in Paris they hired a touring car and a chauffeur and visited the sights. They toured the châteaux of the Loire, which Bill found boring, though some of them had moats where he could fish while his parents inspected the staterooms. They drove through the high Pyrenees and across to the Riviera, where they spent two weeks in a grand hotel on the Croisette in Cannes, where all Bill had to do was cross the road to the beach. He used to hire a kayak and row out to sea. In the evening they dined at all the expensive gourmet restaurants.

Bill and Mort had attended the Los Alamos Ranch School summer camp for three years running, 1925, 1926, and 1927, so the school pitched for them to attend full-time. The director, Albert James Connell, spent much of his vacations traveling the country, meeting with parents, hoping to persuade them of the benefits of sending their boys to his rugged, outdoor-life school, which also happened to be the most expensive school in the United States: $2,400 a year, double the cost of the prestigious eastern schools. After three summers, Connell knew Bill's parents quite well, which must be how he came to be left at Price Road with Bill when he was in St. Louis recruiting. Burroughs remembered an extraordinary story, which we must assume is true: "I was left in the rather dubious company of Mr. Connell. He says, 'I'd like to see this gibbon stripped!' In my own house. Nobody was there." Bill obediently went to his room and took off his clothes. "God, it's enough to make you puke when you think back on it." Bill got a hard-on. "He wanted me to get a hard-on, so I did. He then says, 'Do you play with it gibbon? Do you play with it till it goes off?' and all this creepy talk, oh my God. He made no effort to touch my prick or anything like that. 'Well, have you ever done this with other boys?' And I hadn't. But I remember after he left and everything, that I was thinking that idea of doing it with other boys would seem to me the most exciting thing. I remember I was coming back [from school] and I was walking up the hill and I got a hard-on thinking about it."[18]

In the summer of 1930, Bill, his father, and a guide made a canoe trip in Minnesota, up near the Canadian border, crossing through lakes, back and forth across the border, which was not controlled in those days, just fishing for bass and pike, exploring and seeing the sights. They continued on to Missoula, Montana, where they met up with some of Mote's friends from St. Louis and then took a pack trip up into the mountains, once again with a guide, fly-fishing for Dolly Varden, a large salmon trout.[19] Bill caught them up to six pounds. The fishing was too easy, since the streams had not been fished; he threw in his line and pulled out a fish. The limit then was twenty-five a day. He and his father built a smokehouse and smoked some of their catch, they had so many. Then, at the end of the summer, Bill was enrolled in Los Alamos Ranch School. He was sixteen.

Chapter Four

Far away and high on the mesa's crest. Here's the life that all of us love the best. Los Al-amos.

—Los Alamos Ranch School song

1. "I Know What's Best for Boys!"

"Boys become men more easily when separated from oversolicitous mothers" was the motto of Ashley Pond, who founded the Los Alamos Ranch School in 1917. Pond believed that the rough outdoor life was just what the pampered children of the rich needed. He was succeeded by Albert James Connell, known to everyone as "the Boss," who recognized that these boys were not destined to be farmhands but to run the large prestigious corporations that their fathers owned, and that consequently the school should prepare them for the top universities. The boys stopped doing all the manual labor and staff was brought in to do it. Lawrence Hitchcock ran the academic program and Connell took care of business, recruitment, discipline, and field expeditions such as the overnight excursions to the high valleys and full-day Saturday trips. Connell discouraged married teachers—he wanted an all-male society—however, Pond's daughter Peggy and her husband, the science teacher Fermor Church, lived there with their three children. Half the day was taken up by studies and the other half by scouting activities. Many of Connell's ideas were taken on board by Burroughs, such as that there was no such thing as an accident: if something went wrong, it was someone's fault, probably yours. As an adult Burroughs found amusement in Connell's frequently used line, "I know what's best for boys!"

Every month all the boys were subject to naked physical examinations in the nurse's office by two of the teachers. They were weighed and measured to see how much they had grown and to check their muscle tone. Connell took a close personal interest in this and was almost always there to supervise, touching their arms, chests, and buttocks though never anywhere else. His sexual interest in boys was generally recognized by the

41

staff and boys, and many of the masters were concerned by it.¹ "A closet queer, not so goddamn closet either. A. J. Connell. Confirmed bachelor my dear, confirmed. He had decided that this was all wrong. But he was very superior for having these tendencies and not giving in to them,"² Burroughs opined.

When they arrived at Lamy, New Mexico, the boys were met by the school station wagon and driven across the arroyo and up the switchback turns of the bumpy dirt road cut into the solid tuff of the canyon, emerging eventually on the Los Alamos mesa like something in a western movie. Los Alamos is named after the few cottonwood trees that manage to grow on the Pajarito Plateau (it translates as "little bird"), part of the volcanic Jemez mountain range. Gore Vidal, who attended Los Alamos ten years after Burroughs, wrote, "As they approached the top of the mesa, the road became narrow and rocky. Tall juniper bushes on every side and the air sage-scented."³ The station wagon bumped across the desert, finally arriving at the Big House, a large three-story pine-log structure with a high roof and a veranda supported by smooth round wooden columns. In the distance the Sangre de Cristo Mountains glowed red in the lowering sun.

New arrivals were weighed and inspected by Connell, who assigned them by size and physical development to one of the four patrols, Piñon, Juniper, Fir, and Spruce (older boys); forty-four boys altogether in khaki Boy Scout shirts and short shorts. There were three sleeping verandas on the top floor of the Big House, unheated roofless terraces where the boys slept all year round, with removable awnings that could be lowered in case of rain or snow and screens around them to stop wind. The nights were cool in summer but freezing in winter. There were shower stalls on the ground and third floor, but the boys dressed as soon as they got up and showered later, usually after being outside all day. There was just one toilet on each floor. Connell, Hitchcock, and a number of the other masters had rooms on the second floor of Fuller Lodge, but an unmarried master usually slept on each of the three porches with the boys. He did, however, have an adjoining room to retreat to if he required privacy. Bill had a room that he shared with another boy in Spruce cottage with a sleeping porch attached, but sometimes up to eight boys could be sleeping on the porch.

Lessons were held on the ground floor of the Big House. The ground floor of Fuller Lodge housed the kitchen and large dining room, one end of which had a stage for theatrical productions. Once a year they performed a Gilbert and Sullivan operetta, which called for considerable rehearsal and stage work. Burroughs played the lead role of A. E. Scott-Fortescue, "the Toff," in *A Night at an Inn* by Lord Dunsany. He particularly enjoyed it because he had to flourish his .32 revolver and act the hard man. Occasionally the room was cleared and the girls from Santa Fe's Brownmoor School for Girls or from Bishop's Lodge were invited up for a dance. There was a trading post that sold clothes, ammo, toiletries, and candy: Milky Way, Baby Ruth, Oh Henry!, Hershey Bars and Mars Bars and Denver Maid, chocolate with a pink crème center. O'Connell ordered Life Savers for the whole school by mail.

The Big House and Fuller Lodge were surrounded by ground staff quarters for the forty or more workers at the school, a huge barn, a guesthouse, huts and storage sheds, and the corrals that stabled the sixty riding and ten workhorses that served the ranch. Each boy had a horse assigned to him. On riding days they had to catch their horse—Bill had a strawberry roan—saddle it up, and curry it down afterward. Burroughs often rode bareback "just for laziness. [...] I could stay on, riding along, galloping, trying to hang on to the horse. I fell off a couple of times."[4] There was a ski lift and in the winter months they did ski-oring, towed behind a horse like waterskiing except on snow. Bill liked that.

The school day began at 6:30 a.m.,[5] and at 6:45 sharp the boys did calisthenics on the exercise field outside, push-ups and jumps; if it had been snowing Connell always made sure the field was shoveled clear. If you wanted to get up earlier and work that was permitted. Breakfast was at 7:00 a.m., then beds were made according to Connell's strict regulations. Classes were from 7:40 a.m. until 1:00 p.m. Study hall was at 5:00 p.m., followed by dinner at 6:00, more study, and early to bed. Sometimes movies were shown in the Big House after dinner. A priest would come and talk to them on Sundays in the main lodge. The school library was equipped with the complete Yale Shakespeare, one volume for each play, and all the standard classics.

English, French, Latin, history, mathematics, and chemistry were taught at a number of different levels, and each of the forty-six boys had an individually determined timetable according to his age and ability. Lawrence Hitchcock taught Latin; he was a traditionalist who believed that Latin was essential for speaking and writing English. Fermor Church taught algebra; he was a good teacher but Bill had a blind spot against it. Someone named Waring taught French, but didn't really know the language. The English teachers changed frequently; one named Mr. Chase taught Browning, Shakespeare, David Hume, and the classics. "I was very into it." Bill would escape to his room, light incense, lean against the radiator, play records, and read the Haldeman-Julius Little Blue Books: Guy de Maupassant, Anatole France, Remy de Gourmont, Baudelaire, Oscar Wilde's *Dorian Gray*, and others. Periodically Connell would come around and confiscate some of them as being unfit to read. "Insufferable man!"[6]

Lunch at 1:00 p.m. was the main meal, followed by a half-hour siesta. The food was homegrown and extremely healthy; they had a big vegetable garden and Bill particularly liked a cornmeal cereal made from blue corn. They kept chickens to eat and for their eggs and there was a dairy that provided both milk and fresh beef. They kept their own pigs. Bill recalled throwing them a dead rabbit, of which they ate every morsel. On Monday afternoon the boys mostly did maintenance work, "community service," rolling the tennis courts, weeding the garden. The boys had to do one hundred hours during their time there, which Burroughs thought was pointless. He thought the Mexican staff should do the jobs. The other weekday afternoons were spent on horseback riding and athletics, sports such as boxing or tennis. Or the boys could go to the range and shoot. Bill arranged shooting expeditions. He had a .32 Smith & Wesson with a four-inch barrel that he bought secondhand from a mail-order catalog for fifteen dollars when he was fifteen. Anyone could order guns through the mail. Other boys had .25 automatics, .22 Woodsmans, and one boy had a .38 Colt Long. There was not a lot of interest in shooting, but Bill was usually able to get a group of four or five boys to go out. The guns were kept in a locked drawer in the counselor's room but ammo could be bought from the trading post.

On Saturday the whole school went on an all-day horseback excursion starting at 8:00 a.m. When they reached their destination they cooked their meals in groups of two or three, usually steak and baked potatoes with blueberry jam and bread. Connell had his methods, and if anyone used anything other than glowing coals and got soot on their mess tins from an open flame there was trouble. They were taught to toast marshmallows to a golden brown but never let them catch fire.[7]

The trips were sometimes extended to an overnight camping expedition to Camp May, up near the Jemez crest, the men and boys leading a trail of ranch hands with a mule train of tents and supplies. Connell ran around screaming and hollering at the boys as they attempted to erect their tents, hindering more than helping. At night, seated around a roaring campfire, Connell would lead the storytelling and singing. In the mountains there were deer, black bear, coyote, raccoons, skunks, and gophers, and a few mountain lions and rattlesnakes. Bill used a box trap to catch animals, and had several chipmunks for pets. Sometimes there were swimming parties to hot springs and to the nearby Rio Grande, but the boys generally resisted such trips because Connell liked to share a bed with the prettiest boy and had been known to make advances to them.

Despite the school's location, Native American history was not on the syllabus. In front of Fuller Lodge were the visible remains of an eight-hundred-year-old Pueblo Indian ruin, but it was not excavated until after Burroughs's time there. Sometimes the Indians from San Ysidro were invited to the ranch to perform their traditional dances, dressed in their totemic eagle costumes, but the school did not include their story in their history studies. Burroughs always thought it was a missed opportunity that the school did not teach the Spanish language or Mexican cooking, as the ground staff would have made good teachers and the chefs were all Latinos.

In February, not long after his seventeenth birthday, his mother came to visit and took Bill and a school friend into Santa Fe for a day's outing. In his avid study of gangster books Bill had come across knockout drops—chloral hydrate—and managed to slip, undetected, into a drugstore and buy some. A few days later he took an almost lethal dose and finished up in the school infirmary. His explanation was simply that he wanted to see how it worked. It was his first investigation of mind-altering drugs, albeit a very crude one.

There was one strange episode where Bill hanged one of the teachers in effigy. Henry Bosworth was the algebra teacher, a heavyset sergeant type with very intense, hypnotic brown eyes. He hated Bill on sight even though Bill was not in his class. It manifested in many small ways. On a mountain walk they disturbed a yellowjackets' nest and Bill was stung four times on his back. Bosworth had medicine for insect stings in his backpack but would not help him. Once at shooting practice, Bill hit the target and Bosworth didn't. Bosworth was always insulting Bill, calling him a "worthless little punk." Bill hung a two-foot-high plaster-of-Paris figure of a Boy Scout by a noose over the fireplace with a sign saying, "Bozzy bitch goddamn him!" Before Bill's guilt was detected, Bosworth was dismissed: he had been fooling around with three brothers, and they reported him to Connell. Bill once saw his cock sticking out of his pajamas when he was roughhousing with another boy. He had to go. Connell finally found out that the effigy was by Bill and summoned him to the office. He said it might have been grounds for expulsion, but queried, "Why did you have to make it so vulgar?"

Twice a week Connell made trips to Santa Fe and the specially chosen would accompany him, usually the older children of the richest parents, who could act as drivers. They would stay at the Hotel La Fonda, the adobe-style inn on the plaza. During one of these trips Bill wrote a pulp fiction story on hotel notepaper. It concerned four jolly murderers:

A middle aged couple very brash and jolly...

"Sure on I'd kill my own grandmother just for a little kale."

"We have regular rates of course..." the woman observed tartly.

A soft plump pearl gray man stands there with a sickly smile. He is flanked by a skull face Mexican also smiling.[8]

The Mexican reappeared years later as Tio Mate in *The Wild Boys*. Other characters were developed: there was a vicious old tycoon who kept pretending to die and listening to what people said about him, then leaping up out of bed and cutting people out of his will. The old tycoon later became Mr. Hart in *Ah Puch Is Here*. Bill read Oscar Wilde's *The Picture of Dorian Gray* and "soon languid young aristocrats were making epigrams on my pages."[9]

Bill had a crush on one of the other boys, William Russell Fawcett: "you align yourselves to people you feel attracted to in some way or another. He was [nice-looking] he had pimples, I find pimples quite attractive. [...] we did actually jack off together under the sheets with flashlights on. [...] Then he said that he thought that this was all wrong. He said 'I think you are going to be the sort of person that will be revolted by a naked woman.' He finally got to hating me completely. [...] You see with boys like Kells and Russell Fawcett when I was attracted to them, I became extremely subservient and actually made myself an object of contempt to the boy. For being so much more interested in him than he was in me. Abject. It was horrid! It was horrible, I don't blame them."[10]

In the end it was Fawcett who was the cause of Burroughs leaving the school. Bill had known he was homosexual since he was thirteen, but didn't know how to do anything about it as he seemed attracted to heterosexual boys. Burroughs wrote that he "formed a romantic attachment for one of the boys at Los Alamos and kept a diary of this affair that was to put me off writing for many years. Even now I blush to remember its contents."[11] Home for the Easter vacation in 1931, he convinced his family that his feet were giving him pain. They were unusually long, and later when he lived in London he had shoes specially made to fit him. He managed to persuade his parents to let him stay home. He then told his mother that he felt miserable because he had a fixation on a boy at school and the boy had become "very hostile." He was very unhappy there and just wanted to leave. His mother was terribly upset and traveled to New Mexico with Bill to talk to Connell about it. Connell agreed that it would be best if Bill withdrew from the school. He left two months early, after staying on long enough to appear in a dramatic production he had rehearsed.

Laura was very understanding about it, but to her homosexuality was a terrible, frightening illness. She said, "We'll send you to a doctor who will fix this up. We'll spend every penny if necessary!" They got back to St. Louis and she sent Bill to a psychiatrist friend of theirs, Dr. Sidney Schwab, for a psychiatric evaluation. "We talked a little bit about the Greeks and decided that it wasn't to be taken too seriously, and he assured my mother that it was a phase and that I would grow out of it. He was a nice enough old man."[12]

This first encounter with the official opprobrium toward homosexuality from school, family, and the object of his affection unnerved Burroughs and contributed to his future secrecy about his sexual inclinations: the development of his persona as *el hombre invisible* was all to do with his fear of exposure and his horror of being the object of contempt and ridicule. The school packed his things, including the incriminating diary, and sent them to him. "I used to turn cold thinking that maybe the boys are reading it aloud to each other. When the box finally arrived I pried it open and threw everything out until I found the diary and destroyed it forthwith without a glance at the appalling pages. [...] The act of writing had become embarrassing, disgusting, and above all, false. It was not the sex in the diary that embarrassed me it was the terrible falsity of the emotions expressed. The sight of my words on a page sickened me and this continued until 1938. I had written myself an eight year sentence."[13]

Bill's two years at Los Alamos made a huge impression upon him, featuring in many of his utopian fantasies about all-male societies, particularly in *The Wild Boys*. After Bill left the school, Connell visited St. Louis and they had dinner. Some years later Bill drove out to Santa Fe and spent several days on the ranch; old boys were always welcome. The school came to an abrupt end, however. One spring morning in 1942 a small reconnaissance aircraft circled around and around the ranch. Connell knew something was up, as only the military could afford to use that much aircraft fuel in wartime. Then they received two visitors: Dr. J. Robert Oppenheimer and General Leslie Groves carrying a set of plans. The school was requisitioned, sentries were posted all around, and a team of scientists moved in. It was at Los Alamos that the atomic bomb was invented. "It seemed so right somehow," wrote Burroughs.[14]

Back in St. Louis Bill spent two months at the Evans Tutoring school. That summer he went on a fishing holiday with his father and older brother, which he assumed was intended to make him more "manly." In fact, this was an activity Burroughs loved, and not just on vacation. He would sometimes tag along with a group of rabbit hunters often including his brother, Mort. Max Putzel, one of the group, remembered, "One evening, we drove down to an estate in the Ozarks in an ancient Cadillac town car likewise belonging to a prosperous St. Louis attorney, the father of our host. Avid for sport, we were armed not only with shotguns but with assorted target pistols and drove merrily down the mud highways, stopping from time to time to drink from a large tea kettle of sour wine known as 'Dago red.' We pulled up at a tavern near Kimmswick, unaware that it had been the scene of a hold-up a few days earlier. Unwilling to leave our weapons in the car, we toted them along—five boys with guns, puzzled at the hostility of the host and customers at the bar. The only game we encountered that weekend were two miserable possums treed the next night and happily presented to a tenant farmer partial to fatty meat. The shotguns accounted for one rattlesnake and, I believe, a copperhead cornered near the entrance to a cave."[15]

In the fall of 1931 Burroughs started at the Taylor School. Edgar Curtis "Joe" Taylor was a faculty member of Washington University in St. Louis and saw the need for a small private school for boys that would parallel the East Coast preparatory schools. In 1930 he opened the Taylor School in a fourteen-room house on North Central Avenue to teach grades six through twelve. At its maximum capacity the school had fifty students, and gave individual tuition with classes limited to four or five students per class. It had only been open a year when Burroughs joined. He was not impressed by Taylor. "He was a Rhodes scholar, real bumptious. I didn't like him at all, he was a hustler. But the school was alright, he got some good teachers in." Taylor employed staff from Washington University, including an excellent English teacher called Jellinek who had a deep understanding of literature and was able to communicate it to Burroughs. Thanks to him Burroughs was able to quote at length from Milton, Wordsworth, and Shakespeare throughout his life. "He was a terrifically good teacher. He told me once, 'I know you despise Joe Taylor, I can see it in your face,' but he said, 'Don't despise him, he's hooked, he's got a wife and kids, don't you understand?'"[16] Bill got good grades on the college board and graduated in the spring of 1932 and was able to go on to Harvard.

Even then Burroughs saw beyond the surface of things, and sensed the dread beneath the veneer. Years later he wrote, "When I lived in St. Louis and drove home past the bare clay of subdivided lots, here and there houses set down on platforms of concrete in the mud, play-houses of children who look happy and healthy but empty horror and panic in clear gray-blue eyes, and when I drove by the subdivisions always felt impact in stomach of final loneliness and despair."[17]

2. Billy Bradshinkel

After a summer in Majorca with the family, where Bill enjoyed some serious swimming and diving, he went up to Harvard. Prohibition was still in force when Bill arrived, and he and his friends used to make bathtub gin. Grain alcohol was not hard to get and you just bought flavorings to add to it, usually "gin" (juniper berry juice) or "whiskey," and added water. The results were terrible, but drinkable if you added plenty of soda or quinine water or mixed it with fruit juice. Prohibition was repealed on December 5, 1933, with the passage of the Twenty-First Amendment. There had been plenty of speakeasies in St. Louis, one of which held special memories for Bill: "I remembered a prohibition era road house of my adolescence and the taste of gin rickeys in a mid west summer. (Oh my God! And the August moon in a violet sky and Billy Bradshinkel's cock. How sloppy can you get?) [...] P.S. Billy Bradshinkel got to be such a nuisance I finally had to kill him."[18]

James Grauerholz has provided persuasive proof that Billy Bradshinkel was in reality Prynne Hoxie, Bill's first cousin, neighbor, and his best friend at John Burroughs School.[19] The dates fit, as does Burroughs's use of the material. It is a convincing portrait of eighteen-year-old Burroughs's confused emotional state as he grows into manhood and prepares for Harvard.

The first time was in my model A after the Spring prom. Billy with his pants down to his ankles and his tuxedo shirt still on, and jissom all over the car seat. Later I was holding his arm while he vomited in the car headlights, looking young and petulant with his blond hair mussed standing there in the warm Spring wind. Then we got back in the car and turned the lights off and I said, "Let's again."

And he said, "No we shouldn't."

And I said, "Why not?" and by then he was excited too so we did it again, and I ran my hands over his back under his tuxedo shirt and held him against me and felt the long baby hairs of his smooth cheek against mine and he went to sleep there and it was getting light when we drove home.

After that in the car several times and one time his family was away and we took off all our clothes and afterwards I watched him sleeping like a baby with his mouth a little open.

[...]

I remember the last time I saw Billy was in October of that year. One of those sparkling blue days you get in the Ozarks in Autumn. We had driven out into the country to hunt squirrels with my .22 single shot, and walked through the autumn woods without seeing anything to shoot at and Billy was silent and sullen and we sat on a log and Billy looked at his shoes and finally told me he couldn't see me again (notice I am sparing you the falling leaves).

"But why Billy? Why?"

"Well if you don't know I can't explain it to you. Let's go back to the car."

We drove back in silence and when we came to his house he opened the door and got out. He looked at me for a second as if he was going to say something then turned abruptly and walked up the flagstone path to his house. I sat there for a minute looking at the closed door. Then I drove home feeling numb. When the car was stopped in the garage I put my head down on the wheel sobbing and rubbing my cheek against the steel spokes. Finally Mother called to me from an upstairs window was anything wrong and why didn't I come in the house. So I wiped the tears off my face and went in and said I was sick and went upstairs to bed. Mother brought me a bowl of milk toast on a tray but I couldn't eat any and cried all night.

After that I called Billy several times on the phone but he always hung up when he heard my voice. And I wrote him a long letter which he never answered. Three months later when I read in the paper he had been killed in a car wreck and Mother said, "Oh that's the Bradshinkel boy. You used to be such good friends didn't you?"

I said, "Yes Mother" not feeling anything at all.

Prynne had been killed in the early hours of Monday, December 17, in New York City when the car he was in swerved to avoid wet trolley tracks and struck a pillar. There were four other Princeton students in the car. Later that day, Bill's father cabled Harvard to ask that his son be excused from classes for three days, December 19–21, to attend Prynne's funeral in St. Louis on Thursday, December 20, 1934.

Homosexuality was so forbidden that many people, like Bill's grandmother, had never even heard of it. His sense of alienation and being different put him into a mental turmoil. He didn't know "why I couldn't go out and get boys, which I didn't at all...I just somehow didn't know how to do it! It wasn't a question of being forbidden. I was scared of everything, practically, and no wonder."[20]

Chapter Five

Veritas

1. Harvard

It was the done thing for someone of Burroughs's class and background to go to Harvard, but he had not reckoned with the attitude of the boys from the East Coast prep schools who wanted nothing to do with him. He was unable to get into a club; "those were a very snobbish thing, they were all people from the eastern prep schools. They got into the clubs and other people didn't and that was that."[1] He could have involved himself in the Harvard *Advocate*, the *Lampoon*, or the *Crimson*, the daily student newspaper, but chose not to, nor did he join the Dramatic Club. The 1932 Harvard academic year began on September 25. Burroughs lived at Straus dormitory in room D-41, a new block in Old Yard, overlooking Massachusetts Avenue and Harvard Square. The suites had wood-burning living room fireplaces and the use of a mahogany-paneled common room furnished with leather armchairs and oriental rugs. It was a world away from the Ranch School's outdoor bedrooms. He ate at the Freshman Commons and joined the Harvard Coop to buy his books and equipment. Freshmen were required to do at least one afternoon a week of athletic activity. Burroughs did swimming and individual sculling. He loved swimming; he was buoyant and able to lie still in the water without sinking. He complained that there was nowhere to do target practice, but he could have joined the Harvard Rifle Club, which had facilities for pistol shooting at their Walnut Hill Range in Woburn.[2] He sometimes saw movies, still mostly silent, such as Charles Chaplin's *The Floorwalker*, at the large Common Room of the Freshman Union. Mostly he spent his time reading until the Widener Library closed at six.

Burroughs delved into witchcraft and Tibetan tantricism and read numerous books on the subject. His professor, George Lyman Kittredge, had published *Witchcraft in Old and New England* three years before, and Burroughs also read his *Notes on Witchcraft* (1907). "I was interested in any kind of witchcraft and the occult to learn more about my own visions. If your totem animal is a deer, this will be revealed in a vision of a deer. Now that means for one thing you're not allowed to kill the totem animal. Technically you shouldn't eat the totem animal, but I have eaten venison frequently, but I would never kill a deer. My other vision was of little men playing in the blockhouse. I think of these in cinematographic terms: one is slow-down, and one is speed-up. The little men were moving fast, speeded-up; the deer was in that slow-down medium."[3] He read *The Tibetan Book of the Dead* in the W. Y. Evans-Wentz translation and Sir John Woodroffe's translation of the *Mahanirvana Tantra*. His mother had introduced him to the Buddhist concept of the Four Noble Truths in their long talks together (she later gave him her copy of *Siddhartha* by Hermann Hesse, published in 1951). He was years ahead of Ginsberg and Kerouac in his study of Buddhism, but though he was interested in many of the ideas, he rejected Buddhism as requiring too much scholarly study for an individual from a Western background. He studied astrology and took up yoga, sometimes locking himself in his room for several days. Friends heard him mumbling to himself, and Bill told Bill Gilmore it was subvocal speech, part of his yoga training. He had a French book describing various forms of torture and delighted in shocking people with it and explaining in detail what went on in medieval torture chambers. Many of the Radcliffe women found this objectionable.

The biggest subject of debate on campus at the time was communism and the "Russian experiment"; all the Harvard bookshops were filled with books about it. The idea never appealed to Burroughs at all; in fact, as he put it, "I was never tempted by any political program. [. . .] I don't want to hear about the fucking masses and I never did."[4]

Burroughs was an English major. He graduated with honors and got an A in every course. "I've never seen a course that I couldn't pass the exams with an A after three days' study. My technique was to memorize certain sections so I could quote them verbatim. So there was just nothing to it when it came to getting ready for an exam, it was a snap."[5] He went to hardly any lectures, nor was he required to attend classes. He was taught ethnology by Carlton Coombe, who concentrated on the most sensational things like homosexuality and anything of a violent nature to make his lessons entertaining. Burroughs thought Professor Greenhaup's lectures on seventeenth-century literature were the dullest he had ever heard, but went to everything by John Livingston Lowes, who wrote *The Road to Xanadu*. Another professor whose lectures he found to be a real pleasure was the young Bartlett Jere Whiting, who taught his Chaucer course. "He was marvelous!" Burroughs attended Kittredge's lectures on Shakespeare

and delighted at his showmanship: Kittredge started his class on the dot
and did not tolerate coughing or sneezing. At the end of a talk he would
come down from the platform, still talking, and deliver his last lines from
the door just as the bell rang. Kittredge assigned a lot to be learned by
heart, several hundred lines for an exam, and Burroughs remembered
them all his life. When he published *The Exterminator* in 1960, he provided an epigram for the title page. Though misquoting (not corrected by
the publisher), he pulled from memory an apposite line from *The Rehearsal*
by George Villiers, Second Duke of Buckingham, published in 1672.

T. S. Eliot was the Charles Eliot Norton Professor of Poetry during
1932–33 and delivered eight lectures under the general title "The Use
of Poetry and the Use of Criticism." Burroughs attended one of them.
"He had a very conservative attitude but well presented, and he was quite
humorous and knew how to talk. Very dignified, very decorous, he gave
teas every week that were open to the undergraduates as part of his duties,
but for some reason I never went."

Harvard could have been a lonely place; it was possible to stay in your
rooms and be completely isolated. Fortunately Bill knew a half dozen or
more people. At Harvard he was reunited with Kells Elvins, who had
gone from the John Burroughs School to the University of Missouri and
then transferred to Harvard. But Kells was living off campus; he had married a red-haired woman named Brick ("Brick top") Orwig after getting
her pregnant, and the couple lived with their son, Peter. Several of Bill's
other classmates from John Burroughs were also there, including Jay Rice,
who also went to Los Alamos and whose parents owned a large department store in St. Louis; and Eugene Angert, a beautiful fragile boy who
became a hopeless schizophrenic. Angert had already begun to display
the symptoms that would eventually hospitalize him. He was sent to the
Blaine Sanatorium outside Boston, where Burroughs visited him several
times, but by then his conversation did not make much sense and he gig-
gled compulsively.

Bill's brother, Mort, also arrived at Harvard. He had gone to Princeton
and studied architecture in Paris before taking an architecture course at
Harvard. Bill saw him once a week for dinner. "Mort was much more
interesting in those days, he even read some. We talked about Freud and
neurosis and psychoanalysis, things like that. But as time went on he
became less and less interested in anything. Morose, sort of sullen. Not
at all fun."[6] Bill's friends called his brother Glum Burroughs because he
was so dour. Mort graduated but never practiced architecture. He married Miggie when he was twenty-three, got a job with Emerson Electric
in St. Louis as a draftsman working initially on the B-17 Flying Fortress

bomber aircraft, and stayed there for the rest of his life until he retired. "My brother is a cipher, a blank, a zero. We had some talks about the past and about this nurse that we had together and things like that, but if I ever got close to anything that would mean anything he would immediately break off the conversation."[7] Mort had no small talk and little sense of humor; nothing seemed to really interest him except his family and fishing. "He was a pretty square, regular sort of a guy, so we didn't have all that much in common. He couldn't read my books."[8]

In 1933 Bill was still adjusting to his new surroundings. He read Kafka and continued his studies of tantra and witchcraft. That summer his parents permitted—and paid for—him to go on his first trip to Europe without them. He was accompanied by his friend David Kammerer, whom he had known from the Community School and the Burroughs School and who was now at Washington University in St. Louis. Kammerer was three years older and presumably trusted to take care of Bill. They went to England and to Paris and had a great time. Bill knew that Kammerer was gay, and Bill had probably revealed his own interest in men to Kammerer. One of their subjects of conversation was Kammerer's obsession with an *apache* they met at a bar on the rue de Lappe, probably at La Boule Rouge at number 8, where knife-wielding young petty criminals liked to gather, plying for trade with tourists. His attraction is unlikely to have been reciprocated, given the vigorous heterosexuality of most *apaches*, though money may have exchanged hands. Bill and David were not lovers; it was a friendship based on mutual experience and interests, and Bill enjoyed being with him because Kammerer had a great sense of humor and was always fun to be with. While in Paris Bill added a few items to his arsenal, including a sword cane and a shotgun cane that fired deadly .410 cartridges.

For his sophomore year, Burroughs moved to Adams House, one of the private "Gold Coast" dormitories built around 1900 to provide luxurious accommodation for Harvard undergraduates. Russell, the block containing the dining rooms, kitchen, library, and common room, was not completed until 1932, just before Bill moved in. Unlike most of the dormitory blocks, Adams had multiple, unguarded entries, making it difficult to enforce the college's strict nightly curfews, and was therefore a desirable place to have rooms. He was required to eat two meals a day in house. Most halls shared central kitchens, but Adams had its own, as well as a reputation for the best food on campus. This was not the view of Burroughs, with his epicurian tastes, but he could do little about it.

Bill sometimes drove to New York to see Rex Weisenberger, his friend from John Burroughs. That summer, 1934, Bill planned to go down to Mexico with Rex, who was at Yale. That trip did not work out and instead they went to Paris together and then down to Algiers. It was then that Bill found out that Rex was gay. "We wouldn't make it together, he was not my type."[9] They continued on into the Sahara. It was summer and so hot and dry that they couldn't drink hard liquor and instead drank enormous beers called *Formidables*. They went as far south as Touggourt in the desert, spent one day there, and returned to Biskra. Next they stayed at a little place in the mountains, which was a relief because it was cool. From there they traveled to Malta, where they split up and Rex returned to the States. In Malta Burroughs read a German newspaper report of how Hitler came upon Ernst Röhm, the *Sturmabteilung* chief of staff, "in a disgusting position." The story read: "A shameful sight greeted the eyes of the Führer, there was Röhm with his *Lustknabe*—his pleasure boy." That June 30 was the Night of the Long Knives, when Hitler purged the entire leadership of the SA, murdering eighty-five or more members, including Röhm, and arresting thousands. Bill's normal indifference to politics was breached by the homosexual element in the story.

By now Bill was beginning to make friends at Harvard. He met James Le Baron Boyle, who was also studying English and who later went to the Sorbonne and got his PhD with a thesis on Proust. He was a member of the *Advocate* team. He had a big red Irish face, full lips with crooked teeth, and smoked a pipe. He had developed a number of idiosyncratic manner-isms, all designed to amuse and entertain. He claimed to descend from royalty, but his mother was a cleaning woman. He was gay and Burroughs went to bed with him once, but not until after Harvard. Boyle's mother wouldn't let Bill in the house because she thought he was sinister.

About a year after getting to know Boyle, Burroughs met Richard Stern, of the Stern investment bank family, who was at Harvard Business School. Although it was illegal to have a gun in Massachusetts, the Harvard authorities never searched the students' rooms and Burroughs had with him the .32 Smith & Wesson revolver that he had bought at Los Alamos. Not long after their meeting, Richard Stern and Burroughs were both drunk in Bill's rooms and Bill began waving his gun around. He pointed it at Richard's stomach, some three feet away, and pulled the trigger, sure that it was not loaded. Fortunately Stern was in the fencing club, and as soon as Bill pointed the gun he turned to the side. The gun went off, blowing a hole in the wall. It was a close thing. Another time, Bill invited Stern over for a drink and James Boyle was already there visit-ing. Bill introduced them and they hit it off right away and became lov-ers. James had no money but Richard had plenty. They lived together at

Harvard and on and off the rest of their lives, spending summers together and making foreign trips. Boyle turned up in Tangier in the fifties when Burroughs was there and spent two weeks.

Through Stern, Bill met the Honourable Graham Eyres-Monsell,[10] whose father was then the First Lord of the Admiralty. He was nine years older than Burroughs (born in 1905) and doing postgraduate studies at the Harvard Business School. "Ears" was the social arbiter of the queer set at Harvard, such as it was, and he knew everyone on the international gay scene: Somerset Maugham, Noël Coward, Dwight Fiske. Burroughs saw him with Baron Wolfner in Budapest in 1936 and later in Tangier with Lord David Cecil. He was very grand and used to being deferred to. Though Burroughs saw quite a bit of him at Harvard, they were never really close.

A good friend was Robert Miller, whom Bill met in his first year. Miller later became a priest, but not until after he had accompanied Burroughs on a trip to Vienna and Eastern Europe. Bill described him as "a sort of a high Episcopalian pederast type-person, all very precious."[11] Miller described Bill as a tall, lanky, pleasant guy, amusing, with a dry wit, and wrote that he had nothing but good memories of Bill: "he was placid and good natured, easy to get along with and entertaining."

There were speakeasies in Boston, and Bill used to sometimes cruise Scollay Square, which catered to sailors and gay men, but it was safer for Harvard boys to go to New York to get drunk and have sex. It was also the Big City in a way that Boston never could be. "In the early 1930's, when I was studying at Harvard University, New York was a glamorous, sophisticated, romantic, glittering metropolis. The place where things were happening. Anyone trapped in the provinces with artistic or theatrical or deviant tastes was inexorably drawn to New York. Greenwich Village in that time, that remote epoch, was peopled by real artists and bohemians. Rents were low, restaurants were cheap. Used to drive down to drink at the speakeasies on 52nd Street, to visit Harlem night clubs, to eat in the Village."[12] Richard Stern, James Boyle, Robert Miller, and Bill went to Tony's on 52nd Street and Jimmy Daniels's, a high-class place with a floor show. Daniels was a good-looking young man and every evening would sing "Miss Otis Regrets." Burroughs remembered, "He had a very low key and gentlemanly delivery of his songs." But music was not the point there at all; these were gay clubs.

Clint Moore's place in Harlem was not so luxurious: up three flights and knock three times. It cost a dollar to get in, which entitled you to drink some terrible-tasting liquor from a punch bowl. Most people brought their own rather than drink what was offered, and smoked pot and sniffed coke. Moore had a dimly lit flat, with everyone circulating around, both black and white, making contacts. They met some older people: Bernard Pyle and Thomas Jeffreys, both art teachers at Barnard. It was Clinton Moore who gave Burroughs one of his best lines: "A wise old black faggot said to me years ago, 'Some people are shits, darling.' "[13] There was a cheap "anything goes" apartment hotel on Central Park South at four dollars a night where they always stayed.

In his junior year Bill took refuge from the food at Adams House by moving to rooms in Claverly Hall, just up the street. Built in 1892–93, it had fifty expensive suites, and when it opened it offered the young gentlemen such modern improvements as private baths, electric bells, speaking tubes, valet and maid service, steam heat, a swimming pool on the ground floor, and squash courts. Bill ate in the various nearby cafeterias and tea rooms, and in the evenings he would drive his Ford V8 into Boston to places like the Locke-Ober at Winter Place,[14] Parker House on School Street, or the Union Oyster House on Union. Most of all he liked eating communally at the long paper-covered tables at Durgin-Park in the Faneuil Hall area; it was in the market and catered to the stallholders, there was sawdust and "one of the best chicken pies I've ever eaten."[15] Burroughs's memories of places and situations often involve food, and Harvard was no exception. Bill and Robert Miller often ate at the Bowl Waffle Shop and sometimes at the grill at Harvard's Eliot House, which sold hamburgers and beer. It was at Harvard that Burroughs began his habit of eating all his meals out.

That year, at Claverly, Burroughs and Richard Stern sent away for a ferret. It cost two dollars from the ferret farm, and though it was jointly owned, it lived in Bill's rooms. It was a nice little animal, quite tame, and they fed it dog food. It would curl up in the fireplace in the summer where it was cool. Bill called it Sredni Vashtar, after the little boy in Saki who uses his pet ferret to kill his grandmother.[16] Bill held an open house on Sunday afternoons and the ferret would hide under the couch and nip at the ladies' heels. He had it for more than a year, but there were too many complaints from the cleaners and eventually he put up a notice on the house board and gave it away. There were three girls from Radcliffe in the group, but Bill never had any luck with them; there was just something about him they found wrong. "Rex Weisenberger told me, 'the girls are down on you.' I don't know what for. It wasn't any particular thing. It was just my emanations, they felt were not...I didn't feel bad about it."[17]

That summer, 1935, Bill did not go abroad but instead took a job at the *St. Louis Post-Dispatch*, thanks to his father's friend, the managing editor, O. K. Bovard. Bill was a poor reporter. He would be sent to get a photograph of a dead child, but if the grieving parents saw no reason why they should give him one he was inclined to agree. He would not pressure or cajole them like most reporters. He hung around the police courts and called in any stories that seemed possible. Bill found the editor, Bill Reese, to be a very disagreeable person; the whole job went against the grain and he was glad when it was over.

Bill was twenty-one, but he had never had a lover. His sexual experience was restricted to mutual masturbation and blow jobs. He wanted a boyfriend, but had no idea how to find one. The final realization that he preferred boys had resulted in a complete paralysis of action and no sex at all. None of his visits to New York had resulted in full sexual relations, although his friend Bill Gilmore claimed that Bill was very promiscuous in his first years at Harvard, but much less so in the last two years. He was socially inept; he didn't know how to act, and didn't know the right things to say in order to pick someone up, even in a gay bar in New York. He obtained temporary relief in the traditional manner, by visiting the whorehouses of St. Louis. The best one was on Westminster Place. It didn't have a name. The madam knew who everyone was, and if someone was coming in or out, she would shunt Bill into an alcove and draw the curtain in case it was the judge, or his uncle or a friend of his father. There was one African American woman whom he really liked and whom he would always ask for. "She was real motherly, big boobs. She was gentle and receptive. It wasn't what I wanted but it was better than nothing." Coming from a family where there was little in the way of hugging, the best thing was the physical contact. It was five dollars for half an hour. "I did all kinds of things, I came between her breasts."[18]

He remembered, "It was alright. You get a sense of release and pleasure and you feel you've done a very socially acceptable thing. I used to drive from there over to Culpepper's bar on the corner of Euclid and Maryland. Go there and talk to your buddies and get a little drunk, made you feel a man."[19] The extent of Bill's sexual ignorance emerged when he was in his senior year. "Until the age of twenty-two I thought that children were born through the navel. I did. It was an evening with James Le Baron Boyle, Richard Stern, and Graham Eyres Monsell that I expressed this theory, which I thought was a fact, and they said, 'What?!' Then they enlightened me to the horrible fact, the facts of life. I knew about female genitals, I knew they had a hole down there, but I did not know that the baby was born down there. [...] I never had one of those man-to-man talks with my father. He would have been shit scared. He was the most prissy heterosexual I have ever known."[20]

In his final year of college Bill still had no idea what to do with his life. Mort had done postgraduate studies, and Bill must have been considering some further study. He made plans for another trip to Europe that summer, this time with Robert Miller. Harvard meant so little to him that he left before commencement. His parents were clearly still concerned about him, because they arranged a follow-up meeting with their psychiatrist friend Dr. Sidney Schwab to see how he was doing.

Chapter Six

The sky over Vienna was a light, hard, china blue.[1]

1. Mitteleuropa

Although the trip to Vienna began as another summer vacation, it turned out to have profound repercussions for Burroughs. By the time he returned to the States he had studied medicine in Vienna and was a married man. Burroughs and Robert Miller left for Europe in the early part of June 1936, sailing on SS *Bremen*, which made the crossing in under five days. They went first to Paris for a week, staying on the Left Bank near boulevard Saint-Germain, where they spent most of their time in cafés, people watching. From there they continued to Vienna, arriving on July 4. Gay friends had recommended them to the Hotel König von Ungarn (King of Hungary), at Schulerstrasse 10, on a narrow medieval street close to the twelfth-century St. Stephen's Cathedral. It is supposedly Vienna's oldest continuously operated hotel, first opening to guests in 1746. Mozart lived there from 1784 until 1787 and there composed *Die Hochzeit des Figaro*. Once a pied-à-terre for Hungarian noble families visiting the city, by the time Burroughs stayed there it had become notorious as the place the international queer set took their boys any time of day or night. Burroughs liked to tell the story of someone bringing back a queen in drag to the hotel to be told, "I am sorry, sir, you simply cannot bring a woman into the hotel." The man took off his wig and the doorman quickly apologized—"Terribly sorry, sir!"—and welcomed them in. An arched doorway led to a central courtyard and a maze of small rooms, each of which had a porcelain stove almost the height of the room.

They swam at the beaches on the Danube and met up with Bernard Pyle and Tom Jeffreys, whom they had first met in New York. Bernard and Tom introduced them to the Romanische Baden, the huge Turkish baths complex at Kleine Stadtgutgasse 9, with its marble hot-water pool, its hot and cold showers, Roman sweat room, and wide colonnaded central hall. Burroughs remembered it fondly. "Vienna was a great gay place

[...] they had beautiful boys in the afternoons, the most beautiful boys from twelve to twenty, so it was great from that point of view."[2] Bill had no hesitation in taking advantage of the situation, in fact quite the opposite. He enjoyed Vienna.

They took a short trip to Salzburg, where they saw Mozart's *Don Giovanni* and *Così fan tutte* and also encountered a parade of banner-waving Nazi sympathizers. On July 19, they left the König von Ungarn for Budapest, where they took a pension in Buda on the west bank of the Danube for a week. Bernard Pyle and Tom Jeffreys came with them and they all met up with Graham Eyres-Monsell, who was in Europe for the summer. Monsell introduced them to Baron Janos "Jansci" Wolfner, a well-known character in the international gay set whom Monsell had known in London. Wolfner was a Hungarian nobleman with a monocle, described by Burroughs as "a very purposeful fascist-minded elitist." He was the Baron in Isherwood's *Mr. Norris Changes Trains*, which Burroughs claimed was a lifelike portrait. Wolfner was who you went to to get boys. Many of the Hungarian noblemen were gay, with big estates where they had the pick of all the boys. They would be brought in, made to take a bath, and then be paraded for the guests. Wolfner took his work seriously. Bill often reenacted him in later days: "Vee vill haff FUN. Vee vill haff an ORGY!" Bill went with him to a bar with loud gypsy music. "Do you see anybody here that you want?" Wolfner asked. Burroughs pointed to a boy across the room and Wolfner snapped his fingers. Burroughs had been worried that he would be unable to perform, frozen in self-conscious embarrassment, but "in that case there wasn't any block," he said. "No block there." Burroughs found Wolfner rather dull; still, it was Wolfner who informed him that vitamin A in megadoses of between 200,000 and 500,000 units is a cure for the common cold, something Burroughs swore by as being effective for the rest of his life. With the rise of the Nazis, Wolfner obviously had to get out. He returned to London, but his old famous friends who had been delighted to receive his hospitality in Budapest shunned him, and he ended his life in much-reduced circumstances.

⁓

Dubrovnik in Yugoslavia was an important stop-off for the international gay set. Bill and Robert arrived on July 29. The medieval walled city occupies a promontory overlooking the Adriatic with a harbor on either side. It is a town of stone steps and alleys where even the roads are made from white marble. Cars were banned completely, and there were many wonderful bars and restaurants. Sometimes they took trips out to the beaches at Lapad and spent the night in a pension. Burroughs loved it there.

Graham Eyres-Monsell introduced him to Romney Summers, an English remittance man who moved on the gay circuit and knew everyone. He was a heavy drinker who was sometimes abusive when drunk. He had been a great friend of Somerset Maugham's until they had a falling-out over cards. Through Monsell Burroughs also met Jock Jardine, another wealthy, well-connected Briton. They showed Bill and Robert all the best places to go.

"Ears" Monsell had given Bill a letter of introduction to Ilse Herzfeld Klapper, who made a career out of playing hostess to the visiting gay set, mostly English. She was someone whom everyone called upon when in Dubrovnik. She always knew who was in town and who was expected. She saw Bill and Robert every day, showed them the sights, and introduced them around. Ilse was born on April 19, 1900, fourteen years before Burroughs, and came from a very wealthy haut-bourgeois Jewish family in Hamburg. She knew the cream of the Weimar Republic. Kurt Weill and the American actress Lillian Gish were friends of hers; in fact, Gish was a witness to Ilse's U.S. naturalization petition in January 1944. Burroughs had grown up watching Lillian Gish's films and later met her in New York through Ilse.

Ilse had married Dr. Klapper, a German physician, and they had moved to Dubrovnik, but they were divorced and no longer saw each other. He was Aryan, but had been an outspoken anti-Nazi and was now practicing medicine illegally in a small Croatian community some miles out of town. Ilse had lived in Dubrovnik for many years and had made it her own. She was the city's social arbiter, and she knew all the countesses and artists, all the intrigue and scandal, but had continual problems with the social split between her Serbian and her Croatian friends. Her affairs had taken a downturn: recent developments in Germany meant her stipend from her family was cut off and she was forced to give English lessons and take other odd jobs to earn an income. She was living in a tiny room in a hotel when she met Burroughs and Miller.

She was small-boned but of average height, with brown eyes in a small, birdlike face that was framed by a tight bob of brown hair. Burroughs described her as having "definitely a shrewd birdlike look." He liked her complete lack of any pretense and the fact that she could see straight through any phony. He said, "Ilse was a terrific person. She wore a monocle. She was very straightforward and mannish. Partly a dyke but not really, she was much more into men. She told me a lot about her affairs."[3] Burroughs thought she was "terrifically intelligent" and they became very good friends. He liked the way that no one could put one over on her: she was a survivor. She told him about an affair she had with a White Russian taxi driver, a tough Cossack type. One day in conversation he referred to her hotel room as "our little room." She immediately thought, "I must get rid of this man! It's not 'our little room,' it's *my* little room," and he soon went on his way.

2. Mrs. Burroughs

On August 21, Bill left for Vienna. Bill and Robert had been due to return to the States from Dubrovnik in September, but Bill had always considered becoming a doctor, and in order to get into American medical school he needed pre-med qualifications in biology, chemistry, and mathematics. In Vienna, all he needed was his high school diploma as the university system in Europe meant anyone could enroll in a course and keep taking the examinations until they eventually qualified, although the dropout rate was considerable. Bill enrolled at the fourteenth-century University of Vienna Medical School for the winter term, October 1936 until mid-February 1937, and paid his half-yearly fee of three hundred schillings, the most expensive course on offer. The anatomy was in Latin, which he knew from Los Alamos and Harvard, and he spoke decent enough German. He improved his reading using a method he discovered in one of Somerset Maugham's books: taking a book he knew in English, and a copy of the book in translation, then reading a page from each with the aid of a dictionary. He used books by Maugham. After three books, he could read the language.

The Nazis were growing increasingly more powerful and he followed their rise with deep fascination. He read the local Austrian newspapers, the daily *Völkischer Beobachter*, owned by Hitler and published by the German Nazi Party, and the weekly downmarket *Der Stürmer*. "[I] saw the emergence and manipulation of these fiendish archetypes. A Jew head with a spider body. Picture of a Jew accused of some crime: 'From his horrible Jew eyes speaks the crime world of the Talmud.' And this image was then grafted onto the homosexual."[4] He found that almost all the students he talked to at the medical school were pro-Nazi and anti-Semitic, unless of course they were Jews. It seemed obvious that the Nazis were going to take over Austria with the massive support they had among the population and the police, and in Vienna, despite its left-wing traditions, there was growing support for them, with swastikas on buildings and marches and demonstrations. Only eighteen months later, on March 12, 1938, Austria was annexed into the German Third Reich.

Before starting his studies Burroughs took a bus trip south through Albania, first to Tirana then Durrës on the coast. He and a German were the only tourists. The Albanians were not used to foreign travelers and were unfriendly. There were no proper restaurants or hotels and the food was awful. Burroughs thought it was a very strange, primitive country; the thick forest on the coast did not look Mediterranean at all, but as if it had come from elsewhere.

After another week in the König von Ungarn, Burroughs rented a large flat near the university at Garnisongasse 1, flat 26 on the fourth floor in a huge ornate building overlooking Universitätsstrasse with a rusticated doorway complete with an elaborate pediment. Sigmund Freud lived about four blocks away, but although many Americans visiting Vienna made a pilgrimage to visit him, Burroughs was not among them. Though living in "the City of Dreams," he had not yet realized the importance of his own dreams, which were to provide him with about half of his characters.

As was usual for Burroughs, he moved around a lot, relocating on October 1 to the Hotel Dianabad, at Obere Donaustrasse 93, on the recommendation of friends. It was a huge wedding-cake building with 125 rooms, taking up a whole block on the Donau canalside just over the Marienbrücke bridge. Rooms started at eight schillings a night but the main attraction was that the whole building was essentially one huge Turkish bath. It was clean and very well heated and had a dining room where Burroughs took most of his meals even though he was not too keen on wienerschnitzel or any of the local cuisine. Burroughs described it as "a spa with queer sections." There were quite genuine health baths, but "you could rent a whole section of the Turkish bath for sexual orgies, all the waiters were queer, oh it was a *marvelous* place!"[5] There was a swimming pool on the roof, and Bill had a room two floors below. He spent his twenty-third birthday there. Some days he would walk to the Prater, the huge amusement park that was on his side of the canal. He went on the Riesenrad, the giant Ferris wheel built in 1897 and featured in Carol Reed's 1949 film *The Third Man*, but the Prater itself was equally well known as a gay cruising area. Then Bill found that he had contracted syphilis from a boy in New York and now had secondary symptoms. He initiated a course of intravenous Salvarsan injections but felt that he was "unclean." He became wary of sexual entanglements, not knowing at the time that after a month of treatment using Salvarsan he was no longer contagious. This dampened his appetite for sexual adventures.

In his fourth and final move in Vienna, Burroughs now took a large flat at Auerspergstrasse 21, flat 5 on the fifth floor on the corner of Josefsgasse just one block from the parliament building and still close to the university. He shared it with a man in his fifties who worked as a civil servant at the nearby Rathaus Wien (Town Hall), who appears to have been a sexual partner rather than just a roommate. There was a marble staircase, wrought-iron balusters, and huge double doors leading to his apartment with an elaborate husk garland and cartouche above. His two hundred dollars a month meant that he could live in style. By the end of term, in the middle of February 1937, Burroughs could see that the situation in Vienna was now so unstable that he would never be able to complete his medical education there. He also felt that "I could never have been a doctor. I did right to quit. My heart is too soft and too hard, too quickly moved to love, anger or indifference. I would care too much for some patients and nothing for others."[6] On March 1 he enrolled instead in the Diplomatische Akademie, a postgraduate school founded in 1754 that provided training for careers in international business, public service, and political science. There were courses in German language, French, economics, and international relations, and it might have been useful if Burroughs was intending to join the Burroughs Company, but it was a stopgap move and short-lived.

While visiting Prague, Burroughs came down with acute appendicitis and quickly returned to Vienna. A Dr. Thibes examined Bill, told him, "We can't wait a second," and took him straight to the Sanatorium Hera.[7] They operated that night. In those days before antibiotics, peritonitis was lethal, so he was fortunate. The Sanatorium Hera, at Löblichgasse 9, was a maternity hospital, and it is likely that Bill was the only male patient. He recuperated for seventeen days before being discharged on April 4. He dropped out of the Diplomatische Akademie, and on May 1 he returned to Dubrovnik to recuperate from the operation. There he naturally contacted Ilse.

She was frantic with worry. Her Yugoslavian visa was about to expire, but as a Jew she could not renew it. She would have to return to Germany. There the Nuremburg Laws[8] had already excluded German Jews from Reich citizenship, prohibited them from holding public office and from marrying or having sexual relations with persons of "German or German-related" blood. She could see what was coming. She asked Bill to marry her. For her it was a matter of life or death, whereas for Bill marriage meant nothing; he knew he was gay and unlikely ever to want to marry. He told Ted Morgan, "Obviously she was pushing this, I guess I was pretty malleable. I said, 'Well, it wouldn't hurt anything.' Remember there's a lot of pressure coming from a very experienced woman who knows how to exert pressure, on someone who at that time had no very clear orientation. And she was also being pushed by a desperate need."[9] Bill was twenty-three and she was thirty-eight, but they were genuinely good friends so, as he said, "I was doing it to be a nice guy."

Predictably, Bill's parents went berserk. To them she was a grasping European gold digger, an older femme fatale who had ensnared their naïve young son. They bombarded Bill with phone calls, telegrams, and letters. His mother understood why he was doing it and attempted to find other means of getting Ilse into the country without resorting to marriage, but Bill was determined.

The American consul in Athens, Henry A.W. Beck, was an old friend of Romney Summers's. On July 26, Ilse, Bill, and Romney took the steamship *Prestolonaslednik Petar* from Dubrovnik down the Adriatic coast to Athens, where Beck arranged all the paperwork with no trouble. Americans marrying abroad had to complete a number of forms. It turned out that Beck was living with Fritz Tunnell, an old acquaintance of Bill's from Harvard. Next they needed to find someone to marry them. The first priest refused to do it: he said he had "scruples" and wouldn't have anything to do with it. He thought there was something suspicious about this callow youth wanting to marry a monocled, mannish woman who looked old enough to be his mother. Undaunted, they quickly found a priest with no scruples who was prepared to take the ten-dollar fee, and on August 7, 1937, at the American embassy, they were wed. They had forgotten to buy a ring, so during the ceremony Ilse had to pull a large turquoise ring from her finger and give it to Bill, who then replaced it on her wedding finger. Beck and Tunnell showed them all around Athens, where they ate in a number of fashionable restaurants, drank a good deal of retsina, and walked in the parks full of pepper trees.

Bill's family were still sending frantic messages, and so he returned to New York. Marrying an American citizen does not automatically make you American, and there were a number of obstacles to be overcome before Ilse could join him. Burroughs contacted Mrs. Lipp, a powerful Jewish matron in a hotel in Park Avenue who had known Ilse in Dubrovnik. She remembered Ilse as a charming, magnetic person and that Ilse had once helped her out. "We want to get this straightened out, Bill," said Mrs. Lipp.

"We certainly do," Bill told her.

"I'll send you to see the man," she said.

Bill went to see the man, a dignified white-haired old gentleman in an office in a hotel with an American flag on the wall behind him. He asked Bill, "Young man, this was a perfectly sincere marriage, wasn't it? It wasn't in any sense a marriage of convenience."

"Certainly not!" said Bill. "I love my wife and I want to have her in the United States with me."

Bill answered all the questions and the man said, "Well, all right." Bill let himself out. Three weeks later Ilse had her entry visa and traveled to the United States as a non-quota immigrant. Burroughs had saved her life.

The marriage caused considerable tension between Bill and his parents, but it never erupted into a row; Bill never ever witnessed a raised voice or argument in the Burroughs household, just resignation, disappointment, and sad looks.

Bill had exhibited various types of compulsive behavior ever since he left Los Alamos. From the age of eighteen he always had to have a coin in his pocket, which he took out and looked at frequently. Since marrying Ilse he had compulsively stuck bits of torn newspaper beneath his nails. Bill knew that his behavior was neurotic, but couldn't stop himself. He enrolled in a psychology course at Washington University in St. Louis, hoping to cure his neurosis, but he was soon unhappy with the tuition and looked for somewhere better.

3. Enter Dr. Benway

Burroughs had always been interested in the whole area of psychology, sociology, and anthropology. He enrolled in a psychology course at Columbia University for the winter 1937 term, intending to write a dissertation. When he decided to move to New York, his father contacted James Wideman Lee Jr., Laura's brother, who worked for Ivy Lee in New York and belonged to a lot of clubs. Mote asked him if he could get Bill into the University Club. Uncle James pulled a few strings, Bill was interviewed by the club secretary, and he was in. The club, in a nineteenth-century mansion at 1 West 54th Street at Fifth Avenue, was founded in 1861, originally for the "promotion of literature and art," and housed a magnificent library and art gallery. Bill moved in.

Bill had already read most of Freud, and now extended his studies to Carl Jung on alchemy, archetypes, and the psychology of the unconscious, Otto Rank on dreams and "Will Therapy," and Theodore Reik on masochism.[10] He read the *Psychoanalytic Quarterly* and theoretically he was very well informed. He worked hard in class but was stopped cold by statistics. They were a very important part of psychology studies but he was unable to master them.

The Manhattan that Burroughs entered in 1937 is long gone: when jazz played on the radios in corner stores, the Third Avenue Elevated shook the windows when it passed, and everyone wore a hat. Even the light was different then; John Cheever called it "river light," when Manhattan had working piers all along the Hudson and the harbor was filled with ships. Great transatlantic liners—RMS *Queen Mary*, SS *Normandie*—docked on the Hudson. The recently completed Empire State and Chrysler buildings towered over Midtown.

Burroughs headed for Greenwich Village where there was a run-down block directly across from the Provincetown Players on MacDougal Street between Washington Square South and West 3rd Street that housed a row of gay bars, collectively known as the Auction Block. The San Remo and the Minetta Tavern were both in the next block, and he soon got to know all the regulars like Maxwell Bodenheim, a successful author back in the twenties—Burroughs liked *Replenishing Jessica*—who was now down on his luck. Another was Joe Gould, who was supposedly compiling an *Oral History of the World*, a tiny toothless figure who, when plied with enough liquor, would do his seagull imitation, flapping his arms, skipping from one foot to another, and screeching.

Bill saw a lot of his Harvard friend Bill Gilmore, the notorious check dodger. Gilmore was always sponging off Bill, asking to dine at the University Club, where he knew all Bill had to do was sign the tab. Bill sometimes had a pickup stay over. As long as you wore a jacket and tie "you could take anyone you wanted there. I've seen some guys in the dining room with screaming faggots. You could do pretty much anything you wanted."[11]

Bill remained in touch with Rex Weisenberger and together they would make the rounds of gay bars. Sometimes Rex would hock his stamp collection to get money to go out and get drunk. Rex lived in the family house in Bronxville, and he commuted every day to his job at McGraw-Hill. Rex hated his mother and Burroughs remembered, "Staying at Rex Weisenberger's family's house was something. He was quite likely to have two sailors for breakfast and his parents frowning over their coffee and orange juice as if to say, 'You know what happens to people who go out with sailors.'" Rex had a model electric train set arranged in the family basement, and Bill was visiting one day when his mother threatened to throw it out. Rex retaliated by saying, "If you do, I'll saw the legs off your goddamn antique table."[12]

That summer Burroughs moved back to Harvard to do graduate work in anthropology and Mayan archaeology. He did a summer course, then enrolled for the fall term. Kells Elvins was also at Harvard, doing graduate work in psychology. Bill, Kells, and "a snippy queen" named Alan Calvert rented a wooden suburban frame house on the outskirts of Cambridge in a tree-lined street behind the Commodore Hotel. They had a black manservant who did the cooking and cleaning while they attended to their studies. Kells was still married but he and his wife were no longer together.

Ever since the Los Alamos diary, Burroughs had disliked the whole process of writing; however, in Cambridge writing was a frequent subject of discussion, and Kells persuaded Bill that they should write a hard-boiled detective story together in the style of Dashiell Hammett, Carroll John Daly, and the writers in *Black Mask* magazine. They read Felix Riesenberg's *The Left-Handed Passenger* about the sinking of SS *Morro Castle*, which caught fire and burned off the New Jersey coast with loss of two hundred lives on September 8, 1935. The first mate was in the first lifeboat to leave the burning ship, and the official inquiry condemned the crew's behavior. Similarly they researched the sinking of the *Titanic* in the Widener Library and found that one of the survivors in a lifeboat was a man dressed as a woman.

Sitting in the screened porch of their house, they acted out the different roles of their characters, laughing uproariously as they did so. It quickly became a Burroughs routine, marrying shocking stories of cowardly behavior with elements of his recent medical training. This was taken to a grotesque extreme in a story called "Twilights Last Gleamings" that Burroughs later used, almost verbatim, in *Nova Express*.[13] "We acted out every scene and often got on laughing jags," Burroughs wrote. "I hadn't laughed like that since my first tea high at 18 when I rolled around on the floor and pissed all over myself."[14] They decided that acting out the parts was the best way to gain understanding of the characters and their physical actions. "Acting things out is a very very good practice. Somebody came into the room, where did he come from? What door? Lots of times there's something wrong with a scene and what's wrong with it is, it couldn't possibly have happened. You've got someone coming through the wall. [...] That's a very useful exercise that I started when we were writing this story together. Kells was great, he was funny. That was the first appearance of Dr. Benway. Kells just dredged him up, the name and the personality: a completely irresponsible doctor that gets into the first lifeboat. 'You all all right? I'm the doctor.'"[15] Dr. Benway, who became one of Burroughs's best-loved characters, was based on a real doctor whom Elvins once knew.

The writing of "Twilights Last Gleamings" cemented Bill and Kells's friendship for life, and Elvins always encouraged and supported Burroughs in his literary endeavors, long before he was published. They sent their story to *Esquire* magazine, which rejected it saying, "Too screwy, but not effectively so for us." "I see now that the curse of the diary was broken temporarily by the act of collaboration," Burroughs wrote.[16] It was a temporary respite and Burroughs wrote nothing more until 1945, when once again a collaboration raised him from his torpor.

On September 21, Bill was having a nap in his room when Alan Cowley knocked on the door and said, "Well, Bill, I think the *house* is being blown down, in case you're in-ter-ested."[17] Bill got dressed and they went out into the street. Trees were uprooted and they saw the wind disintegrate a shop window and blow a great cloud of broken glass down the street, so they hurried back inside and stayed away from the windows. It was the great hurricane of 1938. Boston was only on the outer edge of the storm, which killed approximately six hundred people in New England, mostly in Rhode Island, and destroyed over forty-five hundred homes, damaged twenty-five thousand more, and uprooted an estimated two billion trees.

Around this time, Burroughs finally achieved the sexual experience he had been looking for. He told Victor Bockris, "I don't think I was fucked until 1938, in Cambridge. [...] I'd known Lloyd Hathaway before, and we jerked off together, and this particular occasion he fucked me. I asked him to."[18] Life in their frame house was enjoyable, but in the spring of 1939 Kells left to do graduate work in the state prison in Huntsville, Texas, where he had been offered a place as prison psychologist. The household broke up.

Bill was at a loose end and, after giving Kells time to settle in, went down to visit him in Texas, where he was now living with a woman named Jean. Huntsville was a tough jail; the prisoners were kept in stockades and worked at the prison farms, but Burroughs proclaimed the food as excellent. Kells did the psychological evaluations. Elvins's master's thesis in psychology was titled "Forty-Four Incestuous Fathers of Texas," based on interviews with the prison's inmates. There was one man who had gone through three generations, getting his daughter pregnant and then his granddaughter. He got out of jail when he was about eighty years old, and said, "I don't see anything wrong with raising your own tail. I guess the other one's about right now."[19] The prison authorities were not pleased when Kells presented his thesis to the university.

Ilse Herzfeld Klapper Burroughs arrived in New York on MS *Vulcania* on January 19, 1939, and found herself a small apartment at 230 West 61st Street. Her first job was as secretary to Ernst Toller, the leftist German dramatist whom she almost certainly knew from Dubrovnik or Berlin. Toller had escaped to the States and was living in the Mayflower Hotel at 61st Street and Central Park West. Developments in Europe had left him very depressed, and several times Ilse had returned from lunch at two o'clock sharp to find that he had tried to hang himself. She was back in time to cut him down, as he obviously intended. Then one day, May 22, 1939, she ran into a fellow German Jew whom she had been concerned about, not knowing if he had escaped. They discussed who got out and who was in the camps and she was a half hour late getting back. She told Burroughs, "I sit down and get my notes, and then it comes up the back of my neck and I know he is hanging up somewhere." She opened the bathroom door. He'd hung himself with his bathrobe cord, expecting her to be back in time to prevent him from dying. She cut him down and called the hotel manager, whose first reaction was, "We don't want any scandals here and…" She said he was "like ice." Toller had actually broken his neck, so even if she had been back on time it would have made no difference.

At Toller's funeral she met Kurt Kasznar, a penniless Austrian actor who had married the American heiress Cornelia Woolley, an admirer of Toller's work. Ilse moved in with them and became the Kasznars' social secretary. They were multimillionaires and gave big parties to which Bill was occasionally invited. He met John La Touche there and also Mrs. Mathews, his old next-door neighbor from Pershing Avenue, who was there with a young gigolo. Bill saw Ilse from time to time, whenever he was in New York, meeting at modest French restaurants she knew where they could get a good meal for a dollar. Never once did she ask Bill for money or make any claims or demands on him.

When Kasznar's wife died unexpectedly in June 1944, the maid accused Kasznar of having poisoned her. She was exhumed, but it wasn't true; she had died of liver failure from years of excessive drinking.

Ilse next worked as a secretary for John La Touche, a close friend of Brion Gysin's, though Burroughs and Gysin did not meet for another decade. La Touche wrote the lyrics for such hits as "Taking a Chance on Love" in the musical *Cabin in the Sky* (1940) and acted in *Dreams That Money Can Buy* (1947). Ilse did not think much of La Touche's songs but conceded, "He has a tremendous talent—for this shit." John La Touche did an act about Burroughs; prancing around the room he would say, "I am Bill Burroughs. I've got a gun here, don't come near me!"

Bill and Ilse divorced amicably in October 1946, after she moved back to Europe. They last met in New York in 1965. On his return to New York in 1974 he looked up all the Burroughs names in the phone book without success. Then he heard from his friend Timothy Baum that he had met her in Zurich. Bill was never able to locate her. She died in Ascona, Switzerland, in August 1982.

Chapter Seven

If we enquire about the "meaning" of a word, we find that it depends on the "meaning" of other words used in defining it.
—ALFRED KORZYBSKI[1]

1. Count Alfred Korzybski

That summer, 1939, Burroughs attended a weeklong seminar given by Count Alfred Korzybski at his Institute of General Semantics in Chicago. He first heard about Korzybski at Harvard and then read his enormous book, *Science and Sanity: An Introduction to Non-Aristotelian Systems and General Semantics*, first published in 1933. In it Korzybski attempted to show how "factors of sanity" can be tested empirically using modern scientific methods, and illustrated his findings with hundreds of pages of material drawn from all the many different branches of science from biology to mathematics, psychics to semantics. Intrigued, Bill applied for Korzybski's course. In order to be accepted he had to submit an essay, and chose as his subject the eighteenth-century London dandy Beau Brummell, examined in the light of the work of Trigant Burrow, John W. Dunne, and Korzybski. The paper, written in July 1939 and unfortunately now lost, is described as an examination of Brummell as an "oral personality" in the context of "projection" that touched on the future possibilities of television, the new media introduced to the American public two months earlier when Franklin D. Roosevelt became the first person to address the American public live on television. Baudelaire's famous 1863 essay "The Painter of Modern Life" proposed the dandy, or flâneur, as a model for the modern artist; he was opposed to bourgeois society and was aloof from the everyday crowd, having no interest in everyday trivialities—"the soccer scores are coming in from the Capital...one must pretend an interest"—he was distant, detached, removed, an observer, and, of necessity, emotionally cold. These are all traits that Burroughs must have recognized in himself.

Korzybski was a sixty-year-old Polish war hero who emigrated to the

United States after the Armistice. Described by Burroughs as a heavy, vigorous gentleman looking somewhat like Picasso, he was an emphatic and energetic teacher. He would begin his lectures by banging down his fist. "Whatever this is, it is not a 'table.' It's not the label table." That things were not their labels was one of his main points. The other was the fallacy of Aristotelian either/or logic: that a proposition is either true or false; hereditary or environment; instinct or emotion. He said the either/or contradiction does not correspond with the human nervous system at all. It is not either/or, it is both/and; not intellect or emotion, every act is both intellectual and emotional. There is no way that you can split the human organism into two halves. In fact this is a rather crude reading of Aristotle, who wrote, "It is not necessary that of every affirmation and opposite negation one should be true and the other false."[2] Another memorable Korzybski line, often quoted by Burroughs, was that the "I" is not just confined in the brain. Korzybski always told his class, "You think as much with your big toe as you do with your brain—and probably more effectively."[3] As usual, Burroughs took from it what he wanted, namely the idea that words should mean what they say. In conversation, and when he was teaching, Burroughs railed against all generalized words like "justice" and "communism," "art" and "culture" because they have as many definitions as there are users.

It was a small class of fifteen to twenty people. It lasted for five days and everyone had a one-on-one tutorial. Bill's was unfortunately timed for the early afternoon of September 1, 1939. Korzybski could have been forgiven if he was distracted. That morning, at 4:45 a.m., just before dawn, 2,750 tanks, supported by 2,315 aircraft, led an army of more than a million Germans into Poland in the opening action of World War II.

Burroughs took his fall 1939 and spring 1940 anthropology courses at Harvard but made an abrupt move to New York City before completing the course. On February 1 he wrote asking Harvard to send his papers to Columbia to enable him to study anthropology and psychology there. At first he lived in the Harvard Club on West 44th Street, a private club to which anyone who had attended Harvard could apply and which was less expensive than the University Club. He stayed there over the years when he was moving from one apartment to another. Bill moved seamlessly between the world of his upper-middle-class background and his newly found bohemia, and continued to do so throughout his life. After getting settled at Columbia, he moved around from hotel to hotel, finally selecting the huge, anonymous Taft Hotel at 761 Seventh Avenue between 50th and 51st Streets, just north of Times Square.

Bill connected up with Bill Gilmore again, who was living with W. H. Auden in an apartment at 1 Montague Terrace in Brooklyn Heights. Auden was already seeing eighteen-year-old Chester Kallman,[4] who was still living at home. Gilmore was working as a publicist and had plans to write the "Great American Novel," but nothing ever came of it. Burroughs met Auden several times while visiting Gilmore, but he was not impressed: "He talked all the time...He was very pedantic. I was to some extent impressed by his poetry. He's a good poet. Although it gets so far, it's almost profound and doesn't quite make it." Unfortunately he met Auden just as the poet began to go regularly to church again. By October 1940 Auden had joined the Anglican Communion, so Burroughs caught the full force of his conversion period. "He got religion so then he was talking as a Christian. His whole life he was always talking as something." Bill thought that *The Age of Anxiety* was the best thing he did. It was Gilmore, in Burroughs's recollection, who also introduced him to Jack Anderson, in a downtown queer bar.

2. Jack Anderson

Eighteen-year-old Jack Anderson lived in an old redbrick rooming house at 55 Jane Street in the West Village near the Meatpacking District. Bill described him as having "a beautiful face and very mediocre body, and a sort of chorus girl, shop girl mentality. Cheap. Essentially cheap. Completely oriented towards money and that was it; money and having everything he wanted. He was a hustler. Not educated at all and with a great inferiority complex." Anderson had a job as an office boy, but hustled on the side and wasted most of his money betting on the horses. He and Bill made it sporadically. The Taft turned out not to be anonymous enough. One night, Bill and Jack were having sex in Bill's room when a hotel security man, patrolling the corridors to make sure all the rooms were locked, looked in and caught them in flagrante. Bill had forgotten to lock the door. Ten minutes later, the house detective and the hotel manager burst in and found them both stark naked. Outraged at the intrusion, Bill demanded, "What's going on here?"

"Well, we want to know what's going on here!" they replied. Bill's imperious manner didn't daunt them and the house detective said, "You're the wisest prick I ever walked in on." Bill regarded this as quite a compliment. The detective asked, "Didn't anyone ever kick the shit out of you?" Bill was given ten minutes to pack his things. He was told to go to the cashier's window, where he was given a refund, and they were thrown out in the middle of the night. They took a cab back to Jack's rooming house on Jane Street and the next day Bill took a room in the same building. It was a dollar a day, a considerable savings on the Taft.

But Jack was hustling, the walls of the apartment building were thin, and Bill could hear Jack having sex with pickups. What really disturbed Bill, however, was that Jack had a girlfriend and Bill could hear them together. Bill was racked with jealousy; he became obsessed with Jack, constantly remonstrated with him, putting himself through hell. One reason for this may be that the sex was good. Burroughs said on several occasions that he had three memorable orgasms in his life, and one was with Jack Anderson.[5] One of the few violent episodes of his life occurred when Jack and his girlfriend were visiting with Burroughs in his room at Jane Street:

> His girlfriend who was wildly jealous suddenly hit me and knocked my glasses off and I just hauled off and hit her one. [...] She kept complaining, "I happen to love Jack, I happen to love Jack..." Drunk out of her mind. This went on for hours, then all of a sudden the bitch hauled off and hit me. Instead of acting like a professor, I just hauled off and whammed her one and knocked her across the room onto the couch. Jack did nothing. I hit her real hard, slammed her in the face. I was amazed to see this happen from my fist. I'm stronger than I know I am. She got up sort of subdued. She assumed this was her due. It really stopped the whole scene.[6]

Bill was becoming irrational. He warned Jack that if he didn't give up the women he would cut off a finger. At the same time, he recognized that his obsession with Anderson was neurotic and that he needed help. The idea was reinforced when a professor told him that no one could do really good work in social anthropology without first being psychoanalyzed. Bill looked up the New York Psychoanalytic Institute in the phone book and made a blind appointment, resulting in analysis with Dr. Herbert Wiggers. Dr. Wiggers had received his medical degree from McGill in 1934 and was only seven years older than Burroughs. He was a strict Freudian and had a research appointment at Bellevue to study suicide. Bill liked him. He was very tall, six foot three or four, and ineffective-looking. He was in poor health; he had had rheumatic fever as a child and was to die suddenly at the age of forty-six. Bill's parents thought analysis was a good idea and agreed to pay.

They had good reason to think so. Their son was growing more dissociated from reality and unable to function normally. Anderson was his first real lover and had triggered in Burroughs a torrent of suppressed feelings that he was unable to control. He was powerless in his efforts to make Anderson return his love, and his emotions were overwhelming him: a seething mixture of rage, frustration, feelings of betrayal, erotic fantasies, and revenge. On April 23, 1940, Burroughs walked up Sixth Avenue from 42nd Street looking for a cutlery store among the pawnshops. He wanted to buy poultry shears like the ones his father used to cut through the joints when he carved the turkey at his grandmother's Thanksgiving dinners. He found them: stainless steel, one blade curved and sharp, the other serrated to hold the meat in place. They were $2.79 plus tax. Paying a dollar in advance, he booked into the Ariston Hotel, an apartment hotel on Sixth Avenue famous for its gay bath scene. He unwrapped the brown paper package and placed the end joint of his left little finger between the blades. In his short story "The Finger" he wrote:

> He took a deep breath, pressed the handle quick and hard. He felt no pain. The finger joint fell on the dresser. Lee turned his hand over and looked at the stub. Blood spurted up and hit him in the face. He felt a sudden deep pity for the finger joint that lay there on the dresser, a few drops of blood gathering around the white bone. Tears came to his eyes. "It didn't do anything" he said in a broken child's voice.[7]

He crudely bandaged his finger, put the finger joint in his waistcoat pocket, and left. He felt a wave of euphoria and stopped at a bar and ordered a double brandy. "Goodwill flowed out of him for everyone he saw, for the whole world. A lifetime of defensive hostility had fallen from him."[8] He had originally intended to present the finger to Anderson in some sort of Van Gogh gesture, but he had a meeting scheduled with Dr. Wiggers and a half hour later he was seated next to him on a park bench in Central Park. Clearly Burroughs's real aim had been to present the finger to Wiggers, maybe as proof of the depth of his feeling for Anderson. Wiggers was terrified by Bill's self-mutilation. He said, "Really Bill, you're doing yourself a great disservice. When you realize what you've done you'll need psychiatric care. Your ego will be overwhelmed."[9] He persuaded Bill to come with him to his office in Bellevue to have the finger dressed to avoid infection, but once he got there Bill was tricked into signing some papers and found himself in the psychiatric ward. He was interviewed and committed. The finger stub had to have its own burial and death certificate in case someone found it and the police spent time looking for the rest of the body.

Bill's father flew in immediately, and the next day Bill was transferred to the private Payne Whitney Clinic. Bill arrived in a taxi accompanied by his father, his wife, Ilse, and Bill Gilmore. Mote didn't say anything but he was terribly upset. He didn't want to talk about it any more than Bill did. Bill was in Payne Whitney for a month under the care of Dr. Lincoln Rahman and Dr. Oskar Diethelm. Wiggers came to see him and Bill called him a "Son of a Bitch!" But his resentment toward Wiggers diminished after his visit. Some years later, a more experienced analyst, Dr. Paul Federn, discussed it with Bill, saying, "Don't you understand Wiggers's position here? He was a young analyst and he was just scared to death? He didn't know what would happen, and he would be held responsible. You can't blame him for that. He panicked, that's all."[10]

Bill remained aloof from the other patients. He spent most of his time in his room playing solitaire or reading. The nurses went through his belongings and found several joints of marijuana, which they confiscated. They also found a series of strange Brueghel-like symbolic drawings of torture and sex organs, the expression of what was going on in his head. His admission interview was unsatisfactory because Bill did not want his parents to know that the event was triggered by a homosexual relationship and told the doctors a story about being jilted by a girl. Bill's mother arrived and Bill told her that he was interested in perceptions of pain and had cut off his little finger to be able to prove to himself that if one concentrated on not feeling pain one could cut off a finger and feel nothing. He told her he felt no pain in doing it. Laura, as usual, believed every word. On April 30, on being assured of patient confidentiality, he finally told the doctors about his homosexual affairs. Throughout his interviews the doctors reported that he spoke in an affected manner of exaggerated politeness as though condescending to explain something to someone of a lower intellect. He told them that his yoga breathing had sometimes given him hallucinations and given him feelings of unreality that lasted up to twenty hours, a state that he enjoyed. Dr. Wiggers told the doctors that he saw Bill three times a week and that Bill sometimes went into periods of catatonic rage, sat with his arms fixed rigidly, staring into space or with his eyes crossed.

Burroughs discussed the episode with Ted Morgan. "If I was to do an analysis of the situation, I would say that Jack had very little reality so far as I was concerned, but was just a figure in some sort of psychodrama, that's all. At any rate it was obvious that it had little to do with reality. Silly, silly. You look back on this and say, 'What in the hell was the matter with you? To do such a stupid thing?' I remember a dream I had of a child who had a bleeding finger, and I said, 'Who did this, who did this?' and the child points at me. It's also the same hand where I had all these other injuries from the explosion. It healed quite easily."

Bill was discharged from Payne Whitney on May 23[11] with the statistical diagnosis of dementia praecox (schizophrenia), catatonic type. A note on his discharge paper says, "The patient is likely to have further difficulty. Will probably have to be hospitalized again at some later date." Bill had been very underweight and disheveled when he was admitted; now he had gained weight and looked five years younger.

3. St. Louis Return

Bill's parents wanted him to spend some time in St. Louis after his discharge. Mort was married and living in his own place, so it was just Bill and his parents; they were very concerned about him but didn't talk about it. Bill for his part was still acutely worried that they might find out he was a homosexual, so he dared not try to find a gay bar in the city. He continued his psychotherapy in St. Louis, first with Dr. Sidney Schwab, whom Burroughs now disliked, and then Dr. John C. Whitehorn, whom he saw until January 1941.

Despite his anxiety that his parents would find out about his homosexuality, Bill invited Jack Anderson to visit. The story "Driving Lesson" is based on a real car crash that Burroughs had during that visit when he borrowed his father's car to go drinking in East St. Louis, drove it too fast, and wrecked it. He was very bored and dissatisfied. His parents, who were supporting him, thought it would be good for him to help out while he was at home and set him to work as a deliveryman, driving the truck at Cobble Stone Gardens, their garden supply and gift shop. Bill found his situation almost intolerable. "I was twenty-six, working in the shop at Cobble Stone Gardens, which I hate to remember, when this Jew woman sent me around to the servants' entrance and I drove away clashing the gears and saying: 'Hitler is perfectly right!' So you want it honest? You vant? You vant? You vant?"[12] He was unused to being in the servant class.

Another poignant memory dates from around this time. One night Bill went down to raid the icebox at Price Road in the night. "(I was wretchedly unhappy. No sex. No work that meant anything—nothing.) Dad was there eating something... 'Hello, Bill.' It was a little-boy voice pleading for love, and I looked at him with cold hate. I could see him wither under my eyes as I muttered, 'Hello.' Looking back now, I feel an ache in the chest where the Ba lives. I reach out to him: *'Dad! Dad! Dad!'* Too late."[13] Bill saw his main problem as sexual. "Most of my ideas about loneliness and meeting other people were sexual. I was very sexually prostrated. I didn't have a lover. I was looking, but with such a built-in ineptitude I wasn't getting anywhere."[14]

Bill's friend David Kammerer had attended Washington University in St. Louis and stayed on to become an English instructor there. His senior thesis was titled "The Boy in English Fiction: To Defoe." He was very popular with the students, probably for his adolescent sense of humor, and was eventually dismissed for a silly student prank turning on the fire hoses. Bill enjoyed his humor. "He was always very funny, the veritable life of the party, and completely without any middle-class morality. No conventional behavior at all. He was very witty, very charming."[15] While working at Washington University, Kammerer ran a Cub Scout play group. When he saw thirteen-year-old Lucien Carr he was immediately reminded of the *apache* he had become obsessed with on the rue de Lappe when he and Bill had traveled to Paris in 1933. Kammerer transferred his obsession to Lucien. David was more than twice Lucien's age.

Lucien was an exceptionally attractive youth, matching Proust's description of Saint-Loup: "slim, bare-necked, his head held proudly erect, a young man with penetrating eyes whose skin was as fair and his hair as golden as if they had absorbed all the rays of the sun."[16] Burroughs told Ted Morgan, "Dave had some sort of a blond image that was perfectly fitted by Lucien Carr. I know that he didn't get Lucien. Lucien Carr was a beautiful boy, he was blond, he had perfectly molded features, slender and wiry, just a beautiful young upper-class kid."[17] Bill told him, "This is silly, this is awful. It's also completely selfish, you're not really interested in him, you're interested in some idea of him that you have. And what you're trying to do is not at all to his advantage." But Kammerer couldn't see it; he just said, "Oh well, it's my obsession." Burroughs frequently remonstrated with him, even though he didn't feel that it was any of his business, but in vain. He could see the harm that Kammerer was doing to young Carr. There was an early incident when Kammerer's motive for running a Cub Scout pack was revealed: once a week he would fill his Model T with the den, six to eight grade-school boys, and drive out to St. Charles County for the afternoon. On one occasion, after some romping around in a hayloft, Kammerer burst a blood vessel in his penis and had to be taken to hospital.

Lucien's father, Russell Carr, had walked out on his family when the boy was only two years old, and Lucien had been very young when he died so he never knew him. Lucien was a child looking for a father figure and was flattered by Kammerer's attention. He used to visit Kammerer at home, and Lucien's mother, Marion Gratz—she reverted to her maiden name after divorcing Lucien's father—welcomed him into the household. Kammerer restrained himself for some time, until Lucien was fourteen, when he and Kammerer spent the summer together in Mexico. As David was a scout leader, Marion Gratz saw nothing wrong in this in those pre-Freudian days before World War II. It was in Mexico that Kammerer revealed his feelings toward Lucien. Lucien, shocked and confused, rejected him.[18]

Lucien felt that his friendship had been betrayed by the older man, and Kammerer told Bill that Lucien never once allowed him to do anything sexually. Lucien sometimes taunted Kammerer over his obsession. On one occasion in St. Louis, when Lucien was fifteen or sixteen, Bill, Lucien, and David visited someone's empty house. Bill and Lucien got under the rug and Bill began kissing him and feeling him up while David stood across the room, wringing his hands in despair. "Lucien was just taunting him," Burroughs said. "We didn't really make it, but it just drove Dave crazy. If you give a young boy an opportunity to be cruel, he'll sure as hell take it all the way. Lucien was a very attractive boy. I would have been pleased to make it with him."[19] Bill may have been attributing too worldly an interpretation to Lucien's rough-and-tumble games. Speaking about Bill's homosexuality, Carr said later, "He was very deceptive. Either that or I was very naïve. When I'd known Burroughs in St. Louis he was chasing after girls, as far as I know. He had one lovely affair going with some woman. I spent a long time before I realized that Burroughs was into homosexuality. Allen probably told me as a matter of fact. I think I was sort of naïve on the subject. I don't think I really realized what Burroughs was into until, God, after Joan was dead!"[20] In Howard Brookner's Burroughs documentary, Lucien Carr remembered Bill as a womanizer and Bill concurred:

> Lucien Carr: "I was just thinking of Willie in the old days when Willie was more robust of figure and used to speak of a thunder in his chest as he chased skirts around St. Louis."
>
> WSB: "Yes, I used to be quite a woman chaser."
>
> Allen Ginsberg: "You were!?"
>
> LC: "Oh, Willie the lover, I'll tell you. There was a line that always got 'em. He tore open his shirt screaming, 'There's a thunder in my breast' and they all fell flat on their backs!"
>
> WSB: "Every time!"

Burroughs later said, "It is quite true that I did try to lay this girl and nothing happened really, but, 'Thunder in my chest,' that was something that Lucien concocted. I might have said it, who knows. It was a joke."[21] However, stories still circulate about Burroughs in St. Louis. One New York editor from St. Louis remembered that Burroughs would drive across their lawn, leaving great skid marks, when he picked up the young lady of the house.[22]

Lucien Carr told Barry Gifford and Lawrence Lee how he first became friends with Burroughs. He was very young and wanted to visit the whores in East St. Louis. He borrowed Bill's 1938 Ford. It was the middle of winter, and when Lucien was through at the brothel he returned to the car, which was ice-cold. He revved the engine to get it hot. "I was gonna get it *warm* in there. Until the fucking front of the car *exploded!*" The car was destroyed. Lucien and his friends found a hotel and got back across the river in the morning. After about a week he thought he should tell Bill that his car was totaled and abandoned across the river:

> So I call him, and I say, "Hey Bill, you know your car…"
> And he says, "Yasss—"
> I said, "Well, let's see. I had it across the river, and I think I blew the head off it, anyway it all came flying out the hood, and…it's over there and I don't think it's worth goin' over to pick up."
> And he said, "All right."
> And I said, "Well I thought I better tell you," and he said, "Fine"—Click, click. Hang up. And that was it.
> But later the word got back to me that Burroughs really appreciated that I hadn't bothered to apologize. I really didn't *feel* any apology. I thought I oughta tell the guy where his car was—y'know? Ever since then Burroughs and I have been real friends.[23]

4. A Very Private Pilot

With a war appearing inevitable, Burroughs decided to get a pilot's license. He had wanted to go into commercial aviation but could only get a private license because his eyesight wasn't good enough without corrective glasses, but he thought that if the United States joined the war the standards would be relaxed a little. In the spring of 1941 he enrolled at the Lewis School of Aeronautics in Lockport, Illinois, and lived in the school near Joliet. The academy was run by a dozen Catholic Brothers and had started life as the Holy Name Technical School, designed to train wayward boys from Chicago for a profession. With the war approaching they began to emphasize programs that might be of direct use to the armed forces. While Bill was in Joliet, he transferred his psychoanalysis to Dr. Edoardo Weiss at the Chicago Psychoanalytic Institute. Once a week he sped, "doing a hundred on the level," in his black V8 Ford to downtown Chicago to see Dr. Weiss after lessons, returning the same night. Sometimes Bill would take some of the boys from the dormitory where he slept with him to Chicago and "go to a massage parlor and get laid, get jacked off."[24]

He flew Piper Cubs, which cruise at sixty miles per hour. They land at about twenty-eight miles per hour, so if they crash there is a good chance of walking away. He enjoyed it and found it not much more difficult than driving a car, although a completely different operation. He had good coordination and became reasonably competent at it. The school also had gliders, a subject that crops up in Burroughs's work, but he doesn't seem to have actually flown one. The instructor has to decide when the pupil is ready to solo. In Bill's case he'd had ten hours of dual flying when the instructor told him to take it up. After flying for at least one hundred hours he could take the examination. His instructor knew what questions would be asked and trained him in dead reckoning and the other essentials. Bill passed it the first time and got his Class A pilot's license. The course took three months and he did some flying after that. Regulations did change a bit during the war, but Bill never met military requirements and was unable to fly for his country.

Determined to join the war, he got a letter of recommendation to Colonel Donovan from his uncle James Wideman Lee. Franklin D. Roosevelt had appointed Colonel William J. "Wild Bill" Donovan as the "Coordinator of Information" in July 1941 because the United States did not have an intelligence agency. The CoI was based on the British Secret Service and Special Operations Executive and was transformed into the Office of Strategic Services in June 1942, the forerunner of the CIA. Burroughs got on well with Donovan, who said, "We can use this guy," and sent him down to see the head of recruitment. It turned out to be Baxter, Bill's old housemaster from Adams House at Harvard. He was a big man with a black mustache and purple cheeks. Bill had never liked Baxter, and Baxter just hated Bill. Bill took one look at him and knew he didn't stand a chance of being recruited. It was another road not traveled; instead of writing *The Naked Lunch*, Burroughs might have been head of the CIA.

In New York, before the finger incident, Burroughs had tried unsuccessfully to get a job, usually sabotaging the effort by turning up unshaven or late. Now his father stepped in, calling in a favor from a friend in New York. Lieutenant Colonel Massek had known Bill's father in St. Louis. Mortimer asked him to give Bill a job with his advertising agency Van Dolen, Givaudan & Massek. Bill returned to New York in September 1941. Bill liked Colonel Massek very much; like Bill he was a confirmed atheist and they used to go out drinking together. Bill was hired as a copywriter. His memorable campaign was for Cascade, a high colonic consisting of a bag that the customer filled with a special mixture. Bill wrote the copy. He explained:

> It had a nickel in the middle, so you stick the nickel up your ass and sit down on the bag and it's something like a hot water bottle. Your weight forces all the liquid up. Its an enema: "But it's no more like an enema than a kite is like an aeroplane. 'Well done thou true and faithful servant,' that is how many people feel about their Cascade. Sometimes immeasurable relief sweeps over

them as waste matter that has accumulated for years is swept away. You feel as if reborn." Which is absolutely crap. Unfortunately some 300lb woman sat down on this bloody thing and her guts burst open. That wasn't good. Little trouble with interstate commerce at that point.

Bill's parents were still very concerned for his welfare and made sure he lived comfortably. They installed him in a luxurious apartment on West 11th Street in the West Village. It was small but had a compact kitchen, a bathroom, and two comfortable beds; everything Bill could want. "My parents were paying the rent. They always did these things. This is terrible for me to think about it. The point is they gave me a hell of a lot. I gave them fuck all! That's all. No use pussyfooting around when you know you've been a miserable bastard and say that you're anything else." He felt guilty about living off them, but also hated them for the control it gave them over him. The guilt stayed with him for the rest of his life.

Burroughs started psychoanalysis with Dr. Emmeline Place Hayward but soon reached an impasse because Dr. Hayward objected to the early hour that Bill wanted. After three months he transferred to Dr. Spitz, with whom he had a much better relationship. He stayed with Dr. Spitz until April 1942, and Gilmore and Bill's other friends said that Bill became distinctly more sociable during this period.

On arrival in New York he immediately invited Jack Anderson to live with him. It was one of the few times in his life that Burroughs shared a bedroom with anyone. But within a few days of their being together, Bill found that his sexual attachment to Jack was over. At some point, probably at this time when his emotions had subsided, Bill had a threesome with Jack and his girlfriend. After the initial reunion, Burroughs and Anderson had no more sexual relations; however, Bill felt obliged to continue to share the apartment with him. Jack was afraid to be in a room alone at night; it gave him hallucinations and nightmares. Still, life was pleasant. They would eat out at various places around the Village, Chumley's on Bedford Street in particular. Jack was working as an office boy and Bill was earning thirty dollars a week, so between them they had enough money to live very well. As time went by, Anderson began to show signs of mental instability and became unemployable. Burroughs wanted out, but felt a peculiar obligation to Anderson. In April 1942 Bill developed a case of jaundice and was advised to return to St. Louis. There his physician at Washington University diagnosed acute infectious mononucleosis. Burroughs often ended relationships by running away. He would leave the flat, keep paying for it, and consider the case closed. When he stopped paying the rent, it became someone's else's problem to evict the tenant.

In the meantime, America was attacked at Pearl Harbor and joined the war. Bill, with his pilot's license, applied to join the newly formed Glider Corps, but he was rejected because he did not have 20/20 vision. He had earlier applied as a volunteer ambulance driver to the American Field Service when they were sending units to France before Dunkirk, but he was rejected: "this snotty English school tie says, 'Oh, uh, by the way Burroughs, what were your clubs at Harvard? No clubs?' He goes all dim and grey like the room was full of fog. 'We'll consider your application...'"[25] He applied for a naval commission. At his physical examination the doctor told the nurse to write, "His feet are flat, his eyesight bad, and put down that he is a poor physical specimen."[26] The doctor said to him aside, "You may get your commission, if you can throw some weight around." But Bill didn't have the weight.

In May, when he recovered from his mononucleosis, in an attempt to escape from his parents and break from Jack, he went to Jefferson Barracks and enrolled. They gave him a very cursory examination and certified him 1A. "They took me, I did not think they would."[27] He was billeted at the barracks, on the west bank of the Mississippi, just south of St. Louis. As soon as he realized what he had done he looked for a way out. He had volunteered as an officer and been rejected so he didn't see why he should serve as a private. "I liked the idea of danger and killing and living in a very alert fashion. But I am not self-destructive at all. If I find that things are not working, I will find a way out." On his first two-day leave he explained his problem to his mother, who took him to see Dr. John C. Whitehorn, Bill's psychoanalyst until January 1941. Whitehorn had a well-connected friend, Dr. David McKenzie Rioch at the Department of Neuropsychiatry at Washington University. Rioch had a private practice. He was a huge man who looked like Alfred Hitchcock and had a commanding presence. He sent to Payne Whitney for Bill's papers, and consulted with Lieutenant Colonel J. R. McDowell, the medical officer at Jefferson. Bill was admitted to the post hospital to await his honorable discharge. The paperwork took about four months to go through. In the meantime Bill was excused from any military duties and spent his time reading the complete C. K. Scott Moncrieff translation of Marcel Proust's *Remembrance of Things Past* that he found in the camp library. He thought it was a great work.

He had nothing to do. He sat around playing poker, walked around the grounds, and stared out at the Mississippi. He had his own little food club. He made friends with four or five people who were also awaiting their discharge papers, and his parents would drive out with food for them all. One of his new friends was Ray Masterson from Chicago, who was the same age as Bill. Like Jack Anderson, Masterson had been arrested when he was young and spent six months in jail, which may have been why he was being discharged. He told Bill lurid stories about the Chicago criminal underworld, lowlife, unsuccessful burglars, characters out of Jack Black's *You Can't Win*.

Bill left the army in the summer of 1942 with an honorable discharge, entitling him to veterans' benefits but no pension. By now his parents expected nothing of him; all they required was that he continue his psychoanalysis, which they paid for. This was when they fixed the monthly allowance that he lived on until he was fifty years old. Dr. Rioch did not treat people himself, but he was connected with Chestnut Lodge, a well-known sanatorium in Rockville, Maryland, as well as with the Washington school of psychoanalysis started by Harry Stack Sullivan. Dr. Rioch and Bill's mother both felt that he should undergo analysis at Chestnut Lodge.

Bill went out to talk to the doctors and stayed there three days. They considered a year to be more or less the minimum time needed for a complete analysis. Patients could stay at Chestnut Lodge, which had previously been a large hotel, or in D.C. or Baltimore. Bill decided against it. "Obviously there was something wrong psychically, but I just didn't want to do it. I would say I needed it. I really feel that the people at Chestnut Lodge were a great deal better than the others that I had. I might have benefited."[28] Rioch was very much into behavior modification techniques. In retrospect Burroughs considered he may have had a lucky escape. "Who knows what I might have lost? I might never have written at all, I might never have gotten into this whole situation that led to *Junky* or addiction or *Naked Lunch*. None of that might have happened. It was one of those points at which a decision is made, the road not taken."[29] More than half a century later Burroughs mused, "Back at Chestnut Lodge. If I had stayed? Where would I be now?"[30]

Burroughs had tried to serve his country: "Before Pearl Harbor I wanted to be in the fuckin' army, I wanted to do some fighting." He didn't care too much who was giving the orders but would just as soon be giving them himself. He thought the war would shake him out of his lethargy. But he was not permitted to fly into combat with a glider full of raw troops, or to be a naval officer. They didn't want him as a spy nor even as an ambulance driver. As James Grauerholz put it, "If the regular army showed him no respect and tossed him out for being an obsessive, self-mutilating homo—then he would be a queer gangster. And would show them."[31] He moved to Chicago to join the lowlife that Ray Masterton had told him about.

Chapter Eight

Everywhere the smell of atrophied gangsters.[1]

1. Mrs. Murphy's Rooming House[2]

Burroughs arrived in Chicago in the autumn of 1942 and found a room in the Buena Apartments at 4144 North Kenmore Street, managed by Mrs. Hattie Murphy, a "set" known in Burroughs's books simply as "Mrs. Murphy's Rooming House." It was one of the old-style wooden Chicago buildings with three wooden porches above each other at the back, overlooking the elevated rail line on the eastern edge of the Graceland Cemetery. It appears to have had sixteen apartments in all. "Mrs. Murphy's rooming house remember red-brick building on a corner of the alley there it is just ahead Rooms to Let curtain grey as orphanage sugar a grey shadow always peeking out she opens the door a crack."[3]

Bill met up with Ray Masterson, who was newly married but appears to have been sexually involved with Burroughs, at least in the opinion of his wife. Burroughs told Ted Morgan:

> He wanted to stay over at my place to avoid going home to avoid having this shrew leap upon him, so she said, "You're having an affair with him! God, you're keeping him there, living with you."
>
> "I'm not keeping him here, for God's sake."
>
> "Living with you!"
>
> I said, "Look, he's a grown man. He can walk out of here anytime he wants to. He just wants to stay over probably because he can't stand you!" She just went hysterical, berserk with that, screaming, "I'm coming over there with the cops" and all this kind of stuff. It was ridiculous. . . .
>
> She didn't come. She hated me, she kept saying, "I hope he dies, I hope he gets torn in pieces."[4]

Masterson was Bill's only contact in Chicago and it was to be near him that he came to be living in the Near North Side. Burroughs described him as "Small thin black Irish" and later told James Grauerholz that he reminded him of his London boyfriend John Brady: "The same unreliable, charming, black-Irish [...] the 'handsome face of a lousy kid.'" Masterson introduced him to his friends. It was a poor neighborhood and practically every kid on the block had some sort of criminal record. It was Burroughs's first contact with small-time criminals. "They weren't interesting at all, they were Studs Lonigan characters, lowlife, unsuccessful burglars, ward healers. They'd have crap games on Sunday and the cop would rush up. Down there, his ass sticking up in the air, grabbing all the change that was left on the concrete sidewalk. That's a regular Sunday afternoon in Chicago."[5] Nonetheless it appealed to Bill's *nostalgie de la boue*, his romantic ideal of gangsters and the Jack Black characters of his childhood reading: "There on the Near North Side at Dearborn and Halsted the feel of the Twenties will hit you."[6]

The wartime labor shortage meant that anyone could get a job. Burroughs first worked as a clerk at the wartime plant of Inland Rubber, but he was fired after just a few weeks because his manager found that he had been falsifying inventory to cover up his sloppy paperwork.

Bill was taken by the idea of being a private detective and next joined the staff of Merit Protective Services Incorporated at 612 North Michigan Avenue, but the job was not as romantic as he had imagined it. They were hired by stores to check on their employees. Because it was so hard to get staff, rather than fire known thieves they preferred to scare them into honesty. Burroughs worked in a team of four with two middle-aged women and the team leader, Bob Schremser. They worked in Ohio and Iowa where they were unknown. One of the women would buy something and get her change, then the other woman would follow on close behind and give exact change. They would wait for another customer to be served, then Bill and Bob Schremser would approach the clerk and examine the till roll. If the money from the exact-change customer was missing they had their man. They would do their scare routine: "This isn't the first time this has happened at all, is it? We've had you under surveillance for a long time." They had no guns, they were not police, and they had no authority apart from being hired by the employers, but they did protect themselves in case of violence. Bob had a flagstaff and Bill had a springstaff. He never got to use it. After three months he was bored by the work and left. He had taken enough from it. Twenty years later Bob Schremser and Merit were resurrected in *Nova Express*:

> I was travelling with Merit Inc. checking store attendants for larceny with a crew of "shoppers"—There was two middle-aged cunts one owning this Chihuahua which whimpered and yapped in a cocoon of black sweaters and Bob Schafer Crew Leader who was an American Fascist with Roosevelt jokes—[7]

Next came a position as an exterminator with the Nueva Fumigating Co. operating out of the branch at 2947–49 North Oakley Avenue, by the North Branch of the Chicago River. As he described in *Exterminator!*, "During the war I worked for A. J. Cohen Exterminators ground floor office dead-end street by the river."[8] Burroughs liked the job because he was working on his own time and he never knew what he would run into next. Qualifications for the job included having your own car; Bill had a black Ford V8. "A fat smiling Chinese rationed out the pyrethrum powder—it was hard to get during the war—and cautioned us to use fluoride whenever possible."[9] He was given a list of addresses and it was up to him to get his ten signatures a day to show work done. It usually took him about two hours, then he would have the rest of the day free until he checked out at 5:00 p.m.

> I'd go to the apartment and yell, "Got any bugs, lady?" I used to bang on the door real loud, hoping to attract the neighbors so that she might lie and say she didn't have any, and she would sign my book and I would get through my list early.
>
> "Ssh! Ssh! Come in, come in." The old Jewish woman would try and pull me in the door real fast, and there it would be, her bedroom with the covers all pulled back.
>
> "Can't spray beds, lady. Board of Health regulations."
>
> "Oh. You vant some more wine? It wasn't enough before?" and she'd pour me another glass of horrible sweet wine. So I'd hold out and eventually she'd hand me a crumpled dollar bill.
>
> Of course in the negro district it was different. I didn't carry the Board of Health regulations there. I used to carry a gun. You never knew what might happen if one of those spade pimps woke up off the nod: "Hey, what's this white boy doing in the apartment?"
>
> "Shaddap, he's the exterminator!"[10]

He had pyrethrum powder and sodium chloride for roaches, phosphorus paste for waterbugs, and arsenic for rats and mice that he used for warehouses. Nueva advertised "Scientific fumigation of buildings with liquid cyanide and other gases by licensed fumigators." Whether Burroughs was licensed or not, he often worked with cyanide. Bill wore a gas mask and the room had to be carefully sealed to prevent the gas seeping into adjoining apartments, as there had been dozens of deaths caused that way. For bedbugs he used kerosene. According to a Board of Health regulation they were not to spray beds, but they lived in the ticking of the mattress. They would also get in the springs and the screw holes of a wooden bed. He would spray the bed with kerosene for a couple of dollars. Burroughs was proud of his ability to know where all the bedbugs were. "I used to have a spray gun and I could adjust it from a fine spray to a stream, and go in a room and get a bug, Phattt! From across the room, like that." His favorite job was exterminating roaches. Bill knew just where they were. "I just go in there, to a new apartment and give them a spray with pyrethrum powder and they all rush out and die instantly on the floor. You have to get a broom to sweep them up. It's a great sight!" He stored the information away, ready to reappear decades later in *Naked Lunch*:

> They call me the Exterminator. At one brief point of intersection I did exercise that function and witnessed the belly dance of roaches suffocating in yellow pyrethrum powder. ("Hard to get now, lady...war on. Let you have a little... Two dollars.") Sluiced fat bedbugs from rose wall paper in shabby theatrical hotels on North Clark and poisoned the purposeful Rat, occasional eater of human babies. Wouldn't you?[11]

Bill's landlady, Mrs. Murphy, makes a number of appearances in Burroughs's work. She was in several cut-up texts, and was the landlady of a boardinghouse in Nome, Alaska, in 1898: "'That will be two dollars extra per week,' she said when the Frisco Kid told her I would be sharing the room."[12] Her biggest part comes when Burroughs uses her for a dialogue when he was working as an exterminator:

> From a great distance I see a cool remote naborhood blue windy day in April sun cold on your exterminator there climbing the grey wooden outside stairs.
> "Exterminator lady. You need the service?"
> "Well come in young man and have a cup of tea. That wind has a bite to it."
> "It does that, mam, cuts me like a knife and I'm not well you know / cough/."
> "You put me in mind of my brother Michael Fenny."
> "He passed away?"
> "It was a long time ago April day like this sun cold on a thin boy with freckles through that door like yourself. I made him a cup of hot tea. When I brought it to him he was gone." She gestured to the empty blue sky "Cold tea sitting right where you are sitting now." I decide this old witch deserves a pyrethrum job no matter what the fat Chinese allows. I lean forward discreetly.
> "Is it roaches Mrs. Murphy?"
> "Is it that from those Jews downstairs."
> "Or is it the hunkys next door Mrs. Murphy?"
> She shrugs "Sure and an Irish cockroach is as bad as another."[13]

Bill was making about fifty dollars a week: thirty dollars' salary and twenty dollars for cheap fumigation jobs on the side and for breaking the rules. He could go out to dinner and buy decent liquor and didn't really need his monthly allowance. He worked as an exterminator for about nine months, his longest-ever regular employment. He recommended the job to Ray Masterson, who was unemployed, and Masterson took a post with a rival firm. "I got him onto that job. I was the first one into this easy thing."[14]

In Chicago, Burroughs appears not to have contacted Korzybski's Institute of General Semantics again; rather, he turned his interest in language to learning Egyptian hieroglyphs, a subject he had approached earlier when he was studying Mayan hieroglyphs, and which he attributed to Colonel Sutton-Smith in *The Place of Dead Roads*, forty years later.[15] He visited the Oriental Institute of the University of Chicago to make contact with some Egyptologists. As he entered he suddenly heard a voice inside him, shrieking in his ears, "You don't belong here! You can't do this!" He said, "Of course, subsequently I have had many experiences of such voices, that was an early experience. Someone wanted to block me from having any contact with Egyptian hieroglyphs."[16] However, Burroughs did get assistance and was put in touch with a woman tutor. He armed himself with the two immense volumes of E. A. Wallis Budge's *An Egyptian Hieroglyphic Dictionary* and would send her his hieroglyphs and she would reply with her reports.

Burroughs was nearly thirty, but after almost a year in Chicago he still harbored fantasies about the gangsters in Jack Black's *You Can't Win*, and the tommy guns and shootouts of the Chicago mobsters of the twenties. According to Lucien Carr, who was prone to exaggerate in order to tell a good story, Burroughs tried to enter the criminal underworld himself. Carr told two stories, both of which he heard from David Kammerer and were therefore likely to be exaggerated to begin with. Burroughs planned to rob a Brinks armored truck. The idea was to place a large quantity of dynamite in a manhole and blow up the truck as it passed over it. Bill and his collaborator would then rush out and grab the money. He got as far as visiting city hall to inspect the sewer maps and reconnoitering the route of the truck. He drew a map of the robbery site but it went no further than that. Carr doubted that Bill got as far as buying dynamite for the job.

Another plan was to rob Jack's Turkish Baths at 829 North Dearborn Street, which in the late forties was the best-known gay bathhouse in Chicago.[17] Burroughs was a regular at Jack's, which was the venue for one of his more memorable homosexual encounters. He told James Grauerholz, "The redhead was in Jack's Baths. That was a whole set that I've used so frequently; see, it was mirrors, red carpet, red-haired."[18] Bill snooped around and found that the safe was emptied each day at 6:00 p.m. when the maximum amount of money was on the premises. But in order to work up the courage to pull the heist, Bill spent the afternoon drinking. When he finally pulled his gun on the cashier, the man laughed and said, "Bill, you know the money leaves here at six o'clock; it's six-fifteen." Burroughs was able to make fun of himself later in telling the story, but he must have been humiliated at the time, and was lucky that the cashier knew him. The cashier could well have shot him or called the police. Clearly Burroughs would not have lasted long as a criminal.

Bill still didn't feel good about himself. He knew there was something wrong, something was inhibiting him, stopping him from realizing his potential. He decided to get more psychoanalysis and his parents agreed to pay for it. Rene Spitz referred him to Kurt Eissler, a member of the Freud seminar who for many years ran the Sigmund Freud Archives in Vienna. He later emerged as an authority on juvenile delinquents—appropriate, given Burroughs's obsession with the criminal classes. He was tall, gaunt, and unmistakably European.

Burroughs got on well with Mrs. Murphy and once helped her break down the door where a woman was trying to kill herself with gas. "Kitchen gas often causes vomiting and uncontrollable diarrhoea. [...] She has shit all over herself. Ray [Masterson] took advantage of the confusion to steal her wristwatch."[19] But his good relations with Mrs. Murphy came to an end thanks to the hijinks of two of his old friends from St. Louis, David Kammerer and Lucien Carr. Carr was at the University of Chicago for two semesters in 1942, taking their famous "Great Books" course. Lucien would have stayed and completed his studies were it not for David Kammerer, who had followed him to Chicago and stalked him day and night.

David was fourteen years older than Lucien, tall, with rangy features and a big nose. He was not good-looking. He had long muscular legs and wherever he went he almost ran, rushing along with his thick, curly red hair flying, his red beard jutting forward, and his coat undone and flapping. He took stairs two at a time and arrived breathless, wringing his hands in anxiety. He had a high-pitched, fluting voice that got quieter as he spoke until he was barely audible.

Before the University of Chicago, Lucien had been sent from St. Louis to the Phillips Academy, in Andover, Massachusetts, but Kammerer followed him there. The headmaster soon became aware of Lucien's stalker and ordered Kammerer out of town. But he simply moved to the suburbs and was able to encourage Lucien to visit him and go on trips. Lucien was eventually expelled for staying out after hours with Kammerer. When Lucien was sixteen, Marion Gratz found more than fifty love letters from

Kammerer in Lucien's bedroom. Appalled, she enrolled Lucien in Bowdoin College, in Brunswick, Maine, but once again Kammerer followed. Now he had followed him to Chicago.

Lucien was in an impossible position. He couldn't get rid of Kammerer; in fact he quite liked him and was still flattered by his attention. He had known nothing else in his adolescent life, and Kammerer ingratiated himself by writing Lucien's term papers for him and buying alcohol. (Lucien began drinking heavily from the age of fourteen, presumably largely to assuage Kammerer's pressure.) Lucien was still a kid and enjoyed the wrestling, the fooling around and stupid games that seventeen-year-olds enjoy and that Kammerer encouraged. It was one of these pranks that outraged Burroughs.

On one visit to Bill's room they pissed out of his window and tore up the Gideon Bible that Mrs. Murphy thoughtfully placed in all her lodgers' rooms. She evicted him. This was serious because in addition to full employment, there was 99.5 percent occupancy in Chicago, and rooms were extremely hard to get. Burroughs got his own back by shooting her with a poison dart in *The Place of Dead Roads*.[20]

Shortly after this, Kammerer persuaded Lucien to go on a trip with him. They drove to Princeton in Kammerer's Model T Ford. Shortly after their return to Chicago, Lucien put his head in the gas oven and attempted suicide; a "drunken impulse," he later called it. He was discovered when his landlady smelled gas. His mother flew in from New York, but Lucien had gone to hide out at his girlfriend's apartment. His mother found Kammerer and gave him hell, but it still didn't occur to her to seek legal redress to stop his stalking. Lucien was discovered when his girlfriend, who had gone to see what was happening at Lucien's flat, ran into his mother. Lucien was tricked into visiting Cook County Hospital to make sure he was all right and only realized that he had been committed when he found there were no doorknobs on his side of the doors. He was sent to a psychiatrist and after two weeks was released into his mother's care in New York City where she could keep watch over him. David Kammerer followed him there shortly afterward.

Burroughs was adrift. There was no direction to his life, he had no ambition, no drive. He was lonely, looking for a lover. He had an adolescent fixation on gangsters and petty criminals that had yet to play itself out. He had an inchoate interest in the language systems of Native Americans, pre-Columbian civilizations, and the Egyptians, but it would be some time before this focused in on language itself as the vehicle for received ideas and societal control. He was bored. Most of the recent excitement in his life had been caused by David Kammerer, whose ebullience and humor he enjoyed. He decided to follow him to New York.

BOOK TWO

~

The Beat Generation

Chapter Nine

To me the Beat Generation just means that little group at Columbia and very little else.

—LUCIEN CARR[1]

1. Greenwich Village 1943

Burroughs moved to Manhattan in September 1943. New York was on a war footing, with the Brooklyn Navy Yard employing seventy thousand people, twenty-four hours a day, building and repairing warships. The docks had become high-security areas. The old forts were upgraded and the harbor defenses bolstered; an antisubmarine net and a floating boom ran from South Beach, Staten Island, to Coney Island in Brooklyn. The boom was only opened to authorized shipping and was closed at night. At Pier 88, off West 49th Street, SS *Normandie*, once the largest of the transatlantic liners, now lay capsized in the mud of the Hudson after an incompetent attempt to fit her as a troopship. The bars and streets of Manhattan were filled with servicemen. From April 1942, New York was partially blacked out: all the neon signs, including Times Square and the Times building's electronic news bulletin, were doused, all windows above the fifteenth floor to be shaded, traffic lights and street lighting dimmed, car headlights hooded, because the glow from the city was silhouetting ships offshore, making them easy targets for the German submarines that patrolled off Manhattan. (On February 28, the destroyer *Jacob Jones* had been torpedoed off Cape May, New Jersey, with only eleven survivors of the crew of 150, so the navy was taking no further chances.) At street level, exterior lighting on the shops, restaurants, and bars was reduced, though New York was still well lit compared to the blackout of European cities.

It was during this period in New York that Burroughs met the people with whom he would always be associated and who would forever change his life: Allen Ginsberg, Jack Kerouac, Joan Vollmer, and Herbert Huncke; the so-called Beat Generation. Lucien Carr was the key, as they were essentially his group of young college friends. Carr had enrolled at Columbia in the summer of 1943 and was living near the college in the Union Theological Seminary on upper Broadway where his mother hoped he would be safe from the predatory attention of David Kammerer. Columbia students had been displaced from their usual halls of residence by wartime V-7 naval cadets who paraded every Saturday on South Field.

Kammerer found himself a studio apartment in a rooming house at 48 Morton Street in the Village, working as a janitor in exchange for rent, and washing windows for a living. The building was shabby: steps led up to a double door with glass protected by an iron grille. Beyond this was a dirty hallway leading to a double French window. Kammerer's room was large but low-ceilinged. A small writing table stood against another French window that looked out over a courtyard littered with old tin cans. At the other end of the room a comfortable sofa sat against an ugly black partition that separated off a kitchenette. There was a disused white icebox with its doors open to reveal empty whiskey and soda bottles. The sink was littered with can openers, half-eaten food, and strands of red hair. Adjacent to the sofa was a large open fireplace, packed high with newspapers, half-burnt wood, cigarette butts, and used matches. On the mantel was an open copy of Rimbaud in which was placed a small drawing of a dark windswept, swirling sea with a rock jutting out of the waves. Above the pillow on the bed, a strip of wallpaper had been torn away, and heavily penciled in the white plaster was the inscription "Lu-Dave." Dave was very gregarious and quickly got to know a wide group of people, though his main purpose in being in New York was the pursuit of Lucien.

Burroughs found a place just around the corner from Dave at 69 Bedford Street, a three-story 1901 brownstone on what is now one of the most attractive streets in Greenwich Village. The comfortable living room was quite small and overlooked the street. It was furnished with a couch and a carefully selected library of about a hundred books. Burroughs always traveled light. He had a separate bedroom and a bathroom and there was a little walk-in kitchen with a fridge, work top, and gas stove, though Burroughs rarely ate in. Bill saw Kammerer almost every night for dinner and regarded him as his best friend. They would often be joined by Ruth Louise McMann, a lesbian who lived upstairs from Dave, who had joined their group. Burroughs described her to Allen Ginsberg as being "straightforward, manly, and reliable."[2]

Also living in Kammerer's rooming house was the novelist Chandler Brossard, a precocious literary talent who began writing for the *New Yorker* at the age of nineteen. His first book, *Who Walk in Darkness*, used his experiences in the bohemian Greenwich Village of the forties, but he denied that it was one of the first Beat Generation novels, saying it was closer to the French "New Wave." Brossard saw Kammerer constantly and they were close friends. Bill would sometimes go with them to Brossard's favorite French restaurant, Au Bon Pinard, which had a huge back room where people could dance. It was much frequented by French sailors and you could get a good dinner for $1.50. There Burroughs introduced Brossard to eating calf's liver rare.

Burroughs quickly settled into something of a routine: drinks before dinner—Bill used to drink Dubonnet and soda in the summer, something stronger in winter—followed by wine with dinner. Lee Chumley's, a former speakeasy at 86 Bedford Street, was just up the street from Bill's. It was a literary bar, the walls lined with framed dust jackets of books written by its patrons, which included Cummings, Faulkner, O'Neill, Dos Passos, and Steinbeck. There was no exterior sign, and in Prohibition days customers entered through an unmarked entrance on Barrow Street, via a nondescript courtyard (the "garden door"). The term "86" originated when the police would give advance warning of a raid, telling Leland Chumley to "86" his customers, meaning they should leave through the Bedford Street door while the cops came in the garden door.

Being close to both Little Italy and to Chinatown, there was an abundance of cheap good local restaurants to choose from. Bill, Dave, and Louise particularly liked MacDougal's on MacDougal Street, which was close by, and the Grand Ticino on Thompson for an inexpensive Italian meal. Wartime rationing—everyone had points—affected the menus of New York's restaurants, and most set Tuesday and Friday apart as meatless days, but it was not yet law. Then there was Romany Marie's at 64 Washington Square South at West 4th Street, where in addition to the usual fare, you could have your fortune told. She was famous for helping out struggling artists, writers, and scientists. R. Buckminster Fuller provided the stainless steel furniture and gave impromptu talks. Paul Robeson, Edgard Varèse, and Marsden Hartley were all regulars, as well as most of the early abstract expressionists such as Willem de Kooning, Joseph Stella, Stuart Davies, and Arshile Gorky. Bill liked to watch the sidewalk crap games in front of the café. "It requires a very quick mathematical mind."[3] He appears to have gambled there, remembering shortly before he died, "The vague watery blues of an old man's eyes looking back to Romany Marie's, and once I won a double—about $103. The bookie paid me with no smile."[4] Throughout his life, Burroughs was always drawn to European-style cafés and bars where he could make casual acquaintanceships and run into friends.

There was a good deal of drinking, mostly at the Minetta Tavern and the San Remo, both on nearby MacDougal Street. The Minetta had murals painted by Alex Katz, whom they got to know. He could always be found there in his smock and beret, drinking red wine, looking for commissions. They liked Minetta's because there was a lot of meat in their spaghetti sauce, rare when meat was rationed. People sat around playing chess and drinking. Humphrey Bogart, who lived nearby, was a regular. The San Remo was more like a Village approximation of a Parisian literary bar with people flitting from booth to booth, and surly, sometimes violent waiters. At these two bars Burroughs ran into people like Maxwell Bodenheim and Joe Gould, whom he knew from his previous time in New York. He also saw Bill Gilmore, though he became increasingly irritated by Gilmore's habit of leaving the table just before the check arrived. Though Burroughs had his allowance from his parents, he sometimes supplemented his income with occasional jobs. For a couple of weeks he worked as a bartender at Barrow's Bar, a little hole-in-the-wall near Times Square named after the proprietor, but he did it mostly for the experience as he had plenty of money.

2. Derangement of All the Senses

It was through David Kammerer that Burroughs met Kerouac and Ginsberg. Lucien met Edie Parker in September 1943 at George Grosz's life drawing class at Columbia. She was from Grosse Point, Michigan, where her father had a Packard dealership and her mother owned a chain of shoe stores. Edie found Lucien very attractive; she couldn't keep her eyes off of him. The other girls felt the same way. "I was spellbound by him; he moved like a cat. His movements were like mercury over rocks. His eyes were slanted, almost oriental, and pure green, so green they dazzled you. Above all, he was unaware of the effect he had on the girls, which made him all the more attractive."[5]

Although Edie found Lucien to be arrogant, sarcastic, and precocious, he was from the same wealthy background as her and they quickly became friends. She invited him back to her nearby apartment. Carr described her as "birdlike, cheerful, one of the boys, a lot of fun to be with. [...] Full of the excitement of life," and he was soon stopping by to take a shower or make himself a snack in between classes. He heard all about her boyfriend, an ex-Columbia student named Jack Kerouac, who was away at sea in the merchant marine shipping war materiel to Liverpool. Lucien introduced Edie to his girlfriend, Celine Young, from Westchester. She was half French—her mother was from Alsace—and Carr described her as having "long blonde hair, built like a brick shithouse, regal carriage." Edie was more complimentary: "We had the same background and we dressed the same way [...] had nice boobs, solidly built. Celine had a shining glow to her complexion. Her greatest asset was her gorgeous, slightly curly, natural blond hair. [...] Celine, like anyone who is attractive and has the world by the tail, loved to flirt. She had big blue eyes and was full of energy and fun. That's why Lucien adored her so much."[6]

Edie lived at 421 West 118th Street, in the single block between Morningside Park and the Columbia University campus. The stairs were at the back of the building; there were two apartments on each floor, and number 62 was on the top floor at the back. There was no elevator. The flat was huge, with six rooms. A long corridor led past the kitchen to a small bedroom, then passed a large white-tiled bathroom containing a huge freestanding bathtub and on to another, larger bedroom. A pair of sliding wooden doors opened into a sunny double-sized living room. The rent was forty-two dollars a month plus utilities, split between Edie and her roommate, Joan Vollmer, who had recently graduated from studying journalism at Barnard.

Joan was born on February 4, 1923, in Ossining, Westchester, New York, and raised in Loudonville, an exclusive suburb north of Albany. She was thin, with an oval, slightly heart-shaped face, fine features, fluffy brown hair, and pale blue eyes.[7] Edie described her as "Dutch-looking"— the name Vollmer is of Dutch origin—and said she was "the type of person that her personality made you think was beautiful. She had heavy legs and when she walked her calves would wiggle." Burroughs described her as "pretty, but not striking looking." She went to St. Agnes High School in Albany and graduated from Barnard College. She was married to a Columbia law student, Paul Adams, who was now in the army, doing basic training in Mississippi. She had regretted the marriage from the very first day. Though technically married, they were no longer a couple. She did, however, receive his military allotment checks, which, in addition to a generous allowance from her father, allowed her to live well. Her father, David Vollmer, was the manager of the Gevaert photographic film factory. It had been sold to him for a nominal fee, but the Alien Property Custodian agency seized it in 1941 because there was no clear proof that there was a separation of interests from the original German owners. Joan had been overprotected by her father when she was younger; no matter where she went, he would follow her in his car. Adams was her second marriage. Burroughs told Ted Morgan, "She had been married twice, as a matter of fact, and she hated both husbands. She married them and then hated them, for the simple reason that they were ordinary stupid people, way below her level. She was about seventeen when she married the first time."[8]

Each day she bought a half dozen daily newspapers[9] and studied them while relaxing in a perfumed bubble bath. There she received any visitors who might stop by and discussed the papers' treatment of the progress of the war as the pages grew soggy and wet from the bubbles. She read slowly and thoroughly, as Edie said, "savoring every moment." In those days Joan dressed fashionably and enjoyed a complicated love life.

In November 1943, when Edie and Joan still had their previous apartment at 420 West 119th Street, apartment 28, Joan discovered she was pregnant. The child's father has been variously named by Edie Parker as Herbert Kiesewetter, a fellow student, and by Lucien Carr as John L. "Fitz" Fitzgerald, from Poughkeepsie, with whom she had an affair around that time (he is called "Fitzpatrick" in Kerouac's books). Fitz's best friend, also from Poughkeepsie, was a tall, large, silent man named Duncan Purcell, known to the group as Uncle Dunc. As Edie Parker put it, "Uncle Dunc was very fond of Joan. The two would discuss Freud, Kafka, Marx and politics over kummel and listen to Bach."[10] Allen Ginsberg once indicated that Dunc might have been the child's father.[11]

It was difficult to get an abortion in those days and Joan was frantic. She decided that she had better get Paul Adams back, as they were still married, and have sex with him in order to pretend that the child was his in order to give it some security. She talked it over with her friends Geraldine Lust, Ruth Clark, and Edie, and came up with a bizarre plan. She thought that if she pretended to go crazy, he would come back and reclaim her. They took her to Times Square and Joan walked in the rain with one foot in the gutter and the other on the sidewalk, then sat propped up outside a Horn & Hardart cafeteria, playing with her hair, talking to herself, and acting really goofy, all the time being watched from across the street by Edie, Ruth, and Geraldine. After a while someone reported her and people from Bellevue arrived and took her away in an ambulance. Edie went to visit the next day: Paul Adams had been telephoned and was on his way with two weeks' furlough. She told him that she had gone crazy because she missed him so much. He took her back to the apartment that she and Edie then shared on West 119th Street and they were temporarily reconciled. Joan returned to Albany to have her child and on June 24, 1944, gave birth to Julie.

In the meantime, Edie and Joan spent a lot of time at the West End Bar on Broadway, which although it was across the street from Columbia at 113th Street, was mostly full of seamen, Native Americans (who lived nearby), and local lowlifes instead of college students. There were a lot of young war wives whose men were in training or fighting overseas. The white-tiled floor was sprinkled with sawdust and there was a row of dark wooden booths across from the bar that seated six, or eight if they crowded up. Bill the bartender parked his motorcycle outside when he was on duty. He enjoyed talking with the students and always remembered to give them their fourth drink free. The other bartender was a right-wing Irish Catholic named Johnny who regarded all students as communists but would give them free meals if they looked hungry. Among the regulars was a woman dressed entirely in black who sat motionless in the same place at the bar every evening saying nothing and a hooker who stopped by for a couple of hours a night to play the jukebox. There was a cafeteria to the left of the entrance with inexpensive steam tables of mashed potatoes, corned beef, knockwurst, and cabbage, run by a prickly Dane named Otto. Lucien Carr remembered that Edie drank with a whole series of men at the West End, including a huge Manhattan Indian who used to get "drunk as he could possibly get."[12] Everyone called him Chief, and he felt very protective toward Edie and her friends: if anyone caused them trouble, Chief would pick them up bodily and smash them down on the floor.

A few days before Christmas 1943, Lucien Carr was in his room on the seventh floor of the Union Theological Seminary. Most of the boarders had gone home for the vacation, so he was surprised when someone knocked at his door. He had been playing music and it was a stranger from down the hall, wanting to know what he was playing. "I thought it might be the Brahms Trio No. 1," ventured the young Allen Ginsberg.[13]

"Well, well! A little oasis in this wasteland," exclaimed Carr, and invited him in. Ginsberg was seventeen and was enrolled in pre-law at Columbia, intending to be a labor lawyer. He was skinny with large lips, sticking-out ears, and thick horn-rimmed eyeglasses. He was intrigued by the contents of Carr's room: on the walls were prints of *The Bohemian Girl* by Franz Hals, *The Sleeping Gypsy* by Rousseau, and a Cézanne landscape. The bookcase contained Flaubert, a critique of Toulouse-Lautrec, and Rimbaud's *Une saison en enfer*, all in French, as well as a worn copy of Spinoza's *Ethics* and Hardy's *Jude the Obscure*—all heady stuff for Ginsberg. Lucien opened a bottle of Burgundy, filled two glasses, and they began to talk. Allen thought that he was "the most angelic-looking kid I ever saw, with blond hair, pale and 'hollow of cheek as though it drank the wind and took a mess of shadows for its meat.'"[14] It was the beginning of a life-long friendship.

Lucien took Allen on his first ever excursion to Greenwich Village, visiting both David Kammerer and the Minetta Tavern. Ginsberg was in heaven: "It was an un-charted, historic no-man's-land wilderness to me, particularly entrancing as I was a closet queen and had not come out yet, so going down to the Village, where all the fairies were, but in disguise, with a beautiful friend, it was both romantically glorious and at the same time completely repressed, frightening, and frustrating."[15]

A few days after Christmas they made another trip to see Kammerer. This time Burroughs was visiting, lying sprawled across the sofa. Bill had no enduring first impression of Ginsberg, who was shy and hardly said a word. Ginsberg, however, remembered the visit with clarity. Carr described how he had provoked a fight between Kammerer and a gay portrait painter at the artist's Village studio a few days earlier, during which the studio had been totally demolished. Lucien had bitten off part of the painter's earlobe and had sunk his teeth into Kammerer's shoulder. Burroughs was censorious: "In the words of the immortal bard, 'tis too starved a subject for my sword.'"[16] Ginsberg was amazed, never having heard anyone quote Shakespeare in everyday conversation before. In fact it was one of Bill's favorite expressions, one he used frequently.

Lucien's exploits have become part of Beat Generation lore: how he pulled the plugs from a row of yachts and sank them; how he threw a veal parmigiana over his shoulder at the Minetta Tavern, saying, "This is crap," and the waiters rushed to clear up the mess without remonstrating with him; how he stole a cape and a large upright vacuum cleaner from backstage at the Metropolitan Opera House after seeing the Royal Ballet[17] perform *Swan Lake*; and the time he spotted a hole in Bill's seersucker suit, stuck in his finger, and tore the whole suit apart. With Kammerer joining in they tore the jacket into strips, which they tied together and festooned around the room like bunting while Burroughs tut-tutted. Once when Bill was cooking a large steak for four of them, Lucien grabbed it from the pan before Bill could divide it into portions and began gnawing at it, blood running down his face. Naturally, Kammerer quickly joined in. Lucien was a natural leader, but also a disagreeable drunk and loud and insistent in arguments. His emotional and intellectual balance had been distorted throughout his adolescence by the continuous presence of David Kammerer, whom he was both trying to impress and break away from. At that time he was very influenced by Arthur Rimbaud, as were they all:

> The poet becomes a seer through a long, immense, and reasoned derange-ment of all the senses. All shapes of love, suffering, madness. He searches himself, he exhausts all poisons in himself, to keep only the quintessences. Ineffable torture where he needs all his faith, all his superhuman strength, where he becomes among all men the great patient, the great criminal, the great accursed one—and the supreme Scholar! For he reaches the unknown![18]

Looking back, Lucien Carr considered, "It's a wonder they didn't throw us all out of Union Theological Seminary, because our pastimes there were to unroll the fire hose from the top floor, drop it down the stairwell, and turn it on, full blast; to start fires in the incinerator shed; all those things naughty college boys do."[19]

Lucien was often at the West End with Celine Young, but the only way they could escape from Kammerer was to spend their nights together at Edie's apartment at 421 West 118th Street, sleeping on the couch in the living room. When Kerouac returned from sea in June 1944, he was initially, and understandably, very suspicious of Lucien, and when he first saw him in the West End he told Edie, "Looks to me like a mischievous little prick,"[20] but the two of them became immediate friends and drinking buddies. In *Vanity of Duluoz*, the most fictionalized of his memoir books, Kerouac describes their meeting:

> That first night we got really drunk and I don't know whether it was that first night or not, it was, when he told me to get into an empty barrel and then proceeded to roll the barrel down the sidewalks of Upper Broadway. A few nights later I do remember we sat in puddles of rain together in a crashing downpour and poured black ink over our hair. [...] I got to like him more and more.[21]

Jack Kerouac brought energy and boundless enthusiasm to the group, and he also provided its literary direction. He loved jazz and could accurately scat-sing instrumental solos such as "Lester Leaps In" and "Lady Be Good" by Lester Young. He and Edie had lived together, on and off, since 1940. He was stocky, solidly built, with dark, brooding Breton good looks. Ginsberg, when he finally met him, found him physically very attractive and admired his "sturdy peasant build." Jack's parents were from Quebec, but he was born on March 12, 1922, in Lowell, Massachusetts. He grew up speaking French *joual*, the French of the Canucks, with English as his second language, and throughout his life always spoke to his mother in patois. He had been a football hero at Lowell High, and went to Columbia on a football scholarship after spending a year at Horace Mann Prep to bring him up to Columbia's entry standards. At Columbia he argued with the coach, Lou Little, and his standing was not improved when his father came to the college and informed Little that a "cabal of kikes and commies" were controlling the school. Jack flunked out with a leg injury and in December 1942 enlisted in the U.S. Navy. This didn't work out, so he joined the merchant marine, and he was still a seaman when Lucien first met him. But all this came second to his writing. He had a notebook with him at all times and at school he had been nicknamed "Memory Babe" for his prodigious ability to remember whole paragraphs from books, as well as every significant move in a football game. In addition to drinking, he and Lucien discussed writing and literature. As Lucien Carr explained it, comparing his relationship with Jack to Allen Ginsberg's:

> I'd read a lot more books than Jack so I introduced him to a lot of people like Rimbaud, so he always had a great respect for me, which was probably undue, but nonetheless was there. I think Jack and I had a similar love for the English language in a way that Allen doesn't have. As far as language went their communality of language was more in terms of bop-prosody and all this kind of bullshit. Jack was a true genius when it comes to the language. He had a real feel for it. The difference is really that Jack and I shared Shakespeare, say, where Jack and Allen shared Blake.[22]

Burroughs met Kerouac through Lucien, who told him all about this good-looking, hard-drinking, literary seaman who could quote Thomas Wolfe. Perhaps inspired by the D-Day landings in June, Bill wanted to get merchant marine papers in order to ship out. One afternoon in July 1944, he paid Kerouac a visit to find out how to do it. Bill was accompanied by David Kammerer, who had already met Jack at the West End. They arrived at Kerouac's door just as he had taken a shower. Kerouac lounged in an easy chair wearing just his pants while Bill perched on a hassock in the middle of the living room. Bill's first impressions were not strong enough to stay with him, but he recalled that "Kerouac looked like an athlete, good-looking in a sort of a heavy masculine way."[23] He was not really Bill's type. Kerouac, however, remembered the meeting in enormous detail and devoted several pages of *Vanity of Duluoz* to it, providing a picture of how Burroughs looked at the time:

> Tall and bespectacled and thin in a seersucker suit [...] strange, inscrutable because ordinary looking (scrutable), like a shy bank clerk with a patrician thinlipped cold bluelipped face, blue eyes saying nothing behind steel rims and glass, sandy hair, a little wispy, a little of the wistful German Nazi youth as his soft hair fluffles in the breeze.[24]

Allen Ginsberg, meanwhile, had also met Kerouac, having been encouraged to go and visit him by Lucien. Kerouac had not taken a lot of notice of Allen at first because he was so much younger and jejeune, but remembered their meeting in *Vanity of Duluoz*, "spindly Jewish kid with horn-rimmed glasses and tremendous ears sticking out, seventeen years old, burning black eyes, a strangely deep voice." Jack was waiting for a midafternoon breakfast of bacon and eggs and offered Allen a beer. Allen, nervous and seeking to imitate Burroughs, replied, "No, no. Discretion is the better part of valor."[25] Kerouac's narrative continues, "'Aw where's my food' I yelled at Edie, because that's precisely all I had on my mind at the moment he walked in. Turns out it took years for Irwin to get over a certain fear of the 'brooding football artist yelling for his supper in big daddy chair' or some such."[26] They soon became good friends, finding they had much in common despite their four-year age difference.

And so the core of the original Beat Generation was now complete: Jack Kerouac was spending about half his time at Edie's apartment and the rest with his parents in Ozone Park. Whenever he was in the city they would meet up with Lucien and Celine, or everyone would congregate in the big living room at 421 West 118th Street and listen to records on Edie's large aluminum Victrola. Allen Ginsberg was in the middle of long soulful talks with both Lucien and Jack about art and literature, and Kammerer was, as ever, fawning around Lucien. Joan spent much of her pregnancy with her parents and then, after Julie was born in June, remained with them upstate to spend the summer months with Julie away from the city heat. That summer, the group could be found most nights in a booth at the West End, the huge jukebox playing "You Always Hurt the One You Love" by the Mills Brothers,[27] that season's big hit, with Lucien sporting a red bandana, very much their leader, drinking Pernod, imagining themselves in fin de siècle Paris. Burroughs had now met them all except Joan, but he was not yet a part of the group; they were a good ten years younger than him, and he was still living in Greenwich Village and unlikely to make a hundred-block subway ride except by arrangement.

Bill had been taking jujitsu lessons up in Yorkville at 86th Street, learning how to defend himself, learning how to fall. The gym was run by someone known as Henry who also worked for the Shorten Detective Agency. He told Bill, "You go round there. He's shorthanded and he'll probably give you a job." Bill signed up and spent July and August 1944 serving processes and making sure that the beneficiaries named in a will were who they claimed to be. He only stayed for two months.

Although this young, middle-class group of students and graduates were not deprived in any way by the war, apart from the rationing of food and gasoline, they were not unaffected by it: in January 1944, Kerouac's best friend, Sebastian Sampas, had died after being wounded in the Allied landing at Anzio in Italy, and they all knew people in the armed forces. They recognized the futility and waste of war, but most of all they felt that once it was all over, there must be a better way to live, a new set of values to live by. They were vague discussions, unfocused, but they called these new values A New Vision, named after W. B. Yeats's mystical text, *A Vision*,[28] but also taking in undigested mouthfuls of Nietzsche, Rimbaud, Rilke, and Dostoyevsky. Lucien Carr was the leader in these discussions, with Ginsberg his "closest student friend,"[29] as Kerouac called him. Kerouac himself played a very active part. Years later Lucien recalled:

> I suppose in those years at Columbia we really did have something going. It was a rebellious group I suppose, of which there are many on campuses, but it was one that really was dedicated to a new vision. It's practically impossible to define. Maybe it's just a term we sold ourselves. But it was trying to look at the world in a new light, trying to look at the world in a way that gave it some meaning. Trying, I suppose, to find values that were different and not accepted values but at the same time that were valid. And it was through literature that all this was supposed to be done. And it was through Jack and Allen principally that it was gonna be done.[30]

Chapter Ten

Death of a friend. To describe how mixed with one's grief comes the
thought that the witness of some foolish word or act of one's own is gone.
—W. B. YEATS[1]

1. The Gathering Storm

The situation with David Kammerer was becoming critical. Lucien had moved from the Union Theological Seminary to the Warren Hall Residence Club, a small hotel on West 115th Street at Amsterdam Avenue next to the campus. One night Kammerer climbed the fire escape and slipped in through Lucien's third-floor window left open in the hot summer night. He told Bill that he stood silently watching Lucien for half an hour as he slept in the moonlight. But as he climbed back over the fence, the hotel guard held him at gunpoint and the police were called. Lucien was summoned to the lobby and had to testify that Kammerer had been drinking all night in his room. Burroughs laughed—"S'pose you'd'a found the wrong room and hovered over a perfect stranger?"—but it was becoming obvious that Kammerer was allowing his obsession to get out of control.

One time Burroughs and Kammerer stopped by Edie's apartment, where Kammerer hoped to find Lucien, who lived there most of the time with Celine. No one was at home, and to express his disappointment, Kammerer tried to hang Kitkat, a little kitten that Jack and Edie had recently bought, using Burroughs's necktie. Bill fortunately put a stop to it, but Jack was furious when he heard about it. Burroughs's passivity in the face of all this clearly aberrant behavior is extraordinary, as if he were completely withdrawn from life. In later years he adored cats and would never have permitted a kitten to be hurt.

In her memoirs Edie Parker said, "I always felt that David was creepy and might as well have had cloven hooves and horns growing out of thick, curly red hair. He was the dark cloud that hovered over our lives. [...] He drove us all to silence because all he ever wanted to talk about was Lucien.

[...] Needless to say, he was uncomfortable to be around so we avoided him, in fact Burroughs was the only person who could tolerate him."[2] But Kammerer was Bill's best friend, and though Bill liked Jack and Lucien and Allen, they were a decade younger than he and David, and so they had less in common.

Edie describes a small but telling incident at the Minetta Tavern, when Kammerer and Burroughs joined Edie, Jack, Lucien, and Celine at a table. When Kerouac went to visit the toilet, Kammerer immediately left his seat and took the space Jack had vacated between Edie and Lucien. Edie and Lucien both spoke at once—"That's Jack's seat"—then Lucien told him, "Beat it!" and Kammerer stood up and returned to his original seat, completely unfazed. "My God, he was a pest," wrote Edie.[3]

Kammerer's behavior was beginning to scare Lucien; he seemed so obsessive, always hovering on the fringe of the group, staring intently at him. Lucien and Jack decided to ship out together. Jack had been working as a script reader for Columbia Pictures, but that job had come to an end. The best money was in going back to sea with all its attendant risks. Lucien had seaman's papers from a summer vacation job on New York Harbor transporting aircraft fuel, so they decided they would find a boat heading for France, jump ship, and walk to Paris. Jack would speak French and Lucien would pretend to be a deaf-mute. They would be two poets, there for the liberation of Paris. Best of all, Lucien would escape from Kammerer. They found a ship, SS *Robert Hayes*, but as they approached, the crew were all leaving, tumbling down the gangplank to petition the union to remove the chief mate, whom they accused of being a fascist and whom they refused to work with. The bosun told Jack and Lucien to go on board, stow their gear, eat, but not to sign on. Jack and Lucien told the chief mate that they would not sign on until they had made a trial run to Albany, so he threw them off the ship. Every effort of Lucien's to get away from Kammerer seemed to be thwarted. Events seemed to be moving, inexorably, to a climax.

2. A Death in the Family

The night of Sunday, August 13, 1944, was hot and humid, making it almost impossible to sleep. People dragged mattresses out onto fire escapes and sat around on stoops, talking and drinking. By the early hours Kammerer had located Lucien at the West End, where he had gone after dropping off Celine. Lucien was already very drunk. When the West End closed at 3:00 a.m., they took a bottle and walked over on 116th Street to Riverside Park, crossed the Henry Hudson Parkway,[4] which separates the whole of upper Manhattan from its narrow strip of riverside, and settled themselves on the bank of the Hudson looking across to the Palisades in New Jersey. Lucien told Ginsberg that Kammerer insisted that he let him give him a blow job, and in the ensuing struggle Lucien pulled out a scout knife with a two-inch blade and stabbed him. This was basically the story used in court, but Lucien also claimed that Kammerer had threatened to injure Celine if he did not let David blow him. Lucien later told Burroughs that he had been so angry he told Kammerer, "I could kill you!" and Kammerer replied, "Well, why don't you, then?" And Lucien did.

According to Kerouac's novel, Lucien stabbed him twelve times in the heart, then he tore Kammerer's white shirt into strips and tied rocks up with the strips, which he attached to Kammerer's arms and legs. He pushed rocks down his trouser legs and fastened his arms with his belt, but it was all a hasty, inept, panicky job and most of the rocks fell out. Lucien pushed him in but he wouldn't sink. Lucien stripped off all his clothes and waded neck deep into the river and pulled him in. The body floated off downstream, facedown. Lucien mopped himself down as best he could, put on his dry clothes, and made his way back to Riverside Drive, where he found a cab.

Burroughs was woken at dawn on Monday by an urgent tapping on his door at 69 Bedford Street. He pulled on his bathrobe and went to answer it. Lucien was agitated and incoherent. He handed Bill a bloodstained pack of Lucky Strikes and said, "Have the last cigarette." Bill knew at once what must have happened. "So this is how Dave Kammerer ends," he thought out loud.[5] He crumpled up the pack and cigarettes and flushed them down the toilet.

Lucien gave him a garbled, still drunken account of events. Bill told him, "Well, you'd better turn yourself in. You could plead some sort of self-defense." Lucien kept repeating, "I'll get the hot seat," but Bill paced the room. "Don't be absurd. Turn yourself in. Get a good lawyer. Do what he tells you to do. Say what he tells you to say. You'll make a case for self-defense. It's pretty absurd, but juries have swallowed bigger ones than that!"[6] Bill didn't fully believe him, but Lucien was in such a state of anxiety that no coherent explanation of what happened was possible, and when Lucien left, Bill still didn't know whether it was true or not. Bill gave him five dollars to get home. Bill dressed, then walked over to Morton Street to see if Dave had come back, but his room was empty. Bill went upstairs to tell Louise McMann what Lucien had said had happened. She gasped, "My God, how horrible!" and asked, "Do you think it's true?" Bill said he was beginning to think that it was.

At dawn Lucien shook Jack awake. "I got rid of the old man last night," he told him.

"Why'd you go and do that?"[7] asked Jack, then dragged himself out of bed and woke himself up with a shower, leaving Edie to sleep. Lucien still had Kammerer's eyeglasses and the murder weapon. He asked Jack to accompany him while he disposed of them. In fact, as he already intended to turn himself in, there was no reason to dispose of the evidence, but no one was thinking clearly. In Morningside Park, Jack pretended to take a piss while Lucien buried the glasses, and in Harlem, at 125th Street, Lucien rather ostentatiously dropped the knife through a deep subway grate. Next they took a cab to Park Avenue, where Lucien borrowed another five dollars from his psychiatrist, who "washed his hands" of him. On Third Avenue they saw Korda's *The Four Feathers* before continuing on to the Museum of Modern Art. Lucien dawdled before a portrait by Modigliani and spent time studying Tchelitchew's *Cache Cache*. All the time Lucien was screwing up the courage to go to his mother, confess what happened, get a lawyer, and turn himself in. They passed through Times Square and even visited the Maritime Union Hall where, had things gone differently, they would have taken a ship to Europe. They headed back uptown and eventually, after a few drinks, Lucien said goodbye to Jack and turned off Third Avenue onto 57th Street where his mother lived. That afternoon Lucien, accompanied by his lawyer, Vincent J. Malone, presented himself at the office of District Attorney Frank S. Horan and told his story to Jacob Grumet, the assistant DA in charge of the Manhattan Homicide Bureau.

There was no body, and no one had reported Kammerer missing, so at first the police didn't believe him, but after Lucien showed them where he had buried the glasses both the Detective Bureau and the Homicide Squad assigned men to the case. Lucien was kept in custody at Horan's office and spent most of the night reading Rimbaud and Yeats's *A Vision*. At 2:30 p.m. on the fifteenth, the Coast Guard reported a body floating off 108th Street. By the time the Marine Police and Coast Guard had towed it in, Lucien, Vincent Malone, and the police were all waiting on the shore. A shaky Lucien identified the bloated corpse and was taken straightaway to the Elizabeth Street Police Station and booked on a homicide charge. The next morning the *New York World-Telegram* headline read, "Student Admits Killing Teacher."[8]

Lucien told the police the full story: how he went first to Burroughs, then to Kerouac, and how Jack helped him dispose of the evidence. The *New York Herald Tribune* reported that "Carr rocked his questioners in the district attorney's office with liberal use of polysyllable words and deep philosophical observations."[9] Whenever there was a pause in the questioning, he returned to his copy of *A Vision*. The press reported the same withdrawn, distracted attitude in court, saying that he "listened lackadaisically to the proceedings" and "showed little interest" in what magistrate Anna M. Kross was saying in Homicide Court.

When the police arrived at Bedford Street to question him, Bill was not home. He was in a room at the Lexington Hotel on a divorce case, listening for amorous noises through the walls. The client's wife didn't check in, so nothing happened. Hearing that the police were looking for him, Bill presented himself the next day at the DA's office with his lawyer in tow to give his deposition. He was asked what he knew about the relationship between Kammerer and Carr and quite truthfully told them, "I don't think there were any sexual relations." They asked him if he knew that Kammerer was homosexual and Bill said, "Well yes, I frequently remonstrated with him, but in vain." Bill's lawyer then asked him, "Did he ever make a pass at you?" and Bill replied tartly, "Certainly not!" Bill was formally arrested as a material witness, even though his lawyer protested that he had done no wrong as Lucien had told him he was going to turn himself in. He was held for eight hours in the city prison, the Tombs, and was bailed out the same night by Mote, who flew in and paid the $2,500 bond. Bill flew back to St. Louis with his father.

Jack and Edie were also arrested, but it did not take long for the police to establish that Edie had nothing to do with it. When Jack appeared in court he was told that he came very close to becoming an accessory after the fact, and had his bail set at $5,000. Jack whistled. He was not as fortunate as Burroughs; instead of paying his bail bond, Jack's father exploded in rage. "No Kerouac was ever involved in murder before," he yelled, and refused to help. He and Edie had to get married—which they were intending to do anyway—in order for Edie to get the money from her family to pay for Jack to get out. On August 22, 1944, Jack was taken from the Bronx jail to the Municipal Building, where he and Edie were wed, with Celine Young as the maid of honor, and two detectives acting as witnesses. The police bought them several rounds of drinks before escorting Jack back to jail. It fell to Jack to formally identify Kammerer's bloated body, in the basement morgue of Bellevue Hospital. Jack was released on the thirtieth and went with Edie to her mother's luxurious home in Grosse Pointe, Michigan.

Jack had to borrow a hundred dollars from Edie's mother and needed a job in order to pay her back. Their next-door neighbor in Grosse Pointe was Dick Fruehauf, owner of the plant that manufactured Fruehauf trucks. He gave Jack a job inspecting ball bearings. Jack was able to spend most of his shift reading and taking notes and made enough to pay Edie's mother back twenty-five dollars a week.

On August 24, a Manhattan grand jury returned a second-degree murder indictment against Lucien and on September 15 he appeared in court before Judge George L. Donnellan in General Sessions Court. Lucien looked visibly nervous, shifting from one foot to another, dressed in a conservative light brown suit with his hair slicked back with hair cream. He pleaded guilty to manslaughter in the first degree. Lucien's counsel, Kenneth M. Spence, told the court how Kammerer had "hounded" nineteen-year-old Carr from city to city for the past five years and said that "the older man exercised a strong influence over the boy." Assistant DA Jacob Grumet told the court that Lucien was "emotionally unstable as a result of the improper advances" that Kammerer was alleged to have made, and said that Carr was intoxicated when he finally pulled the knife. The usual term for manslaughter was five to twenty years, but Judge Donnellan said that the sentence would depend very much on the "autobiography" that he wanted Carr to write for him. Sentencing was set for October 6.

Bill returned from St. Louis to attend the trial. When he left the courtroom, he walked out with Lucien's lawyer, who told him that they made the guilty plea because they had not wanted to take the case before a jury. Lucien would have had to be rehearsed in a story of attempted rape and might have ended up with ten years for second-degree murder. The lawyer told Bill, "I think it would have been very bad for his character for him to get off scot free," which astonished Bill as it meant his heart wasn't in the case at all. He had not wanted to get him off. As can be imagined, the West End group could talk of little else other than the subject of Kammerer's death and Lucien's sentencing. On October 1, a few days before sentencing, Celine Young wrote to Jack, who was still working in Grosse Pointe, outlining her anxiety that Lucien might get a long sentence because he showed no remorse:

> Had Lucien felt less pride in having Dave dog his footsteps he might have gotten rid of Kammerer before this and in a socially acceptable manner. The chief criticism of Lucien, and his probation officer observed this too, is that Lucien's values are all intellectual ones. [...] If he persists in the idea that he has done a messianic service by ridding the world of Dave, he is becoming too presumptuous a judge. When he loses that pride in doing away with Dave, then I hope he is let out immediately. I know he is very remorseful at times. [...] Mrs. Carr has pictured [Dave] to me as a veritable Iago, who at every turn in Lucien's life, has appeared and dissuaded him from the proper course, as she puts it, "purely for love of evil." [...] His influence on Lucien, this past year at least, was definitely to be destroyed at all costs.[10]

Judge Donnellan sentenced Lucien to an indeterminate term in the Elmira Reformatory, saying, "It is my opinion that this boy might not have been convicted of anything had he gone to trial. Even if he had been convicted, I doubt if it would have been anything but manslaughter in the second degree." A second-degree murder conviction could not be obtained because the knife used in the killing had not been recovered by the police and there was no eyewitness. However, the judge said, "I feel this boy deserves some punishment, but in an institution where he will be under good medical care, not in a prison where he will be constantly associated with hardened criminals." The court was told of Lucien's alcoholism, how he had been drinking to excess since he was fourteen years old, and was told that Lucien was unstable and had a split personality but that he could be "turned into a useful citizen" under the supervision of psychiatrists and educators. The judge explained that by giving Lucien an indeterminate term, it meant that Lucien's release was entirely dependent upon his behavior and rehabilitation. He was warned that though he might be released within eighteen months if his behavior warranted it, he would be shifted to Sing Sing to serve a possible fifteen-year sentence if he did not comply with reformatory regulations. Lucien was taken from City Prison on October 9 and eventually served a little less than two years at Elmira Reformatory.[11]

According to Edie, Bill showed no emotion at the death of his best friend, nor did he blame Lucien in any way. At first his only concern was for Lucien to get off. He regretted very much that Lucien had come to him, because had he kept his mouth shut and told no one, the murder would have been passed off as a mugging. As soon as one other person knew, then the truth would get out. Bill told Lucien, "You shouldn't blame yourself at all, because he asked for it, he demanded it!" Burroughs said, "The real engineer of the whole thing was Dave. He was the manipulator. He was a lot older than Lucien, much older. It was Kammerer's doing really, Kammerer's obsession that provoked the killing. He maneuvered and engineered this whole climax."[12]

Chapter Eleven

My emotions became like so many strange guests. As if chapter after
chapter of your life, panel after panel of your psychology were opening
and shutting in the twilight.

—Virginia Woolf[1]

1. New Romantics

After Lucien's trial Burroughs spent several months in St. Louis with his
parents, only returning to New York City in December to be psychoanalyzed. Edie Parker maintains that his parents made his monthly allowance conditional upon him attending his analyst regularly, as they were
concerned about him being in the city. Burroughs began seeing Dr. Paul
Federn, who had been, along with Anna Freud, Sigmund Freud's official
representative as well as the vice president of the Vienna Psychoanalytic
Society. He had escaped to the United States in 1938. Federn had a bald
head, an Old Testament beard, and was once described by Freud as having
"patricidal eyes."[2] It was not until 1946 that he was officially recognized
as a training analyst at the New York Psychoanalytic Institute. It had been
Bill's idea to see him, and his parents agreed. In the course of his analysis,
Bill had a dream about Federn, that he had been offering candy to little
girls without realizing he would be regarded as a pervert. When he told
it to Federn, Federn said that this had actually happened. He had offered
candy to children and then later worried what people would think.
Apparently Federn had recorded more than thirteen hundred instances of
telepathic contact between him and his patients.

Federn shot himself in 1950. His wife had died and he was suffering
from incurable cancer. He differed from Freud in thinking that it was
an absence rather than an excess of narcissistic libido that determined
the psychotic's problems in life. As a result his approach involved supporting the patient's efforts at integration by trying to prevent the emergence of repressed events and by strengthening the patient's defenses,
an approach hardly conducive to identifying the event involving Nursy

that so disturbed Burroughs, although Federn was perplexed by it, asking Bill, "What is this? This that could have affected you your whole life long? What happened?" All Bill could say was, "Well, Doctor, I just don't remember, I don't know. I don't know." Bill saw Federn for several months but was not particularly impressed. He had been reading a lot of Freud and was getting more and more dubious about the whole process. He saw that his analysis wasn't going anywhere, so Federn transferred him to Dr. Lewis R. Wolberg, a hypnoanalyst and specialist in the recall of buried memories.

Burroughs was resistant to hypnosis, and in these cases, Wolberg used narcoanalysis instead, nitrous oxide or sodium pentothal to get him to a state between waking and sleeping. Many of Wolberg's cases were battle shocked and had repressed memories because they were so horrifying. Sodium pentothal or nitrous oxide induced a light degree of anesthesia, which enabled repressed memories to surface and be dealt with. Burroughs had both treatments: when Wolberg administered nitrous oxide Bill had control of the mask, which enabled him to regulate the dose, whereas sodium pentothal, known as "the truth drug," was administered intravenously. It is a barbiturate and knocks people out. The treatment revealed various identities or alter egos that all appeared to mirror his family upbringing: there was an English identity, derived from his Welsh nanny and his own ancestors; a southern gentleman, which was not surprising as his whole upbringing was white southern; and a Negro, which also related to his southern upbringing and Negro servants. Burroughs felt that the results, once they came, were rather banal. He did some talking in accents, but imitations of other accents and mimicries had always been one of his specialities from his college days and these were later carried over into his writing. "You have to hear your characters talking, and they talk in different voices. You have to be in a sense a medium. But in these particular sessions nothing very interesting was coming through, nothing usable."[3]

Burroughs said, "He struck me as being very nice, a very well-intentioned man. He was following more or less the Freudian line, which means that the patient must provide all the information and that the analyst should not attempt any interpretation and try to force it on the patient."[4] In the end Bill said, "Well, I don't see anything more to be gained by this." He felt that where it could lead, it had led.

Burroughs had given up his Greenwich Village apartment and now moved into an apartment on Riverside Drive, lent to him by an absent friend from Harvard. It was small but had spectacular views out over the

Hudson, with wonderful sunsets. He was now living close to the West End and the circle of friends he knew through Lucien.

Jack had returned to New York in October 1944 after staying with Edie and her parents, and signed on to SS *Robert Treat Paine* as an able-bodied seaman. While waiting to ship out, he stayed with Allen Ginsberg in his small room at the Warren Hall Residence Club and devoted his time trying, unsuccessfully, to seduce Celine Young. The *Robert Treat Paine* sailed from New York in mid-October, but Jack soon got into trouble. The burly boson took a fancy to him and began calling him "Pretty Boy," "Baby Face," and "Handsome." Jack, fearing that he would be raped in his bunk, jumped ship in Norfolk, Virginia, and was blacklisted by the Maritime Union for a year. He returned to New York in disgrace.

Jack moved in with Ginsberg while he waited for a room to come up in Allen's building. It was during one of their long late-night conversations that Ginsberg finally confessed to Jack that he was gay, that he was in love with Lucien and with him and wanted to sleep with him. It was the first time he had told anyone. Jack let out a long groan, not in anger but of dismay, knowing what complications were in store. In fact Allen remained a virgin for another six months, until Jack finally allowed him to blow him.

Only Allen and Celine knew that Jack was back in the city. Allen borrowed books for him from the Columbia library, and he holed up in his new garretlike room at Warren Hall and wrote. Lucien's ideas still influenced the group, and Kerouac was voraciously reading Rimbaud, Yeats, Huxley, Claudel, Louÿs, Nietzsche, and, most particularly, *Les chants de Maldoror* by Isidore Ducasse, the self-styled comte de Lautréamont. Jack wrote by candlelight, and one evening he solemnly tied string around his arm as a tourniquet and cut his finger in order to inscribe "BLOOD" on a calling card, which he then labeled "The Blood of the Poet" and tacked on his wall to remind himself of his high ideals. He told Ted Berrigan, "I had a ritual once of lighting a candle and writing by its light and blowing it out when I was done for the night [...] also kneeling and praying before starting—I got that from a French movie about George Frederick Handel."[5] In order to prove to himself that his art was not being produced for any commercial or practical use other than the highest artistic expression, he burned his work in the flame of the candle at the end of each day. This was because he felt he had been using the image of himself as a writer to impress people and enhance his self-image. He wrote in his journal, "Art so far has rationalized my errantry, my essential Prodigal Son behavior. It has also been the victim of an ego craving fame and superiority. I have been using art as a societal step-ladder—which proves that my renunciation of society is yet incomplete. Self-Ultimacy I saw as the new vision—but I cravenly turned it to a use in a novel designed to gain me, the man of the world, respect, idolatry, sexual success, and every other thing that goes with it. Au revoir à l'art, then."[6]

When Burroughs returned to New York from St. Louis he contacted Ginsberg, who told him that Kerouac was living in the same building. Kerouac remembered, "He showed up early that December after much candle-writing and bleeding on my part, 'My God, Jack, stop this nonsense and let's go and have a drink.'"[7] Bill took him to dinner and, since he was into blood and writing, to see Jean Cocteau's 1930 film *The Blood of a Poet*.

Until then, Burroughs had always remained in the background, meekly accompanying Kammerer in his endless quest to find where Lucien was holding court. Bill only became central to the group over dinner; he was the one with the most money and was happy to buy dinner for Louise McMann, Jack and Edie, Allen, and the group. He was then receiving $150 a month (it went up later). Despite being only nineteen years old, Lucien Carr had always led the West End group, but with him away, both Allen and Jack felt adrift and lacking in a mentor. This led them to visit Burroughs with the conscious intention of finding the source of Lucien's ideas, or, as Ginsberg put it, to "investigate the state of his soul."[8]

2. An Alternative Education

Jack and Allen visited Bill's apartment on Riverside Drive, where he showed them his library, introducing them to many authors they had never heard of. They knew Rimbaud, of course, and Melville's *Moby-Dick*, Louis Untermeyer's poetry anthologies, the works of John O'Hara, and Raymond Chandler and other crime novelists. Bill told them that he had a scientific approach to reading, which was both functional and pragmatic. "I read for information, I read each book for a special purpose, for instance, I read Chas Jackson's *Lost Weekend* to see what alcoholism is like and St.-John Perse for the foreign perfume, the juxtaposition of strange experience and the images of cities glittering in the distance." Burroughs particularly liked the T. S. Eliot translation of Saint-John Perse's *Anabasis*. He had books on boxing and jujitsu, which he was still studying; on parlor tricks, card games, and formulas; E. A. Wallis Budge's *Egyptian Grammar*; Kovoor Behanan's *Yoga: A Scientific Evaluation*; and Abrahamson's *Crime and the Human Mind*. There were books on psychoanalysis and psychotherapy, including hypnoanalysis. It was the literature that interested Jack and Allen most. Here they discovered Cocteau's *Opium*, Louis-Ferdinand Céline's *Journey to the End of the Night*, Baudelaire's *Poésies*, and Kafka's

The Castle. At a time when William Blake was little known in the United States, Burroughs thought Blake was a "perfect poet" and showed them *Songs of Innocence and Experience*. Bill's complete Shakespeare was well used and had many marked passages. Also on his shelves were *The Ox-Bow Incident* by Walter Van Tilburg Clark; *Nightwood* by Djuna Barnes—one of Burroughs's favorite books; *The Folded Leaf* by William Maxwell; Gogol's *Dead Souls* and Nabokov's study *Nikolai Gogol*. He showed them the Fischer edition of *Maiden Voyage* by Denton Welch, which had just been published and was to have an enormous influence on Burroughs's work, and explained the Mayan calendar system, using a large volume of illustrations of the Mayan Codices.

Burroughs was happy to lend them books—Lucien had Bill's copy of Yeats's *A Vision* with him in jail—and gave Jack and Allen books as gifts. Jack received Oswald Spengler's *The Decline of the West*, from which he got his notion of the fellaheen. "Edify your mind, my boy," said Burroughs.[9] Allen was given an old red clothbound Liveright edition of Hart Crane's *Collected Poems*; Crane's "The Bridge" became one of the influences on "Howl." In addition they borrowed books by Cocteau, Blake, Kafka, Joyce, and Céline.

At that time Burroughs was very keen on the work of Vilfredo Pareto, the Italian economist and sociologist, and often carried with him his *Mind and Society*,[10] as well as *New Science*, Giambattista Vico's circular theory of history. Lucien Carr remembered, "Bill used to say, 'Literacy is the curse of mankind. If, however, you are cursed with literacy, all you should read is Korzybski, Pareto, and Spengler.' And of course everyone rushed out to find out who these wonderful people were and no one could put up with Korzybski and Pareto, but Spengler we managed to fight through."[11] Korzybski, Pareto, and Spengler are virtually impenetrable to the modern reader and posterity has returned them to obscurity, but they are interesting in that they are early examples of Burroughs's fascination with alternative social and medical systems.

Throughout his life Burroughs tried dozens of forms of self-improvement, from Scientology to est, ESP, psychoanalysis, Wilhelm Reich's orgone box, and Reich's vegetotherapy. He practiced the Alexander posture method, studied general semantics, Robert Monroe's out-of-body seminar, Konstantin Raudive's paranormal tape experiments, Major Bruce MacManaway's Pillar of Light, the Psionic Wishing Machine, and Carlos Castaneda's fictional Don Juan. He believed in UFOs and Whitley Strieber's alien abductions and used the "Control" computer in London that answered questions for twelve shillings and sixpence a time. He felt that they all had something of value, but that none of them came near to really helping him.

Ginsberg and Kerouac came away with the image of Burroughs as Gainsborough's "Blue Boy." They found him to be courteous and dignified, a perfect gentleman, but very shy and sensitive. "Delicacy and melancholy, fragility and vulnerability, sweet and sad like a little boy,"[12] was how Ginsberg remembered him. Burroughs quickly replaced Lucien Carr as the "leader" or mentor of the Columbia group. They discussed art and literature, and he soon introduced them to his other interests: psychotherapy, weapons, lowlife and *nostalgie de la boue*. Burroughs was usually the one with money and he was always happy to pay for meals and taxis. In those days traces of Bill as *jeunesse dorée* still came through, and he could be obstreperous when drunk and exhibit the bad behavior of a privileged Harvard schoolboy. Kerouac wrote, "the way he'd spit his bones out & snarl over chicken in elegant French restaurants, wrenching pollitos apart with his great healthy Anglosaxon teeth—'Bill, we're in a polite French restaurant!'—'Full of la belle gashes, hey? Whup?'"[13] Bad behavior in restaurants—picking food up in his hands and generally offending the other patrons—continued until he became friends with Brion Gysin in the late fifties, who soon put a stop to it, regarding it as the height of bad manners.

Burroughs always credited Kerouac with encouraging him to become a writer, and it was Kerouac who first created the public perception of Burroughs as Old Bull Lee. The humor, the intelligence, the idea of William as sage, as guru, all first came from Kerouac's books. Kerouac was already a dedicated writer. He told Bill, when they first met, that he had already written over a million words and showed some of his writing to Bill, who thought it was terrible and said so. Bill Gilmore agreed with him. "I must say I didn't think he showed any talent at all," Burroughs said. "I don't think he could ever have published that early stuff. It wasn't good. It wasn't just my opinion because when I saw *On the Road* I could see he really had something." Burroughs said later, "He didn't have much of a mind. I don't think he had a mind at all. Like so many writers, a writer that thinks is a great rarity. He had talent and he had a voice. He never had any doubt at all about what he was going to do."[14]

Jack had been working on a text based on the Kammerer killing called *I Wish I Were You*. He showed a short version to Burroughs and they came up with the idea of collaborating on a book, which was to be written as a hard-boiled detective story with Bill and Jack writing alternate chapters, Bill as "Will Dennison" and Jack as "Mike Ryko." The book was credited to William Lee and John Kerouac. They began writing it that December, initially at Riverside Drive, then when the flat's occupant returned to the city, the majority of it at Bill's new apartment above Riordan's Café at Columbus Circle. They called the book *And the Hippos Were Boiled in Their Tanks*, after a radio report of a circus fire they heard while writing the book.

Bill attempted the hard-boiled style with some success: "At this point the buzzer rang. It's a loud buzzer that goes right through you." There was a clear separation of material and who wrote what. They would meet and read their latest section to each other. Bill would normally only grunt a noncommittal "It's alright" or "Good," whereas Jack wanted a more enthusiastic response. Jack's friends were astonished that Bill had managed to get Jack to do so much work; he was famous for walking off the job. Duncan Purcell—"Uncle Dunc"—wrote to Edie to say, "I suppose [Burroughs] should be commended for keeping Kerouac at work for a longer period than ever before in history." Their perceptions, however, were based on work other than writing. In fact, it was Kerouac who deserved the praise, because he broke Bill's aversion to writing. "He encouraged me to write when I was not really interested in it. But stylistically, or so far as influence goes, I don't feel close to him at all."[15] By March 1945 the book was finished and Kerouac took it to his agents, Ingersoll & Brennan, who sent it to Simon & Schuster for consideration. They were both hoping for commercial success, with Kerouac describing it to his sister as a "portrait of the 'lost' segment of our generation, hard-boiled, honest, and sensationally real"[16]—almost a definition of the Beat Generation. Alas, publishers were not overwhelmed. In August Kerouac, who was a fast, accurate typist, retyped it, possibly with a few changes. Burroughs said, "It wasn't sensational enough to make it from that point of view, nor was it well written or interesting enough to make it on a purely literary point of view; it fell in between."[17] Nonetheless, Bill had "fun" doing it and it helped establish writing as his creative outlet. When Lucien heard what they were doing he objected vociferously, which dampened their later attempts to sell it. Years later, in discussion with Carr, James Grauerholz on behalf of the Burroughs estate agreed not to permit publication until after Carr's death. The Kammerer killing was one of several incidents to inspire James Baldwin's second novel, *Giovanni's Room*, published in 1956, and in 2013 *Kill Your Darlings*, a film by John Krokidas, was made of the incident.

Bill's apartment was above Riordan's Café at 42 West 60th Street at Eighth Avenue, just to the west of Broadway at Columbus Circle, a rundown neighborhood on the edge of Hell's Kitchen. The apartment opened onto an air shaft and never received sunlight; it was dirty and filled with cockroaches, although Bill soon disposed of them, and he sometimes killed a bedbug. The wallpaper was peeling away because the radiator leaked steam "when there was any steam in it to leak."[18] Bill sealed the dirty windows tight with a caulking of newspapers against the penetrating cold. He had moved there specifically to study the denizens of Eighth Avenue: the gamblers and honky-tonk types who hung around nearby Madison Square Garden; the old men's bars; the hustlers' bars; the junkies and tea-heads, narcotics agents and agent-provocateur bars between 44th and 42nd Streets; and Times Square itself.

Tens of thousands of servicemen passed through Times Square nightly; many were lonely country boys, in New York for the first time, all looking for booze and broads, wandering bewildered down dimmed-out Broadway until they caught the excitement of the Square, which was like a permanent celebration, a daily New Year's Eve, watched over by the giant Camel sign at 44th and Broadway, which now featured an airman blowing smoke rings (actually steam). There were giant movie palaces and dancehalls, Loew's State, Radio City Music Hall featuring the Rockettes dance troupe, the Palace, the Capitol, and the four-thousand-seater Paramount featuring the Benny Goodman Orchestra with its vocalist Frank Sinatra. Times Square had another, less salubrious population who preyed upon the servicemen and tourists. It was haven for the hustlers and thieves, pickpockets and amphetamine-heads, the pimps and junkies who hung out for hours talking over cold cups of coffee or dunking pound cake at Bickford's twenty-four-hour cafeteria on 42nd Street and the twenty-four-hour Horn & Hardart Automat. There was a twenty-four-hour pinball palace there called the Pocarino where nighthawks, high on amphetamine, played pinball with speed-freak intensity illuminated by undersea, greenish-blue fluorescent light. The cinema marquees lit up the whole area, though they were dim in comparison to prewar levels, making it into a huge frenzied stage set.

3. Junk

Burroughs's interest in lowlife began with Jack Black's *You Can't Win* and grew with his introduction to petty criminals in Chicago. He always took on the protective coloring of his friends, and in New York he had mostly socialized with Kammerer and his bohemian circle in Greenwich Village. Now that Dave was gone, Burroughs returned to his original interests. While drinking at the West End, Jack Kerouac had met Bob Brandinburg, who had moved to New York from Cleveland. He claimed to have connections in the underworld, and Kerouac introduced him to Bill. Brandinburg worked as a soda jerk at the Hamburger Mary cafeteria near Columbia, and Bill liked to stop by there in the afternoon and listen to his stories of heists and stickups. Brandinburg looked like some-one from a Humphrey Bogart movie with his padded shoulders, felt hat, and flashy tie,[19] and he became something of a role model for Burroughs, who took to imitating his purposeful way of walking, shoulder up as he turned a corner or sliding sideways through a doorway. Bill admired his single-minded approach to life: how he would enter a bar for a drink, have his drink, and leave with no wasted time. Bill was still in touch with Jack Anderson, and a friend of his, Hoagy Norton, had managed to steal a quantity of morphine syrettes and a tommy gun from the navy dockyard. He broke the gun into parts and took one piece a day until he had the whole thing. He never left the yard without something. Bill contacted Brandinburg to sell the stolen goods. Brandinburg said he knew someone who would want them and invited him to stop by his apartment.

Brandinburg lived with his girlfriend, Vickie, on Henry Street on the Lower East Side, under the giant steel span of the Manhattan Bridge. Their roommates were Herbert Huncke, Phil "the Sailor" White, and Bozo. Henry Street was a canyon wall of tall crumbling "old law" tene-ments, with tiny rooms and little light, built to house immigrants, iron fire escapes crawling over their fronts like vines. Bill stamped the snow off his feet, climbed the worn black metal stairs, and knocked at a narrow metal-fronted door. It was opened by Bozo, an overweight, flabby middle-aged queen, with tattooing on his forearms and backs of his hands.[20] Bozo was the original owner of the apartment before the others moved in. He was a failed vaudeville performer who now worked as an attendant at a Turkish bath.

"Good evening," said Bill politely, and handed him his gray snap-brimmed fedora, his gloves, and his fifteen-year-old Chesterfield overcoat with the velvet collar. Confronted by a man of obvious wealth and taste, Bozo immediately began apologizing about the state of the apartment. It was a railroad flat, with the front door opening straight onto the kitchen. Brandinburg came to greet him and introduce him to the other occupant of the room, Herbert Huncke. They sat Bill down at the kitchen table. Huncke took one look at Bill and was convinced that he was a federal nar-cotics agent. "Waves of hostility and suspicion flowed out from his large brown eyes like some sort of television broadcast. The effect was almost like a physical impact," Burroughs wrote.[21] Huncke was small and thin, his shirt collar too large for his neck. His skin had a spotted, translucent quality like vellum, as if a suntan were fading into a mottled yellow color. Pancake makeup had been heavily applied to cover a skin eruption. Bur-roughs wrote that his mouth was drawn down at the corners "in a gri-mace of petulant annoyance."[22] Huncke passed up the opportunity to buy the morphine and Brandinburg took Bill through a red corduroy curtain into the next room where there was a votive candle burning in front of a china Buddha.

Phil White, known as "the Sailor" because he was in the merchant marine, was lying on a studio couch but swung his legs off to say hello and smiled, showing discolored brownish teeth. Burroughs described him in *Junky*: "The skin of his face was smooth and brown. The cheek-bones were high and he looked Oriental. His ears stuck out at right angles from his asymmetrical skull. The eyes were brown and they had a peculiar brilliance, as though points of light were shining behind them. The light in the room glinted on the points of light in his eyes like an opal."[23]

Bill explained that he was trying to dispose of seventy-five half-grain morphine syrettes. Unlike Huncke, Phil White trusted Brandinburg's judgment that Bill was all right. Bozo appeared with a quart of Schenley's bourbon and Phil got down to business and explained that the normal price for morphine was two dollars a grain but people wanted tablets; the syrettes had too much water in them and people had to squeeze the stuff out and cook it down unless they wanted to inject it. He offered Bill $1.50 a grain. Bill said that was all right. In the next room Bill could hear raised voices as Brandinburg assured Huncke that Bill was not a narc. The apartment was not only littered with drug paraphernalia but also contained an arsenal of weapons as well as stolen goods. Bill gave Phil his telephone number.

A few nights later, Bill used one of the syrettes.[24] It was his first experience of junk. Syrettes are like toothpaste tubes, only with a needle on the end. A pin has to be pushed down the needle to pierce the seal and ready the syrette for use. Huncke later described how Burroughs had his own, fastidious way of shooting up, which consisted of rolling his shirtsleeve as high as he could get it up his arm. Then he would take a bottle of rubbing alcohol and a cotton swab, dab the cotton into the alcohol, and clean off a likely spot on his arm. "He'd look at the point on the end of the dropper to make sure that the point was good and sharp. And he'd sort of feel around his arm until he'd located the spot he thought he wanted to use. And then he'd inject the needle and squirt it in."[25]

Morphine hits the backs of the legs first, then the back of the neck, a spreading wave of relaxation slackening the muscles away from the bones so that you seem to float without outlines, like lying in warm salt water. As this relaxing wave spread through my tissues, I experienced a strong feeling of fear. I had the feeling that some horrible image was just beyond the field of vision, moving, as I turned my head, so that I never quite saw it. I felt nauseous.[26]

Phil White came over a few days after their first meeting and bought five boxes of syrettes for four dollars a box. He shot up one of them in his leg before he left. The next day he came back for ten boxes. Bill laid them out and put two to one side, saying, "These are for me."

Phil was surprised and told him that using junk was "the worst thing that can happen to a man. We all think we can control it at first. Sometimes we don't want to control it." The next day he showed up and asked if Bill had changed his mind about selling the two remaining boxes. Bill said no but sold him two syrettes to use right then. Bill shot the eight remaining syrettes over the next month, then, after six weeks, he telephoned Phil to see if he had any to sell. The price had gone up to three dollars a grain. Bill bought twelve half-grain tablets in a thin glass tube and Phil apologized for the retail rate. He introduced Bill to a drugstore that sold needles without a prescription and showed him how to make a collar out of paper to fit the needle into an eyedropper: easier to use than a hypodermic syringe. He took him to a writing doctor on 102nd Street and Broadway—"making the croaker"—with a story about kidney stones. The doctor's wife slammed the door in Bill's face, but Phil managed to talk his way past her and get a script for twelve grains. Every few weeks Phil would ship out for two- or three-week trips. Bill was using junk, but not enough to have a habit. He was fascinated by the criminal circles he was now moving in and took to spending time at the Angler Bar where Herbert Huncke liked to hang out.

The Angler Bar, on the eastern side of Eighth Avenue at 43rd Street, wrapped itself around a jeweler on the corner, with another entrance on 43rd Street, hence its name. It was around the corner from Times Square and was, according to Ginsberg, who accompanied Bill on many of his anthropological expeditions, the hottest social-melting-pot venue in the area, filled with 42nd Street male hustlers, car thieves, second-story men, burglars attempting to offload hot goods, dealers in grass and heroin, junkies looking to score, black chauffeurs killing time, and undercover cops keeping tabs on everyone.[27]

Bill had bribed Huncke with spare change, drinks, and meals, and his animosity toward Bill had quickly evaporated. Kerouac described him as "a small, dark, Arabic-looking man with an oval face and huge blue eyes that were lidded wearily always, with the huge lids of a mask. [...] He had the look of a man who is sincerely miserable in the world."[28] Huncke sat at the window, his half-closed eyes fixed on the street, like an alligator flopped on a mud bank waiting for prey, tracking every movement. He looked for johns to fuck, looked for marks to steal from, pockets to pick, drunks to roll, waited for dealers, waited for fences, watched for suckers, anticipating the movements of the cops. The Times Square cops despised Huncke because he lacked even the questionable morality of a thief: he would steal from anyone, friend or stranger, no matter how sick or hungry or down-and-out they were. The cops nicknamed him "the Creep," and sometimes, when his behavior was particularly despicable, they would ban him from the Square.

Burroughs described him: "Huncke's very prickly. I got along with him over a period of time. I saw a lot of him but he was always mooching off of somebody else, he hated to live in his own place. I didn't dislike Huncke, we had difficulties at times. He was an argumentative, nagging sort of person, always was, always starting arguments and complaining all the time about this and that. Very much a whiner. He's a great storyteller when he gets on a pure anecdotal, picaresque thing, about how he's always getting the worst of it, but when he got on his self-pity kick he was terrible. It was a question of keeping him off that, then he was quite amusing."[29]

At this time, Burroughs's interests were mostly in his criminal cohorts. Of the West End crowd, he was closest to Kerouac, whom he saw all the time because they were working on the book together. When Kerouac was in Manhattan they would bar hop together. He saw something of Ginsberg but they were not as close. Kerouac had traveled, he was a seaman, he was married, whereas Allen was only nineteen, and had been no farther than New Jersey. But Allen was anxious to learn, and that Christmas he spent as much time as he could with them, when he was not studying at Columbia. He described the Times Square scene: "Times Square was the central hangout for Burroughs, Kerouac and myself from about '44 to '46, probably the most formative period of early, Spenglerian mind, where that language of, Zap, Hip, Square, Beat, was provided over the Bickford cafeteria tables by Huncke. I would say Herbert Huncke is the basic originator of the ethos of Beat and the conceptions of Beat and Square."[30] Ginsberg said, "I was hanging around and tried out some of those syrettes at the same time. I took a lot of junk over the years thereafter but always irregularly and mechanically. Needle in vein and all. I made sure I didn't take it twice in the same week, never on the same day, and always with ten days in between, or nine days or a month. Just irregularly. But I'm not a habit type—I'm a workaholic. So I started taking junk the same time as Burroughs and I observed him building a habit."[31]

Bill was, in a sense, living two lives, and purposely separated them by renting a small apartment a few doors from Phil, Bozo, and Bob's apartment on Henry Street, where he could take drugs and hang out with under-world types whom he didn't particularly want to mix with his West End Bar friends. The rent was only ten dollars a month. Bill installed an old Victrola and a few basic amenities but it was never intended as a permanent address.

One night Bill and Jack went to Phil White's Henry Street apartment to see if he had any morphine. The door was answered by a slim, six-foot-tall redhead, who was the only one at home. Vickie Russell, whose real name was Priscilla Arminger, was the daughter of a Detroit judge and, like Edie, was from Grosse Pointe, Michigan. She was Bob Brandin-burg's girlfriend, having got off the bus at the Port Authority terminal and walked straight into the arms of a pimp named Knuckles. He held her prisoner then broke her in with a couple of 42nd Street whores. She soon got away from him and set up on her own. She wore a knuckle-duster under her glove and bought a switchblade.

She took them through to the sitting room. It had been transformed into something resembling the illicit gambling room in back of a Chinese restaurant. The walls were painted black, with black drapes over the windows. A large Chinese character was painted in red lacquer on one wall. There was a black, L-shaped couch, several red-and-black lacquered tables, and a red light bulb. On the ceiling Brandinburg had painted a large color wheel: a mosaic of triangles and squares in crude primary colors. "We get some frantic kicks out of that wheel when we're high," she told them. "We lay on our backs and dig the wheel and pretty soon it begins to spin. The longer you watch it, the faster it spins."[32]

She suggested that they go to Times Square and score. Bill paid the cab fare, but after she tried several likely places she concluded it was too late and suggested they buy some Benzedrine inhalers and get high on them. The Smith, Kline & French Benzedrine brand inhaler, in the new plastic tube introduced in 1943, cost twenty-five cents and contained 250 milligrams of racemic amphetamine, 75 milligrams of oil of lavender, and 25 milligrams of menthol. They were perfectly legal and advertised in the press. Bill and Vickie bought a number of inhalers and went to an all-night coffee shop near 52nd and Sixth Avenue where musicians hung out after their gigs. Vickie showed them what to do. Inside the inhaler there were six white strips of blotting paper impregnated with amphetamine. They were awful to taste, but the effect of just one of those strips came on quickly and lasted for eight hours. Vickie expertly extracted the strips and gave three to Bill, telling him to roll them into a pill and wash it down with coffee. In *Junky* Burroughs uses this event as the subject for one of his hilarious set pieces:

[Vickie] selected some gone numbers and beat on the table with the expression of a masturbating idiot. I began talking very fast. My mouth was dry and my spit came out in round white balls—spitting cotton, it's called. [...] I was full of expansive, benevolent feelings, and suddenly wanted to call on people I hadn't seen in months or even years, people I did not like and who did not like me.[33]

They got so high that Kerouac became completely disoriented on the subway back downtown and didn't know where he was. However, he recovered enough to spend twenty-four hours in bed with Vickie at Bill's seedy apartment.

Chapter Twelve

She was in all probability one of the most charming and intelligent women I've ever met.

—HERBERT HUNCKE

1. Joan

Joan Vollmer returned to New York with her daughter, Julie, early in September 1944 looking rested and having lost fifteen pounds. Within three weeks she found a place to live: apartment 35 at 419 West 115th Street between Morningside Drive and Amsterdam Avenue, a huge, old-fashioned apartment with six big rooms and a sun-filled living room. She signed the lease for $150 a month under her married name of Mrs. Paul Adams and gave as her cosignees Mr. and Mrs. Jack Kerouac. Edie had given up the old apartment when she went to Grosse Pointe after marrying Kerouac but had followed her errant husband back to New York and was living with him in his cramped room at Warren Hall. She arranged to share the place with Joan but then broke up with Jack again and returned to Grosse Pointe, so Joan needed to find more flatmates to share the rent. Her old friend Ruth Clark spent a few months there but became pregnant and soon went to join her marine husband where he was stationed. An advertisement in the *Columbia Spectator* student paper found Hal Chase, who took the first room by the door. Haldon Chase was from Denver and was studying anthropology at Columbia, specializing in American Indian culture. He had been in the ski troops but was already discharged and was on a somewhat different wavelength from Joan, Edie, and Jack, but he fitted in well enough. Ginsberg described him as a "brash innocent mountaineering Denver boy, 'Child of the Rainbow' with pretty golden blond hair and good physique, an all-Indian hawk nose and American boy State Fair fresh manners." His role in the Beat Generation saga was to introduce them all to his hometown friend Neal Cassady, but in the meantime he began seeing Celine Young.

On arrival in New York Joan began an affair with Bruce Mazlish, later the celebrated psychohistorian. Through Mazlish she met John Kingsland, a nineteen-year-old Columbia student who was in Ginsberg's year and had originally been on the same floor of the Union Theological Seminary as Allen and Lucien. He was thrown out of the seminary in January 1945 for being drunk and having once taken Joan to his room. He and Joan got together and he moved into 115th Street. Despite their age difference, Kingsland assumed it was a serious, long-term relationship and that this disparity would diminish in time. He arranged to have his classes in the afternoon so he could watch over Julie in the mornings while Joan worked in a nursery school. Then he would go to class and work evenings at the library. Joan often wrote his class papers for him, and there was one term paper on Dryden and eighteenth-century English literature that she wrote in the style of Dryden that his professor, Joseph Wood Krutch, admired so much that Kingsland was concerned he would be found out. Joan was very well read: her bookshelves were filled with the works of Goethe, Marcel Proust, James Joyce, and Karl Marx, and she was clearly a good writer.

Allen Ginsberg, meanwhile, had been having a difficult time. Johnny the bartender—presumably a paid informant—had reported to Dean McKnight's office at Columbia that Allen had been drinking with Kerouac at the West End Bar and the dean summoned Allen's father; Louis left the dean's office in tears. Allen studied hard and had straight-A grades, but Columbia wanted complete control over their scholarship students and the West End was out of bounds. Allen had to leave Warren Hall and move to Livingston Hall, on campus, where he shared with Bill Lancaster, whose father was a banker and a director of the Foreign Policy Association.

On March 16, in the course of one of their long discussions, Burroughs told Jack bluntly that he would never free himself from his mother's pernicious influence unless he made a proper break with her instead of running home every time he had a problem. Bill said, "The trouble with you is you're just tied to your mother's apron strings and you are going in a wide circle around her now, but it's going to get a narrower and narrower circle and sooner or later you are going to be right in there, unable to move away from your mother. That's your fate, that's your Faustian destiny."[1]

Appalled by Burroughs's prophecy, Jack went straight to Livingston Hall to discuss it with Allen. Ever since Edie had returned to her mother in December, Jack had been spending at least half of his time in Ozone Park, Queens, where his father was dying. Jack had not connected his separation from Edie, and his inability to commit himself to their relationship, with his mother's strenuous efforts to be the only woman in his life. Jack recognized that Burroughs was right: he had internalized many of his mother's ideas and was too closely tied to her. It got so late that Jack stayed over with Allen. Jack was aware of Allen's erotic feelings for him, but they slept chastely in their underwear.

Allen suspected that the Irish woman who cleaned his room harbored anti-Semitic feelings, and had used this to draw her attention to the dirty window that she never cleaned. He had written "Butler has no balls" (a reference to Nicholas Murray Butler, president of Columbia University), followed by an eye-catching "Fuck the Jews" with a skull and crossbones beneath it. But instead of a clean window, Allen's graffiti resulted in a report to Dean Furman. At 8:00 a.m., after Bill Lancaster had already gone to class, Furman, the assistant dean of student-faculty relationships, burst into Allen's room. Jack leapt from the bed and ran to Lancaster's empty bed in the next room, pulling the covers up over his face. Allen was made to wipe the offending words from the window, but he knew that Furman was thinking the worst. Allen later found two notes in his box. One charged him $2.35 for entertaining an unauthorized guest overnight, and the other, from Dean McKnight, informed him that he was suspended and suggested that he spend the weekend with his father, "since the privilege of residence at Livingston has been withdrawn from you." McKnight wrote to Allen's father saying that he had been suspended for obscene writings on his window and giving overnight housing to a person who was not a member of the college and whose presence on the campus was unwelcome. Kerouac had been branded as "an unwholesome influence on the students" ever since he was charged as a material witness in the Kammerer case.

On Monday morning, Dean McKnight glared at Allen across the desk and said, "Mr. Ginsberg. I hope you understand the *enormity* of what you have done!"

Allen remembered the lines in Céline on dealing with madmen and knew that the only way out was to humor him. "Oh I do, sir! I do! I do!" he said. "If you can only tell me what I can do to make up for this..." McKnight decreed that Allen could not return to Columbia until he had worked at a job for a year and had a psychiatric report to confirm that he was now mature enough to be a responsible member of the academic community. Allen was out and the purity of Columbia was assured. With nowhere to live, Allen moved into West 115th Street with Joan, Julie, and Hal Chase.

Jack and Allen got it into their heads that Burroughs should meet Joan Vollmer because, in Ginsberg's words, "Joan was a very intelligent woman, somewhat sardonic, curious-minded, learned, and an intellectual lady with a very fine mind and a high noble brow and wittier than any lady I'd ever met. So Kerouac and I thought, 'Gee, we should introduce her to Burroughs 'cause she's real smart and Burroughs would appreciate her humor.' "[2] Joan had been in Albany from the beginning of 1944 and missed the chaos and excitement surrounding the death of Kammerer, and Bill had been away until December, so they had not had much opportunity to meet thus far. Jack and Allen did not know at that time that Bill was gay, so there was a degree of matchmaking going on as well as a genuine feeling that they would get on. They invited him over to 115th Street and he and Joan hit it off. Their humor clicked and they clearly enjoyed each other's company. Burroughs said, "She was a very extraordinary woman and we got talking, exchanging ideas, she was the smartest person around." He compared her to Allen, saying that she was in many ways smarter because she didn't have any limits to her thinking, whereas Allen did. "That was the basis of the attraction, an intellectual, not the usual talks about nothing. She had a sense of humor. It was more humor my style. She had an immediate insight into anyone's character. Just one look and she knew."[3]

This was a trait that Bill felt she shared with his mother, who could also tell someone's character with just one glance and knew instantly if someone was lying. Bill said, "Joan was exactly the same. For example, on Kerouac's character she said, 'He has a natural inborn fear of authority and if the cops questioned him his mouth would open and out would come the information.' She had a great deal of insight."[4] Clearly the shared attributes with his mother were part of her appeal. They became good friends and Bill often visited her. His relationship with Joan did not become physical until later. They often ate out together, though this was becoming more difficult in New York as the war effort finally started to have an impact on the general population. In January 1945, Mayor La Guardia had instituted meatless Tuesdays and Fridays; no butchers could sell meat on those days and all restaurant meals had to be meatless. Hot dog stands were exempt. Then in February the federal government introduced a midnight curfew on all restaurants and bars and nightclubs, which hit Manhattan hard as so many people worked in late-night bars and clubs. Only places that were traditionally open twenty-four hours were exempt; night workers had to eat somewhere.

Jack brought Vickie Russell around to 115th Street and, inspired by Joan's bathing habits, she began taking a perfumed bubble bath in the kitchen bathtub at Henry Street, her hair piled high on her head like Nefertiti's crown, the men lunging forward, attempting to blow away the bubbles, avoiding her slaps. For her part, Vickie quickly introduced

Benzedrine to the group. Joan had a huge bed with an oriental rug draped across it, and soon Allen, Jack, and Joan, often accompanied by Vickie, were spending evenings high on amphetamine, sprawled over the bed as little Julie slept in the corner of the room.

On V-E Day, May 8, 1945, Bill and Jack went to join the crowds in Times Square to celebrate; they tried to pick up women but failed. Bill later thought that Jack's heart wasn't really in it; Jack thought that Bill scared them off. Later that month, around Memorial Day, people began to drift away for the summer. Joan went with Julie to her parents; Hal Chase went back to Denver; Allen eventually signed up for training at the U.S. Maritime Service in Sheepshead Bay, Brooklyn, an idea that Bill had several times toyed with because that was the fastest route to the coveted Seamen's Union card. Bill returned to St. Louis to spend the summer with his parents. In July he made a trip to Chicago, "on business," probably to buy drugs, and was back in New York by the end of August. He had given up the West 60th Street place when he left for the summer and moved into a $4.50-a-night hotel on Park Avenue. Joan was still in need of flatmates, and so around Labor Day, Bill moved into 115th Street.

Joan and Julie had one room; Hal Chase had another. Allen Ginsberg had his things there, but as he was away for three and a half months' training he had stored them all in Hal's room. Bill took over the spare bedroom and installed his library and few other belongings. By now it was obvious that Joan was very attracted to Bill, but it would be a little while before he reciprocated. He had, however, already told her—and Jack and Allen— that he was homosexual. Edie was back in New York and working for an agency that supplied cigarette girls, selling Chesterfields at "21," the Kit Kat, Zanzibar, and the Stork Club. Jack was unemployed so he lived off her wages, dividing his time about equally between 115th Street and Ozone Park looking after his father, who was dying of stomach cancer. With Edie away each night until 3:00 or 4:00 a.m., Jack was free to run around town seeing other girls. According to Ginsberg, who was prone to exaggerate these things, Kerouac was also seeing men. He was certainly bisexual, and Allen claimed to have had sex with him as many as fifty or sixty times:

> Mostly I blew him. He blew me once. [...] Mainly he was interested in getting blown, with men and women! That was probably his main sex life with girls was getting blown too. It became a burden in our sexual relationship because I wanted more response. [...] Except I really loved him so I was happy to [go along]. [...] It was a very ambivalent relationship with him sort of deny- ing interest but allowing it so it was sort of, a little bit in the pattern of John

Rechy…in the sense of Rechy's feelings of triumph, if he could get somebody to blow him. But refusing to blow anybody. [Kerouac and Burroughs] were in bed a couple of times. [...] I think Burroughs would get desperate and say, "Oh, c'mon Jack," and Jack'd say, "How about blowing me?" and Burroughs'd say, "No, c'mon Jack." The thing was so funny it wasn't even homosexuality.[5]

In September Bill took Jack to a homosexual orgy, but Jack's Catholic guilt was so great that he canceled a meeting with Bill the next day. He wrote to Allen, who was still training for the merchant marine at Sheepshead Bay in Brooklyn, telling him:

Since then, I've been facing my nature full in the face and the result is a purge. [...] Remember that the earlier part of my life has always been spent in an atmosphere vigorously and directly opposed to this sort of atmosphere. It automatically repels me, thereby causing a great deal of remorse, and disgust. [...] As to the physical aspects, which as you know, disgust me consciously, I cannot be too sure [...] whatever's in my subconscious is there.[6]

Kerouac's notebooks were filled with drawings of crucifixes and references to God and Jesus; he never left the faith, and his homosexual flings filled him with remorse. However, shortly after the orgy, Jack, Bill, and Allen spent a night at the notorious Everard Baths at 28 West 28th Street where Jack disappeared into the Turkish baths with a group of French sailors who gave him a blow job. Allen commented, "I think he just dug the idea of a bunch of French sailors. He was quite sociable and happy [...] he was very gay about it."[7]

As the end of 1945 approached, the little band at Henry Street had dispersed and Huncke had moved into Bill's Henry Street apartment, which he had kept on because it was so cheap. The idea was that Huncke would pay half the rent and look after the place, but naturally that never happened. Ever since he first met Phil White, Bill had been slowly developing a habit until he was now shooting every day. Phil White and his girlfriend, Kay, moved into an apartment in the same building, and every morning after breakfast they would meet to plan how to get that day's supply of junk. Bill, now short of money from his habit but still looking respectable, began touring doctors recommended by Phil as being likely to write a script. Burroughs often said that *Junky* is extremely accurate concerning events around this time, and it spells out in meticulous detail his inexorable slide into addiction. He wrote, "As the habit takes hold, other interests lose importance to the user. Life telescopes down to junk, one fix and looking forward to the next."[8]

2. The Wolfeans and the Non-Wolfeans

Joan was still married to Paul Adams, but had written saying she no longer wanted to be with him. He clearly still had feelings for her, as Joan
revealed in a letter to Edie: "I got two letters from Paul this morning—
quite nice ones. First I'd heard from him since I wrote. Didn't seem too
upset, and asked what I wanted to do. Don't know quite what to answer.
He didn't suggest divorce, but said we might separate and 'begin court-
ing again.' Poor little soul. But honestly I think he might be just a little
relieved."[9] Their relationship was finally terminated one night in September 1945, when Paul came striding down the hall of 115th Street in
his big army boots, fresh home from the front. He was appalled to find
six people, all high on Benzedrine, cross-legged and sprawled across the
bed, surrounded by overflowing ashtrays, discussing skepticism and deca-
dence. He stared at them in horror and exclaimed, "Is *this* what I fought
for?" Joan just looked up and told him to come down from his "character
heights."[10] He filed for divorce shortly afterward.

It was around this time that one of the set-piece Beat Generation events
occurred, later known as "The Night of the Wolfeans and the Non-
Wolfeans." Kerouac was enormously influenced by Thomas Wolfe and
talked constantly about his overlong celebrations of American provincial
life. In the Benzedrine-fueled discussions at 115th Street this evolved into
a split in the household between the Wolfeans and the non-Wolfeans. The
Wolfeans were the heterosexual all-American boys, Kerouac and Hal
Chase, and on the other side were Burroughs and Ginsberg, characterized
by Allen as "the sinister European fairies, me and Burroughs, fairy-Jew-
communists non-Wolfean cynics who didn't believe in the wide-open
dewy-eyed lyrical America that they did and who were always trying to
make it with the Wolfean boys."[11]

On the night in question, they wound up talking all night, Bill in bed
with Kerouac and Allen in bed with Hal Chase, speeding their heads off.
Allen got very upset with the way the conversation was going; he felt as
if a huge cellophane curtain had come down between them, and protested vehemently, "It's not fair to be divided like this." He felt the non-
Wolfeans were being discriminated against. "Homosexuality was one of
the attributes of non-Wolfeans, and among other things, intellectuality
and fear of the body and manipulativeness and Jewishness. International
concern rather than appreciation of America and homeyness and family
and normal values."[12] That night became a reference point between them
for many years. Ginsberg said, "If I had been the only non-Wolfean I
would have felt like a jerk, but with Burroughs as one of us, I felt there

was some dignity and possibility in the situation despite our deficiency in earthiness."[13] In many ways, the roles and relationships defined by them that night determined how they saw each other for the rest of their lives. These roles were reinforced in games of charades where the Wolfean and non-Wolfean roles were acted out.

Ginsberg played "The Well-Groomed Hungarian" with an atelier full of worthless paintings. Burroughs would play his shill, wearing one of Joan's skirts and a wig. Kerouac borrowed his father's straw hat and played the wide-eyed, innocent American in Paris. Allen would rub his hands together and affect a thick Middle European accent: "Ah, my young man, you vant to buy some culture? I haff these masterpieces that we brought with us when we flee the Nazis."

Jack would cross his legs and step from one foot to the other, clutching his hat: "Aw gee, fellers. I cain't. I got a girl. I have a date with my girl at one of those coffee houses you got out here."

At this, Burroughs rather broke role, saying, "You want to stay away from those, Jack. Those ladies got poison juices. Your cock falls off and sometimes they got teeth up there!"[14] Bill later remembered his role. "I was playing, er-hum, an Edith Sitwell part. I got in drag and looked like some sinister old lesbian."[15]

This was at the height of Burroughs's analysis with Dr. Wolberg, and Bill was reading a great deal about hypnoanalysis, narcoanalysis, and Freud. He attempted to put his ideas into practice by analyzing Allen, beginning in August 1945. Ginsberg claimed that he and Kerouac spent a year, an hour a day, five or six days a week free-associating while Burroughs acted as a psychiatrist, sitting in a straight-backed chair while they in turn lay on the couch.[16]

Burroughs challenged this, telling Ted Morgan that "perhaps there were ten sessions in all. He unburdened himself to me to no purpose at all. There were various traumatic events, but on the whole nothing of much significance. 'Nobody loves me, nobody loves me, nobody loves me!' Now I felt, even at the time, that this was sheer histrionics. It just didn't ring true and it didn't mean anything. Now I'd say, 'Why should anyone love you? And why do you want anyone to love you? That's the most important question. Why do you want to be loved, why do you need to be loved?'"

Ginsberg, however, felt that the analysis was something of a success. "Mine came to a conclusion when there was some kind of breakthrough of feeling and I finally burst into tears and said, 'Nobody loves me!' which I think was what was bothering me at the time. And when I finally came out with it and wept Burroughs sat there, sort of impersonally, friendly, listening, commentating, welcoming. So it was kind of a breakthrough for me, a realization of my actual feelings." As Ginsberg was just nineteen, and somewhat adrift, Burroughs does seem to have helped him.

With all the talk of analysis, and the acting out of "routines," Bill next attempted to act out the different layers of his own alter ego that his narcoanalysis with Dr. Wolberg had identified. The top personality was easy, that of the distinguished scion of the respectable St. Louis family, so he went straight on to the nervous, possibly lesbian English governess, which once again involved getting up in drag. Ginsberg said that this "was more or less what Burroughs was like naked, when he was in bed making out; that is, kind of prissy, self-conscious, simpering, middle-aged feminine." As the English governess he was very prim, serving tea, shrieking in a high voice, "My dear, you're just in time for tea," and rapping people on the knuckles if they said something untoward: "Don't say those dirty words in front of everyone."

Bill loved acting out the old tobacco farmer, sittin' on his front porch on the banks of the river watching the catfish go by. He would slowly build his monologue while people held their breath in anticipation. "See that catfish comin' down the river? Well it's just like one catfish after another going down. Comes down from there and goes right down here, and I jest sit and watch 'em all day long. Once in a while I get out my fishing tackle and I catch me a catfish. EVER GUT A CATFISH?" And he'd leap up and go completely mad with psychopathic bloodlust with his capping line while everyone roared with laughter.

Beneath all the personality layers was a silent, starving, skull-headed, yellow-skinned Chinese, crouched on the banks of the muddy Yangtze; a character with no hope, no ideals, no beliefs, and no words, that Bill felt might be his ultimate persona.

In addition to his experiments in lay analysis, for many months Bill attempted to hypnotize Ginsberg, with no success. They conducted experiments in telepathy, marking crosses and circles and squares on sheets of paper at predetermined times. Ginsberg remembered that "there was a whole year we did that for fun. We would not see each other and match them every two days."[17] This was something that Bill and Joan would do together for many years to come.

It was inevitable that the other residents of 115th Street would get to know Huncke. Burroughs first took him around in October 1945, thinking that his stories might amuse them. They did, and Huncke made enormous efforts to ingratiate himself into their society, knowing they were all from solid middle-class backgrounds, like himself, and that there was money there. Huncke recalled, "I used to visit there constantly. Sometimes I'd stay overnight. Sometimes I'd cut out, stoned out of my gourd, at the crack of dawn, walk downtown, down to forty-second Street."[18] Jack was particularly intrigued by him, seeing material for his writing: "Then there was Herbert Huncke—he's the greatest story teller I've ever known. I don't like his ideas about mugging and all that stuff, but he doesn't do the mugging himself. He's just a little guy."[19]

Huncke recognized that he had to sing for his supper. "I guess I represented the underworld. They were curious about the underworld and I was certainly much closer to the underworld than they were at that point, such as it was. Well, one thing they all had in common is that they wanted to write. They talked about writing and they knew of writers and so forth. They were very thoroughly trained academically."[20]

Bill also brought round Phil "the Sailor" White, whom he was seeing on a regular basis to get morphine. The Sailor also had a good line in stories, and to the 115th Street group these were romantic, outsider figures, free from the normal constraints of society. In fact they were just self-serving criminals with no thought for other people who would do anything as long as it was to their advantage. Shortly before Burroughs met them, Huncke and Phil White were on board ship; both had merchant marine papers. They stole all the morphine syrettes from the medical supplies in the lifeboats—identical to the ones Burroughs sold them, and probably from the same source—and shot them up. Had the ship been torpedoed and injured men taken to the lifeboats, there would have been no morphine to ease their pain, but no one made a moral judgment about them. They were characters.

There was a diverting interlude in late 1945 when Huncke was approached by a researcher in Times Square and asked to participate in Dr. Alfred Kinsey's study on sexual behavior. Huncke immediately asked to be paid and after the usual wrangling was given ten dollars. He was also offered fifty cents for every new subject he could get to do it. Huncke knew an enormous number of people who would be willing, mostly junkies and thieves, and Kinsey and his assistant, Wardell Pomeroy, were thrown out of one hotel because the manager didn't like the line of seedy-looking people visiting their rooms, suspecting them of dealing drugs. The questionnaire had 521 items, but depending on the subject's particular experiences, usually only about three hundred questions were asked. Tape recorders did not yet exist and so the answers were taken down by hand. The questions were extremely detailed and the whole thing took about an hour. Bill, Jack, and Allen all agreed to do it. Bill was very interested in the project and was introduced to Dr. Kinsey, but it was Pomeroy who asked the questions. Bill was paid five dollars. After fifty-three hundred men had been interviewed, the findings were published in 1948 as *Sexual Behavior in the Human Male*[21] —something of a generalization, as all the participants were white and American.

Joan and Bill spent hours in Joan's room, lying on the bed talking. "We had all these really deep conversations about very fundamental things," Burroughs recalled later, "her intuition was absolutely amazing."[22] Ginsberg had fond memories of spending long hours in Joan's room talking, with Bill lying on the bed, propped up with pillows, and Joan at his side with her arm around him. Because Bill was so involved with it, Joan tried morphine (she didn't shoot it), but she hated it. She said it was just awful, she hated the sensation and couldn't understand how anyone could take it. She had a complete intolerance for opiates. However, as Burroughs drifted deeper into addiction, so Joan took more and more Benzedrine. By Christmas 1945, she was using an entire tube a day. Bill used to line up the empties and shoot them with an air pistol.

Joan claimed to have very acute hearing and told the others what the Irish couple living in the apartment below were saying. She reported quarrels over the old man's sexual demands and petty squabbles. Several times they debated whether Joan was a whore, and whether they should report them all to the police as drug addicts. Then one evening she heard a bad quarrel going on and said the man was threatening to stab his wife. She insisted that Jack and Allen, the only ones there, do something. They ran downstairs and pounded on the door. There was no one home. For the past five months Joan had been having auditory hallucinations caused by the amphetamine.[23]

Ever since Hiroshima and Nagasaki, Joan and Huncke, who was also a heavy user of Benzedrine at that time, had been talking about the effects of atomic radiation and believed (correctly) that radiation caused mutation and skin cancers. They spent hours discussing the radioactive spores that they saw emerging from their flesh and believed that the effects of radiation could be most clearly seen among the nighttime inhabitants of Times Square where the diseased skin and cellular breakdown was illuminated in the brightly lit all-night cafeterias.

Jack, too, used so much Benzedrine that his health deteriorated. He started to have hallucinations, his hair began to fall out, and one day he looked so deathly pale that Vickie Russell slapped makeup on his face before she would go on the subway with him. Finally, in December, he collapsed with thrombophlebitis, painful swelling of the veins caused by blood clots, and was admitted to Queens General Hospital on the VA program, where he had to lie with his legs up on pillows swathed in hot compresses for several weeks.

Jack was released to the care of his mother, who was already looking after her husband, Leo. Burroughs went to visit him for dinner; he had been out to Ozone Park before and Mrs. Kerouac had always been civil to him, even though he could tell that she hated him. Allen was forbidden to visit because he was a Jew, and Jack went along with that. Leo's face was a lifeless gray color and his stomach was purple and swollen hard like a watermelon; every two or three weeks the doctor would come and drain it into a bucket. As soon as Bill entered the room Leo began an anti-Semitic, antiblack diatribe. Bill was appalled: "He was just a horrible mess of a Catholic consciousness." Back at 115th Street, Jack told Bill and Joan that his mother had put a curse on his father strong enough to kill him. He said that as he lay there dying she would taunt him: "Pretty soon I'm going to be saying, 'Ya ya ya' to you, six feet underground!"[24] He lived another month after Bill's visit.

After his father died, Kerouac turned up at 115th Street with a distant, spaced-out look on his face and said, "You know, Joan, I realize that my mother is the most marvelous woman in the world!" As far as Burroughs was concerned, he was running scared. His mother had killed his father and he was next if he stepped out of line. She wanted him all to herself; she did her best to undermine every relationship he ever had with a woman, including his wives, and tried hard to separate Jack from the pernicious influence of Bill and Allen. As far as Bill was concerned she was a stupid, superstitious, vindictive, hateful Breton peasant: "They know what they want and by God they're going to get it. They're just *there* like a real hunk of hard evil shit."[25] Bill did not disguise his opinion of her. "Jack was under her thumb. A real mama's boy."[26]

Kerouac was going through a very hard time. His father had made him swear that he would look after his mother after his death, an oath that potentially meant that Jack would have to get a job instead of pursuing his career as a writer and living off her earnings from the shoe factory until he had finished his book and was able to live off his writing. But fortunately she agreed to support him, at least until his book was published, recognizing the power that gave her over him. In fact, Leo's death focused Jack's energy and precipitated him into a writing frenzy. Once more using Benzedrine, though in more moderation this time, he began writing a massive Wolfean bildungsroman, *The Town and the City*, about Lowell and New York, which occupied him until September 1948. Supported by his mother, he prayed each day to Jesus, placed his Bible next to his typewriter, and began a long work session. The final manuscript was indeed Wolfean, with over twelve hundred manuscript pages and more than 300,000 words. It was published by Harcourt, Brace & World in 1950. He had always known he was a writer, and he had achieved his aim.

Meanwhile Bill's addiction had reached the stage where his monthly allowance did not cover the cost of his drugs. He concentrated instead on getting scripts from doctors, and when that got difficult, he began forging them. Edie's grandmother had put someone named Morris Martin through medical school, and when he died, he left her some property in Brooklyn. She never threw anything away that might be useful, such as the dead doctor's prescription pads, which Edie was now using for grocery lists. Phil White talked Bill into forging prescriptions and Bill spent ages practicing a signature in an illegible hand. They used the prescriptions to get junk, but then the others began using Dr. Martin's pads as well. Then Bill misspelled "Dilaudid," using two l's, attracting the attention of the pharmacist. As Edie put it, "some druggist checked and found out that the croaker had croaked." The inspectors examined the scripts and found they were in different handwriting.

Bill was not surprised when two detectives, Shein and O'Grady, arrived at 115th Street, as Huncke had already been arrested. Bill was charged with violation of Public Health Law 334, giving the wrong name on a prescription. He remembered in *Last Words*, "(When you see a Jew can an Irishman be far behind?) Just cops. Trying to be as nice as they aren't. No push. No slap. Just a few snarls from Shein."[27] Bill used them as the models for Hauser and O'Brien in *The Naked Lunch*. He was taken to the Tombs, fingerprinted, and his mug shot was taken. Bail was set at $1,000. Joan arrived accompanied by Dr. Wolberg; she didn't have any money, but as a physician, Dr. Wolberg could sign a bond. Bill's parents were notified and his father flew to New York. Joan told Edie, "The only way I could get him out on bail was to call his psychiatrist and he promptly informed Bill's family which led to a good deal of unpleasantness."[28] They were very upset. They had not seen Bill for six months and had no idea that he was using drugs. Mote didn't lecture him, he just said, "It's a terrible habit." He got Bill a lawyer, who advised them to get a doctor to say he was under treatment for this "affliction," as he put it. They secured Dr. Milton Feltenstein, who later almost killed Dylan Thomas with the wrong drugs. He gave Bill a prescription for Demerol but that was all. He was only hired to say he was treating him. Bill was busted in April 1946, but his case would not reach magistrate's court for two months.

And he still needed money for drugs. He began working as the Sailor's accomplice as a lush worker, rolling drunks on the subway, known as "working the hole." The first line of the revised edition of *The Soft Machine* reads, "I was working the hole with the Sailor and we did not do bad." He acted as a shill and stand-up man for Phil, respectable in his suit and tie, holding his *New York Times* open, spread wide, while Phil reached behind Bill, his fingers feeling for the inside breast pocket, looking for the man's wallet, or "poke," as Phil called it. They would never wait for more than three trains to pass before moving on to another station, but when they found someone slumped, asleep or dead drunk on a bench, they would home in on them. If the drunk opened his eyes, he could see that Bill had both hands on the newspaper and his suspicions were allayed. Huncke wrote, "Somehow there was something ludicrous about a man of Bill's obvious educational background becoming a business partner with knock-around, knock-down, hard hustling Phil."[29]

The partnership did not last long. Bill did not have the stomach for the violence involved. One time the drunk woke up and grabbed them. "Okay you guys, ya been in my pockets, we're going downtown." Burroughs remembered, "The Sailor hit him and he fell down, but he was still hanging on to the Sailor and the Sailor said, 'Get this mooch off of me.' So I hit him once in the jaw and kicked him once in the ribs. Well, the rib smashed. I had to get outa that, man. I hadda get out of that situation."[30] The next day Bill told Phil he was retiring as a lush worker. "I don't blame you," he said.[31]

Bill's next move was to go into pushing heroin with Bill Garver, another of Huncke's criminal friends. William Maynard Garver, known as Bill Gains in *Junky* and as Old Bull Gaines in Kerouac's *Desolation Angels* and *Tristessa*, was yet another thief from a "good family": his father was a bank president in Philadelphia. Garver was a tall, thin, distinguished-looking man, with a gaunt face, thinning hair that was turning gray, and a very elegant manner of speech. Burroughs described him as having "a malicious childlike smile that formed a shocking contrast to his eyes which were pale blue, lifeless and old."[32]

He had been thrown out of Annapolis Military Academy for drunkenness and received a hundred dollars a month from his father to stay away from the family, the result of some reprehensible occurrence in his youth. Unfortunately this was not quite enough to maintain his drug habit, so he supplemented it by stealing overcoats from the coatracks in restaurants and coffee shops, which he then pawned. He could get ten to fourteen dollars for a good hundred-dollar overcoat, but he had to travel to the farthest reaches of the city to pawn them, otherwise the pawnbrokers would have turned him in. He recruited all his friends and acquaintances to help out, giving them a percentage of the deal. Allen Ginsberg liked to watch him in action and even sold one of the pawn tickets to Eugene, his lawyer brother. Garver first met Huncke when he was allocated a bed next to his in the dormitory of Rikers Island jail where Huncke was doing three months for robbery. Huncke suggested that he look up Burroughs when he got out, as they were of similar background and interests.

Garver had a ten-dollar-a-week room on the fifth floor of Hotel Globe, a theatrical hotel at 42nd Street and Fifth Avenue, very convenient for Bickford's and Horn & Hardart on 42nd Street where he scored his heroin. He had the same utter callousness as Huncke: when he worked as a medical orderly in a mental hospital during the war he substituted milk sugar for the morphine given to help patients in pain. He saw nothing wrong in it: "After all, they're crazy anyway. They don't know the difference."[33] In fact, he delighted in schadenfreude, getting pleasure from others' misfortune. Burroughs wrote that Garver "was one of the few junkies who really took a special pleasure in seeing non-users get a habit. [...] [He] liked to invite young kids up to his room and give them a shot [...] and then watch the effects, smiling his little smile." Burroughs liked him nonetheless.

Garver had an Italian connection on the Lower East Side who sold them a quarter ounce for ninety dollars. They cut it one-third with milk sugar and put it in one-grain caps that they sold for two dollars each, retail. They were offering the best deal on the street as their caps were about 16 percent pure. They got about eighty caps out of a quarter ounce because their connection constantly gave them a short count. Burroughs now spent hours at a time in cafeterias and bars, waiting, watching, until his customers found him. It was all used later, to great effect, in *The Soft Machine*, where his powers of observation, his delight in the underworld characters of his acquaintance, and their names and parlance outweigh the harrowing descriptions of junk sickness and kicking:

> There is a boy sitting at the counter thin-faced kid his eyes all pupil. I see he is hooked and sick. Familiar face maybe from the pool hall where I scored for tea sometime. Somewhere in grey strata of subways all-night cafeterias rooming house flesh. His eyes flickered the question. I nodded toward my booth. He carried his coffee over and sat down opposite me.[34]

Bill's case came before the magistrate early in June 1946. Bill was there with his lawyer and Dr. Feltenstein, but the doctor wasn't even called. It was a first offense, a misdemeanor; obtaining narcotics by the use of fraud. The judge made a joke of it, and said he was going to inflict a terrible punishment on him. "I'm going to sentence you to go back to St. Louis for the summer. Which is terrible." To make a disposition of the case, he said Bill was on general probation, but there was no suspended sentence. Bill walked free. He went straight to the U.S. Narcotic Farm in Lexington, Kentucky, to take the cure. They gave him a reduction cure, using Dolophine, a brand of methadone, but he only stayed ten days, so he was not completely cured. Joan was pleased for him and wrote Edie, "That was pretty good of course, but it left me in rather a spot, emotionally as well as financially."[35]

Even before Burroughs was sent to St. Louis, the apartment at 115th Street had been going downhill. Now it took a turn for the worse. Hal Chase left to spend the summer in Denver, intending to room in Livingston Hall on campus when he returned, leaving just Allen and Joan to share the rent. Huncke moved into Hal's room. He and Phil White began using the place to stash weapons and stolen goods. A gum machine was brought up and broken open, so they all had free gum for a week. They borrowed Bill's blackjack and his gun to use in robberies, and hid their own "piece" there. After Bill left for St. Louis, things got worse and worse. Fritz the elevator man told Huncke, "It's all right you steal the stuff in the cars, but don't bring the car here and leave it in front of the building!" As Burroughs said, "It wasn't very smart. No wonder Huncke did so much time. One time they'd made a good haul, they'd gotten away clean, then the other guy says, 'Huncke, we missed some stuff, let's go back.' He went back for five years. Imagine anyone being as stupid as that? Huncke said, 'I didn't want to go back,' but he let the other guy talk him into it. It's completely stupid. The basic stupidity of the criminal mind."[36]

Then one time, Phil got very high on goofballs—a pentobarbital sold under the brand name of Nembutal—took Bill's .32, and set out to hold up a store. He asked Huncke if he was coming, but Huncke could see the deranged state he was in and wisely declined. Phil burst into a furrier's showroom, pulled his gun, and demanded money. Phil shot the furrier in the stomach, killing him in cold blood. The *New York Journal-American* headline read, "Mad Dog Noonday Killer." He and Huncke dismantled the gun and scattered bits of it all over Brooklyn. Years later, in May 1951, Phil was picked up on a junk offense, and in order to reduce his sentence he squealed on a pusher. While in the Tombs, awaiting transfer to another jail, he hanged himself. He knew what happened to informers. He would be beaten, tortured, and possibly even killed when he reached a regular prison. Unable to face years of fear and violence, he killed himself. Bill wrote Allen, "I was sincerely shocked to hear about Phil. He was so uncompromising and Puritanical about stool pigeons. He used to say: 'I can't understand how a pigeon can live with himself.' I guess Phil couldn't after what he did."[37] He told Allen, "It was quite a shock to me as I always thought a lot of him."[38]

Huncke introduced Joan to a friend of his, known as Whitey because of his white-blond hair, and she began living with him, "that sweet but stupid character with whom I was having a light affair at the time," as she described him to Edie.[39] Jack stopped by one day to see how she was and found her "out of her mind" on Benzedrine. She came in and immediately stripped off her clothes. Jack said, "Joan, what are you doing?" Joan said, "Who are you, strange man, get out of this house." Confused, Kerouac pleaded with her, "I'm not a strange man, Joan, I'm Jack!" She started yelling at Huncke, "Jack is trying to rape me!" but Huncke just lay in bed, saying, "Well ba-by, I don't know what to do," and "I'm all hung up baby, I . . ." In the end Joan went into Huncke's room to discuss it and shut the door. Jack fled.[40] Allen, meanwhile, was engrossed in a ten-page, amphetamine-driven introduction to his enormous poem "Death in Violence," as the apartment disintegrated around him.

Joan wrote Edie, "After a while we began taking in a few desperate characters as boarders and before long I was running quite a pad. Everything in the damn place was hot, as were of course, a couple of cars parked out front. Inevitably people kept going to jail."[41] When the police arrived at 115th Street with the victim of a suitcase crime, he identified Huncke, who was promptly arrested because he had in his pocket the keys to a stolen car parked right outside. He soon found himself in the Bronx jail. Joan was evicted for nonpayment of rent and she and Julie and Whitey began living in a series of sleazy hotels; there were no apartments available in the city. Then Whitey was arrested, caught trying to crack the safe at a Howard Johnson's, leaving Joan alone and broke. He got five to ten years in Sing Sing. A gay black friend of Huncke's named William "Spence" Spencer took her in at his apartment at 250 West 47th Street. It was a nice place with a huge record collection, but the neighbors took up a petition against him and got him evicted for too much traffic to his apartment. Joan was almost at the end of her tether. Kingsland ran into her that October and wrote to Edie Parker, "I saw Joan last weekend. She seemed to be losing her mind. It's a shame, don't you think?" Shortly afterward Joan cracked up completely and was picked up wandering around Times Square. She was admitted to Bellevue Hospital suffering from acute amphetamine psychosis—the first female case on record—and they kept her there for ten days. Her father came from Loudonville to get Julie.

BOOK THREE

~

Down Mexico Way

Chapter Thirteen

I never saw any place in Texas I want to see again given the fact of Texans there.[1]

1. Farmer Bill

Bill's parents were very concerned. His uncle Horace had been a morphine addict and he had ended up slitting his wrists. They complained and cajoled, but could never understand why Bill was doing it. Burroughs said they were "compassionate and understanding, a mixed reaction." Upon arrival in St. Louis, he was delighted to find his old school and Harvard friend Kells Elvins there.

Kells was back from serving as a marine in the Pacific theater, where he had lost the hearing in one ear thanks to a Japanese shell. He told Bill his war stories, which were filed in Burroughs's writer's memory. Kells's radio code name was Big Picture, and his colonel was called Shifty Shaeffer. He had just hit the beach with Major Ash, whose radio name was Clinker, and there was a lot of machine-gun fire. Kells tugged at Ash's trouser leg, urging him to get down. At that point machine-gun fire took off the top of Major Ash's head. Colonel Shaeffer called on the radio and said, "Howya Elvins. Put Major Ash on the phone." Elvins delivered the memorable line: "Big Picture calling Shifty, Clinker is dead." Throughout the mid-sixties Burroughs did scores of cut-ups on the theme of the Clinker Squadron, and Shaeffer became a doctor in *The Naked Lunch*.

Kells was a macho Rhett Butler figure, a heavy drinker, virile, enormously attractive to women, good-looking, with deep black eyes, curly, wiry brown hair, and strong, well-defined features. He was well built, athletic, and was described by his son Peter to Rob Johnson as "an alcoholic playboy of the Western World." His second wife, Marianne Woofe, described him as "charismatic, cultured, well-read in many fields. He had a superb vocabulary and he was like the Pied Piper when he spoke, holding everyone spellbound with every word and gesture. He was the most graceful man I ever met." But his wife also saw a downside. He was "alcoholic, volatile, and had a sadistic side.

[…] He did not really like women. He required them, but didn't like them; he had no close woman friends."[2] Kells had always been on Bill's wavelength, particularly his humor, and thought he was the funniest person he knew.

In St. Louis the old camaraderie kicked in, and they immediately began thinking up crazy moneymaking schemes. Burroughs told Kerouac that he was variously engaged in patent medicines and household appliances. It seems that the Food and Drug Administration, established in 1907 to control patent medicines, took a dim view of Bill and Kells's "Death County Bill's Tooth and Bone Tablets from the County Without a Toothache." Deaf Smith County, near Amarillo, was famous for the high lime and phosphate in the water, and it was said that the lime built up under your fillings and pushed them out. Whether Bill's medicine ever existed or not, it was a good example of their thinking. They also came up with a fluorescent mouthwash for dentists and a home dry-cleaning machine, the research and development of which destroyed the washing machine belonging to a friend of Kells's mother. Kells's influence helped Bill to continue his cure. He wrote Joan, "Off the habit. Kells wanted to associate only with dynamic people, and I'm forced to admit that junk seriously hampers my dynamism."[3]

Kells's father, Politte, owned property in the Rio Grande Valley in South Texas, and had moved there in 1936. Kells followed him and had bought ten acres of citrus groves and a hundred acres with cotton allotments for $5,000 near his father's land. He suggested that Bill join him and they would both make some money as cotton farmers. You couldn't really lose with cotton farming because there was a government wartime support price of $150 a bale that was still in place, and allotments went with the land. It was a bizarre situation, because no matter how good a piece of land was, without allotments it was virtually worthless until the end of the war; the price of cotton went from nine cents a pound in 1940 ($45 a bale) to thirty-two cents a pound ($160 a bale) in 1947. Bill's parents, who knew both Kells and his parents, were delighted with the idea and advanced him enough money to buy fifty acres of "the finest land in the Valley," complete with cotton allotments.

The Rio Grande debouches into the Gulf of Mexico just outside Brownsville, Texas. Across the river is Matamoros, in Mexico. A strip of land known as the Valley, twenty miles across and a hundred miles long, extends upriver from Brownsville as far as Rio Grande City. Thanks entirely to the massive irrigation system begun in 1904, it is now some of the richest farmland in the United States. Before that it was a desert of mesquite and cactus. There were no proper towns in the Valley in the forties, just a "vast suburb of flimsy houses" surrounded by endless fields of citrus. Burroughs was not flattering in his description of it: "The whole Valley has the impermanent look of a camp, or carnival. Soon the suckers will all be dead and the pitchmen will go somewhere else. [...] A premonition of doom hangs over the Valley. You have to make it now before something happens, before the black fly ruins the citrus, before support prices are taken off the cotton. [...] The threat of disaster is always there."[4] There was always the disquieting knowledge that it was once desert and will be desert again, just as soon as the pumps are turned off.

Kells's land was in Hidalgo County about sixty miles from Brownsville just off U.S. 83, a three-lane highway that straggled through a series of towns and communities named after the men who settled the area in the early part of the twentieth century. Kells had fields all over the area, from the Redlands, north of Edinburg, right down to the "lower lift," the lowest of the irrigation pumping stations on the Rio Grande. In the center was Pharr, just south of Edinburg, where he had property on the city line between Pharr and McAllen on Morningside Drive (now César Chávez Road). Bill bought fifty acres at Monte Cristo and Morningside Drive, in Edinburg.

He first went to see it late in June 1946. Kells was already out there. Kells and his girlfriend, Obie Dobbs,[5] and his friend Ted Marak and Ted's date for that night were all drunk and lying naked on the veranda in front of Kells's house on South Jackson Road at the corner of Kelly, looking out at a real Texas gullywasher. Kells told his friends that he had a friend coming that day, and fifteen minutes later a pair of car headlights showed through the pouring rain. A GI surplus jeep pulled up, driven by Bill wearing a fedora and his usual suit and tie. He was so wet from driving the open jeep that his tie hung down between his legs. Kells didn't stir, just called out, "Come on in, Billy." Bill pushed open the screen door and stood with water pouring off of him. "You better get out of those wet clothes," Kells told him. Bill stripped naked and carefully placed his wet clothes in a pile before joining them for a drink.[6]

Neither Burroughs nor Elvins knew anything about farming. They had a farm manager to organize everything. He hired the farmhands, bought the plants, organized the trucking, and received a monthly wage and a percentage of the profit. Burroughs explained in *Junky*:

> The farmer did all the actual work. [Kells] and I would drive around every few days to see how the cotton was looking. It took us about an hour to look at all our cotton because the fields were scattered around from Edinburg to the lower lift, almost on the river. There was no particular point in looking at the cotton since neither of us knew the first thing about it.[7]

They all did very well out of it. There was more profit to be made in vegetables, but if you hit a bad year you could be wiped out; a drought or a hailstorm could do it. Kells had a citrus orchard of about twenty acres of ruby red grapefruit, a hybrid from Barbados, then quite rare in the United States. He also grew limes and had ten acres of citrus—grapefruit, oranges, and lemons—that he bought for $5,000. Bill grew carrots, peas, lettuce, and cotton and appears to have had some sort of land-sharing arrangement with Kells, possibly determined by which plots had support allotments on them. Allotments were usually for half or a percentage of your land and the rest would be given over to fruit or vegetables.

When Bill got there his land was planted with tomatoes. They were huge, beautiful to look at, but tasteless; no one wanted them, so they plowed them in. Bill and Kells intended to plant cotton on the land and the tomatoes made good fertilizer. One bale an acre is a good yield for cotton, but Bill's land was so good it made two bales at $300 an acre. He and Kells had 150 acres in cotton between them. A good cotton picker could pick five hundred pounds in a twelve-hour day of exhausting, back-breaking work, and some could double that, but most managed between three hundred and four hundred pounds. Children could only manage a hundred pounds a day. If the cotton was picked—the fluffy cotton pulled off the bolls—then eight hundred to fifteen hundred pounds was needed to gin a five-hundred-pound bale. If it was pulled—the bolls were pulled off because they were too tight to pick the cotton off—then it took sixteen hundred to eighteen hundred pounds to make a bale. Sacks varied from three or four feet long for children to a maximum of twelve to fifteen feet for experienced pickers. Most were about nine feet, as they were heavy to drag around when almost full. Ginning cost three to five dollars a bale, and white farm laborers in Texas received a maximum of five dollars a day, but most refused to do it, preferring to seek factory work instead. Bill and Kells, like all the farmers in the region, relied on "wetback" labor, paying two dollars or less for a twelve-hour day. During the picking season, Bill and Kells employed up to two hundred laborers. They had one bad setback when their tractor driver killed their best worker, hitting him over the head with a tire iron. The driver got five years.

Cotton picking began on July 4 and was over by September 1. It was perfect cotton weather, but Bill still only broke a little better than even. He reckoned it was costing him $700 a month to live in the Valley, without out a maid or a car, which took most of his profit.[8] This mysterious figure suggests an enormously profligate lifestyle: at a time when the average yearly salary was $2,900, Burroughs was spending three times that. Where did it all go? Bill's overheads were negligible. He first lived with Kells and his girlfriend, Obie, at South Jackson Road, then house-sat for Walter Benson at his house at 321 Kelly Street in Pharr, followed by house-sitting for someone named Philip; only then did he rent a small house on Kells's land. He was not on drugs at the time, boys in nearby Reynosa cost three pesos, or forty cents, and they were making their own alcohol. A good life was cheap; Burroughs did co-own some equipment with Kells, which probably accounts for the difference—a tractor, for instance, cost $19,000—that or he must have been paying large increments of his loan back to his parents.

Whatever social life there was happened on Kells Elvins's front porch: Kells and Obie, Ted Marak, Walter Benson, Gene Terry, and T. L. Reed. Obie, from nearby Mission, was renowned for her outstanding beauty and apparently finished up in Hollywood; she was with Kells because he was rich and handsome and they both liked a lot of sex. Ted Marak had been a dealer in a Las Vegas casino, where he also worked the cage, overseeing the count. He had been framed by a con man whom he had caught skimming the take, but the owner believed the con man and Ted felt it prudent to leave town as fast as possible. He was laying low in Texas. Eugene "Gene" Terry was a popular, excitable, and unpredictable young man who had been thrown out of the University of Texas for too much partying. He drove a 1936 black Ford pickup nicknamed the Black Death and once screeched to a halt in it, leapt out, and did a tightrope balancing act on the top strand of a barbed-wire fence to entertain his friends. A sharp dresser, he had first used junk in the army, raiding first his own, then other people's morphine kits, so he and Bill had common interests. Walter Benson had a brilliant brain but was described as a "Jekyll and Hyde alcoholic."[9] The immaculately dressed T. L. Reed had previously been a pimp in New Orleans.

During the day, Bill and Kells drove around inspecting the land just to pass the time until 5:00 p.m., when they started drinking. Burroughs wrote, "There were five or six regulars who gathered every afternoon at [Kells's] house. Exactly at five, someone would bang a tin pan and yell 'Drinking time!' and the others would jump up like fighters coming out at the bell."[10] They made their own gin from Mexican alcohol as an economy measure. Kells would send his headman over the border to buy five gallons of sugarcane alcohol that they would dilute, half and half, with Ozark water to make ten gallons of gin. It tasted terrible so Bill made his own drink by adding sugar, limes, seltzer, and a tiny pinch of quinine to make an approximation of gin and tonic. No one in the Valley had ever heard of quinine water. In addition they broke open inhalers for the Benzedrine, sometimes staying up forty-eight hours, and smoked powerful "red dirt" marijuana grown by Kells in a tin barn on his property even though he himself didn't use it because it made him paranoid; he was strictly an alcohol man. They ate hallucinogenic mushrooms, except Marak, who didn't care for them. They tried hard not to be stoned or drunk during working hours and established a set of working rules: a turn-on time of 5:00 p.m. and a turn-off time of 4:00 a.m. except for Saturday and Sunday when they had to stop imbibing at 6:00 a.m.[11] They indulged in a variety of mad schemes. These ranged from a cockroach farm to "provide food on the hoof for chickens" to growing a test plot of Egyptian ramie, which they had Burlington Mills turn into five to ten yards of "indestructible" fabric. They made a shirt from it that was so "indestructible" it would not even burn. According to Marak, DuPont heard of the potential for ramie and quickly buried it by using their political influence to get the plant banned from the United States. Ramie received a brief mention in the "International Zone" section of *The Adding Machine,* and a longer one in *Interzone*: "hardest fabric known, beat ramie hands down and cocks up."[12]

Bill absorbed all the stories about the local wheeler-dealers, con men, and wildcat oilmen, such as David "Dry Hole" Byrd, who emerged as Dry Hole Dutton in *Queer.* The Valley is in fact completely flat, being the floodplain of the Rio Grande, but land speculators in the twenties coined the name as part of their sales pitch when they brought potential investors to the Valley and let them pick grapefruit straight off the trees and eat them. There was one promoter who constructed an artificial lake and sold plots of land all around it, telling his clients that "the lake will sub-irrigate your crops." As soon as the last plot sold he turned off the water and disappeared, as did the lake, leaving the investors sitting in the desert. Bill stored all these characters and stories away for future use. That one did not reemerge for forty years, when he used it in *The Western Lands*: "the area is infected with every variety of faker and swindler selling spurious Western Lands plots and villas and condominiums. There you are in your beautiful villa, straight out of Disneyland, on a clear blue lake that drains away, while you sit, with a last derisive gurgle . . . '*suuuuuugggger.*' "[13]

Kells was a member of the McAllen Country Club, and Bill sometimes did a round of golf with him or swam in their pool. The country club was very puritanical and had a rule that ladies had to wear one-piece bathing suits, so Kells went with Obie to San Antonio and had a body stocking made for her from the new synthetic materials that were just appearing on the market. It was the same color as her skin, and several times, after they had been up forty-eight hours on Benzedrine and were completely drunk, they showed up at the country club with Obie in her body stocking so that she looked completely naked. They also caused controversy by putting her on the back of the fire department truck in her body stocking for the Fourth of July parade in McAllen.[14]

But the real action was across the border in Reynosa's Zona Rosa, about eight miles away, where Kells, Obie, and Burroughs often went to drink. It was usual to bar hop, but the most favored spot was Joe's Place, at Miguel Alemán and Paseo de los Virreyes, an enormous establishment that featured a revolving bar, a large patio, a bandstand, and a dance floor. There were two huge fireplaces, tall enough to stand up in, where they would build fires and roast potatoes when the weather was cold. Whole families would attend the ten o'clock show, which was suitable entertainment for kids. The midnight show ended with a stripper, the two o'clock show was more risqué, and the 4:00 a.m. show included drag acts and nakedness. The cook, Berto Guajardo, told author Rob Johnson that the place was wide open. No one cared if you took off your clothes and danced on the tables and did whatever you wanted.[15] José "Joe" Ortega was always looking for a new attraction to pull in the customers. He loved animals and had peacocks and coyotes there. Behind the bar he kept a brown bear that drank scotch. Plenty of people fell for the idea that they could outdrink the bear. Sometimes Joe would walk through the restaurant with a fully grown lion on a chain. There was a lion pit in the patio that sometimes had as many as five lions in it, a mother and her fully grown cubs.

One time Gene Terry got drunk and went into the lion's cage to pet them. One leapt up and clawed his back, leaving some nasty scars. José and the waiters were always warning Terry to stay away from the lions, but he was fascinated by them and wouldn't listen. On the night of November 9, 1950, Terry boasted to two friends how he would "pet the lions" over in Reynosa, but they didn't believe him, never having been to Joe's. They drove over the border, went to a few bars, and finished up at Joe's around 1:30 a.m., where Terry showed them the lion cage. The waiters warned him to stay away, but they were busy and Terry eluded them. He lifted the large wooden bar that secured the door and dragged his terrified friends inside. His flashlight startled the lioness and she attacked him. His friends rushed to safety, but the door slammed behind them. He scrambled up the door, but the lioness slashed open the main artery in his leg, then dragged him down by his neck. His horrific screams brought the staff running. They pushed the door open and several of them went in, throwing bottles and glasses at the lioness. She dropped Terry and Roberto Perez, the lions' trainer, held her back with a chair as he leveled his .45 and fired, hitting her in the chest, killing her. Burroughs was living in Mexico City by this time and no doubt got the story from Kells, who knew how much Bill would love it. Burroughs was intrigued not only by the bizarre nature of the story but also the fact that Terry drove himself to his death in a car named Death, thus the reference to Conrad's *Heart of Darkness* at the end of the quote when he used it in "The Word":

> Young friend of mine name of Terry have this 1936 Ford he call the Black Death. One night he get in the Black Death and cross the Rio Grande to Reynosa. Where a mangy old lioness stood in Joe's patio. So Terry goes in the cage, throw a flashlight in the lioness' face, who leaps on him and break his neck, and the bartender vault over the bar with a forty-five blast the lioness. But Mr. Terry, he dead.[16]

Five years later Bill wrote a short story about it that he sent to Allen Ginsberg, who was trying to sell Bill's work to magazines, telling him, "I enclose the story I wrote about Terry who was killed by the lion. I don't like it too much. I am not cut out to write anything so separate from myself."[17] The story has unfortunately been lost, but it shows Burroughs searching for a commercial subject with popular appeal. But as he wasn't there, he couldn't get his imagination working on it, even though he had known Terry. However, the incident became one of Bill's favorite set pieces for dinner parties.

It was in Reynosa that Bill found his boys; it would have caused too many problems to have approached any of the field hands, and none of Kells's friends were anything other than straight. In Reynosa, however, Bill was known as "Willy El Puto" or Willy the Queer, outed by a cabdriver named Carlos El Pelacuas who got to know Bill pretty well from the times he drove him the eight miles back to Pharr when he was dead drunk. Carlos liked to talk with his fares, and Bill may have asked where to get boys or even made a drunken pass at him. When they saw him in Reynosa the cabdrivers would call out to him, "Hello Willy! Hello Willy!" and Bill would quicken his pace to get away from them; he was sometimes called *Patas Largas*—long legs—because of this. They would tell the street kids, "If he takes to running he's going to catch you," and the kids would circle around him, taunting him. Bill would make perfunctory lunges at them, cursing them in English and Spanish: "Cabrón, chinga tu madre."[18] He tried to pretend it was a game, to show that he could join in, but according to Ernesto Garza, another Reynosa cabdriver interviewed by Rob Johnson, Burroughs "would try his best to ignore them but you could see he would get rigid— and red as a fire truck. You would think his blood was going to pop out of his ears he got so red. You could see his jaw clenched and grinding."[19] This was a nightmare scenario for Burroughs, who did his best to always keep as low a profile as possible. To be taunted in the streets by children for being homosexual must have been excruciatingly embarrassing for him.

Early in October 1946, Bill heard the disturbing news from Allen that Joan had been admitted to Bellevue suffering from amphetamine psychosis. They had been living together in a sexual relationship at 115th Street but Burroughs does not appear to have regarded it as a particularly ongoing affair or else he would have made more effort to contact her in the ensuing months. He immediately sent her some money and told her that he would be in New York later in the month. He was just off to St. Louis to formally divorce Ilse Herzfeld Klapper, whom he had married nine years before, and to obtain financial backing from his parents for more land.

At Bellevue they cured Joan of her Benzedrine psychosis within a few days, but because she kept telling the doctors about "junk neighborhoods," they thought she was still hallucinating. Eventually they called in Shein and O'Grady, the detectives who had arrested Bill for forging a script, and they confirmed, "Sure, there's a junk scene at 103rd and Broadway." Joan told Bill she had never been so relieved as to see these two decent people slouch in instead of the idiot psychiatrists who thought that everybody was nuts except themselves. With no basis for their diagnosis they were forced to discharge her. She was met by Burroughs, who, after spending a few days in New York, took her to Pharr on October 31, to begin a new life in Texas.

They stayed at the magnificent Casa de Palmas hotel, on Main Street in McAllen, not far from Kells's house on the Pharr-McAllen city line. In Pharr, the local people thought Joan was "nice" but were dismayed at her neglect of Julie. But they were not around for long. Shortly after arriving with Joan, Bill set off to buy land to grow pot. The Valley was too flat, too visible, and filled with far too many people who all knew each other's business for him to even contemplate such a project there. Instead he looked for a remote, thickly forested area where there were few neighbors and the ones who were there minded their own business. Bill had visited Kells in Huntsville, Texas, in 1939, and remembered that the land around there was ideal for his purpose.

Chapter Fourteen

Sometimes you get, sometimes you get got.
—OLD TEXAN SAYING

1. Burroughs in East Texas

Burroughs bought ninety-nine acres outside Huntsville in Walker County, East Texas, in November 1946, for $2,000. The nearest community was New Waverly, a town of a few hundred people, Conroe was the nearest town of any size, and Houston was sixty miles away. The farm was at the end of a logging road cut through the woods and lacked both electricity and running water. There was a weathered silver-gray single-story cabin that had two enormous rooms, subdivided into four, with a porch taking up the long side and several vine-covered tumbledown barns, all surrounded by wild berry thickets. Huncke once described the structure as having an open passage through the middle; this would have been a traditional Texas "dog trot" designed to cause a breeze and cool the building in the summer. A black potbellied stove in the kitchen provided the only heat. They instigated repairs on the house then drove to New York ten days before Christmas, where they stayed for a few days before Bill went to see his family and Joan went to Loudonville to collect Julie and take her to her new home on January 2.

The house needed work and they obviously needed help. Before they even moved in they decided to invite Herbert Huncke to come and help fix the place up, and he agreed, having just come out of the Bronx jail with nowhere to live and no source of income. Bill sent fifty dollars for a train ticket and meals on board, but Huncke dipped into the money and finished up taking the bus, which took much longer. He started out high and forgot the marijuana seeds that he was supposed to bring; by the time he reached Texas he was in withdrawal. Fortunately Bill had been receiving supplies of powdered pantopon from Garver and was able to fix him up.

Bill, Joan, and Julie were staying at a tourist camp while slowly hauling provisions into the farm. Joan told Allen, "We have a Jeep, which while it bounces intolerably, is an incredible blessing as it actually navigates our road, flooded as it is by five days of steady rain. So now we can carry loads in, things are looking up."[1] The priority was to provide water. Bill installed a seven-hundred-gallon water cistern on a wooden stand to collect all the rainwater that fell on the corrugated iron roof and a filter system to strain out any bugs. Next he investigated the possibility of a well. Nobody in that part of Texas would ever dig for water without having the "water witch," so Bill hired one to come and dowse the land. The water witch walked around until his wand dipped. He told Bill, "Go down there so many feet and there's the water." The amount the wand dipped indicated where the water was and how deep down it was. This ability apparently ran in families; Bill tried using the wand and felt nothing. The water was exactly where the water witch said it would be. The well was dug by a tethered mule, walking in an endless circle, digging out the earth, and was lined with concrete tubes that fitted onto each other. In the house the porch had to be screened to keep out bugs, and the roof leaked. It was several months before the plumbing worked properly.

As usual, Burroughs got a few routines out if it. In the "County Clerk" section of *The Naked Lunch*, possibly one of the funniest as well as the most powerful indictments of Texas small-town racism, anti-Semitism, and prejudice ever written, Arch, the County Clerk, rambles on about the local good ol' boys: "Feller name of Hump Clarence used to witch out wells on the side... Good ol' boy too, not a finer man in this Zone than Hump Clarence."[2]

The land sloped away from the house down to a bayou filled with frogs, toads, crawfish, and catfish, surrounded by semitropical undergrowth and swampland and home to all manner of chiggers and mites, mosquitoes and tics, scorpions and water snakes. Armadillos wandered across the paths in the woods and chameleons would mate in the trees, their rose-colored throats blowing up like huge bubbles. The dirt road leading in was so narrow at times that you could reach out and touch the trees on either side. There was a rickety plank bridge over a stream. Bill fenced part of the land to keep out deer and planted tomatoes as a cover crop to divert attention from the marijuana plants and opium poppies hidden among persimmon trees and oaks draped in Spanish moss. The tomatoes must have been planted by hired hands, but he would not have trusted anyone else to plant pot seeds for him, so the notion of Bill's pot farm is most certainly incorrect. It is unlikely that any more than a quarter acre of his ninety-seven acres could have been planted with cannabis; hardly a "pot farm."[3]

Each morning, at about 10:30, Bill would appear on the porch from his room, dressed in his suit and tie. He would take the Jeep into New Waverly to collect the mail and buy the local newspapers and then sit on the porch in his rocking chair and read. Huncke, not surprisingly, was not much good as a field hand, so his job was to collect kindling and firewood from the woods for the outdoor grill and to cook the steaks in the evening. He was also in charge of the wind-up Victrola, changing the needle from time to time. Joan built a pinewood cabinet to amplify the sound. They sometimes argued over the records, Bill preferring Viennese waltzes and Louis Armstrong's Hot Fives and Hot Sevens, whereas Huncke and Joan liked Stan Kenton and Lester Young, Josh White's version of "Cotton-Eyed Joe," Hoagy Carmichael's "Baltimore Oriole," Coleman Hawkins's "Low Flame," Dizzy Gillespie's "Night in Tunisia." The music was absorbed into the trees as they sat on the porch by the light of the kerosene lamps, the records accompanied by cicadas, night birds, and strange cries of animals in the forest.

The idea of Huncke, the skinny, sallow-faced Times Square hustler, working as a farmhand is as extraordinary as Burroughs's idea that he could hide away in the woods without everyone in a hundred-mile radius knowing about it. Huncke was incompetent at most things but does seem to have made himself useful. Bill remembered, "He got on my nerves to some extent. He gets on anyone's nerves, but not to an overwhelming extent because he's a minor irritation." In fact Huncke settled in surprisingly well. He wrote to Allen, "Bill is a good friend. He is exceedingly interested in guns. He has allowed me to shoot and I find them much less awe inspiring. Bill is quite a guy."[4] Bill was using a .22 target pistol. He stood in back of the cabin and aimed at the barn. The sound echoed through the woods. One time Huncke and Joan got talking to the pharmacist in a small town some distance away and the man said, "You guys must be the fellows I hear through the woods. We thought you were shooting off machine guns over there." Huncke reported, "That just tickled the shit out of Burroughs. Such strutting was never known."[5] It had been Joan's suggestion that Huncke should come to the farm; she wanted the Benzedrine company.

Naturally Bill's neighbors were very curious to know what brought this Harvard-educated gentleman to live as a subsistence farmer in East Texas, and Bill soon got to know them. Arch Ellisor was very friendly indeed. He loved whiskey and Bill would invite him onto the porch, get out a bottle, and encourage him to tell stories. Arch's grandmother was dying of cancer and Arch would tell Bill, "Her breast is all eaten away." He hoped that she would die soon. Arch Ellisor is a character, under his own name, in The Place of Dead Roads, where his old grandmother gets swept away by a tornado. "Everybody was glad to see the last of her, she'd been clear out of her mind the past five years, her breasts all eated away with the cancer and Arch kept buying morphine to finish her off but she had such a strength for it no amount would kill her and Arch said it was like buying feed for a hawg."[6] The day she died Arch came over to tell Bill and they celebrated with a big slug of whiskey. The Ellisor family also make an appearance in *Cities of the Red Night*. "Only two families hereabouts, the Bradfords and the Ellisors."[7] Steve Ellisor comes to help clean and repair a riverside shack that seems to have arrived in the novel from a future book. The title of the section perhaps gives a clue: "I can take the hut set anywhere." It does not appear again.

Bill had another neighbor, Mr. Gilley, who was always coming onto Bill's property looking for his "brindle-faced cow." One time he encountered Bill when he was out with his axe in the pot plantation. Bill immediately steered him to the house, offering him some whiskey. Gilley knew something suspicious was going on but didn't know what. He said, "Well, pretty good stand of it you got there, whatever it is." Gilley was very much a rural mooch. When Bill bought a second car, as well as his Jeep, Gilley opined, "A rich man who got himself another car, I figure he'd just about give that Jeep to a poor man."

Judging by his letters to Ginsberg, Burroughs seemed to be enjoying himself. On March 11, he boasted to Allen, "It is practically summer down here, and king size scorpions, Tarantulas, Ticks, chiggers and mosquitoes are emerging in droves. I killed 10 scorpions yesterday. The house is overrun with huge rats as big as possums."[8] Bill shot one that was so fat it got wedged in its hole. He said he was contemplating the purchase of a ferret. It was a worthy challenge for an experienced exterminator like Burroughs. Joan wrote Allen, "Already we're being attacked by hordes of all sorts of dreadful bugs, including scorpions, to which William has taken quite a fancy."[9]

In the summer the fields were ablaze with flowers, hibiscus bushes, huge blossoms, everything lush and fecund. There was a large pond not far from the cabin where some previous occupants had built out a spit of sand into the water. Joan liked to sit down on the sand with the water up to her belly and play with Julie. It was her favorite place during the heat of the summer and sometimes she and Huncke would take a lunch basket with them and spend all day there. Two-year-old Julie followed her everywhere she went, barefoot, hair matted, chewing on her arm, a nervous habit she had developed that left a large scar in the crook of her arm.

But this sylvan idyll was flawed. Joan was still seriously strung out and, if anything, her Benzedrine habit increased. She looked after Julie and shared the cooking with Huncke, sometimes shopping with him, but much of her time was spent obsessively cleaning, first the cabin and porch, then in sweeping lizards off the tree in the yard. The moment she turned away, they would climb back. In New Waverly Joan and Huncke continued the same speed-freak discussions about white filaments that they could see coming out of their skin that they'd had at 115th Street; typical amphetamine hallucinations. Joan had an animated vision, similar to her audio hallucinations. She would look down the sidewalk and see everyone moving as a unit, like a shoal of fish, then she would say, "Next thing you'll see them going down that side," and to her they'd be going the other way. Bill never paid much heed to it, recognizing it for what it was, Benzedrine psychosis.

Joan's two-inhaler-a-day Benzedrine habit meant that they soon cleaned out the nearby pharmacies, and it was Huncke's job to make runs into Houston every two or three weeks, where he had found a drugstore that would supply inhalers by the gross and paregoric by the half gallon. He also scored for pot and shopped for liquor. They were living in a dry county and had bought all the rum, tequila, and gin in the nearby towns, so had to drive the twenty-five miles to the big liquor store in Conroe to stock up. Unfortunately Houston proved an enormous attraction to Huncke, and sometimes he would not return to the Jeep at the appointed time. Once they waited so long for him that the ice, which they had come to town to buy, had all melted. Another time he scored and disappeared for days.

Huncke had grown very close to Joan in New York and had initially been surprised to find that she and Bill had a physical relationship. Living with them in Texas enabled him to further observe them together, and in his memoirs he wrote:

> I believe he did respect her, as she was very intelligent and could match him wit for wit. But as far as love—in the accepted sense of the word—I'm sure he had little or no deep affection for her. She was interesting to him in some way, that was all. He did not like to be annoyed by her too much, though she demanded he give her a little attention each night. Just before we'd all go to sleep she would spend maybe an hour with him in his room and they'd talk. She'd leave and go into the front of the cabin, which she used as her room.[10]

One night Huncke heard Joan tap on Burroughs's door. The door opened and he heard her tell Bill, "All I want is to lie in your arms a little while." There was never any outward sign of affection between them. Bill for his part said, "Joan was a very extraordinary person. We got along very well. I wouldn't say I was in love. It was a very close relationship."[11]

When they did have sex, it was apparently very good sex. Joan had said that though he claimed to be a faggot "you're as good as a pimp in bed." Burroughs revealed this in Howard Brookner's documentary about him and afterward regretted it. "I'm terribly embarrassed about that bit about being as good as a pimp in bed, that sounds awful! I thought it was awful. I was a pretty good lay in those days, I had all my teeth, well anyway..."[12] Still later he thought, "Goddamn it, I *was* a fuckin' good lay even if I was a queer. Believe me, I could satisfy a woman! Nothing wrong with that. I'm thinking it over, I thought, 'What the hell was I talking about?'"[13]

After Joan left Bellevue, she and Bill had stayed in a cheap hotel near Times Square, which was where Billy Jr. was conceived. Burroughs said, "They say women always know when they conceive, well I knew too. That was it."[14] When Joan confirmed that she was pregnant she asked Bill if they should get an abortion, but he said that he would not consider it under any circumstances. "I certainly would never have consented to an abortion. I'm against abortion, absolutely. I think it's murder."[15] Despite such high-minded views about termination, he made little or no effort to get Joan to restrict her consumption of amphetamine, alcohol, and pot, even though it was obvious that they posed a considerable danger to the developing fetus. It was so against his principles to interfere in anyone else's life that he would have regarded it as impertinence to criticize her behavior. As a consequence, Billy Jr. was born an amphetamine addict and went straight into withdrawal, crying all the time and very distressed. Joan was unable to breast-feed him because of her addiction.

They had made no arrangements for the birth. At 3:00 a.m. on July 21, 1947, Joan tapped on Bill's door and told him it was time to go. They climbed into the Jeep and drove the eighteen miles to the hospital in Conroe. Instead of waiting around, biting his nails in the hospital, Bill returned to the Jeep, where he had a bottle. Someone had left a puppy on the seat. It was whining and barking. Billy was born at 4:10 a.m. and the next day Bill drove Joan back with their baby.

Bill's parents paid a visit to the farm shortly after Billy was born, bringing with them all manner of baby clothes and equipment, including a cradle, delighted that Bill had produced a grandchild for them. Burroughs had been worrying about the visit but it went well, and he was able to tell Allen, "No complications arose from the parental visitation, on the contrary a shower of benefits."[16] Huncke was made to wear a cowboy hat and pretend to be a local, and Joan must have somehow hidden her amphetamine use from them.

We get a good, though possibly exaggerated, picture of Burroughs's attitude to the new child from an interview with Joan conducted two years later at the New Orleans sanatorium, where Bill was detoxing. She was reported as saying that Burroughs was "a good father, and absolutely devoted to his young son. He is good to his stepchild, also, but 'adores' his own son, and seems almost as if he is seeking to be both mother and father to the child—has assumed most of the responsibility for feeding, washing and walking baby. [...] Informant states that the patient 'wasn't aware' that he wanted the child until it arrived, and now devotes himself to it almost completely."[17]

On hearing of the birth of Billy Burroughs Jr., Allen Ginsberg set out to write a birthday ode. It took him six days, working late at night on Benzedrine. Like much of his work in this period, it was an epic work consisting of many sections, written in highly artificial rhymed verse and almost unintelligible. The section on bebop began, "The saxophone thy mind had guessed / He knows the Devil hides in thee; / Fly hence, I warn thee, Stranger, lest / The saxophone shall injure thee."

Allen arranged to visit Bill and Joan that summer, bringing with him Neal Cassady, with whom he had been having an unsatisfactory love affair in Denver. Neal, a compulsive womanizer, ran between several women and very occasionally spent time in Allen's bed. Using his considerable powers of persuasion, Allen managed to convince Cassady to accompany him on a visit to Burroughs's farm, and they set out to hitchhike there. Rides were hard to get, but they finally arrived on August 30, 1947. Allen wrote, "When we got here, I expecting this happy holiday of God given sexuality, where was the royal couch?" There was no couch; in fact there was no bed at all. Huncke was still trying to build it. Huncke normally slept on the screened porch, so he thought that Allen and Neal might like to have his room, but his bed was not big enough for two people. Huncke explained that there were some army cots and wooden planks in one of the barns, and "I conceived of getting these sideboards together in some kind of bed situation. The only place to work was dead in front of the cabin, everybody could see me working with that fucking bed. [...] I did work on it because I figured I had a practical idea. Unfortunately while I was working on it, they arrived."[18]

Neal, who was never very keen on the prospect of sleeping with Allen, refused to help, so Huncke and Allen struggled with the beds. Huncke had managed to get the headboard off one and together they eventually got the other headboard off, which at least made the bed level on the ground, but it sagged in the middle and was very uncomfortable. It was also dangerous, as scorpions could reach it. "I was absolutely outraged with Burroughs for not having the sense to get a decent bed or make provision," Ginsberg remembered. "We didn't make out much, and that was the whole point of it. We were gonna go down there and I was finally gonna get satisfied for the first time."[19] Two days after they arrived, Allen finally accepted that Neal was not interested in men. He wrote in his journal, "The sacramental honeymoon is over. I have a drag against turning my mind to a practical, non-romantic set of arrangements a propos Cassady. Since it has at last penetrated my mind and become obvious to me that, without angling, he means what he says when he says he can't make use of me sexually, it requires turn of mind."

Allen's physical demands of Neal were just as off-putting as his emotional ones. Neal told Kerouac, "I got so I couldn't stand Allen to even touch me, you know, see, only touch me. It was terrible. And man, I'd never been that way, you know, but, man, he was all opening up and I was all..." But despite all this evidence of Neal's real feelings, Allen wrote quite seriously in his journal, "I am wondering what will happen to Neal if I really withdraw my active queer love and leave him alone emotionally." Neal insisted that they split up, and Allen decided to ship out from Houston to make some money, whereas Neal would stay on and help with the marijuana harvest and then drive Bill back to New York. Bill had decided that the family would be better off spending the winter in the city.

Joan and the children, accompanied by a load of baggage, went ahead by train while Bill, Huncke, and Neal Cassady drove the Jeep to New York, the back loaded with Mason jars of pot wrapped in duffel bags to sell in the city. The Jeep was not made for highway driving and when pushed beyond forty-five miles per hour everything burned out. By the time they reached New York on October 2 the car was a wreck. Burroughs said that nobody but Neal could have driven it and that he was a marvelous driver. The trip sounds a strange one. Cassady was obviously intimidated by Burroughs and his long, contemplative silences. Burroughs said, "Jack makes out Neal as a compulsive talker, but actually I've driven with him for eight hours and neither of us said a word. Going back to New York to sell the pot."[20] Bill never liked Cassady; he thought he was a cheap con man and didn't see the sexual attraction that Allen felt. Relations, however, remained cordial.

Bill had arranged to meet Joan at a railroad station in New York, but they were so late that the police picked her up and took her to Bellevue for observation, thinking that she was planning to abandon her children. When Bill arrived, all it took was for him to give his address as the University Club for her to be released with apologies.

2. Texas Justice

Bill and Neal had only brought a few kilos of pot to New York; the majority of the harvest remained in Texas. The pot had not been properly cured: it was green and tasted sour, so no one was very enthusiastic about buying it. Eventually, with Huncke's help, Bill found a buyer and made about $100. There were a few complaints that it was green, but a few hours in a low oven would have fixed it.

Bill's parents came to see the baby at Christmas and set Bill and the family up in a beach club in Atlantic Beach on Long Beach Barrier Island, across the strait from Far Rockaway. It was an affluent summer resort and, being winter and off-season, they could get a large, comfortable room very cheaply. Bill met up with Garver and almost immediately got a new habit. He spent much of his time in the city hanging out with Garver and scoring heroin, usually with Joan in tow. One night, visiting an Italian friend of Huncke's in Yonkers, he overdosed and passed out. Joan managed to revive him, gave him coffee, and walked him around the room until he was fully recovered.

In the spring of 1948, disappointed at his own lack of willpower in getting hooked again, Bill tried to kick using the reduction cure while driving back down to Texas from New York with Joan, but it naturally did not work. He had a sixteenth of an ounce of heroin in solution with him and a bottle of distilled water. The plan was that each day for twelve days he would take his shot and replace the same amount of junk with distilled water. After twelve days he would be shooting pure water. But it never works that way, each shot calls for an exception for some reason, and after only four days they had reached Cincinnati and he was out of junk and suffering from withdrawal symptoms. He and Joan continued to St. Louis, where Laura Burroughs tried to get him to go to "a private nut house." Instead he opted to take the straightforward withdrawal cure again at the U.S. Narcotic Farm in Kentucky. Laura described Joan as "like a tiger" in her insistence that Bill not go to a private clinic; presumably she thought he was more likely to be cured in Lexington. He put the car in storage and took the train. He already knew the routine. Afterward he wrote to Allen from New Waverly, "Back here for several weeks and feeling O.K. at last. I had to go to Lexington for the cure. Stayed 2 weeks and was sick 3 weeks more after I got out."[21] This is the cure he describes in such acute detail in *Junky*.

After Lexington he managed to stay off junk for about four months. Bill tried to cut down on expenses at the farm by growing some of their own food. He contemplated buying his own chickens, and in February

1948 Arch gave him two female pigs, telling him, "You keep feedin' 'em and they'll be worth a heap of money." Bill fed them on garbage. The pigs loved it and they hollered and squealed for more. "More! More! More!" They didn't have enough garbage so they had to start buying feed at three dollars a bag. The more they fed them, the more they wanted. Finally Bill told Arch, "Look Arch, we've carried these fuckers as far as we can. Take 'em back!" By this time they weighed about 150 pounds. Bill said, "It got so once a week we had to buy three dollars' worth of feed to feed these fuckers. Otherwise they'd squeal, you've never heard such squeals. So Arch came and took 'em back."[22] Bill enjoyed Arch's company and went with him to the livestock market with five acorn-fed hogs in the truck. Arch would call his hogs once a day and they would come running.

On April 27, 1948, Bill, Joan, and little Billy were driving the four hundred miles south from New Waverly to Pharr, where Bill was intent on buying more land. Bill was driving and was really drunk. Staying off junk for so many months clearly had a potent effect upon his libido, because at one point, between San Antonio and Corpus Christi, they stopped the car and he and Joan got out to fuck by the side of the road, leaving Billy in the car. Someone drove past and reported them to the police, and the next thing Burroughs knew Sheriff Vail Ennis and his deputy were on the scene. They put Bill in the prowl car and took him to the Beeville jail. Bill was in overnight, and the next day Sheriff Ennis told the local magistrate, "This here feller was disturbin' the peace while tryin' to get a piece." He was charged with drunken driving and public indecency, fined $173, and lost his driver's license. Bill quickly telegrammed his parents: "For God-sakes send the money or I will be here in Beeville jail." He was anxious to get out of there because he had fallen into the hands of one of the most vicious, brutal lawmen in the whole of Texas.

Sheriff Ennis had killed eight people, mostly Mexican American or African American, and singled out Mexican Americans for abuse: beatings, pistol-whippings, torture. Burroughs knew of him from a recent *Time* magazine article describing how Ennis had arrested two men for forgery and manacled them together. As he was telephoning for reinforcements one of the men pulled a concealed weapon and shot Ennis four times in the gut. *Time* reported, "Bleeding but upright, Vail turned from the phone, pulling his Colt from his hip holster; he pumped six shots into his manacled prisoners. Deliberately, he reloaded and pumped six more. When the smoke cleared away, both men were dead." Ennis survived and was not charged.

He was guilty of an even more outrageous murder. On July 7, 1945, Ennis drove to the farm of Geronimo Rodriguez to serve a child custody order for not returning his children to their mother after a weekend visit. The family refused to give Ennis the children until Rodriguez returned from the fields and gave his consent. They ordered Ennis off the property. He returned with a Texas Ranger and a civilian he had deputized on the spot. He was carrying a Thompson .45 submachine gun, which he set up on a tripod outside the farm before calling to the inhabitants to come out. Felix Rodriguez, the grandfather, opened the door to see what the problem was and Ennis opened fire on him, throwing him back into the house. Felix's two brothers, Domingo and Antonio, heard the gunfire and ran around the side of the house, only to be mowed down by Ennis. Felix's terrified twelve-year-old granddaughter ran from the house and Ennis tried to kill her as well, but his bullets hit the water cistern. Ranger Frank Probst then threw a tear gas grenade into the house. When the gas cleared the three lawmen entered the farmhouse, finding only unarmed men, women, and children gathered around the grandfather's body. Ennis kicked and beat them, fracturing one man's skull with a rifle butt. In court he claimed self-defense and got off. Such was law and order in Texas in 1945. No wonder that Kells Elvins, when he heard that Bill had been arrested by Ennis, feared for his life.

Prompted by his brush with Ennis and Texas justice, Bill decided that he had had enough of Texas, and on June 5 he wrote to Allen from New Orleans to say that he and Joan were moving there. He sold the farm on June 23, 1948, for $2,000, exactly the amount he paid for it. By then the Burroughs family was living in a rooming house at 111 Transcontinental Drive in New Orleans, and on August 2 Bill bought a house at 509 Wagner Street in Algiers, Louisiana, just across the Mississippi from the French Quarter.

Chapter Fifteen

I'd just go across the river to score, just go across and come back, that's all.[1]

1. The Big Easy

The house on Wagner Street cost $3,800 and was a single-story white clapboard Greek Revival ranch house with a sagging porch on two adjacent sides. There was a collapsing old barn in back, weeping willows, and waist-high uncut grass in the yard. It was a few blocks of swampy fields from the Mississippi levee and a short drive from the ferry across to Canal Street and the French Quarter. Burroughs took his responsibilities as a father seriously, and his first priority had been to find a place to "stash these brats."[2] He also began looking around for cheap land near New Orleans, intending to grow enough pot for his own use with enough left to sell, and on October 14, 1948, he bought a tract of land in the Woodland Acres subdivision in Kenner, west of New Orleans, and told Kerouac, "I am buying a small tract of land in a swamp near N.O., where I will build a house."[3]

Bill's parents came down to visit and took a dislike to the Wagner Street property, which was very run-down and in an insalubrious area. Bill and his father looked around the French Quarter for something more suitable to buy. They found a house they liked but it was occupied by a black family and Bill's lawyer told him it would take an act of Congress to get them out. They settled on two houses and a patio at 1128–1130 Burgundy Street in the French Quarter, the plan being to live in one and rent out the other. The tenants who were already renting were, not surprisingly, upset at their potential eviction and refused to move without a fight. Burroughs told Kerouac, "I am having tenant trouble already. Two insufferable fruits live in the back house on my new property, and I find to my surprise and indignation that I cannot evict them without removing the premises from the rental market. I tell you we are bogged down in this octopus of bureaucratic socialism."[4] He told Allen, "I am now a landlord body and soul. Scrap rent controls, I say. [...] To dictate to a man what he can and can't do with his own property is *Un-American Socialism*. Such insidious measures leave the back door of the Ship of State ajar so that cur of Communism can slink in and plunder the American ice-box. My tenants are fat and sassy now, but come March 31 at midnight RCED Day (Rent Control End Day)—and I'll be waiting up with a stop watch to raise the rent or out they go."[5] This diatribe borders on becoming a routine, so it is hard to know just how much it reflects Burroughs's real viewpoint, and how much he was posturing for Ginsberg's benefit. Bill and his family never did get to live on Burgundy Street.

Bill had been getting awfully bored by Texas, but on arrival in New Orleans he had his usual period of disillusionment, telling Allen, "I am very dissatisfied with living conditions here. There seems to be no-one of interest around, or if such people exist, I can not find them."[6] This was a pattern repeated in many cities around the world, including Tangier and London: Burroughs would arrive in town, find it difficult to meet people, and cure his loneliness by lapsing into junk. He was in New Orleans during the great early days of rhythm and blues, but clearly did not visit any of the famous music clubs. When Jack Kerouac and Neal Cassady came to visit he insisted, "The bars are insufferably dreary,"[7] and claimed that it was against the law to go into the colored section of town. Bill's New Orleans was not Mardi Gras, red beans and rice, and fish fries. He was not interested.

Inevitably, soon after he moved to New Orleans, Burroughs returned to his old ways. He quickly became readdicted and began picking up boys. Junk was just too easy to get, and the French Quarter had "several queer bars so full every night the fags spill out onto the sidewalk."[8] Just walking around New Orleans, Bill identified junk neighborhoods: St. Charles and Poydras; the area around and above Lee Circle; Canal and Exchange Place. In a bar off Exchange Place he ran into a junkie named Joe Ricks—called "Pat" in *Junky*—who offered to score for him if Bill would buy him a cap. If *Junky* is accurate, Bill appears to have had an apartment in town as well as the house for his wife and kids. He and Joe went to his place, and despite Joe's warning that it was strong stuff, Bill measured himself two-thirds of a cap. He overdosed and passed out. When he came to he was lying on the bed with his collar loosened. He stood up and fell over. Ten dollars was missing from his wallet; Ricks had assumed he wouldn't be needing it. When Bill ran into him a few days later, Ricks said he had thought Bill was dying; he had rubbed ice on his neck but he turned all blue. A week later and Bill was hooked. He fell into his boring junkie routine, shooting up three times a day and pottering around the house, fixing things up in a desultory way, hardly ever going out except to score. He and Joe began pushing in a small way, just enough to pay for their habits, and *Junky* goes into exhaustive descriptions of their clients: Lonny the Pimp, Seltzer Willy, and Old Sam.

Bill had a minor run-in with his Italian neighbors. They lived farther down the block, but their children liked to hang around and taunt Billy, who often ran around the yard naked—"Little Beast," Bill called him. One day they threw a rock and hit Billy on the head so Bill went round to see them. Their father was at work but their mother was at home. Bill told her to keep her kids off his goddamn property. She told him her husband would come over and beat him up. Bill produced his gun and told her, "Well, if he does, he won't walk home." Nothing ever came of it.

Around the new year of 1949, the Burroughs household got swept up in one of Jack Kerouac and Neal Cassady's trips across the States that were eventually compressed into *On the Road*. Ten days before Christmas 1948, Jack Kerouac had received a telephone call from Neal Cassady in San Francisco to say that he had just bought a new 1949 Hudson and wanted to drive it to New York to "break it in." Al Hinkle, a fellow railroad brakeman, was coming along for the ride as he had never been to New York. The only problem—apart from the fact that Neal had a three-month-old child and had just spent his wife's savings, leaving them both destitute in San Francisco—was that Neal was broke. Jack said he would send him ten dollars and asked to be picked up at his sister's house in Rocky Mount, North Carolina, where he and his mother were spending Christmas. The next person to be conned was Al Hinkle's girlfriend, Helen, who was asked along on the trip because they thought she had money. But Helen refused to travel with Al unless they were married, so the trip was delayed until a quick marriage could be arranged. Then, to Neal and Al's dismay, it turned out that she wasn't rich after all.

They set off, but Helen, who was so innocent that she had not been permitted to wear lipstick or see a movie until she was twenty-one, objected to Neal smoking marijuana in the car. She also wanted to stop to use the bathroom, whereas Neal crudely told her to piss out the window. She wanted to spend the nights in motels; it was, after all, her honeymoon. But Neal was manic and wanted to drive all night, stopping only for gas and food. Helen thought that Neal was "the devil incarnate," and when they reached Tucson, Arizona, she insisted on leaving the car. It was arranged that Al would continue with Neal and see New York, then they would drive back in a week's time and collect her from New Orleans. Al gave her his railroad pass to get there. Neal gave her Burroughs's phone number and address as she knew no one in New Orleans.

Helen booked herself into a hotel, but was unable to stay there indefinitely because it was Sugar Bowl week and fully booked. Someone eventually got her a room in a brothel. Though she had never met him, Helen was so desperate that she called Burroughs. "I told him my plight and he replied with a long, long speech on prefabricated housing."[9] Bill met Helen at a Chinese restaurant and invited her to come and stay.

Meanwhile, Neal had detoured to Denver, where he picked up Lu Anne Henderson, his previous wife, to join in the trip. Jack was collected en route, and on arrival in New York, Neal and Lu Anne stayed with Allen Ginsberg at his apartment on York Avenue. Allen was working the night shift at the Associated Press, so they used his bed while he was out, and he would crawl in with them both when he returned home. Leading up to the new year, life was a continuous round of parties, except for Lu Anne, whom Neal sent out to work while the men sat around stoned. The Beats may have been revolutionary in some areas, but they were irremediably backward in their attitude toward women.

A series of increasingly irritated letters and telegrams arrived at York Avenue from Burroughs demanding to know when the party were coming to collect Helen. He told Allen, "Mrs. Hinkle is here for the past week. 'Gathering her brows like the gathering Storm, Nursing her wrath to keep it warm.' Tam O'Shanter—Robert Burns. Can't say as I blame her much." Bill said he did not object to her staying there as she was a most considerate guest, but "I seriously consider this kind of irresponsible behavior intolerable."[10] After another letter and a cable, he wrote again, "Does this Hinkle character expect to billet his wife on me indefinitely? His performance is an all-time record for sheer gall and irresponsibility."[11] However, he noted again that she had been a perfect guest and was very conscientious about helping out and paying her way as far as she was able. Bill knew that Neal never had any intention of picking her up in a week's time; he had conned her as he conned everyone.

For Helen the Burroughs household was astonishing. First of all she told Bill how dreadful Neal was because he smoked pot. Bill demurred and gave her the 1944 La Guardia Committee Report on marijuana to read, which contradicted government claims that pot was addictive, resulted in insanity and mental health problems, and led to criminal behavior. Then she was co-opted into buying an inhaler tube for Joan each day when she was out sightseeing; when a pharmacist offered to let her have a dozen because he could see she wouldn't "misuse" them, she still only bought one. Joan showed her what she used them for. Helen found Joan's behavior most peculiar. Joan washed the kitchen walls and mopped and scrubbed the kids' room to hospital standards and yet the children themselves were filthy; they were never washed. "You bathed that little girl, and you could tell she hadn't been washed in ages. That little girl—she bit her arm all the time. She had great, terrible scars on her arm."[12] The children were allowed to use Joan's Revere Ware pots instead of the toilet, and the same pots were used for cooking in the evening. Joan never slept; she would be out in the yard at 4:00 a.m., sweeping lizards off the dead tree in the yard where they lived, the moon reflecting in her oval face, high on amphetamine. Helen described Joan to Barry Gifford and Lawrence Lee, saying she was very quiet and "looked like an overworked, dreary housewife. Straight hair tied back with wisps hanging. She never wore a bra. There was something naked about her. I don't think she ever wore shoes or hose. She looked rather childlike." Kerouac, when he finally arrived with Neal and Hinkle, said, "Her face, once plump and Germanic and pretty, had become stony and red and gaunt. She had caught polio in New Orleans and limped a little."[13]

Helen also found Burroughs peculiar. He and Joan had thirteen cats and Bill liked to tease and torture them, tying them up with string and holding them over a bath of water so they screamed and tried to bite him. One day the white cat was sick and lay under the kitchen table. It died in the night. At breakfast of boiled eggs the next morning, Bill put his foot under the table and the cat was stiff and cold. In order not to traumatize the children, Bill spelled it out for Joan. "The white cat is D-E-A-D." Julie looked at the dead cat blankly and said, "Take him outside because he stinks."[14] Bill wore a gun in a holster and would line up a row of Joan's empty inhaler tubes and sit on the couch and shoot them, often with baby Billy asleep on his lap. At least they always ate good, well-balanced meals. Burroughs always enjoyed his food and ate heartily.

After Neal stole two dollars from Lucien Carr and began beating up Lu Anne, it seemed that the New York party was over, and on January 19, 1949, as the sun set over the New Jersey swamps, Neal Cassady, Jack Kerouac, Lu Anne Henderson, and Al Hinkle set out for New Orleans. Ever since Helen arrived to stay, Burroughs had fulminated against Cassady, telling her all the things he was going to say to him, blaming him entirely for the pointless trip. But when they did arrive, to Helen's surprise, "he didn't say a damned thing." However, Bill was very good at letting his feelings be known, and Neal kept a wary distance throughout their stay. As Lu Anne Henderson put it, "I got the definite impression that Burroughs wasn't all that pleased about seeing Neal."[15] Bill did, however, give Jack the benefit of his views. Lu Anne wrote that she felt Jack change when he reached Algiers. "He was doing a lot of talking alone with Bill, and there was a lot of stuff being discussed between them that they didn't share with us. I got the impression when we were there that Bill was very unhappy with Neal. Bill didn't show it in any way, or say anything particular to us. [. . .] It was something I felt more than he expressed directly. [. . .] I perceived something subtle change inside Jack. Jack was still excited about the trip, and clearly happy being on this trip, but I felt something had begun to trouble him [. . .] maybe Bill putting Neal in a little bit different light for him. [. . .] He was no longer quite as exuberant over the whole trip."[16] Bill was trying to get Jack to leave the trip and stay with them and get to know New Orleans. On their arrival Helen Hinkle led her wayward husband firmly into her back bedroom to give him a piece of her mind. Lu Anne followed, sat on one of the twig benches, and asked, "Aren't you going to screw? I'd like to watch." Helen's opinion of her husband's friends sank even lower.

Kerouac in *On the Road* recalled getting up one morning to find Burroughs and Neal Cassady yanking hundreds of rusty nails from a large wooden beam. Bill told him, "When I get all these nails out of this I'm going to build me a shelf that'll last a *thousand* years."[17] Warming to his subject, he told him there were plastics by which they could build houses that last forever, there were everlasting tires, everlasting fabrics, and even a certain gum that if you chew as a child you will never get cavities. These were ideas that he was still chasing in the seventies and eighties.

Bill was delighted to see Jack. He had been starved for intelligent company, and apart from Joan, he'd had no serious discussions since he got to New Orleans. He would sit in his rocking chair in his corner where the shades were always drawn, a copy of the Mayan Codices and an air gun at his side, little Billy on his lap, while the others sat around his feet and listened as he discussed literature—directing most of his conversation to Jack—and pontificated upon his other current concerns. Lu Anne said Jack was "in need of Burroughs at the time. The fact that we were going down by Burroughs really meant a great deal to Jack. When we would talk or anything, Burroughs was very much a part of him, like a teacher."[18]

Jack was clearly fascinated by Bill, and in *On the Road* he gave several pages to Bill's biography, leading to many inaccurate presumptions about him, but he also described Bill and Joan's relationship in some detail:

His relation with his wife was one of the strangest: they talked till late at night; Bull[19] liked to hold the floor, he went right on in his dreary monotonous voice, she tried to break in, she never could; at dawn he got tired and then Jane talked and he listened, snuffing and going thfump down his nose. She loved that man madly, but in a delirious way of some kind; there was never any mooching and mincing around, just talk and a very deep companionship that none of us would ever be able to fathom. Something curiously unsympathetic and cold between them was really a form of humor by which they communicated their own set of subtle vibrations. Love is all; Jane was never more than ten feet away from Bull and never missed a word he said, and he spoke in a very low voice, too.[20]

Bill and Allen had been engaged in a lively correspondence ever since Bill left New York, and now Ginsberg introduced the touchy subject of Bill's sexual relationship with Joan. He clearly suggested that Burroughs was "living a lie" with Joan, because of his preference for boys, which provoked a vigorous response from Burroughs:

> I never made any pretensions of permanent heterosexual orientation. What lie are you talking about? Like I say I never promised or even implied anything. How could I promise something that it is not in my power to give? I am not responsible for Joan's sexual life, never was, never pretended to be. Nor are we in any particular mess. There is, of course, as there was from the beginning, an impasse and cross purposes that are, in all likelihood, not amenable to any solution.[21]

Allen had questioned the validity of Neal's cross-country trip, but Burroughs expressed his feelings more forcefully, comparing the trip, for its sheer compulsive pointlessness, to the mass migrations of the Mayans. He told Allen in no uncertain terms his low opinion of Neal: "He is the Mover, compulsive, dedicated, ready to sacrifice family, friends, even the very car itself to the necessity of moving from one place to another. Wife and child may starve, friends exist only to exploit for gas money. [...] Neal must move. [...] Then he arrives here and has the unmitigated gall to expect me to advance $ for the continuation of this wretched trip. [...] I would not have contributed one cent, if I were wallowing in $s."[22] When Neal realized that Bill was not going to be conned, his friendly attitude toward him cooled considerably. As Bill put it to Allen, obviously quoting Allen's words, "He didn't unlock and 'charm' or 'graceful human nature' around here."[23] But Jack managed to get twenty-five dollars from his mother, so they were soon off again, this time to Tucson, where they hoped to borrow money from Alan Harrington. Al and Helen decided to stay in New Orleans, and Bill and Joan had grown to like Helen so much that they suggested doing up the chicken house in the yard as an apartment for them to live in.

When Joan did finally go to sleep she was out to the world. Burroughs, who was a very light sleeper, recalled one occasion in a New Orleans rooming house when Joan had been smoking in bed and fallen asleep, dropping her cigarette, setting her mattress on fire. It was Bill who was immediately wide awake. It took four metal wastebaskets of water to stop the smoldering and the mattress was ruined.[24] Bill paid the landlady fifty dollars.

On April 5, 1949, Bill found he was broke and took a pistol into town to pawn. He visited Joe Ricks at his hotel room and made a deal with one of Joe's visitors to exchange two ounces of pot for four caps. They all piled into Bill's Chevrolet and with Ricks driving went to get the pot, then set out to score the heroin. Around Lee Circle a cop recognized Joe in the car as a junkie well known to them and began following them. Bill told them to throw out the pot, which they did, but when the cops boxed them in on Calliope Street, one of the other passengers still had a joint in his pocket. That was enough to get Bill's car confiscated. They also found a gun in the glove compartment. There had been a law passed recently in New Orleans that in effect made it illegal to be a junkie. Bill had a needle welt on his arm. "All right, let's see your arms"—Burroughs remembered their command forty years later in "A Thanksgiving Prayer."[25] They were all taken to the Second Precinct and locked in a cell together.

Bill accompanied three detectives to his house and allowed them to search it without a warrant. They seized half a dozen firearms, a Mason jar of pot, as well as letters to Jack Kerouac and Allen Ginsberg, both containing references to drugs. It was a state matter, not federal, but the law provided a sentence of twenty months to five years in the notorious Angola State Prison if convicted. It was fortunate that Bill was not carrying when he was arrested, also fortunate that the house was searched illegally and his statement obtained through coercion. Bill had a very good lawyer named Robert S. Link who managed to get Bill's bail set before he was even charged—most irregular—and who quickly found a group of witnesses to give evidence of coercion; that Bill was in a bad state of heroin withdrawal at the time and was not in his right mind. Bill's father put up the bail of $1,500 and Link put Bill in the De Paul Sanatarium to get cured. He was in his third day of withdrawal and not in good shape. More importantly, Link arranged with the DA that Bill could leave the state for an indefinite period before the case came to trial on October 27. Bill, in hospital, was almost clear within eight days.

Three days after Bill's arrest, papers were drawn up to sell the Burgundy Street property to Mote, suggesting an emergency substitution of Bill's father for himself, and on July 11, 1949, the purchase was complete. Two weeks later the Algiers house was sold back to the Eureka Homestead Society, the people he first bought it from. Bill defaulted on the swampland in Kenner where he was intending to build a house and it was put up

Mortimer, Laura, and Billy, St. Louis, 1914. *[William S. Burroughs Estate]*

Laura Lee Burroughs, 1942 *[William S. Burroughs Estate]*

Mortimer Perry Burroughs ("Mote") fishing, a love he passed on to his sons. *[William S. Burroughs Estate]*

Mort and Billy in front of the family firm. *[William S. Burroughs Estate]*

Billy and Mort around the time that Billy saw the green reindeer. *[William S. Burroughs Estate]*

Billy with Nursey, who was to cause him so much angst. *[William S. Burroughs Estate]*

Bill at Los Alamos School, where the A-bomb was later invented. *[William S. Burroughs Estate]*

Bill's Harvard ID photograph. *[William S. Burroughs Estate]*

Hal Chase, Jack Kerouac, Allen Ginsberg, William S. Burroughs, New York, 1944. *[photographer unknown, Allen Ginsberg Estate.]*

Joan Vollmer on the Upper East Side, c1944. *[Allen Ginsberg, Allen Ginsberg Estate]*

Joan Vollmer, Barnard University graduation, 1943. *[William S. Burroughs Estate]*

William S. Burroughs III *[William S. Burroughs Estate]*

Julie Adams. *[William S. Burroughs Estate]*

Herbert Huncke on the Burroughs farm in East Texas, 1947. *[Allen Ginsberg, Allen Ginsberg Estate]*

Burroughs and Joan on the farm in East Texas, 1947. *[Allen Ginsberg, Allen Ginsberg Estate]*

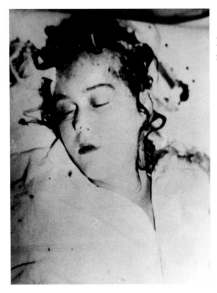

Deathbed photograph of Joan from the local press.

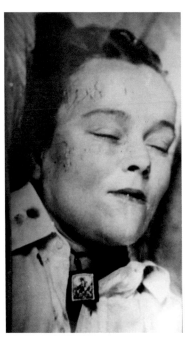

Joan in hospital. A religious medal had been placed at her throat.

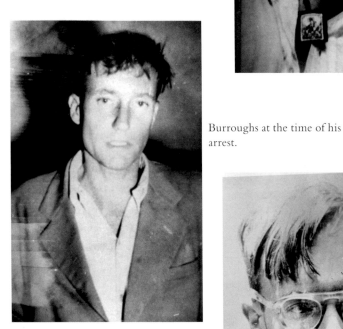

Burroughs at the time of his arrest.

Burroughs the day after the murder.

Burroughs with "Old Dave" Tesorero, Mexico City. *[Photographer unknown, William S. Burroughs Estate]*

Burroughs reading the reports of Joan's death.

Burroughs in Search of Yagé, Peru, 1953. *[Photographer unknown, William S. Burroughs Estate]*

Burroughs, fully armed, in the Amazon jungle, 1953. *[Photographer unknown, William S. Burroughs Estate]*

William S. Burroughs II and III, Palm Beach, Florida, 1953. *[Photographer unknown, William S. Burroughs Estate]*

Burroughs on a Lower East Side rooftop with Alene Lee, who typed the manuscripts of *Queer* and *Yage Letters,* fall of 1953**.** *[Allen Ginsberg, Allen Ginsberg Estate]*

Burroughs and his new friend Alan Ansen outside the San Remo in New York, fall of 1953. *[Allen Ginsberg, Allen Ginsberg Estate]*

Burroughs explains to Jack Kerouac how he must get away from his mother's apron strings. *[Allen Ginsberg, Allen Ginsberg Estate]*

Burroughs and Kerouac come to blows! *[Allen Ginsberg, Allen Ginsberg Estate]*

for sheriff's sale and repurchased by the original developers.[26] James Grauerholz threw an interesting new light on Burroughs's real estate ventures when he uncovered Joan's answers to questions posed by an interviewer named Joyce Adams, who took a social history from her when Burroughs was admitted to the De Paul Sanatarium. She said that Bill's parents meant well but attempted to arrange things for him and always got him out of trouble, which caused the patient to violently oppose them as he would rather deal with his problems himself. They phoned frequently and the father frequently sent substantial checks. "Recently, the parents came to New Orleans—visited the patient at his home in Algiers, were not fond of the house, and purchased a new one for patient in the city at Burgundy Street. They had purchased the Algiers home for [the] couple when patient and his wife came to New Orleans about a year ago." All of which rather contradicts the impression that Burroughs had been giving Kerouac and Ginsberg in his letters of himself as a tough businessman. Burroughs was playacting, perhaps unconsciously, acting out a role-playing game as the rapacious landlord, and before that as the cotton farmer, just as he acted out character roles back at 115th Street with Kerouac, Ginsberg, and Chase. It was all inauthentic. He was trying to be the adult, the grown-up that his parents so desperately wanted him to be.

Burroughs often compared Joan with his mother, saying they had many of the same characteristics: "[Joan] had an immediate insight to anyone's character. Just one look and she knew. My mother had that. Just glance at someone and say, 'He's a crook, he's no good'";[27] "Like Joan there are no conventional words or categories to describe either one of 'em. My mother was this very intelligent person, very psychic. Quite a lot like Joan";[28] "[Joan] had just a complete intolerance for opiates. My mother did too."[29] There was even an instance where a calico cat in the room, "very delicate, very special and completely unaggressive," reminded Burroughs of Jane Bowles, "also mother, and Joan. All three in Calico. Same quality of ethereal delicacy."[30] Bill's relationship with Joan was more than intellectual compatibility and friendship; she was also a mother figure to him. The assessment of Dr. John W. Bick at the sanatorium was that "the patient [...] gives me the impression of being grossly immature, lacking all adult sense of responsibility, and being grossly dependent on his wife, who seemed to enjoy taking care of the serious problem which he represented." Dr. Bick tried to persuade Joan that a long period of hospitalization should be considered, but she did not agree and Bill was discharged into her care on April 15, 1949, against hospital advice.[31]

Bill's relationship with his mother was infantile and narcissistic. He entwined his life with hers, took her name, Lee, for his own, and later even delivered her a son to bring up. He liked whores because they were "motherly." He relied on his parents to get him out of trouble—legal and financial—for fifty years. There never was a trust fund, their money was all earned. Bill had incest dreams[32] and felt guilty about not visiting, yet Laura always adored him. He remained her favorite son. Bill was a mama's boy, always whining and complaining about the conditions and service. Many people filled this role later in his life, to a greater or lesser extent: Allen Ginsberg, Brion Gysin, Ian Sommerville, James Grauerholz, and numerous others supported him and helped him to organize his life, just as Laura Burroughs had done, but in Joan's case she was actually a woman.

For Bill and Joan, the biggest problem was where to go next. A second felony in New Orleans would draw seven years in the state penitentiary and he could be pulled over at any time under the new drug laws. In Texas a second conviction for drunken driving would be almost as bad. Bill's family was prepared to use their financial clout to prevent him from returning to New York. Joan told Allen, "It makes things rather difficult for Bill, as for me, I don't care where I live, so long as it's with him."[33] They thought of a cruise, to get Bill completely away from drugs, but in the end Bill decided that he would first return to Texas to oversee the sale of his farming interests and spend more time with Kells; he had missed good conversation in Algiers. He had already decided to move on to Central or South America.

Chapter Sixteen

It was down in Texas that I made an orgone box with Kells Elvins.[1]

1. Return to the Valley

Bill, Joan, and the children moved to the Valley in April 1949 to sell Bill's landholdings there. He and Kells had earlier combined their operation and Bill owned a share of the farm equipment as well as land. In May he sold his original fifty acres to Kells, but the family stayed on in Pharr until October, waiting to see how Bill's trial was shaping up. Bill hated it there. "All the worst features of America have drained down to the Valley and concentrated there. In the whole area, there is not one good restaurant. The food situation could only be tolerated by people who do not taste what they eat."[2] He felt that the Valley was plagued by DOR, Wilhelm Reich's "Deadly Orgone Radiation," a negative debilitating energy that brought on depression and lack of vitality. "Death is absence of life. Wherever life withdraws, death and rot move in. Whatever it is—orgones, life force—that we all have to score for all the time, there is not much of it in the Valley. Your food rots before you can get it home. Milk sours before you can finish the meal. The Valley is the place where the new anti-life force is breaking through. Death hangs over the Valley like an invisible smog. [...] The dying cell gravitates to the Valley."[3]

The notion of orgones came from Wilhelm Reich's recently published *The Cancer Biopathy*,[4] in which he argues that cancer is caused by an inability to discharge sexual energy. Reich calls it orgone energy, natural energy, the life force, cosmic energy, what Henri Bergson called élan vital, which exists everywhere in the atmosphere and in all living and dead matter. It can be concentrated and used to help relieve a stasis of energy in the body, and Reich manufactured a simple device known as an orgone accumulator in which the patient sat and absorbed life energy. Burroughs thought that anything that energized the body would be good for the after-effects of junk sickness. His approach to the orgone was essentially that of Bergson's notion that "life is essentially a current sent through matter."[5] Bill wanted to keep himself charged up.

Reich's ideas on the role of the orgasm in healthy functioning, a natural extension of Freud's theories, were seriously taken on board by New York intellectuals (and elsewhere). Reich was a long-standing member of the Freud seminar in Vienna, and his book *Character Analysis* on psychoanalytic technique was a standard work, so his ideas were carefully considered. Reich's books were then extremely popular and people were hiring orgone accumulators from Reich's institute or building their own. Burroughs took exception to the amount of paperwork attached to renting an orgone accumulator, so in June he built his own in the yard behind Kells's house. The principle was very simple. Orgones are absorbed and retained by organic matter but pass freely through metal. A metal box with organic material on the outside will have a higher concentration of orgones inside than out because the layer of organic material will retard the escape of orgones from the box. The more layers of metal and organic material, the higher the concentration of orgones. Bill ordered sheet metal, wood, and a roll of rock wool. He told James Grauerholz, "Kells and I made it, and it was a sloppy job too. [...] We had some kind of jerry built hut to start with and sloppily nailed sheet iron inside that. Then inside that we had another orgone box made out of an old icebox which you lowered down over yourself, and then we had a little accumulator made out of one of those jerry cans, we just covered that over in burlap and various stuff—we were getting three levels."[6] He felt it did him good: "My skin prickled and I experienced an aphrodisiac effect similar to good strong weed. No doubt about it, orgones are as definite a force as electricity. After using the accumulator for several days my energy came back to normal."[7] Kells and Bill's accumulator was a popular new toy for the front porch set. Bill wrote Kerouac, "The gimmick really works. The man is not crazy, he's a fucking genius."[8] From then on, whenever he was settled somewhere, Burroughs usually built himself an orgone accumulator. He had them in Tangier, London, New York, and Lawrence, Kansas.

His reasons for selling in Pharr were largely financial rather than lack of orgones. He and Kells were gentleman farmers and had never won the respect of the local farmers. They were always having problems with their field hands; the border patrol kept returning their wetbacks to Mexico. Other farmers had an arrangement with the border patrol. The patrol would arrive and say they were under pressure to deport a certain number of Mexicans and then they would discuss how many would go and would take them to the border and deport them, but always with the understanding that they would be back in time for work the next morning. Trucks would be waiting at the riverbank to collect them as they swam or waded over. The quotas would be met and everyone was happy. Bill and Kells never colluded enough, or else they were unaware of such arrangements, so they were sometimes left shorthanded.

Burroughs went along with the views of the local landowners, claiming they were all on the verge of bankruptcy and that if they paid the higher minimum wage demanded by government bureaucrats they would not make any profit and go out of business. But these farmers were very wealthy, and farmers in the rest of the United States managed to make a profit without employing illegal labor. This became the subject of an intense correspondence with Allen Ginsberg, who had originally enrolled at Columbia in order to become a labor lawyer. He accused Bill of complicity in preserving a corrupt system and paying what amounted to slave wages. Bill disagreed, saying that he provided medical care, clothing, and food for his laborers, who were on an hourly rate, and that he had devised a system of profit sharing, though it is hard to know how he would have known who to include as sometimes he and Kells had more than two hundred field hands, hired and paid by agents, not by themselves.

At first Bill housed his family in a dilapidated motel in McAllen at Ash and 10th Street. Julie was dirty, barefoot, and wore no underpants. Joan also eschewed underclothes and wore button-front dresses that gaped revealingly. Whether this was intentionally provocative or not, Bill's friends had to try hard to avert their eyes. She still ate the strips from two Benzedrine inhalers a day and yet hardly said a word. Bill appears to have spent most evenings on the front porch, drinking and carousing with Kells or else visiting the boys in Reynosa. Joan, presumably, stayed home with the kids and her Benzedrine.

After the motel they moved to a run-down house located on the north side of Kells's orange groves on South Jackson Street. Bill spent some time doing it up. Bill's idée fixe that American manufacturers were intentionally making second-rate goods, designed to wear out and fall apart in just a few years, was still foremost in his mind. He thought that there was a conspiracy against the American consumer. A concrete house could be made to last a thousand years but American houses barely lasted for twenty-five; R. Buckminster Fuller's 1933 Dymaxion car was fast and energy-efficient but was blocked by Chrysler. There were light bulbs that lasted a lifetime but the patents were bought up by the Phoebus cartel and purposely shelved. The same with everlasting car tires; all had been bought up by big business and shelved. Doing his bit to counteract this trend, Bill constructed for the house sturdy side tables and a dining table of huge railroad ties bolted together with rebar. When they had fixed up the house, Joan gave a dinner party for all their friends. In the middle of dinner, Bill jumped up onto the table, scattering food and dishes, and stamped his foot on its indestructible surface. "Now, by God, this is functional!" he assured them.

Bill was of course armed, and continued to practice by shooting Joan's empty inhaler cases off a wall. Ted Marak told Rob Johnson that one of their games consisted of Bill getting him or Kells to throw oranges or grapefruit into the air. Bill would aim and hit them in the air almost every time. Marak was a qualified marksman from his time in the U.S. Army cavalry and said that Bill was an expert shot. Marak also told Johnson that Bill would sometimes put a grapefruit or other fruit on Joan's head and shoot it off in a reenactment of the William Tell story. This is in direct contradiction to Burroughs's later story that they had never played the William Tell game before, but there is no reason to doubt Marak's recollection of that time.

Bill enjoyed being with his best friend Kells. There were weekend trips to Corpus Christi and South Padre Island on the coast, then still undeveloped, and long evenings drinking and smoking on Kells's porch or at his own house. Kells loved to feed Bill stories just to see what he would make of them. He told Bill about his friend the Texas oilman Clint Murchison, and how he would sit around with his cronies and ask, "Hey Clem, when are you gonna get yourself cured?" Kells explained this meant get rich, properly rich, not the two or three million that Clem already had. He always said he would help Kells if he asked him, so Kells was well disposed toward him. Kells also respected the "second sight" that Bill and his mother supposedly possessed. He asked Bill, "Tell me about the man, Burroughs, tell me about his hands." Bill concentrated on Murchison: "And I could see his hands were twisted, he had terrible arthritis. And with second sight I saw, I said, 'His hands are twisted. Being down there with all that shale.' And Kells says, 'Yes, the man's got arthritis, that's right, Burroughs.'"[9]

In between his drinking and farm management, Kells was also trying to write the Great American Novel, but he never devoted enough time or attention to it. In later years he did have a short story published in *Esquire* and another in *Dude*, but most of his writing remains unpublished. Burroughs recalled, "He didn't write all that much. He always encouraged me. Kells felt, in a way, that without my influence he would never have realized anything, that's the idea, that I turned him on to possibilities beyond that he wouldn't have realized unless he had known me: a less conventional life, less conventional ways of thinking, and his whole interest in writing came from the work that we had done together."[10] Kells kept all of Burroughs's letters, which he considered the most fantastic writing he had ever seen.

In September, Bill made a trip to Mexico City with Kells and rented an apartment at río Lerma 26, preparatory to moving there with his family. His lawyer had warned him that there was every indication of an unfavorable outcome in his drug case, and he had decided to skip the country. He was delighted by Mexico City, telling Kerouac that a single man could live well on two dollars a day, liquor included. "Fabulous whore houses and restaurants. A large foreign colony. Cock fights, bull fights, every conceivable diversion."[11] He told Allen that he wanted to live in Mexico City, "and don't see how I can afford to live anywhere else."[12] Bill told Kerouac that he thought he would be in Mexico for some time as the statute of limitations was five years.[13] By October 1949 they were there. With the exception of relatively short visits, Burroughs would live outside the United States from then until 1974.

Chapter Seventeen

Nothin a junkey likes better
Than sittin quietly with a new shot
And knows tomorrow's plenty more
　　　　　　　—JACK KEROUAC, MEXICO CITY BLUES[1]

Many hundred years ago, the Valley of Mexico, an oval seven thousand feet above the seas, walled and sheltered by porphyry and immense volcanic rock, was a valley of great lakes and flowering tropical forests. Here on fifty islands and the shore of Lake Taxcuoco rose the city. Waterways fronted by low-roofed palaces of pink stone, plazas at anchor, floating gardens: Tenochtitlán, waterbound, canal-crossed, bridge-linked, ablaze with flowers... And amid the soft magic, a huge temple, a pyramid, squat, vast, solid. [...] Then the Spaniards came and changed everything. They couldn't have been more thorough. After four years the city is destroyed and rebuilt, the lakes drained, the waterways filled in, the canals dry, the forests decimated.

　　　　　　　—SYBILLE BEDFORD[2]

1. Mexico City

After the Mexican Revolution virtually anything was permitted under the first civilian president, Miguel Alemán. American corporations flooded across the border, eager to make money, Ford and General Motors, Kodak and RCA, Singer sewing machines, American comic books, Quaker Oats, Walt Disney, and Hollywood movies. Corruption was rife; these were the years when the *mordida* was at its height. Burroughs rented a place for his family at paseo de la Reforma 210, house 8, in Colonia Cuauhtémoc, a fashionable residential suburb to the west of the historic center of the city, close to the Angel of Independence monument. He still retained his bachelor apartment on nearby río Lerma. The family apartment was not far from Chapultepec Park, said to date back to Montezuma, with its huge old trees, over two hundred feet tall and forty-five feet in circumference, hanging with Spanish moss. There was a castle on the rock above and little boats on the lake.

Mexico City had an inescapable physical impact on the senses: noise, smell, color, movement, altitude, and sun. Mexico City is in the oval Valley of Mexico. It is in the *tierra fría*, the cold zone, which is anywhere in Mexico above seven thousand feet. At 7,350 feet above sea level, the air was thin, and any quick movement caused dizziness until acclimatization. Vultures circled in a sky so blue it hurt to look at it. Three active volcanoes surrounded the city, Popocatépetl, Iztaccíhuatl, and Xinantécatl, with three curls of smoke rising into the air. There was also Peñón, a small hill, which according to geologists will one day erupt and destroy the entire city. Bill and his family arrived in the rainy season, which runs from the end of May until October. The sky is always clear, except for the swirling El Greco clouds that build up to the day's rain at 4:00 p.m. It is always warm, never hot, never cold except at night. Business begins again around eight o'clock after the noisy early evening rain. Darkness comes suddenly. Dinner was at ten.

Burroughs, not normally interested in art, architecture, or history, was keen to see the Aztec and Mayan artifacts. In the plaza Mayor, the great Aztec pyramid, the only building the Spanish were unable to destroy, lies belowground. With the ecological destruction of the city by the Spanish, the ground became boggy and by its own great weight, after a few years, the great pyramid sank out of sight. The Spanish built a garish cathedral on top of it, the oldest Christian structure in the New World. The greatest treasure of the National Museum of Anthropology was the Aztec Calendar Stone, the Stone of the Sun, discovered when Mexico City Cathedral was being repaired. Across the square, the enormous edifice of the National Theater, El Teatro Nacionál, on Alameda had slowly sunk five feet into the subsoil.

Bill and Joan looked around the university quarter, with its high dark stone streets like the Left Bank of Paris. Everywhere were tramways and new American hotels. Many baroque churches and convents had been converted into warehouses, libraries, garages, newspaper offices after the government closed down 480 Catholic churches and establishments in the 1931–36 antireligious clampdown. It was a society in rapid transition. In 1949, the population was less than two million, one-tenth of today's total, but travelers give us a picture of an enormously busy, vibrant, exciting city. The pavements were narrow and crowded: people carrying basins of glowing charcoal, women with water in small earthenware vessels strapped to their backs, a peasant with a tethered chicken slung casually over one shoulder, mules carrying clay jars wrapped in straw, a baby mule born in the street, a chain of mules carrying boulders in panniers, men weaving a cage of twigs for a waiting parrot, parrots shrieking from upper windows, everyone pushing and shoving. Beggars displaying deformities, waving stumps and crutches, lottery tickets thrust in the face, sellers of puppies and straw hats, flowers, hot chestnuts and candies; fruit sellers covered the pavement with piles of mangoes, plums, avocados, pineapples, and papayas. Overflowing trams dominated the streets, and peasants with donkey carts jostled with mules, goats both live and dead, huge American automobiles, and pedestrians. Grubby babies with faces like an Aztec carving grasped at passersby. The all-pervading smell of confectionery drifted down the avenida Juárez.

The shops were, then as now, filled with tourist junk, hideous elaborate silver filigree, bad serapes, gourds, dead fleas dressed up as people inside walnut shells, skeleton figures in sombreros. It was a city of bookshops filled with Spanish editions of the classics from Emily Brontë to Sigmund Freud, but a quarter of the people were illiterate, and another quarter had considerable difficulty in reading, despite a new law that anyone who was literate must teach at least one person to read.

Joan adjusted to the new situation with her usual equanimity and told Allen, "I shan't attempt to describe my sufferings for 3 weeks after the Benzedrine gave out, but with thyroid tablets, Reich and faith, I made it." She told him that she was "somewhat drunk from 8 am on. Evil people here sell tequila for 40c (U.S.) a quart," and that she tended to "hit the lush rather hard."[3] She also told him, "The boys are lovely, easy and cheap (3 pesos—40c) down here, but my patience is infinite."[4] Clearly Burroughs was making no effort to hide his boys from her. Shortly after arriving in Mexico City, Burroughs began to frequent a particular queer bar, named in *Junky* as "the Chimu Bar," most likely the Linterna Verde—the Green Lantern—on Monterrey not far from Mexico City College. It was here he later met Angelo, his long-term Mexican boy, but in the meantime he had no particular favorite. Burroughs did not bring them into the family home, but initially retained his small apartment at río Lerma 26, and later used hotels.

Whether Joan was allowed, or insisted upon, the same sexual freedom we do not know. Bill had his boys and, at least initially, thought he was living in a free and easy society where everyone minded their own business. This he pontificated upon to both Allen and Kerouac at some length: "It really is possible to relax here where nobody tries to mind your business for you, and a man can walk the streets without being molested by some insolent cop swollen with the unwarranted authority bestowed upon him by our stupid and hysterical law-making bodies. Here a cop is on the level of a street-car conductor. He knows his place and stays there."[5] Inevitably Bill's early impressions were rose-tinted, but his initial reaction to Mexico was positive and he talked of opening a bar near the U.S. border, of farming in the south, and of becoming a Mexican citizen. One of his first moves was to build an orgone accumulator to aid Joan in her Benzedrine withdrawal. Benzedrine was easily available in Mexico City— Burroughs speaks of using it himself in *Queer*—so Joan must have decided to kick the habit, though it sounds as if she thought that she would not be able to get any: "Benzedrine gave out."

They settled into an approximation of normal family life. Neighbors were hired as child-minders and to do the laundry, and Joan cooked: American food early in the month, Mexican food later. Burroughs was not keen on Mexican food. The Aztec diet of frijoles and tortillas, black beans, hand-ground corn cakes, and chili pepper was something they resorted to only when his parents' allowance ran low. The Aztecs had no cattle and therefore no dairy products. It took four hours to grind the corn for one person's daily tortillas. Staff were paid one or two pesos a day. Traditional Mexican restaurant fare was also not to his taste, particularly the service, where, after a lengthy wait, all the courses appeared in quick succession, long before the previous one had been eaten, until the table was full and the coffee waiting, getting cold, at the end of a line of as yet uneaten courses. There was a very good Viennese restaurant and several French ones that they patronized when they could afford it.

Burroughs was still under indictment in New Orleans for possession of narcotics, and having jumped bail his first move was to find a lawyer to block any possibility of being extradited. He was using the pay phone at the Reforma Hotel, asking someone at the American embassy if they could recommend an English-speaking lawyer, when he was overheard by a flashily dressed, husky Italian American with a big diamond ring on his finger, a stereotype mafioso named Tony, who said, "Pardon me, I couldn't help overhearing what you said. The man for you to see is Bernabé Jurado." Then he asked Bill, "What's your trouble? Embezzlement?" Bill told him it was narcotics. "Oh," he said. "Well, he's your man."

Bernabé Jurado had his office in the most fashionable business quarter, at calle de Madero 17, but often saw his clients at a bar, La Opera, at the corner of Cinco de Mayo and Filomeno Mata, famous for its celebrities and politicians. Jurado was a big, confident middle-aged man, very well dressed, with black greased hair, a mustache, and a piercing gaze. As a child he had witnessed the execution of his father by Pancho Villa, who seized the family hacienda. He worked in a mine until he was twelve, when he moved with his mother and sister to Mexico City. He studied accounting, medicine, and law and specialized in labor law, defending striking workers. He was the essence of machismo and was reputed to have married fourteen times, twice to one woman. He liked cocaine, alcohol, and cantinas. He was a formidable lawyer and would do anything to win a case: buy off judges, alter documents, challenge his opponents to a duel, and on one memorable occasion he asked the judge to show him the proof against his client. The judge passed him a bounced check and Bernabé popped it in his mouth and ate it. His client got off for lack of evidence. He was clearly perfect material for Burroughs, who used him as a character in a number of books, including *Junky, The Naked Lunch, Cities of the Red Night*, and *The Place of Dead Roads*.

Burroughs intended to study at Mexico City College. Most foreign students got one-year student immigrant visas that could easily be renewed, and the college even provided a student registration service, but Burroughs preferred to use Jurado in case the U.S. authorities attempted to extradite him. Jurado immediately filed a petition for Mexican citizenship even though an immigrant must normally live in Mexico for five years before becoming eligible for actual citizenship, and must have an "immigrant" rather than "tourist" visa. In fact Burroughs did not need Jurado's services immediately, because though his lawyer in New Orleans said, "Frankly, I wouldn't advise you to come back," he also told Bill that the U.S. authorities had no intention of extraditing him. No papers were ever filed. Burroughs told Allen, "Mexico is my place. I want to live here and bring up the children here. I would not go back to the U.S. under any circumstances. This is basically an oriental culture (80% Indian) where everyone has mastered the art of minding his own business. If a man wants to wear a monocle or carry a cane he does not hesitate to do it and no one gives him a second glance. Boys and young men walk down the street arm in arm and no one pays them any mind. It is not that people here don't care what others think. It simply would not occur to a Mexican to expect criticism from a stranger, nor would it occur to anyone to criticize the behavior of others."[6]

On November 21, 1949, Burroughs enrolled in the Mexico City College School of Higher Studies in the department of anthropology and archaeology, specializing in Mexican archaeology. He was on the GI Bill; the U.S. government paid for his books and tuition, and gave him a seventy-five-dollar-a-month living allowance. He was formally admitted on January 2, 1950, and the next day he began his courses in Spanish language, the Mayan language, and the Codices. At this time, about 70 percent of the college's eight hundred-plus students were Americans on the GI Bill, though many were there just for the bursary to supplement their income and attended few lectures. Although Burroughs had a genuine interest in Aztec and Mayan culture, it was the money that interested him most. As he told Kerouac, "I always say keep your snout in the public trough."[7] Burroughs studied the Mayan Codices under Robert Hayward Barlow, the chairman of the distinguished Anthropology Department. Barlow committed suicide in January 1951 with an overdose of goofballs after a disgruntled student outed him as being gay. Burroughs joined the Sahagun Anthropology Club and went on field visits with them, including one in July 1950 led by Barlow and Professor Pedro Armillas to the Temple of Quetzalcoatl in Teotihuacan. Burroughs had studied a copy of the Mayan Codices in Algiers; now he examined them in depth and they became one of the topics that he and Joan discussed. From the things Bill told her, Joan suggested that the Mayan priests must have had some sort of telepathic control over the population, which started Burroughs thinking in that direction. Burroughs sometimes quoted her thoughts on the Mayans as a good example of her intelligence. Clearly, despite their other problems, theirs was a true meeting of minds. For her part, Joan finally convinced Burroughs of her theory that atomic explosions had polluted the atmosphere and were causing a mild radiation sickness worldwide.

2. Back on Junk

One day, after being in Mexico City for several months, Bill went to see Bernabé Jurado and found the office closed. A shabby, short, middle-aged man was waiting outside who said Jurado hadn't arrived yet. Burroughs immediately identified him as an old-time junkie, and the man obviously could tell that Burroughs was the same. After they had both conducted their business with Jurado, Burroughs asked David Tesorero[8]—"Old Ike" in *Junky*—to join him for supper. At a restaurant on San Juande Letràn, Tesorero flipped back his coat lapel and showed Bill the spike stuck on the underside. "I've been on junk for 28 years," he told Bill. "Do you want to score?"[9]

Dave Tesorero was scoring through María Dolores Estévez Zuleta, the powerful, obese boss of the Mexico City trade from the twenties until the end of the fifties. Burroughs based his character Lola la Chata directly upon her: "There is only one pusher in Mexico City, and that is Lupita."[10] She began dealing marijuana, morphine, and heroin from a fried-pork-skin and coffee-with-a-shot stall in La Merced for her mother in 1919 when she was only thirteen years old. At nights she would cruise the colonia, where she earned her own money. She quickly became adept

at figures but never learned to read or write. She established her headquarters on calle San Simón and began bribing officials in the Office of
Narcotics and the higher-ranking police. At Lent she always bought a
truckload of fish to distribute to the people of her neighborhood, La Merced, where they loved and respected her. Each year she took some of them
on a pilgrimage to the Virgen de San Juan de los Lagos, all expenses paid.

Hers was a risky profession and she spent seven terms in jail. In 1945 she
was arrested and transported to las Islas Marías, making it impossible to
visit her. Using her connections she was able to build a hotel and a landing
strip suitable for small planes on the islands so that her two daughters could
visit, but soon managed to get herself relocated to Lecumberri in Mexico
City and was set free. Her drugs were hidden in religious paper medals,
plastic yo-yos, and other ingenious places, and distributed by a team of
salesmen to locations like her husband's auto repair shop. She never took
drugs herself; it was María who gave Burroughs the line, "dealing is more
of a habit than using."[11] When Burroughs was in Mexico City she ruled
the drug scene. She had spies in many of the police stations feeding her
information, and all the top court officials and police were on her books.[12]

Burroughs never met her, always scoring through Tesorero. He wrote,
"I had been off junk three months at this time. It took me just three days
to get back on."[13] Joan was horrified. It may be that they had a deal where
she would get off Benzedrine in Mexico and Burroughs would get off junk;
she had gone through a painful withdrawal and now he was using again.

Buying junk through María was more expensive than it was in the
United States. Her papers cost fifteen pesos each—about two dollars—and
they were half the strength of a two-dollar wrap in New York. Bill needed
two papers to fix and four to get really high. Bill and Dave tried getting
scripts, but doctors were only allowed to prescribe two and a half grains
maximum each time, but that was cheaper than María so they made the
rounds of doctors. They found several who would write scripts for five
pesos, but it was a problem to get them filled. Sometimes the pharmacist
would give them distilled water, and sometimes, if they were out of stock of
morphine, they would use anything that came to hand. "Could have killed
myself trying to shoot this crap," Burroughs wrote.[14] Then one of the doctors suggested that Dave apply for a government permit. This entitled the
bearer to a fixed quantity of morphine each month at wholesale prices. For
one hundred pesos the doctor said he would put in an application. Bill gave
him the money. To their astonishment, in fifteen days they had a government permit to buy fifteen grams of morphine every month, at about two
dollars a gram. Burroughs wrote, "Like a junkie's dream. I had never seen
so much morphine before at once." Bill put up the money and he and Dave

split it. Seven grams a month allowed Bill about three grains a day, more than he had ever had in the States, and all for thirty dollars a month.

Now that they had a regular supply of junk, they began getting prescriptions for cocaine, but they were even harder to fill. There is no medicinal use for cocaine except as administered by a doctor and a lot of pharmacists threw them back at him. "No prestamos servicio a los viciosos!" It was a yellow prescription, like a dishonorable discharge from the army. They used coke to make speedballs, a mixture of cocaine and heroin. Burroughs remembered, "Of course your veins wear out. Dave was very good at hitting a vein, he could find a vein in a mummy. Sometimes I couldn't. Your veins retreat and you can't hit 'em."[15] He and Dave became friends, or at least comrades. When Tesorero got fifteen days in jail for vagrancy, Bill visited him there, knowing he would be junk-sick. Dave hadn't taken a shot in seventy-two hours and was in bad shape. Bill gave him an orange that had been injected with morphine and also managed to transfer a piece of opium to him that he had smuggled into jail under his tongue, wrapped in cellophane.

Bill decided to accompany Dave on his annual visit to Our Lady of Chalma, the saint of thieves and drug addicts. The small pilgrimage town of Chalma is about a hundred kilometers from Mexico City, a few kilometers from the Malinalco ruins. It was a pre-Columbian pilgrimage site where Indians worshipped their gods in a cave. It was no surprise then that an image of the Virgin Mary appeared in the cave in 1539, two years after the Augustinian fathers arrived. It became so popular that in 1550 a chapel was built and the image was moved to it. It attracted huge crowds on Sundays and religious holidays. It took Bill and Dave two days to get there, partly on foot. Naturally, with a target clientele, Dave took along twenty bags of morphine to sell. All along the track there were beggars slithering along on boards, holding out their withered hands for alms. Bill enjoyed himself immensely.

It appears that his latest addiction was a tipping point for Joan. In *Junky* he wrote:

> When my wife saw I was getting the habit again, she did something she had never done before. I was cooking up a shot two days after I'd connected with Old Ike. My wife grabbed the spoon and threw the junk on the floor. I slapped her twice across the face and she threw herself on the bed, sobbing, then turned around and said to me: "Don't you want to do anything at all? You know how bored you get when you have a habit. It's like all the lights went out. Oh well, do what you want. I guess you have some stashed anyway."
> I did have some stashed.[16]

That summer, the *On the Road* gang turned up again. Neal Cassady, Jack Kerouac, and Frank Jeffries crossed into Mexico at Laredo driving a clapped-out 1937 Ford sedan. Neal wanted to get a quick Mexican divorce and Jack was keen to visit Bill and Joan. They arrived in Mexico City on June 24, 1950, and celebrated with a wild night on the town, but Jack immediately came down with dysentery and a fever that confined him to bed for several days. By this time Bill and Joan were living at Cerrada de Medellín 37,[17] a third-floor flat at the rear of a run-down white apartment building in a small dead-end passage in Colonia Roma, behind the Sears Roebuck building. Jack and Neal rented a cheap two-bedroom apartment next door in the same building, but as soon as Neal got his divorce he shot off to New York to marry for the third time. Jack gave up the room and moved in with Bill and Joan for two months, drinking and smoking pot alone in his room every day, trying to revise his first draft of *On the Road* and writing nothing new. He was depressed because his first novel, *The Town and the City*, had received a lukewarm reception; poor sales left one-third of the first printing unbound. After working four years on the book he had naively expected to be welcomed into the literary community, but little had happened except that a few editors had tried to seduce him. He had never before indulged in so much pot and also began to experiment with morphine with Burroughs. Bill spent so much time taking drugs with Kerouac that his coursework suffered and he was forced to temporarily withdraw from MCC. After Kerouac left in October to stay with his mother, Bill, who would not normally attempt to influence the behavior of his friends, wrote him a tactful letter suggesting that he cut down on the pot and morphine, saying, "You are a young healthy man with no habits, and I can not understand why you are not more active."[18]

That August Lucien Carr and his girlfriend, Liz Lehrman, came for a brief visit. While they were there, Lucien witnessed Bill and Joan playing their telepathy game. They would sit in opposite corners of the room, each take a pencil, and draw a square divided into nine equal-sized squares on a piece of paper, and in each of the squares they would draw nine images, to be compared at the end. According to Lucien the results were astonishing, with more than half of the images the same. Lucien thought that there existed a very special and profound level of communication between them, caused by the power that Joan had over Bill. Joan was the sender and Bill the receiver.[19]

Lucien loved to hear Bill recount his experiences with Huncke and Phil White and suggested that the stories would make a very commercial book. They discussed the idea, and as soon as Lucien and Liz left, Bill set to work. Bill employed a young woman named Alice Hartman to type his manuscript. She was enrolled in the Writing Center at MCC and had married Jack and Neal's friend Frank Jeffries. The manuscript was written by hand, but Bill complained that she insisted on making editorial changes. Every time he wrote "junk" she would change it to "opiates," and according to Hal Chase, Bill would whine, "But I want to use the word 'junk,' I don't want to call it 'opiates.'" Burroughs worked diligently so that by January 1, 1951, he was able to tell Allen that he had sent the completed manuscript to Lucien and asked him to try and sell it to a New York publisher for a $1,000 advance. "Very likely it won't sell at all. But you never know."[20] He had been writing *Junk*—as the book was then called—largely for money because, as he told Allen, "Of course, being responsible not only for myself, but also for Joan and the children, I have an absolute duty to place their welfare high on the priority list."[21] He had also to pay for his junk and cocaine. Burroughs on junk was very boring to be around, and not long after Lucien and Liz returned to the States, Joan went to Cuernavaca and filed for divorce. She'd had enough. They owned joint property and were technically man and wife in a common-law marriage.

3. The Mexican Dream Unravels

Burroughs had by now begun to encounter Mexican bureaucracy and corruption. Foreigners were not permitted to own land in Mexico, which meant farming was out, nor were they allowed to own businesses unless one of the partners was Mexican, which ruled out the bar idea. He decided to look farther south, to Panama or Central America, telling Allen, "I prefer to settle in a country where they want Americans to come in and farm,"[22] and told Jack at Christmas 1950, "It looks like I will abandon Mexico very soon."[23] In early January, Kells Elvins paid a visit. It turned out that it had been prescient of Burroughs to sell his land in Texas, because 1950 and 1951 saw the worst freezes in the Valley for fifty years, decimating Kells's citrus groves and almost putting him out of business. He had always told Burroughs, "I want to make a lot of money. I think that's a good solid clean thing to do." He had sold his land and, using the tips given him by Clint Murchison, invested wisely in oil enough to provide himself with an income of more than six hundred dollars a month. He arrived with his new wife, Marianne, who took an instant dislike to Burroughs, and Burroughs to her. The couple rented a new apartment on the boulevard Ávila Camacho out on the road to Guadalajara near the golf course. Some years earlier Elvins had been in Cuernavaca studying with Erich Fromm; he had some Spanish and now wanted to continue his studies. He enrolled in Fromm's psychology course at the medical school of UNAM, the Universidad Nacional Autónoma de México.

In addition to writing for money, Bill was still toying with the idea of drug dealing again, telling Allen he had bought a quantity of opium at forty dollars a pound that he expected to have off his hands in a matter of days. He had sold the land in Texas, but was unable to move on farther south to buy land because the buyer was unable to pay him all at once. He told Allen that he was not intending to leave Mexico until he had enough capital to buy a ranch, and until he had kicked his habit. His fantasies about how life was going to be in Central America knew no bounds. "You live like a king on a ranch while you are making the $. Hunting and fishing and a hacienda full of servants for about nothing a year in expenses."[24]

Perhaps in an effort to reconcile his relationship with Joan and hold together his family, Burroughs made a superhuman effort to get off junk in the new year. He used the reduction method, and managed to kick junk in two months. By the end of February 1951 he was clean. It was made more difficult because he was kicking on the street, where junk was readily available at any time, tempting him to get back on. He joked to Allen, "Doctors came to the house and waved their prescription pads under my nose. People were pushing junk through the transom and shelling it under the door. Now I am completely off, *I couldn't get back on the junk even if I wanted to. [. . .] If you kick of your own choice you can't go back.*"[25] Strong, confident words that were true at the time. He was, of course, still smoking opium twice a week, but in Burroughs's view, "You can hit the pipe that often with no risk of habit."[26]

During the course of the cure he was drunk for a month, lost two guns to the law, and almost died from uremic poisoning. The incident with the guns could have resulted in his getting shot had it occurred in the United States. He was drunk at the Ku Ku bar on the corner of Coahuila and Insurgentes, got into an argument with a fellow drinker, and pulled a gun on him. A policeman standing next to him grabbed his arm and Burroughs turned and pushed the gun into his stomach. "I was flabbergasted by this insolence and asked him what he was putting his two cents in for."[27] Fortunately the bartender reached across the bar and twisted Bill's arm, with the gun, across the counter. Burroughs wrote in *Junky*, "The cop stolidly hauled out his battered .45 automatic, placing it firmly against my body. I could feel the coldness of the muzzle through my thin cotton shirt. [. . .] I relaxed my hold on the gun and felt it leave my hand. I half-raised my hands, palm out in a gesture of surrender."[28] The bartender took the gun and commented, "Esta cargado"—"It's loaded." The cop took Bill by the arm and told him, "Vámonos, señor," and walked him to the bus stop. The cop kept the gun.[29] On another occasion a cop took his gun away, unloaded it, and gave it back to him.

By mid-April he had stabilized on a three-cocktail-a-day schedule. Joan, who had seen it all before, appears not to have been particularly sympathetic. Hal Chase, the Wolfean roommate from 115th Street days, who was now living in Mexico City studying the Zapotecan language at MCC, told Ted Morgan, "Joan was such a castrator. Bill was constantly being disarmed. The Mexicans were armed, and he went to Mexican bars and got into arguments with these *políticos* with great *pistoles* and cartridge belts, and in the course of these altercations he would get his gun taken from him. And Joan would say, 'So they took your gun away from you, did they?' [...] She loved to see Bill get embarrassed. Bill had to posture before the whole world, but he didn't have to in front of her."[30] Although Joan had abandoned her divorce petition, she clearly no longer had the worshipful attitude toward Burroughs that she began with. Joan was twenty-six, a bout of untreated polio in Algiers had left her limping and using a cane, and she was an alcoholic. She did her best with the children, and had decided to give the relationship another chance, though Burroughs as a permanent drunk was almost as bad as Burroughs the junkie. He gives a very disparaging description of himself in *Junky* that is probably very accurate:

> I had deteriorated shockingly. My clothes were spotted and stiff from the drinks I had spilled all over myself. I never bathed. I had lost weight, my hands shook, I was always spilling things, knocking over chairs, and falling down. But I seemed to have unlimited energy and a capacity for liquor I never had before.[31]

Burroughs writes about this entire period in *Junky* with remarkable candor; he is unsparing in his recounting of embarrassing scenes and reveals surprisingly intimate details about his life that are often overlooked because of the book's superficially hard-boiled style: "My emotions spilled out everywhere. I was uncontrollably sociable and would talk to anybody I could pin down. I forced distastefully intimate confidences on perfect strangers. Several times I made the crudest sexual propositions to people who had given no hint of reciprocity." Kells Elvins grew concerned for his well-being, and there is a scene in *Junky* where Elvins—called "Rollins" in the book—remonstrates with him for his behavior: "You're going to get your head blown off carrying that gun. [...] Everyone is fed up with the way you've been acting lately. If there's one thing I don't want to be around, and I think no one else particularly wants to be around, it's a drunk with a gun."

Bill's favorite bar at that time was the Bounty at Monterrey 122 at the northeast corner of Chihuahua, which had opened that February 1950, just five blocks from his apartment. It is known as the Ship Ahoy in both *Junky* and *Queer*. It was in a five-floor building largely inhabited by gringos studying at Mexico City College or who worked in the city. Clientele included American and Mexican students from the School of Plastic Arts and the medical school, but it was basically a gringo college hangout. The decor was nautical, with a mural featuring odd-looking fish running around the walls and chair backs spoked like the wheel of a ship that poked you in the back if you leaned back to relax. There were colored lights strung around the walls and over the bar. Bill and Joan quickly adopted the Bounty as their own. They would arrive just after five o'clock in the afternoon and take seats near the door so that they could watch Julie and Billy play in the street. Bill would drink vodka or tequila, and Joan was already far gone on tequila. If they didn't finish a bottle of tequila, they would put their name on it for the next day. But while Bill was drinking his way through the cure, this never happened.

The Bounty was owned by three Americans, Luis Carpio, John Healy, and Marvin Apt. Luis was born in Mexico, which enabled the U.S. citizens' ownership, but he had been brought up in North America. Burroughs got on well with him. Marvin Apt was a Jew from Miami who had come in with Healy as a business venture. John Healy lived above the bar in apartment 10 and had at one time been the lover of Juanita Peñaloza, the manager of the building. He was Irish American, "a good Irish drunk" according to Burroughs, who had worked all over the States and had been in the air force without achieving much. One day in Minneapolis he went to the bus station and asked how far south he could get on the money he had. He was told "Mexico City." Once there he met the former Chinese consul to Mexico, who invited him to run a restaurant called the Good Ship Bounty. The Chinese businessman left the picture somehow, and other partners appeared. Bill regarded Healy as a "Johnson" and they became good friends.

The Bounty and the apartments above were like a stage set, the kind of bar that Bill loved, with people wandering in and out, having dinner in each other's rooms with whoever happened to be there. The Beat Hotel in Paris, the Empress in London, and the Café Central in Tangier that all featured in Bill's later life were just such places. Among the regulars at the Bounty was Eddie Woods, a thin young crew-cutted blond American who was at MCC. Bill saw him at the Bounty almost every day and often at Juanita's, a nearby hole-in-the wall beer joint that people used in the daytime. Another regular Bill saw there was Bill Dobson, an ex–army

officer on a disability pension; one arm was practically incapacitated. He
was an ex-Mormon, completely irreligious at this time, and could be a
difficult drunk. "Dobson was a very ambivalent person. At a certain stage
of drinking he would become very insulting. He pulled it on everybody.
Not a fight, just verbal abuse. I didn't respond."[32] Burroughs was not the
only drinker in the Bounty who was armed. Arnold Copland carried a
.25 automatic in his belt and was always starting trouble with Mexicans,
staring at them, trying to provoke them. Bill enjoyed his company. "He
always had these recurrent things he said, 'We will die like dogs! I tell you
we will all die like dogs!' and his marvelous imitation of the Mexicans
looking up at the heart being cut out: 'You know when the heart is cut
out, the rising sun says it's still, uuuughhh!!!' He did this horrible imper-
sonation. Oh man, he was something."[33]

Bill's friends were amused by his obsession with guns, which was seen
as a macho attempt to counter any effeminacy he felt might be associated
with his homosexuality. One time John Healy was organizing a farewell
party for Marvin Apt, who had decided to return to Miami, and met Burroughs in the street. Healy and Apt invited him to the party but asked him
not to bring any weapons. "Not even a little one?" Burroughs asked. At
the party the next day Healy noticed that Burroughs was still wearing a
small automatic pistol under his belt. Sometimes they encouraged him as
a joke. The busboy at the Bounty had caught a mouse. He tied a string to
the mouse's tail and held it out at arm's length against the wall. Bill pulled
his .22 and shot it, blowing its head off.[34]

During the month he was drunk all the time he propositioned Hal
Chase. Chase turned him down, loudly and in front of a witness. Burroughs told Kerouac, "Hal Chase is down in Salina Cruz allegedly building a boat that is going to have golden sails to match his hair. Enough to
make a man spew. So far as I am concerned the sooner he sails off into the
sunset the better, from which you may conclude that I don't like him no
more."[35] Burroughs excused his behavior to Allen, saying that he was both
drunk and junk-sick and adding, "After all, how could anyone expect me
to act any way but crummy, me having all these traumas and complexes?
Well, drunk or sober I acted like a fool."[36] Ginsberg was delighted by
these revelations, and others in this important letter, commenting to Neal
Cassady, "Heaven, heaven, things I've been waiting and wondering about
for years."[37] Burroughs continued to write, carrying on from *Junky* into
Queer and now dealing with Ginsberg, who had taken over from Lucien
Carr as his agent.

As a result of allowing Huncke to use his apartment to store stolen
goods, and then getting busted, Ginsberg, in a deal brokered by Columbia

University, had inadvertently found himself in the Columbia Psychiatric Institute instead of facing a possible jail term. He shared with Burroughs his lengthy discussions with the psychiatric staff about his sexuality, resulting in a long exchange of views. Unfortunately, up until the seventies Burroughs threw away his correspondence, so we only have his side of it. A letter from May 1951 discusses Burroughs's attitudes to homosexuality and his relationship with Joan in some detail:

> I have been laying women for the past 15 years and haven't heard any complaints from the women either.*1 What does that prove except I was hard up at the time? Laying a woman, so far as I am concerned, is O.K. if I can't score for a boy. But laying one woman or a thousand merely emphasizes the fact that a woman is not what I want. Better than nothing, of course, like a tortilla is better than no food. But no matter how many tortillas I eat, I still want a steak.*2[38]

Footnotes were added by Joan, who commented:

*1—Correct!
*2—Around the 20th of the month, things get a bit tight and he lives on tortillas.

Bill's conviction that Mexicans believed in minding their own business was overturned when Bill and Joan's neighbors complained to the police about Bill's drug taking, their late-night drinking, and their loud parties. An arrangement was made and Bill had to bribe the immigration inspector two hundred dollars because his papers were suddenly not in order. He looked for somewhere else to live. John Healy suggested he speak to Juanita Peñaloza Gonzalez, the manager of the building where the Bounty was located, who lived with her niece Eva in one of the apartments above the bar. She was single, a mestiza (Mexican-Spanish) about forty years old. She had been Trotsky's maid and had worked in Europe for five years, where she learned English, French, and Italian. On returning to Mexico she used her savings to lease entire apartment blocks, which she sublet as furnished apartments. She was short, single, and good-natured, always willing to help people. Burroughs calls her "Jerri" in *Queer*. In addition to the block housing the Bounty, she also leased a courtyard apartment block two blocks from the Bounty at 210 Orizaba. Juanita offered Burroughs a place there. In June 1951 they moved in.

Apartment 8 was in a little courtyard. Julie and Billy spent the day playing with the local children, all running barefoot around the flat roof, which was fenced in by a wire cage. Doña Marina Sotelo, who lived on the top floor, said, "They passed the whole day sleeping, and all the nights they drank—they slept all day—the children [...] spent the whole day playing here on the rooftop terrace, but they didn't go downstairs." They ran around in little pajamas, around the roof, up and down the stairs. "Who gives them breakfast? Who gives them anything?" she asked. "And for the most part, they ate up here, because those others were hungover from their sprees that they did every night, and the children more or less lived up here."[39] Joan paid Sotelo and the other women in the building to do her laundry—she never did it herself—and it is assumed she must have paid her neighbors for Billy's and Julie's food. Both Joan and Julie had learned Spanish very rapidly, so they could communicate with the neighbors; Burroughs just got by. When Bill and Joan went out, they left the children in the charge of the lady porter. We get the occasional glimpse of Burroughs's family life and his concern for the children. For instance in *My Education* he wrote, "The quake in Mexico City: I am on the bed with Billy beside me and I notice the light shade on a cord from the ceiling is shaking and I think one more quake and I'd better take Billy out to the Sears Roebuck parking lot half a block away."[40]

Burroughs's money from the Texas land sale came through in June 1951, finally giving him the cash needed to buy a farm. But his first move was not to explore the agricultural possibilities of Panama, but to go in search of yagé ("ya-hay"), a hallucinogenic vine used by the local Indians, with his new paramour, Lewis Marker. Throughout his life, his modus operandi when receiving a cash injection was to go on a trip with a boy.

Lewis Adelberg Marker, called "Eugene Allerton"[41] in *Queer*, was from a "good" family in Jacksonville, Florida. He was twenty-one when he met Burroughs, who was then thirty-seven. Marker was studying, in a dissolute way, at MCC on the GI Bill, having left military counterintelligence in postwar Germany with a pension. Most people did not find him attractive, but Burroughs did. He described him to Ted Morgan as having "a slim youthful look, actually the sort of helpless look of a baby bird about him, this innocent slightly surprised look. His eyebrows were like pencil lines and black whereas his hair was almost blond. His eyes were almost brown, thin nose, small face. He was six feet tall and weighed about 125 pounds, but very healthy and surprisingly confident physically."[42] Marker had been given training in unarmed combat, and his friend Eddie Woods from the Bounty told Burroughs of a time when he and Marker were in Jacksonville and a barroom drunk started an argument with Woods and began getting aggressive. Marker pretended to drunkenly stumble against this man, who yelled, "Hey, get away from me, skinny!" Marker hooked his finger in the man's belt, holding him down, and brought the heel of his hand up under his chin, dropping him to the floor. Marker then stepped on his face. Burroughs said, "He had that innocent very American look, but something really cold and fishy behind it. Very cold person, a real agent type. He was receptive to a point, he was unshockable."[43] *Queer* is the story, in great detail, of Burroughs's doomed love affair with him. Burroughs regarded him as likable, loyal, interesting, and very intelligent. He was very competent, good at making arrangements, probably as a result of his Intelligence Corps training. He drank a lot but never before the late afternoon. He seemed to be adrift. According to Burroughs he didn't have any particular talents or interests. His stated ambition was to "get rich, sleep till noon, and fuck 'em all!"

Marker was not homosexual, so Burroughs had to seduce him with amusing stories, the promise of adventure and distractions, and financial gain. *Queer* is filled with routines. Some, like "Corn Hole Gus's Used-Slave Lot," are quite long, and presumably they are the ones he told Marker to amuse him, making a clear connection between the book and *The Naked Lunch*. With his Texas land-sale money, at the end of June or early in July, Burroughs was able to invite Marker to accompany him on a trip to Ecuador in search of yagé, a new interest stemming from his experiments in telepathy. Yagé was supposed to increase telepathic sensitivity. Burroughs had read—no doubt in one of the fringe-science magazines he loved—that the Russians were using yagé in experiments on slave labor to induce states of automatic obedience. Rather than research the project before leaving, Burroughs was confident that he would find a scientist in Ecuador who could point him in the right direction.

4. In Search of Yagé

Marker had never been enthusiastic about the sexual aspect of their relationship, but he enjoyed the company of older men and he found Bill's exaggerated humor funny. They had made an agreement that Bill would pay all expenses in return for sex twice a week. No more. All along Burroughs knew the relationship was doomed. He described it in *Queer*: "Allerton was not queer enough to make a reciprocal relation possible. Lee's affection irritated him." First they took a bus to Panama, where they headed for El Ganso Azul—the Blue Goose—a cabaret that *Argosy* magazine said was supposed to be the center of drug traffic. It naturally proved to be nothing more than a sleazy bar, and if there ever were any drugs there, they would have been long gone after a mention in a mass-market magazine like *Argosy*, but throughout his life Burroughs often took tabloid reports seriously, particularly if they were of a pseudoscientific nature. He remained tremendously naïve in that way.

According to *Queer* they flew on to Quito, Ecuador, in a tiny plane. There Burroughs fell ill, possibly from altitude sickness: at 2,850 meters Quito is the highest capital city in the world. They shared a room there but not a bed. Quito is a town of steep narrow streets set against the high Andes and overlooked by Pichincha, an active volcano. Trash blew through the main square and lines of Indians sat against the dirty walls, wrapped tightly in blankets in the cold sunlight. From Quito they flew on to Manta, a port, where they stayed at the Hotel Continental, a rickety establishment made from rough boards and split bamboo. Bill plugged the knotholes in the wall, not wanting the neighbors to witness anything untoward. All the houses along the shore were made from split bamboo on wooden frames, elevated six feet above the ground. The streets were mud. Thousands of vultures roosted on the roofs and hopped about the litter-strewn streets, pecking at offal, squawking and flapping their wings in disagreements over choice items. It was a classic Burroughs set, of the sort that recur in virtually all of his books. The sea was warm and he and Marker swam for an hour, helping to dispel Bill's residue of junk sickness.

From Manta they flew on to Guayaquil, on the west bank of the Guayas River estuary. The waterfront had Spanish-style buildings, built out over the sidewalks to form arcades, mostly wooden, with louvred shutters. A formal promenade, broken by statues and gardens filled with shade trees, followed part of the shoreline. Stone benches were shaded by umbrella pines and huge banana palms and the squares were filled with palms, tropical trees, shrubs, and vines. Small boats were stranded on the mud banks when the tide was out. Chimborazo volcano could be seen on a clear day. Marker had been irritated by Bill's pressure for sex even before they reached Panama. A revealing dialogue from their time in Guayaquil gives a good indication of Marker's ambivalence in the face of Burroughs's pleading:

"Oh, go away."

"But, Gene...I am due, you know."

"Yes, I suppose you are." [...]

[Lee] could see that Allerton was a little excited.

Allerton said, "Maybe it would be better now. You know I like to sleep alone."

"Yes, I know. Too bad. If I had my way we'd sleep every night all wrapped around each other like hibernating rattlesnakes."

Lee was taking off his clothes. He lay down beside Allerton. "Wouldn't it be booful if we should juth run together into one gweat big blob?" he said in baby talk. "Am I giving you the horrors?"

"Indeed you are."

[After having sex, Lee to Allerton:]

"But you do enjoy it sometimes? The whole deal, I mean?"

"Oh, yes."[44]

Burroughs and Marker continued their trip along the coast, first to Playas, which they hated, then to Salinas, which was more to their taste, being more upmarket with better food. They spent most of their days relaxing on the beach; the sea, however, was too cold to swim: the Humboldt current cools the water in the summer months. Burroughs returned to Quito for five days to gather information on yagé. He found that the Indians also called it ayahuasca, and that its scientific name was *Banisteriopsis caapi*. It was a vine that grew in the high jungle on the Amazon side of the Andes. They had to go to the center of the country to Puyo, on the Puyo River, a tributary of the Pastaza River, which itself eventually leads to the Amazon.

This was a proper jungle expedition. First they took a riverboat from Guayaquil up the Guayas River, then the Daule River to Babahoyo. On deck they lay in their hammocks watching the jungle slide by. Palms leaned out over the water beneath huge canopy trees often over two hundred feet high, kapok, gum, fig, and capironas, draped with lianas and vines. They passed clear tumbling mountain streams and the occasional clearing in the thick jungle with raised bamboo and straw huts. Babahoyo was only three years old, having been founded by legislative decree in September 1948. Previously it had been on the opposite side of the river.

From Babahoyo they took a fourteen-hour bus ride in a converted flatbed truck, up over the Andes to San Juan de Ambato. At the pass, high above the tree line, the bus stopped for a snack of chickpeas and brandy. They passed the 20,700-foot peak of Mount Chimborazo in the cold moonlight and pulled their blankets tighter around them. The high mountain wind cut through their clothes. Ambato, on the banks of the Ambato River, surrounded by high mountains, was still recovering from the huge earthquake of August 1949, which had almost completely leveled the cathedral and the town.

The road from Ambato to Puyo wound along the edge of a thousand-foot gorge. It was wild jungle country with waterfalls and streams washing over the roadbed from the cliffs above. Several times the driver stopped to push aside large fallen stones blocking the road. They passed the abandoned buildings of Shell Oil, which spent $20 million in two years there but found no oil and pulled out. It was late at night when they arrived in Puyo. They found a room in a decrepit hotel near the general store and fell asleep at once, too exhausted to speak.

The name Puyo means "cloudy" in the local Kichwa language. Puyo is often overcast and there is heavy rain every day. The hotel was damp and cold and the houses across the street from the hotel were blurred by torrential rain splashing up from the cobblestones. Burroughs met a Dutch farmer who told him there was an American botanist named Dr. Fuller living in the jungle a few hours from Puyo. Bill packed supplies to visit the man: a small frying pan, tea and flour packed in cans and sealed with tape, two quarts of Puro alcohol, his .22 automatic, and some cartridges wrapped in oiled silk. Next morning they set off, Bill carrying the supplies in a rubberized sack, Marker wielding a new machete from the market.

The trail through the jungle was laid with wood, but covered with a film of mud that made walking treacherous. They cut walking canes to help them. High jungle and hardwood forests impinged from both sides, with very little undergrowth. Rivers, streams, and springs of cold clear water ran everywhere. Each time they encountered a house they asked the way, and were always told "about three hours." They walked all day and it was dark when they surprised Dr. Fuller in his house. Bill explained he was interested in medicinal drugs, and tried to draw Dr. Fuller out, but the doctor was suspicious and clearly did not like this unexpected intrusion.

Bill produced his gifts and they all had a drink. The doctor's wife, a large, powerful red-haired woman, made some cinnamon tea to cut the kerosene taste of the pure alcohol. Bill got drunk on three drinks and began talking hipster, junkie slang, which made the doctor even more suspicious. The doctor gave them a cot on the porch made from bamboo slats and rigged up a mosquito net against vampire bats. When Bill attempted to snuggle up to Marker he pushed Bill's arm away, saying, "Slack off will you, and go to sleep." Burroughs wrote in *Queer*, "Lee drew his arm back. His whole body contracted with the shock. Slowly he put his hand under his cheek. He felt a deep hurt, as though he were bleeding inside. Tears ran down his face."[45] That night Bill dreamed that he was standing in front of the Bounty and heard someone crying. He saw his son, Billy, and knelt down and took the child in his arms. The sound of crying came closer and he felt a wave of sadness. He began crying and pulled little Billy close to his chest. A group of people dressed in convict suits stood watching him. He awoke still feeling a deep sadness. Was Burroughs feeling guilt for abandoning his wife and children for Marker? It was not Billy Jr. who was crying; possibly it was Joan. The dream was memorable enough to go into *Queer*.[46]

Fuller kept two small monkeys and a two-toed sloth. The house was guarded by a five-foot viper. He was attempting to extract curare from the poison that the Indians used to tip their arrows and use it as a muscle relaxant. He told Burroughs a lot of jungle lore: about the yellow catfish with extremely poisonous spines and how the area was so deficient in calcium that people lost their teeth, their bones were brittle, and chickens were unable to make shells to lay eggs. Both Fuller and his wife were toothless. Burroughs listened, his antenna out. All these details, along with the jungle settings, appeared in later books. Fuller was civil but ultimately unhelpful about ayahuasca. After three days, it was apparent they could get no more from Fuller and they had overstayed what slight welcome they had received. The visit had not produced any yagé, but it had brought home to Burroughs the futility of his pursuit of Marker. Nonetheless, he kept trying. They had been away for two months; now they returned quickly to Mexico City, arriving at the beginning of September 1951.

While Burroughs sought yagé, Allen Ginsberg and Lucien Carr, accompanied by Lucien's dog, Pasky, made a surprise visit to Mexico City. Lucien had wanted to attend the wedding of a friend from UPI. Kerouac had pulled out at the last minute, so Lucien simply drove around to where Allen was living and told him, "Al, it's time to take a couple of weeks off and go to Mexico." Allen said, "Fine, I'll have to pick up a sweater." Allen didn't drive, so it was down to Lucien, fueled by alcohol, to get them there. They only stopped to sleep in the car and grab quick meals. The top of the Chevrolet's thermometer blew off as they drove through a Texas heat wave. They were disappointed to find that Bill was not there, but gathered up Joan and took her to the wedding. Lucien remembered, "Joan and I immediately paired off in a sort of protracted drinking contest, or whatever."[47] Lucien drove the bride and groom to the airport and was so drunk he got out on the tarmac and tried to direct the plane in with his arms. This naturally attracted the attention of the police, who followed him to his car. He bumped a few parked cars trying to leave and was arrested. He might have got off as a gringo had not one of the party, a Mexican general's daughter, started telling the cops how important she was and what would happen to them. The cops were not impressed. Lucien quickly gave all his money, driver's license, and papers to Allen before he was whisked off to the cells to spend the night. Sure enough, his drunken Indian cellmate went through all his pockets in the middle of the night as Lucien pretended to sleep.

Joan wanted to go to Guadalajara because she had a pot contact there she wanted to see. Lucien's driving appears to have been as reckless as

Neal Cassady's. "We were so drunk, Joan and I, we were driving these mountain roads. I was much too drunk to drive and so was she but she could at least steer. She had this polio-shriveled leg so that she couldn't work both the gas pedal and the brake, so I was lying on the floor of the front seat pushing down on the gas pedal and she had her one good leg on the brake and we would scream round the corners." They were drinking *ginebra* out of the bottle. Joan was yelling, "How fast can this heap go?" while in the backseat Allen cowered on the floor with Billy and Julie, absolutely terrified.

They came to a river where the bridge was washed out. It was night, but fortunately somebody had put a bush in the road; otherwise they would have driven into the water. They managed to find a Mexican to help them push the car back on the road. Lucien remembered, "Allen took his pants off and got out to push. And suddenly, out of nowhere, appeared a lot of Mexicans to help push, and as they were helping to push, they stole Allen's pants, along with all his money and whatever he had in there."[48]

They eventually reached Guadalajara and Joan met her connection. On the way back they decided to visit Paricutín, the new volcano in Uruapan that had lowered the level of Lake Taluca by twelve feet. Paricutín came up in a farmer's cornfield in 1943, and within a week was eight hundred feet high and had buried the land and homes of fifteen thousand people in fire and ash and lava. By the time Joan and party were there only the tops of the church spires could be seen. Lucien and Joan fortified themselves with more *ginebra* and drove out onto the lava field at night. "I can remember the car falling into crevices, and having to get it out with the jack and Joan saying, 'Go on! Go on! Let's get to the volcano,'"[49] Lucien remembered. Finally they got within a mile of the eruption, but molten lava and rocks landing all around them and hitting the car roof forced them to turn back.

Lucien was very fond of Joan; in fact it seems very likely that they spent the night together while in the hotel in Guadalajara. Lucien said, "Joan and I were close, and as a matter of fact, we were so close that little Willie at one point bit me in the leg for paying too much attention to his mother. Little Willie didn't like it.

"I remember how sad Joan was when we left because there she was, stuck in Mexico, not much money and a hell of a liquor habit, two kids to keep an eye on and Bill off in South America. And we were driving away and leaving her [...] she really was the most mournful, sad-looking woman that I've ever seen. I was really of half a mind not to leave. But unfortunately I'd gotten engaged before I left, so I had to go back."[50] Lucien clearly had regrets about leaving her. "There was something, in a wistful way, there was something tremendously compelling about Joan. She was very very bright and very exciting and very much in command of the various tight situations she got into. She was sort of in command of everything but herself, you know. She was quite a woman."[51]

Ginsberg said they were so moved by her state that they invited her to return to New York with them, but she declined. Burroughs had been away for two months and she was expecting him back in a few days. Hal Chase reported to Ted Morgan that he met her in the street around this time and was shocked at her deterioration. He said that he put his arms around her because she looked so awful. He said she had lost some of her hair and carried herself a little awkwardly, swinging one arm more than the other. She said that she had an incurable blood disease. She had open running sores, and told Chase she knew she was dying. "I'm not going to make it," she said. It should be noted that Burroughs disputed many of Chase's recollections to Morgan and this may also be exaggerated.

Chapter Eighteen

She was an extraordinary person, one of the more perceptive and intelligent people I've known.[1]

1. The Low Shot

Burroughs returned to Mexico City deeply depressed at the failure of his attempt to gain Marker's love. Joan, we assume, did not let his two-month jaunt go by without suitably scathing comment, so we can assume a certain amount of rancor between them; she knew just how to prick his ego. In addition, the weather was terrible; it was pouring with rain, the aftermath of Hurricane Dog, which had already inundated large parts of the city in the famous "Flood of '51." The neighborhood just south of Bill and Joan's apartment, the Colonia Roma Sur, was under a meter of water and five thousand workers were trying to clear the flooding in the old part of the city. There was an angry sky, with fierce gusts of wind and intermittent squalls of rain.[2]

Marker was living at 122 Monterrey, above the Bounty bar. John Healy and Luis Carpio, co-owners of the Bounty, together with an American couple, Glenn and Betty Jones, lived in apartment 10 on the third floor, a six-room apartment on the northwest side of the building. Marker's childhood friend from Jacksonville, Edwin John "Eddie" Woods, who had arrived in Mexico City in mid-August, was also living there. Betty Jones appears in *Queer* as "Mary" and was the cause of much jealousy on the part of Burroughs, who could see that Marker was very attracted to her; in the book they spend a lot of time playing chess together and were possibly having an affair. She was thirty-five in 1951 and reportedly she and Glenn had something of an open marriage. Bill's jealousy was more in the form of frustration; he had nothing against Betty herself, whom he liked, describing her as a "good-looking young woman. She was stacked and she was sexy-looking, she was a blonde. She had a long affair with Marker. She was a nice woman, I liked her, she was easy to get along with."[3]

Healy's room had a bed at one end and a living room and dining room at the other with a sofa, armchairs, and tables used by all the residents, divided by two wall partitions that jutted several feet into the room on either side. Joan liked Healy and would often join him at the Bounty. Healy explained, "I used to drink with her a lot, she would come over for a drinking partner. She didn't like to drink alone. [. . .] She was an alcoholic. When she came in, she would give me the high-sign and I would sit down and talk to her, and she liked that. She was as smart as a whip, she was no dummy, but she was just wearing out, she didn't look healthy at all. [. . .] She used to put [Bill] down."[4]

The story is that Bill had arranged to meet Bob Addison in Healy's apartment on the evening of Thursday, September 6, 1951. According to Eddie Woods, Marker had told him that Burroughs was short of cash and wanted to sell some guns to someone, but didn't want to do it at his place. He wanted Marker and Eddie to be there in case there was a problem; he also didn't want the man to know where he lived. Woods, who had only been living in the apartment for about three weeks, didn't feel he could object. But Bob Addison was a friend, who lived in the building and presumably knew perfectly well where Burroughs lived. Burroughs, however, used this story of wanting to sell the gun himself in later interviews. Also, he could not possibly have squandered all the money from the sale of the Texas land on two months' traveling in Ecuador with Marker. They had stayed in cheap hotels and traveled largely by bus. In fact Burroughs said that he was able to pay his lawyer several thousand dollars from the money he had from the land sale. Marker, with his background in military intelligence, may have been trying to impress his friend by building Burroughs up as a mysterious, sinister character.

Joan arrived at the Bounty before Burroughs, at either 1:00 p.m. or 3:00 p.m.—eyewitness reports differ. She ordered a *ginebra*, the cheap gin, and *limonada*, a carbonated limeade, which she took upstairs to Healy's apartment. Marker and Betty Jones were already there with Eddie Woods.

At about three o'clock in the afternoon, three days after he got back from Ecuador, Burroughs heard the familiar whistle of the knife sharpener in the street: a simple glissando up and down the scale on an Andean pan pipe. He took a clasp knife that he had bought in Quito and took it to be sharpened. He was depressed, a feeling of loss and sadness, and had a sense that that day something awful was going to happen, so much so that he could hardly breathe. As he walked toward the knife sharpener's cart he felt a dampness and, brushing his hand across his face, felt tears streaming down his cheeks. He thought, "What in hell is the matter? What in hell is wrong with you?"[5] Burroughs, interviewed for Howard Brookner's 1980 documentary, said:

You see, I've always felt myself to be controlled at some times by this com-
pletely malevolent force, which Brion [Gysin] describes as the Ugly Spirit.
My walking down the street, and tears streaming down my face, meant that
I knew that the Ugly Spirit—which is always the worst part of everyone's
character—would take over, and that something awful would happen. [...]
I went back to the apartment where we were all meeting, with this terrible
sense of depression. And foolishly, of course, in order to relieve the depression,
I started tossing down the drinks.

Then I said to Joan, "It's about time for our William Tell act." And she put
a glass on her head.

I had this piece of .380 junk. I fired the shot. The glass hadn't been touched.
Joan starts sliding down towards the floor. Then Marker said—[he] walked
over and took one look at her—he said, "Bill, your bullet has hit her forehead."

I said, "Oh my God..."[6]

Burroughs had arrived at Healy's about twenty minutes after Joan, after
leaving off his knife. He had with him a Czech-made Star .380 automatic
in a holster in a small overnight bag. It was a cheap gun and he knew that
it fired low. Healy was not present; he had presumably gone downstairs
to work at the bar. Marker and Eddie Woods were there—though there
is some dispute over whether or not Betty Jones was also there. Eddie
Woods's recollection is that Joan's drink was the only drink he saw all
afternoon, but the likelihood of either Joan or Burroughs socializing for
four or five hours straight without a drink is extremely remote. Also, we
have Burroughs's consistent recollection that he began throwing back
drinks immediately after he felt the tears on his face, so we can assume that
he was very drunk by the early evening. For her part, Joan was a maintenance drinker; she took small sips regularly, and got through between
one and two bottles of tequila or gin a day. By 7:15 in the evening she
would have been drinking for twelve hours straight. Bob Addison and his
seventeen-year-old Mexican girlfriend stopped by briefly early on but he
did not buy the gun, if the sale was ever even mooted. Addison's friends
discount the idea, saying he was always broke.

Marker and Eddie Woods were sitting on the sofa. Burroughs was sitting in the dining room, separated from Woods by an arm's length by the
room division. Joan was sitting across from him with her drink at her side.
Although Burroughs was not addicted at that time, the conversation appears
to have turned to the subject of how to get through a cure when there are
so many ways of getting junk to threaten the addict's resolve. One idea Burroughs discussed was to retreat to an island that was reachable only by summer tides, and that there would be no way to leave until the water was once

again high enough, by which time he would be long cured. There were apparently such places in the Amazon and the Orinoco. Bill said they would survive by eating wild hogs. Joan dismissed the idea, saying, "We'd starve to death! Because you won't be able to shoot, you'd be so shaky if you try to come off it, you'll shake, you won't be able to shoot anything."[7]

"Nonsense," Burroughs said. Provoked by Joan's remarks, he said he didn't get the shakes, and was still a good shot. It was then that he said, "Put that glass on your head, Joanie, let me show the boys what a great shot old Bill is."[8] According to Eddie Woods:

> That's exactly what happened, so she did, and she said with a giggle—and she turned her head, she is balancing the glass on her head, and she said, "I can't watch this, you know I can't stand the sight of blood."
>
> I remember this vividly, and that's exactly what she said. And then it dawned on me, he was actually going to pull the trigger. [...] So I started to reach for the gun, as he actually aimed it, and then I thought, "You'd better not, because if it goes off just when you reach it, and it hits her—" [...]
>
> So I didn't grab it, and then *bang!*—the noise, that's the first impression I had, was the noise. Next thing I knew, the next impression I had was that glass was on the floor, [...] rolling around in concentric circles on the floor. [...]
>
> Then I looked at her, and her head was over to one side. Well, I thought "She's kidding," you know. That's the first thing you think, and then I heard Marker say: "Bill, I think you hit her."
>
> And then [Bill] said, "No!" And he started towards her, you know, and Marker got there first, and I got over there, too, and then I saw the hole in her temple, a little blue hole, and Burroughs jumped on her lap and he said, "Joan! Joan! Joan!"
>
> I mean he was out of it, in shock that this happened. Again, to me, that's evidence it was absolutely an accident. He was shocked that he had hit her, and he was trying to wake her up. This guy was out of it.[9]

Marker got to her first and saw the red trickle of blood. He rushed to the roof, where a Mexican medical student lived, but he wasn't in, so they found Juanita Peñaloza, the building manager, and told her. Marker knew that Bernabé Jurado was Burroughs's lawyer, so Peñaloza called him first, who said he would be right over. Next she called the Cruz Roja (Red Cross) hospital just four blocks north at Durango and Monterrey, and finally called the nearest police headquarters at the Octava Delegación (Eighth Delegation). She told Marker that Jurado's advice to him and Woods, as the eyewitnesses, was to lay low, move to a hotel, and call him that evening when he would tell them what to do.

The Red Cross received the phone call at about 7:30 p.m. and ambulance No. 4, manned by Lieutenant Tomás Arias, was dispatched to 122 Monterrey, where the emergency personnel found Joan slumped in an easy chair with a wound in her forehead flowing with blood. She was unconscious but still breathing. Her cane was on the floor to the right of the chair. The medics took her straight to the hospital, where she was given a blood transfusion, serum, and oxygen. The type-O blood was taken from twenty-year-old Manuel Mejía, the porter at 122 Monterrey, who had run to see what was happening when the police and ambulance arrived. He had accompanied Burroughs on foot to the hospital along with the reporters, and after the transfusion he asked the Red Cross how much his blood was worth. Later, when Burroughs was out of jail, Mejía told Burroughs that he owed him money for the blood, and a month or so later, Burroughs gave him 250 pesos.[10] It is unclear how long Joan survived at the Red Cross hospital: some reports say an hour, others just a few minutes.

In addition to the ambulance, the police arrived accompanied by a number of reporters whom they had presumably tipped off. Burroughs reached the hospital on foot shortly after Joan, followed by a pushing, jostling group of reporters. In his confused state he was interviewed by Lieutenant Luis Hurtado, in front of the reporters in the courtyard of the hospital, giving them a more or less accurate account of what happened. This was later contradicted by Jurado. The report in El Nacional, on September 8, 1951 read:

> At first the killer declared that in the said gathering, after there had been a great consumption of gin, he tried to demonstrate his magnificent marksmanship, emulating William Tell, and to that end he placed a glass of liquor upon the head of his wife, and aiming over the glass, at a distance of two meters, he fired, but as a consequence and result of the state of drunkenness in which he found himself, he missed the shot lamentably and injured the forehead of his wife with a bullet.[11]

While Burroughs was being interviewed by Lieutenant Hurtado, a message came from the doctors that the wounded woman had died. Excelsior reported that at that moment Burroughs "cried bitterly, tearing out his hair in desperation."[12]

Just as Burroughs finished giving his account of what happened to Lieutenant Hurtado, Bernabé Jurado arrived and told Burroughs, in front of all the reporters, that he would not be saying that before the authorities, only that the pistol had fired accidentally—and if he didn't, he would surely go to jail: "Don't say anything Bill, this is a shooting accident!"[13] The newspapers reported the entire proceedings. *La Prensa* wrote:

> Minutes later he changed his mind, as the result of a chat that he had with a lawyer. He stated to the journalists that this professional told him: "Don't be stupid; don't say you wanted to make a target [of the glass]. Testify that you were examining the pistol, very drunk, and then the shot went off, that penetrated the forehead of Joan."
>
> From that moment on, William changed his first testimony, but not without first arguing, "But how am I going to say that the shot went off [that way], when several people saw the facts?" [...] Then, on the way to the scene of the crime, Bernabé Jurado himself went on saying to the reporters that he, in his capacity as the killer's defender, was obliged to do everything possible so that the punishment would be the least possible for his client.
>
> "I will prove that it was an accident," said Jurado. "The point is, William has not testified before the authorities [yet], and before he does, he will know perfectly what he has to say."[14]

Lieutenant Hurtado then arrested Burroughs for murder and he was taken to the Eighth Delegation police headquarters, where he was questioned by investigative agent Lieutenant Robert Higuera Gil. The police also arrested John Healy and John Herrmann, who had walked in on the scene later. Joan may have gone to Healy's that day to visit with Herrmann; Herrmann was an older writer, born in 1900, and had been part of the expat scene in Paris in the twenties. Herrmann and his wife knew Joan and he told the police he had visited with her both in Mexico City and Guadalajara. Joan probably visited him in Guadalajara, where he lived, when she went there with Allen and Lucien. He appears to have been in the wrong place at the wrong time, but he was not held for long, as it soon become known that he wasn't a witness to the shooting, nor did he know Burroughs.

As the police were interrogating John Healy, they set up the apartment ready for the news photographers, making it look as though much more of a party had been going on. There were thirty empty bottles in the cupboard, evidence of a party some days before, and some of these, bottles of Glorias de Cuba rum, were put on the tables, ashtrays tipped over, and dirty glasses placed around the room. Then the reporters were let in. Healy was released that night.

Late that night, with the aid of Bernabé Jurado, Burroughs worked on a written statement, which he read aloud to Lieutenant Higuera Gil, in front of a group of news reporters. *La Prensa* reported his statement verbatim. His revised statement read:

I am 37 years old. Three days ago I arrived in Mexico, accompanied by my wife, with whom I have been married for five years. We installed ourselves in 210 Orizaba, Colonia Roma.

At 3:00 P.M. I went to apartment 10 in 122 Monterrey to visit my friend John Healy. Hours later, we were all drunk.

I took my pistol from a valise and put it on the table; then I picked it up again, to demonstrate to those present how to handle it, and while I was playing with it the shot was produced that killed my wife, who was seated before me.

She fell to the floor and I thought she was playing a trick, but one of my friends informed me that she was hit. Then I lifted her up and seated her on an easy chair.

All my friends left. After that, my wife was taken by persons from the Red Cross. I went to that institution to find out her condition.

Later, from a friend of mine, I knew that Joan had died.

Joan's body was formally identified by Juanita Peñaloza and John Bensmiller Rogerson, a student who lived at 122 Monterrey, who knew Joan from the Bounty but was not a close friend. The next day, Joan's body was transferred from the Red Cross Hospital to the old Juarez Hospital for the legally required autopsy. It was found that she died from a bullet that entered her brain 4.5 centimeters to the left of the middle line of her forehead. There was no exit wound, consistent with a short-load shell. At some time after her death, someone had placed a religious medal at her throat as a blessing for the dead.

That same day Burroughs was transferred from the police station, where he had spent the night, to the infamous Black Palace of Lecumberri, on the avenida Eduardo Molina. He was admitted to Cellblock H, the remand wing, detained as being "presumed responsible for the crime of homicide." Meanwhile, Bernabé Jurado swung into cocaine-fueled action. On September 8, Burroughs was questioned in his first formal hearing. He testified from behind a wire cage as his lawyers and the prosecution, led by Mexican novelist Rogelio Barriga Rivas, augmented by translators, argued it out. He was questioned first by Judge Eduardo Urzaíz, the *juez instructor*, and then by Lieutenant Barriga Rivas. Barriga Rivas was an old friend of Bernabé Jurado from law school. The whole procedure was new to Burroughs, who recalled, "The judge has his office there in the prison. He and Bernabé Juarado would be pushing each other away from the typewriter. He'd say, 'Well,' Bernabé would say, 'Strike that out.' And the judge would say, 'Leave it in,' and they would sort of tussle at the typewriter to get something in or out. The prosecuting attorney said nothing, it was really so strange a procedure."[15] It was at this hearing that it was revealed that Bill and Joan had filed for divorce in Cuernavaca the previous year on the grounds that "they were tired of each other," with two newspapers reporting "continual arguments" and Burroughs's drunkenness as the reason. But it was also noted that they had reconciled and dropped the formal proceedings.

At the end of the day, Jurado told Judge Urzáiz that he was going to petition for Burroughs's release from prison, because "he only committed a crime in a manner mostly accidental, or through imprudence." But the judge did not agree and ordered Burroughs to be bound over for more hearings and also issued subpoenas for Marker and Woods to appear for questioning. Marker and Woods were coached by Jurado in what to say, and they made two or more visits to his apartment, where they were followed, rather obviously, by plainclothes policemen when they left. Mexican law required that the exact charges against the prisoner must be determined within seventy-two hours of his arrest. At the hearing on September 10, Eddie Woods, Lewis Marker, Betty Jones, and John Healy testified, in that order, all sticking to the same story; that Burroughs had been handling a gun that fell onto the table and discharged. At the end of the hearing Judge Urzáiz determined that, all things considered, Burroughs could rightfully be held for *formal prisión*, saying, "In the opinion of the undersigned, the investigation lays out enough facts to make possible the legal guilt of the detainee William Seward Burroughs in the crime of murder that is imputed to him, for he himself confesses that the shot that wounded and caused the death of Joan Vollmer Burroughs was produced by the pistol that, in the event, he had in his hands." Burroughs was charged with *homicidio*—murder.

In the event, Burroughs spent only two weeks in the Black Palace of Lecumberri. Jurado obtained his release and he walked free on September 21. His release on bail may have been granted by the director of the penitentiary, who had no legal necessity to consult Judge Urzáiz, who had intended him to be held until trial. It is possible that his release may have been assisted with a bribe. It is possible, also, that Jurado's petition cast enough doubt on the case to free him on bail. There is certainly no evidence that the two presiding judges, Judges Urzáiz and the first judge of the Distrito Federal for penal matters, Lieutenant Antonio Fernández Vera, were in any way corrupt. They made every effort to uncover the facts of the case in the face of an ever-changing story.[16] Burroughs put up a bond of $2,312 and paid Jurado a fee of $2,000 plus $300 "to bribe the four ballistics experts appointed by the court," though there is no evidence that any such experts were in fact appointed.[17]

Burroughs was eventually sentenced, in absentia, to two years in jail—suspended. He was ordered to report each Monday, before 8:00 a.m., to the Lecumberri prison until his case was settled. If he was only a minute late he could have been put right back in jail. He could get permission not to sign in, or to sign twice to go on a vacation, but otherwise he had to be there. His two weeks in jail do not appear to have been arduous, and his experience changed his previously derogatory views about Mexican police. He told Jack Kerouac, "While sojourning in the box I was greatly impressed by the kindness and decency of the Mexican people. Can you imagine during my preliminary interrogation at the precinct the cops were telling me what to say: 'You must deny that. You must say this.' And in prison a man gave me one of his 2 blankets, and believe me it is cold in there at night sleeping on a slab of tin."[18]

Meanwhile, the children had been looked after by Doña Marina Sotelo and the other women who had previously cared for them when Bill and Joan were asleep all morning or too out of it to feed them. Billy Jr. claimed to have been present at the shooting, but he was not. When Bill was in the Lecumberri, John Healy and Marker, at Burroughs's request, went to his apartment and cleaned out anything that might be incriminating. They had to climb up the back and get in through the window because there were squad cars patrolling the area all the time. They found a pipe and a couple of syringes, which they took away. Mort had reluctantly flown down on September 9, the third day of his brother's incarceration, sent by his parents to see what he could do to help. His first action, on the day he arrived, was to make arrangements with the Tangassi funeral parlor for Joan's body to be interred that day at Panteón Americano. Her body was placed in *fosa* 1018 in Section A/New, where it remained for seven years for a fee of 320 pesos. The cemetery had no way of contacting Burroughs subsequently, and in August 1990 they published an official notice in the *Diario Oficial de México* asking the family to renew the interment arrangements as more than thirty years of back rent were due.[19] When no one came forward, her remains were moved to a *nicho* marked only with a chalked reference number: Number 82, Class R, Section PR. Burroughs was eventually made aware of the situation, and in January 1996 paid for a stone covering to be made, inscribed with the words:

> *Joan Vollmer Burroughs*
> *Loudonville, New York*
> *1923*
> *México, D.F.*
> *Sept. 1951*

In August 2000, on a visit to the grave, James Grauerholz paid for gold leaf to be rubbed into the lettering.

From his room in the Reforma Hotel, Mort dealt with Jurado and his partners and also had the uncomfortable task of confronting Joan's parents, who had flown down from Albany. They remained in Mexico City long enough to have a meeting with Burroughs himself when he was released on bail. Burroughs never forgot this excruciatingly painful confrontation. It was arranged that Mort would take the children to St. Louis, where Bill's parents had offered to raise them both, but in the end the Vollmers decided to take Julie to Albany and raise her themselves. Mort was also present in court when Eddie Woods and the other eyewitnesses testified, and he was able to visit Bill in jail, where the visiting rules were very lenient. Burroughs had not seen Mort for about three years, not since Bill passed through St. Louis on his way to the Lexington Narcotic Farm in 1948. Mort was under a lot of stress in Mexico City, a city he did not know, dealing with a foreign bureaucracy in an unfamiliar language, and was, by all accounts, drunk much of the time. Burroughs's friends were not impressed by him.

On one occasion, on Jurado's instruction, Mort, John Healy, Lewis Marker, Betty Jones, and Eddie Woods went again to Burroughs's flat to make sure that nothing had been overlooked, because the police had a reputation for entering and planting evidence, as well as taking away anything that they fancied. Eddie Woods said, "He made a very ungraceful direct pass at Betty Jones, who was also a little drunk, and I felt insulted on behalf of my friend, Glenn, the absent husband, and said something to that effect to Mortimer—and Mortimer referred to her as 'just another cheap broad,' or something like that."[20] Mostly they found him to be arrogant and a whiner, denigrating Bill and complaining that Bill got all the breaks and was the favorite. Woods remembered him griping, "But *I* had to go to night school and get my degree, and I've always worked [...] and that son of a bitch has never worked." No doubt these were very real complaints, but this was not the occasion, with Bill in jail possibly facing a long prison term, to air them.

Bill and Mort had never been close as adults, and Mort clearly resented that Bill was his mother's favorite. But the unusual nature of the situation, its gravity and otherworldliness, caused a breakdown in their usual reserve, and apparently, when Bill was released, the two brothers had an emotional, highly alcoholic rapprochement before both passing out on Mort's bed in his hotel. Bill was staying with him temporarily, rather than go back to the empty apartment.

Bill remained at 201 Orizaba, but Juanita Peñaloza arranged for him to move downstairs to apartment 5, in the rear on the ground floor, to escape the memories of living with Joan. However, she was clearly concerned about this gringo, and whenever she saw him she impressed upon him, "We can't have another scandal, we can't have another scandal." One can only imagine Burroughs's feelings, faced with the arduous task of sorting through Joan's clothes and possessions and disposing of them in order to move to another apartment. Mort left for St. Louis, taking both children with him. Joan's parents came to collect Julie from there. It was a strained, unpleasant interview. Joan's mother told Bill's parents, "I hope that Bill Burroughs goes to Hell and stays there." The children never saw each other again.

~

There has been much comment and speculation about Joan Vollmer Burroughs's death, ranging from the obvious—killed by a dangerous drunk with a gun—through a jealousy angle, Burroughs's claim of being in a state of possession by "the Ugly Spirit," to the notion that Joan had a death wish. That she was killed by a drunk with a gun seems the most obvious explanation and the one the court accepted. As Burroughs said, "Of course I was drunk. It was an utterly and completely insane thing to do. I mean quite apart from the fact, if I'd hit the glass, it would have been terribly dangerous for the two people sitting there! Glass splinters would have been flying everywhere. So it was literally an insane thing to do."[21]

According to Burroughs, the jealousy angle was first spread by John Herrmann, Joan's friend from Guadalajara. Joan knew both Herrmann and his wife, and for purely logistical reasons, if no other, it is unlikely that anything had occurred recently between Herrmann and Joan. The only suggestion that Joan had seen someone else was identified by James Grauerholz in a passage in *The Naked Lunch*; the first-draft typescript used Joan's real name. Grauerholz said that when he asked Burroughs about it in August 1991, Burroughs had asserted, "not very convincingly," that the scene was entirely fictional. It now reads:

> In Cuernavaca or was it Taxco? Jane meets a pimp trombone player and disappears in a cloud of tea smoke. The pimp is one of these vibration and dietary artists—which is a means [by which] he degrades the female sex by forcing his chicks to swallow all this shit. He was continually enlarging his theories...he would quiz a chick and threaten to walk out if she hadn't memorized every nuance of his latest assault on logic and the human image.

Joan may have had a brief fling with Lucien Carr when he and Allen Ginsberg visited, and may have told Burroughs in the course of an argument when he finally returned from Ecuador with Marker; it would have been one way to hurt Burroughs. But Burroughs had always maintained a no-jealousy rule with his boyfriends such as Ian Sommerville, and if Joan did see anyone else he could hardly blame her, and in any case, it is extremely unlikely to have provoked such a strong reaction, even unconsciously. James Grauerholz proposes that of "Joan's possible extramarital liaisons, the only scenario that would have elicited Burroughs' jealousy is the least likely: Joan having sex with Marker. Burroughs could demonstrably be possessive of Marker—but probably not of Joan."[22] Again, this is extremely unlikely.

The "Ugly Spirit" idea was not mooted until Burroughs was conducting occult experiments with Brion Gysin at the Beat Hotel some years later. In his much-quoted introduction to the 1985 edition of *Queer*, Burroughs wrote:

> Brion Gysin said to me in Paris: "For ugly spirit shot Joan because..." A bit of mediumistic message that was not completed—or was it? It doesn't need to be completed, if you read it: "Ugly spirit shot Joan *to be cause*"—that is, to maintain a hateful parasitic occupation. [...] I am forced to the appalling conclusion that I would never have become a writer but for Joan's death, and to a realization of the extent to which this event has motivated and formulated my writing. I live with the constant threat of possession, a constant need to escape from possession, from Control. So the death of Joan brought me in contact with the invader, the Ugly Spirit, and maneuvered me into a lifelong struggle, in which I have had no choice except to write my way out."

Grauerholz suggests that Burroughs might be being a little devious here and wrote, "Other commentators have taken Burroughs' statements in the *Queer* introduction as a sort of 'key' to the writer's *oeuvre*, again taking his words at face value: to redeem himself of the sin of murder, William Burroughs dedicated his life to writing. But this *apologia* may be just a bit disingenuous, because Burroughs had already written a nearly-complete draft of *Junkie* by December 1950, eight months before Joan's death."[23]

Burroughs was aware that the Ugly Spirit would not wash with many people, that it would be seen as a way of blaming someone else, something else, for something he had done. He wrote in a late journal entry on December 2, 1996, "Tell any feminist I shot Joan in a state of possession, and she will scream: 'Nonsense! No such thing. HE did it.'"[24]

Though it in no way redeems Burroughs's culpability, the idea that Joan was feeling suicidal was widely felt. Allen Ginsberg's impression of Joan's state, from his visit with Lucien Carr shortly before her death, was "that there was something scary about her—suicidal. [...] Just as she had said to Lucien, 'How fast can this heap go?' I think she said to Bill, 'shoot that off my head.' I always thought that she had kind of challenged him into it—that it was sort of like using him to [...] that she was, in a sense, using him to get her off the earth, because I think she was in a great deal of pain."[25] Ginsberg would always do his utmost to defend and excuse his friends, but his view was shared by a number of people who saw her at the time.

Lucien Carr felt the same way: "After Joan was killed, I remember thinking that she was much more the Sender than Bill was...that the shooting was really her doing."[26]

Hal Chase, who basically disliked Burroughs and had been very close to Joan, told Ted Morgan, "She wanted to die, and she offered Bill a chance to kill somebody. That William Tell stuff was a sham. [Her] death was a put-up thing to release Bill, to let him commit 'the ultimate crime'—he was childish about things like that. [...] Joan gave her life for Bill."

Burroughs rejected all this: "Allen was always making it out as a suicide on her part, that she was taunting me to do this, and I do not accept that cop-out. Not at all. Not at all."[27] Burroughs said he thought of Joan every day of his life; she was a permanent presence in his life. He took full responsibility for her death: "That is to say, if everyone is to be made responsible for everything they do, you must extend responsibility beyond the level of conscious intention."[28] Almost forty years later, Burroughs explored the terrible idea that there might have been an unconscious desire to kill her. In *The Black Rider: The Casting of the Magic Bullets*, an opera written by Robert Wilson, Tom Waits, and William Burroughs in 1990, Burroughs wrote, "Now a man figures it's his bullets, so it will hit what he wants to hit. But it don't always work out that way. You see some bullets is special for a single aim. A certain stag, or a certain person. And no matter where you aim, that's where the bullet will end up. And in the moment of aiming, the gun turns into a dowser's wand, and points where the bullet wants to go."[29]

Chapter Nineteen

And I'll direct thee how thou shalt escape
By sudden flight: come, dally not, be gone.
—SHAKESPEARE, *HENRY VI, PART 1*,
ACT 4, SCENE 5

1. Marker Comes Through

Many people thought Marker was dull. He was the butt of jokes and unable to really instigate a conversation. Healy thought he was a "moocher." However, despite the disastrous trip to Ecuador, Marker proved to be a good friend. He testified on Bill's behalf in court and ran errands and helped out when Bill was in jail. When Burroughs moved to apartment 5, Marker moved in as his flatmate. Burroughs said, "Any actual affair with Marker was mostly all after Joan's death. Naturally sex with a straight guy is doomed to failure, of course it is. I think, 'What in the hell was the matter with you? What nonsense was here?' But he always said that himself, Marker always said that love is a bunch of bullshit and I would agree with him in that sense."[1]

In December Marker came down with hepatitis, almost certainly caught during their trip to Ecuador, so Burroughs had to nurse him. This must have helped turn his thoughts away from Joan's death. At some point Bill gave Marker an injection of penicillin and then used the same needle to shoot up morphine. He came down himself with hepatitis about a month later, so they had overlapping illnesses. To recuperate, they went to Veracruz, where they stayed in a hotel where, instead of mattresses, they had only canvas stretched tight over a wooden frame. It was very uncomfortable.

It might have been expected that after killing Joan, Burroughs would have got over his puerile infatuation with guns, but this was not the case. He had with him in Veracruz an 1896 German Mauser, an early semiautomatic that fired a high-velocity 7.63-millimeter bullet. They hired a boat and went upriver with it and used it to shoot melons, "And boy that thing would tear a melon apart."[2]

As relations between them had evidently improved, Burroughs still nursed his ambition of a jungle expedition with Marker but this time proposed taking four-year-old Billy with them. Marker went home to Jacksonville, Florida, for Christmas, having made arrangements to meet up with Bill in Ecuador in a month's time. Burroughs continued working on *Junk*, as the book was still called, sending revised sections to Allen. He no longer saw Dave Tesorero, who had mysteriously disappeared around October, but this did not matter too much as Burroughs got off junk just before he and Marker went to Ecuador. In March he told Allen, "I chippy around but haven't been hooked in a year now."[3] A month later he was hooked, claiming it was for his health: in order to cure his hepatitis he wanted to stop drinking completely for a few months. He heard nothing from Marker.

In March 1952, Bill told Allen that he had begun work on a new novel that could be seen as part two of *Junk* or read complete in itself. He said Dennison was still the main character but he had shifted to third-person narrative. It was about his relationship with Marker, known in the book as Allerton. He passed the time by writing and attending bullfights and cockfights. "I like my spectacles brutal, bloody and degrading."[4] In April, Allen Ginsberg finally persuaded Carl Solomon to publish *Junk* as an Ace paperback original for an eight-hundred-dollar advance; it was to be called *Junkie*, since the publishers thought *Junk* might be taken as a value judgment on the text. In 1977, Burroughs changed the spelling of the revised edition to *Junky*, which it has remained ever since. Now began months of prevarication and stalling on the part of Ace, who demanded to see the new material Burroughs was writing and to incorporate it into *Junkie*.[5] One complication came over Solomon's suggestion that part two of the book be called *Fag*. Burroughs told Allen he did not mind being called queer: "T.E. Lawrence and all manner of right Joes (boy can I turn a phrase) was queer. But I'll see him castrated before I'll be called a Fag. [...] That's just what I been trying to put down uh I mean *over*, is the distinction between us strong, manly, noble types and the leaping, jumping, window dressing cocksucker. Furthechrissakes a girl's gotta draw the line somewheres."[6]

As usual Bill had plans for buying houses in Panama, farming, and traveling. The one thing he was sure of was that he did not want to return to the United States. He told Kerouac, "I have been happier down here than I ever was before in my life. I feel like I took off a strait jacket. You don't realize how much the U.S. is dragging you until you are out of it and feel the difference."[7] He was still suffering from hepatitis and had no energy and no appetite. He told Allen, "I do get hungry but I can't bring myself to sit down alone in a restaurant and eat through a meal, so break two eggs in milk and that is dinner. How I miss Joan!"[8]

After Marker left for Florida, Bill formed a relationship with Angelo—he used his real name in *Junky*—with whom he began a fourteen-month casual affair, seeing him twice a week unless he was on junk, and always paying him twenty pesos. They went at first to hotels until Burroughs trusted him enough not to steal from the apartment, as pickups were prone to do, then he brought him back to 201 Orizaba, where he "insisted on sweeping the apartment out whenever he spent the night there."[9] Angelo was not queer, he was doing it for the money. He conformed to a romantic stereotype "boy" in Bill's mind that he later applied to boys in South America, Tangier, and Paris. In *Junky* he describes Angelo as having an Oriental face, "Japanese-looking except for his copper skin."[10] Burroughs was not promiscuous; once he found a suitable boy he stuck with him. "I always tended to do that. Get one that was satisfactory, I saw no necessity to change. His name was Angelo and he was of very good character. I'm not one of these people who likes to be exploited, or taken or used in any way. He had a very good character, he was a good person."[11] Bill fervently hoped that Marker would return, or that they would meet in Ecuador, but even though he wrote him numerous letters, "with fantasies and routines in my best vein,"[12] and sent him books and presents, he received no reply.

Jack Kerouac arrived at the end of April. In an enormously long letter to Allen, Kerouac wrote, "Bill was like a mad genius in littered rooms when I walked in. He was writing. He looked wild but his eyes innocent and blue and beautiful. We are the greatest of friends at last." Their days were spent working on their respective books, with each of them having a high regard for the other. Kerouac was on a creative roll: he had completed *On the Road*—the version now called *Visions of Cody*—and had just started work on *Doctor Sax*. Burroughs, meanwhile, was working each day on *Queer*. The apartment resounded to the clacking of typewriters. Bill wrote Allen, "I'm very impressed by ON THE ROAD. He has developed unbelievably. He really has tremendous talent. No doubt about it."[13] At the same time, Kerouac wrote Allen saying, "His 'Queer' is greater than 'Junk'...Bill is great. Greater than he ever was."[14] It was a mutual admiration society, but rightly so.

In the course of his long correspondence with Ginsberg concerning the publication of *Junkie*, Burroughs explained the genesis of the two main "routines" that appear in *Queer*, which Ginsberg was also trying to sell. This form of extended, wildly exaggerated extrapolation of a simple story was to become Burroughs's trademark form. He told Allen, "The

Oil-Man and Slave Trader routines are not intended as inverted parody sketches [...] but as a means to make contact with Allerton and to interest him. The Slave Trader routine came to me like dictated. It was the turning point where my partial success was assured. If I had not achieved the reckless gaiety that charges this fantasy, Marker would have refused to go with me to S.A. The point is these fantasies are a vital part of the whole set-up."[15]

In May, Bill and Jack went on a weekend trip to the mountains to Tenancingo to attend a fiesta with Dave Tesorero and his young girl-friend, Esperanza Villanueva, who was to become the subject of Kerouac's novel *Tristessa* in 1956. Bill and Dave were friends again, even though Tesorero had stolen three hundred pesos from him before disappearing. They did some shooting while they were there. Kerouac told Allen that Burroughs "misses Joan terribly. Joan made him great, lives on in him like mad, vibrating."[16] They went to bullfights, Burroughs making sure that Kerouac wore a straw hat to deflect the bottles the crowd liked to throw at gringos in the lower seats. They also visited the pyramids of Teotihuacán. Kerouac recalled, "The last time I was in Teotihuacan, [Burroughs] said to me 'Wanna see a scorpion, boy?' and lifted up a rock—There sat a female scorpion beside the skeleton of its mate, which it had eaten—Yelling 'Yaaaah!' [Burroughs] lifted a huge rock and smashed it down on the whole scene."[17]

Kerouac, always parsimonious, delighted at how cheap everything was: filet mignon sixty cents a pound, hamburger eighteen cents a pound, cigarettes six cents a pack, and teenage girls just one peso—twelve cents—at the whorehouses on Organo. By the beginning of June he had already written forty-five thousand words of *Doctor Sax*. They met a gang of young American hipsters who persuaded them to take peyote with them. Bill had a miserable time of it and stopped himself from vomiting only by recounting a long, depressing story about a penal colony in a town not unlike Quito in the high Andes.

After a few weeks staying with Burroughs, Kerouac ran short of money and grew surly and petulant when Burroughs declined to support him indefinitely in food and board: Burroughs had been paying the rent, buying the food, the drink, and the drugs. Their biggest arguments were over drugs: Burroughs had to live an exemplary life in Mexico City and give the authorities no excuse to return him to jail. He even stopped wearing a gun when he went out. He also kept his rooms free of drugs and hid his stash outside, away from the apartment, and told Jack to do the same except for what he was using. Bill did not want a whole big bag of it there because, as he put it: (1) he was out on bail; (2) it was his apartment, Jack paid no rent; and (3) Bill had a habit and did not want to spend time in a police cell after a shakedown. He might have added that the pot was also bought by him. But Jack secretly asked Dave Tesorero to bring the bag to him so that he could hide it somewhere in the apartment without telling Bill. Fortunately Dave told Bill of Jack's request. Kerouac ignored Bill's entreaties and not only filled the place with clouds of pot smoke that could be detected outside, but continued to store his marijuana and a supply of peyote there. Burroughs was outraged that Kerouac would endanger his freedom and behave in such a selfish and careless manner. His thoughtless action could have resulted in Burroughs serving a long jail sentence.

Kerouac did what he usually did when he was broke and had overstayed his welcome; on July 1 he went home to his mother, who was now living with Jack's sister in Rocky Mount, North Carolina. On July 13, Bill wrote to Allen, complaining that he had heard nothing from Jack, who had borrowed his last twenty dollars of rent money, which he had promised to pay back immediately on arrival in the United States. "To be blunt, I have never had a more inconsiderate and selfish guest under my roof."[18] Bill told Allen that he could no longer get along with Jack and unless he underwent some radical transformation he did not want him to visit again. Burroughs wrote Allen, "He needs analysis. He is so paranoid he thinks everyone else is plotting to take advantage of him so he has to act first in self-defense. For example, when we were out of money and food, I could always rely on him to eat all the food there was if he got the chance. If there were two rolls left, he would always eat both of them. Once he flew into a rage because I had eaten my half of the remaining butter. If anyone asks him to do his part or to share on an equal basis, he thinks they are taking advantage of him. This is insane."[19] By August 20, Bill had still not heard from Jack or been paid, and was so exercised by Jack's behavior that he devoted a whole other letter to his misdeeds. "Recall I was picking up the tab in toto. After the first week he was flat and did not put out centavo one. During the brief time he had $ it was like pulling an impacted molar to get any money out of him. I may add that at least 50% of the time his manner was surly and ill-tempered [...] selfish, inconsiderate and downright insufferable behavior and he doesn't drop me a line."[20]

In July, Bill received the first quarter of his eight-hundred-dollar advance from Ace Books for *Junkie*, less Ginsberg's 10 percent for acting as agent. Allen had found New York publishers particularly reluctant to publish the book, given its subject matter and its neutral—to them—position toward addictive drugs. Even so, the deal was a particularly poor one at a time when Gold Medal, a rival mass-market paperback company, was attracting authors with royalties based on print runs rather than actual sales: a $2,000 advance on an initial print run of 200,000 copies; $3,000 on a run of 300,000. Ace printed 150,000-plus copies of *Junkie* when it was finally published in 1953.[21] Years later Burroughs called them to account and collected over $2,000 in overdue royalties.

Early in July, Bill Garver, the overcoat thief and junkie with whom Bill once sold heroin in New York, arrived in Mexico City, acting on Burroughs's recommendation as to the availability of junk and cheapness of living. His father had died and he inherited an income of $400 a month, enough to live in considerable comfort in Mexico City. He came off the plane with blood all over his pants where he had given himself a fix using a safety pin in his leg.[22] Bill got him a cheap room, which Garver made extra secure by padlocking the door. He sat, hunchbacked and thin, with his white hair combed sleekly back with water like a teenager. His room was filled with books of classical history, volumes of poetry including Rimbaud and Mallarmé. His walls were covered with reproductions of the work of José Clemente Orozco, one of the leaders, along with Diego Rivera, of the Mexican Mural Renaissance, that he had cut from magazines. Every day he had to go upstairs to empty his chamber pot. Each week he bought *Time* and *U.S. News & World Report* from Sears Roebuck and read them from cover to cover, nodding off after every few pages. In September, Bernabé Jurado bought an ounce of cocaine that he didn't like the look of and thought might be heroin. He offered it to Burroughs. It was gray and metallic-looking, so Bill passed and offered the deal to Garver, who paid Jurado five hundred dollars for it. Garver took some. At seven in the morning he came into Bill's room and asked, "Are you just gonna lay in your bed with all these shipments coming in?" Bill said, "Shipments? What is this, a fucking farm? I'm getting up at 6:30?" Garver said, "Pure drugstore in." Burroughs recalled that "he had on his overcoat and he had a strange look in his eye. And then he got into bed with me. I said, 'What's the matter, are you, crazy?' He says, 'Hee-hee-hee-hee!' I edged out of bed and got on my clothes, and Dave and I got him back to his room."[23] Old Dave and Bill were concerned that the drug was poisoned and that Garver was going to die. Just in case he did, they searched his room for the five hundred dollars that he had not yet paid Jurado rather than leave it for the Mexican police to steal, but they couldn't find it. However, the next day Garver was fine; his money was still there but he threw away the bad stuff. According to Alan Ansen, when Garver died as the result of junk in Mexico City in 1957, Bill was taken aback and didn't want to believe it. His romantic notions about junk and junkies did not include death.

Marker returned to Mexico City but did not contact Bill for five days. Bill was hurt and made something of a scene. Marker told him, "Why can't we just be friends with no sex?" but Bill said the strain would be intolerable and put so much pressure on him that he finally agreed to have sex once or twice a month. Bill told Allen, "The strain is still considerable, but since he is here I can't help but see him even if it is ruining my digestion, sleep and nerves" (as well as his bank balance).[24] But the strain was too much for Marker, and in October he left once more, without writing Bill as much as a card. In a final attempt to reestablish the relationship—such as it was—Burroughs flew up to Jacksonville and managed to persuade Marker to accompany him back to Mexico City. Bill told Allen, "He likes me well enough in his way. I know how far his way is from my way," then crossed out in the original letter, "[we] have sex even if he doesn't like it, and does it just to oblige once in a while."[25]

Fourteen months had passed since Joan's death. The court case was still pending, the dates constantly being moved; Ace was dithering over publishing *Junkie*, demanding extra sections, wanting to see his latest writing about Mexico; Jack had shown him a complete lack of consideration, and had not supported him as a friend; he was despondent over his failed affair with Marker, which was obviously not going to work long-term; he was off junk and not drinking but his health was clearly not good—he couldn't hold down anything solid, only milk, and he had to force that down. He was marking time. His letters from this period suggest that he was severely depressed, perhaps buffeted by gusts of memory, plagued by nightmare feelings of remorse. He just wanted out. He constantly speaks of moving to Panama, of making his fortune as a farmer, of achieving the good life. In his letters to Ginsberg he tries to harden himself, saying he wants to make a lot of money and he is not choosy how he makes it: "Most people simply aren't human so far as I am concerned. I don't care what happens to them. I have not learned any lessons of charity."[26] Even Garver "bores me to death."

Things suddenly came to a head when on November 13, 1952, Bernabé Jurado had just parked his brand-new Buick Roadmaster outside his apartment on avenida México when he was sideswiped by a car full of drunken teenagers. Outraged, he let off a few shots at the departing car, hitting seventeen-year-old Mario Saldaña Cervantes in the leg. The injury was not immediately fatal, but septicemia set in and the boy died on November 29. His family moved in high political circles, and even the newly elected president, Ávila Camacho, got involved. Jurado went into hiding, first to Brazil, then the United States, and on to Europe, where he stayed for several years. Jurado's legal partners immediately demanded more money from Burroughs, saying that everything had changed, and Bill realized he was no longer protected. Less than two weeks later, Burroughs was safely ensconced in the bosom of his family in Palm Beach.

Kerouac arrived in Mexico City at the beginning of December, a few days before Bill left. He had been laid off by the railroad where he had been working in San Francisco and was driven down by Neal Cassady, who went straight back to the States. Burroughs was in no mood to host Kerouac again, so Jack took a little two-room apartment on the roof of his building. Kerouac wrote to Neal complaining that twelve dollars a month was a high rent, even though he could have lived in a cheaper neighborhood, then went on to say how he had bought three dozen oysters to cook in butter, imported Chianti, and French bread. He told Neal he started each day with steak and eggs, so he was clearly in funds. He reported that Burroughs left Mexico City on December 8, after closing down the apartment, telling John Clellon Holmes, "I saw him pack in his moldy room where he shot M all this time—Sad moldy leather cases—old holsters, old daggers—a snapshot of Huncke—a Derringer pistol, which he gave to old dying Garver—medicine, drugs—the last of Joan's spices, marjoram, new mould since she died and stopped cooking—little Willie's shoe—& Julie's moldy school case [...] throwing in his bag, at last, picture of Lucien & Allen—Smiled, & left."[27]

Chapter Twenty

I was travelling because I was a man trying to escape from himself. I felt guilty about my wife's death in a shooting accident in Mexico. We had both been under the influence of drugs. I was acquitted by the Mexican authorities but I hadn't acquitted myself in my own mind. From Mexico I went on to Colombia and Peru.[1]

1. Yagé Found

Bill's parents had moved from St. Louis to Palm Beach in the spring of 1952, ostensibly to avoid the harsh St. Louis winters. But they were also no doubt embarrassed by the extensive coverage given in the St. Louis papers of Burroughs's murder trial, which had severed their little remaining connection to St. Louis society, already strained by Bill's role in the Kammerer murder. Burroughs had thought he might feel differently about the United States on revisiting it after a three-year absence—apart from a brief trip to collect Marker—but he didn't. He told Allen, "I don't like it here. I don't dislike it. I feel that my home is South of the Rio Grande."[2] He determined to stay a few weeks, spend time with his parents and little Billy. Early in January 1953 he set off on his long-mooted trip to Panama. He was to spend eight months, essentially alone, in search of yagé in the jungles of South America, an exploration that would take him to Panama, Colombia, Peru, and briefly back to Mexico City. He was thirty-nine years old.

Burroughs ends *Junky* with the lines, "Maybe I will find in yage what I was looking for in junk and weed and coke. Yage may be the final fix."[3] After his period of stasis in Mexico City following the death of Joan, he was searching for something other than yet another high: Burroughs was almost taking Rimbaud as his textbook, as Lucien Carr and the others had done so long ago in the West End Bar, embarking on a "long, intimidating, immense and rational derangement of all the senses. The sufferings are enormous, but one must be strong."[4] He was searching for something that would kick him bodily out of his present condition into a new place, with new potentials and new possibilities. His first visit with Marker was basically an excuse to get Marker alone in the jungle. The second visit was more like Burroughs's dark night of the soul. The trip was as much an exploration of himself as of the South American jungle, a controlled midlife crisis, to find what led to his addictions, his alcoholism, his love lack, the irrational behavior that led to the killing of Joan. To do so he searched out the most powerful mind-altering drug known to man, yagé, hoping it would cut through the layers of ego, of prejudice, of received behavior and thought, cut through all illusions, to reach the very core of his being. It was an arduous trip, but a necessary one. He was not traveling for "material," but out of it came a book—*The Yage Letters*—and a series of characters and sets that informed his writing for the rest of his life.

The Hotel Colón in Panama was built in 1915 to house Panama Canal workers. It had an ornate Moorish tiled lobby, a hand-operated Otis elevator, and a pleasant terrace overlooking the bay. Bill was junk-sick and trying to kick, and wasn't helped by Bill Garver, also in Panama, who kept nagging him to get back on, "once a junkie always a junkie." One night when Bill got drunk and bought some paregoric, Garver was delighted. Bill reported that "he kept saying over and over, 'I knew you'd come home with paregoric. I knew it. You'll be a junkie all the rest of your life' and looking at me with his little cat smile. Junk is a cause with him." Eventually Garver said something untoward about Joan and Bill stopped seeing him.

Bill checked into a hospital to have an operation for hemorrhoids. He told Allen that "my skivvies disappeared in surgery, a sinister conjuncture of circumstance."[5] He was there four days and still in withdrawal, but they only gave him three shots of morphine so he couldn't sleep for the pain, the heat, and junk sickness. Why he did not have the operation in Florida, where the hospital conditions were likely to have been better, is not known. Burroughs did not like Panama, telling Allen, "The Panamanians are the crummiest people in the western Hemisphere and the U.S. Civil Service and Armed Forces stationed here are the ultimate shit."[6] He took a room on the beach near Panama to recuperate until he was in fit condition to travel on to Colombia. Panama was a classic Burroughs set, with albatrosses and vultures roosting on the buildings. There was a vacant lot filled with weeds and trees across from the American embassy where boys undressed and swam in the polluted waters of the bay, which was home to a small venomous sea snake. "Smell of excrement and sea water and young male lust. [...] Same old Panama. Whores and pimps and hustlers."[7]

Burroughs arrived in Bogotá on January 20, and put up at the Hotel

Mulvo Regis. The city was cold and wet, "a damp chill that gets inside you like the inner cold of junk sickness. There is no heat anywhere and you are never warm."[8] This was caused by its elevation, high in the Andes at 8,600 feet (2,620 meters), with mountains as a constant backdrop; the nearby Cerro de Montserrat is 10,000 feet (3,030 meters). The altitude is well known to have a mildly unpleasant effect, creating gas known as "Bogotá belly" and a general feeling of anxiety.[9] Bill found Bogotá to be gloomy and somber, weighed down by its Spanish heritage. His hotel room was a windowless cubicle with walls made from green composite board and the bed too short. He wrote, "For a long time I sat there on the bed paralyzed with bum kicks."[10]

Things improved the next day when he met Dr. Richard Evans Schultes—known as Dr. Schindler in *The Yage Letters*—who worked out of the Botanical Institute, an office building filled with crates of stuffed animals and specimens, with people constantly shifting things around like a scene from *The Naked Lunch*. Schultes received his doctorate from Harvard in 1937 for research into peyote, the year after Burroughs graduated. He was an ethnobotanist, a specialist in the hallucinogenic drugs of South America, and was connected to the U.S. Agricultural Commission. He showed Bill dried specimens of yagé vine and said when he tried it he saw colors but had no visions. He gave him its scientific name, *Banisteriopsis caapi*, but said there were various Indian names for it, including ayahuasca in the Quechua language and yagé in Tucanoan. The active ingredient is in the inner bark of the vine, which has to be scraped out. Every Indian tribe had a different way of making it, mixing the yagé with other vines and drugs, some making an infusion, others spending a whole day cooking it up.

Schultes said he liked to smoke opium and had chewed cocaine and experimented with various hallucinogenic drugs. He was very much opposed to all attempts to regulate cocaine, which he said was nonsense; he advocated its free sale. He told Bill that the Putumayo region was the most readily accessible area where he might find yagé and explained exactly what he would need for his expedition: medicines; snakebite serum, penicillin, enterovioform, Aralen (chloroquine) to counteract malaria, a hammock, a blanket, mess tin, tea, a canteen, and a primus stove so that he could cook anywhere, and finally a waterproof rubber bag known as a tula to carry it all in.

After five days Bill left Bogotá for Pasto, en route for the Putumayo, first taking the bus to Cali because the *autoferro* was booked solid for days. Colombia was in the grip of a civil war between the ruling Conservatives and the popular Liberals. The bus was stopped several times by the

Policía Nacional, the palace guard of the Conservative Party, and the bus and everyone in it searched. Burroughs had a gun in his baggage, hidden beneath his medicines, but they only searched his person at the stops. Burroughs quickly took sides in the war, he told Allen: "This [the PN] is the most unanimously hideous body of young men I ever laid eyes on, my dear. They look like the end result of atomic radiation. There are thousands of these strange loutish young men in Colombia and I only saw one I would consider eligible and he looked ill at ease in his office. If there is anything to say for the Conservatives I didn't hear it. They are an unpopular minority of ugly looking shits."[11] The bus passed through the Tolima region, close to a war zone, and the numbers of PN increased. In the late afternoon Burroughs bought a bottle of brandy at a coffee stop and got drunk with the bus driver. He spent the night in Armenia and continued to Cali the next day on the *autoferro*, a colorful tram/train that ran on rails and was considerably more comfortable.

Burroughs liked Cali; it had a pleasant climate and semitropical vegetation with bamboo, banana palms, and papayas. Next day he took the *autoferro* to Popayán, a quiet university town with beautiful, distinctly Spanish colonial architecture. Bill walked out of the town to see the country: rolling meadows, very green, grazed by sheep and cattle. He saw some propaganda movies celebrating the Conservative Party; the audience sat in dead silence. The next day he took the bus to Pasto, a high Andean town 8,290 feet (2,527 meters) at the foot of the Galeras volcano, the most active in Colombia. Pasto's other claim to fame was as the leprosy capital of Colombia. In Pasto he lodged at the Hotel Niza.

Bill wrote Allen, "Driving in the place hit me in the stomach with a physical impact of depression and horror. High mountains all around. High thin air. The inhabitants peering out of sod roofed huts, their eyes red with smoke. The hotel was Swiss run and excellent. I walked around the town. Ugly crummy looking populace. The higher you got the uglier the citizens."[12] He went into a cantina, played mountain music on the jukebox, and drank anise-flavored aguardiente (literally "fire water"), the local version being made from sugarcane.

Dr. Schultes had given him an introduction to a German wine producer who knew Putumayo well and told Burroughs that there was a bug there like a big grasshopper that was a powerful aphrodisiac. "If it flies on you and you can't get a woman right away you will die. I have seen them running around jacking off from contact with this animal. [...] Another thing I have been trying to get information on [is] a vine you chew and all your teeth fall out."

"Just the thing for practical jokes on your friends," Bill said, filing the story away.[13] He left Pasto a couple of days later for Mocoa, the capital of Putumayo and the end of the road. From there transport was by mule or canoe.

Burroughs arrived in Mocoa late at night. It was a small town of muddy cobbled streets and single-story buildings, surrounded by towering mountains part covered by low clouds and encroaching jungle of palms and canopy trees. Bill wrote Allen, "For some reason these end of road towns are always God awful. [...] But in all my experience as a traveller—and I have seen some God awful places—no place ever brought me down like Mocoa. And I don't know exactly why."[14] No one knew anything about the jungle or yagé, and he couldn't even buy citronella to ward against bugs. Mocoa had four streets, which were constantly patrolled by a member of the Policía Nacional on a motorcycle that could be heard from any part of the town. The police also had a brass band that paraded around the town three or four times a day, starting early in the morning.

Bill bounced about in the back of a truck thirty miles to Puerto Limón, near the meandering Rio Caqueta, where he found a helpful Indian and within ten minutes had a yagé vine. But the Indian refused to prepare it, insisting that was the monopoly of the *brujo*. Essentially a *brujo* is a black magician, combining witchcraft with Spanish Catholicism, whereas a *curandero* is the inheritor of the folk medicine techniques of the Mayans and deals in white magic. Bill's *brujo*—"a drunken fraud"—was crooning over a man prostrate with malaria when Bill found him. Bill believed that the *brujo* drove the evil malaria spirit out of his patient and into the gringo, because he came down with malaria exactly two weeks later. The *brujo* explained that he had to be half drunk in order to work his witchcraft and cure people, so Bill bought him a pint of aguardiente, which is 25 percent alcohol. He agreed to prepare the yagé for another quart. He made a pint of cold-water infusion, but only after he misappropriated half the vine so that Bill got very little effect. One of the telepathic effects of yagé is supposed to be visions of a city. That night Bill had a vivid dream in color and saw a composite city, part New York, part Mexico City, and part Lima, which he had not yet seen. He told Allen, "I was standing on a corner by a wide street with cars going by and a vast open park down the street in the distance. I can not say whether these dreams had any connection with Yagé."[15]

He spent the next day with an Indian guide, exploring the jungle and looking for yoka, a vine the Indians used to prevent hunger and fatigue during long trips in the jungle. It took them four hours to reach the high ground where yoka grows. The Indian cut a vine and shaved off the inner bark with his machete. He soaked the bark in a little cold water then squeezed the water out and handed the infusion to Bill in a palm leaf cup. It was faintly bitter but not unpleasant, and in ten minutes Bill felt exhilarated, as if he had taken Benzedrine but "not so tight." He walked the four hours back to Puerto Limón without stopping and said that he could have walked twice that far. The jungle views were spectacular. He told Allen, "The trees are tremendous, some of them 200 feet tall. Walking under these trees I felt a special silence, a vibrating soundless hum. We waded through clear streams of water."[16] He said that the Upper Amazon jungle had fewer disagreeable features than the midwestern Ozarks in the summer. Insect repellent discouraged the sand flies and jungle mosquitoes. Unfortunately he had run out of citronella. The whole time he was in the Putumayo he never got any ticks or chiggers.

Burroughs spent about a week in Puerto Limón before continuing by truck to Puerto Umbria and canoe to Puerto Asís. The canoes, the standard method of travel, were about thirty feet long and powered by outboard motor, but the motors were often out of commission because their owners took them apart and left out pieces they regarded as inessential. They also economized on oil so the motors often burned out. The Indians loaded them right down beyond the gunwale so they were almost at the water level. Puerto Asís consisted of a mud street along the riverbank, one cantina, one hotel, a few shops, and a Capuchin mission. Bill checked into the Putumayo Hotel. It was run by a middle-aged couple with seven daughters. "This giggling brood of daughters kept coming into my room (there was no door, only a thin curtain) to watch me dress and shave and brush my teeth. It was a bum kick,"[17] he told Allen. The day after he arrived, the governor found an error in Bill's tourist card. In Panama the Colombian consul had mistakenly put down "52" instead of "53" as the date. It was an obvious error, as Bill's other papers, his passport, air tickets, and receipts, all showed clearly enough that 1953 was the correct date, but the man was obdurate. Bill was placed under town arrest pending a decision from Mocoa. A cop searched his luggage, missing the gun, but decided to impound all the medicine where the gun was hidden. Fortunately a father from the Capuchin mission interceded and he was not held in a cell. After the interrogation, Bill returned to the mission, where the fathers gave him good food, wine, and liquors; "they live the life of Riley, man, they lived good [. . .] they snap their fingers and people jump around. But they're always helpful."[18]

Bill was stuck in Puerto Asís with nothing to do but sit around and watch the wide flowing river and get drunk in the cantina in the evenings.

One day he was sitting on an upturned worn-out canoe on the riverfront when a boy joined him there. That evening they walked into the jungle. Afterward Bill reported to Allen, "I beat him down to $10 bargaining under increasingly disadvantageous conditions. Somehow he managed to roll me for $20 and my underwear shorts (when he told me to take my underwear all the way off I thought, a passionate type, my dear, but it was only a maneuver to steal my skivvies)."[19]

After eight days, word came that Burroughs had to be returned to Mocoa, so, accompanied by a cop as he was technically under arrest, he went back upriver. In Puerto Umbria he came down with chills and fever. Next day they arrived in Mocoa and the second-in-command threw Bill in a cell without even a bucket to piss in. They threw all his baggage, unsearched, in with him, including of course his gun. He took some Aralen and lay shivering all night. The next morning the commandante saw him, immediately recognized the error, and set him free. Bill returned to his hotel, called a doctor, and went straight to bed. He had chills, fever, and was aching all over. The doctor took his temperature, which was 105, said "Caramba!" and gave him an injection of quinine and liver extract to offset secondary anemia. Bill continued to take the Aralen and used codeine tablets to counteract the malaria headache. His temperature came down and he spent most of the next three days sleeping. The Aralen knocked the malaria right out of his spleen and bone marrow and Burroughs never had a recurrence.

By February 28 he had reached Pasto and was back in the Hotel Niza. Two days later he was in the Hotel Nueva Regis in Bogotá. Dr. Schultes and the U.S. embassy helped him, and he was now armed with a paper signed and sealed by the minister and secretary of the Colombian Foreign Office. The trip was not a complete waste, however, because thanks to Dr. Schultes he was now a member of an expedition. This included Schultes, three Swedish photographers intent on capturing a live anaconda, two English broom rot specialists from the Cocoa Commission, two Colombian botanists, and their assistants. They were followed by a truckload of equipment including tents, rations, movie cameras, and weapons. They were to go to Putumayo in convoy, retracing Bill's journey through Cali, Popayán, and Pasto to Mocoa. The expedition received regal treatment, with free boat and plane transport, free food served in the officers' mess, and accommodation in the governor's house. Officials were under the misapprehension that Bill was a representative of the Texas Oil Company traveling incognito. He gave them no reason to doubt it. Bill got on extremely well with Schultes, and told Allen, "He likes to chew coke with the Indians, and is not above amorous dalliance with indigenous females."

Schultes later became world famous for his work protecting the Amazon jungle and its peoples, identifying more than three hundred new species of plants, and for isolating the active principle in curare, now used as a muscle relaxant in operations.

Bill's next experiment with yagé nearly killed him. The expedition had broken up, and Bill carried on with Dr. Schultes, the two Englishmen from the Cocoa Commission, and the two Colombian botanists. In Mocoa, Bill's German connection made an appointment for him with a medicine man. At dusk they went to a thatched hut with a dirt floor in the jungle, about ten minutes out of Mocoa, to meet the *brujo*. The *brujo*, a smooth-faced old man of about seventy, first took a long drink from the quart of aguardiente that Bill brought with him, then squatted by a bowl set up on a tripod before a crude shrine. He sat in silence for a long time, then took another swig from the bottle and began crooning and shaking a little whisk over the bowl. Eventually he poured some of the black liquid into two dirty red plastic cups. The liquid was oily and phosphorescent. He handed one to Bill, who drank it right down, anticipating the bitter taste. The *brujo* downed his. The effect on Bill was instantaneous; within ten seconds the room began spinning. Blue flashes passed in front of his eyes, and he saw Easter Island heads carved in the support posts of the hut. He rushed for the door, banging his shoulder. He leaned against a tree and vomited violently. He was completely delirious for four hours, vomiting at ten-minute intervals, crouching on all fours by a rock, gasping, thrown by waves of nausea. It turned out that the *brujo* had given a similar dose to a man just a month before; the man ran into the jungle and they found him in convulsions. He died. The *brujo* had given Bill an overdose that, had he not puked it up within twenty seconds, could well have been fatal. Clearly the *brujo* had built up a large tolerance for yagé himself. Finally Bill was coordinated enough to find his Nembutal. It took him ten minutes to shake five tablets from the bottle, but he couldn't swallow them because his mouth was so dry. He managed to crawl to a stream and gulp enough water to get them down. He recovered, but it was a horrible experience. He crawled into the hut and pulled a blanket over himself, blue flashes still igniting in front of his eyes. The next morning, feeling fine, he walked back to town.

The expedition continued next day to Puerto Asís. Dr. Schultes had two assistants to carry his equipment and help collect specimens, one of whom was an Indian from the Vaupés region where they had a very different method of preparing yagé. In Putumayo the vines were crushed with a rock and boiled all day in a small amount of water together with a double handful of another plant to make a small amount of the beer. The

Vaupés method consisted of scraping about three feet of bark to make a double handful of shavings. These were soaked in a liter of cold water for several hours and the liquid strained off. Nothing was added. The liquid was sipped over a period of an hour. The *brujo* in Mocoa told Bill that if a woman witnesses the preparation of yagé it spoils and will poison you. Bill resolved to try the Vaupés method. In the Putumayo Hotel there was no way to avoid the landlord's seven daughters, who poked sticks into the mixture, breathing down Bill's neck and giggling. The infusion was a light red color. He had blue flashes and a slight nausea but no hallucinations or vomiting. The effects were like marijuana.

The next day they continued downriver to Puerto Espina, where the governor put them up, allowing them to sling their hammocks in an empty room on the top floor. There was supposed to be a Catalina flying boat service out of Puerto Espina, and Bill and Dr. Schultes were ready to return to Bogotá, but the agent had no radio, or any way of finding out when the next plane would arrive. Each day the river was getting higher and all the canoes in Puerto Espina were broken; desultory attempts to repair them could be heard all day as motors started up and failed.

The Englishmen from the Cocoa Commission went up the San Miguel to collect specimens. Dr. Schultes continued downriver to Puerto Leguizamo hoping to catch a military plane. Bill decided to stay in Puerto Espina in the hope that the Catalina would arrive; if it didn't he would go back with the Cocoa Commission. The Cocoa Commission returned and Bill joined their voyage downriver to Puerto Leguizamo, where the commandante put them up on a rusty gunboat anchored in the Putumayo River. Puerto Leguizamo was the inspiration for many of Burroughs's descriptions of South American river towns: rusty abandoned machinery scattered here and there, unlighted streets deep in mud, the town's five whores sitting out in front of blue-painted cantinas in the humid night beneath a naked electric bulb, waiting, the town's young kids clustered around them, watching "with the immobile concentration of tom cats."[20]

After a week on the gunboat Bill was able to get a military plane to Villavicencio. Then he traveled to Bogotá by chauffeured car, provided by the U.S. Point Four scheme to assist underdeveloped countries; the driver rejected Bill's advances. He arrived with a crate of yagé, but after the long journey it was no longer fresh. At the Botanical Institute Dr. Schultes helped Bill to extract the alkaloids in the lab, but it didn't work, even though he followed the extraction directions carefully. Bill thought that some of the other ingredients usually added by the Indians might act as a catalyst to the drug. He only had fifty dollars to last two weeks because his monthly check had been stolen while he was away. To get drunk he stole pure alcohol from the university lab, went to a café, and poured it in a Pepsi-Cola. He moved into the cheapest possible flophouse accommodation. Burroughs was increasingly convinced by the Liberal cause, and even donated his gun—which he could have sold for $150—to a "pretty young Liberal." He told Allen, "It is *impossible* to remain neutral, and I will help this boy no matter what. Always was a pushover for a just cause and a pretty face. Wouldn't surprise me if I end up with the Liberal guerrillas."[21]

2. Into Peru

His visa expired, so Burroughs had to leave Colombia. He flew to Quito and from there made his way south down the coast by sea. The ship broke its propeller at Las Playas, halfway down the coast between Manta and Guayaquil, and on April 29, Burroughs made one of his more celebrated landfalls, by riding ashore at Las Playas on a balsa raft accompanied by a beautiful boy.[22] The Ecuadorian police arrested them as soon as they reached the beach, thinking they must be Peruvian spies or smuggling contraband, but only detained them for fifteen minutes. "I rode ashore on a balsa raft. Arrested on the beach suspect to have floated up from Peru on the Humboldt Current with a young boy and a tooth brush (I travel light, only the essentials) so we are hauled up before a dried up old fuck, the withered face of cancerous control. The kid with me don't have paper one. The cops keep saying plaintively: 'But don't you have any papers *at all*?'"[23]

Guayaquil, where he had stayed with Marker on his first South American trip, must have raised some memories. He was stuck there until May 4, when he flew to Lima. There was a letter waiting from Bernabé Jurado, informing him that Judge Eduardo Urzaíz Jiménez had found him guilty of homicide and sentenced him in absentia to two years in prison, less the thirteen days served, with no reparations to be paid. The sentence was suspended, but Burroughs doesn't appear to have learned that until later; in the meantime he felt he was unable to visit Mexico. The formal sentence was not actually handed down until December 14, 1953, seven months later, by which time Burroughs was in New York.

Lima was enough like Mexico City to make Bill feel homesick. Lima is famous for its flowers, and even roadworks were indicated by red carnations on a pole stuck in the road. A ceiling of cloud hung over the city, rarely breaking. He spent his first night in the Gran Hotel Bolívar before looking for cheap lodgings. He rented a little shop with a pull-down front shutter at 930 José Leal out near the public dump, in an area of empty lots and one- and two-story buildings. There was a long adobe wall where at all hours people were lined up shitting, vultures wheeling in the violet sky. Burroughs recalled, "You walked out of there and there were vultures right on the sidewalk because there was the public dump and the vultures came there by the hundreds to eat fish-heads and stuff like that. And you're walking down there and kick the vultures aside. They flap away. They'll even snap their beaks at you. I've never seen a city with more vultures in it than Lima. They are all over the public buildings and Bolivar Square. And here's a statue of Bolivar with vultures perched all over it."[24] The vultures were useful in a city with rudimentary sanitation; they ate all the garbage.

In his little storefront apartment he could do anything he wanted. He wrote Allen, "Lima is the promised land for boys. I never saw anything like it since Vienna in '36. [...] in the bars around the Mercado Mayorista—Main Market—any boy is wise and available to the Yankee dollar. Last night I checked into a hotel with a beautiful Indian to the great amusement of the hotel clerk and his friends."[25] Making up for lost time, he told Allen that the older he got the less wisdom, maturity, and caution he had. He shadowboxed with a young boy in a louche Peruvian bistro—"Haven't you any dignity at *all*? Obviously not"[26]—and made a pass at a thirteen-year-old Indian right in front of his family, dragging home two "ragged brats." He told Allen, "All I remember is they were young. Woke up with the smell of youngsters on my hands and body." The extreme poverty in Lima meant that sexual tourism was common, though it was not yet a fixture on the international pedophile route. Burroughs preferred to think it was cultural, describing Peruvian boys as "the least character armored people I have ever seen. They shit or piss anywhere they feel like it. They have no inhibitions in expressing affection. They climb all over each other and hold hands. If they do go to bed with another male, and they all will for money, they seem to enjoy it. Homosexuality is simply a human potential as is shown by almost unanimous incidents in prisons."[27] Lima and the Mercado Mayorista is used as a set for the "We are the language" section of *Cities of the Red Night*.[28]

Back in civilization Burroughs reveled in the good food of Lima's Chinatown and drank so much that one morning he couldn't get out of bed. He found an American doctor who said, "You've been drinking pisco." Bill said, "Yes." The doctor told him, "You have pisco neuritis. Another week and you'd have been in hospital for six months." He shot Bill with huge doses of vitamin B. He told Bill, "These people can drink it but you can't." Pisco is a raw sugarcane distillate that drains the vitamins right out of the system. He suggested that Bill switch to rum or Chilean brandy instead, so he drank that or plain aguardiente. Still, Bill liked Lima and its people very much, telling Allen, "The Peruvians are charming. These people down here are so much nicer than Americans."[29] It was in Lima, while recovering from his neuritis, that Bill wrote the *Roosevelt After Inauguration* routine that came to him in a dream. He enclosed it in a letter to Allen Ginsberg on May 23, 1953. Burroughs left for the high jungle on June 6.

The six-week trip to Pucallpa in the high Andes took him first to Tingo María, where he spent a couple of days at the Hotel Touriste, a well-run mountain resort hotel. From there he took a fourteen-hour car ride, squeezed in the back with two sisters who sprawled all over him. The road from Tingo María to Pucallpa had only been built nine years before, and was continually being repaired by bulldozers, pushing aside rocks from frequent landslides. If the road was left for a month it became impassable. Bill journeyed through some of the highest towns in the world, cold windswept places in the Puna, high above the tree line, where the houses were made of sod with just a hole in the roof to let the smoke out, and everyone dressed in animal skins and goat hats and ate a diet of chickpeas and cavies—guinea pigs. Bill thought they were the most depressing places he had ever seen.

Pucallpa, however, was "the pleasantest end of the road town I have seen in S.A." Situated on the banks of the Río Ucayali, a major tributary of the Amazon, Pucallpa was still a small river town with just a couple of hotels and a shopping street, but even the smallest drugstores had penicillin, codeine, and a range of antibiotics and antimalarial drugs. The big news was "the Russians were here." In 1927, the Russians had shipped a ton of yagé back to Moscow, the origin of all the stories in the Cold War pulp magazines.

The hotel put Burroughs in touch with the local *curandero*. Bill visited his hut in the early evening, taking with him Nembutal and codeine. He was a young man and there were two women there and another man; unlike in Colombia, women were allowed to participate. They sat around for hours, slowly sipping the potion. "It was a nice relaxed occasion. I was there for hours, hours and hours. It was great. Then I came back to him several times and then he gave me some that he'd fixed up, in a bottle, to take whenever I wanted. And I took it in my hotel room a couple of times, its really great. Great experience."[30] He was given the yagé in a large cup, and he sipped it very carefully. "Everything is blue, it's a blue drug and you only take it at night. It's a night drug and everything is just beautiful, sort of Easter island masks or something. Blue, colors, cities, vistas, very beautiful."[31] Burroughs was very impressed and told Allen, "It is the most powerful drug I have ever experienced. That is it produces the most complete derangement of the senses. You see everything from a special hallucinated view point."[32] He enclosed some notes on the yagé state:

> The room took on the aspect of a near Eastern whore house with blue walls and red tasselled lamps. I feel myself change into a Negress complete with all the female facilities. Convulsions of lust accompanied by physical impotence. Now I am a Negro man fucking a Negress. My legs take on a well rounded Polynesian substance. Everything stirs with a peculiar furtive writhing life like a Van Gogh painting. Complete bisexuality is attained. You are a man or woman alternately or at will. [...] There is a definite sense of space time travel that seems to shake the room.[33]

He added that it had occurred to him that the preliminary sickness of yagé was the motion sickness of transport to the yagé state, and referred to H. G. Wells's *The Time Machine*, which speaks of the indescribable vertigo of space-time travel. He found that he quickly developed tolerance and could have easily handled the dose given to him by the first *brujo* in Colombia.

Unfortunately his last five days in Pucallpa were a nightmare because he wanted to leave but was trapped by torrential rain and impassable roads. Everyone in the hotel had frayed tempers. The biggest blight on the landscape were the Protestant fundamentalist Christian missionaries from the so-called Linguistic Institute, based at the University of Oklahoma in Norman. Unlike the Catholic fathers, who lived high on the hog, and on all other local foodstuffs, the missionaries lived on Spam and canned pineapples as they were afraid of the local food. They had no medical knowledge and had no medicines with them to help the local people. Burroughs met them all over Peru. There are thirty-five Indian languages in Peru, and they were learning them all, not for scientific research to analyze and preserve their culture, but in order to translate the Bible into all those languages. In Pucallpa one missionary told Burroughs, "I'd like to see a law against yagé with teeth in it because it comes from the Devil." He believed this literally. They had six Indians with them and they were slowly working their way through the Bible, word by word, doing a literal translation. Burroughs hated them. "They were all horrible people, horrible."[34]

On the bus ride back to Tingo María in the back of a converted truck Bill got so drunk he had to be helped to bed by the assistant truck driver. There was a two-day delay in Huànuco that he hated, "sad little parks with statues of generals and cupids, and Indians lolling about with a special South American abandon, chewing coca."[35] Bill tried it a couple of times, but coca leaves are only one percent cocaine and the absorption is so slow that there is little systemic reaction; all it did was freeze up his mouth.

The yagé experience freed Burroughs from the stasis of the previous year and introduced imagery that was to occur in all of his subsequent books. He had set out to change his life and had done so. "Yes Yagé is the final kick and you are not the same after you have taken it."[36]

Yage is space time travel. The room seems to shake and vibrate with motion. The blood and substance of many races, Negro, Polynesian, Mountain Mongol, Desert Nomad, Polyglot Near East, Indian and new races as yet unconceived and unborn, combinations not yet realized, passes through your body. You make migrations, incredible journeys through jungles and deserts and mountains (stasis and death in closed mountain valleys where plants grow out of your cock and vast Crustaceans hatch inside you and grow and break the shell of your body), across the Pacific in an outrigger canoe to Easter Island. The Composite City, Near Eastern, Mongol, South Pacific, South American where all Human Potentials are spread out in a vast silent market.[37]

Chapter Twenty-One

*What the American male really wants is two things: he wants to be
blown by a stranger while reading a newspaper and he wants to be fucked
by his buddy when he's drunk.*

—W. H. AUDEN[1]

1. Reunion in New York

Burroughs flew to Panama, where he was reconciled with Garver—"After
all, it was just a junky spat you know"[2]—then spent several weeks in Mexico City, looking for Marker. He had sent him ten letters but received
no reply. Apparently Marker had left Mexico City by car for Guatemala,
working as a guide to a major and his wife very shortly after Burroughs
himself had left. Burroughs felt the pain ease a little. Then an acquaintance said he had seen Marker in the street about a month before. "A wave
of misery and pain hit me like a main line shot, settling in the lungs and
around the heart. Then I knew I was hung up on M just the same as ever."[3]
He searched for Angelo and wrote in his journal, "Can visualize Angelo
sharp and clear as overdue pusher. His eye brows. His smile. The way
he would stop when he saw me with both hands in his pocket his green
sweater. His young male gentleness. [...] He was the best boy I ever had,
and I didn't know it. I used to give him $20. Now I would give him $100.
I want to help him. No one else had the same young male gentleness like
an affectionate animal. Almost saintly in his freedom from viciousness,
hostility, conflict."[4] But Bill had changed; he used to love Mexico, now
he hated it. "It's like I came back to Mexico City after being away 5 years
instead of 5 months. Everybody. Gone."[5] But Mexico City hadn't changed
that much; people were always moving around when he lived there. It was
Burroughs who had changed. He continued his journey.

In August he stopped briefly in Palm Beach to see his parents and young
Billy. Although the purpose of publishing *Junkie* under a pseudonym was to
prevent his parents from seeing it, he could not help but mention that he had

published a book. He told them it was written under a pseudonym but said that he didn't think they would be interested in reading it. While in Florida he located Marker, who had returned to his hometown of Jacksonville, where he had bought a house and divided it into apartments for sale. Bill still found him attractive but now knew he had to move on and control his feelings.

Allen Ginsberg was living at apartment 16, 206 East 7th Street, a tenement building built in 1900 in the Lower East Side between Avenues B and C. He was working as a copyboy at the *New York World-Telegram* earning forty-five dollars a week writing up share prices. He had previously shared a flat with Dusty Moreland in one of his rare heterosexual relationships, and she had moved with him to his new apartment. Allen wanted her to get a job and contribute to the costs, but this led to a tempestuous breakup and she walked out leaving all her clothes and furniture behind. When Burroughs arrived in town in late August, her place had been taken, in part, by the young poet Gregory Corso, who was prepared to trade the occasional blow job from Allen for somewhere to sleep. Gregory had not been very responsive to Ginsberg's advances and Allen had complained to Burroughs, who wrote to him from Lima saying, "Get rough with your little beast of a poet. They're all alike, ingrates every one of them ingrates."[6] Now, with Burroughs sitting across the room giving him bloodcurdling looks as he slowly and methodically used his machete to shave the bark from the two suitcases' worth of yagé vines he had brought back from Lima, Gregory found it prudent to seek accommodation elsewhere.

Bill and Allen had not seen each other for six years, the time Allen and Neal Cassady had visited Bill briefly in East Texas, but they had been in continuous correspondence and had worked closely on the editing and publication of *Junkie* with Ace Books. They were delighted to see each other. Ginsberg told Neal Cassady, "He is really exciting to talk to, more so for me than ever. His new loquaciousness is something I never had the advantage of. I'm older now and the emotional relationship and conflict of will and mutual digging are very intense, continuous, exhausting and fertile. He creates small usable literary symbolic psychic fantasies daily. One of the deepest people I ever saw. He is staying with me. I come home from work at 4:45 and we talk until one AM or later. I hardly get enuf sleep, cant think about work seriously, am all hung up in great psychic marriage with him for the month—amazing also his outwardness and confidence, he is very personal now, and gives the impression of suffering terribly and continuously. I am persuading him to write a really great sincere novel.

He is going to Tangiers. [...] The new impression of Bill that I get is that he is very great, greater than I ever realized, before even."[7]

By the end of the forties, the bar scene had moved from the Minetta Tavern and Burroughs's usual haunts to the San Remo Café at 189 Bleecker Street at MacDougal. The San Remo attracted the young, hip crowd who were more into experimenting with drugs than the straighter crowd that was just beginning to popularize the White Horse Tavern over on Hudson. According to Michael Harrington, "The Remo was a sort of Village United Nations. It was straight and gay; black, white, and interracial; socialist, communist, Trotskyist, liberal, and apolitical; literary, religious, pot smoking, pill popping, and even occasionally transvestite."[8] It was a classic old-time New York bar with a stamped-tin ceiling, black-and-white tile floors, a brass rail at the foot of the bar, booths, and salads for a dollar with all the bread and butter you could eat. Allen Ginsberg, Jack Kerouac, Gregory Corso, and their crowd hung out there, but the cool crowd rather disapproved of Kerouac because, according to Burroughs, "he was too frantic." There were many comparisons made between the San Remo and the Café de Flore or La Coupole in Paris, and the analogy held: Village nightlife after the war took inspiration from the Left Bank, the liveliest *quartier* in Paris after the Liberation—the home of *les caves existentialistes*, as Boris Vian called them.[9] The Village promised the same combination of alcohol, sex, jazz, open marriages, and highbrow conversation. John Cage, Miles Davis, Mary McCarthy, Delmore Schwartz, James Agee, William Steig, Julian Beck and Judith Malina of the Living Theatre, and the editors of *Partisan Review*, whose office was on Astor Place, were all regulars at the San Remo. The only crowd not well represented there was the painters, who preferred the Cedar Street Tavern.

Burroughs dropped right into Ginsberg's social scene. During his four months in New York he consolidated his friendship with Allen, got to know Gregory Corso, and met Alan Ansen, who was to become one of his lifelong friends. When Burroughs arrived in New York Ansen was one of the first people Allen told him about. Burroughs wanted to meet him and so Ginsberg dialed Ansen's number and put Bill on the line. "Come on in, man," Bill said. "Take a cab. We'll pay at this end." Ansen thought that was a delightful gesture. Ginsberg first met Ansen at one of Bill Cannastra's notoriously wild parties. At one of them, Ansen gave Cannastra's dog, a boxer, a blow job. The other guests responded with ennui. "Oh, *that* again!" It took a lot to astonish the guests at Cannastra's parties. Ansen also met Lucien Carr at Cannastra's, so he was closely involved with the Beat Generation at an early date. Ginsberg was interested in Ansen because he was W. H. Auden's secretary. Ansen's father was a jeweler and had left him a trust fund income of six hundred dollars a month, a lot of money in those days. Burroughs described him. "He is a very strange, very brilliant person. He was very Jewish-looking with a big nose, typically Semitic features, fat, and a semi-spastic, he didn't have any strength in his arms. I remember in Venice he couldn't pull himself up into a boat from the water. He would get in a panic." Ansen was a San Remo regular and several times invited Bill and Allen, and sometimes a crowd of people, out to his house in Woodmere, Long Island. Ansen introduced Burroughs to the work of Jean Genet. In 1948, Bernard Frechtman, an American living in Paris, had translated *Our Lady of the Flowers* into English for a limited edition of five hundred copies illustrated by Jean Cocteau. When Frechtman began living with Annette Michelson, a friend of Ansen's, she gave him a copy and Ansen lent it to Burroughs. Burroughs was astonished and came to regard Genet as one of the two twentieth-century writers whose work would stand the test of time (the other was Samuel Beckett).[10]

Kerouac was also around, living with his mother out in Richmond Hill, New York, but frequently coming into the city to see Allen and Bill. Ginsberg had recently bought a Kodak Retina camera, and many of his most famous early photographs date from this period: Burroughs on the roof of 206 East 7th; Burroughs lecturing a puzzled-looking Kerouac or engaging him in a mock fight; and the portrait of Burroughs behind a row of books, taken from the fire escape outside the window that was used on the front flap of the first edition of *The Naked Lunch*. Burroughs was thirty-nine, still young. There is a picture of him standing outside the San Remo with Alan Ansen, both smoking, Burroughs immaculately dressed in a double-breasted, off-white suit with wide lapels and shoulder pads, dark shirt and light tie, with his dark hair greased back, looking a bit like an Italian film director.

Bill had originally intended to spend a month in New York, before moving on to Rome or Tangier, but he found the company so congenial, and was getting such a lot of writing done, that four months passed. He and Allen typed up his long letters to Allen from Peru and Ecuador and rearranged them to make a continuous narrative, taking parts of one letter and adding it to another. The dates in the book are not necessarily the date the letter was written. These became an epistolary novel then called *Yage*, filled with his ruminations on the effects of the drug and its significance, as well as hilarious descriptions of his trials and tribulations in search of it. They also retyped *Queer*, adding in new material. Clean manuscript copies were then typed by Allen's friend Alene Lee, who later featured as Mardou Fox in Kerouac's *The Subterraneans*, a novel based upon his short affair with her.

Burroughs's life from 1944 until 1953, with the obvious omission of his marriage to Joan, was now written. "Everything happened as it is [...] they are as autobiographical as I could make them from memory, *Junkie, Queer,* and *The Yage Letters* [...] those are all just precisely as it happened."[11] *The Yage Letters* was the most accurate, because it was based on contemporary documents. He was pleased to have it all on paper, but still did not see himself as a writer, and could not conceive of the two final books ever being published. *Yage* was later modified to incorporate letters from Allen Ginsberg, who also visited Pucallpa and experienced yagé. It was published by Lawrence Ferlinghetti as *The Yage Letters* in 1963. *Queer* was not published until 1985.

Allen's tenement window looked out over fire escapes and backyards with laundry lines strung from building to building, level upon level of metal stairs and wires all connected. Burroughs saw a woman reach out over the fire escape and start pulling in the laundry and conceived the futuristic city of *Interzone,* with its levels connected by a web of catwalks, boardwalks, and fire escapes, a great labyrinth of alleyways and passages, squares and tunnels, like a medina; a city so old that it had collapsed on itself and been rebuilt one building upon another, layer upon layer. As he described the idea to Ginsberg he gave the city a vibrating soundless hum, like insect wings and larval entities waiting to be born. The imagery of *The Naked Lunch* was being developed, in this case drawing heavily upon Arthur Rimbaud's visions of cities in *Illuminations,* always one of Bill's favorite books. Both Burroughs and Ginsberg later agreed that the "Interzone Meet Café" was the seed of *The Naked Lunch.*[12]

Allen's role as the receiver of the long, intimate letters from Central and Latin America, and now as his confidant, collaborator, and editor in New York, had quickly led to an affair. Allen had been a teenager when they both shared the apartment in New York with Joan and had regarded Burroughs as his mentor, if not his guru. He was only nineteen when Burroughs left New York. As the result of their conversations his respect for Bill had grown and he was prepared to do anything he wanted. "I thought he was my teacher, so I'd do what I could to amuse him. In bed, Bill is like an English governess, whinnying and giggling, almost hysteric. [...] He liked to come while being screwed," Ginsberg said. "Burroughs fell in love with me and we slept together and I saw a soft center where he felt isolated, alone in the world and he needed [...] a feeling of affection, and since I did love him and did have that respect and affection, he responded. I kinda felt privileged."[13]

Ginsberg's affection released a huge reservoir of pent-up feelings in Burroughs, to Allen's great alarm and consternation. He said, "Bill became more and more demanding that there be some kind of mental schlupp. It had gone beyond the point of being humorous and playful. It seemed that Bill was demanding it for real. Bill wanted a relationship where there were no holds barred; to achieve an ultimate telepathic union of souls."[14] Ginsberg explained, "Schlupp for him was originally a very tender emotional direction, a desire to merge with a lover, and as such, pretty vulnerable, tenderhearted and open on Burroughs' part."[15]

Burroughs's concept of schlupping—the complete merging of soul mates into one entity—came from his close, and imaginative, reading of Wilhelm Reich, who saw that the point of the orgasm was to fuse the two orgone fields of the sex partners into one "orgonome"—to use Reich's term—in an explosive, rejuvenating recharge of natural universal energy. Reich explained, "The sexual embrace, if abstracted and reduced to its basic form, represents superimposition and the bio-energetic fusion of two orgonotic systems. Superimposition follows orgonotic penetration. The pre-orgastic bodily movements and in particular the orgastic convulsions represent extreme attempts of the free orgone of both organisms to fuse with one another, *to reach into one another.*"[16] It was not a question of one partner dominating the other; there was no invasion, no usurping the masculine status of the other person. The intention was *schlupp,* the complete fusion with the other person, "to enter the other's body, to breathe with his lungs, see with his eyes, learn the feel of his viscera and genitals."[17] Burroughs didn't want to become the other person, he wanted to fuse with the other person, the two of them making one. This is a common theme in Burroughs, particularly in the later writing where Mayan priests conduct various rituals to join two bodies. Of course complete schlupp was impossible, but a temporary flash of it was very desirable and partial occupation perhaps possible by cultural means. The flash of orgasm was when Bill was outside time and space. The orgasm flash where two orgone fields fuse into one is accomplished with no top and bottom, no domination or effeminacy, and Burroughs had always stressed that he saw his sex role as normal and male. "Like all normal citizens, I ejaculate when screwed without helping hand, produce a good crop of jissom, spurt it up to my chin and beyond. I have observed that small hard cocks come quicker slicker and spurtier."[18] This rather aggressive stridency suggests that Bill was not at all sure that "all normal citizens" did in fact come that way. There was also the matter of his small cock. "My cock is four and one-half inches and large cocks bring on my xenophobia."[19] Ginsberg thought that Bill's small penis accounted for his obsession with guns,[20] a subject that many academics have mulled over.

Years later, Ginsberg revealed all the intimate details of Burroughs's sex life in an interview in *Gay Sunshine*,[21] saying, "His particular sexual thing is being screwed, because Burroughs can come when he is screwed; he is one of the few men that can." Then, realizing that Bill might be embarrassed by it, he wrote to tell him what he'd done. Bill replied, "Yes I saw the interview in Gay Sunshine. No, I was not at all upset by the reference to my love life. I cannot understand why you think it at all remarkable to come when fucked. Lots of people do I find. Also people come from being beaten, kissed, etc. It's all electric brain stimulation. As you may know you can now make someone come by pressing a button."[22]

Just as he had with Marker, Bill kept making up weird routines about the idea of parasitic symbiosis, like Bradley the Buyer in *The Naked Lunch*, who schlupps up the District Supervisor in some unspeakable manner. Bill was hoping to please and attract Allen with these routines, and in normal circumstances Allen would have found them highly amusing, but this was sending chills down his spine. Ginsberg said, "Burroughs will gross out in all sorts of situations that other people would think would be untouchable to begin with. He not only touches them, but he grosses out on them and turns them into comedy so that what is created is that attitude of everything is permitted, or at least as much is permitted in writing as is permitted by the mind in private."[23] Bill's routines were turning Allen off. Ginsberg's own sexual preference was for younger, straight young men who were "making an exception" for him; Bill was twelve years older and gay. It was Allen who was making the exception because of his love and respect for Bill. When Bill began talking seriously of taking Allen with him to Tangier, Allen blurted out, "But I don't want your ugly old cock." Bill froze.

Ginsberg later said, "It wounded him terribly because it was like complete physical rejection in a way I didn't mean. Like a heart blow that severed the trust, because I'd freaked out for that moment and regretted it ever since."[24] Bill began to actively plan his move to Europe. He told Alan Ansen that he wanted to move to Tangier or Rome and steep himself in vice. Ansen, who was gay and about to move to Rome, liked the sound of this and decided Bill would be a good traveling companion. In the end they traveled separately and agreed to meet in Rome.

Relations with Kerouac, though amicable, were no longer as close as they once were. Allen had asked him for a blurb and for a quote to be used in a *New York Times* literary column to help publicize *Junkie* but Kerouac, despite living off Burroughs in Mexico, refused to help his friend, telling Ginsberg, "I do not want my name used in conjunction with habit forming drugs while a pseudonym conceals the real name of the author thus protecting him from prosecution but not myself. [...] Especially I do not want to be misquoted as saying that 'I dig the pseudonymous William Lee as one of the key figures of the Beat Generation.' My remarks on the subject of either pseudonymous author or the generation are at your disposal through the proper channels, from my pen and through my agent."[25]

Burroughs's relationship with Kerouac had always contained an element of suspicion and hostility, probably from as far back as his warning to Kerouac of becoming tied to his adored mother's apron strings. Burroughs said, "It would be typical of him to use a name for me in a book that I didn't like. He called me Old Bull Lee in *On the Road*. It was a peculiarity of Kerouac's, this undercover, covert hostility that he had. I don't think he thought of it as being hostile but it certainly was. [...] Kerouac always liked to do things to annoy me. So someone who hated what I had written, he would be sure to bring that person around. He brought around some jerk who said that the prose in *Junkie* stinks. He did that quite deliberately. More so, this jerk was known for his violence, his physical attacks on people. [...] I was just leaving for Europe the next day, going to Tangier. He did it a number of times, people who didn't like my work, or didn't like me, or were insulting and insufferable."[26]

Burroughs left for Rome on TS *Nea Hellas* on December 1, 1953. As usual, he found fault in the service. "In all my experience as a traveller I have never encountered such food and service and accommodations. Long greasy hairs in the scrambled eggs, no hot water, dirty state rooms, unwashed dishes. This is the crummiest line in the industry."[27] He was getting himself into shape, ready for Europe: "As for Rome. In all my experience as a traveller I never see a more miserable place."[28]

Ginsberg was left to close down the apartment. He intended to move to California, taking a scenic route through southern Mexico to visit the Mayan ruins at Chiapas. He sold the furniture, stored his books with his father, leaving the apartment empty except for the huge orgone accumulator that Bill had built in the bedroom, taking up much of the floor space. An unpublished Ginsberg poem despairs over it:

> And the great blue pool of bedspread running from
> my torso down the bed.
> And the inaudible stupid snout of the unbelievable
> homemade orgone accumulator sticking over the foot of
> the bed.
> Empty valises over the door on shelves—but not
> to be used.

2. When in Rome

It was winter and it was cold when Burroughs arrived in Rome on December 12, 1953, and he did not like it at all. He was unable to find a Roman equivalent of the San Remo and he was not permitted to have visitors in his hotel room. He told Allen, "A Roman 'bar' is a hole in the wall soda-and-ice-cream joint, no toilet and no place to sit down, with the door propped open or missing altogether where you can gulp a drink with a cold, blue hand."[29] He huddled in his room in his overcoat, reading *The Invisible Man*. Alan Ansen finally arrived, which cheered Bill up a little. Burroughs had not bothered to see any of the Roman sights, but Ansen managed to drag him out, telling Allen, "The fountains are wonderful (even old Cactus Boy melted at the sight of Trevi)."[30] Burroughs was not convinced and booked passage to Tangier. Alan went on to Venice, where he lived for a number of years, making frequent trips to Tangier to visit Bill. Burroughs was about to make a fresh start in a country where he knew no one.

BOOK FOUR

The Classic Stations of the Earth

Chapter Twenty-Two

We are torn between a nostalgia for the familiar and an urge for the foreign and strange. As often as not, we are homesick most for the places we have never known. All men are lonely. But sometimes it seems to me that we Americans are the loneliest of all. Our hunger for foreign places and new ways has been almost like a national disease. Our literature is stamped with a quality of longing and unrest, and our writers have been great wanderers.

—Carson McCullers[1]

1. Bill and the Boys

Tangier was very important. It was here that Burroughs really became a writer. Most of *The Naked Lunch* and *Interzone* was written here; the "Talking Asshole" routine, Dr. Benway, Marv and Clem, A.J. were all developed here. It was where Bill achieved happiness for the first time since the killing of Joan, but it was also where he was to endure his worst ever phase of drug addiction.

From Rome Bill had gone to Naples, then taken a boat to Algeciras from Sicily on January 4, 1954, docking en route at Syracuse, Malta, and Barcelona. It was a ten-day voyage, tourist class, and Bill had to share a cabin with four other people. It was awful. From Algeciras he took the ferry across the strait to Tangier. From the sea, Tangier looked like a collection of whitewashed blocks, like a box of sugar cubes scattered over a series of low hills; an animated Cézanne. At the port, he was met by the usual squabbling mob of "guides," who soon directed him to a hotel. The population at that time was more or less segregated: the Moors, *Tanjawis*, in the Medina, and the Europeans, *Tangerinos*, living in the New Town, where the Moroccans rarely went. Bill opted for the Medina.

Tangier then was unique in the world: an international zone in a French colony, run collectively by eight nations and with local representation. It challenged the very notion of the nation-state; it also challenged the financial certainties that most countries, including the United States, operated under. In Tangier there was freedom from taxes, freedom to exchange the

251

world's currencies, there were no customs duties on goods in transit, and anyone could trade in gold or start a company and trade in secret. No visa was needed to enter and you could stay as long as you liked.

The International Zone was run by the Big Four Committee of French, British, Italian, and Spanish ministers. The committee had the final say on all issues, though the Zone was nominally controlled by the administrator, a puppet governor. By law he had to be Dutch, Belgian, Portuguese, or Swedish, and held office for two years on a rotating basis. Each nation had its own judge: two French, two Spanish, one each from Belgium, Britain, Italy, Spain, Portugal, Sweden, Morocco, and the United States. They were responsible for the administration of the law regarding disputes between foreigners and Moroccans, and foreigners with each other. The Americans, who were not part of the committee, had a unique system in which they alone tried and judged their own people (meaning that a Moroccan was bound to lose in a dispute with an American). As capital of the International Zone, Tangier had fifty-two banks, and the boulevard Pasteur was lined with the booths of money-changers.

Tangier had a population of 180,000, of which 100,000 were Moors. The city was surrounded by *bidonvilles*, shakily constructed from sheets of cardboard and petrol cans, with old rags to caulk the ramshackle walls. There was no drainage, water, heating, or light, and little protection from the incessant rains of winter or the icy nights. There was no income tax and therefore no money for social services. Fewer than one in ten children attended primary school. A laborer's wage was capped at thirty pesetas a day, leaving no possibility for advancement. At the time of writing this book, more than 60 percent of the population is still illiterate.

Americans of Bill's generation arrived in Tangier with a preconceived notion of Morocco, based in part upon popular fiction and Hollywood films: Robert Hichens's *Garden of Allah* (1904), set in Algeria, and the classic 1936 version starring Marlene Dietrich; P. C. Wren's French Foreign Legion adventure *Beau Geste*, filmed in 1926 with Ronald Colman and William Powell, and again in 1939 with Gary Cooper and Ray Milland; Edith Hull's *The Sheik* (1919), which launched Rudolph Valentino's career when filmed by Paramount in 1921; and many others, including Michael Curtiz's film *Casablanca* (1942); Alfred Hitchcock's *The Man Who Knew Too Much* starring Peter Lorre (1934, remade by Hitchcock in 1956 with James Stewart and Doris Day); and a torrent of popular novels such as Edith Hull's *Sons of the Sheik* (1925) and *The Captive of the Sahara* (1931).

Bill headed for the Socco Chico to look for boys. His hotel would not permit visitors to his room and there were no cheap hotels for the purpose; as soon as the proprietors saw what the deal was, they upped their prices, and the boys didn't like hanging around in public. Burroughs told Ginsberg, "Ali is getting worried about his standing in the shoe-shine set. [...] He thumps his little scrawny chest and says 'I am a man.' Oh God! Such shit I could hear in Clayton, Mo." He was unable to score for opium, and the marijuana he bought was rough and burned his throat. He told Allen, "I like Tanger less all the time."[2] (Burroughs always used the official French spelling: Tanger.)

He didn't know anyone at all. He had gone to Tangier, attracted by reading Paul Bowles's *Let It Come Down* and *The Sheltering Sky*, but Bowles was away and Burroughs was unable to find the supposed writers' colony. His immediate reaction was to blame Bowles: "What's all this old Moslem culture shit? One thing I have learned. I know what Arabs do all day and all night. They sit around smoking cut weed and playing some silly card game. And don't ever fall for this inscrutable oriental shit like Bowles puts down (that shameless faker). They are just a gabby, gossipy simpleminded, lazy crew of citizens."[3]

Within a few days he met a Spanish boy who rented him a room in a small house in the cerrado de Medellin, a dead-end passage among the narrow alleyways and workshops of the medieval walled city. He lived there for about a month while he took his bearings. A week after arriving he attended an art opening of paintings by Brion Gysin at the Hotel Rembrandt on boulevard Pasteur but couldn't connect with him. Burroughs: "He didn't exactly snub me but he made it quite clear that he didn't want anything to do with me. He later said it was because he was into Arabs and I was into Spanish, and that was a bad mix."[4] Bill had both Spanish and Moroccan boyfriends but after so much time in Mexico found it easier to speak Spanish than French, the colonial language of Morocco, and was more at home with Spanish culture.

By now Burroughs had found the right bars—Dean's and the Parade—but had not yet adopted his chameleon role and adjusted to fit in. "The most loathsome types produced by the land of the free are represented in the American Colony of Tanger. There are like 2 American bars. No 1 I hit dead cold sober at 1 o'clock on a Sunday afternoon. Horrible vista of loud-mouthed, red-faced drunks, falling off bar stools, puking in corners, a Céline nightmare. Bar No 2 is stocked with the dreariest breed of piss elegant, cagy queens. [...] Nowadays I spend my time smoking weed with shoeshine boys in Arab cafés. Their manners are better and their conversation quite as interesting."[5]

However, things quickly improved: "I have a room in the best district for 50 cents a day,"[6] a meal in the Medina was twenty cents, boys cost a dollar or less. Bill always protected himself with Aureomycin pro(phylactic), an antibiotic cream, which was expensive at three dollars "for adequate pro coverage fore and aft." The room was in Anthony "Tony Dutch" Reithorst's male brothel at 1 calle de los Arcos, now renamed rue Khay-attine. It was on the corner with the rue des Chrétiens, now the rue des Almohades. Calle de los Arcos was a narrow alleyway beginning in an archway in the Socco Chico, then running behind the Café Central. Tony ran a string of Spanish boys but could get you anything you wanted. He was pale and portly, with a cherubic face, dressed neatly in a suit and tie, and was often seen sitting outside cafés in the Medina or walking his two poodles. He was sometimes accompanied by a beautiful woman, a friend of his who provided young women for other women. Tony rented two of his small colorless rooms to guests, lived in a third, and used the backroom kitchen-restaurant as the waiting room for the assignations he set up for English, American, and German tourists. There he offered lunch to all the madams from the Black Cat and the legal whorehouses. There was little that went on in the Tangier sex business that Tony didn't know about or have a hand in, and it didn't do to cross him. He had a heavy Dutch accent and spoke of the Arabs as the "Arabics." Burroughs remembered Tony once told him a story that ended, "And in this house there was living also one dirty whore and she sleep with my *poy*. But the police come and take her to the prison and that's what she get to sleep with my *poy*."[7] A month after he arrived Bill was able to report to Allen Ginsberg that he had been to bed with three Arabs since he arrived but was unable to tell them apart. In fact he wondered if it might have been the same boy. "Next time I'll notch one of his ears."[8] By April 22 he was already with Kiki, a Spanish boy who was to feature in his dreams for the rest of his life.

Typically, we are never told Kiki's surname; he is just a boy. His father had been killed in Spain by the Fascists in the Civil War, and the persecution continued in Morocco: the Spanish occupied Tangier in World War II and shot all the Republican supporters they could find. Burroughs, normally the most apolitical of men, was always clear in his condemnation of Franco: "And America supports that lousy bastard who is no better than Hitler!"[9] If his father had died then, Kiki must have been fifteen to eighteen years of age when he met Burroughs.

⁓

One of the first people Burroughs met in Tangier was David Woolman, who lived in the room next to his at Tony Dutch's brothel. He was an adopted boy from a well-off family in Indiana who had been an air force captain during the Korean War. He was tall, slim, muscular, with fair hair and a high-pitched, whiny voice, described by Alan Ansen as "very outer-directed, also liked small boys." He appears in *The Naked Lunch* as Marv.

He was effeminate and superficial, or at least pretended to be. He wrote two columns for the Casablanca-based weekly *Moroccan Courier*: "Socco Chico" about Tangier, and "Chips Off the Old Rock" about Gibraltar, and, as Barnaby Bliss, contributed a weekly gossip column, "The Spirit of St. Louis," to the *Tangier Gazette*. He was to write the standard history of the Rif Wars, *Rebels in the Rif: Abd el Krim and the Rif Rebellion*.[10] Bill found him fun to be with. To fill his columns Woolman was always out on the town, and Bill often accompanied him. Restaurants always gave them a 10 percent discount in the hope that Dave would mention them. Bill enjoyed Woolman's company, but was always disturbed by his preference for very young boys. Bill told Allen, "No lower age limit on boys. An American I know keeps a 13 year old kid. 'If they can walk I don't want them.' "[11]

Bill and Dave paid sixty cents to watch two Arab boys screw each other. The boys protested, saying, "Molo," it's bad, it's bad to do this, then they began giggling. David said, "Sí, molo schmolo, todos molos," all bad.[12] Bill reported the incident at length to Allen Ginsberg: "We demanded semen too, no half-assed screwing. So I asked Marv: 'Do you think they will do it?' and he says: 'I think so. They are hungry.' They did it. Made me feel sorta like a dirty old man."[13] Bill used his report almost verbatim in the "Black Meat" section of *The Naked Lunch*.[14] "We took the two boys back to Dave's room and told them what we wanted. After some coy giggling they agreed, and took off their ragged clothes. Both of them had slender, beautiful boy bodies. Dave was M.C. he pointed to Boy 2 and said: 'All right, you screw him first' pointing to Boy 1. Boy 1 lay down on his stomach on the bed. Boy 2 rubbed spit on his prick and began screwing him. Dave said: '*Leche* we want *leche*.' Leche means milk, Spanish for jissum—the boy contracted convulsively and his breath whistled through his teeth. He lay still for a moment on top of the other boy then shoved himself off with both hands. He showed us the jissum on his prick and asked for a towel. Dave threw him one and he carefully wiped his prick. Then he lay down on his stomach and Boy 1 took over. He was more passionate. He got mad because Boy 2 kept his ass contracted and pounded on his buttocks with his fist. Finally he got it in and began screwing violently. Boy 2 groaned in protest. Boy 1 came almost immediately, his buttocks quivering in spasms. He sighed then rolled free...I see both boys every day. They will do it anytime for forty cents, which is standard price."[15]

Bill described this in full to Ginsberg partly because he knew it would excite him, and partly because he knew Allen would have serious reservations because of the boys' poverty. Bill used this in *The Naked Lunch* to purposely annoy his readers, a Swiftian gesture to reveal their prurience and to undermine their middle-class values. It was an illustration of the well-known Thomas Macaulay adage: "The Puritan hated bear-baiting not because it gave pain to the bear, but because it gave pleasure to the spectators." This is true of most of the erotic scenes in *The Naked Lunch*, which are based on the idea that sex is usually some kind of exploitation—the hanging scenes are both a critique of pornographic movies and the racist policies then pertaining in the southern states. Alan Ansen felt that Burroughs was a very moral writer and that the most important quality in his writing was in fact tenderness. "It is a great key to what makes his work so wonderful. It's what I call the melody as opposed to the fugato. That enormous compassion is very very basic."[16]

2. Bar la Mar Chica

After less than two months in Tangier, Bill was able to write to Allen, "Tanger is looking up. Meeting the local expatriates. Junkies, queers, drunks."[17] Bill's kind of people. His social life now centered around the Parade, the Café Central, which was just around the corner from his room, and the Bar la Mar Chica, at 19 calle Bordj, a dim dockside Andalusian bar open twenty-four hours a day. At one end was a small rickety stage with a badly painted backdrop of a Spanish patio with an open window in the center and a window box filled with half-dead geraniums. There were two more or less permanent performers. One was Malaguena, a dumpy middle-aged flamenco singer who had often drunk so much brandy that she was unable to climb onstage and resorted instead to begging for money from the audience. She was nicknamed "Miss Pits" because she smelled so bad. The other was Louis, a slim, elegant gypsy dancer who performed to the clicking of castanets, a violin, and Spanish guitar. The proprietor was, according to Burroughs, "a man of great strength and exceedingly evil disposition. Beautiful Arab boy behind the bar. Languid animal grace, a bit sulky, charming smile. Every queer in Tanger has propositioned him, but he won't play." The bar was filled with young Spaniards and the occasional Arab dockworker. The American bullfighter known as El Rubio de Boston was a regular; though scarred by the horns of the bulls, he was admired for his courage reentering the ring. The British writer Rupert Croft-Cooke was there most nights, and the Honourable David Herbert took his guests there as an example of "local color." Though he disapproved of Herbert's slumming, Croft-Cooke reported one bon mot from Herbert:

> "Tell me," said a young woman who was just learning about the sexual complications of Tangier. "Which is the one who has just come in? Jack or Jill?"
> "That? Oh *that's* just the pail of water," said David.[18]

The Parade Bar, a single-story building on the rue de Fez, just off the boulevard, had a garden, offering a respite from the constant attention of passing beggars found in street cafés. This quiet courtyard was filled with shade trees, a large palm, and eight wobbly iron tables. There was a bitter orange tree from which Rupert Croft-Cooke made marmalade each year. The trio of owners were Jay Haselwood, from Kentucky, tall, handsome, and mustachioed; Bill Chase, a suave New Yorker who managed the kitchen, producing some of the best cuisine in Tangier; and Ira Belline, an older woman, a White Russian, unsmiling and wearing a turban, who was supposed to have been Stravinsky's favorite niece and a designer for the Ballet Russe. All three had worked for the Red Cross in France during the Second World War. Their financial backer was Phyllis de la Faille. The bar was lit by gold reflecting balls, like old-fashioned gas lamps, and there were always fresh flowers. Later, in the sixties, the décor included three highly varnished oil paintings by Stuart Church of half-naked Nubian adolescents wearing feathers and rowing Venetian gondolas ("fruity gondolier murals," as Burroughs put it).

Among the regulars was Leslie Eggleston, from Philadelphia, who often appeared arm in arm with alcoholic women whom no one else could stand, glad to squire them for drinks and food. Bill would sometimes buy him drinks—"he was very very amusing, in a very strange horrible way. Not self-deprecation, no, just shameless mooching."[19] Sometimes Haselwood would order, "That one has been scrounging all evening, don't buy him a drink!" Another regular was Bill Findlay, also from Philadelphia, who together with Eggleston moved in on the mother of Brian Power, another Parade regular, in Málaga, claiming to be Power's friend. Findlay and Eggleston made indecent proposals to her servants, drank all the wine, brought back sailors, and refused to leave. Eventually a retired colonel of her acquaintance arrived and bodily threw them out. Bill loved these kinds of stories.

All these people were observed by Burroughs and added to his cast of characters. One old reprobate was Gerald Hamilton, the original Mr. Norris from Christopher Isherwood's *Mr. Norris Changes Trains*. It was not until *The Place of Dead Roads* that he made an appearance, but then it was deadly: "An old-queen voice, querulous, petulant, cowardly, the evil old voice of Gerald Hamilton."[20]

The view from Tangier across the strait was sometimes so clear you could see the mountains of Spain and even the village houses. Sometimes it was lost in white glare. The *levante*, the *ech cherqi*, could blow for days, making the beautiful wide beach impossible to visit. Still, the summer lasted

until November and it was rarely unbearably hot. The air had a particular luminosity that had delighted painters such as Matisse. In spring the
breeze sang in the palm trees of the Villa de France. Tangier before independence was a smaller, quieter city. You could sit in the terrace of the
Café de Paris and listen to the sounds of the cicadas in the eucalyptus trees
before they were drowned out by the noise of traffic. The atmosphere had
a particular smell, a mixture of burning charcoal, excrement, sweat, kif,
and other fugitive elements that was unmistakably Oriental. Bill began to
like the city.

He lived just around the corner from the Socco Chico, which was then
lined on both sides with cafés: the Café Fuentes, the Tingis, the España,
Pilo's, and the Café Central. Bill became an afternoon regular at the Café
Central, which served beer and wine, as well as coffee and the ubiquitous
glasses of sweet mint tea. It was open twenty-four hours. The stagelike
architectural features of the nineteenth-century façades were perfect for
the ongoing show, which was like a Brueghel come to life. Elderly Moors
in white djellabahs and white beards, Jews in skull caps, peanut-sellers,
bootblacks, money-changers, and beggars crowded the street. Young
boys, eyes eaten by trachoma, were led by the hand by the eldest among
them who tapped the way along the cluttered alleys with a long stick. Evidence of tuberculosis and syphilis was everywhere. Berber women carried
enormous loads of charcoal on their backs, their noses frequently eaten
away by disease possibly associated with their trade, followed by their
menfolk riding donkeys. Trains of mules, laden with building materials
or charcoal, pushed through the crowds. Bill's new friend Brian Howard
described Bill at the center of it all in a letter:

> Everyone within sight, from the tiny children to the elderly, fat waiters in tar-
> booshes, is for sale. And the hubbub is appalling. The lights are just coming on
> in Mangharan's Celebrated Shirts opposite me and the smell of Kief cigarettes
> is asphyxiating. [...] The other person at the table is a nice, if slightly long-
> winded, ex-Harvard creature of forty who is endeavouring to cure himself of
> morphinomania by taking this new medicine which the Germans invented
> during the war. There are several trade names for it. He uses two. Eukodol
> and Heptanal. Unfortunately the effects are so much stronger, and much more
> delicious than morphine itself that he now spends his whole time running
> from chemist to chemist buying it—and spends all his money on it, too.[21]

Bill discovered Eukodol within days of arriving in Tangier and in less
than two months he reported to Allen, "I am hooked. [...] Some stuff
called Eukodol which is best junk kick I ever had. Start Dolly cure in a
few days now."[22] (Dollys were Dolophine, now known as methadone.)

Eukodol was dihydroxycodeinone, a morphine substitute made by Merck in Darmstadt as a painkiller, but they found that it was euphoric, an unfortunate side effect that stopped them manufacturing it. It was made from codeine with its strength increased six times by dehydration. It was a short-acting drug, with the high only lasting three or four hours, which made it particularly addictive as the euphoria made the user want more. According to Bill, "it had a sort of a lift like a combination of cocaine and morphine. It was great."[23] By the beginning of April, Bill was shooting Eukodol every four hours. He told Allen, "God knows what kind of habit I am getting. When I kick this habit I expect fuses will blow out in my brain from overcharge and black sooty blood will run out eyes, ears and nose and staggering around the room acting out routines like Roman Emperor routine in a bloody sheet."[24]

Most people found Brian Howard impossible. He had no tolerance for alcohol and was thrown out of every bar and hotel in Tangier, including the Minzah, the Parade, the Mar Chica, Tony Dutch's, and Dean's Bar, where he called the proprietor a "pretentious West Indian nigger." Eventually he and Sammy, his Cockney boyfriend, finished up at the Maybrook Hotel on the outskirts, which was the only place that would have him. Burroughs introduced Howard to Dolophine. "He was impossible when he was drinking so I said, 'Why don't you try a little junk instead?' and that made a great improvement. Instead of drinking he got onto morphine and methadone and some kind of junk; it calmed him down and he was still fine."[25] However beneficent this was for Howard, it proved to be a big mistake for Bill. "He sweeps into drug stores, 'chemist shops' as he calls them, and says, 'Give me four tubes of M tablets quickly.' He has decided that M is after all more 'amusing' than Dolophine. 'And you know, the strangest thing. I simply don't *feel* right in the morning until I've had my medicine.' "[26] Brian Howard burned the town down, and whereas before Burroughs could buy junk over the counter, scripts were now required.

Burroughs found Howard very sweet when sober and enjoyed his literary connections. He was an old friend of Auden's and Isherwood's and was one of the characters in Evelyn Waugh's *Brideshead Revisited*. Howard was quite a comfort to him in the absence of communication with Allen, extravagantly praising Bill's writing. Bill told Kerouac, "Right now I am in urgent need of routine receivers. Whenever I encounter the impasse of unrequited affection my only recourse is routines. (Really meant for the loved one, to be sure, but in a pinch somebody else can be pressed into service.) And Brian really digs my routines. But he is leaving tomorrow."[27]

Chapter Twenty-Three

Looking down at my shiny, dirty trousers that haven't been changed in months, the days gliding by, strung on a syringe with a long thread of blood, it is easy to forget sex and drink and all sharp pleasures of the body in this Limbo of pleasure, this thick cocoon of comfort.[1]

1. Morphine Minnie

Bill's neighbor the gossip columnist David Woolman knew everyone, and in April he took Burroughs to meet Paul Bowles at the Hotel Marsillia in the Medina where he was living. Bill took along his contract from Ace Books, hoping to discuss it with a published author. Unfortunately Bowles was recovering from a dose of paratyphoid and was on his sickbed. He reclined in his dressing gown, smoking a cigarette in a holder. As Bill had already signed the contract, which was terrible, Bowles simply suggested that Bill get an agent for his next book.

Bowles didn't follow up on the contact and in July Bill grumbled to Allen that perhaps Bowles wished to avoid him because of his narcotic associations, "fearing possible hassles with customs inspection and authorities in general if he is known to be on familiar terms with me—guilt by association."[2] This assessment was probably partially correct, as Bowles had a terrible fear of being expelled from Tangier, but Bowles was also very passive and mostly responded to situations rather than creating them.

Rumors soon spread that Bill was a drug addict. The newly appointed British police chief, Gerald Richardson, already referred to him as "Morphine Minnie." All this upset his landlord. Bill told Kerouac, "So Tony, this old Dutch man who runs this whore house I live in, keeps casting me reproachful glances in the hall and saying: 'Ach thirteen years and never before I haff such a thing in my house. And since two weeks are here in Tangiers two good English gentlemens I know since long times. With them I could make good business except my house is so watched at.' However I am still his star boarder and he hesitates to evict me."[3] Bill had been in Tangier less than four months and the police were aware of him. Kiki's mother had disapproved of their relationship and reported him, bursting into Tony Dutch's with a policeman while Bill tried to push Kiki into Dave Woolman's room like a bedroom farce.

In the second week of May, Bill tried to kick. He was shooting Eukodol every two hours. So he paid fifty dollars to an Englishman named Eric Gifford to bring him food and dole out Dolophine over ten days. Gifford took away Bill's clothes to prevent him sneaking out to score. But Bill went into Dave Woolman's room and stole his clothes, bought some Eukodol ampoules, and glutted himself. Gifford of course found out, confiscated the remaining ampoules, and insisted that Woolman lock his door in future. He also took Bill's money away. Bill told Allen, "I am really stuck now. [...] Gifford, he's a hard man. No use trying to coax an extra ampoule out of him. 'By God,' he says, 'I'm being paid to do this and I'm going to do it right.' "[4]

Gifford was a public-school boy[5] first heard of during the war when his house in Tangier, the Villa Harris, was used as a billet for Spanish soldiers. He was arrested by a Spanish patrol, hanging around the building, "offering himself with lowered garments to a long queue of infantrymen who, deprived of womenfolk, were impatient to find relief." Since the Spanish could not reveal the real nature of his offense he was charged with spying. However, as this could not be proved, he was set free. He worked for the British Council in Syria during the war. He was known to the Tangerines as "Calamity" Gifford because he attracted disaster. He had written a guidebook to Greece that didn't sell, then went in with a friend in a scheme to make honey in Trinidad where no honey was produced. They soon found out why: a species of large moth that invaded the hives. The bees flew out and stung the moths to death, an action that caused their own demise, so that soon the hives were surrounded by mounds of dead bees and moths. He returned to Tangier and stopped by Dean's Bar for a drink before returning to the Villa Harris. At the mention of Villa Harris, his friends went quiet and studied their drinks. When he got there he saw why. As it was apparently not being used, the locals had helped themselves to the roof tiles, the windows, the walls, until nothing was left but the foundations; even the floor and doorstep were gone. He then taught English until Tanjawi thieves broke into his new apartment and stole all of his possessions. This gave rise to his sobriquet "Calamity." Even his social column for the *Tangier Gazette* came to an unfortunate end when he had a pointless argument with the editor. By the time Burroughs arrived, he was impecunious. He became a good friend of Burroughs's, who saw a lot of him and used him as the model for Leif the Unlucky in *The Naked Lunch*.

Gifford's best efforts to help Bill kick did not work, and by June 16 Bill was back shooting up every two hours. It was the worst habit he ever had. "A shot of Eukodol hits the head first with a rush of pleasure. Ten minutes later you want another shot. Between shots you are just killing time. I can't control this stuff any more than I can control the use of coke. [...] From taking so many shots I have an open sore where I can slide the needle right into a vein. The sore stays open like a red, festering mouth, swollen and obscene."⁶ In an outtake from *The Naked Lunch* Burroughs wrote, "put leeches on my needle scars to suck out the poison,"⁷ which sounds like a report of actual experience. He scoured Tangier, looking for any remaining supplies of Eukodol. "I think I bought all the Eukodol in the place, then I had to shift to methadone in ampoules. I got all there was."⁸

Bill had quickly found drugs, boys, and drinking companions in Tangier, so the severity of his addiction was not caused by loneliness or unfamiliarity with his new surroundings. But he was still heartbroken by Allen's rejection and what appeared to be an attempt to ignore him completely by not replying to his many letters. When Bill left New York for Europe, Allen had gone south. He hitchhiked to Florida and spent Christmas with Bill's parents in Palm Beach. From there he continued to Havana and reached Mexico in time for the New Year celebrations. His intention was to investigate Mayan culture, and he had made arrangements to stay free of charge in archaeological camps. He went first to Chichén Itzá. All this time he wrote regularly to his family and friends, including Bill, but unknown to him, the Mexican postal service had lost all but a few of his letters. In Tangier Bill grew desperate. He wrote to Jack, "Allen's neglect will drive me to some extravagance of behavior. I don't know what I will do, but it will be the terror of the earth. You must remonstrate with him. I didn't expect him to act like this (not a line in four months) and I didn't expect I would feel so deeply hurt if he did."⁹ He asked Jack to write to Allen and tell him of the pain he was causing.

Allen had told Bill to write him care of American Express in Mexico City, but his letter was returned unclaimed. "I don't mind he doesn't write if he wants to feel completely free for a while," Bill told Jack, "but he could have spared me all this hurt—(which I am not playing up, which is worse than I describe in my letters to him)—by simply dropping me a line (as he apparently did to you) saying he would be out of touch for a while. [...] P.S. No matter what Allen says I want to hear it understand? If he says something that you know would hurt me, please don't keep it from me. I want to know. Nothing is worse than waiting like this day after day for a letter that doesn't come... THIS IS SERIOUS JACK, DON'T let me down."¹⁰

After visiting Uxmal, Allen had set off for the ruins at Palenque in Chiapas, where he met Karen Shields, a writer and actress. She invited him to stay on her coca *finca*, deep in the jungle, and he spent most of April and the beginning of May there writing poetry. Storms washed out the track from the *finca* to Salto de Agua, the nearest town, and made the rivers impassable so they could not get their mail. Allen had written to Neal Cassady on April 6, urgently requesting money, which Neal had sent at once, but the funds were returned from Salto de Agua as "unclaimed." Bill asked his parents to cable Allen thirty dollars from his next month's allowance, which they did, but the money disappeared en route. Bill wrote to Allen's father, asking him to make inquiries at the U.S. embassy in Mexico City, and asked Lucien to contact the Mexican branch of UPI. Bill told Jack, "I am afraid he may be in serious trouble, perhaps held incommunicado in jail. To stupid people he *looks* like a communist."[11] He concluded, "I don't know what I would do if anything happened to Allen. I guess you have seen the letters I wrote to him and have some idea of how much he means to me." Neal Cassady was also concerned; three letters in a row had been returned. Allen, of course, was happily writing to his family, to Bill, Neal, Lucien, and Jack, from Salto de Agua, but the letters were all lost. Then one finally reached Bill and put his mind at rest.

Bill told Allen how worried he had been at his disappearance. On May 11 he wrote, "I will send along two more letters. You haven't seen anything yet. There were even some letters I destroyed as too extreme."[12] The intensity of Bill's feelings concerned Allen deeply. He wrote Neal, "He sure is lonely or imagines himself such and I guess it drives him off the road at times. [...] This kind of need, with which I cannot but sympathize & try to do something real about [...] will be a real problem. But of our friendship, so complicated now & in some ways difficult [...] I hardly know what to do to straighten out and think probably the loco elements too deep to resolve and so must be put up with—too ingrained with the genius."[13] But Bill saw Allen as the key to dealing with his demons, and Burroughs could not shake loose from his obsession. In July he told him, "You're one of the few people I would want around me if I was dying. [...] That is a special compliment."[14] Burroughs certainly knew how to flatter people. A few days later he told Allen of a dream he had. "We were in the country somewhere like Texas, red clay, roads and farms. I wanted to be with you, but you kept saying like 'today I'm spending with Jack, tomorrow with so and so' and I said 'What about me?', feeling hurt and rejected. Finally I packed my suitcase and went away. [...] Later started down Amazon alone in a canoe."[15] Further sad proof that Burroughs's bluff that he never felt loneliness was untrue.

2. Kells in Morocco

In May, Kells Elvins came to visit from Rome, where he was living with his third wife, the Danish actress Mimi Heinrich. According to Burroughs, Kells "just hated Tangier. Thought it was insane, schizophrenic."[16] Kells wanted Bill to accompany him on a trip across Morocco but it didn't work out. They got as far as Casablanca before parting ways. "Well, I didn't have enough junk. I went back to Tangiers." Kells disapproved of Bill's addiction and decided that it was impossible to travel with him if he was continually seeking out Arab pharmacists to buy junk. Kells went exploring alone. On his return to Tangier, the hard-drinking Elvins soon found a tolerable roost in Dean's Bar. Burroughs very rarely went there. "Dean and I just never hit it off." Bill made an exception for Kells and described a visit to Allen: "We had just been in Dean's Bar where I encountered a barrage of hostility. [...] Dean wanted not to serve me, rolling his eyes in disapproval, but there was Kells, a good customer. (Dean has heard that I am a dope fiend. More than that, he instinctively feels me as a danger, far out, an ill omen.) So I sat there, loaded on tea, savoring their disapproval, rolling it on my tongue with a glass of good dry sherry." Kells, as usual, was very supportive of Bill and clearly concerned about his drug addiction. Bill complained, "I don't think I have much talent for writing," but Kells told him, "You know what I think? I think you're better than Paul Bowles and Peter Mayne, I think you're better than all these people, you just don't know it." Bill was very sorry when Kells left for Madrid to join his wife in Copenhagen in the beginning of July.

Just as Kells left, Bill was stricken with a painful swelling of his ankle so that it was difficult even to walk around the room. His monthly check was unaccountably delayed so he was not only sick but broke as well. Kells's departure left him in a deep depression, relieved only by visits from Kiki, who sat with him, stroking his head, feeding him on soup and tea, arranging his bedding. It was a week before Dr. Apfel came and diagnosed an acute attack of rheumatic fever, drew off the pus, and prescribed penicillin. "Just like me to contract an adolescent illness."[17] Bill was lucky that no damage to the heart ensued, as many people are invalided for life by such an attack. Even before he was sick, Bill had found himself growing fonder of Kiki, buying him nylon socks, underwear, a toothbrush, and a knife on his saint's day, June 25, as a present. Now Bill told Allen, "(Remember I am broke now and have no money to give him.) Find me an American kid like that. Not that they are easy to come by any place, but Angelo in Mexico was very similar. What I feel with them is not the same as I feel with you, but it is definitely a *relationship*. That is, it involves real affection on both sides and some protoplasmic contact. [...] Actually U.S. provides no counterpart to my relation with Kiki or Angelo."[18]

What Burroughs was looking for in a sexual partner was a "boy" who was "straight"—that is to say who had sex with men for money but whose real preference was for women—and "Oriental." In *Queer* he described Marker as "delicate and exotic and Oriental,"[19] and while in Quito he had told Ginsberg, "The best people in S.A. are the Indians. Certainly the best-looking people. My boy is at least 70% Indian."[20] He described Kiki to Allen as looking like "a South American Indian"[21] and Angelo as having a face that was "Oriental, Japanese-looking, except for his copper skin."[22] In *Interzone* he wrote that "both had very straight black hair, an Oriental look, and lean, slight bodies. Both exuded the same quality of sweet masculine innocence. Lee met the same people wherever he went."[23] By "Oriental" Burroughs meant people whose distant ancestors had arrived in the Americas from Asia. Thus to Burroughs, both American Indians and Mexicans were "Oriental." In boys of Spanish or Indian ancestry he identified "real uncut boy stuff," the essence of adolescent naturalism, fertility, and masculinity. Kiki fit the bill.

As Burroughs wrote in "Lee and the Boys," "Lee was well pleased with Kiki." Bill did not like the process of looking for boys; he was not compulsively promiscuous and did not lose interest in his boys. He had sex with Angelo in Mexico City twice a week for more than a year, and now that he had found Kiki, he was content to stay with him. It was in many ways a sybaritic life, but he found himself getting dangerously fond of Kiki, as he told Jack Kerouac: "I find myself getting jealous of Kiki—he is besieged by importunate queens. In fact, I am downright involved, up to my neck in Maya. He is a sweet kid, and it is so pleasant to loll about in the afternoon smoking tea, sleeping and having sex with no hurry, running leisurely hands over his lean, hard body, and finally we doze off, all wrapped around each other, into the delicious sleep of a hot afternoon in a cool darkened room, a sleep that is different from any other sleep, a twilight in which I savor, with a voluptuous floating sensation, the state of sleep, feeling the nearness of Kiki's young body, the sweet, imperceptible, drawing together in sleep, leg inching over leg, arm encompassing body, hips hitching closer, stiffening organs reaching out to touch warm flesh."[24]

He was so pleased with his description that he repeated much of it in a letter to Ginsberg the same day, adding, "Kiki would be quite at home in 'sophisticated' company. He simply wouldn't try to compete. The only danger would be that he would be pampered and spoiled. Example of his health and simplicity: he had some sort of swelling or infection in his rectum, and I gave him four shots of penicillin. The other day he was sitting on the bed naked and I asked him if his ass was alright. 'Yes' he said with a boyish grin, and putting his hands on his knees rolled himself back showing me his ass. It was done without a trace of prissiness or exhibitionism, beyond a natural joy in his body that any young human male has."[25] Sometimes Bill and Kiki spent as much as sixteen hours together in bed, the room lit by flickering candlelight in a big brass holder, dozing, eating sweet grapes, smoking kif. Kiki said that Bill talked in his sleep and sometimes awoke with a cry.

Inevitably Bill fell in love with him. The realization came toward the end of August when Kiki came in late one night and described in great detail the designs that he proposed to have tattooed on his chest, shoulders, and arms. Bill had hysterics, cried, and begged him not to do it. He had to give him his sports coat, a combat jacket, and ten dollars to promise not to do it. Bill reported to Allen, "I was shocked into an awareness that in a way I love him. Now I know I should not allow myself to be emotionally involved. He doesn't understand and looks at me in bewilderment when I embraced him with special intensity. It is exasperating. I can't really get near him. I feel all-out attempt would be disastrous for me. I know I should let matters rest in status of liaison, fond of him in an offhand way, but it's so dull like that. I notice that sex is much more enjoyable since I feel some variety of love for him."[26]

In a matter of hours after writing those lines to Allen, Bill was brought down to earth about the reality of the situation. In a postscript he wrote, "Kiki was here and hurt me so I am quivering all over. Oh, he'll come around all right because of the $. It hurts me to know that is the reason, at the same time glad that I have that advantage. A complete shambles of feeling. [...] I simply can't take these details lightly: if I do, it's no more than masturbation; if I don't, I get hurt like this."[27] Kiki could be very sulky at times and sometimes shocked Bill with tirades of abuse. Bill told Allen, "I always have a fear with anyone I love that they really hate me and I will suddenly be confronted with their hate,"[28] which was of course what had happened in his sexual relationship with Allen.

All around him he could see Europeans and Americans falling in love with their boys in untenable situations. His friend David Lamont, a Canadian writer, used to weep on Bill's shoulder because he couldn't find his boy, "who was a real little horror, actually." Dave Woolman experienced pangs of jealousy at the thought of his boy going off with another European or American (Arabs were okay). Bill hardened his heart.

Decades later, Burroughs revised his memory of those years, saying, "I didn't really get too much attached to any boyfriend. I preferred it that way, just a perfectly simple relationship. All these people that I saw making fools of themselves over some Arab boy, with their boys, with all this emotional nonsense. Obviously this is a confusion of levels; the boys aren't thinking in these terms at all. They are thinking in very simple terms of advantage, of bettering themselves, and why shouldn't they?"[29] He recognized that the boys were just doing it for money, and that if a better opportunity came along they would take it. There were also certain rules to be followed, as Harold Norse explained to Winston Leyland. "They often put a restriction on the amount and kind of sex they have with you: three orgasms a week, no kissing, and you can't fuck them."[30]

That summer Bill attempted another cure, at Kiki's urging, perhaps because junk had made Bill's sex drive almost completely disappear and Kiki felt his services would no longer be required. Kiki confiscated all his clothes, and they began a reduction cure, using new substitute preparations prescribed for him by Dr. Apfel. Rumor had it that Dr. Apfel was in fact a concentration camp doctor who only pretended to be a German Jewish refugee. Bill didn't care which; he was a good doctor, the best in Tangier.

He was rather looking forward to noon prayers for Friday, August 20, the anniversary of the day the French had exiled the old, much-loved sultan. He happily reported to Allen that in 1952 there had been a riot, with twelve Arabs killed by French police and a Swiss tourist mistaken for French and torn to pieces by the mob. In readiness, Bill had purchased a meat cleaver and a razor-sharp knife; he also had two weapons of his own invention: a Flit gun filled with ammonia, and a piece of lead on the end of a leather thong. "And me caught short without a pistol the one time in my life I really need one!"[31] There was no riot, but Bill demonstrated his weapons when a plague of black rats suddenly infested Tony Dutch's rooms. As Tony screamed and carried on, Bill killed one with his cane. Tony's Chinese orderly killed another in the toilet bowl with a Coca-Cola bottle. Eric Gifford believed they came up out of the sewers. Bill said he felt very "manly."

At this point Bill had not yet become friends with Paul Bowles, and though he spent a lot of time with Dave Woolman, Dave Lamont, and various other members of the Socco Chico set, he still felt that he hadn't properly connected with what was really happening in Tangier. He was also badly strung out on Eukodol, he was depressed, and he yearned for Allen Ginsberg's company. In addition, he was plagued by rectal warts, which, considering he was a "bottom" in sexual relations, meant that this was a particularly troublesome inconvenience. He determined to have them operated on in New York, and from there visit Allen Ginsberg in San Francisco. If circumstances seemed propitious, they would share an apartment.

Chapter Twenty-Four

The book grabs you by the throat. [...] It leaps in bed with you, and performs unmentionable acts. Then it thrusts a long cold needle deep in your spine and gives you an injection of ice water.[1]

1. Looking for Ritchie

Bill boarded the *Saturnia*, on the Italian Line, in Gibraltar, bound for New York, on September 7, 1954, and arrived on the sixteenth at 8:00 a.m. He planned to have his operation, then visit his family in Florida before continuing to San Francisco to see Allen. Kerouac had foolishly written to Bill telling him that Allen "secretly wants to be with you as before otherwise you see Bill he wouldn't write and discuss and rehash so much," something that Kerouac regarded as a "poor little kind white lie I told Bill—to make him feel good." This now resulted in a wasted trip to the United States by Burroughs (who could have had his operation in London or Paris) and tremendous stress and anxiety on Ginsberg's part, who was on the point of moving into an apartment on Nob Hill to live a straight life as an advertising executive with his girlfriend, Sheila Boucher. The thought of Burroughs arriving to demand his time and love and attention threw Allen's life into chaos. He told Kerouac, "I will do everything I can for and to Bill, anything he wants, but the impossibilities of his demands are ultimately inescapable unless I let him carry me off forever to Asia or something to satisfy his conception of his despair and need."

The news that Allen had fallen in love with Sheila and wanted to live with her came as a huge shock to Bill. He told Kerouac, "Now Allen is talking about making it with a chick, and I am really upset and worried. If I get out to Frisco and he is making it with a chick I might as well turn around and start back. You know how U.S. chicks are. They want it all. It would be the end of my relationship with Allen. At this point I couldn't stand to be around him all the time with no sex. It would be too much of a strain on me."[2] Allen pleaded with Kerouac to try and set Bill straight. "The situation with Sheila will be a madhouse. I don't know how to man-

268

age it. Bill will enforce his idea so much he will *make* me reject it [. . .] he still puts all his life in my hands. [. . .] I can't be his one sole and only contact forever, I can only be his nearest and best." Although it pained him to do it, his fear of sharing a place with a frantic, jealous, and possessive Burroughs forced Allen to write him a stiff, formal letter explaining that he loved him but that he could not be his sexual partner. Allen reported to Kerouac, "Confusion reigns! After an exchange of shocking letters, Bill seems to have come off the distraction-intensity. [. . .] My letter to him was perhaps too strong but subsequent correspondence has straightened out some of the bad feeling and left the whole situation a lot relieved." Bill reported to Allen that Kerouac was angry at him for writing such a hurtful letter, but as Allen explained, "If I had not written so he would continue in state of tragic self-pity absorption perhaps. Even Bill knows at heart."

Burroughs ran into Alan Ansen, who was back in New York, arranging to rent his house to the novelist William Gaddis. Ansen was staying at the Hotel Saint George on Henry Street in Brooklyn Heights, and Bill joined him there. Bill was clearly very broke and kept asking Alan for money, about ten dollars at a time. Alan kept giving it to him. "Then I saw him consulting with a man with a moustache, who turned out to be Ritchie, the famous drug peddler, and after about four or five times the penny dropped, and I said 'Oh, that's what you want it for.'" Ansen recommended him to Dr. David Protetch, Stravinsky's doctor, who was able to fix Bill up with something. Ansen: "I thought he was a kind of guru and it was a good work to give him money. He was always very very impressive. Not so much as a writer but a personality."[3]

Meanwhile, while all the letter-writing was going on, Bill had his operation with Dr. James Leake. Dr. Leake asked him how he was fixed for money and Bill explained that he had an income of about two hundred dollars a month. Leake said he would do it for $150, and when he heard that the hospital room would cost twenty dollars a day, he told Bill he thought he could get him out of there in two days. "Got rid of the problem forever." Bill was upset that Kerouac did not visit or telephone the hospital.

As soon as he had recovered enough to travel, Bill visited his family in Florida. It was not a success. He could not stay with them at 202 Sanford Road in Palm Beach because they had converted the spare bedroom into a television room, so he had to make do with a mediocre hotel nearby at five dollars a day. His parents, faced with their strung-out son, whose child they were bringing up at their expense, kept asking him what made him return to the States in the first place. Even worse, his parents were not doing as well as they used to with their garden supply business and wanted to reduce his allowance by half. Bill was faced with the awful possibility, at forty years of age, of having to find a job. There was little in his résumé that would appeal to a future employer. In fact the only thing he could think of was dealing heroin with his old friend Ritchie. As usual, Bill looked for someone else to blame for his predicament. He told Allen, "Understand I forgive you the letter, but for the record, I still think there was a lot to forgive."[4] He wished Allen had changed his mind about their sharing an apartment before Bill had left Tangier, in which case he would still have been there and not trapped in Florida. "Well, maybe *you* have some suggestions as to what I should do now," he told Allen, making it very clear. "Not to mince words, I *did* come back to U.S. to see you. Just wanted to be sure you knew that, and to put you in cognizance of my generally altered situation." In the end he thought, "Maybe I can blackmail them into sending me back to Tangier."[5]

Marker was in Miami, looking for a job, and Bill went to visit him. They went to visit Betty Jones, his friend from the Bounty in Mexico City, who had separated from her husband, Glenn, and was living in Hollywood, Florida. But soon Bill was back in New York City and booked to sail for Gibraltar on November 20, 1954, having presumably extracted the fare from his long-suffering parents, who, perhaps relieved to see him go, had relented and kept his allowance at two hundred dollars a month. He wrote Allen, "They have a bad conscience about me. Besides they've been giving me money so long it's a habit. They don't have what it takes to kick the habit and me out on my ass which is what I would do in their place."[6]

2. The Socco Chico Set

Back in Tangier Burroughs immediately resumed his life with Kiki at Tony's brothel: "back in the Promised Land flowing with junk and boys."[7] Presumably no provision had been made for Kiki when he left, and as Burroughs had expected to live with Ginsberg in San Francisco, Kiki had not been expecting to see him again. However Bill and Kiki were soon spending fifteen to twenty hours every day in bed. He told Allen, "I didn't realize what a drag the U.S. can be, until I hit a free country and get relief in every direction." Unfortunately much of that relief came from Eukodol, which he began using again as soon as he hit town. Though convenient in many different ways, Tony Dutch's had its disadvantages, one of which was the taunting by the street boys—"You like Beeeg one Meester?"—but the main one being the small room he occupied. By Christmas 1954, Kiki had moved in with Bill and they were looking for a bigger place so that Kiki could have a bed of his own and a place to store his things. Bill seemed to have now accepted that Tangier was his home. By the middle of January 1955, he had moved to a larger apartment in the Kasbah—four rooms for twenty-three dollars a month— owned by Jim Wyllie, the watercolorist and children's author. Wyllie, a British expat who moved to Tangier in the 1920s to learn Arabic and then stayed for sixty years, could be seen each day pottering down to the Petit Socco in his tattered brown burnoose for mint tea. Wyllie rented out his house, Dar Zero on the place de la Kasbah, when he was away (it was here that Samuel Pepys wrote his *Tangier Diaries* in 1683 beneath an ancient fig tree in the courtyard). Wyllie also owned a nearby property built into the walls of the Kasbah, and it is unclear which house Burroughs rented.[8] "I have my own house now," he told Allen. "Can't get up energy to clean it, and live here in slowly accumulating dirt and disorder."[9]

Paul Bowles had a house near the place Bab Amrah, which was rented by Burroughs's friend David Lamont while Bowles was away in Ceylon. The houses in the Kasbah wall overlook the rue Amrah, and Burroughs was able to write to Allen and tell him he was so close to Paul Bowles that he could lean out the window and spit on his roof "if I was a long range spitter and I wanted to spit there"—a reworking of Hemingway's lines "and a hole in back you could put your fist in, if it were a small fist and you wanted to put it there"—one of Burroughs's favorite lines and one he often reworked in conversation. This gave Burroughs access to Paul Bowles's library, with unfortunate results. Bill borrowed a bound script copy of Tennessee Williams's *The Angel in the Alcove* and in the course of reading it dripped blood on the pages while shooting up. Bowles was most displeased as it was the 1943 original.

Burroughs never cooked for himself, so he became very much a member of Tangier café society, soon getting to know all the restaurants, cafés, and bars. Most Arab cafés consisted of one room with a few tables and chairs with a raised dais at one end covered with mats and rugs where the patrons lounged about with their shoes off, smoking kif and playing *ronda*, a card game. A radio played Arab music loudly and at the counter was a huge copper or brass samovar for mint tea or coffee. Often, in the course of his walks around town, Bill sat in one of these cafés for a mint tea, to people watch or talk to the inevitable boys who would approach him. Mostly during the day he sat in the Socco Chico, watching the passing show. Cars were banned from the square from 8:00 a.m. until midnight and anyone not ordering between 5:00 p.m. and 8:00 p.m. had to relinquish their seats in the cafés. A never-ending stream of beggars targeted anyone sitting outside, or even those seated at the bar: "Two girls paralyzed from the waist down, swing around on blocks. They bar the way, clutching at my pants leg." Many people whiled away the entire day there waiting for job offers, selling or buying drugs, smoking their kif, looking at the boys, panhandling, and mooching for loans: "A nightmare feeling of stasis permeates the Socco, like nothing can happen, nothing can change."[10] It was out of this mix that *The Naked Lunch* was born.

David Woolman dubbed its denizens "The Soco Foreign Legion": Rupert Croft-Cooke, George Greaves, Dowell Jones, Paul Lund, and many other regulars. In his essay on Tangier, Burroughs gave the Café Central as "the official meeting place of the Socco Chico set." Burroughs now found himself in an almost completely homosexual community. The prolific novelist and biographer Rupert Croft-Cooke had moved to Tangier with Joseph Susei Mari, his Indian "secretary," after a stretch in prison in Britain on homosexuality charges. He was solidly built with black swept-back hair and freckles. He was pompous and smoked cigars. Croft-Cooke gives his impressions of Burroughs in *The Caves of Hercules*: "He was a pleasant enough fellow when I knew him [...] in those days, when I first came to Tangier, he used to moon around the Socco Chico in suits which, he told me, he bought from supplies of used clothing sent from American charities for the poor Moroccans and sold by them to anyone who could pay for them. He was unnaturally gaunt, hollow-cheeked, meagre in body, and the Spaniards used to call him *el hombre invisible*. [He] was always asking to borrow my typewriter. He wandered down to the beach and sat, six foot two of palsied white flesh, nursing his knees and giving out wisdom to an artless young Canadian who encouraged him."[11] The Canadian was David Lamont, a painter who had moved to Tangier for the boys.

Welshman Dowell Jones was the owner of the Passapoga, a gay bar in the arcade on the rue de Fez, a block from the Parade. He was a pedophile, already in his seventies in the late 1950s, who had arrived in Tangier one step ahead of Scotland Yard. His bar was the rival to Tony Dutch's for very young boys, but though this trade was illegal, he survived for several years before being closed down by the police. He spent time in the Kasbah jail, but such was Tangier that he was permitted to order in gourmet food and other amenities and was soon set free to open once more for business.

Bill found Paul Lund, one of the few straight members of Burroughs's circle, to be particularly amusing. Lund was a professional criminal from Birmingham, though he appeared to have more of a London accent when imitated by Burroughs. He came from a wealthy shipping family, so a life of crime was a deliberate choice on his part. He came to Tangier because he was now liable to preventive detention, a law introduced in 1948 which meant that anything between five and fourteen years in jail could be given for any felony, however slight, as long as the accused was over thirty years old and had served three terms of imprisonment. When he was charged with conspiracy to defraud—selling cases of sawdust as stolen tobacco—he faced a ten-year stretch. He jumped bail and headed for Tangier.

Australian George Greaves was described by Burroughs as "the most completely corrupt person you could possibly imagine."[12] He was generally thought to be a police spy and not to be trusted. He sprawled his huge bulk in a cane chair outside the Café Central and had a word of salacious gossip to pass on about everyone who passed by. He would invite people over for breakfast to his place on the rue Alexander; that was his meal of the day. Burroughs was there one morning while Greaves was importuning Paul Lund: "Listen, Paul, if you just give a little information about arms shipments, I think a lot of things could be forgotten." Paul said, "How could I look at meself in the mirror if I did something like that?" And George said, "Well, Paul, you have to take a broad general view of things." It was almost thirty years before George Greaves appeared in Burroughs's prose. He is one of Kim Carsons's dinner guests in *The Place of Dead Roads*:

> Well there's old George Hargrave the Aussie, and a rottener man never drew breath. He takes a broad general view of things...nothing too low or too dirty for old George. [...] Got his fat greasy fingers into all the pies and puddings.[13]

3. The Talking Asshole

Despite his initial dislike of Tangier, Burroughs had begun writing almost as soon as he arrived. His quick mind filled with routines, all of them directed toward Ginsberg, but Ginsberg was not replying, being stuck in the Mexican jungle. At first, only a month after arriving there, Bill contemplated setting down the most difficult story of all. He wrote Allen, "May yet attempt a story or some account of Joan's death. I suspect my reluctance is not all because I think it would be in bad taste to write about it. I think I am *afraid*. Not exactly to discover unconscious intent, it's more complex, more basic, more horrible, as if the brain *drew* the bullet toward it. Did I tell you Kells' dream the night of Joan's death? This was before he knew, of course. I was cooking something in a pot, and he asked what I was cooking and I said 'Brains!' and opened the pot showing what looked like 'a lot of white worms.' I forgot to ask how I looked, general atmosphere, etc. To summarize I pass along one of my specialized bits of wisdom like 'always use poultry shears to cut off fingers' '*Never* participate in active or passive role in *any* shooting things off of, or near one or knife throwing or *anything similar*, and, if a bystander, always try to stop it.'

"I told you of a horrible nightmare and depression and anxiety I had that whole day so that I asked myself continually 'What in God's name is the matter with me?' [...] One more point. The idea of shooting a glass off her head had *never entered my mind* consciously, until out of the blue as far as I can recall (I was very drunk, of course) I said: 'It's about time for our William Tell act. Put a glass on your head, Joan.' Note all those precautions, *as though I had to do it* like the original William Tell. Why, instead of being so careful, not give up the idea? Why indeed? In my present state of mind I am afraid to go too deep into the matter. [...] I aimed carefully at six feet for the very top of the glass."[14] Many years would pass before Burroughs once again dared to address the issue.

Writing poured out of him in an inexorable torrent. On April 7 he wrote, "Routines like habit. Without routines my life is chronic nightmare, gray horror of Midwest suburb. [...] I have to have receiver for routine. If there is no-one there to receive it, routine turns back on me like a homeless curse and tears me apart, grows more and more insane (literal growth like cancer) and impossible, and fragmentary like berserk pin-ball machine and I am screaming: 'Stop it! Stop it!' Trying to write novel. Attempt to organize material is more painful than anything I ever experienced."[15] By May 11 he was able to write to Allen enclosing the "beginning of novel," and two weeks later he sent Kerouac a four-page text titled "Dream of the City by William Lee." This was a routine based on a dream Kerouac had described about the huge overcrowded cities of the future, but it has some elements of the narrow winding alleys of the Medina where Bill was living and of the vision he had of a multileveled city looking at the clotheslines on pulleys and the fire escapes behind Allen's building in the Lower East Side a few months before. It was also clearly influenced by Arthur Rimbaud's cities in *Illuminations*:

> A strange design of bridges, some straight, some arched, others descending at oblique angles to the first. [...] A few of these bridges are still covered with hovels, others support poles, signals, frail parapets.[16]

Ginsberg later retitled the text "Iron Wrack Dream," but it was not finally published until it was included in *Interzone*.

That same day, May 24, 1954, Bill sent Allen a "routine about purple-assed baboons, and Tangier miscellanea." This was, of course, the celebrated *Roosevelt After Inauguration* that Lawrence Ferlinghetti's English printers, Villiers Publications, found so disturbing that they insisted it be excised from *The Yage Letters*. (City Lights eventually published it as a separate text in 1979.) Bill had been delighted to find that there were purple-assed baboons in the mountains a few miles from town and that it was claimed that Paul Bowles was set upon by them and forced to flee for his life. The editor and poet Kenneth Rexroth was then a reader for New Directions so Ginsberg showed it to him at one of his San Francisco literary evenings, but Rexroth appears to have completely missed the point. Burroughs asked, "What does Rexroth mean by his remarks on the Roosevelt skit: 'by one who had no touch with the higher ups'? It's not supposed to be *accurate*. Does he think it has anything do with *Roosevelt*?"[17]

More sections of *The Naked Lunch* emerged. In December, Bill claimed to have sat down to write a Best-Seller-of-the-Month piece on Tangier, but the first sentence that came out was, "The only native in Interzone who is neither queer nor available is Andrew Keif's chauffeur, which is not an affectation on Keif's part but a useful pretext to break off relations with anyone he doesn't want to see: 'You made a pass at Aracknid last night. I can't have you in the house again.' (People are always blacking out in the Zone whether they drink or not. No one knows for sure what he did last night.)

"Aracknid is the worst driver in the Zone. On one occasion he ran down a pregnant women from the mountains with a load of charcoal on her back, and she miscarriaged a bloody, dead baby on the street, and Keif got out and sat on the curb stirring the blood with a stick while the police questioned Aracknid and finally arrested the woman."[18] This routine was used almost verbatim as the opening of the "Interzone" section of *The Naked Lunch*. Andrew Keif (Burroughs's spelling of the drug) was of course Paul Bowles, and Aracknid his driver Mohammed Temsamany. Burroughs once claimed it was based on a true incident.

Warming to his task, Bill told Allen, "Have written 1st chapter of a novel in which I will incorporate all my routines and scattered notes. Scene is Tanger, which I call Interzone. Did I write you anything about novel in progress? Starts with a deal to import and a sell 'a load of K.Y. made of genuine whale drek in the South Atlantic...' As you gather, in my most extreme line. I am going to attempt to complete work."[19] This opening text later appeared in the Marvie and Leif the Unlucky section of the "Interzone" chapter in *The Naked Lunch* (two characters based loosely on his neighbors Dave Woolman and Eric Gifford).[20] However, in the same letter, Burroughs asked Ginsberg if there was any possibility of "publishing *Naked Lunch* I have some notes on cocaine that belong in it, but in the *Junk* section." This was when the celebrated title was still being used for a three-part book comprised of three sections called "Junk," "Queer," and "Yage."

The "Tanger novel" dominated his work to the extent that he even wrote the jacket blurb, "getting a bit previous, I admit," which immediately turned into a routine parody of jacket blurbs: "The book grabs you by the throat..."[21] The first chapter, the section comprising part or the whole of the "Interzone" section, was sent to Ginsberg on December 30, 1954. When he was not inspired to write the novel, Bill wrote what was intended as a conventional travel article about Tangier that he hoped Ginsberg might sell to the *New Yorker* (eventually published as "International Zone" in *Interzone*).

Bill now recognized the significant role that Tangier played in his writing, not just in providing characters, incidents, and the stage set for many of the scenes, but as inspiration for the whole book. It came to Burroughs in a flash while writing to Allen Ginsberg on January 6, 1955: "I have just conceived, at this second, the way to achieve my work, solving the contradictions raised by dissipation of energy in fragmentary, unconnected projects. I will simply transcribe Lee's impressions. [...] The fragmentary quality of my work is *inherent* in the method and will resolve itself so far as necessary. Tanger novel will be Lee's impressions of Tanger, discarding novelist pretext of dealing directly with his characters and situations. *I include the author in the novel.*" In the same letter he enclosed further notes on the South American letters and a new introduction to *Yage Quest*— destined to become *The Yage Letters*.

It was not until he returned, emotionally shattered, from the United States that one of his most celebrated—at least by academics—routines emerged. Sent to Ginsberg on February 7, 1955, it was all part of his "latest attempt to write something saleable." First of all he would busy himself with displacement activities: reading magazines, making hash fudge, cleaning his shotgun, washing the dishes, going to bed with Kiki, before he would finally sit down, smoke some pot, "and out it comes all in one piece like a gob of spit: The incredible obscene, thinly disguised references and situations that slip by in Grade B movies, the double entendres, perversion, sadism of popular songs, poltergeist knockings and mutterings of America's putrefying unconscious, boils that swell until they burst with a fart noise as if the body had put out an auxiliary ass hole with a stupid, belligerent Bronx cheer. Did I ever tell you about the man who taught his ass hole to talk?"[22] And he launched into the famous routine. The man's asshole begins to take over; it would get drunk and have crying jags because nobody loved it. Eventually his mouth sealed over, leaving just the man's eyes. "This is my saleable product," Bill told Allen. "Do you dig what happens? It's almost like automatic writing produced by a hostile, independent entity who is saying in effect 'I will write what I please.'"

This routine, addressed to Allen Ginsberg, who had rejected Burroughs's asshole—Burroughs was a "bottom"—is literally the rejected orifice sending routines to the loved one, both in an attempt to amuse and please him and so to reclaim his affections, and also to register complaint. Burroughs's asshole becomes quite strident in its objections to the way it has been treated. The Talking Asshole routine empowers the asshole, giving it the same active status as the penis, overcoming Bill's problem with effeminacy. The routine was derived from Alberto Cavalcanti's "The Ventriloquist's Dummy" story in the 1945 British portmanteau horror film *Dead of Night*. "Like when you have a ventriloquist's dummy and suddenly the dummy starts talking for you."[23]

In the same letter he described a new routine that was to become the opening and closing sections of *The Naked Lunch*, framing the book: "I have started writing a Chandler-style straight action story about some super Heroin you can get a habit in one shot with it or something similar. [...] But it starts out 2 detectives come to arrest me. [...] To save myself I kill them both. That is where I am now. On the lam."[24] The Hauser and O'Brien section was a wildly exaggerated account of Burroughs's bust for possession in New York in 1945. He didn't remember their actual names, but the good cop was an Irishman and the bad cop, who came on heavy, was a Jew. The shootout was pure fantasy, Burroughs had nothing against them as people, and besides, it would have appalled him to do such a thing. "They were just cops." Eight months later he tried to explain how the drifting, unsettled status of Tangier was affecting his book and told Allen and Jack, "Tanger is the prognostic pulse of the world, like a dream extending from past into future, a frontier between dream and reality—the 'reality' of both called into question."[25] This he extended to Interzone, the territory of his novel: "The meaning of Interzone, its space-time location is at a point where three-dimensional fact merges into dream, and dreams erupt into the real world [...] the very exaggeration of routines is intended to create this feeling. In Interzone dreams can kill—like Bangutot—and solid objects and persons can be unreal as dreams. [...] For example Lee could be in Interzone, after killing the two detectives, and for various dream reasons, neither the law nor The Others could touch him directly" (just as the law couldn't touch Americans in Tangier, as they had their own courts).[26]

4. Remittance Men at Large

In the middle of March 1955, Alan Ansen arrived for a two-week visit. Bill arranged for him to stay at Tony Dutch's, which was convenient in every way. Ansen: "Tony was a good cook with lovely boys coming in." Bill enjoyed Alan's company enormously; together they did the rounds of the numerous good French restaurants in town. Bill cited a sample menu that included snails à la Bourgogne, chicken cooked in wine with lima beans, frozen chocolate mousse, camembert, and fruit, all for one dollar. One of the best and most expensive restaurants was Brion Gysin's 1001 Nights, housed in a narrow wing of the Menebhi Palace in the Marshan. As Alan Ansen really did have a trust fund—six hundred dollars a month, unlike Burroughs's parental allowance—they spent a number of evenings there sampling the black couscous, chicken tajine with dates stuffed with walnuts, lamb roasted over a wood fire, *bisteeya pastilla*, a cinnamon-flavored pigeon pie made with boiled eggs and sugar, all washed down with copious quantities of North African wines. Gysin had burned the menu onto a wooden tablet using a soldering iron. There were Moroccan lanterns of brass and colored glass that threw patterns on the walls and ceiling, and a huge fireplace burned most of the year round. A five-man Joujouka orchestra sat on a small corner dais, and there were adolescent dancing boys in gowns, slippers, and turbans from the Ahl Serif tribe in the Jibala Hills south of Tangier. There was usually a fire-eater or a sword-swallower. The performance ended with a dancing boy prancing around the room with a large brass tray set with ten glasses of tea and a lighted candle balanced on his head, never touching the tray or spilling a drop. At the end he would squirm and writhe until he was lying on the floor, then he would somehow turn completely over and slowly regain his feet as the music rose to a crescendo of flutes and drums, prompting large tips from the clientele. One evening Bill and Alan both got completely drunk and began throwing money at the dancing boys. This probably did little to improve Burroughs's standing in Gysin's imperious eyes.

It was Ansen who first met Charles Gallagher and introduced him to Burroughs. Gallagher was an intellectual who was thrown out of the CIA when a lie detector test showed he was homosexual. However, he continued to work for many organizations that were long seen as CIA covers, including regular reports on the situation in North Africa for the American Universities Field Staff in New York. He later wrote several books on Morocco, including *The United States and North Africa: Morocco, Algeria, and Tunisia* (1963). He was a linguist, speaking French, Spanish, Czechoslovakian, very good Arabic, and Japanese. He was in Japan during the war and had returned with a large collection of valuable Japanese art, enough to retire on.

Burroughs said he looked just like a CIA man, an analyst not a field man, fat but powerful with "very cold gray eyes." He was something of a gourmet, hated children and animals, and could be found at the Parade Bar most evenings. He was good friends with Paul and Jane Bowles. When he and Burroughs met he was writing a history of Morocco for the Ford Foundation, something that entailed spending a lot of time in the national archives in Rabat. He liked to drink and had a lot to say about local politics. He kept Burroughs up to date with all the latest political developments in Algeria, Tunisia, and events in the Sahara. He explained to Bill why the French should get out of Algeria, and why the independence movement in Morocco would eventually win. Burroughs found him very interesting to talk to and as a consequence was far more cognizant about local affairs than most critics have believed. Burroughs had also met Paul Bowles a few more times at parties and was getting to know him, and had met Peter Mayne, author of *The Alleys of Marrakech*. In addition he had become friendly with Christopher Wanklyn, a Canadian writer. He told Allen that there were now quite a few people of interest around.

At the end of March Bill had to give up Jim Wyllie's place because of the high utility bills. David Woolman had left Tony Dutch's at the same time, and Bill now joined him in renting rooms on the Terrace Renschausen on the east side of the Medina overlooking the port. This arrangement did not last long, and the pair decided to return to the shelter of Tony Dutch's establishment.

In May Bill tried yet again to kick junk. He was treated by Dr. Apfel in a clinic in the Marshan. It was an unpleasant cure. Bill was knocked out for four days with huge doses of sedatives—thorazine, barbiturates, and chloral hydrate, used in rotation to keep him in a semiconscious state— followed by cold turkey. He lost thirty pounds. He told Allen he'd had "a substantial case of the horrors," and days later he was still sick and sensitized to the point of hallucination. "Everything looks sharp and different like it was just washed. Sensations hit like tracer bullets. [. . .] Junk is death. I don't ever want to see it or touch it or commerce in it."[27] He almost fainted in the street and had to be helped by Dave Woolman. But he did not have enough self-control, and by the beginning of July he was using again: "After that awful cure it is really heartbreaking to find myself hooked again." He recognized his problem: "I am so disgusted with my prevarication—always some excuse for one last box—I have been buying absolutely the last box of demerol ampules every day for the past 3 weeks. Such a dreary display of weakness."[28]

As usual, when exposed to a medical environment, Burroughs wrote medical routines. In his letter to Allen of July 3, Burroughs extrapolates on Eric Gifford's bad luck, which included an operation without anesthetic, in what was to become a precursor of the Dr. Benway routine:

"Or the old German Practitioner who removed his appendix with an old, rusty can opener and tin shears: 'The germ theory is nonsense.' Flushed with success, he then began snipping and cutting out everything in sight: 'The human body is a most inefficient machine. Filled up vit unnecessitated parts. [...] You can get by with von kidney—vy have two? Yes dot is a kidney. The inside parts should not be so close in together crowded. They need Lebensraum, like der Vaterland...' This German cat practices something he calls technological medicine."[29]

Things got so bad with Bill's addiction that he had to consider entering a clinic for a cure. The critical point came in the middle of September when he got hold of some ampoules each containing one-sixth grain of dolophine and one-hundredth grain of hyoscine. He shot six ampoules in the main line. He was found by Dave Woolman at 2:00 a.m., sitting in the hallway, stark naked on the toilet seat, which he had wrenched from its moorings, playing with a bucket of water and singing "Deep in the Heart of Texas" in his cracked voice. At the same time he complained to Woolman, "in clearly enunciated tones," about the high cost of living: "It all goes on razor blades." He tore up his sheets and threw bottles about his room looking for something and attempted to go out on the street but was restrained. "What a horrible nightmare if I had succeeded and came to myself wandering around the Native Quarter naked."[30] Dave Woolman and Tony Dutch were hugely relieved to find him fully dressed and in his right mind the next morning, as they had worried if this was a permanent state.

Bill tried several doctors and every hospital and clinic in Tangier but no one would take on an addict. Help came from an unexpected source. Several times a week for about five months Bill had been giving Leslie Eggleston, the mooch at the Parade, a little money for food, but it was all worth it when Eggleston gave Bill a note of introduction to a woman in the Office of Social Assistance, an office Bill passed every day without noticing it. Within ten minutes she had found a doctor to treat him and booked him a room in the Benchimol Hospital, where he had his own room for two dollars a day and was permitted to use his new portable typewriter. Bill told Allen, "I am already paid back for the money I gave him and the meals and drinks I bought, by this introduction."[31]

Benchimol Hospital, known as "the Jewish Hospital," was founded by Haim and Donna Benchimol in the New Town. Oliver Harris reports that one of its rooms was called Salle Salvador Hassan, surely the origin of "Hassan's Rumpus Room" in *The Naked Lunch*. This was not the only idea that sprang from Benchimol. Dr. Apfel became another of Burroughs's characters. Bill reported to Allen and Jack, "Just went to the head again. Still locked. Locked for six solid hours. I think they are using it as an operating room,"[32] which became the opening lines of the Dr. Benway routine. Other sections used in Benway appear in a letter of November 2: "I'm afraid she's gone, doctor" and much of the "Black Meat" section of *The Naked Lunch* comes from this same letter.[33] Pages of the book were piling up, almost all inspired by Tangier. This time the cure appeared to work, because Bill's sex drive reasserted itself: "Figure to start at one end of Interzone and screw my way through to the other. I am tired of monogamy with Kiki,"[34] he told Allen.

In addition, Bill was beginning to appreciate more of his surroundings. He took a walk on the Old Mountain in the outskirts of the town, wandering through low hills covered with trees, tangled vines, and shrubs, overlooking red sandstone cliffs topped with pines. The beauty of the landscape astonished him and he told Allen he could write fifty pages just about that walk. He also took notice of the society he was living in, saying he was "beginning to dig Arab kicks. It takes time. You must let them seep into you."[35] This appreciation would grow and grow.

In the summer of 1955 the political situation in Tangier began to heat up, as the independence movement grew in strength. "I simply must see some of this bloodshed," Bill told Allen after a small riot in which there were four casualties, all Arabs. "All I saw was people running, shop shutters slamming down, and women jerking their babies inside off the street."[36] He went home and loaded his shotgun, but the riot had been promptly quelled.

That summer Bill attracted the unwanted attentions of a local eccentric named Manushi, a member of a very puritanical Muslim sect. On his first approach, the man addressed him as his "Dear friend" and asked for fifty cents. Bill retorted, "with some asperity," that he was not his friend and that no money was forthcoming. Next Manushi told both David Woolman and Bill, "I hear you like little boys, Allah doesn't like that." He began selling cakes and was abusive if people didn't buy them. Over the weeks, Manushi's communications became more cryptic. He was convinced that the U.S. embassy was the root of all evil and that Bill was a U.S. agent. He asked Bill, "Why does the American embassy have wires in my head?" Bill said he didn't know. Bill always kept their conversations as short as possible, holding himself ready for any violence, but Manushi never made a hostile move.

Then on Monday, August 1, Manushi ran amok with a sharp butcher knife. He charged through the Medina, slashing at people, down past the American embassy, where they locked the door before he got there, and onto the beach. He killed five people and wounded four before the police shot him in the stomach and dragged him away. Bill missed him by ten minutes and wondered if he would have been one of his victims had he been there.[37]

Bill made another attempt to move from Tony Dutch's establishment, this time to the Hotel Muniria on the calle Cook in the New Town. He took room 7, a top-floor apartment with a balcony and a view out over the harbor. David Woolman, reporting as Barnaby Bliss in the *Tangier Gazette*, wrote, "Twas the rain-riddled late afternoon of December 13, 1955, at the Villa Muniria Calle Cook. Author Bill Burroughs was writing a letter in his penthouse quarters. Suddenly a stream of men, some carrying guns, opened Burroughs' door and looked in. The explanation is that the Villa Muniria is for sale and these were guides for the 'Black Bernous,' none other than the ex-Sultan of Morocco Mohammed ben Arafa. Burroughs, the most politically neutral man in Africa, said: '¿Ben Arafa, Quién es?'"

Burroughs demonstrated considerable sangfroid, as "¿Quién es?" were the last words of Billy the Kid before he was shot by Sheriff Pat Garrett on July 14, 1881. Burroughs of course knew who Ben Arafa was, but to admit it might provoke a line of questioning with unfortunate results, as he did not know who these men were or what line to take. Or he may have just wondered who was at the door.

Inevitably, Bill drifted back into addiction. By now Kiki realized that his situation with Bill was untenable. Bill was taking huge amounts of junk and had little money left over to give him. Kiki met a Cuban bandleader who came through Tangier, and as this looked like a better opportunity, he went with him first to Gibraltar, then to Madrid, where the bandleader was based. Bill didn't blame him. "And Kiki went away. Like a cat, somebody gives him more food and one day he is gone. Through an invisible door. You can look anywhere. No good."[38] Kiki began playing drums in the band, which was made up mostly of women players. This was to be his undoing. The bandleader found him in bed with one of them in their hotel. At the beginning of September, 1957, Bill told Allen, "Poor Kiki was murdered last week in Madrid by that shit of a Cuban singer. Seems the frantic old fruit found Kiki in bed with a girl and stabbed him in the heart with a kitchen knife. Then he attacked the girl, but the nabors rushed in and the Cuban took off, but was shortly afterwards detained by the Civil Guard."[39] The singer killed himself before the case reached court. Kiki remained in Bill's thoughts for the rest of his life, transformed into one of his characters. We were never told Kiki's real name. The only hint comes from a line in *Nova Express*, which suggests that his family name was Henrique, from which came his nickname Kiki, otherwise inexplicable among the macho Spanish boys as it is a girl's name.

...met Paco by the soccer scores and he said: "Que tal Henrique?"

And I went to see my amigo who was taking medicina again and he had no money to give me and didn't want to do anything but take more medicina [...] so I said, "William no me hagas cas." And met a Cuban that night in the Mar Chica who told me I could work with his band.[40] [...] and KiKi went away like a cat."[41]

Chapter Twenty-Five

Was Weston glad to get rid of his evil and downright insolvent roomer.
Never take a tenant with a monkey.[1]

1. Dr. Dent

Bill's parents were dismayed to discover he was back on junk and insisted that this time he take a cure in England, but they prevaricated about sending the fare in case he used it to score. Bill was in a bad way again. At the end of February 1956 he told Allen, "Taking so much I keep going on the nod. Last night I woke up with someone squeezing my hand. It was my own other hand."

Thirty years later he recalled those times: "I was on almost 50 grams a day living in the slimiest one room you could have found in the native quarter of Tangier. I hadn't shaved or bathed or had a good meal in months. People would shy away from me in the streets—it must have been the body odour. I had some good friends, like writers Jane and Paul Bowles, but even they threw up their arms in disgust. Walking to the American Express office to pick up my monthly check from home [...] I caught a reflection of myself in a shop window. It was not pretty. I could hardly recognise the person. To this day I cannot explain how I managed to pull myself together and get on that plane to London for a cure. I know I have my friends in Tangier to thank."[2] His father insisted on making the arrangements in London to ensure that Bill followed through, and finally, in the middle of April, Bill set out for England.

Mote had arranged through his local doctor, Dr. Murphy in Palm Beach, for Bill to contact Dr. MacClay in London—Bill marveled at the address: Queen's Gate Place—but addiction was not his line at all. Bill was immediately referred to Dr. John Yerbury Dent, author of *Anxiety and Its Treatment*, because he had a good rate of success with addicts. Bill telephoned and went over to his house at 44 Addison Road, off Kensington High Street, a large comfortable house, separated from the road by a stuccoed stone wall, with a garden and a dog kennel for his Scottish terrier. Dr. Dent was known for his energy and his good humor. Over a cup of tea, Dr. Dent, a short-set, heavily built man with an untidy shock of white hair and mustache, asked, "Would you feel more comfortable so we can talk if you had an injection first?" Bill said, "Well, that would help." Dent told Bill about the apomorphine treatment that obviated the need for morphine, but said that if he really needed morphine he could have it. Bill had been using methadone, but Dent said he'd rather he switched to morphine for two days because he would be using that in the treatment. "Magnificent man," said Bill. Dr. Dent's entire practice was drug addiction and alcoholism. He was the pioneer in the use of apomorphine, a metabolic regulator, to treat addiction, and soon convinced Bill of its efficacy.

Bill was sent to a nearby nursing home at 100 Cromwell Road, a four-story building where Bill had a room with rose wallpaper on the third floor. He had a day nurse and a night nurse and was given an injection of one-twentieth grain of apomorphine every two hours, day and night, reducing to every four hours. The withdrawal from opiates meant that he was unable to sleep for five days and nights as he went from thirty grains of morphine a day to zero in seven days. "You'll sleep when you're ready to sleep," Dent told him. Bill told Allen, "The cure itself was awful. [...] But I had a real croaker, interested in Yage, Mayan archaeology, every conceivable subject, and would often come to see me at 2AM and stay till 5 since he knew I couldn't sleep."[3] Dent gave him three tubes of apomorphine tablets to use if the withdrawal pain became too intense. Bill enjoyed his company and had dinner with him at his house several times in the days following his cure. Dr. Dent shared the house with a civil servant and his wife, the Brenans, the brother of Gerald Brenan, the writer, whose books on Spain Bill knew. On release from the nursing home, Bill stayed on in a rooming house at 44 Egerton Gardens near the Victoria and Albert Museum. This address became one of Burroughs's "sets," appearing in *Cities of the Red Night* and in his dreams.[4] Burroughs formed a long-standing friendship with Dent, whom he described as "the least paranoid of men, and he had the full warmth and goodwill, the best the English can offer."[5]

Bill attempted to connect with writers in London. He tracked down poet George Barker in order to give him a copy of the manuscript of Ginsberg's "Howl," but Barker wasn't interested. "Mutual disinterest," Bill reported. "London is about the most God-awful place I was ever in. Barker is a bore. I never want to see England again,"[6] he told Allen before moving on to Venice to stay with Alan Ansen at the beginning of June.

Venice could not have been more different. "Venice is perhaps the greatest place I ever see. Such a cornucopia of available ass. I mean, too much. Since the cure I been sexy as an eighteen-year-old and healthy as a rat."[7] He stayed at Ansen's top-floor apartment on the calle delle Carrozze. They took a motorboat out but broke down in the middle of the lagoon. Fit and well after the apomorphine cure, Bill learned to row Venetian fashion so you faced the direction you were going. He rowed around Venice for two or three hours each day, usually with Ansen on board, and also swam in the lagoon. Learning to row this way was difficult; thirty years later he still remembered the pain:

> Remember when you first tried to row a gondola? The way you couldn't possibly get it, and your muscles knotted up and you were just making spastic gestures with the oar and the feeling in your stomach and groin, that sort of packing dream tension almost sexual...? And then suddenly you could do it.[8]

He walked all over the city, exploring the little squares and canals. Ansen introduced him to a lot of people, including the gay American poet James Merrill. Bill met Mary McCarthy and her husband Bowden Broadwater. He found her "most pleasant" and they had a number of agreeable dinners together. Ansen introduced him to Harry's Bar and they made the round of parties. At a cocktail party given by Peggy Guggenheim for the British consul, Bill was told that it was customary to greet Guggenheim by kissing her hand. Burroughs replied, "I will be glad to kiss her cunt if that is the custom." Unfortunately this was overheard by her assistant, Bob Brady, who nearly swooned with excitement before running to report it. Burroughs and Guggenheim had gotten along well up until that point, but now Bill was banished forever from the premises. Guggenheim's daughter Pegeen was there with her husband, Ralph Rumney. Bill was probably introduced to Rumney, who was a founding member of the Situationist International, but as Bill was very drunk at the time, it is unlikely that much in the way of political discussion occurred. Rumney was a friend of Ansen's and sometimes put up his visitors, such as Allen Ginsberg, when Alan's place was already full. Rumney, when later asked about Burroughs, simply said, "I liked Burroughs. But he lived in a different world from me. But he was a great man. Our attitudes were very different."[9]

They established a regular routine and Bill spent a lot of time in his room writing. He hated Ansen playing solitaire, which he thought was very idle. To Ansen it was "a Puritan reaction to a harmless amusement—all right to take heroin but not to play solitaire." They cooked curries and picked up a lot of boys together. Bill became dissatisfied with the sex scene in Venice: "As soon as I came off hard drugs I got randy as a fucking goat but there were slim pickings in Venice, slim pickings. There were lots of them willing to do almost nothing at an exorbitant price." They did get involved with a couple of U.S. Army boys, but Bill surprised Ansen, saying, "We're too old for them." Ansen said, "A bit of friction at the end because we'd been more or less sharing boys but at the end there was one called Bruno that he wanted to keep for himself and I didn't feel that was fair—there were no ultimatums but it was shortly after that that he decided to leave for Tangier."[10]

According to Burroughs, "There were no quarrels over Bruno. Alan did feel that my presence there and my carryings on was imperilling his position. Two people is worse than one." Ansen told Allen, "It was too bad he was leaving, he had been an ideal guest diffusing endless calm." Ansen was trying to get permanent-residence status, but the Italian authorities refused because his neighbors had reported his behavior to the police. Then, some months after Burroughs left, there was a terrible scandal. Ansen brought two sailors home and they attacked him. He rushed into the street stark naked and ran to a bar at the corner, where he seized a chair to defend himself. This proved too much for the authorities, who threw him out of the country. He moved to Athens.

Bill left Venice for Naples on August 10, 1956, and from there took a boat to Tripoli. He didn't like it, telling Allen, "Tripoli utter nowhere. Fraternizing between Arabs and Europeans is literally spat upon. I mean the Arabs spit on the sidewalk when you pass and yell: 'Cock suck 'Mericans go home.'"[11] The Suez Canal had been nationalized by Egypt in July, and there was an ongoing crisis that eventually led to war. In Tripoli there was a general strike and everything was closed. The American embassy was expecting trouble and all the vice consuls were walking around with pistols in their belts. They begrudgingly gave Bill a cup of coffee and told him to stay indoors. Bill's hotel was just inside the Medina, and he soon found a black-market restaurant that was open. The local police were there eating steaks. Bill wandered around the Kasbah and the Medina with no trouble. He spent about a week in Tripoli before heading to Algiers, but there he was really stuck.

The Algerians had been fighting a war of independence for almost two years and there had been recent disturbances after an Arab had thrown a bomb into a crowded café in Oran and had been torn to pieces by an infuriated French crowd. All the flights were booked up for weeks in advance. Bill summed up the local feelings toward westerners:

Sample conversation between your reporter and a nameless Arab asshole:
A.A. "Hey, Johnny, feelthy pictures?"
Lee: "No."

A.A.: "See me fuck sister? Me rimmy you?"

Lee: "No."

A.A.: "Fuck you son bitch. Go back to your own country."

In short, to deal plainly, I am definitely anti the Arab Nationalists and pro-French as far as the Algerian setup goes. You can't imagine what a pain in the ass these Nationalists are. Bastards, sons a bitches.[12]

The American consulate explained how Bill might get a permit to take a train to Morocco, and eventually he was able to find the right bureau and the right bureaucrat to stamp his papers. Despite the war, Bill was able to wander unharmed around the Medina. The worst experience came at night because his hotel was full of bedbugs. The train ride was long and uncomfortable and the sleeping soldier seated next to him kept slumping over onto his shoulder. At Oujda, a dreary border town, the French official stamped his passport with no problem. The train went to Casablanca and from there he had to take a bus to Tangier. The trip from Algiers to Tangier took twenty-four hours, nonstop. He was pleased to be back and told Allen, "There is no town like Tanger town. The place relaxes me so I am subject to dissolve. I can spend three hours looking at the bay with my mouth open like a Kentucky Mountain Boy. Man, I don't *need* junk."[13]

2. Villa Delirium

On September 16, 1956, Bill wrote to Allen to say, "So me and Dave [...] have found us the original anything-goes joint. Run by two retired junky whores from Saigon."[14] The Hotel Muniria was at 1 rue Magellan, on the corner of calle Cook. Madame Aquarrone, the Frenchwoman who had just bought the hotel, used to run a brothel in Saigon and had brought her Vietnamese servant with her. "You can be *free* here, you understand?" she said, digging Bill in the ribs. Bill, Dave Woolman, and Eric Gifford took the three rooms on the ground floor. They opened onto the hotel garden and had their own private entrance onto calle Cook. Bill paid fifteen dollars a month for room 9, which contained a large comfortable bed, a dresser, and a washstand. He had a small oil stove on which he used to cook his own hashish candy, of which he was very proud. There were no maids to interrupt his work, but the Vietnamese servant used to bring him afternoon tea in a tea cozy, well made and very hot. He decorated the room by covering one wall with his snapshots taken in the South American jungle, all stuck together to make a giant collage. Another wall was pockmarked from target practice: shooting matchboxes off the shelf with his air gun. "I don't see how anyone could be happier than I am right now,"[15] Bill wrote.

It was an ideal situation: just a stone's throw away from the main artery of Tangier, close to the Medina, and a stumble down the steep unpaved track to the beach. In those days the hillside was completely rural; there were a few goats and some gardens, many of them abandoned. The walled garden of the hotel was filled with sparrows twittering, the air thick with the scent of datura blossoms. Bill was so relaxed that he had a spontaneous orgasm while doing the special abdominal exercises that he received from a man named Hornibrook in London, who learned them from the Fijian islanders. "Now a spontaneous waking orgasm is a rare occurrence even in adolescence. Only one I ever experienced before was in the orgone accumulator I made in Texas,"[16] he told Allen. "And another thing. I find my eyes straying towards the fair sex. (It's the new frisson, dearie [...] women are downright piquant.) You hear about these old characters find out they are queer at fifty, maybe I'm about to make the old switcheroo. What are these strange feelings that come over me when I look at young cunts, little tits sticking out so cute? Could it be that?? No! No! He thrust the thought from him in horror. [...] He stumbled out into the street with the girl's mocking laughter lingering in his ears, laughter that seemed to say 'Who do you think you're kidding with the queer act? I know you baby.' Well, it is as Allah wills."[17]

Bill led a very healthy life. After his breakfast egg he would usually go rowing for an hour with a relaxed easy motion, Venetian style, in the deep blue water of Tangier Bay, looking straight ahead. He was soon very fit. The water was usually too cold for him to swim; there are cold Atlantic currents sweeping in through the strait, and you also have to wade out several hundred yards before it is deep enough. Sometimes he would stroll around the town, a flâneur, sitting in either the Café de Paris or the Normandie, the two grand cafés facing each other across the place de France. "These things give me pleasure," he told Allen. "I think I must be very happy."[18] Now that he was no longer on junk he loved Tangier. He wrote, "Tanger extends in several dimensions. You keep finding places you never saw before. There is no line between 'real' world and 'world of myth and symbol.' Objects, sensations, hit with the impact of hallucination. Of course I see now with the child's eyes, the Lazarus eyes of return from the gray limbo of junk. But what I see is there. Others see it too."[19]

Around midday he would take majoun—hash candy—and begin writing. Generally he would take a lot of majoun every other day, alternating with smoking a lot of pot on his days off. "That helped a great deal, there's no doubt about it, it helps anybody, it stimulates the flow of images. And the whole associative process is very useful. I think it's very useful for writing."[20] He wrote through until the evening drink and would sometimes take a little notebook with him to dinner and write down a few ideas, which he would type out after dinner. It was a period of a tremendous outpouring of material. "I am really writing Interzone now, not writing about it."[21] Routines clamored to be written down and were duly mailed off to Allen in San Francisco. In the afternoon he would take a break when Paco or Nimón would come over; he had several steady boys at this point.

Dave Woolman, who lived next door, and Eric Gifford, who was on the other side, said they could hear his "strange wild laughter" through the doors. He would sit hunched over his typewriter, pounding the keys furiously, hair tousled, often cackling with laughter at his own routines, throwing the pages onto the floor as they came out of the carriage, where the sea breeze would sometimes blow them out into the garden through the open door. Paul Bowles described the scene: "The litter on his desk and under it, on the floor was chaotic, but it consisted only of pages of Naked Lunch at which he was constantly working. When he read aloud from it, at random (any sheet of paper he happened to grab would do) he laughed a good deal, as well he might, since it is very funny, but from reading he would suddenly (the paper still in hand) go into a bitter conversational attack upon whatever aspect of life had prompted the passage he had just read. The best thing about Bill Burroughs is that he always makes sense and he is always humorous, even at his most vitriolic."[22]

Now that he was clean, Bill found himself spending more and more time with Paul Bowles and getting on well with him. In October 1956 he told Allen, "[I] dig him like I never dig anyone that quick before. Our minds similar, telepathy flows like water. I mean there is something portentously familiar about him, like a revelation."[23] Unfortunately Bowles was just off to Ceylon again, not to return until February. Though Burroughs often found him icy cold and parsimonious, they had very many things in common. Bowles was only four years older than Bill, they were both expatriates, both somewhat disoriented individuals in voluntary exile in a potentially hostile environment. They were both escaping from an America where they could not live freely and about which they were both disparaging. They both became writers late in life, though they did not often discuss writing except to praise Conrad, whom both cited as their favorite author. Both had an interest in magic, and both took drugs. Not surprisingly they had much to talk about. They both used kif to unlock the doors to imagination: Bowles said of the final section of The Sheltering Sky that it was written "without any thought of what I had already written, or awareness of what I was writing, or intention as to what I was going to write next, or how it was going to finish."[24]

They both also shared an interest in boys, though Bowles was much more reticent about his homosexuality than Burroughs and may have been much less active in Tangier than in his youth. He and Burroughs were pragmatic about sex, both pretending that they had no emotional involvement with the boys they used, but both feeling emotional attachments, then angrily denying them.

Bowles appears to have had the more promiscuous past. He complained to the composer Aaron Copland in the summer of 1933, "Where in this country can I have thirty-five or forty different people a week, and never risk seeing them again? Yet, in Algeria, it actually was the mean rate. [...] I think it's what I want, so it must be."[25] Another time he joked to Copland, "Did you tell me *to* or *not* to sleep with someone different every night? I have forgotten."[26] By the late forties, however, he had stopped having several boys a day, and when Bill met him he had fallen for Ahmed Yacoubi, the model for the young Arab boy, Amar, in Bowles's *The Spider's House*. They met in Fez in 1947. It was Yacoubi whom Burroughs referred to when he reported to Ginsberg on his initial lack of success in meeting Bowles: "Paul Bowles is here, but kept in seclusion by an Arab boy who is insanely jealous, and given to the practice of black magic."[27]

In the spring of 1953, Bowles had taken Yacoubi to Ceylon and India, then back to Italy, where they stayed with Peggy Guggenheim in Venice. This was followed immediately with a trip to the States, where they stayed with the singer Libby Holman in Connecticut. Montgomery Clift was another houseguest, and when he left, Holman transferred her affections to Yacoubi, who responded with enthusiasm. Bowles had derived satisfaction in seeing how an illiterate boy from the Medina in Fez reacted to India (he hated it), but was deeply upset when the experiment of seeing how he fared in American high society went badly wrong. Yacoubi had loved being with Holman; he enjoyed visiting the Stork Club, Cartier's, the Blue Angel, and stayed on when Bowles returned to Tangier. Unfortunately, Yacoubi apparently felt up Holman's seven-year-old adopted son, then pushed him in the pool and tried to choke him, clearly seeing him as a rival. Soon Yacoubi was on SS *Constitution*, first class, bound for Tangier. Astonishingly, Bowles made up with Yacoubi and next took him to Rome with Tennessee Williams, where Williams reported, "Ahmed is torturing Paul by not sleeping with him."[28] In December 1954, Paul took Yacoubi to Ceylon, then on to Singapore, Malaysia, Hong Kong, and Japan.

Bowles told Simon Bischoff, "All relationships I ever had, from the beginning, had to do with paying. I never had sexual relationships without pay, even when I was much younger. So I took that for granted. [...] [With Yacoubi we] were friends, yes, naturally. But I never expected him to care one way or the other. He didn't."[29]

Burroughs, however, played a different, more difficult game: he liked to get to know his boys, but not get emotionally involved. He reported to Allen, "I never been so horny in my life as right lately. Like yesterday I had two-hour set-to with Nimón, my latest heart-throb—that's a way of putting it."[30] Bill used to alternate between an Arab and a Spanish boy, Nimón and Paco. Said Burroughs, "They were hot to go. Of course they want money, they don't have any money. These old queens that object to paying, its really disgusting."[31] He described Paco to Allen: "My latest number is Spanish, 16, with a smile hit you right in the nuts. I mean, that pure, uncut boy stuff, that young male innocence."[32] He thought that one reason he received so many offers—he claimed ten "attractive" propositions a day—was that everyone knew how generous he had been with Kiki and so he was the "most eligible queer in Greater Tangèr." This much sexual activity began to take its toll. On a visit to his doctor, after finding his buttocks were a bright purple-red color, he was diagnosed with ringworm. "Then he looked at me over his glasses and smiled discreetly... 'And there seems to be a certain amount of, uh, chafing.'"[33] Mycota cured him at once.

Paco was callow, guileless, he had no tact. When Alan Ansen visited, Paco used to tease him by taking off his clothes and sitting in provocative poses, hoping to disconcert him so that he would give him more money. Alan and Bill both had sex with him. In the end Bill succumbed and allowed Paco to move in. It didn't work, and two months later, by Christmas 1956, Bill told Allen, "Paco, this Spanish kid wind up buggin' me like I throw him out already."[34] In fact it probably upset Bill a lot to have to do so. Sadly Paco, like Kiki, came to a horrible end. In September 1967, he visited Lourdes, where he robbed and murdered a taxi driver. When the police arrived, he committed suicide. Ansen found it extraordinary that he was in Lourdes, but Paco was a poorly educated Spanish boy, almost certainly Catholic, and therefore racked with guilt and remorse for his "sins." He went with men out of necessity not desire, which must have caused him enormous conflicts.

Moroccan prostitutes felt less guilt, although they were also forced into homosexuality by poverty, rather than out of sexual preference. In Moroccan society, to be called a *zamel*—to take the passive homosexual role—was the worst possible insult. Many of the boys refused to do it. Despite the formal disapproval of religious authority and the strict segregation of men and women in Muslim societies, the strong emphasis on virility leads adolescents and unmarried young men to seek sexual outlets with males younger than themselves. It was not so much the action, "getting fucked," that was disapproved of—this was often done from economic necessity—what was regarded as bad was enjoying it.

Homosexuality is forbidden in Islamic law: "For the unmarried, one hundred lashes and exile for a year, for the married, one hundred lashes and stoning to death" (Sura IV:15), but "And there shall wait on them [the Muslim men] young boys of their own, as fair as virgin pearls" (Sura LII:24), and "They shall be attended by boys graced with eternal youth, who will seem like scattered pearls to the beholders" (Sura LXXVI:19). In any case, the Moroccans always had a more relaxed attitude toward homosexuality than most other Muslim countries (or Christian ones). Long before the arrival of sexual tourism by westerners, as far back as 1632, the Scottish traveler William Lithgow reported that in Fez there were twelve thousand allowed brothels and "three thousand common stewes of sodomitical boyes. Nay, I have seene at mitday, in the very market places, the Moores buggering these filthy carrions, and without shame or punishment go freely away."[35]

Their friends and neighbors understood why they did it: they were poor and their families were hungry. Tahar ben Jelloun in *Leaving Tangier* quotes the concierge, in what is obviously Paul Bowles's building, observing the predatory sex tourists who came to Tangier: "This I know that poverty—our friend poverty—leads us to some very sad places. People have to make do with life, that's how it is, and me, I see everything but I don't say everything."[36] This was a Moroccan's critical view of Paul and Jane Bowles. She continues, "They want everything, men and women from the common people, young ones, healthy, preferably from the countryside, who can't read or write, serving them all day, then servicing them at night. A package deal, and between two pokes, tokes on a nicely packed pipe of kif to help the American write! Tell me your story, he says. I'll make a novel out of it, you'll even have your name on the cover: You won't be able to read it but no matter, you're a writer like me, except that you're an illiterate writer, that's exotic!" A tough critique, but in the decade they were together, there would have been plenty of time for Bowles to teach Yacoubi how to read and write.

As Bowles didn't drink, Bill would either visit him at his new apartment in the Edificio San Francisco, at plaza de Navarra, overlooking the Spanish consulate, or they would sometimes meet in a café such as Mme. Porte's Salon de Thé, in the rue du Statut around the corner from the place de France, an establishment renowned for its pastries. In the morning men outnumbered women but in the afternoon it was the reverse. It was used as a headquarters by Abdelkhalek Torres, the popular Moroccan nationalist leader who appeared at 10:00 a.m. with his faithful acolytes, and many other local and foreign politicians and journalists gathered there. Bill would have observed many of the nationalist leaders here whom he parodied so mercilessly in *The Naked Lunch*. Sometimes, when asked a difficult question, Bill would quote Mme. Porte: "Je n'ai pas un opinion." She was the model of discretion and Bill could be too.

3. "The Jihad Jitters"

It would have been impossible for Bill to overlook the struggle for independence going on all around him in Morocco, and though he was nominally in favor of it, inasmuch as he found the treatment of the Moroccans by the French utterly repellent, Bill disliked the puritanism and right-wing attitudes that went hand in hand with nationalism. Watching the politicians at work, however, was guaranteed to give rise to some routines. The "Ordinary Men and Women" section in *The Naked Lunch* came straight from the Socco Chico:

> Luncheon of Nationalist Party on balcony overlooking the Market. Cigars, scotch, polite belches...The Party Leader strides about in a jellaba smoking a cigar and drinking scotch. He wears expensive English shoes, loud socks, garters, muscular, hairy legs—overall effect of successful gangster in drag.
> P.L. (pointing dramatically): "Look out there. What do you see?"
> LIEUTENANT: "Huh? Why, I see the Market."
> P.L.: "No you don't. You see men and women. Ordinary men and women going about their ordinary everyday tasks. Leading their ordinary lives. That's what we need..."
> A street boy climbs over the balcony rail.
> LIEUTENANT: "No, we do not want to buy any used condoms! Cut!"
> P.L.: "Wait!...Come in, my boy. Sit down...Have a cigar...Have a drink."
> He paces around the boy like an aroused tom cat.
> "What do you think about the French?"
> "Huh?"
> "The French. The Colonial bastards who is sucking your live corpuscles."
> "Look mister. It cost two hundred francs to suck my corpuscle. Haven't lowered my rates since the year of the rindpest when all the tourists died, even the Scandinavians."
> P.L.: "You see? This is pure uncut boy in the street."
> "You sure can pick 'em, boss."
> "M.I. never misses."
> P.L.: "Now look, kid, let's put it this way. The French have dispossessed you of your birthright."[37]

The Sargasso was Bill's name for the Café Central on the Petit Socco facing the Fuentes, a restaurant with a long narrow balcony above the café of the same name where people could eat and drink. Burroughs's attitude was nonjudgmental, noncommittal, like that of Mme. Porte herself. The independence movement grew in size and by October 29, 1956, Bill was able to report to Allen, "This town really has the jihad jitters—jihad means the wholesale slaughter by every Moslem of every unbeliever. Yesterday I am sitting in the Socco and suddenly people start running and all the shop keepers are slamming down the steel shutters of their shops [...] so at this point about thirty little children carrying the Moroccan flag troop through the Socco. [...] I have a strange feeling here of being outside any social context. I have never known anyplace so relaxing. The possibility of an all-out riot is like a tonic, like ozone in the air: 'here surely is a song for men like wind in an iron tree.'—Anabasis, more or less."[38]

Bill composed a long song called "The Jihad Jitters": "The *Istiqlal* hates me / The guides all berates me / I'm nobody's sweetheart now..."[39]

He told Allen, "I have purchased a machete. If they stage a jihad I'm gonna wrap myself in a dirty sheet and rush out to do some jihading of my own like 'I comma Luigi. I killa everybody.' I say it's nothing but a half-assed jihad that confines itself to unbelievers. [...] Like there's this awful queer guide here name of Charley who keeps insulting poor Dave on the street, saying: 'Just wait. We're going to take care of you fucking American queers.' So come the jihad I will scream 'Death to the queers!' and rush out and cut Charley's head off. And I will shit sure avail myself of the next jihad to take care of the nabor's dog, the bastard is barking all night. [...] I hereby declares the all-out massacre of everybody by everybody else. [...] Perhaps come the Jihad I will have to yell 'Death to the American queers!' and cut off Dave W's head."[40]

The Istiqlal Moroccan independence party was founded in 1944 but really became a significant force in April 1947 when Sultan Mohammed V made a historic speech in Tangier calling for freedom and independence from France. After a series of increasingly violent protests and demonstrations, the French reacted in 1952 by deporting Mohammed V and his son, Crown Prince Hassan, to Madagascar. For the first time in forty years there was a riot in Tangier; the police fired on demonstrators in the Grand Socco, killing nine people and injuring eighty or more. A Swiss teenager was beaten to death by a mob who mistook him for being French. In the summer of 1955, fifty-five Moroccans and eleven Europeans died in a riot in Casablanca. Police opened fire on the crowd in Fez and there was a riot in Tangier on August 20. The French could see that their protectorate would not hold, and in October 1955 Mohammed V was recalled to Paris and in November, on the twenty-eighth anniversary of his accession as sultan, he made a triumphant return to Morocco. The anti-Western rhetoric of the independence movement made it obvious that the days of the free zone were numbered and banks began transferring their assets abroad. Tons of gold were flown out and more than 250 businesses closed, causing mass unemployment in what was still a small town. The former luxurious shops on the boulevard Pasteur stood empty, to be taken over in part by cheap tourist outfits. The British and Spanish post offices closed and all bars within a certain distance from mosques were closed: there were a lot of mosques in Tangier, so most bars were near one. Kif was made illegal, making criminals of half the population. Westerners left in droves, and the international banks closed their doors for good. Foreign imports of food and wine were now taxed, putting many foreign provision stores and luxury shops out of business. The days of the old Zone were now over forever, but officially at least the sultan wanted to maintain Tangier's international community.

Given that it was becoming increasingly difficult for Europeans in Tangier, it was a good thing that Burroughs had been cultivating his anonymity. He was famously known as *el hombre invisible* to the Spanish boys in Tangier; this came from a conscious effort on his part to blend in so well that people would not see him, as well as the fact that, in his junk phase, he was gray and spectral-looking. To the Moroccan writer Choukri Mohamed he was rather more sinister than invisible, and possibly to be avoided: "There was always something severe about his bearing. Anyone who saw him then would get the impression that he was a spy surreptitiously gathering information, the collar of his overcoat perpetually raised, his fedora tilted slightly downwards on his forehead, his gaze steady, one hand clutching the front of his coat, the other in his pocket, or both hands plunged deep in the pockets of his coat."[41] But invisibility was the intention.

Burroughs said that Stuart Gordon, who was now living in Jim Wyllie's house in the Kasbah, taught him two ways to make yourself invisible as practiced by a mafioso in Columbus, Ohio. The first was to give no one any reason to look at you, and the other was to see everybody before they saw you. Bill practiced getting from the Villa Muniria to the place de France without being seen. He walked down the street, his eyes swiveling, checking everybody out. He found the latter method to be a very effective exercise. Sometimes he could get through a whole line of guides without anyone seeing him, which in Tangier was a very good test. "You don't give anyone any reason to see you. There are people whose job it is to see you. If you see everybody before they see you, they won't see you!"[42] He wrote in *The Wild Boys*, "Disguise is not a false beard dyed hair and plastic surgery. Disguise is clothes and bearing and behavior that leaves no questions unanswered...American tourist with a wife he calls 'Mother'...old queen on the make...dirty beatnik...marginal film producer...Every article of my luggage and clothing is carefully planned to create a certain impression. Behind this impression I can operate without interference for a time. Just so long and long enough. So I walk down Boulevard Pasteur handing out money to guides and shoeshine boys [...] Nobody gets through my cover I assure you. There is no better cover than a nuisance and a bore. When you see my cover you don't look further. You look the other way fast."[43]

He told Paul Bowles that he had perfected a system of rays by which he could remain invisible. Said Bowles, "I said, 'How, Bill, I don't understand. I mean, you realize it sounds impossible.' 'I know it sounds impossible,' he said, and then explained that he would put himself in such a state at a certain moment that he was literally invisible and no one could see him. Thanks to low-grade violet rays. He claimed he could go all the way to the place de France without being seen." Bowles assumed it had similarities to Moroccan trance dancing where the dancers leave their body behind and have an out-of-body experience.[44]

Bill's invisibility did him little good in December, however, when three men followed him home and produced a twelve-inch shiv. Instead of swooning and giving in, Bill—no doubt drunkenly—hauled out his blade, "which opens with a series of ominous clicks and it got six inches." Remembering his close reading of *Commando Tactics*, he advanced in a knife fighter's crouch, left hand out to parry. The would-be robbers retreated, then they burst out laughing, "and one of them comes back to mooch a dime off me which I hand him at arm's length."[45]

Chapter Twenty-Six

I figure it will require the orgones of ten thousand boys to finish my sexology. I assume the frightful responsibility of the creative artist.[1]

1. More Orgones

For some time, Bill had been asking Allen to come to Tangier to help him edit his book. When Allen suggested bringing Peter Orlovsky and Jack Kerouac along, Bill said "by all means" and assured him, "I will not be jealous. In fact jealousy is one of the emotions of which I am no longer capable. [...] Self pity is also impossible for me."[2] Kerouac had wanted to accompany Allen and Peter but had seen reports of the independence riots and now had cold feet. That October Bill assured them, "Jack must not be afraid of Arabs. I am in the position to officially abolish fear. The chaos in Morocco is beautiful."[3]

Kerouac took a lot of persuading that he would be safe, and Bill had to write a number of times to reassure him. In January he was still dithering. Bill wrote, "I will say it again and say it slow: TANGER IS AS SAFE AS ANY TOWN I EVER LIVE IN. I feel a chill of fear and horror at thought of the random drunken violence stalking the streets and bars and parks and subways of America. [...] ARABS ARE NOT VIOLENT. [...] They *do not attack people for kicks or fight for kicks like Americans.*"[4]

Now that Bill had enough space, in January 1957 he began to build an orgone accumulator. He had been deprived of the benefit since he stayed with Allen in New York. He kept it in the garden of the Muniria and would sit in it, doubled up, smoking kif for an hour a day. Said Paul Bowles, "He kept after me to go out and sit in it. 'Just sit there and you'll feel different when you come out,' he said. It was a bitter cold winter night, and I did, and of course I did feel different when I came out—I was shivering. The box was like a dog kennel—I'll never know why he believed in that. Some people believe in astrology too. It doesn't seem compatible with what one knows about science."[5] Strange stories circulated around Tangier about Bill's orgone accumulator. In the summer of 1954 he had made "an amazing discovery." When he was high on kif and lying next to Kiki, his ideas came faster, and better than at other times. "It's like he is some kind of orgone battery that tunes me in," he told Allen. "I have tested this many times. The difference is palpable. Trouble is I don't feel like, and it isn't appropriate, to get up and write them down."[6] He did commit enough ideas to paper to be convinced of the theory. He reported that "he is sort of a *medium* through which I get ideas."

Naturally Bill turned the whole thing into a routine: "One after the other his boys were drained of their orgones and cast aside, dragging themselves about like terminal hookworm-malaria-malnutrition cases.

"I don't know why, but I just feel sorta tired after I make it with that writing feller..."[7]

Bill appears to have extended this theory—that boys have an abundance of orgones—and attempted to store them, at least temporarily, in his orgone accumulator. The evidence comes from Colonel Gerald Richardson, the British chief of police, who wrote, "One of them was known as Morphine Minnie. He was an educated American, a remittance man, like so many of them. It was sometimes said that he was putting up a fight against the habit. I suppose many of them did. [...] Morphine Minnie certainly got up to some strange tricks. He had a large box specially made for him with holes punched in the sides: in appearance it was like a very long cabin trunk. On occasions he would induce a young boy to enter the box and lie down in it—fully clothed, I hasten to add—and he would put the lid back on. After he judged the boy had been in there long enough he would open up the box again, let the boy out and send him on his way. He would then get into the box himself, and lie down. When he later emerged, so far as I was able to understand it—and he was a strenuous advocate for the practice—he was supposed to be rejuvenated."[8] Clearly Richardson had not seen the device, as you sit in it, not lie down, but it helped confirm Bill's reputation for eccentricity in the town.

One of the revelations that came to Bill in his junk-free state was that he now found how emphatically he disapproved of stealing, or of any criminal activities, carefully distinguishing between criminal acts and illegal acts. He despised crimes against property and against the person of others. "And I used to admire gangsters. Good God,"[9] he exclaimed to Allen. This was quite a profound change in position given his background in petty crime and association with Huncke, Phil the Sailor, Bob Brandinburg, and the rest.

He was also tuning in to the all-pervasive spiritual atmosphere of Tangier, and made the surprising confession, "My religious conversion now complete. I am neither a Moslem nor a Christian, but I owe a great debt to Islam and could never have made my connection with God ANY-WHERE BUT HERE. [...] And I realize how much of Islam I have absorbed by Osmosis without spitting a word of their appalling language. I will get to that when I, ah, have a free moment. [...] I have never even glimpsed peace of mind before I read the real meaning of 'It is As Allah Wills.' Relax, you make it or you don't, and since realizing that, whatever I want comes to me. If I want a boy, he knocks on my door, etc."[10]

This appears to have been the high point of Burroughs's writing career in terms of ease of writing. Never before had he been so possessed of the muse. "It is coming so fast I can't hardly get it down, and shakes me like a great black wind through the bones," he told Allen, and, "I live in a constant state of routine. I am getting so far out one day I won't come back at all. [...] There is something special about Tanger. It is the only place when I am there I don't want to be anyplace else. No stasis horrors here. And the beauty of this town that consists in changing combinations."[11]

Not only that, but his sex life was also going strong. "Interzone 150 pages, all new, comes like dictation—I hardly get time out to eat and fuck. [...] Tanger is the place in the World today where the dream breaks through. [...] I had two boys that afternoon come to my room, and I am about throw them out they interrupt the Great Work [...] So one says let's make it—'Let's make it three ways.' So Pepe fuck me, I fuck Pepe and Poco fuck me at the same time—it's great in the middle, just relax and let the man behind shove you up the front ass hole. [...] So that's Africa, son. [...] Many times I don't have the slightest memory of what I wrote yesterday until I read it over, it is practically automatic writing."[12]

By mid-February 1957, Bill was writing "The Word," a long prose poem of such majoun-inspired density that most people found it unreadable. He told Allen, "As you see I am running more and more to prose poems and no straight narrative in over a month."[13] Two weeks earlier he had revealed, "I have been hitting the majoun pretty heavy of late,"[14] and it showed. He edited "The Word" down severely, but only a few pages of it finished up in *The Naked Lunch*, unlike most of the routines from Tangier, most of which entered the book more or less intact as written.

Everything seemed to be going his way. The introduction of the Moroccan franc to replace the peseta as currency went in Bill's favor. "The dollar is going up like a beeyutiful bird," Bill reported. "I really love Tanger and never feel like this about any other place. Such beauty, but more than that, it's like the dream, the other dimension, is always breaking through."[15] He appeared to be in good form to receive Jack Kerouac, Allen Ginsberg, Peter Orlovsky, and Alan Ansen, who were about to descend on him to knock *Interzone*—as *The Naked Lunch* was still known—into shape.

2. *Interzone*

In mid-February 1957, Jack Kerouac left New York Harbor on SS *Slo-venija*, a Yugoslavian freighter, bound for Tangier. On arrival, his initial mood was elation as Bill showed him around the Kasbah and they sat smoking kif in outdoor cafés without fear of arrest. Bill arranged for Jack to have room number 8 on the roof with a terrace facing the bay for twenty dollars a month, and Jack unpacked his knapsack and settled in. He wrote excitedly to his editor Malcolm Cowley, "Together we take long walks over the green hills in back of the Casbah and watch the fantastic sunsets over Moroccan fields where little burros trot, men in robes, women in veils [...] we brew tea and have long talks, go rowing in bay."[16] He developed a taste for Málaga wine at twenty-eight cents a liter that he designated "the most delicious wine in the world" and brewed coffee and boiled eggs in his room over an alcohol stove. He complained that the veiled Arab whores charged three dollars to come to his room when he was used to paying only fifty cents in Mexico City but told Cowley, "O they are passionate & sweet." He wrote up his experiences, thinly disguised, in *Desolation Angels*. He described hanging around in Bill's room while he wrote; "often, while typing out his story, he'd suddenly double up in laughter at what he'd done and sometimes roll on the floor." Sometimes Bill would whip out his pen and start scribbling on the typewritten pages, annotating them with further ideas, which he then threw over his shoulder as he finished each one. The floor was littered with pages of manuscript, covered in his spidery handwriting. He told Kerouac, as reported in *Desolation Angels* and so maybe elaborated upon, "I'm shitting out my educated Midwest background for once and for all. It's a matter of catharsis where I say the most horrible thing I can think of. [...] By the time I finish this book I'll be pure as an angel, my dear."[17] Jack was a fast, accurate typist and offered to help type up Bill's manuscript but found himself strangely affected by Bill's prose. "When I undertook to start typing it neatly double space for his publishers the following week I had horrible nightmares in my roof room—like of pulling out endless bolognas from my mouth, from my very entrails, feet of it, pulling and pulling out all the horror of what Bull [Burroughs] saw, and wrote."[18] Jack tried to get out of typing any more, but Bill persuaded him to keep at it, and as a reward for completing the first two sections bought him a small kerosene stove in the Medina because Jack's room was cold at night.

At 4:00 p.m., Bill would reach for the Fundador, a Spanish brandy from Jerez. His friends Paul Lund, Dave Woolman, and Eric Gifford would stop by, and the evening would begin. Over the years Paul Lund had become one of Bill's best friends. Bill found his stories of Britain's criminal under-world particularly amusing: "He had all his funny stories: 'Don't worry about 'im, we've put 'im down the marl hole.' The English gangster scene is so hard and brutal, compared to the American."[19] Bill knew about marl holes because they were also found in the limestone country outside St. Louis. Kerouac called Lund "John Banks" in *Desolation Angels*. He said that Bill "just loved him" and recalled that Bill "always had a favorite *raconteur* he'd found someplace to regale him with marvelous stories at cocktail time."[20] After numerous drinks and tall stories from all involved, Jack and Bill would head off to dinner in a good French restaurant. Ker-ouac mentions eating at the Paname, a tiny basement restaurant run by Paul Toton, who had previously worked at La Pyramide in Vienne. He specialized in steak tartare and langouste. Burroughs commented that Paul Bowles thought it was "an outrageous extravagance going to the Paname and paying two dollars to get a magnificent partridge because he doesn't eat, doesn't care anything about food." Bowles said, "He spends more money on food than most of us Tangerines, I've noticed; perhaps he has more to spend—I don't know—but the fact remains that he insists on eating well."[21] Bowles, who was famously parsimonious, regularly dined at Tony Dutch's café, where Burroughs also often ate, because there a meal only cost thirty cents. Other places Burroughs liked at the time included Michel Maslenikov's Volga in the Rif Hotel on the bayside ave-nida de España, which specialized in borscht and chicken Kiev. There Bill liked the smoked fish and beef Stroganoff, and another favored French place was Grenouille on rue Rembrandt.

Bill's experience with the would-be muggers who had backed off laughing when he retaliated by pulling his own knife appears to have unsettled him. Possibly as a way of showing off to Kerouac, he behaved in such a belligerent way in public that Kerouac was alarmed. He would take out his switchblade in the street and click it open and shut and push his way rudely through groups of pedestrians. Kerouac wrote that "sud-denly he walked right through a bunch of Arabs on the sidewalk, making them split on both sides, muttering and swinging his arms with a vigorous unnatural pumping motion. 'Just push 'em aside, the little pricks,'"[22] he told Jack. Fortunately his aggression was not reciprocated.

Bill's equanimity was disturbed by the imminent arrival of Allen Gins-berg. Kerouac describes how after dinner, standing on the roof terrace out-side Jack's room, Bill pulled out his binoculars and stared out to sea, asking, "When will he get here?"[23] To Jack's surprise, Bill began crying on his shoulder. "He's really crying and he really means it," Kerouac wrote.

Bill questioned Jack about Peter Orlovsky, demanding to know what he looked like. Kerouac wrote that he drew a portrait in pencil, but Bill was not convinced and instead suggested, "Let's go down to my room and kick the gong around." According to Kerouac, they had earlier scored opium from a man in a red fez in the Socco Chico, which they smoked using an old olive oil can with a hole in it for the bowl and another for the mouth. In fact this was hashish. Burroughs explained that "there's an old black guy that hung around the Socco Chico and he sold us some bad hash and several people either went nuts or became sick from smoking this shit. Now it looked gray, it was kind of metallic-looking, I didn't like the looks of it. And Jack started smoking this stuff and he came down with a violent diarrhea with blood."[24] One person, Jim Monte, had a complete breakdown and had to be repatriated to New York. Kerouac wrote that he lay in bed for twenty-four or maybe thirty-six hours, staring at the ceiling and occasionally getting up to vomit in the hall toilet. The experience reversed his opinion of Tangier completely. "And I had really liked Tangiers," he wrote. But now he wrote, "On the opium overdose I had snarling dreary thoughts about all Africa, all Europe, the world—all I wanted somehow was Wheaties by a pine breeze kitchen in America. [...] So by the time Allen and Peter finally arrived for their big triumphant reunion with us in Africa it was too late."[25]

Burroughs had no memory of Jack's initial positive reaction, only his post–hash overdose reaction. "Jack just hated Tangiers, it made him very paranoid. He wasn't happy there, he just had an awful time. The guides bothered him, he was bothered by the whole thing, he didn't like anything outside of America."[26]

Bill and Jack were waiting, waving, on the harbor wall in the sun on March 23, 1957, when Allen Ginsberg and Peter Orlovsky arrived. The excitement was too much for Bill, who quickly became very drunk. He began waving his machete about until Allen told him to stop because he was frightening everybody.

Ginsberg was at the height of his powers. He was thirty, filled with energy, "Howl" had recently been published and was causing waves in literary circles. Allen wanted to do everything, see all the sights, explore the Medina and the Kasbah, visit the circus, swim in the harbor, explore the countryside, visit Fez. Bill's orderly life of rowing and writing, drinks at 4:00 p.m. and then dinner was turned completely upside down. They washed balls of Bill's majoun down with hot tea and stayed up half the night talking. Bill was very proud of his recipe for majoun: two pounds finely chopped kif, half pound unsalted butter, half pound ground wheat grain, quarter pound finely chopped dates, quarter pound finely chopped dried figs, quarter pound finely chopped walnuts, one ounce caraway seeds, one ounce aniseed, one pound honey, ground cinnamon, and half a ground nutmeg. (Two or three of these flavoring ingredients were usually left out.)[27] Mix together and cook in a frying pan until it was a brown paste or became the "consistency of sticky shit," as Ginsberg described it. Rolled in balls and popped into the mouth or spread on crackers, two spoonfuls would see you through the night.

It had been more than three years since Bill and Allen had seen each other, and there was a lot to talk about. Bill would stumble around the room, visiting the two or three kif joints that sat burning in ashtrays in different corners, stirring his drink with his index and middle fingers, gesturing and interrupting. Sometimes his voice rose high in protest at one of Allen's suggestions and Allen gleefully provided him with ammunition for the sheer joy of hearing Bill shoot it down. Art, literature, the politics of the independence movement, Wilhelm Reich, Tangier were all covered as well as gossip about Bill's neighbors and Paul Bowles. Jack was withdrawn and often retired early to read and pray, his demeanor possibly still affected by the toxic hash. During the day, Peter and Allen would sometimes stand in the garden outside Bill's room and call up to him on his roof terrace, "Jack-eee! Jack-eee!" like children calling up to one of their friends' bedrooms, asking him to come out and play. Allen and Peter explored the Medina, drinking mint tea in Arab cafés, relaxing on the beach, walking on the Old Mountain. They were on a tight budget and hoped to spend a long time in Europe, so they couldn't afford Bill's nightly restaurant regime. Instead they mostly cooked in Burroughs's room on his kerosene stove. Allen shopped at the market, often with Alan Ansen, who had arrived from Venice to help with the typing, and each evening they prepared huge meals: baby tuna or little perch from the harbor, or Allen would make his famous linguini with clam sauce.

Paul Lund shared a lot of the cooking. Lund was going through a bad period financially and Alan Ansen often bought him dinner. Before the meal they usually gathered on the terrace outside Allen's room to watch the sun go down and drink sherry provided by Ansen. It was during one of these terrace sessions that Ginsberg took the famous photograph of Burroughs acting out the hanging scene in *The Naked Lunch* with Ansen.

Shortly after they got there, Allen received news that on March 25, 1957, U.S. Customs had seized copies of *Howl and Other Poems* arriving in the country from Villiers Press, City Lights's British printer. City Lights quickly produced an offset reprint in the States, exempt from Customs control, and announced they would fight the seizure. At the end of May,

Customs backed down, but that was only the beginning of the book's notoriety. It was enough, however, to make Allen famous, and literary Tangier wanted to hear him read "Howl" aloud.

On April 5, two weeks after Allen and Peter's arrival, Jack took the packet boat to Marseille. He had been bored and withdrawn, but shortly before leaving "a lovely flute began to blow around three o'clock in the morning, and muffled drums beat somewhere in the depths of the Medina."[28] It was the beginning of Ramadan. Jack suddenly felt sorry that he had already bought his boat ticket and was leaving Tangier.

Allen and Peter immediately moved from the Hotel Armor, across the street from the Muniria, into Kerouac's wonderful rooftop room. Now they settled into more of a routine. Allen would rise at dawn as the muezzin made the first call to prayer, and write letters or journals sitting out on the tiled patio, watching the sun rise and the city come to life. Each day, the Vietnamese maid brought a delicious lunch to Allen and Peter's room. They spent hours on the patio, looking out at the rooftops of the Medina, the harbor, and the boats, or leaning over the concrete parapet to watch Bill putter about in the garden with the hotel cats. Bill had a Russian blue with a silky gray-blue coat and blue eyes that could catch a scrap of meat in the air between its paws like a monkey. Most days Allen and Alan Ansen would spend five or six hours working on Bill's manuscript, continuing the sterling work done by Jack Kerouac. By late May, they had completed over two hundred pages of *Interzone*, as the book was still called.

Next came the harder task of pulling out biographical material, routines, and narrative fragments from Bill's letters to Allen over the past three years that had not already been developed as part of the main text. As far back as June 1954, Bill had remarked to Allen that "maybe the real novel is letters to you," and though not all the routines and fragments had been sent to Ginsberg, most early drafts of large sections of *The Naked Lunch* first appeared in his letters to him. As time went by, Bill developed a number of people in Tangier—"receivers"—to read the routines to, among them Paul Bowles, Eric Gifford, Paul Lund, and David Woolman, and Allen's role as receiver became less important. But no matter how finished the texts were, it all had to be retyped because Bill's typewriting was so sloppy, filled with misspellings, excisions, and annotations. Allen wrote Lucien, "It's quite a piece of writing—all Bill's energy & prose, plus our organisation & cleanup & structure, so it's continuous and readable, decipherable." But according to Bill, Allen had considerable reservations about the book, despite his later efforts to champion it. "Allen did a lot of typing, retyping parts of the manuscript, which he didn't like at all. He said, 'I don't like it.' He thought it was meaningless. He didn't like it at all."²⁹ Allen believed in Bill's genius, but knew that the book was not yet ready for publication. He had felt the same way about Kerouac's *Visions of Cody*, which in a later draft became *On the Road*.

Inevitably Bill's assertion that he would feel no jealousy toward Peter was proved wrong, and it was not helped by Peter's eccentric behavior, which Bill found acutely embarrassing. Peter would constantly stop strangers on the street and talk to them, drawing attention to himself and therefore to Bill and Allen. Bill hated him. "He was so nutty, he just acted like a retard. I found him extremely annoying. It was embarrassing."³⁰ Bill adopted a contemptuous attitude toward Peter, either teasing him and putting him down, or else completely ignoring him. As well as upsetting Peter, Bill's attitude also offended Allen, and things got so bad that after an evening's mocking and ridicule, high on majoun, Allen's patience finally snapped and he leapt up and, grabbing a hunting knife, ripped open Bill's khaki shirt. But even though this shocked everyone into a momentary sobriety, it did no good. Bill simply loathed Peter and could not see why Allen found him in any way attractive; at twenty-four, Peter was too old to be a kept "boy," and yet as far as Bill could see that was what he was. "I didn't like Peter's looks, never have. He just does nothing for me." Bill was further irritated when Allen and Peter dragged a schizophrenic Swede back to the hotel and insisted on introducing him to Bill.

Allen, of course, tried to mediate between Bill and Peter, telling Bill it would be good for both of them if they got along, but they never did. Bill never liked him, even later in life. Alan Ansen shared his opinion and told Bill that as far as he could see Peter was "a free loading bitch imposing his persistent mahatma on you," a view that was reinforced when Allen and Peter stayed with Ansen in Venice a month or so later. To Jane Bowles, however, Peter was a "saint." She loved talking to him. Jane, on the other hand, harbored a great dislike of Allen Ginsberg. On April 4, 1957, shortly before Allen and Peter got to Tangier, Jane had had a stroke and was in bad shape. She was afraid that she was losing her sight, she couldn't read, and was in a continual dithering panic. Allen told her that William Carlos Williams had just had the same problem, with many similar symptoms, and had been left half blind and deaf. Allen joked that she had better get a good seeing-eye dog. Jane was furious. She never forgave him for his insensitivity and refused to ever see him or talk to him again.

It was through Paul Bowles that Burroughs first met Francis Bacon. Bacon had first come to Tangier in 1955, driven by Paul Danquah in his white Rolls-Royce, and he went annually for the next six years, often renting an apartment. He had a boyfriend there, Peter Lacy, a former Battle of Britain pilot, who finished up a complete alcoholic, playing piano at

Dean's Bar, often until 7:00 a.m. Bill introduced Allen to Bacon and he frequently came over to the Muniria to visit, though Bacon, who was used to drinking from Waterford cut glass, objected when Ginsberg offered him a drink in an empty tin can, retrieved from the garbage. He later said he had been worried in case he caught typhoid. Bacon was a wonderful addition to the late-night conversations and, unusual for Bacon, he talked a lot about art to both Allen and Bill. Burroughs said that he had a lot of interesting things to say about modern painting: "he said so much of it is nothing, it's decoration, it's not painting, and as to what painting actually is, his views were hard to understand but very interesting to hear."[31] Bill asked him how he knew when a painting was finished. Bacon told him that he completed a painting with a chance brushstroke that locked in the magic, a fortuitous thing that he couldn't predict or orchestrate. Bacon found he had much in common with Burroughs, and they saw each other in both Tangier and London for the next three decades.

Paul Bowles had been in Ceylon when Ginsberg and Orlovsky first arrived but returned not long afterward. It was Bacon who introduced them. Francis Bacon first encouraged Ahmed Yacoubi, Bowles's boyfriend, to paint by letting him watch him work and by importing paint from Winsor & Newton in London for him. Allen Ginsberg got on particularly well with Yacoubi and invited him over to the Muniria thinking he might like to hang out with a younger crowd. Yacoubi and Bill became friends and he continued to visit after Ginsberg left for Europe and even after Yacoubi married an American woman writer at the end of the year. Burroughs liked him because he was very much into magic, and Yacoubi thought Bill was a great magic man. They enjoyed each other's company. For the same reason, although Bill did not exactly click with Jane Bowles, he got on fine with Sherifa, her Moroccan girlfriend. "I had no difficulties with Sherifa. She thought I was a sorcerer, I was a magic man, a holy man."[32]

Jane had a stroke. A packet containing a spell was found in a houseplant in Jane's room and the story went round that Sherifa had poisoned her, but Burroughs thought that was nonsense; it looked to him like a plain ordinary stroke. What worried him was Paul Bowles's passive attitude toward Jane's illness. As far as Burroughs was concerned, if there was any suspicion of brain damage that person should not be given electroshock treatment, but Bowles just went along with what the doctor said without getting a second opinion. Bowles told Bill, "Well, if you hire a doctor, and if you pay him, he should know what to do. You have to rely on his judgment!" Bill's reaction was, "Well, that's just bullshit. [...] It just seemed to me outrageous on Paul's part to retreat behind this."[33] With Allen around,

Bill got to see even more of Paul and grew to like him very much. He detected a rivalry between Paul and Jane because many people regarded her as a much better writer. Bill agreed, but liked Bowles's early work. His translations from the Maghrebi he found very slight and uninteresting.

The work on Bill's book progressed. Alan Ansen made a trip to Granada and Córdoba to see the Moorish architecture in early June and then returned to resume typing. Bill had liver trouble and had to stop drinking. He also cut out majoun. The manuscript gradually took shape, and by June 11, when Allen and Peter finally left to begin their exploration of Europe, it was ready to offer to a publisher. They had begun with about six hundred pages of notes, some of it more or less finished, much of it not. Over the ten weeks that they worked on it they concentrated on the finished or nearly finished portions, to get it as much completed as possible. Allen Ginsberg remained concerned that there was no character development, no narrative, and no apparent order. He thought that it was, essentially, unpublishable. But Bill was not prepared to make any compromises. As he wrote in "Ginsberg Notes," "How can I write a 'novel'? I can't and wont. The 'novel' is a dead form, rigid and arbitrary. I can't use it. The chapters form a mosaic, with the dream impact of juxtaposition, like objects abandoned in a hotel drawer, a form of still life."[34] Alan Ansen stayed on a few more days to finish off the final details before returning to Venice. As Bill saw it, leaving aside the "Word" section, the manuscript was ready for presentation to a publisher. "Word" he rewrote as soon as Ansen left, cutting it down to thirty pages, but even this he thought he would split up and scatter the material throughout the other sections. "There will always be time for additional changes," he told Ansen, and he was right.

Chapter Twenty-Seven

I reach Freeland, which is clean and dull my God.[1]

1. Freeland

Bill had planned to join Allen and Peter in Spain at the end of June, but by the time he got to Madrid—after first visiting Barcelona, which he hated—they were already with Ansen in Venice. Bill managed a half hour in the Prado but spent most of his time lying in a curtained room, laid up by a mystery illness. He could not even drink one glass of wine without feeling sick. He went straight from Madrid to London to the only doctor he could trust, Dr. Dent. Dent ran a series of tests and determined that he had a mild atypical form of hepatitis and that there was nothing wrong with his liver. Bill found London dull as ever, and rather than go to Venice, he decided to first visit Kells Elvins in Copenhagen, then join Allen in Paris on his way back to Tangier.

His decision to give up his room at the Muniria was based, to an extent, on the great changes sweeping through Morocco. Bill knew that Tangier would not ultimately be exempt and that the sweet life of the expatriates, with their protected legal status, drugs, and boys, was doomed by the nationalist takeover. He went looking for a new utopia, somewhere cheap where he could live as he liked without censure. He had already investigated Algiers, Tripoli, and the whole Near East "during my last bout of inconvenient, expensive, and totally unrewarding travel,"[2] and now he could cross off Barcelona and Madrid as well.

Bill arrived in the Danish capital at the end of July 1957 and booked into a hotel in the center. Copenhagen was cheap, a room for a dollar and thirty cents for a meal, but alcohol and boys were expensive. Kells Elvins and his wife, Mimi Heinrich, the Danish actress, lived at Jaegersborg Allé 67, a single-story modern building in extensive grounds in the leafy Charlottenlund suburb on the coast north of Copenhagen, and Bill spent many evenings with them. Bill liked Mimi. "She was real nice and said she'd fix me up with a boyfriend."[3] Much of the time, however, it was just Bill and Kells out on the town. They took the ferry to the Swedish town of Malmö, just across the strait. Liquor on the boat was tax-free and people would ride back and forth, getting drunk and not even get off the boat in Sweden. When they disembarked the first thing they saw was a cemetery. Bill said, "Kells, let's get right back on that ferry," a line he used in the "Rube" section of *The Naked Lunch*. Bill had a low opinion of Malmö. "God what an awful place that is. Very bad vibes. It was at that time one of the great centers for the distribution and disbursement of anti-Semitic propaganda."[4] Sweden had very strict liquor laws; people had ration cards allowing them so much a month. There were no bars as such, and if you went to a restaurant and ordered a drink you had to eat. They would put dried-out, curled-up sandwiches on the table to show you had ordered food, but only two drinks were allowed, then people had to find another place. There were doormen who would sniff your breath to see if you had already been drinking. As a result there was a lot of illegal moonshine and people were reeling about and puking on the streets. Bill and Kells quickly returned to Denmark.

After spending three weeks in the Danish capital, Bill reported to Allen, "I cannot say that the present trip has been lost on a connoisseur of horror. [...] Scandinavia exceeds my most ghastly imaginations. Freeland in the Benway section was underdrawn. [...] Curious that I should have known without ever having been here that the place is a series of bars along a canal."[5] It was August, and Bill went with Kells and Mimi to stay at their beach house in the country. Kells loved Denmark and was clearly enjoying his marriage to Mimi. He told Bill that he could still have sex three times a day, and compared himself to the old bull apes, who continue until they drop dead.

As for Bill, he was gathering material for his book thick and fast. He told Allen, "Copenhagen is looking up. I am engaged in most curious affair with young man whose face was destroyed in an accident and completely rebuilt by plastic surgery. His pre-surgery picture is as beautiful as I ever see, and he looks just like a *copy* of it [...] but no life in his face now. In fact I think he died in the accident."[6] The boy wouldn't tell Bill where he lived and appeared at arbitrary and unexpected times like 6:00 a.m. "I seem able to conjure him up like a junk pusher." By the beginning of September Bill told Allen, "This novel is now taking shape faster than I can write it down. [...] I made no mistake to come here. [...] Only Scandinavia could have catalyzed the Great Work, and no other place could be the background." He got an enormous amount out of his monthlong visit that was in such extreme contrast to Tangier. The wealthy Scandinavians were so unhappy compared to the Spanish Moroccans who had nothing.

The visit gave rise to Carl, the "Joselito" and the "Examination" sections, and the idea of Dr. Benway's Reconditioning Center. Scandinavia itself was, of course, Freeland, "a place given over to free love and continual bathing."

Freeland had provided the missing set. *The Naked Lunch* has four main sets, inspired by Burroughs's life experience. One was Interzone, based on his four years in Tangier; another was the whole of South America, all the centipede cults and Mexican imagery gathered in the jungles and his years in Mexico City; the third was the United States, both the good ol' boys in Texas and years in New York City as a junkie and rolling drunks. He had only been in Scandinavia for a month but it gave him what he needed. It marked a turning point when the book began to gel into a whole. He told Allen, "I have always felt that the MS. to date was in a sense notes for a novel rather than the novel itself."[7] He hesitated to leave this source of inspiration and wanted to travel north to see the aurora borealis, but practicalities won out; he was short of money and he was out of marijuana. By mid-September, after a brief eight-hour stopover in Paris, he was back in Tangier, where he was delighted to find that his old room at the Muniria was still available. It was a relief to unpack and organize his papers. He had decided that *Queer* and *The Yage Letters* had no place in *Interzone* and should be published as separate works. *The Naked Lunch* was finally taking shape. "The MS. in present form does not hold together as a novel for the simple reason that it is not a novel. It is a number of connected—by theme—but separate short pieces. My feeling is that it will eventually grow into several novels all interlocking and taking place simultaneously in a majoun dream."[8]

Bill's two months away had broken the spell of Tangier. The biggest change occurred in London, where he found himself again questioning his homosexuality. He told Allen, "I feel myself closer and closer to resolution of my queerness which would involve a solution of that illness. For such it is, a horrible sickness. At least in my case. I have just experienced emergence of my non-queer persona as a separate personality. This started in London where in dream I came into room to see myself not a child but adolescent, looking at me with hate. So I said, 'I don't seem to be exactly welcome,' and he say: 'Not welcome!!! I hate you!' And with good reason too. Suppose you had kept a non-queer young boy in a strait-jacket of flesh twenty-five years subject to continual queer acts and talk? Would he love you? I think not. Anyhoo. I'm getting to know the kid, and we get on better. I tell him he can take over anytime, but there is somebody else in this deal not yet fully accounted for and the kid's not up to deal with him, so I hafta stay around for the present. Actually, of course the kid and all the rest of us have to arrange a *merger. A ver.*"[9]

Bill's heterosexual aspect was the impetus for Benway's Reconditioning Center in *The Naked Lunch*. In the same letter that Bill reported his new insights, he enclosed a routine: "Benway: 'The broken spirits of a thousand boys whimper through my dreams...'Let me out. Let me out.' I can hear their boy images scream through the flesh. Always boy crying inside and the sullen averted boys' eyes and those who still love me, and say: 'What have you done to me? Why did you do it? WHY??'"[10] By November 10, he reported that he was unable to interest himself in boys anymore. The words, however, continued to pour out of him. Sometimes it was like a giant jigsaw puzzle; late in November he realized that the "blue movies" hanging sections belonged in a South American Sodom section he had just written and Benway slotted into the Freeland section. He now had a structure: an American section, a long South American section, Scandinavia, and Interzone, with material switching back and forth between them.

With nothing but marijuana, no alcohol, and no junk, Bill was engaged in a form of self-analysis. He was determined to get to the bottom of the childhood trauma involving Nursy that he felt had distorted his sexuality and shaped his life. Instead of writing all the time, he now spent each afternoon sitting on his bed in quiet contemplation, seeing no one. He told Ginsberg that he became aware of the existence of "a benevolent sentient center to the whole Creation" that gave him the courage to dispassionately examine his entire life, including his obsession with Ginsberg. He wrote to Allen, "The whole trauma is out now. Such horror in bringing it out I was afraid my heart would stop. Did get severe intracostal neuralgia and sciatica." He said he didn't want boys anymore, couldn't make it. "Must have some cunt. I was never supposed to be queer at all."[11] This is when he first identified that Nursy made him suck her boyfriend's cock and when he wrote the section of "Word" about "nature's little white soldiers" that he used to bite it. Having brought the event to consciousness, Bill now wanted to move to Paris, not just to work on the book with Allen, but to see a psychoanalyst to clear up psychic blocks that remained.

Suddenly Tangier was dull. Paul Bowles was away and nothing held him there except that it was a convenient, cheap place to work. Bill told Allen he was sick of Tangier, "and everybody in it, especially B.B. who is now going with eight-year-old Arabs and it is really disgusting, pre-pubescent gooks prowling about the house looking to rush in and steal something. And he says gaily, 'Oh, it's just that I feel *inadequate* with older people,' and *laughs*. The stupid bastard is in the middle of a particularly undesirable section of hell and *doesn't even know it*. 'I just feel *inadequate*. He, he, he.' I mean, too much."[12] Bill booked his plane seat. A new season was about to begin.

BOOK FIVE

The City of Light

Chapter Twenty-Eight

"She has her orders," Brion Gysin always said. And if her orders said NO, you didn't get in and that was that.[1]

1. The Beat Hotel

After working with Bill in Tangier, Allen Ginsberg and Peter Orlovsky explored Spain and Italy, staying with Alan Ansen in Venice throughout July and again on their way back from Rome. They reached Paris on September 13 and went straight to Mme. Rachou's hotel at 9 rue Gît-le-Coeur, recommended by Guy Harloff, a Dutch painter friend of Ansen's who lived there. Harloff introduced them to Mme. Rachou, who said that a room would become available on October 15, when the American tourists all went home after the summer. Pleased to have solved their accommodation arrangements, they continued on to stay with Gregory Corso in Amsterdam, but not before handing Burroughs's manuscript to Maurice Girodias at Olympia Press. Three weeks later they moved into room 25. Mme. Rachou liked Allen and promised him that he could have the next available room for his friend, so when the American writer Kenneth Tindall and his Danish girlfriend, Tove, moved to a larger room with a double bed, Allen began paying the rent on room 15. It took Bill about two weeks to settle his affairs in Tangier, and on January 16, 1958, he flew to Paris.

Burroughs arrived in a city rife with corruption as competing lobbies and interest groups took turns in the government. Between 1945 and 1958 there were twenty-five cabinets, with an average life of seven months, as the French deputies played a game of musical chairs in a seemingly endless series of coalition governments. With no clear leadership, the powerful colonial lobby had managed to thwart all efforts to solve the growing conflict in Algeria, where the French campaign of torture, reprisal, and murder only strengthened the Algerian demand for independence. As long as you had papers, and did not look like a Muslim, the Paris police left foreigners alone; they had too much else on their minds. Between

1947 and 1953, 740,000 immigrants arrived in Paris from Algeria, and the police saw them all as potential terrorists.

For Ginsberg, and to a lesser extent for Corso, Paris was a romantic destination. They saw themselves in the great tradition of expatriate American writers—F. Scott Fitzgerald, Henry Miller, Ernest Hemingway, et al.—living and working in the City of Light. Burroughs was less enthusiastic; he had spent eight hours there on his way back from Copenhagen three months before and it seemed very expensive to him. At that time he said, "Paris looked pretty nowhere to me," but he had several good reasons for being there now. He needed to be in a cultural center; Tangier was still pleasant but becoming problematic, and he felt he was atrophying there. He had changed the novel, added new sections, and wanted to work with Allen to finish it and, hopefully, find a publisher. He had made great strides with his self-analysis and wanted to consolidate these by working with a trained therapist. David Lamont's lay analyst David Steele knew Marc Schlumberger, son of the homosexual writer Jean Schlumberger, who was associated with the early surrealists. He was a well-respected Freudian and agreed to take Bill on. Burroughs signed up for twice-a-week sessions. His parents agreed to pay the ten dollars per visit.

The Latin Quarter of Paris was named after the use of Latin by the scholars attending the university of Paris, the Sorbonne, founded there in the twelfth century. The rue Gît-le-Coeur was a narrow medieval street running from the rue Saint-André-des-Arts down to the quai des Grands-Augustins where it met the Seine, overlooking the île de la Cité and the Palais de Justice. This part of the city has been in continuous occupation for two thousand years. The ruins of the Gallo-Roman *thermes* (baths) from the first to third centuries, when Paris was still Lutèce, are just a block away on boulevard Saint-Michel. The street dates from the end of the twelfth century when it was called rue de Gilles-le-Queux or Gui-le-Queux (*Queux: cuisinier,* or chef), which over the centuries was corrupted into "Gît-le-Coeur." Number 9 was rebuilt on old foundations in 1671 and originally occupied by the duc de Nivernais.

Number 9 was bought in 1933 by M. and Mme. M. L. Rachou, who opened it as a class 13 residential hotel, the minimum standard. They never did give it a name. Mme. Rachou had begun life serving tables at the age of twelve in a country inn at Giverny frequented by Claude Monet. She became one of his favorites and got to know many of the artists and writers who came to visit him. Her husband shared her enjoyment of the company of artists, and they encouraged them to stay at their hotel. All through the Occupation they managed to keep the hotel open, despite the privations and shortages of food. All was well until September 1957, when M. Rachou was killed in a car accident; Madame had no choice but to carry on.

Mme. Rachou had curly blue-rinsed hair and round apple cheeks. Because she was so small she had to stand on an upturned wine case when serving behind the bar, her short arms folded over her pale blue house-coat with a smocked collar, engaging in conversation with residents but always with one ear listening for an unexpected creak of the floorboards or an unauthorized person entering the hotel door. Adjacent to the bistro was the small dining room, no longer used, which had a window onto the stairwell where she could literally reach out and grab someone by the ankle as they climbed the stairs. The hotel entrance was never locked, but the door made a terrible screeching sound when it closed. Someone attempting to close it quietly at night was regarded with great suspicion, and Madame would materialize in her white nightgown demanding, "Monsieur? Que voulez-vous?" Easily visible from Madame's position behind the bar was her switchboard, mounted on the wall across the room: forty-two small light bulbs, each with a ceramic label identifying a room number. If the bulb was dark, no power was being consumed; a dim light showed that the room's 25-watt bulb was on. When a bulb flared, someone was exceeding their 40-watt power limit, and she headed for the stairs. Electricity in France was very expensive and she monitored its use carefully. The use of a tape recorder or other electric appliances inevitably blew the fuses and plunged the hotel into darkness. You could have your power limit extended by a supplementary payment.

There was a Turkish *chiotte* on each floor beneath the stairwell, two raised ceramic footprints to stand on while you squatted. Sheets of news-paper torn from *France-soir* were provided in lieu of toilet paper: most people bought their own and brought it from their room. Someone kept making off with the newspaper, leading Burroughs to leave a sign: "To the nameless asshole who rips off the paper—stop!" The toilets were filthy and smelled appalling; most residents preferred to piss in the sink in their rooms, including many of the women, who used buckets. There was one bath, but advance warning had to be given to allow for the water to heat, and naturally there was a small surcharge. There was radiator heat all week but the plumbing was decrepit, subject to loud clankings and vibrations, and hot water was only provided on Thursday, Friday, and Saturday.

Each room had a small gas stove for cooking, and Mme. Rachou inevi-tably arrived at an inconvenient time with the meter reader. If you didn't want M. Dupré to wander into your room pushing a broom, you could opt out as Burroughs did. Most of the beds had straw mattresses; there was a sink and a large armoire. The curtains and bedspreads were changed each spring and the bed linen once a week. The rooms had no carpets or telephones and the cheapest ones, the "cells," one on each landing, were quite dark as their windows looked out onto the stairwell rather than the outside world. The corridors, which sloped at strange angles, creaked and groaned and smelled strongly of garlic, excrement, and cannabis.

Bill's room was not much bigger than a large cupboard. There was a single bed, two upright chairs, a table, and a single dim, naked light bulb to light the gray walls. The window looked out into the hallway so there was little natural light. He paid twenty-six dollars a month. In many of the surrounding small hotels, residents were often harassed and searched by the police. Madame's clients, however, were spared such treatment. She had little time for the police, remembering their behavior during the Occupation, but several of the local police inspectors were old friends from the war when they had worked together in the Resistance. She occasionally gave them lunches in the small back dining room, separated from the bistro by a curtain, to discuss how times had changed. They made sure that her guests remained undisturbed.

She was, however, unable to control visits from the immigration inspectors. As Burroughs described, "The immigration police made passport checks from time to time, always at eight in the morning, and would often take away some guest whose papers were not in order. The detainee would be back in a few hours, having paid—not a fine—but a tax, attendant on the application for a *carte de séjour*; though few had the time and patience to fulfil the complex bureaucratic regulations required to obtain this coveted document."[2]

Mme. Rachou loved her artists and poets, and unlike a great many Parisian hoteliers, she was delighted when they disappeared up the stairs with a new girlfriend or boyfriend, but always made sure that if they stayed the night they signed the police chit as required by law. She tended to treat her tenants as if they were her children, but as Burroughs later said, "She was very mysterious and arbitrary about who she would let into her hotel."[3] She became one of Burroughs's stock of characters, and even twenty-five years later made an appearance in *The Place of Dead Roads*: "Kim heard the blast as he had an afternoon Pernod with Madame Rachau, his landlady at the theatrical hotel where he lived in his song-and-dance capacity."[4]

2. A Friendship Renewed

Allen and Peter had traveled around Europe for six months, ever since they left Bill in Tangier. Paris had always been Ginsberg's ultimate destination, and he hoped to spend a year or more there. Now that he had secure accommodation he unpacked his papers and portable typewriter and began catching up on his voluminous worldwide correspondence. Peter Orlovsky, for his part, had all along felt guilty about leaving his mentally disturbed family to look after themselves. When they reached Paris he received news that his brother Lafcadio had moved back home but that his mother was having a difficult time containing him. In one bad argument she threw a beer-can opener at him, cutting his arm to the bone. Peter was concerned that Lafcadio would finish up back in the mental hospital, where his brother Julius had been for years. Peter felt it was his role to be the older brother to Lafcadio, to protect his mother and sister and get Julius out of Central Islip hospital. Kerouac owed Allen $225, which would have paid for Peter's transport, but he kept prevaricating and not sending the money. In the end Peter applied for a loan from the Veterans Administration and when it came through booked a ticket on the *Mauritania*.

He left Paris on the boat train from the Gare Saint-Lazare the day after Burroughs arrived. Bill didn't seem much changed to them; he was still mocking and aggressive toward Peter, cynical and distant toward Allen. They both worried that Bill had come to claim Allen, and after kissing Peter goodbye at the station Allen fell into a deep depression. He sat crying on his bed. He smoked some pot, but he had recently been getting anxiety attacks when he smoked it and it only made things worse. He had sex with Burroughs "for old times' sake" and sniffed some heroin, but it did not lift his mood. Bill's first two days in Paris were a nightmare for Ginsberg; they argued and had the usual misunderstandings.

But on the third evening, Bill and Allen had a serious talk, sitting facing each other across Allen's small oilskin-covered kitchen table in room 25. Allen told Bill how stressed and miserable he felt and revealed how anxious he was about Bill's arrival. Bill carefully explained the changes he had been going through in Tangier during the last few months of 1957: how he had stopped drinking, and even stopped writing, and spent his days sitting on his bed, thinking and meditating. He had written to Ginsberg about it at the time but Allen had not realized the significance of what Burroughs had told him. Ginsberg wrote to Peter Orlovsky that it "finally dawned on his consciousness, slowly and repeatedly, every day, for several months—awareness of 'a benevolent sentient (feeling) center to the whole Creation.'"[5] Burroughs had, in his own way, come to a similar understanding to Ginsberg's and Orlovsky's "vision of big peaceful Love-brain." Burroughs told him that it had given him the courage to examine his whole life, including his feelings about Allen, more dispassionately and to devote his days to self-analysis. He explained that his trip to Paris was not to "claim" Allen but to visit him and also to see an analyst to clear up any psychoanalytic blocks left over. They talked until 3:00 a.m. Allen told Peter they "got into tremendous rapport, very delicate, I almost trembled."[6]

They discussed sex, Allen's willingness to have sex with Burroughs even though he really didn't want to, and Bill finally understood his feelings. Allen wrote that Bill "has stopped entirely putting pressure on me for bed—the whole nightmare's cleared up overnight."[7] Allen woke the next morning "with great bliss of freedom & joy in my heart. [...] Bill is changed nature, I even feel much changed, great clouds rolled away."[8] They had breakfast together and talked more; the rapport was real, their relationship now on a new footing. It was a cold day but with a clear blue sky, so they took a long walk together through Paris. The next week saw many more long intimate conversations and a deepening of their understanding of each other. Allen went to bed with him a few times, and now that the tension and fear had gone there was great intimacy and relaxation for them both. Allen felt that soon they would no longer have sex, that Bill really no longer needed it.

Bill explained his method of meditation to Allen in detail: how he cleared his mind to stillness "so he sees his important benevolent sentient soul emerge."[9] He used a method similar to the meditation techniques of Tibetan Buddhism, which he first encountered at Harvard. He would sit and let his thoughts come freely. Rather than combat the chatter and fantasies that immediately filled his mind, he encouraged them. He explored all his hostile fantasies, like killing Ginsberg or his nurse; this latter theme had been much worked over by his various analysts. He recognized that these were a part of himself and that he had to deal with them, rather than rejecting them as unwholesome and suppressing them. No matter how painful they were, he accepted their reality. Burroughs, as a dispassionate observer, watched these feelings take over his mind, change, disappear, and be replaced by new ones. Only when the fantasies were accepted as a component of himself were they drained of their power and lost their horror.

Despite all this, Burroughs recognized that there was something beneath all this that he could not get at, something powerful to do with his early trauma with his nurse. Whenever he got near to it, he would experience such a feeling of fright that prickles ran up his neck and he was afraid to continue, afraid that some horrible ghost would break through into consciousness, a memory of something so horrible that he had suppressed it all his life. He was hoping Schlumberger could help him to reach it. He tried to demonstrate the feeling to Allen. He stood by the bed, looking at him in silence. The air seemed to thicken. Bill looked blank-eyed and strange and Allen began to feel scared himself, worrying that Bill might suddenly up and kill him. He began to fight it but then realized it was better to remain calm. He relaxed, Bill relaxed and soon returned to normal.

They also talked about sex. Bill thought that he might be switching his attention from boys to women. When Allen and Peter arrived in Paris they had been having sex with a girl named Françoise, who was still very hung up on Allen, and before Allen got together with Peter he had been living in a relationship with Sheila Boucher in San Francisco, so the question of his orientation was also something to be worked out.

In the two months Ginsberg had been in Paris he had developed a light heroin habit. Heroin was easily available, cheap, and so pure that they could sniff it rather than inject. By the time Bill arrived it had become more difficult to get, but he soon found that paregoric, an elixir of opium, was available without prescription at any drugstore. By mid-February he had a light habit, but by the end of the month Ginsberg had found him a doctor who would prescribe apomorphine and he began to kick. Ginsberg attributed his lapse to his depression about the state of the world. "He was glooming about state of the world, all them armies & armories & closing down of soul maybe forever, in oncoming civilization."[10]

While Ginsberg was in Paris, he and Bill usually cooked at the hotel, shopping at the market on the nearby rue de Buci. Ginsberg made pea and ham bone stews, lamb stews, dishes that lasted several days. Though Paris was more expensive than Tangier, Burroughs was surrounded by good cheap restaurants. There was Chez Jean at 132 boulevard Saint-Germain down a passageway, one of few cafés that still had sawdust on the floor and where a huge meal was only 250 francs (420 francs was equal to one dollar). It was very popular with the Beat Hotel crowd. Au Petit Source, next door at 134 boulevard Saint-Germain, had charcoal-grilled steaks and frites until 1:00 a.m. and was often crowded late at night with Beat Hotel residents. Bill particularly liked the Beaux Arts at the end of the street, and the Balkan. The local Chinese was Au Dong, at 8 rue de la Place, where a good meal cost 250 francs. Even cheaper was Chez Marta on rue Mazarine, where steak and frites, fried eggs, and omelets cost only 180 francs. It was a bit greasy and usually resorted to late in the month. There were also late-night places like Le Cujas, off boulevard Saint-Michel, open until 4:00 a.m. for onion soup and good, filling *plats du jour*. The hotel crowd and local students used to gather in the back room, often with their guitars. And for really late-night dining, there was the Pergola, behind the

Mabillon Métro station, open all night but 500 francs for a meal. It was crowded with late-night people, mostly gay, effeminate young men and masculine young women and great for people watching. Nearby was the Rhumerie Martiniquaise bar, for punch and hot rum on a cold night, and the Old Navy, on boulevard Saint-Germain, one of Allen Ginsberg's favorites, where the art students hung out.

As his room was so small, Bill spent a lot of time in the bistro, usually seated at the traditional zinc-topped bar, exchanging pleasantries with Mme. Rachou. The room had four cast-iron tables with spindly legs on the cracked red tiles. There were several spiky aspidistra plants in the wide window that Madame peered through to see what was happening in the street. Coffee and croissants were served in the mornings, and hearty, inexpensive dishes of cassoulet or rabbit stew were available at lunchtime. Local workmen would often bring their prepared lunches in for Mme. Rachou to reheat in the stove. Bill often lingered over a forty-centime watery coffee after lunch, chatting to the young Americans and Britons who congregated at the bar.

Unlike his early days in Tangier, Burroughs had dropped right into the middle of a ready-made social scene. Allen Ginsberg, Peter Orlovsky, and Gregory Corso were already installed in the hotel, all living together in chambre 25 on the third floor, and had got to know dozens of the hotel's residents as well as many of the British and American expats and students living in the neighborhood. Allen's room was next door to the Dutch painter Guy Harloff's. Bill met him within days of his arrival and liked him, though he was skeptical about his avowed communism and penury. Bill noticed that Mme. Rachou gave him unlimited credit and that he was able to buy drinks on credit at several local bars. It soon turned out that he came from a wealthy family who gave him a large monthly allowance. He was a big man, towering over most people, and had loud drunken arguments with Sharon Walsh, his girlfriend, though at other times they could hear him through the walls as he read aloud to her from Henry Miller. Burroughs remembered witnessing one argument with a small Japanese man in which Harloff bellowed, "Watch you talk. I beat you down to a pulp."

Bill got to know Graham Seidman, "the foggy hipster," who blew the fuses all the time in his small attic room, five floors up with only a skylight. He painted one wall black, another ochre, and the rest white. Like the rest of the rooms, the floor was made from eight-sided terra-cotta tiles, and when it was really cold in the mornings he would splash alcohol on the tiles and set fire to it, which warmed the room just enough to get up. Even with an increased wattage, his record player caused the electrical system to trip. "I can't give up my hi-fi system," he said, so Madame asked him to leave.

Bill knew Kenneth Tindall and Tove from his first day, because he had taken over their room. Kenneth would often visit Bill to discuss the political situation in America. One of the locals tried to move into Allen's room while he was visiting London. Bill reported, "'NOOOOO' I brayed with inflexible authority. 'Don't like you and don't know you. I need two rooms. When I get tired of sitting in one I go and sit in the other.' Such crust. These Paris mooches would move right in and shove a man out of his own bed."[11]

That March the New York critic and novelist Herb Gold was in Paris and came to visit several times. They all had long talks together. Gold had previously been critical of the Beats, not helped by Allen losing his temper with him virtually every time they met, but with the publication of *On the Road* and *Howl* he was now beginning to show more sympathy for their attitudes. Ginsberg read the then unpublished "County Clerk" section of *The Naked Lunch* aloud to him, "which he dug." Burroughs had read Gold's work and liked it, particularly his novel about heroin addiction in a traveling carnival, *The Man Who Was Not With It*, which was probably the source of the word "rube" in Burroughs's work.[12] Bill told Gold that his was the most accurate description of kicking a habit that he had ever read. Bill invited him to dinner, along with Allen and Gregory. "Beat cuisine," he said. But Gold arrived with a girlfriend, the bourgeois daughter of a French general, which no one was expecting. Gold thought that Bill had silently showed his displeasure by pissing in the sink while preparing the lettuce (which he carefully avoided), but virtually everybody used the sink in this way as the toilets were so disgusting. It didn't do much for Gold's relationship with the general's daughter.[13]

Gregory Corso had been visiting with Alan Ansen in Venice but now returned and on March 26, 1958, celebrated his birthday. Gregory wrote that he received no presents, "only a wild party at Allen's with four girls and Bill Burroughs, two Frenchmen, and the drummer Kenny Clarke. [...] We all took off our clothes and turned on."[14]

Burroughs began accompanying the hotel residents to the local cafés and bars, the Bonaparte on the Palais du Luxembourg and in particular the Monaco near the carrefour de l'Odéon. A number of folksingers hung out there, including Alex Campbell and Derroll Adams. Adams wore a ring through his ear, unusual for the time, and was a close friend of Ramblin' Jack Elliott's. Adams used to visit Bill in his room at the hotel. Ginsberg, normally the gregarious one, was surprised and wrote Peter, "Bill strangely more open & enterprising in seeking out the cats than I am, but he found some nice ones."[15] There was one called B. J. Carroll, described by Ginsberg as a "big tough lookin fellow [...] with wild black hair & weird eyes, young, enthusiastic"[16] whom Bill liked. B.J. was six feet two inches tall with a full black beard and dressed as a biker, modeling himself on Brando in *The Wild One*. He and Bill bought hash at Zizi's Moroccan café, next to the police station near the Hôtel de Ville, or visited Ali's at the Bastille. B.J.'s life was complex. Every time Claude, his live-in girl-friend, got angry about his other women, she retaliated by sleeping with someone famous. She boasted about Gerry Mulligan and Chet Baker and others, and when she found B.J. in bed with GiGi she chased her out with B.J.'s belt and vowed to retaliate heavily. A few days later she shouted, "Guess what? I just fucked Marlon Brando." "Brando," a defeated B.J. exclaimed. "Where is he? I've got to meet him."[17] Brando was shooting *The Young Lions* outside Paris.

B.J.'s best friend was Baird Bryant, an American novelist who had been around the hotel for some time. He had worked on *Merlin* magazine with Alexander Trocchi and his then girlfriend, Jane Lougee, who financed the magazine in its last days. He lived by writing pornography for Olympia and was responsible for the first, 1954, translation of *The Story of O*, which was so bad that a new translation by Austryn Wainhouse had to be com-missioned for all future editions. The next year he turned to fiction and, as Willie Baron, wrote *Play This Love with Me*, while at the same time his wife, Denny, wrote *Tender Was My Flesh* under the name of Winifred Drake. Bill enjoyed his company and Bryant claimed in his memoirs that they shot up heroin together, but unfortunately his memoirs are unreli-able, being semifictional, so this may be invention.[18] Bill enjoyed being around these young people, most of whom were in their early twenties. Allen wrote Peter, "Bill thinks new American generation will be hip & will slowly change things—laws & attitudes, he had hope there—for some redemption of America, finding its soul."[19]

Burroughs kept hearing stories about a mythical character named Peter Webber, a handsome young Englishman, a poet, who had died in 1956 or 1957 at the age of twenty-one. Most of the stories surrounding him were conflicting: he was in a clinic in Paris, in a clinic in London, he had died of an overdose, he died of a brain tumor. Alex Trocchi had known him, so it was probably Trocchi who got him onto junk. One day Webber's girlfriend approached Burroughs at the Camelia Café on the rue Saint-André-des-Arts. She said, "I'm so sick of people asking me about Peter Webber, here, here are his papers, all I've got," and gave him a packet of papers: a few lyric poems, some fragments of prose. The last entry on the last page had scrawled across it, "Sir, a young man is dying..." then trailed off the page. Peter Webber was a comet that burns itself out, and Burroughs tried to reconstruct some of the legends and find out the truth. This proved to be impossible—there were too many conflicting stories—so instead Bill "built him into an idealized character of youth and daring."[20] Several years later, Burroughs made a lot of cut-ups using Webber's poems, cutting them in with Rimbaud and other texts. He also makes an appearance in *Port of Saints*: "Audrey is with Peter Webber and they both can fly about thirty feet in the air above the small trees."[21] His brief biography is told in *Exterminator!*: "W.E.9 could tick off a list of agents who had been murdered because they might learn to read and write Arabic— P.W. a young poet who had learned Arabic in a matter of days—Addicted to heroin by J.S. Died 1956 in Paris... cause of death unknown."[22]

3. Librairie Anglaise and the Mistral

The hotel was situated between the two English bookshops, Librairie Anglaise in a seventeenth-century building at 42 rue de Seine, and the Mistral at 37 rue de la Bûcherie, which had a magnificent view overlooking Notre-Dame and the river. The Mistral used to be an Arab grocery until it was bought by George Whitman in 1951. There was a maze of small rooms on different floors, all crammed with books. One room was a library where the books were not for sale, but where people could settle and read. Whitman held many vaguely communistic beliefs. There were cots and long couches in many of the rooms where "book people" could stay, usually writers or poets, preferably published. It was not uncommon for someone to wake up midmorning and find people reaching over them to take a book from the shelf above. The bedbugs tended to make most residencies short ones, at least until the end of the sixties. Guests were expected to do some work about the shop in lieu of rent. Over the years George acquired more rooms in the building and people began to stay for longer periods. George lived upstairs and was a constant presence. He added strange eccentric features, one of which was a wishing well right in the middle of his main sales room on the ground floor. He would turn on a tap and gas would bubble up through the water. He would throw a lighted match in and the flames would dance on the surface. He was hoping people would throw money into it. People were always stepping back from the shelves and nearly falling in. He cooked huge, cheaply sourced meals for his guests, using a pressure cooker that made a terrifying whistling sound. Burroughs sometimes ate there. George's prices were high and he was notoriously parsimonious, buying all his clothing at the flea market and living very frugally. Although many of the people who spent their days reading in the library, or even living there, were writing porn for Girodias, George Whitman refused to stock any of their books, not even Henry Miller, Lawrence Durrell, J. P. Donleavy, or, later, Gregory Corso or Burroughs. It was quite legal to sell them, but not to display them; all the respectable Right Bank shops had cupboards full of Olympia titles, but George was terrified of getting busted and thrown out of the country, so no Olympia books. Because of its large size and accommo-dation, the Mistral was where American students tended to congregate, and it had something of the atmosphere of an American college campus bookstore.

Although very much smaller, Gaït Frogé's Librairie Anglaise was the literary center of the Left Bank. Many of the Americans and Britons had their mail sent there, and there were frequent book launches, readings, and art exhibitions. According to the artist and poet Jean-Jacques Lebel, "It was a wonderful, friendly place to be, much more of a center than the Mistral."[23] The Librairie Anglaise was inevitably much more Pari-sian, with Gaït Frogé acting as a go-between, introducing French and other European writers and artists to Americans and Britons. She was tiny, pretty, and spoke English with a very proper English accent. She had a great fondness for American writers and lived above the shop with the American author and painter Norman Rubington, the "Akbar del Piombo" of the Olympia Press books. Often there was no one in the shop after lunch, but puzzled visitors could hear the bedsprings going in her tiny flat above. She stocked a full range of Olympia books and held book launches for the more literary titles. She specialized in small-press poetry, literary journals, and self-published volumes; there was not enough room for other subjects. The shop was in a curious triangular-shaped room on the corner of the rue de Seine and the rue de l'Échaudé and was domi-nated by a huge circular table, piled high with books and magazines that were in a constant state of flux as people moved the piles around to see what was underneath. The Librairie Anglaise was the logical successor to Sylvia Beach's Shakespeare and Co. as the Paris literary meeting place, and Gaït was outraged when in 1964, two years after Sylvia Beach died, George Whitman appropriated the name in what Gaït saw as a crass com-mercial move designed to pull in the tourists as if his shop had been the birthplace of *Ulysses*.

In the medieval stone barrel-vaulted *cave*, or cellar, beneath the shop, Gaït used to hold readings and art exhibitions, and it was at one of these, when Bill read some extracts from the work in progress *The Naked Lunch*, that he first met twenty-two-year-old Jean-Jacques Lebel. Gregory Corso was there and approached Lebel, thinking him to be a young American, and asked if he knew where they could score some hash. Jean-Jacques said he did. He had been educated in the States and spoke unaccented English, so when they inquired his name they were surprised to find out he was French. He took them on the Métro to Bastille and from there to the nearby passage Thiéré, off the rue de la Roquette, to Chez Madame Ali. Ali was a rotund Algerian in a wheelchair, and his wife was French. It was her café. Jean-Jacques described the place: "The first room was tables and you would eat couscous and when you entered there you were stoned immediately because the thickness of the smoke, like in a Moroccan place, was so heavy that you couldn't breathe without getting stoned. Madame Ali had a dog, and the dog was so stoned, the dog was very nice, and he would always bump himself into chairs, the dog was totally out of his mind, he couldn't walk straight. The dog was completely wrecked."[24] They bought little cubes of the celebrated black hash from the Rif town of Ketama in Morocco for three francs each. As Jean-Jacques said, it was "really good stuff." There was a second room, a secret room, in the back where they had meetings of the FLN, which tommy-gun-wielding police would sometimes raid. They beat up the Algerians but were uninterested in American passport holders and unconcerned about any drugs they may have had.

It is an indication of how well known Burroughs became at Ali's that one day, when Kenneth Tindall asked Bill if he knew where they could get some kif, Bill told them, "Well maybe I do." Tindall wrote, "When he talked he sounded just like my grandpa from Kansas." He told them to go over to Ali's and say Burroughs sent them. They did, and felt uncomfortable surrounded by Moroccans and Algerians, but sure enough, in came an effeminate American in tight white pants, tennis shoes, and a turtleneck sweater. Tindall wrote, "He came sashaying in and plunked a little plastic bag on the table in front of us, and we gave him the amount agreed on, and that was that. Man, I tell you [...] the types Burroughs knew!"[25]

At the end of March, Allen wrote Peter how on the first "dreamy warm day of spring" he and Bill left their coats at home and went for a long walk through the Jardin du Luxembourg, meeting Gregory Corso and a French girlfriend. They were joined by Iris Owens, an American who wrote pornography for Girodias under the name of Harriet Daimler; a drummer named Al "the Shades" Levitt; someone known as Money; Ramblin' Jack Elliott and his wife; John Balf, who lived at the hotel; and Mason Hoffenberg, the coauthor of Candy with Terry Southern, "out for a junk cure constitutional walk." Mason Hoffenberg, one of the funniest men on the Left Bank, agreed with Burroughs about the new generation. Allen wrote, "Mason also talking about how everyone, underground, getting hip or enlightened while both Official America & Russia put out more shit trying to keep war going between each other."[26] They all bought ice creams and Bill entertained them with stories about man-eating piranha fish and sharks. The meeting with Iris Owens was useful because she was an adviser to Girodias and had already recommended that he should publish Burroughs's work.

There was also interest from the States in Burroughs's writing. Irving Rosenthal, editor of the *Chicago Review*, published an extract from *The Naked Lunch* in the spring 1958 issue and in May wrote that he liked it so much that they would publish it serially if no one else would. Allen typed up a chapter for him and, good to his word, Rosenthal published "Chapter 2 of *Naked Lunch*" in the autumn 1958 issue.

Jean-Jacques Lebel was delighted with his new friends but was concerned that they stayed very much in English-speaking circles. He thought they should meet some of the great French artists and poets, which, coming from an artistic family, he was able to arrange. In mid-June 1958, his parents were giving a party at their house on avenue President Wilson in the sixteenth arrondissement. Among the invited guests were Man Ray, Benjamin Péret, Marcel Duchamp, André Pieyre de Mandiargues, Jean-Paul Riopelle, and other luminaries of the world of art and literature. Jean-Jacques begged his parents to allow him to invite Burroughs, Ginsberg, and Corso, and though they had never heard of them, they agreed. Burroughs, as usual, wore a smart suit and Ginsberg managed a shirt and tie. Lebel got Gregory to comb his hair. The first incident came on the way in, when Gregory vomited on the staircase and Jean-Jacques's mother insisted that her son clean it up, that it was not a job for the concierge. After washing Gregory's puke off the stairs, they joined the party. About fifty people were there, everyone standing. They were introduced to Péret, Duchamp, Man Ray, Breton's wife (Breton was in bed with flu), and all got very drunk, mixing red wine with whiskey.

Then toward the end, as people began leaving, Allen and Gregory, holding hands, approached Duchamp, who was in a chair talking to someone. Allen got down on his knees and began kissing Duchamp's knees. Duchamp looked embarrassed, but worse was to come. Thinking to imitate the Dadaist action of cutting off people's ties, Gregory had gone to the kitchen, found a pair of scissors, and proceeded to cut off Duchamp's tie. Teeny Duchamp started screaming, but Duchamp understood immediately what he was doing and reassured her, "Non, c'est très Dada!" Jean-Jacques's father was less sympathetic. Jean-Jacques remembered, "My father comes up to me and he says, 'Hah, your friends, huh? Where did you pick up these fucking clochards?' He didn't say it but his eyes said it. I was all upset."[27] In fact Duchamp found the whole thing amusing. Jean-Jacques was close to both Duchamp and Man Ray and saw them at least twice a week. They never failed to ask after his American beatniks. Duchamp spoke excellent English, but he was shy, and though Burroughs would have liked to have spoken with him, nothing more than pleasantries were exchanged, though, as Allen wrote Peter, "We got drunk and conversed with Duchamp, finally kissed him and made him kiss Bill, which he did—they are very similar in temperament." Burroughs's embarrassment at the antics of his friends can only be guessed at, though some of Burroughs's perceived lack of exuberance was probably due to the fact that by the end of May he was back on paregoric and addicted again.

Chapter Twenty-Nine

Jacques Stern had psychic powers...I was easily impressed in those days.[1]

1. Enter Jacques Stern

In the middle of June 1958, Ginsberg wrote to Peter to say, "A new strange cripple boy appeared on scene. Frenchman named Jacques Stern, went to Harvard & is very intelligent & serious...he and Bill now good friends & sit & talk junk by the hour."[2] It was Gregory who first met Stern near the Jardin du Luxembourg. Stern had just been to see his analyst, who was supposed to be helping him to kick junk. He was a polio victim and was walking with two canes and two aluminum braces. As he struggled to get into his specially modified dark blue Bentley, Gregory approached and asked if he needed any help. Stern looked at him and asked, "Who the fuck are you?" Gregory could spot a junkie at a hundred meters and they immediately began talking about heroin. They went to a bar on the corner and talked for an hour, then Gregory asked him, "Would you like to meet a very wise man?" They drove to rue Gît-le-Coeur but the car blocked up the whole street so they had to park on the corner, then Gregory carried him to the door. Burroughs was sitting in the bar at one of the tables when they arrived. He remembered, "Now here comes Gregory and this almost transparent green demon on two crutches. It was Jacques Stern. Sinister music in the background."[3] Stern recalled, "And I got to talk to Burroughs. [...] I don't care what you say, but Burroughs is the most fascinating character I've met in my whole life, period!"[4]

Jacques Stern was the son of the Countess Mathilde Simone de Leusse and Jacques Leon Stern, a prominent Jewish banker possibly related to the Rothschild family—Jacques certainly claimed he was. He was twenty-six when he met Burroughs, though even his date of birth is in dispute. He and his American wife, Dini, lived in some splendor in an eight-room apartment at 8 rue du Cirque, one block from the Elysée Palace, complete with butler and maid, a library of first editions, and a crystal chandelier in the dining room. He began visiting Burroughs at the Beat Hotel, carried up the twisting stairs by Gregory or Allen, and would sit on Bill's bed, discussing literature, philosophy, and, most of all, their great shared interest, drugs. Stern held little gatherings at the rue du Cirque in which he would give everyone a joint or a little bag of heroin. He was very generous.

Stern had a great friend named Harry Phipps who was even wealthier. He had the whole second floor of the Hôtel Lambert, a magnificent mansion at 2 rue Saint-Louis en l'Ile built by Le Vau in 1640. Voltaire had lived there for fifteen years from 1742. Now Burroughs found himself leaning against the marble fireplace, drink in hand, blending in perfectly, admiring the piano that had supposedly belonged to Chopin. Either Stern would invite them all to his place, or they would meet at Phipps's place. Phipps became something of a patron to Bill, Allen, and Gregory, supplying them with huge amounts of cocaine, paying Gregory's rent, once showing up with three suits he no longer wore; Bill's didn't fit, but it was a nice gesture. Bill was naturally intrigued to know him because the Phipps family owned a third of Palm Beach, where Bill's parents had their Cobble Stone Gardens antiques shop on Phipps Plaza.

Bill attended a number of dinner parties at the rue du Cirque. The food was mediocre, the butler was rumored to have been castrated by the Nazis, and Jacques sat at the head of the table making unpleasant remarks about his wife. Dini remonstrated by saying, "Well, this isn't very nice for Bill to hear." Bill found himself caught where he least liked to be, in the middle of a domestic argument, but he continued to visit.

Jacques' wife disliked Allen and Gregory, who were too ill-mannered and uncouth for her, but Bill she liked. The feeling was mutual. Bill told Allen, "I think she is a really nice person, and I have come to like her very much."[5] She took him to lunch at Brasserie Lipp to talk about Jacques. Marcellin Cazes, who ran the Brasserie Lipp,[6] hated the sight of Bill, who had dined there several times, but on the strength of Dini's good looks they were seated in the back room—not as good as the front room but not the Siberia of upstairs. She told Bill how unpleasant Stern was to live with. "He's a monster," she said. "Being in the same room with him is like being with death itself. When you are alone with him, the bloom and the feeling of death that comes off him is unbelievable. When you're in his power it's terrible."[7]

She told Bill quite frankly that her profession was marrying rich men. "I don't have very long to go, I'm twenty-seven, I think I made a mistake with Jacques." She said she had had another offer from a St. Louis businessman, but, "Oh my God, the idea of living in St. Louis." However, she now thought it might have been a mistake to turn him down. "It might well," said Bill.

Because Stern handed out so much free, high-quality heroin, Bill soon found himself addicted. Both he and Gregory Corso were shooting up. Stern was much more strung out and had been trying to kick for some time. He volunteered to pay Bill's way if he would accompany him to London to take the apomorphine cure that Bill recommended. Bill made the arrangements and Stern traveled to London, where he rented a two-bedroom luxury flat at 2 Devonshire Street in Marylebone. Bill joined him a few days later in the middle of October, after having stopped off at rue du Cirque to collect two hundred dollars in expenses from Dini.

At first the trip was satisfactory. Burroughs was cured quickly, and they enjoyed being in London together. One evening Burroughs took Stern to the Colony Room, a members-only drinking club in Soho where they ran into Francis Bacon. Stern told Victor Bockris, "I don't know how Burroughs knew Bacon, but he did and Bacon was there. Bacon, who is not only, as far as I am concerned, maybe the greatest painter of his time, he was also fantastically versed in everything. Extremely brilliant who knew everything about everything." Stern was in need of a fix and would not have stayed for more than ten minutes had it not been for Bacon's conversation. He stayed more than three hours, listening to them talk. "Burroughs and Bacon are like Gods. They were friends. I just stood there listening to both of them, but mostly Bacon. It was unbelievable."[8]

Problems arose between them because Bill objected to Stern missing Dr. Dent's appointments and not giving the apomorphine method a fair chance. But Stern argued that in order to give it a fair chance he had to really want to be off drugs and he didn't really. Because he couldn't go himself, he sent Bill out to hustle doctors for morphine. In addition Stern was high on cocaine most of the time, which made communication difficult. Bill regarded Dr. Dent as a friend and could see that he had a strong dislike of Stern even though he continued to treat him. Then Stern began the games that rich people like to play.

Bill, I left some change here on the table. Did you happen to see it?
Well, no I didn't.
I just thought you might have seen it.
No.
Well, listen Bill, if you need any money, don't hesitate to let me know.

Next he accused Bill of being a con man. He suddenly yelled, "You son of a bitch, you're conning me! You sneaked around to Dini and got two hundred dollars off her."[9] This was the money he had originally agreed to pay for Bill to accompany him, but Stern was on a cocaine high. He told Bill to get out. Bill went to his room, packed his things, and wrote him a note saying, "Classifying me as a conniving con man is one of the most grotesque pieces of miscasting since Tyrone Power played Jesse James."[10] Bill walked out onto the street and on the corner of Great Portland Street the *Evening Standard* billboard read, "Tyrone Power Dead in Madrid." It was November 15, 1958.

Back in Paris, Dini could stand it no more and she and Jacques broke up. For some reason, Bill seemed immune to Jacques's lies and tantrums and continued to see him even after the London debacle. With divorce pending, Jacques quickly ran out of ready money and asked Bill to go over to the rue du Cirque to try and smuggle out one of the Molière first editions. Astonishingly, Bill was prepared to be ordered about like this and did as he was asked. He greeted Dini—"Hello, Dini, nice to see you. I hope this whole rift between you and Jacques can be solved"—and began to sidle toward the library. She caught on right away; Bill's play-acting was utterly transparent. "Stop!" she said. "I know what you're here for. You want to get the first editions. Well, instead of that, you're going to get out!"[11] Bill conceded defeat and left. Stern was outraged and called him a "no-good dolt." Bill later admitted that his heart wasn't in it, but he'd done his best.

2. Louis-Ferdinand Céline

For Allen Ginsberg, his season in France rushed to an end. He suggested that Burroughs return to the States with him, but Bill replied, quoting Saint-John Perse, "I have told no-one to wait."[12] Allen wanted to see everyone, but only in his last few weeks did he meet many of the writers and artists he had long read and talked about. He received an invitation to visit André Breton but couldn't understand the French on his postcard and so missed the appointment, but he did run into Tristan Tzara at the Deux Magots, and met all the painters at Robert Lebel's party. Burroughs was largely indifferent to meeting other writers because of the language problem but was enthusiastic at the idea of visiting Louis-Ferdinand Céline, whom he regarded, along with Jean Genet, as one of the most important writers alive. *Journey to the End of the Night* and *Death on the Installment Plan* were two of the books he had lent Allen and Jack Kerouac when he first got to know them back in 1944.

The visit was arranged for them by Michel Mohrt, a journalist friend at *Le Figaro*. All Ginsberg had to do was telephone to fix a time. Céline, speaking hesitantly in a shy, reticent, strangely youthful voice, said, "Anytime Tuesday after four." On July 8, Burroughs and Ginsberg took a suburban train out to Meudon, about halfway to Versailles to the southwest of Paris. Céline and his wife, Lucette Almanzor, lived in a large mansarded villa set on a cliff, overlooking a great loop of the Seine and the distant spires of Paris. Bill and Allen were greeted at the gate by barking dogs. Céline came out and locked the dogs up. "Are they dangerous?" asked Allen. "No," Céline said, "I keep them for the noise," but he did always take them with him on a leash to the village to protect him "from the Jews. The postmaster destroys my letters. The pharmacist won't fill my prescription."[13] The dogs continued to bark and howl in their compound. Burroughs could see that Céline was the sort of person you could put down anywhere and he would immediately be on bad terms with his neighbors.

Although it was the middle of summer, Céline had several scarves wrapped around his neck and wore three unraveling, moth-eaten sweaters. He had long hair and there was brown mold under his fingernails. He was sixty-four years old, tall, thin, and very slight. Burroughs estimated he weighed only 125 pounds. He had gone to school in England and spoke perfectly accented English, but had not used the language for many years so they spoke in a broken mixture of French and English. Bedsprings stuck up from the overgrown grass near the gate and they sat outside on iron chairs at a rusty garden table. Madame Céline brought them glasses of beer. Céline was friendly and Allen and Bill were very respectful toward him. Céline clearly appreciated it, and the visit lasted for several hours; they got the impression that Céline did not get many visitors even though his work was enjoying a critical revival at that time.

Bill told him about his periods of addiction to morphine and Céline told the story of how a boat he was on was torpedoed. To calm the hysterical passengers he lined them up and gave them all a shot of morphine, but they all began vomiting because he'd given them too much. Céline and Bill discussed the various prisons they had been in, and Céline said that one could only truly know a country by seeing its prisons. Burroughs agreed. His outrage at the brutality of the American justice system was a subject that he often turned to in conversation in the sixties, in particular the fact that America was (is) the only country in the world, bar none, in which children are sentenced to die in prison with no hope of parole for homicides committed when they were thirteen or fourteen years old. It was a subject he cared about passionately.

They spoke about having a mother tongue. Céline said that it is very different if you're told you're going to be shot in your own language than in another language. Hearing it in your mother tongue has more impact. Bill was sure he was right about that. Naturally they discussed writing, but every writer they mentioned, Michaux, Beckett, Sartre, Céline would say, "Oh, it is nothing, it is nothing, every year new little fish in the literary pond. It is nothing. Genet is nothing!" As far as Céline was concerned, there was nobody but him. He was not self-centered, he just thought that nobody else's work was any good, that was all. Allen had brought with him copies of *Junkie*, *Howl*, *Gasoline*, and *On the Road*, and Céline said that if he had time he would give them a glance, his English was still good enough to read, but Bill noticed that he put them to one side and doubted if he ever looked at them again.

Allen asked him if he was a good doctor. He said he was "reasonable" and told them that he still practiced, but "all the young women want a young doctor to look at them, and all the old women want to stand naked in front of a young doctor," so what could he do. Besides, "It's too filthy here to practice." He gave them a tour of the house, through huge messy downstairs rooms and upstairs to the study where he wrote, filled with piles of papers and books. At the gate as they left, Allen said, "We salute you from America as the greatest writer in France!" to which Lucette playfully added, "In the universe!"[14]

To Burroughs, Céline was primarily a humorist in the picaresque tradition, and couldn't understand why people often regarded him as a vortex of despair. To him, Céline's books were funny, full of life, and an obvious inspiration for his work. He wrote, "Dead people are less frightening than live ones," taking Céline's famous line, "Sick people are less frightening than well ones," just a little bit further. Bill agreed that Céline had been foolish politically. He saw no point in taking any political position unless you were going to do something about it, like join the Resistance, whereas Céline had antagonized both the Nazis and the French Resistance and finished up being branded as a collaborator.

Allen left for New York in mid-July, but managed to make contact with Henri Michaux before he left. He came to supper at the Beat Hotel, bringing a chicken for them to cook. They were most interested in his experiments with mescaline, and after Allen left, Michaux returned several times to continue the discussions with Burroughs. Gregory Corso wrote to his publisher, Don Allen, "Henri Michaux sees me and Burroughs for supper at our place, he's really inspired, great talks. He and Bill talk about various kinds of effects from nutmeg [...] even with my poor French and his poorer English we had rapport."[15]

Burroughs's everyday life at the Beat Hotel is glimpsed in the journals of the English poet Gael Turnbull:

July 31, 2:30 P.M. I knocked on the door of this other friend of Ginsberg's, called Bill Burroughs—he only just up, in pyjamas, looking like a man dying of cancer, thin, pale, unsteady, the curtains still drawn—he made some tea.

[...] Burroughs dressed, an older man, about 40 I'd say, very slow speaker—two themes in his talk, a hatred of America, the physical culture of it, and also an interest in all forms of drugs of all kinds—eventually monotonous, but despite this, a rather pathetic sort of sad stick, one couldn't help liking him.

August 1, 4 P.M. Went to see Burroughs, and had more tea with him, he must consume as much tea as Dr. Johnson is said to have drunk.[16]

On June 26, before returning to the States, Allen, high on Jacques Stern's cocaine, had written a long letter to Kerouac telling him what was going on: "I'm full of snow right now."[17] Kerouac was living at home with his mother in Northport, New York, and she intercepted the letter. She immediately wrote to Allen insisting that he stop writing to Jack or attempting to contact him through other people, calling Allen an immoral lout not fit to associate with Christians like Jack and herself. She told Allen that on his deathbed her husband had made her promise to keep Allen away from Jack, and she swore that she would honor that promise. She said she had given Allen and Bill's names to the FBI. "You miserable bums all you have in your filthy minds is dirty sex and *dope*," she wrote, and warned them, "Don't ever mention Jack's name or write any more about Jack in your 'dirty' 'books' I'll sue you and have you in 'jail.' [...] We don't want sex fiens or dope fiens around us." She put a six-cent stamp on it, not knowing that overseas mail cost extra, so it went sea mail, arriving in Paris after Allen had already returned to the States.

Allen had asked Bill to open any mail for him before forwarding it in case it was important. Bill sent her letter on to Allen, commenting that she was a "stupid, small-minded vindictive peasant incapable of a generous thought or feeling. I mean, she really is evil in her small way. In your place I would show Jack the letter. If he is content to be treated like a child and let his mother open his mail and tell him who to see and correspond with, he is a lost cause."[18]

But when Jack's mother told him what she had done, instead of writing to apologize, Jack instead quickly wrote to defend her, justifying her position and saying, "I agree with my mother on the point of your not using my name in any activities of yours (other than pure poetry and prose) such as politics, sex, etc." The letter was also sent to France, and this time Bill's reaction was more extreme. He wrote Allen, "I herewith forward Jack's weak and cowardly letter, like some cat explaining to a former friend how he 'can't have him to the house anymore because of the little woman don't like Jews, and after all I am out of "all that" now. Not that we can't meet now and then (not too often) for a glass of beer someplace maybe,' etc. Weak and cowardly, 'and of course you understand I can't help out with Neal or Julius. After all why should I involve myself. Must consider Mother first. She is easily upset you know, and I *did warn* him after all.' And a *Catholic*-Buddhist yet, My God! She really has him sewn up like an incision."[19]

Bill told Allen that he could tell Jack from him that no one could achieve the fence-straddle he was attempting. "No one can simultaneously stand behind those filthy letters of Mrs. Kerouac and be in any meaningful sense a friend of the person to whom those letters were addressed. Jack has reaped fame and money telling Neal's story, recording his conversation, representing himself as Neal's lifelong friend. Maybe the fuzz got onto Neal through Jack's book. In any case he sold Neal's blood and made money. Now he will not lift a dollar to help. I don't see it, Allen."[20]

Bill brooded over Jack's behavior overnight and the next day added a postscript to his letter, still furious at Jack's treatment of Allen: "He seems to forget all your hours of work getting his manuscripts before publishers, agents, etc. I don't like the way he shrugs off the horrible injustice of Neal's imprisonment. All he wants is *security for himself.* A weakling and a coward who cannot be trusted under any pressure. He doesn't want *his name* mentioned. What about *your* name and Neal's and mine in his books??" Jack had not told his mother that Allen was back in New York, so she continued to bombard Bill and Allen with letters in Paris. The last letter Bill received he burned in his bidet, and then wrote to her saying he would not forward any more of her insane letters to Allen but would destroy them unopened. He told Allen, "More I think about it, the *less* I think of him, and the less desire I have to see any more of him." It was the end of Burroughs's fourteen-year friendship with Kerouac. He saw him again, once, a decade later when Kerouac, incoherently drunk, attempted to get him to accompany him to William F. Buckley's television show. Burroughs refused and Kerouac himself was thrown off the show during the ads because he was being so abusive. Kerouac never understood what he'd done wrong. In a letter to Ginsberg five years later he asked, "And Bill, how come I don't ever get to see him anymore and if I journeyed to Paris via Air France or Lufthansa jet would he be kind to me when I rushed up to him? Or laugh at me for being fat? Or WHAT?"[21]

That August, before his trip to London with Stern, Burroughs took a holiday in Tangier. His analyst was on vacation and Bill needed a break from the continual interruptions of the hotel. The full effect of the independence movement's cleanup campaign was now clear. "Tangier is finished," Bill wrote Allen. "The Ouab days are upon us. Many a queen has been dragged shrieking from the Parade."[22] Rupert Croft-Cooke and his boyfriend Joseph had been questioned. Dave Woolman left the country. Tony Dutch fled to Málaga, and his boys, "many beaten to a pulp," gave the police a list of hundreds. Bill thought he might well be on it, but as there was always preliminary warning of interrogation, Bill had his suitcase packed and could leave town in minutes. With most of his friends gone he told Paul Bowles that he had never spent a quieter and pleasanter month, eating majoun and working.

Back in Paris, a month before his cure with Dr. Dent, Bill was shooting up with Gregory Corso, who told Allen that "he is hooked, and his room is black, and fumes of PG, etc. etc.. It is not good for me but then again, I ask for it."[23] This was a period when Bill and Gregory had a close friendship. Gregory described it: "we are very much in closeness; almost a love. How nice, I never thought that possible."[24] They sat up for hours talking. Bill found him very entertaining.

At the beginning of October 1958, Bill ran into Brion Gysin on the place Saint-Michel. Though Burroughs had occasionally eaten at Gysin's restaurant in Tangier, they had never connected, and in fact barely knew each other, but Bill had some pot to sell and muttered, "Wanna score?" They began talking and suddenly found that they had much in common. They went to Brion's place and he showed Bill a large pink painting—one that Bill subsequently owned—and Bill began to have all sorts of visions looking at it. Brion had been removed from his Tangier restaurant and had come to Paris, where he had been lodging with Princess Martha Ruspoli, but after three months he had rather outstayed his welcome on the île Saint-Louis. Bill suggested that he move into the Beat Hotel and took him to meet Mme. Rachou. Brion charmed her and she promised to find him a room. In the meantime, Brion moved into the hotel next door and he and Bill began to see a lot of each other.

Chapter Thirty

The years at the Beat Hotel were full of experiments . . . it was the right time, the right place, and the right people meeting there together, there were lots of experimental things going on.

—Brion Gysin[1]

And all this I owe to one man—Brion Gysin. The only man I have ever respected.[2]

1. Brion Gysin

Brion would have liked to have been a black African prince—tall, finely featured, and wealthy. He was tall, but with large features, curly sandy hair, intense ice-blue eyes, freckles, and an oatmeal-colored complexion. His many years of exposure to the sun in Tangier had given him spider veins on the nose and cheeks that increased with age. He claimed that immediately after his birth he screamed, "Wrong address! Wrong address! There's been a mistake in the mail. Send me back. Wherever you got me, return me. Wrong time, wrong place, wrong colour."[3] Brion mythologized his past. He claimed a Swiss father when in fact it was his grandfather who was Swiss but who immigrated to England at age twenty and married an Englishwoman. Brion's father had been born in London but emigrated to Canada to seek his fortune. He met and married Brion's mother there but returned to Britain to fight for his country in the Great War. Brion was born in 1916 in the Canadian military hospital in Taplow, Buckinghamshire. He never knew his father, who was killed in the Battle of the Somme, six months after Brion's birth.

Brion was a poet, a novelist, biographer, artist, photographer, multimedia performer, and restaurateur but was ultimately best known for his paintings. He attended Downside College, known as "the Eton of Catholic public schools," before moving to Paris in 1934, where he joined the Surrealist Group. A year later, aged nineteen, he was expelled from the group on the orders of André Breton, who told Paul Éluard to remove Brion's paintings from a group show held at the Galerie des Quatre Chemins where he was shown together with Arp, Bellmer, Picasso, Magritte, Duchamp, Dalí, Man Ray, and Yves Tanguy. It seems that Brion's poster for the show, of a large calf's head wearing a *perruque*, abandoned on a deserted beach, resembled rather too closely the surrealists' leader. Decades later, Gysin was still fulminating about his expulsion, which his biographer, John Geiger, has suggested "had the effect of a curse." During the war Brion served first in the U.S. Army and then in the Canadian army, where he studied Japanese and Japanese calligraphy in preparation for the American occupation, but the war ended before he could go east.

After the war he became a naturalized American, changing his name from Brian to Brion at the same time. In 1946 he published *To Master—A Long Goodnight*, a biography of Josiah Hanson, the inspiration for Harriet Beecher Stowe's 1852 novel *Uncle Tom's Cabin*, which also included a related text on *The History of Slavery in Canada*. He continued to paint, and in 1950 he went to Morocco with Paul Bowles and fell in love with the country and its music. He was to live there for twenty-three years. In 1954 Brion opened his famous 1001 Nights restaurant in Tangier with Mohamed Hamri so that every day he might hear the wild flutes of the hill tribe, Ahl Serif, whom he hired as the resident entertainers.

Although Burroughs did not know Brion very well in Tangier, he did include him, and his restaurant—renamed the Baghdad—in one of his routines. "After a shot I went up to the Baghdad and met Leif and Marv. The manager is an artist named Algren. If he has a first name I never heard it. Tall, broadshouldered, handsome with a cold imperious manner. [...] As a fashionable restaurateur, Algren is superb, just the correct frequency of glacial geniality."[4] Brion was a mythmaker, a storyteller. He would lower his voice, lean toward you, and reveal intimate details about the court intrigues of Eleanor of Aquitaine as if he were gossiping about mutual friends. He saw plots and schemes everywhere; he imagined slights and made malicious gossip about his friends, while always remaining loyal to them. The simplest facts were imbued with mystery. His closest woman friend, Felicity Mason, whom he always introduced as his "sister," wrote, "He was by turns hospitable, inhospitable, friendly, unfriendly, misanthropic, misogynous, tolerant and intolerant. He was not an easy man. [...] 'I'm a butch queen,' [Brion] said one day on the porch of the Café de France. 'I can't stand fairies.' He was the most masculine homosexual I had ever met."[5] Burroughs was fascinated by Brion's stories and was drawn close to him, becoming a lifelong friend and collaborator.

Brion believed that it was magic that closed his 1001 Nights restaurant.

When his musicians learned that he had been keeping notes and drawings about Moroccan magic they were furious. According to Brion they twice tried to poison him before resorting to more efficacious means to get rid of him. During a routine kitchen inspection he called for a ladder to see if a kitchen ventilator had really been oiled. In the ventilator he found a magic spell: seven round speckled pebbles, seven large seeds in their pods, seven shards of mirror arranged around a small square packet made from folded paper. The charm was sealed with glue made from gum, menstrual blood, pubic hair, and newt's eyes. Inside was a text, written in brownish ink, from right to left across the paper, which had then been turned ninety degrees and written over again to form a cabalistic grid. It called upon the Djinn of the Hearth, "May Massa Brahim [Brion] leave this house as the smoke leaves this fire, never to return."[6] When the kitchen staff saw it they ran from the kitchen in terror. Seven days later, on January 5, 1958, he lost his business to Jim Skelton and his friend Mary Cook, a couple of American Scientologists who had "only wanted to help him out." They foreclosed on the loan and owned the restaurant. Brion was out. However, some good came of it: Brion was to use this method of creating a calligraphic grid in his paintings from then on. Some of his most beautiful paintings were done in room 25 of the Beat Hotel not long afterward: "I write across the picture space from right to left and, then, I turn the space and write across that again to make a multi-dimensional grid with the script I picked up from the Pan People."[7]

Burroughs began to spend much of his free time in room 25, watching him paint. Gysin told Terry Wilson, "William often sat in on painting sessions, following big oils on canvas from inception to completion. Here was I teaching myself to do something bigger and a lot different from what I had ever attempted and I let him sit in on it. There he was and I just had to get on with it. I never let anyone do that before nor would again in my right mind. The process is more solitary than masturbation, or should be."[8]

Bill had never seen anything like it before, and the experience of watching Brion paint influenced him enormously when he began to paint himself in the early eighties. He wrote to Allen that Brion was doing "GREAT painting. I mean great in the old sense, not jive-talk great. I know great work when I see it in any medium. I see in his painting the psychic landscape of my own work. He is doing in painting what I try to do in writing. He regards his painting as a hole in the texture of so-called 'reality' through which he is exploring an actual place in outer space. That is, he moves into the painting and through it, his life and sanity at stake when he paints."[9]

Burroughs's approach to the paintings, and his use of them, was not that of the usual appreciative observer. Gysin's canvases were a complex overlay of glyphs, painted first one way and then the other to produce a deep picture space, not unlike the work of his friend Matta, filled with passages and tunnels. Burroughs described it as "a three-dimensional frieze in plaster or jade or some other precious material."[10] He told Gysin that to enter the picture he needed a "point of entry": an archway, a special spot of color, something to draw him in. "You can see way deep into all sorts of landscapes," he said, "and then you flash back to what appears on the surface. The substance of the painting exists with a double motion, in and out. When you see one layer of the picture, then you suddenly see it all. The eye which I am using as a port of entry jerks me abruptly into a landscape I never saw before. It is a sort of toy world, and one that is somehow alarming, populated with mechanical insects attacking each other, and men in armor from other planets. Or they may be simply modern welders with bridges in the background."[11]

When Gysin left for a holiday in La Ciotat, an artists' colony near Marseille, Burroughs began drawing glyphs himself, showing the obvious influence of Gysin, first in pen, often as parts of letters to his correspondents, then in blue watercolor on paper. But he was not yet ready to use the visual arts. He was strung out and at a stress point in his analysis. He was still visiting Marc Schlumberger twice a week and told Allen, "Analysis is coming to spectacular climaxes,"[12] but did not reveal what they were. Three months earlier, he had told Allen that his analysis was coming to a head and he now was sure that he had witnessed Mary Evans, his Welsh nanny, have a miscarriage, the results of which were burned in the furnace in his presence. That was the "murder" that his analysis had revealed.[13]

With regards to his writing he said that he was completely dissatisfied with all the work he had done to date and with the whole medium: "Unless I can reach a point where my writing has the danger and immediate urgency of bull-fighting it is nowhere, and I must look for another way."[14]

2. Psychic Discoveries

That November, Burroughs bought himself a key chain with a small stainless steel ball on the end from a magic shop on the rue de la Huchette called La Table d'Emeraude and hung it up in his room as decoration. Seeing it, Brion introduced Bill to the idea of using crystal balls for scrying, a magic technique in which you focus your attention on a shining surface, such as a mirror or crystal ball, until a vision appears; at least twenty minutes were needed for a beginner. To "descry" means "to make out dimly" or "to reveal." Brion stared hard into Bill's stainless steel ball and in its surface saw a Muslim funeral, with crowds of mourners on the streets of Tangier. Bill tried it and saw the same thing. They sought out all the information they could find on scrying and quickly moved on to using a mirror. As it is essentially a meditation technique giving rise to visions, it is important to be as comfortable and relaxed as possible. After some deep breathing, the scryer looks intently into the mirror or crystal ball. It is important not to stare, as that causes tears and blinking. The correct technique is to relax the focus of your eyes, while remaining alert, and to not hesitate to blink if necessary, allowing the lids to close halfway. After a while, a dark mist will cover the mirror's surface, followed by a small light from which clouds form and spread to fill the mirror. The viewer's inner eyes are now said to be open, and the journey into the mirror begins. The clouds clear and the pictures begin. Brion: "We did a great deal of lengthy mirror-gazing at that time. We felt that we had all the time in the world to give to such explorations and we did see some strange stuff, just like 'they' always said we would."[15]

Thus began one of the most intense periods of activity of Burroughs's entire stay in Europe. He told Ginsberg that the events of December were "complex and fantastic to point where coverage is difficult. Like covering events of ten crowded years."[16] In the course of one mirror-gazing session, Bill saw himself with completely inhuman hands: thick black-pink, fibrous, long white tendrils grew from curiously abbreviated fingertips as if the tips had been cut off to make room for the tendrils. Jerry Wallace, a twenty-year-old boy from Kansas sitting across the room, exclaimed in horror:

"My God, Bill! What's wrong with your hands?"
"My hands?" asked Bill.
"They are all thick and pink and something white growing out of the fingers."[17]

As Burroughs put it, "para-normal occurrences thick and fast."[18] He was continuing to add new sections to *The Naked Lunch*, and after completing the "Fats Terminal" section he saw Fats's face in an amber bead that Brion showed him from a magic Arab necklace. It was like a monster virus, frozen in the precious stone, looking for a way out: "a lamphrey disk mouth of cold, grey gristle lined with hollow, black, erectile teeth, feeling for the scar patterns of junk."[19]

Another time, sitting across the room from Jacques Stern, Bill distinctly felt him touch his arm. Bill watched fascinated as Stern appeared to lose seven pounds in ten minutes when he took a shot of heroin for the first time in a week. According to Burroughs the muscle that the body first builds back when coming off junk is soft and ectoplasmic and literally melts away at the first touch of junk. The incident appeared in *The Naked Lunch*, albeit in a slightly exaggerated form: "I saw it happen. Ten pounds lost in ten minutes standing with the syringe in one hand holding his pants up with the other, his abdicated flesh burning in a cold yellow halo."[20]

Burroughs and Gysin quickly involved fellow residents in their experiments. Baird Bryant described staring at the armoire mirror and the use of a half coconut shell filled with water. Bryant reported, "It did not take long for the water to begin glowing, subtly, very subtly, then it became a little window."[21] Their two main collaborators were Jacques Stern and Sheldon "Mack" Thomas, usually referred to as Shell by Burroughs, a tenor sax–playing novelist from Texas. Burroughs, Stern, Gysin, and Thomas all had the same vision of a coffin in a library. Gysin, anxious to retain his leadership of the paranormal experiments, embarked upon a thirty-six-hour session, gazing into the mirror on the door of his armoire. He sat lotus position on the bed and his friends handed him food, cigarettes, and joints to keep him going. He saw scientists in nineteenth-century labs, great battles, and chieftains of unknown races. After twenty-four hours the images disappeared and he wrote that "there seemed it was a limited area that one could see only a certain distance into, uh, where everything was covered with a gently palpitating cloud of smoke which would be about waist high [...] that was the end, there was nothing beyond that."[22]

Every night Bill and assorted residents went to Brion's room to watch all the weird psychic experiences that were occurring. Burroughs told Ted Morgan, "It was a great period, a lot of fun, just a lot of fun. The thing about it for me, about magic, and that whole area of the occult, is that it is FUN! Fun, things happen. It's great. And none of it ever bothers me, you can't get too extreme." Some residents were freaked out by what went on. Nick Smart, a friend of Burroughs's, put his nose around the door when they were all in there and some sort of spirit materialized before his eyes. Burroughs said, "He took one look and said, 'Oh shit!' and walked out."[23] As far as Burroughs was concerned they were breaking new ground and making important new discoveries, and it was all thanks to Brion.

Allen Ginsberg: "So Brion was a kind of shaman."
WSB: "He was a shaman. A very potent shaman."[24]

One of the key findings in all this experimentation for Burroughs was the identification of the "Ugly Spirit" and the concept of occupation and possession by spirits. During one of their psychic experiments in 1959, Brion wrote on a piece of paper in a semitrance state the line, "For ugly spirit shot Joan because..." In his introduction to *Queer* Burroughs wrote, "A bit of mediumistic message that was not completed—or was it? It doesn't need to be completed if you read it: 'ugly spirit shot Joan *to be cause*,' that is, to maintain a hateful parasitic occupation."[25]

Burroughs identified the Ugly Spirit as having to do with his privileged patrician background, received ideas and attitudes that were still lodged in him, controlling him. Now that he could name it, countermeasures could be taken. Burroughs regarded the Ugly Spirit as a "psychic entry" into his being by a malevolent force, and as the years passed, the term entered his personal cosmography. The true cause of Joan's death was again revealed in one of Bill's cut-ups. He wrote, "Raw peeled winds of hate and mischance blew the shot," which he assumed meant blowing a shot of junk, when the junk squirts out the side of the syringe or dropper because of a blockage, until Brion Gysin pointed out that this referred to the shooting of Joan. It was more evidence of possession. Another suppressed area was identified in the summer of 1958. "Brion told me, 'This is not life or death but something in between' and at some point he said, 'What about your brother?' and I burst into tears, realizing the emptiness of Mort's life and my own responsibility."[26] Scrying was as good as psychoanalysis.

In February 1959 Brion had an appendectomy and went to Marrakech to recuperate. That April, Bill decided to follow him to the sun and flew to Tangier, but on arrival he found that he was wanted by the police. About six months before, he had considered the possibility of selling some Moroccan hash in Paris and wrote Paul Lund, asking if he could supply him with any "leather goods"; the idea was to sew it into the lining of Moroccan camel saddles. Nothing ever came of it. Meanwhile, Clive Stevens, the captain of a three-masted topsail schooner called the *Amphitrite* and an old friend of Paul Lund's, had been sailing for the West Indies when he was stopped and held in house arrest for a year in the Canary Islands after hitting a policeman. The boat had been impounded in Gibraltar to await the result of litigation, and when Stevens returned to Tangier he was busted trying to buy a half kilo of opium from "the Old Black Connection" in the Socco Chico.

Both Stevens and "the Old Black Connection" were held incommunicado and in an attempt to shift the blame, "the Old Black Connection" implicated Paul Lund and "an American with glasses" in the deal. Lund had been going straight and had opened a bar called the Novara in November 1957. If he had been repatriated to England he would have faced a long jail sentence. He appears to have concocted a story with Stevens and the Connection to shift the blame to Burroughs—the "American with glasses"—and make out that he was the Paris mastermind of an opium-smuggling plot. This explains how Burroughs's "camel saddles" letter came to be found, improbably, in Stevens's pocket. To further complicate matters, the police had somehow obtained a letter that Bill sent to Shell Thomas from London, saying something to the effect of, "Pooling our knowledge could be of great benefit to both parties," which, although it referred to scrying, suggested to the authorities that Bill was the mastermind behind a narcotics ring.

While searching Paul Lund's premises they found a suitcase of manuscripts that Bill had left there in storage. Bill wrote Allen that "[they] wade through a suitcase of my vilest pornography looking for 'evidence.' (They must figure hanging has a code significance.)"[27] Burroughs was ignorant of quite how much he had been implicated and happily socialized with Paul Lund. One day he was visiting Lund when the police appeared to make another search of his premises. Miraculously they did not ask to see Bill's papers or search him, which was fortunate because he had five grams of opium in his pocket at the time, which would have made the charges all the more difficult to explain.

After the police left, Lund was forced to shamefacedly explain that he had given them the letter and denounced him as a smuggler. Bill was outraged: his freedom was endangered, his holiday ruined. However, he continued to see Lund after that and never raised the issue with him again. One day Lund said, "You know Bill, there comes a point when you're broken. [...] They broke me." Burroughs said, "Those were his words, I didn't press him any further. All my annoyance having evaporated completely."[28]

〜

Bill took the packet boat to Marseille with Alan Ansen, who had also been taking a break in Tangier and had decided to accompany Bill back to Paris. Bill demonstrated his latest psychic discoveries and Alan was suitably impressed. Bill asserted that there was a magnetic attraction between his stainless steel scrying ball and a magnifying mirror he had bought. He claimed that every time the mirror was positioned near the ball, the ball moved away. Alan assured him it was indeed the case. In fact Burroughs was now finding the ball painful to use. In Tangier he had begun to feel a physical pressure operating on his body, pushing him away from the ball, which made him so uneasy that he had to sleep with the light on. Things jumped from his hands. He told Allen, "Well, I will not turn back (even if I could)."[29]

He also told Allen that he no longer thought about sex; he didn't know if he was interested in man or woman, or both, or neither. He said that his analysis had, "with a slow scalpel of fact, cancelled my sado-masochist visa to Sodom. I wonder if any but the completely innocent can enter without a S-M Visa? I don't know." This was not the first time he had expressed doubts about his sexual orientation, but his lack of sex drive was more likely attributable to his severe drug habit. Back in Paris, in order to maintain his addiction but keep himself clean in the event of a police raid, Burroughs began taking box after box of Eubispasme pills. These were codethyline, an alkaloid extracted from opium, small black pills available at any pharmacy in France without a prescription and sold as a cure for the *grippe*. France is still the only country in the world where opium extract is sold freely at pharmacies.[30] He even kept his supply of kif out of his room in case the police visited but was clearly not assiduous enough in his housekeeping because when they eventually came, they found a couple of cubes of hash.

Alan Ansen returned to Venice and Bill found himself more or less alone in Paris: Shell decided to return to the United States. Bill was sorry to see him go because he already regarded him as part of a triumvirate of mystical experimenters: "the three mystics I had hoped to form nucleus and get something definite and useable via cross-fertilization—Shell, Gysin and Stern."[31] Shell told Bill that he was going to buy an ounce of heroin and smuggle it back to the States. Bill didn't want to hear about it. When Shell tried to sell it in Houston, the buyer informed on him and he got twenty years. Burroughs thought he was lucky not to be busted at customs. He told Allen, "Imagine that idiot going back with a saxophone and loud clothes...a *saxophone!!!* My God, how fucking stupid can a man get...?"[32] Bill was sure that the police were watching him from then on. Shell served five years and while in jail had a number of stories published in *Evergreen Review*. When he got out, Grove published his first novel, *Gumbo*,[33] which ran to a number of printings. Burroughs remained in touch with him throughout his lifetime.

Shell's departure coincided with Stern going into complete seclusion, not even answering letters, saying that the presence of people was painful to him. Gysin, meanwhile, was having a paranoid episode, leaving Bill with no one. Bill thought that Brion was afraid of him as "a notorious carrier of Black Fuzz, bad luck and death." He told Allen, "I continue to see visions and experience strange currents of energy, but the Key—the one piece that could make it useable—Stern had part of it, and so did Shell (Gysin more a catalyst or medium in strict sense)."[34] Possibly Gysin's exclusion was because of the four of them, he was the only one not on hard drugs. Burroughs was down to 120 pounds, strung out and in ill health. Two things happened to pull him from his depression: the return of Jacques Stern, and Maurice Girodias's change of mind over publishing *The Naked Lunch*. He also got busted.

Stern was a complete fantasist and regaled Bill with an account of a series of improbable events, all of which Bill believed implicitly, and all of which were complete fabrication. He invited Bill to spend a month with him on his yacht in Monte Carlo (the yacht did not exist). He claimed to have hit a concrete island in his Bentley at 130 miles per hour, rolled over twice, and emerged without a scratch, and to have fallen down a marble staircase (the Bentley was intact, there was no accident). He claimed that Dr. Dent had treated him for an acute case of catatonic shock by injecting him with twelve grains of heroin in two hours, with two nurses holding him down and the pain so bad that he bit a piece of wood in half. He was given an electric shock, came out of catatonia, and wrote a novel in nine days. Burroughs read the novel, called *The Fluke*, which Stern claimed was going to be published by Faber in London, and was astonished by its brilliance. He told Allen that he thought Stern's writing "is better by far than mine or Kerouac's or yours or Gregory's or anyone I can think of. There is no doubt about it, he is a great writer. I think the greatest writer of our time."[35] Ginsberg despaired over his old friend's latest unrestrained enthusiasms. *The Fluke*, written in an inaccessible post–*Finnegans Wake*, post-Céline style, in short sentences, sometimes of one word, prefigures cut-ups in its overall impression but makes very hard reading:

> Taking in the sight of many many people.. Many.. More than I had even seen before from any single vantage point.. At any one time.. There seemed to be...a multitude, I guess one would call it.. A veritable one.. The normal abnormalcy one with ordinary eyesight would see from such a height.. And I tried to count.. For then I could.. But there were so many.. too many.. That I could not.. Not possibly.. Nor choose.. One.. That might instruct me.. As I wished to be..[36]

Faber, of course, did not publish it and probably never even saw it. When Stern eventually decided to print it himself, Burroughs wrote a glowing introduction, concluding, "The real writer is there. And sometimes he can only send back a short wave code message of warning."

Chapter Thirty-One

Can I bring it back, the magic and danger and fear of those years in 9 rue Git-le-Coeur and London and Tangier—the magic photographs and films.[1]

1. *The Naked Lunch*

Although he periodically added new sections to *The Naked Lunch*, not a great deal had happened on the publishing front since Burroughs had arrived in Paris. The first thing Allen Ginsberg had done on arrival was to show it to Maurice Girodias, but Girodias had turned it down. He returned it to Ginsberg and recalled, "It was such a mess that manuscript. You couldn't physically read the stuff. [...] The ends of the pages were all eaten away by rats or something."[2] Ginsberg was very angry with him. Over the months Burroughs had continued to tinker with it, adding some material he found in the medical library on the rue Dragon, and some new routines. Terry Southern and Mason Hoffenberg had tried to interest Girodias in it a second time, but still without success. Then on October 25, 1958, in the Saturday issue of the *Chicago Daily News*, columnist Jack Mabley, in a piece headed "Filthy Writing on the Midway," fulminated against a magazine that he identified only as being published by the University of Chicago, calling it "one of the foulest collections of printed filth I've seen publicly circulated." Mabley concluded, "But the University of Chicago publishes the magazine. The trustees should take a long hard look at what is being circulated under its sponsorship."[3]

It was obviously directed against the autumn edition of the *Chicago Review*, which opened with "Chapter Two of *Naked Lunch*." The article caused little more than a ripple. Some students felt insulted, and the campus newspaper, the *Maroon*, ran an editorial calling Mabley irresponsible, saying his contemptuous remarks about the Beat Generation were "more an attack on the University than a literary criticism of its publications."[4] Mabley quickly responded in his column, writing, "If in criticizing half a dozen University of Chicago students, I reflected on the whole student body, I apologize."[5]

Meanwhile, although there was a tradition of editorial autonomy, the dean asked to see a list of contents for the upcoming winter issue. Among the pieces he objected to were ten chapters from *The Naked Lunch*, Jack Kerouac's "Old Angel Midnight," and three poems by Gregory Corso. In the first week of November, Chancellor Lawrence A. Kimpton called an emergency meeting of the faculty advisory board and told them that he was under pressure from the university's fund-raising and public relations departments, who were concerned "over the possible consequences of continued adverse publicity." On November 11, Kimpton called a meeting of the nine-member committee of the council of the university senate to discuss the *Chicago Review*, but the matter was unresolved. After more discussions, Dean Wilt informed Irving Rosenthal that the winter issue could not be published as it stood and must be "completely innocuous." He suggested that the offending articles could be spread over a number of subsequent issues. Rosenthal and six members of his staff resigned in protest, leaving only one, Hyung Woong Pak, who stepped in as editor as he was prepared to accept censorship from the university authorities.

Rosenthal resolved to publish the offending issue himself, and on January 29, 1959, there was a benefit poetry reading by Allen Ginsberg and Gregory Corso, who traveled to Chicago specifically for it. (Kerouac refused to help even though his piece was one of those instrumental in getting the winter issue suppressed.) Their visit was front-page news in the Chicago press. Society hostesses vied to put them up and even *Time* magazine covered the event. The reading and donations from the Shaw Society of Chicago raised enough money to publish the suppressed issue. The new magazine was called *Big Table*.

And there it might have ended, except for a surprise intervention from an unlikely source. August Derlith, the first publisher of H. P. Lovecraft and the author of numerous horror stories and science-fiction novels, read a review copy of *Big Table* and was so offended by its contents that he contacted the postmaster in Chicago to get the magazine banned from the mails. Under the Comstock Act, the U.S. Post Office had stringent laws to prohibit "obscene, lewd, lascivious, indecent, filthy or vile" articles from going through the mails. Derlith "evidenced a desire" to testify against the magazine in any hearing designed to determine its mailability. Without realizing it, this self-appointed guardian of public morality did Burroughs a huge favor.

In March, the Post Office refused to give *Big Table* second-class mailing privileges and launched an inquiry into its mailability. The American

Civil Liberties Union got involved, appointing Chicago attorney Joel J. Sprayregen to represent them. A formal complaint against the magazine was made suggesting that *Big Table* violated U.S. Code 18, Section 1461, because "'Old Angel Midnight' and 'Ten Episodes from Naked Lunch' were 'obscene, lewd, lascivious, indecent, and filthy.'" A hearing was eventually set in Chicago for June 23 (always a good number for Burroughs). The ACLU was sure that the case could be won, if not at the Post Office level, then at some future federal court level, and began to gather testimonials. On May 30, *The Nation* ran an article on the case, criticizing the Post Office, and other magazines and newspapers began to take notice.[6] Maurice Girodias in Paris saw all the controversy being caused by *The Naked Lunch* and decided that now was the time to publish.

Moving swiftly, he dispatched his assistant, a young South African poet named Sinclair Beiles whom Burroughs had known in Tangier, to the Beat Hotel. He told Burroughs that Girodias wanted the manuscript in two weeks to capitalize on the publicity generated by the court case and news articles. Burroughs already had a lot of it prepared. For instance, no further work was required on the ten chapters published in *Big Table*, and other sections were almost ready. Burroughs had a large suitcase containing six or seven hundred pages of manuscript and he would rummage around in it looking for material that needed the least amount of work to include. Brion Gysin and Alan Ansen were summoned to do the typing. Burroughs: "I'd say, 'Here, this section. I can get that together easily,' and reach into this great suitcase full of manuscripts and assemble it. Nobody had any part in the editorial process. I didn't organize it, I just got the pieces together. I said, 'Here's piece one, piece two...' I said, 'We'll worry about the order later.'"[7] As soon as a section was typed, Beiles took it to the typesetters, and so the order was determined by the arbitrary order in which the pages were retrieved from the suitcase. Burroughs did little or none of the typing; he was coming off paregoric and in no shape to type accurately. In between annotating sections for typing he busied himself with sticking photographs from his South American trip to the wall of his hotel room with adhesive tape. These were to act as an aide-mémoire for his next book, *The Soft Machine*, which was set entirely in South America. Burroughs was already thinking ahead. Eventually this photographic collage, made up of corner-pharmacy-size black-and-white prints, covered a large section of the wall and was the genesis of his photographic collages and the illustrated scrapbooks of the early sixties.

When the galleys came back from the printer, first Sinclair Beiles looked through them, then Brion Gysin took a look and said, "Why change the order at all? It's perfect!" The only change that Burroughs made was to move the beginning to the end so that the policemen Hauser and O'Brien bookended the text. He already had the name *The Naked Lunch*, ever since Ginsberg was reading aloud from the manuscript of *Queer* and misread "naked lust" for "naked lunch" and Kerouac identified it as a good name for a book. At the time Burroughs thought it was a bit pretentious, but when the time came to give the book a name it seemed all right. In July, four weeks after Beiles came knocking on his door, Girodias had printed five thousand copies and it was out in the bookshops. Burroughs himself designed the jacket using some of the calligraphs he had been experimenting with under Gysin's tutelage, and Allen Ginsberg took the portrait of the author on the inner flap.

The Naked Lunch takes place in a number of different locations or sets but is "much more of a surrealist extrapolation than a journalistic account"[8] of these places. Burroughs has described the book as a group of free-association vaudeville routines, and he was later to use them in readings to great comic effect. "A series of episodes, misfortunes, and adventures happening to the protagonist, but no real plot, no beginning, no end."[9]

The book uses the oldest novel format in the world, the picaresque, which developed in sixteenth-century Spain but has roots going back to the *Satyricon* of Petronius. The word *picaresca* comes from *pícaro* or "rogue," and inevitably the protagonist is an antihero, usually living by his wits in a corrupt society. Examples are *Don Quixote* (1605, 1615) by Miguel de Cervantes, *Tom Jones* by Henry Fielding (1749), and *The Unfortunate Traveller* by Thomas Nashe (1594), books well known to Burroughs from his degree studies at Harvard. In *The Naked Lunch*, Lee is the narrator just as Jack Wilton was the narrator in *The Unfortunate Traveller*. The *Adventures of Roderick Random* by Tobias Smollett (1748) has been cited by Burroughs as an influence on the book, particularly on the character of Dr. Benway. Smollett's book contains a description of the sea battle of Cartagena in 1741, in which the ship's doctor is unable to tend the wounded until he has drunk enough rum to completely dull his senses and by then there are limbs flying all over the deck. It was a book that Kells Elvins and Burroughs discussed when writing "Twilight's Last Gleamings" at Harvard in 1938, where Dr. Benway first makes an appearance.

Burroughs's classical education played a powerful but invisible role in much of his writing, particularly his study of the picaresque novel. Modern picaresque novels would include Henry Miller's *Tropic of Cancer* and the works of Céline. Burroughs often spoke of *The Naked Lunch* as being in this tradition, with characters like Dr. Benway, Carl, or A.J. appearing fully formed with no character development; they are what you see. Like

Benway, A.J. had no life model, though it pleased Alan Ansen to think it was based on him. The initials stood for nothing. He was another Burroughs figure of outrage, putting piranha into Lady Sutton-Smith's swimming pool and decapitating Dame Sitlong's Afghan hound at a party.[10] Just as Burroughs found characters waiting in other people's novels, so Terry Southern deliberately appropriated A.J. whole for his book *The Magic Christian*, where he became Guy Grand.

The Naked Lunch introduced a stage full of Burroughs characters, many of whom were to reoccur in subsequent books. Some were taken from real life, others were composites, but most just came from Burroughs's dreams or imagination; he once said that he dreamed at least half of his characters. Real-life characters included Pantopon Rose, an old whore who hung around 103rd Street and Broadway in 1945 who sometimes had pantopon on prescription. Some of the old junkies Burroughs knew then would say, "Maybe Pantopon Rose is holding," a phrase that Burroughs filed away. She charged two dollars per tablet. (Pantopon is opium in an injectable form with all the tars and other insoluble material removed, and is nearly as potent as morphine by weight.) Several characters came from Tangier: Marvie was Dave Woolman and Leif the Unlucky was Eric "Calamity" Gifford. Andrew Keif and Arachnid his driver were based very much on Paul Bowles and Temsamany.

Many of the characters were composites or stereotypes mixed with real characters such as Carl, who was a generic Scandinavian boy, or Hauser and O'Brien, who were the cops who busted him in 1945, but in a wildly exaggerated form. Clem and Jody were stereotype "Ugly Americans," saying the most outrageous things just to annoy the local people.

Among the characters that came from dreams were the mugwumps. The character came to him as a picture: an Egyptian face with purple lips and black eyes with no irises, like a character in Bosch's *Garden of Earthly Delights*. The Mugwumps were a nineteenth-century American political grouping, but Burroughs had no interest in them except to appropriate their name. The final passage in *The Naked Lunch*, where David Lamont throws gasoline over a group of Arabs and sets fire to it, came to Burroughs in a dream in London in 1956.

There are clear models for the book. For instance, the interview between Dr. Benway and Carl Peterson is consciously modeled on the interview between the protagonist of Conrad's *Under Western Eyes* and Councillor Mikulin; Burroughs used Mikulin's broken-off, unfinished sentences and even some of his words. Burroughs mentioned in writing classes that he regarded it as perfectly legitimate to take a scene from someone else's book and use it in another way.

The political parodies in the book included the Moroccan nationalist party, the Istiqlal. Having observed the Istiqlal at close quarters in Mme. Porte's Salon de Thé in Tangier, Burroughs was engaging in light parody and getting back at all the shoeshine boys who would snarl at him and say, "We will push you into the sea!" The other political parties of Interzone were Burroughs's inventions: the Senders who stood for control addicts; the Liquefactionists who were the exploiters and absorbers of youthful energy; the Divisionists who stood for multipliers of their own personality; and the Factualists who were the pure in heart.

The most notorious passages in the book are the hanging scenes featuring John and Mary, which were included in counterpoint to all the idyllic sex with boys. Burroughs had read about autoerotic sex where young men part-hang themselves to enhance their orgasm, but mostly it was the image of hanging itself that he was interested in. Hanging was the form of capital punishment in Missouri and Illinois when he was a child in St. Louis and there were many photographs of hanged criminals in the newspapers in those days. The image of a hanged man was one of his earliest memories; it was the sort of thing children dwell upon. Hangings were often public and the prison authorities could not keep photographers away, so they were often right up close when the prisoner was executed, producing dramatic, if prurient, pictures for the popular press. There were fewer photographs of electrocutions because photographers were not allowed into the chamber.

Burroughs's intention to present a positive image of sex with boys was perhaps hampered by the hanging scenes. Certainly Alan Ansen thought so. He wrote to Ginsberg saying, "There does seem to be a *multiplicatio coitum praeter necessitatum*, or in the vernacular, too many fucks in a little room. And of course, if you're trying to show sex as something nice, obscenity is a very two-edged tool [...] what description wants to do is suggest the physical centrality [...] boy is a sexier word than cock."[11] But Ansen was in awe of the book, which he saw as a giant step in literature.

Bill's friends loved it. Burroughs sent Paul Bowles an inscribed copy and he had it bound in Moroccan leather in Marrakech. "I loved it. Read it through three times. I think I laughed more each time. It's a comic classic. He's one of our greatest comedians. A sophisticated Will Rogers. Nothing since was as funny." It rapidly became a cult book, smuggled through customs into London and New York, passed around until it was in tatters. Girodias quickly printed a second run of five thousand. The only review, if it can be called that, was by Alan Ansen, who wrote a biography of Burroughs and a survey of his unpublished work, plus *Junky*, in the second issue of *Big Table*.[12] Working from a manuscript copy, he refs to *The Naked Lunch* as *Interzone* throughout but gives a very good account of the work, complete with an explanation of the political parties in the book. This was the first critical piece on Burroughs. In the original draft he mentioned Joan's death and showed it to Burroughs. Ansen: "He made me take it out. 'I wouldn't put that in if I were you.'"[13]

2. Busted

One morning at the Beat Hotel at 8:00 a.m. there was a *tap tap tap* on the door of room 15. It was the police with an arrest warrant dating back to April 9. It had taken them three months to find him. They asked a lot of questions and searched his room, finding nothing but a little less than a gram of hash. Bill was bustled into an old Citroën *traction avant* and taken to the prefecture, just across the river, where he spent a junk-sick twelve hours while they typed up forms and took his photograph. When they developed it there was nothing on the plate. They tried again and still nothing. Two hours later, only on the third attempt, were they able to get an image. As Bill told Allen, "Not for nothing am I known as 'The Invisible Man.'"[14] After he was released he made a quick trip back to the hotel for some Eubispasme tablets, then headed over to the rue Saint-Séverin, where Maurice Girodias had his headquarters, interrupting him in the middle of his tango lesson. Girodias arranged for him to meet his lawyer, Maître Bumsell.

In France you are entitled to know who denounced you, and Bumsell obtained copies of Paul Lund's statement. He had told the police in Morocco that Burroughs was an international opium smuggler; this was the reason Burroughs had been arrested. Bumsell spoke good English and coached Burroughs on what to say and how to behave: stand up if the judge addresses you, just answer the question and don't elaborate, never laugh, even if the judge does, keep a calm demeanor at all times. Bumsell knew that the key to the case was to find the right *juge d'instruction* for the preliminary hearing, and he located one whose wife had been an addict. The *juge d'instruction*'s estimation of the case is very important because his assessment of the accused goes on to the court. The judge had the letter referring to camel saddles and asked Burroughs what it referred to. He could have bluffed it, but decided to be honest and told the judge that it did indeed refer to importing hash, but explained that the plan was never put into action. After Bill admitted his guilt everything went well and the *juge d'instruction* sent a favorable recommendation to the court.

At the actual hearing, before three judges, Maître Bumsell used as his defense that Bill was a man of letters who had fallen into bad habits and mixed with the wrong people as so many poets had done before. Back in September 1959, when the case looked more serious than it turned out to be, Burroughs had written a deposition to shield himself from accusations of promoting—or indeed dealing—drugs. Called "Deposition: Testimony Concerning a Sickness," it had been translated by Maurice Girodias's brother, Eric Kahane, and published in the January 1, 1960, issue of *La Nouvelle Revue Française*,[15] the prestigious literary journal. He explained it to Allen as being "essential for my own safety at this point: Naked Lunch is written to reveal the junk virus, the manner in which it operates, and the manner in which it can be brought under control. This is no act. I mean it all the way. Get off that junk wagon, boys, it's going down a three mile grade for the junk heap...If you can help get the Beatniks off the junk route, then maybe other routes won't be so difficult as they are now."[16] He wanted the authorities to understand that he was anti-junk, that he wrote about it as an example of a control system, not as a romantic escape. Maître Bumsell made his speech, explained that Bill was "a man of letters, not a criminal," and read aloud from sections of "Témoignage à propos d'une maladie" before giving copies to the three judges. Bill had to say very little except, "Oui monsieur le juge." He was fined sixty dollars. Bill gasped audibly with relief. It took all of ten minutes. Brumsell's fee was very modest.

Ginsberg reacted critically to "Deposition: Testimony Concerning a Sickness," in which he felt Burroughs was abdicating responsibility for the book by saying, "I have no precise memory of writing the notes which have now been published under the title Naked Lunch," and of adopting an unnecessarily humorless and high moral tone. Burroughs reacted sharply, telling Ginsberg, "The article is intentionally humorless and moralistic, like I say. A loveable hepatitis carrier is no ad for hepatitis."[17]

Burroughs found Maurice Girodias very likable and thought of him as an old-fashioned riverboat gambler, always with a white waistcoat[18] and a dark suit. He had been seeing quite a bit of him socially before the bust and before Olympia published *The Naked Lunch*, and his support during the trial made Burroughs feel even more favorably toward him. Girodias had made a huge sum of money from publishing *Lolita* by Vladimir Nabokov and had used it to start a restaurant and nightclub called Le Grand-Séverin, just a few blocks from the Beat Hotel. There was a dome-covered patio where birds flew around, shitting on the customers, and the headwaiter was always drunk; a large African served up American-style barbecue ribs in a filthy undershirt; Burroughs liked to eat Girodias's blackbird pie.

Ginsberg was concerned that Bill was going to be ripped off by Girodias, which he did of course do, but Bill told him, "I am sure that the deal I made with Olympia was the best deal I could have made. I saw Jack fucking around five years with American book publishers. [...] Of course the two pornographic sections—'Hassan's Rumpus Room' and 'A.J.'s Annual Party' are in, and very important part of the whole structure."[19] Girodias gave him an eight-hundred-dollar advance and took one-third of the foreign rights on the book, which was a very bad deal, but Burroughs didn't realize it at the time. He was very gratified to get a measure of recognition and be published after so many years and to have the assurance that Olympia would publish other books. Supposedly to avoid taxation, all the foreign rights went through Odette Hummel in Switzerland, which made it even harder for Burroughs to get hold of his money. Girodias told him, "This is a complicated business full of angles. I know them—you don't. Let me handle it. You will have to trust me."[20] Gallimard bought the French rights almost immediately and paid an advance. Eric Kahane translated it for them but it was not published until 1964 and even then was to be sold legally only under the counter.[21] Limes Verlag in Wiesbaden published it in Germany in 1962 in a translation by Katharina and Peter Behrens with eight pages left in the original English to avoid prosecution for obscenity. Barney Rosset bought the American rights for Grove Press, giving an advance of $3,000, but the book was not published until March 1962 because Grove had several other obscenity cases to win first and knew that they would have to defend it in court.

3. Ian Sommerville

Toward the end of May 1959, the American poet Harold Norse turned up in Paris intending to write a book. He stayed, rent free, in some luxury on the île Saint-Louis, and within weeks he had found a boyfriend and made friends with James Jones, author of the 1951 bestseller *From Here to Eternity*. He soon ran into Gregory Corso at Les Nuages, Gregory's favorite café on boulevard Saint-Germain. It was at Gregory's insistence that he sought out Burroughs at the Beat Hotel. Burroughs was distant and uncommunicative, but they slowly became friends, and after about six weeks Burroughs asked him, "Where do you go to meet people?" Norse told him about Ian Sommerville, a young Englishman he had met at the Mistral bookshop who was spending the summer in Paris to learn French, working at the bookshop in lieu of rent. Norse had taken him home for dinner but he was not his type. "I've never been able to pick up anyone there," Bill told him, but was clearly interested when Norse described the young man. He was rather attractive, Norse said, but had a provincial working-class Northern accent and mumbled, which made him difficult to understand. He was studying mathematics at Cambridge and was very intelligent. "The kid likes older guys," Norse told him.[22]

Bill went over to the Mistral and engaged Ian in conversation as he tidied the shelves.[23] He found him reserved and "uppity," but when Ian found out that he was the author of *The Naked Lunch*, he said, "Now I feel very humble," and became quite contrite. Sommerville was just eighteen years old, Burroughs was forty-five. It was a relationship that would last until Sommerville's death in 1976. Ian was tall and looked not entirely unlike Burroughs at the same age, with reddish-blond hair that he was continually running his fingers through so that it stood on end. He had pale, almost translucent skin stretched across a bony visage with strong cheekbones, a birdlike nose, and thin lips. Burroughs asked for Ian's assistance in his latest attempt to cure his habit. He explained that he had what he called a drugstore habit; he was addicted to Eubispasme and wanted to get off. He got Ian a room in the Beat Hotel and gave him a rather small amount of money to oversee a reduction cure. Ian was to give him so many Eubispasme pills each morning and so many each night on a reducing scale along with doses of apomorphine. This was oral apomorphine put under the tongue; when you began to feel really nauseous you spat it out.

On August 24, Harold Norse stopped by the hotel with a friend who wanted to meet Bill. He knocked at room 15. The door opened partway and in the dim light he saw a tall thin figure, stripped to the waist. "Bill?" asked Norse tentatively.

"Hey man, Bill's kicking and I'm taking care of him," said Ian. Norse was stunned. "I thought you were Bill," he exclaimed.

"Everybody does," Ian replied. "I'm a replica. Bill can't see anyone," he explained. "I can't tell you what it's been like, man. It's been fuckin' unbelievable. I never want to go through this again. Hallucinations, convulsions, freakouts, the edge of insanity. But it's been worth it. He's getting well."[24] It took eight to ten days, after which Burroughs went to London to complete the cure with Dr. Dent. A codeine habit is considerably harder and more painful to kick than heroin, the symptoms are much more extreme, and Bill swore he would never touch it again. He claimed not to have used it again for three years.

It was a terrifying and traumatic experience for teenage Ian, whose life experience had consisted of little more than growing up in Darlington, in the north of England. His father died when he was ten or twelve years old and his mother had some difficulty in making ends meet. Ian managed to get into Cambridge on a scholarship, which was the making of him, but studying at Corpus Christi College among the quiet medieval streets of Cambridge was no preparation for what he had just been through. "I've spent a season in hell," he told Norse. "I had to hang on to my sanity by my fingernails, and they're bitten down to the moons."[25] Burroughs ran through the full gamut of his various personalities, from the giant centipede to the frog-faced "Nigger-killing" southern sheriff, from the silent icy Chinaman to the Ugly American. Brion Gysin described them as the "all-time grizzlies." "Bone-cracking crustaceans. Mister Ugly Spirit. 'Ah feel Ah'm about to give birth to some horrible critter,' he moaned in front of the pulsing mirror, 'Ah don't feel rightly hooman!' "[26]

Those eight days were a dramatic introduction to a new way of life, and Ian possibly never really recovered from it. He and Bill began a lifelong love affair, Ian's first real affair. They lived together, they were lovers. Bill introduced him to his friends and he and Brion Gysin became close friends. Brion: "Ian Sommerville was skinny and quick as an alleycat with bristly red hair that stuck up all over in pre-punk style. He was crisper than cornflakes and sharp as a tack. He crackled and snapped with static electricity, often giving a strong shock with an icy handshake. He was not fond of water and panicked at the idea of rain on his hair. He was an expert model-maker, handy with tools."[27] Through Bill Ian was introduced to the pleasures of hashish, the sinister writings of Paul Bowles, the world of avant-garde literature, and the attentions of the international bohemian crowd. Brion explained surrealism and modern painting and introduced him to the mysteries of the occult. Ian was completely taken up by this new life and determined to stay on in Paris with Bill and forget about his studies. But Burroughs was adamant that he should return to Cambridge to get his degree, so at the end of the summer Ian packed his bags and left while Bill made plans to visit him. When Ian finally graduated he left Cambridge a more mature individual. His provincial accent had been replaced almost entirely by a Cambridge University drawl, and the deference shown to him in matters scientific and practical by Burroughs, Gysin, and their friends gave him self-confidence. Meeting Ian also had a profound effect upon Burroughs. It was his one great love affair. After Sommerville's death he said simply, "Ian was in every book."[28]

Off junk, Bill now began to play a greater role in the life of the hotel. He was very attracted to a boy named Jerry Gorseline. He had red hair, what Burroughs called "a cosque of curly hair," a mispronunciation of the French *casque*, or helmet. But Bill's attentions caused rather an extreme reaction. At one point Jerry told Burroughs, "There are things that I feel should be destroyed. People like *you* should be destroyed." And he also spread a rumor that Bill had chased him all over Paris with a gun. Bill didn't have a gun at that time, though he did later shoot at potatoes with an air gun in his room. There was, however, a complicated business with Gysin. Burroughs told Ted Morgan that Gorseline was "more than friendly with Brion. This was deliberate. He made it with Brion, he never made it with me. Throwing a jealousy block between me and Brion, but it didn't work at all. He was a beautiful kid, I didn't say I liked him, I wanted him, nothing likable about him. I would have been willing to get very close to Jerry Gorseline. He was interesting, he had glitter and glamour, but nothing special."[29]

Bill liked the young male hustlers in the gay bars of boulevard Saint-Germain, and Mme. Rachou was always very accommodating about overnight guests, as long as they signed the police ledger. Homosexuality was not illegal in France so there was no problem there. Burroughs became something of a connoisseur of the graffiti on the outdoor pissoirs. His favorite, often quoted in his books, was:

J'aime ces types vicieux
Qu'ici montrent la bite.
(I like the vicious types
Who show the cock here.)

To which he added, "Oh oh, whoo hoo, me too!"[30]

Bill spent more time at the local bars drinking with hotel residents. He gossiped at the hotel bar and visited people in their rooms but was still seen as a distant, unapproachable figure. Most of the hotel residents were much younger American and British students exploring Europe and most of them were heterosexual. Burroughs carefully modified his image to fit his chosen role. He cultivated a mysterious, disconcerting aura. One time a group of residents were sitting around in someone's room talking. Burroughs had remained silent for the whole time, then, in a lull in the conversation, he growled, "The most addicting drug of all is silence," and the room went completely quiet. He stood up and walked slowly from the room. They sat in silence, listening to his footsteps down the curving staircase. Then, at the sound of the street door, they threw themselves at the window to watch him turn right, walk down the street, and disappear into the mist swirling in off the Seine. This was how legends were born. The incident likely occurred when Burroughs was working on the "Rub Out the Word" section of The Soft Machine, which concerns itself with silence, ending, "Enemy flak hit him a grey wall of paralyzing jelly. Retreat. Cut Word Lines. Keep Silence."[31] By then Burroughs was working with cut-ups.

Chapter Thirty-Two

Nothing is true, everything is permitted.
—Hassan-i-Sabbah

1. The Writing of Silence

Shortly after the publication of *The Naked Lunch*, Brion Gysin gave Burroughs a copy of the recently published *Le vieux de la montagne* (*The Old Man of the Mountain*), by Betty Bouthoul.[1] It is the story of Hassan-i-Sabbah, leader of the Assassins, in eleventh-century Persia, who sent his killers out from Alamut, his castle, to infiltrate the courts and governments of his enemies. They would lie dormant, sometimes for years, before receiving the signal to cut someone's throat. Brion, of course, claimed, "The book in itself is a mystery," and said he had met the author, who was a society portrait painter in Left Bank Paris, but that "she was oddly vague about why she wrote the book or what her sources of research were."[2] It is possible she didn't remember anymore exactly why she wrote it because it is a revised edition of *Le grand maître des assassins*, published back in 1936, but as far as her sources go, it contains a four-page bibliography. But Brion always tried to make everything strange and mysterious.

Together he and Bill pored over the book, passing it back and forth. Brion wrote, "We read and reread it. The crux of the matter, of course, is: How did he do it? And, beyond that: What is the nature of power? Bouthoul teases the reader enough to make you feel that there must be an answer and in the answer lies the key to Control on this planet. Big stuff." Burroughs was fascinated because here was a control system, operating across time and space. Hassan convinced his followers that by blindly following his orders, they ensured to themselves after death the enjoyment of a "garden of delights," pavilions filled with wine, sumptuous food, flowering trees, songbirds, luxurious furnishings, and beautiful young virgins, anxious to satisfy their every whim. They believed in this dream because Hassan actually had a garden of delights, housed in a series of pavilions near his castle, and would get his followers intoxicated on a beverage

361

made with hashish so that they fell into a deep sleep. When they awoke they were in what seemed like heaven, where everything that Hassan had promised was provided. After several days they were drugged once more and returned to Alamut. They remained loyal ever afterward, intent on returning to that heavenly garden.[3]

Hassan-i-Sabbah himself was a member of the Nizari Isma'ili sect who held to the doctrine that *Qiyamat*[4]—the Resurrection, the day of judgment, the fifth fundamental belief of Islam—has already come, thus obviating all their religious obligations. They could drink wine, use cannabis,[5] have sex during Ramadan, and neglect their prayers. The historian Henri Corbin described the doctrine of *Qiyamat* as "nothing less than the coming of a pure spiritual Islam, freed from all spirit of legalism and of all enslavement to the law, a personal religion of the Resurrection which is spiritual birth."[6] But this was secret knowledge, only imparted to Masters and Fellows, the Dais or emissaries, who were initiated into all the grades of the secret doctrine. For the vast majority of his subjects, Hassan was rigid in his imposition of the strictest Islamic laws.[7] The word "assassin" is a derogatory term, derived from *hashishi*, used by Hassan's opponents to trivialize the assassins' beliefs as being mere cannabis dreams.

That everything was seen to be illusion—"nothing is true"—meant that everything was permitted, a phrase seized upon by Burroughs and Gysin as a summation of the philosophy of Hassan-i-Sabbah. (It was used by Nietzsche in *Thus Spoke Zarathustra* in 1880.) Burroughs used it as a trope, along with Hassan's name, cutting it up and giving it many shades of meaning. Decades later, in *The Western Lands*, he was to confess that perhaps his approach to Hassan-i-Sabbah had been faulty and that, "with a carry-over of Christian reflexes," he had used Hassan's name "like some Catholic feeling his saint medals."[8]

2. Cut-Ups

Around lunchtime on the first of October 1959, Brion Gysin was in room 25 of the Beat Hotel, cutting mounts for some drawings, slicing through the mat boards with his Stanley knife and simultaneously slicing through the pile of old copies of the *New York Herald Tribune* he was using to protect the table. When he finished, he saw that where the strips of newsprint were sliced, they peeled back and the words on the next page showed through and could be read across, combining stories from different pages. He found some of the combinations so amusing that the people in the next room knocked on the door, concerned that he was having a hysteria attack. Burroughs had been to lunch with two reporters from *Life* magazine, and on his return, Gysin excitedly showed him his discovery. Bill agreed that the results were amusing, but immediately recognized its importance as a technique and pronounced it to be "a project for disastrous success." He could see that cut-ups literally enabled you to "read between the lines" and find out what the newspapers were really saying.

Together they began experimenting, initially with the magazines in Gysin's room: the *Saturday Evening Post* and *Time*. They picked the best word and phrase combinations and used the results as poems, but quickly became frustrated by the mundane words at their disposal. They began placing the strips of newsprint on texts by Rimbaud and Shakespeare and the results showed a marked improvement. As Burroughs said, "A page of Rimbaud cut up and rearranged will give you quite new images—real Rimbaud images—but new ones. [...] Cut-ups establish new connections between images, and one's range of vision consequently expands."[9] He recognized the importance of good source material. "I could see right away all the possibilities of cut-ups, where you have one image, you can have six out of that. What cuts up well are images, so you take Rimbaud and start cutting it up you get all sorts of quite good Rimbaud. We made a number of experiments, cut up my own texts, cut up other texts, cut up the Bible and Shakespeare and the classics, cut up experiments."[10]

Cut-ups held an obvious appeal for Burroughs, whose work was already fragmented. *The Naked Lunch*, with its lack of narrative or character development, its episodic presentation and random order of chapters, has sometimes been mistaken for a cut-up text even though it was written before their discovery. Burroughs was well aware of the idea's antecedents: Eliot's *The Waste Land*, the first great cut-up collage; Tristan Tzara's poems made from words pulled from a hat; the "Camera Eye" sequence in *USA* by Dos Passos. Burroughs said, "I felt I had been working toward the same goal; thus it was a major revelation to me when I actually saw it being done."[11]

Slicing lines of text from articles was cumbersome and they quickly progressed to an easier system. A page of text from a book, a magazine, a newspaper, or a letter was simply cut into four sections. The margins were trimmed off and the sections were moved against each other until a likely phrase or sentence was found. This was typed out on a new sheet of paper. The process was repeated for as long as it produced interesting new word combinations. They went through Rimbaud, Ezra Pound, T. S. Eliot, *Life* magazine features, whatever came to hand, and typed out anything that caught their eye. They did not paste up the juxtaposed pages; there was no point. In cutting the pages with scissors, some words were cut in half and could be combined to make not just new phrases but new words: cut words.

There were many different methods of cutting text, but they all had one thing in common: they introduced a random juxtaposition of texts to give new word combinations. Only those lines of literary interest were typed up on a separate page. Sometimes Burroughs would only get one or two lines from the combinations offered and move on to another. These new pages might themselves be cut up, removing the material even further from its source.

Naturally they wanted to share their discovery with everyone, and soon Gregory Corso and Sinclair Beiles were engaged in cut-ups as well. Beiles had been persuaded to move to the hotel by Gysin, who thought that he really belonged there, with them, after his sterling work on getting *The Naked Lunch* into print. Corso was torn between his desire to be part of the experiment and join in the enthusiasm and excitement it was causing, and his core belief in the power of the muse. His contribution consisted mostly in cutting up the work of others: letters from friends, a poem by Allen Ginsberg, a stanza or two of Shelley. When the results of these initial experiments in cut-ups were published as *Minutes to Go*, Corso dissociated himself from the other three contributors, writing, "I join this venture unwillingly and willingly. Unwillingly because the poetry I have written was from the soul and not from the dictionary; willingly because if it can be destroyed or bettered by the 'cut-up' method, then it is poetry I care not for, and so should be cut-up. [...] to the muse I say: 'Thank you for the poesy that cannot be destroyed that is in me'—for this I have learned after such a short venture in uninspired machine-poetry."[12]

Sinclair Beiles took the opposite path and cut up his source texts— articles from the *Observer, Life, Encounter*—again and again until they had such a density as to be bereft of meaning. The arguments between the four of them became so intense that Beiles, who was already in a mentally fragile state, had to sometimes leave the room to throw up. His mother later accused Burroughs of driving her son mad. Beiles has given two similar accounts of what appears to be a conscious imitation of Tristan Tzara's pulling words out of a hat: "The four of us got together in Gysin's room. We cut up bits of books and put them in wooden bowls. We then extracted piece after piece and put them together. The result was *Minutes to Go*."[13] As this is his memory of his involvement, there must have been at least one experiment of this type.[14]

One of the people that Burroughs and Gysin knew from Gaït Frogé's Librairie Anglaise was Jean Fanchette, a psychiatrist from Mauritius, who was also the editor and publisher of *Two Cities*, a bilingual arts and literature magazine. He agreed to publish *Minutes to Go*, and designed it to look like his magazine, using the same format and blue cover. Unfortunately he ran out of money and the book was impounded by the printer. Gaït Frogé came to the rescue. She paid the printer's bill of three hundred dollars and took delivery of one thousand copies of *Minutes to Go* plus ten signed by three of the participants—Corso refused to sign. The book was published on April 13, 1960, with a launch party at the bookshop. Cut-ups were launched on the world. It was clear that from the beginning Burroughs saw cut-ups as weapons. Early copies of *Minutes to Go* were issued with a wraparound band reading, "Un règlement de comptes avec la littérature."[15]

Even before *Minutes to Go* was published, on December 24, 1959, a second batch of material, called *The Exterminator*, was sent to David Haselwood at the Auerhahn Press in San Francisco. At the time Burroughs appears to have seen it more as a bulletin or magazine than as a book. He told Haselwood, "I enclose first issue of The Exterminator which will appear from time to time in response to civic need."[16] The manuscript clearly went through many changes. On February 23, 1960, Burroughs apologized for the delay in sending the completed manuscript, saying, "I found it necessary to make so many alterations, deletions and additions in the MS that it split into separate sections." Some of the material was hived off and later became part of *The Soft Machine*. It was not until March 21 that he wrote enclosing the completed book. It would appear that *The Exterminator* was originally *Minutes to Go*, volume two, as Burroughs explained: "Difficulties with my colleagues resulted in a considerable shift of material, as you can see. Leaves only two names connected with The Exterminator. Brion Gysin who discovered The Cut Up Method. And William Burroughs." It is unlikely that Corso would have wanted to collaborate on a second volume, so this must refer to "difficulties" with Beiles. More corrections followed on May 22 and May 24, but by May 27, Burroughs was pressuring Haselwood to publish the book: "I think you realize how explosive the material is. [...] Are you willing and able to publish?"[17]

The Exterminator was published in July 1960 with an uncredited epigram on the title page: "Let petty kings the name of party know / where I come I kill both friend and foe." This was Burroughs's classical Harvard education at work, though the quotation from *The Rehearsal* by George Villiers, Duke of Buckingham, was misremembered. It should read: "Let petty Kings the name of Parties know: / Where e'er I come I slay both friend and foe."[18] The final form of *The Exterminator* consists mostly of blocks of cut-up prose by Burroughs, occasionally interspersed with single-page permutations upon a single phrase by Gysin. Toward the end of the book, Gysin experiments by replacing the words "Rub Out The

Words" by the typewriter symbols % $ & and #. This was an experiment that Burroughs later appropriated for himself. *The Exterminator* ends with four pages of Gysin's calligraphic drawings, in which words have been replaced by glyphs.

The first extension of the cut-up method was when Brion Gysin applied it to tape recordings. They read aloud texts taken from poems and newspaper articles and recorded them. Then the tape was rewound and new passages were cut in at random. Where these cut-ins occurred the old words were wiped off the tape and replaced by the new ones, often giving some interesting juxtapositions. Burroughs wrote, "I would say that my most interesting experience with the earlier techniques was the realization that when you make cut-ups you do not simply get random juxtapositions of words, that they do mean something, and often that these meanings refer to some future event. I've made many cut-ups and then later recognized that the cut-up referred to something that I read later in a newspaper or in a book, or something that happened. To give a very simple example, I made a cut-up of something Mr. Getty had written, I believe for Time and Tide. The following phrase emerged: 'It's a bad thing to sue your own father.' About three years later his son sued him. Perhaps events are pre-written and pre-recorded and when you cut word lines the future leaks out."[19]

As usual, Burroughs experimented exhaustively: inching the tape past the record heads, superimposing tracks, playing the tape backward and recording the drop-ins in the other direction, speeded-up and sloweddown recordings, echoes, and the addition of music and sound effects. He liked radio static, with its intergalactic origins, the sound of pneumatic drills, and the high-pitched wail of Moroccan flutes. He experimented with playing three tracks at once: "There are all sorts of things you can do on a tape recorder that cannot possibly be indicated on a printed page except very crudely through the use of columns and even so the reader must follow one column down."[20] Unfortunately the technology did not yet exist to publish and distribute these new experiments, and so this aspect of Burroughs's work was to remain unknown to the general public for many decades.

BOOK SIX

London Town

Chapter Thirty-Three

Rub Out The Word "Accent." Rub Out The Word "Class." "Rub Out The Old School Ties."[1]

1. The Western Suburbs

Fulham had been described as one of the visually least attractive boroughs of London.[2] It was dull and anonymous, just perfect for Bill: a bleak grid of late-nineteenth-century streets, broken by bomb sites, within a great loop of the River Thames to the west of Chelsea. It was only developed as a smart annex to Chelsea in the mid-sixties. The Empress Hotel, at 25 Lillie Road, was in northeast Fulham, bordering on Earl's Court, an area known then, as now, for its Australian community and its gay pubs. The neighborhood was shabby and run-down, a few bomb sites covered in buddleia still in evidence, with desultory rebuilding near the main junctions. There was not much traffic as Londoners were still poor, recovering from the war. The Empress comprised a row of low stucco Victorian villas, like the ones still standing across the street, knocked into a labyrinthine series of bed-sitting-rooms, and is long demolished. Bill's rooms were usually quite large—he had a number—over time he lived in rooms 7, 8, 25, 28, 29, 32, 35, and 37, never being particularly concerned to get his old one back. Each had a locking bathroom down the corridor and "a sink to piss in." He moved there toward the end of April 1960. It was to be his headquarters for the next year, and on and off for some time afterward. He preferred the back rooms like number 29, off the street and away from traffic noise, and remembered it still twenty years later: "Room 29 was on the back overlooking back yards with outside stairways and clothes on lines and trees. It is Sunday. There are 3 shillings on the mantelpiece over the boarded up fireplace. My portable on a table overlooking the one window. The bed is comfortable. I am wondering where I can get some more shillings...for the gas meter. Sunday in London is always a gloomy day. The pubs don't open until 7. The Empress is long since torn down."[3]

Not long before, Bill had sworn he would never visit London again.

Now he changed his mind. "I love London," he said, "it was very cheap." Bed and breakfast at the Empress was five pounds a week, and it was the kind of English breakfast Bill liked, with bacon and eggs, toast and tea. (In Paris he had to go over to the Right Bank to get a proper breakfast.) North End Road, with its cheap cafés, was a few blocks to the west, where he could get a home-cooked meal of lamb, roast potatoes, broccoli, bread and butter, a cup of tea, and a pudding for less than a dollar in the working-class cafés. To the east, where Lillie Road became Old Brompton Road, was West Brompton tube station, on the rather inconvenient Wimbledon branch of the District Line. However, Earl's Court station was only another two blocks, with direct links to most parts of town.

Bill already knew a few people, as many British students and writers had visited the Beat Hotel, among them Michael Horovitz, who had published two chapters from *The Naked Lunch* in the first issue of his magazine *New Departures* in Oxford in 1959. Horovitz's coeditor, the partner who put up most of the money, was David Sladen, though Burroughs himself gave them fifty pounds toward the first issue. One day, Sladen mentioned to John Howe, a fellow Oxford graduate, "You know Burroughs is in town, man?" Sladen had already told Bill that Howe might be able to get him some dope. Bill was new to Britain and didn't know where to score safely. John called Bill and visited him in his room at the Empress. They got on well and Bill gave John two pounds. John went to Brick Lane in the East End. Pot there was half the price it was in Notting Hill and almost as good. He bought the equivalent of eight five-bob deals (pot was usually sold in a five-shilling wrap, about 70 cents in those days). He then called Bill, told him he had the stuff, and they arranged to meet at the Venice Restaurant (Bill pronounced it "the Venus"), a cheap Italian restaurant around the corner from the hotel. Bill was excited and went to a red phone booth on the corner and stood hunched up by the receiver. He tore a page from the phone book and wrapped up a portion of pot for John for getting it. Bill was laughing: "Reminds me of my days dealing junk in New York."[4] John was an appropriate person to score from because he had himself been turned on to pot by Allen Ginsberg and Gregory Corso while punting on the Cherwell in Oxford with Dom Moraes and the poet Peter Levi in 1958. It was a full circle.

John introduced Bill to Graham Wallace, who had been his schoolmate at the Jesuit public school.[5] Wallace was energetic, intelligent, with a very quick wit of the kind that Bill appreciated. He was in his early twenties, but had a spinal deformity that twisted his body and had given him a hunchback, something that caused difficulties in his relations with women and was probably one of the reasons he took up heroin. Bill liked him and they became good friends, with Wallace often stopping by the hotel to smoke pot in Bill's room. They collaborated on a number of cut-ups, and Wallace began making his own cut-up texts that Burroughs liked. When Jon Webb, editor of *Outsider* magazine in New Orleans, wrote asking for advice for a cut-up issue, Burroughs listed Graham along with Brion Gysin, Sinclair Beiles, and Stewart Scott as potential contributors.[6] Graham Wallace died in his twenties.

Michael Horovitz was in his final year at Oxford when Bill came up for a visit. The intellectual undergraduates were expecting someone unusual, but they were genuinely shocked when Bill turned up with a rent boy. Homosexuality was illegal and though there was a large gay scene at Oxford, where the majority of colleges were male only, it was very discreet. They were nonplussed by the straightforward way in which Bill introduced the boy to them, expecting him to be treated as an equal. For them it was an unexpected introduction to American democracy.[7]

That summer Horovitz was able to obtain some mescaline and brought it to Burroughs at the Empress. Horovitz had a vivid memory of its effects: "I struggled in vain to keep the swirling Van Goghy changes hitting me distinct from what I fancied Burroughs might be making of it, so was relieved at his suggestion we go out. The waves of near-nauseous claustrophobia ebbed, but I had to pinch my leg to make sure I wasn't freaking when, sat an eternity later in an Earl's Court transport café, he appeared to be bashfully chatting up the buxom waitress. Sure she was 'kind of cute' as he said, but it felt so out of character."[8]

Another person often to be found in Bill's room, sitting in the corner, quietly rolling joints, was Jane Armitage, an attractive young upper-class woman, described by John Howe as "blonde, very cool, not voluble, obviously intelligent." Then there was Nicolette; Burroughs took a number of photographs of her in 1960 at the Empress. Bill's supposed misogyny was clearly not as active then as was later thought.

Burroughs appears to have first met his friend Dennis Evans in Tangier or Paris. He was reading in organic chemistry at Imperial College, London, and famous for his work with a nuclear magnetic resonance spectrometer and on the magnetic properties of oxygen. His colleagues thought him eccentric, partly because he kept locusts, a Lord Kitchener lizard, a cayman alligator named Augustus, a bird-eating spider, a giant black scorpion, and a five-foot-long sand snake named George, which he would feed live toads obtained from his local pub. After George escaped and was found slithering down the King's Road, Dennis donated him to London Zoo.[9] Some friends were also dubious about his interest in the recreational aspects of organic chemistry. Evans used his enormous skills in synthetic organic chemistry to synthesize new derivatives of compounds such as diethyltryptamine in his basement lab at Imperial that he would first test on himself to discover their effects. He synthesized a number of other psychoactive molecules, such as bulbocapnine. Burroughs presumably tried it, as he has Dr. Benway use it in *The Naked Lunch*, which means he first met Evans prior to the summer of 1959. Other hallucinogens were also experimented with, including LSD, mescaline, and psilocybin (Dennis grew the mushrooms and extracted the chemical).

Professor Hannah Gay, who was a PhD student under Evans from 1961 to 1964, remembers that there were a number of experiments conducted with Burroughs such as getting the exact mix of cocaine with heroin to counteract the negative side effects of the coke; the perfect speedball. "Dennis engaged in this too but it did not appear to affect his work or everyday behaviour." Burroughs visited the lab about once a week, occasionally bringing in bags containing several weeks' supply of heroin. Hannah Gay and another student, John Maher, helped to weigh out exact safe individual doses of heroin using the lab's electronic scales. One can assume that some of these doses were for Evans, and of a different strength than those for Burroughs. According to Christine Keeler, Evans was taking heroin in the early sixties when she sheltered from the press in his flat at the height of the Profumo affair.[10] Keeler, a high-society call girl, was found to be having sex with both the Russian military attaché and John Profumo, the UK minister for war; Profumo denied it and when the truth emerged it almost brought down the Macmillan government. Evans gave public lectures on hallucinogenic chemicals and was often called upon as an expert defense witness for those accused of possessing illicit drugs (sometimes proving that the substance was not what the accused thought it was).

Burroughs was sometimes accompanied to the lab by a man whom Hannah Gay took to be his partner: "He was a little flamboyant (carried a fancy walking stick with silver knob, though not needing it to get around)." Burroughs usually wore a cloth cap and "looked rather drab, but well dressed," as befitted someone living in an anonymous area like Earl's Court. Several people say that prior to 1961, Evans once rescued a very ill Burroughs in Tangier and brought him back to London for treatment, but further details are unknown; it was possibly the 1956 trip.

Evans liked to party and was a well-known, well-liked member of the Chelsea Arts Club. He was notorious for his party tricks, often performed at the Imperial College summer fairs. He would "drink" liquid oxygen and exhale the gas through a lighted cigarette, ignite ammonium dichromate, freeze rubber tubes in liquid nitrogen then smash them. He would pretend to eat 78 rpm phonograph records and lighted candles and would munch on wineglasses (he would store the thin-walled glass fragments in the inside of his cheek for later disposal.). He could always get a laugh by speaking in a Donald Duck voice after inhaling hydrogen or helium. Despite his thin, stooped frame, he always stood up to intimidation, like the famous occasion in a Fulham nightclub when he reacted to a physical threat by unscrewing a light bulb and appearing to eat it. His assailants fled. Evans was exactly the sort of person whose company Bill enjoyed. They drank in the beer garden of the Chelsea Arts Club and more formally at the Savage Club, where they dined in splendor in the huge colonnaded restaurant of the National Liberal Club, the premises used by the Savage.

Just down the road from the Empress Hotel was the Lillie Langtry pub, where Bill often drank. The archivist Douglas Lyne tells how he arranged to meet Burroughs there. When he asked Bill if he would like a drink, Bill replied, "That's what we're here for," and managed to get through five triple brandies before Lyne ran out of money. Burroughs would sometimes make reciprocal visits to Lyne and drink with him at the Surprise pub, on Christchurch Street in Chelsea, or at his home at 1 Tite Street.[11]

Journalist Kenneth Allsop met Burroughs at the Empress, where he noted the sagging bed and the peeling wallpaper. Allsop described Burroughs on his way to the pub: "He drifted along the pavement beside me with reedy body effaced in neat but shabby suit and dun raglan, faded trilby lowered over peaky, pink-nosed bespectacled face, with an anonymity so theatrically emphasized that it seemed to shout in the street." At the Lillie Langtry Burroughs told Allsop he was off junk and explained the cut-up method to him. When asked about the Beat Generation he dissociated himself from it. "I don't associate myself with any trends, groups or political programmes, with any standardized way of living or working, and that includes the Beats. Coffee bars and Zen aren't my scene. Ginsberg and Kerouac are friends of long standing, but they subscribe to enthusiasms I don't share. Kerouac actually likes living in America and baseball and all that jazz, and he's now become a Catholic, I learn."[12] Bill was beginning to enjoy being in London. He tried to get Brion Gysin to join him there. He wrote Brion, "London is a much better deal than Paris, believe me. The best thing I ever did was get out of Paris and come here."[13]

Nearer to the Empress, at 265 Old Brompton Road, was the Troubadour, a fifties coffeehouse that served everything from a full English breakfast to wine and restaurant food in the evening. It was a labyrinth of small rooms, making it a favorite for both gay and straight clientele. In the back there was a beer garden, crowded in the summer. In the early sixties performers included Paul Simon, Bob Dylan, and, a little later, Jimi Hendrix. Next door was the Coleherne, at 261 Old Brompton Road, which as far back as the thirties had featured drag acts. In the mid-fifties it became a gay pub, but to avoid trouble, as homosexuality was still illegal, it was segregated by mutual agreement into two bars, one for the straight clientele and the other for gays. Bill often drank there. Many of the other nearby pubs were more or less gay, though less obviously so. "I was picking up people in bars, very good pickings. No trouble. Living cheaply. It was a very good period."[14] Bill had some memorable sex there. One encounter he remembered twenty-three years later: "I have spoken of sexual blockage. Out of thousands of orgasms I can only remember three as being satisfactory to the point of being memorable and to have some approximation to what orgasms are supposed to do. That is to relate the function of the orgasm.

"One was with Jimmy Cookson in the Empress Hotel and just at the crucial moment. A knock at the door. Telephone. It is Kenneth Alsop's secretary to say he twisted his ankle and can't keep the appointment for today. What perfect timing."[15] At other times Bill named the three as one with Jack Anderson and two with Ian Sommerville.

Bill was in London to be with Ian, whom he would visit in Cambridge, only fifty miles away, one hour by train, or Ian would come down to London. He and Ian used to like to walk in the nearby Brompton Cemetery, and they would sometimes take a picnic, spreading a rug out on a tombstone, with sandwiches and wine in paper cups. "I used to go to the cemetery with Michael Portman and Ian Sommerville for a quiet afternoon. You couldn't find a pleasanter place to sit on your June time." Later he and Ian made a number of recordings there, and also in Holland Park, which they played back on location. Most days Bill walked in the cemetery for the fresh air and as a welcome break from his single hotel room. Brompton Cemetery is a huge, thirty-nine-acre garden cemetery opened in 1840. A monumental entrance arch with four columns leads to a long avenue of trees behind which are large family vaults, crumbling mausoleums, stone angels, lions, ziggurats, pylons, and urns, more than thirty-five thousand of them. Everywhere between the trees are leaning overgrown tombstones, alive with squirrels, birds, cats, and foxes. Some way down the avenue are colonnades that become two huge crescents, making an enormous arched circle with catacombs beneath. Bill enjoyed spending a quiet afternoon strolling among the tombstones. It has always been a notorious cruising area and Bill sometimes picked up there.

The Beat Hotel experiments continued with Brion and Ian at the Empress, and forty-five years later, in *The Western Lands*, Burroughs recalled:

> Remember when I threw a blast of energy and all the light[s] in the Earl's Court area of London went out, all the way down to North End Road? There in my five-quid-a-week room in the Empress Hotel, torn down long ago. And the wind I called up, like Conrad Veidt in one of those sword-and-sorcery movies, up on top of a tower raising his arms: *"Wind! Wind! Wind!"* Ripped the shutters off the stalls along World's End and set up tidal waves killed several hundred people in Holland or Belgium or someplace. It all reads like sci-fi from here. Not very good sci-fi, but real enough at the time. There were casualties...quite a number.[16]

But mostly Burroughs worked, seated at his typewriter for hours on end, and during his first six months at the Empress produced about two thousand pages of cut-ups and material for *Novia Express* (as it was then called) and *Towers Open Fire*. This was also a period of intense tape cut-up activity, particularly cut-ups centering around the so-called last words of Hassan-i-Sabbah.

There was an old Irish woman working at the hotel and she must have subconsciously reminded Bill of the Irish maid who worked for his parents. "I had a terrible nightmare when I was staying in the Empress Hotel, that a white worm was crawling out of my eye and I woke up screaming and clawing at it, then I remembered, what I'd forgotten all these years, the blinding worm. It all came back to me."[17] He later wrote about it.

In July, through Brion who was visiting, Bill met Nicholas Guppy, the naturalist and explorer, author of *Wai-Wai: Through the Forests North of the Amazon*. His ancestor Robert Lechmere Guppy had discovered the tiny guppy fish in Trinidad in 1866 and it was named after him. Guppy asked them, "How does it feel to know that you're one of the last human beings?" He said, "Life won't be so bad on the reservation. We must accept the fact that women are more suited for space conditions than men, and men are going to be relegated to a reservation."[18] This was an idea guaranteed to appeal to both Brion and Bill, although Burroughs later reversed the idea completely. Guppy was a close friend of Francis Huxley's, who had explored the Amazon basin and documented the use of psychedelic snuff by the Yanomami Indians. Huxley and Bill had much to discuss. Another friend of Huxley's and Guppy's was Charles Hatcher, a qualified but nonpracticing doctor, described by Burroughs to Gysin as "most interesting character here."[19] Hatcher wanted to open an "institute of far out studies" to be located in Tangier. He later became one of the directors of Alexander Trocchi's Sigma [non] organization.

At the beginning of August 1960, Burroughs made a one-night trip to Amsterdam for the purpose of reentering Britain with a new six-month entry permit. He thought Amsterdam was charming, enjoyed the restaurants, and thought the Indonesian people on the streets were very beautiful. He met some Dutch chemists who had developed powerful hallucinogenics but were not releasing them because they thought it was too dangerous. Back in London, he continued his investigations into drugs. Through his friend the poet Melville Hardiment he took LSD,[20] but he didn't like it. He always had bad acid trips, never a good trip.[21] Allen Ginsberg sent him some mescaline from the States, where it was legal, but he did not like that or psilocybin. It was not the loss of control of his mental process he objected to, but the way it made his hands shake and the lack of coordination. Yagé was the only psychedelic he liked even though it was much stronger.

There was also a new method of altering consciousness to hand. Ian Sommerville had now more or less perfected his design for a "flicker-machine." On December 21, 1958, when Brion Gysin was taking a short break in La Ciotat, an artists' colony on the Mediterranean midway between Marseille and Toulon, he experienced a spontaneous hallucination as his bus was passing through an avenue of trees. "I closed my eyes against the setting sun. An overwhelming flood of intensely bright patterns in supernatural colours exploded behind my eyelids: a multi-dimensional kaleidoscope whirling out through space."[22] The vision stopped the moment they left the trees. The regularly spaced trunks had produced a stroboscopic effect as they interrupted the sunlight on Brion's eyes, approximating the 8- to 14-hertz oscillations of alpha rhythms, which can cause hallucinations. Brion was intrigued, but it was not until Burroughs met Ian Sommerville that he found an explanation for it and was able to reproduce it.

Ian was familiar with the literature of the effects of stroboscopes, as much of the research had been done at the Psychological Laboratory in Cambridge by John R. Smythies.[23] He had also read W. Grey Walter's 1953 study *The Living Brain*, which had an entire chapter called "Revelation by Flicker." Brion wrote to Sommerville asking if it would be possible to reproduce the effects at home, using everyday materials. For Ian the problem was quite simple. There were undoubtedly many ways to create a stroboscopic flicker at between 8 and 13 cycles a second, but he came up with the simplest: a record player with the tone arm removed, a light bulb, and a cardboard cylinder with holes cut in it. On February 15, 1960, he wrote to Brion from Cambridge saying he had made "a simple flicker machine." He set the record player to revolve at 78 rpm and made a cardboard cylinder about twelve inches across, the size of an LP. He cut slits in the cylinder so that a 100-watt light bulb suspended in the middle of it would flash through them at between 8 and 13 cycles a second. It worked. Ian told Brion, "Visions start with a kaleidoscope of colours on a plane in front of the eyes and gradually become more complex and beautiful, breaking like surf on a shore until whole patterns of colour are pounding to get in. After a while the visions were permanently behind my eyes and I was in the middle of a whole scene with limitless patterns being generated around me. There was an almost unbearable feeling of spatial movement for a while but it was well worth getting through for I found that when it stopped I was high above the earth in a universal blaze of glory. Afterwards I found that my perception of the world around me had increased very notably."[24] Using Ian's instructions Brion constructed a flicker machine, which he called a Dream Machine, later changing it to one word, Dreamachine. He added calligraphic designs to the inside of the cylinder that made it more attractive, but as the effects were obtained with eyes closed, they added nothing to its functioning. On July 18, 1961, Brion patented the device in Paris as a "procedure and apparatus for the production of artistic visual sensations."[25] Many people felt that the patent should be in Ian Sommerville's name as Brion had nothing to do with its invention, but Ian was surprisingly passive about matters like this.

Burroughs spent hours sitting, eyes closed, in front of the spinning cylinder, and mentioned the Dreamachine in both *The Ticket That Exploded* and *Nova Express*. It also featured heavily in *The Cut-Ups*, the film he made with Antony Balch.

2. Mikey Portman

In late September, a teenage boy of about seventeen presented himself at the Empress. This was Mikey Portman, a fan who had read *The Naked Lunch* and wanted to meet its author. Bill thought he was "fantastically attractive" and invited him in. He came from a very wealthy family, but the family had sold their grand country house in 1928 (it became Bryanston school) and Mikey grew up with his sister, Suna, and his parents, Marjorie and Winky, in the lodge, a white Regency house in the village of Durweston, Dorset, in the west of England. He was a nephew of the Seventh Viscount Portman, heir to the Portman Estates, a huge tranche of Marylebone that includes Bryanston Square, Baker Street, Portman Square, and Durweston Street, and worth over £1.2 billion in 2006. Mikey's older brother got the bulk of Winky's money when he died, and Mikey came into a trust fund for life, enough to mean he never had to work.[26]

Mikey was slovenly and irresponsible; he was very selfish, greedy, and weak. He was undisciplined, he couldn't do anything for himself, he never cleaned up, he had never known what it was like to *do* anything. He would borrow clothes and money and never return or repay them. Cabs were left outside, forgotten about and unpaid, holes burned in expensive carpets, checks bounced. As Michael Wishart put it in *High Diver*, "During his occupation of my house, gramophone records became ashtrays, sheets tourniquets. The house became a rallying ground for *le tout Marseilles (quartier Arabe)*."[27] The problem was, Mikey would not take a hint. He latched himself on to his current object of fascination and would not go away. He hung about Bill for years, at the Empress, at the Beat Hotel, and in Tangier. He was gay, and he and Bill became lovers—"Very briefly, in an unsatisfactory way, because he just didn't like anyone who wasn't black." Ian knew immediately when Bill and Mikey made it, which was not for a number of months after first meeting. Ian didn't like him at all. Ian, who was dirt poor, thought that Mikey had had every opportunity and had bungled them all; he had made nothing of his life. Bill, however, was clearly flattered by this disciple, who imitated his every action. If Bill had mint tea Mikey would have one too; he walked like Bill and ordered the same meals as him in restaurants. Bill was obviously a father surrogate but was prepared to take on this role. He drew the line, however, at allowing Mikey to move into the hotel. "Mrs. Hardy has her orders,"[28] he told Brion. This caused Mikey to disappear for a few months, but he soon bounced back.

Bill was interested in this entree to dysfunctional British upper-class life. He got to know the family. Mikey's mother, Marjorie, had been a Norwegian ice-skating star and had a tempestuous relationship with her younger son. Bill's friend Christopher Gibbs remembers him chasing her around the kitchen at Portman Lodge with a carving knife. Her husband, Winky, died when Mikey was about fifteen, and when Bill met her she was going out with a Greek travel agent. Bill and Mikey would have dinner with her in London and on several occasions in subsequent years she visited Bill at the Beat Hotel in Paris.

The family estate was looked after by Lord Goodman, who was Mikey's godfather. Arnold "two dinners" Goodman, as he was known for his girth and appetite, looked remarkably like Alfred Hitchcock. He lived in some splendor, attended by his manservant, in a flat at 79 Portland Place, a 1780s row house by James Adam in Marylebone, an address that occurs in several of Burroughs's texts because it is also the name of the next street to his childhood home in St. Louis; he often mixed the two in a text. In *My Education*: "Radio silence on Portland Place [...] a remote curtained drawing room. Marble mantelpiece. Decanter of port. A table. Maps and blueprints."[29] Portland Place is also home to the BBC headquarters, thus "radio silence." Goodman was the senior partner in the legal firm Goodman Derrick, and was still on the rise when Burroughs met him. By the mid-sixties he was Prime Minister Harold Wilson's private lawyer, the chairman of the Arts Council, director of the Royal Opera House and Sadler's Wells, and held dozens of other important positions in the arts. He was a clever negotiator and Wilson used him to solve union disputes and tricky behind-the-scenes political problems. Goodman administered the affairs of the entire Portman family, including those of the Seventh Viscount Portman, who was left £275 million when he was in his early twenties. For thirty years members of the family puzzled over the figures, but Goodman was a family friend and they were more inclined to accept his explanations than query them. Suspicions mounted, however, and in 1993 Portman issued a writ. It was discovered that all through the sixties and seventies Goodman had embezzled over £1 million from Lord Portman, worth more than £10 million in the mid-nineties. Since the family did not wish to drag the family or the dying Goodman through the courts, a secret settlement was struck in 1995 whereby Goodman paid back £500,000 and Portman wrote off the rest. Goodman died shortly afterward, age eighty-two. A family member, who did not wish to be named, said, "Everyone thought he was so kind, but underneath it all he was a conniving old crook."[30]

Burroughs, of course, did not know any of this, and even thought that Goodman was subsidizing the profligate Mikey from his own pocket. Bill enjoyed knowing Lord Goodman and often dined with him at Portland Place. Goodman, for his part, liked Bill and thought that he was a good, calming influence on Mikey, an adult whom Mikey respected and listened to. Goodman was later to use his own influence to help Bill out in an important way.

Bill and Ian spent several weekends at Portman Lodge with Mikey, always when his mother was up in town. It was a substantial house with five bedrooms and a cottage in the grounds for the servants. The housekeeper very much disapproved of Mikey and his friends and made no secret of it; sometimes she would refuse to speak to Mikey in the mornings. Bill was astonished to see that Mikey was scared of her. Christopher Gibbs recalls visiting Portman Lodge with Michael Wishart, whose son was at Bryanston. They collected the thirteen-year-old from the school, who asked if anyone else was staying. Wishart said, "Yes, my darling. There's a Nigerian tap dancer practicing in the wine cellar.'"[31] This was Mikey's family house and the housekeepers had no doubt been told to look after him but to take no nonsense from his unsuitable friends. It was English upper-class life as Bill had always imagined it from reading Saki, P. G. Wodehouse, and Evelyn Waugh: the sulky servant, the petulant young master. He was gathering material.

Mikey wanted to be like Bill in every way, and by October 1960 he was making cut-ups. Burroughs acknowledges two collaborations with Michael in *The Ticket That Exploded*, "In a Strange Bed" and "The Black Fruit." Bill said, "He'd written this thing, it wasn't too bad so I included it. He'd written something for it. I fitted it in. A favor to a friend." Although he was not a lover, except briefly, Mikey joined the pantheon of friends and characters who inhabited Bill's dreams, and long after Mikey's death he was still there. Bill wrote in *My Education*, after dreaming about Mikey, "Death hasn't changed him a bit; the same selfish, self-centered, spoiled, petulant, weak Mikey Portman." The fact was that Bill saw a lot of himself in Mikey, the same eternal adolescent, foot-stamping sulky child, rebelling against his mother. It was the fictional character that Burroughs would later develop using Denton Welch and Saki's Comus Bassington as models.

That October Bill ran short of money. He had to sell his tape recorder and moved to Cambridge in order to economize. He said he found the dreaming spires of Cambridge more congenial for work than the bustle of London.[32] He rented a large room, containing a sofa and one narrow bed, for four pounds a week, including a full English breakfast, on St. Mary's Street overlooking the market, "and the landlady was always snuffling around when we made it, so one could never relax."[33] It was in this room, looking out over the awnings of the market stalls, that Bill got his idea of color separation. "Look out there and pick out all the reds; now all the blues; now the green shutters on the stalls, and trees, and a sign; the yellows, a truck, a license plate, a fire hydrant; the reds, a stop sign, a sweater, some flowers; the blues the sky a coat, a sign on the side of a truck...later elaborated into the 'color walk.' I recall the feeling of strain, of not quite being able to do it."[34] The idea of categorizing one's observations by color was used as the organizing feature of his next book, *The Soft Machine*, which was divided into four sections, each given a color "theme."

John Howe visited Bill in Cambridge, but he found Ian Sommerville very difficult to deal with. He was not only overly protective of Bill but also spoke in an elliptical, confusing way that only the initiated could understand. He had a blond young man with him, also studying at Cambridge, whom he appeared to be seeing. They came on very gay, introducing themselves to people as one another, and generally playing mind games. John was glad to get back to London.

Burroughs made a quick trip to Paris in order to reenter Britain on another six-month permit. He stayed at the Beat Hotel, where he found a number of manuscripts he had thought lost stored in the hotel attic. He returned to Cambridge, where on November 24, 1960, at Ian's instigation, he gave a talk to the Heretics Society. He read his article on "The Cut-Up Method of Brion Gysin." It was a very prestigious event. The Heretics Society was founded in 1909 and previous speakers included T. E. Hulme, Bertrand Russell, Virginia Woolf, Rupert Brooke, George Bernard Shaw, G. K. Chesterton, and Ludwig Wittgenstein. Bill was possibly a bit nervous as he told Allen he felt rather like Gertrude Stein.

The locals claim that there are supposedly no hills between Cambridge and the Urals on the eastern edge of Russia to stop the icy wind and rain that lashes the city in winter.[35] Bill believed them and in December decided he couldn't stand the weather much longer and moved back to Paris to the comfort of the Beat Hotel. Allen Ginsberg sent him some mescaline. Burroughs shot it up in order to avoid the nausea associated with swallowing it, this time with very satisfactory results.

3. *L'Homme Invisible*

At the end of the Cambridge term, Ian joined Burroughs in Paris. There they put on one of their performance pieces. In order to boost the idea of Burroughs as *el hombre invisible*, or *l'homme invisible*, Bill undertook to literally become invisible. One day Ian Sommerville visited all their friends in the hotel and informed them that in two hours' time, Bill would become invisible, and at the same time gave them all a substantial piece of hashish. At the appointed time, a dozen or so mostly stoned people gathered in room 15, where Bill sat in a chair set against a white wall. Ian projected a color slide of his face, actual size, onto him, then moved it out of focus. The projection moved slowly in and out of focus for a while, then a black wooden frame crossed by strings like a Venetian blind was lowered in front of Burroughs. The projection now focused on the strings, then on Burroughs, the strings, then Burroughs, slowly back and forth. At one point, when the image was focused on the strings, Bill lowered himself to the ground, so the projection focused instead on the white wall behind him. Bill slid along the floor and behind a curtain while the audience continued to stare first at the string frame, then at the wall, thinking it was still him. Then the lights went up and Bill vanished. Photographer

Harold Chapman, who was in the audience said, "It was absolutely brilliant, and well rehearsed. Burroughs is a brilliant performer." Chapman had sensibly not taken any of the hash because he wanted to see how the trick worked.[36]

In 1961, Paula Wolfert, later the author of numerous celebrated cookbooks, spent six months in room 23. She had a small two-burner gas stove in the corner and often used to cook a hearty soup as an evening meal for her friends in the hotel. She described how much Mme. Rachou "loved the American and English writers and artists who inhabited her hotel," which she said was "not a usual response to 'Anglos' in Paris at that time." She lived across the hall from Brion Gysin. Burroughs lived in a tiny back room on the floor below. "I was attracted to the bohemian lifestyle," she wrote, "but theirs was a gay or guy 'thing,' so I was never really welcome in their circle. There were plenty of other younger poets, painters, and jazz musicians staying at the hotel to befriend."[37]

However, Burroughs was not entirely uninterested in women. Felicity Mason described how one evening she dined at a cheap Greek restaurant on the rue de la Harpe with Brion and William. In the middle of it Brion had an attack of coughing, the first sign of his emphysema. Bill was already quite drunk and Felicity found herself supporting both men as they staggered back up the quai toward the rue Gît-le-Coeur. When they reached the hotel Brion had recovered but Bill was still tipsy. She wrote, "Bill was still not himself. To my amazement he said, 'Why don't you come up to my room with me, Anne?'"

"What for?" she asked in astonishment.

She tactfully told him that she had given up sex, and after a while he replied, almost inaudibly out of the side of his mouth, "You'll never give up sex, man. Sex becomes a habit—the most difficult of them all to kick." She gave him a hug and went home.[38]

If the American actor and writer John Gilmore's memoir is to be trusted, Burroughs was drinking a lot during this stay in Paris. He wrote, "Burroughs knew where to find the best absinthe in a section of Paris he called 'the sewer' and I went with him and another poet named Frank Milne, from Hoboken, who wore some sort of turban on his head with a bunch of fake jewels stitched to the front above the eyes. Burroughs kept staring at my crotch and almost obscenely licking his lips, or making strange remarks about 'a penis colony in the desert.' He drank quickly, painfully, and at one point began sweating and shaking. His eyes rolled up like an epileptic's, and he seemed to go into a kind of fit. I got up and away from him when he started frothing at the mouth and shitting his pants. Frank Milne's turban fell off as he tried to pull Burroughs back into a sitting position and get him out of the café. The turban was dirty inside and I didn't pick it up, but as I followed them out I noticed Frank's bald head had a square scar like a flap on the crown, as though he had a metal plate in his head, or his skull had been operated on."[39]

Burroughs also seems to have been short of money at the time, because he was borrowing money from his fellow residents. Bob Gardner, an American in the hotel, loaned him money on several occasions. He told John Gilmore, "I didn't mind giving Burroughs money, even though I figured I probably wouldn't get it back. But I did, you know. Years later I wrote him in New York, and he actually sent me a money order."[40]

When Australian poet and musician Daevid Allen moved into the hotel in 1961, he was approached by Burroughs to play music at a performance organized by Jean-Jacques Lebel at the American Center on boulevard Raspail. "I was more than a little intimidated by him," Allen said in a later interview. "But he wanted me to play music at his poetry readings—I was a jazzer back then—so he suggested we first go up to his room where he got behind this desk like some Brooklyn insurance salesman. 'Well, Daevid,' he said, 'there are two ways of doing this. One way will take ten minutes, the other will take the rest of your life.' I assumed the first way might have involved sodomy so I opted for the latter."[41] Burroughs told him, " 'I've got this job and I want you to play.' We put on the show and there was the weirdest collection of people in the audience. Burroughs had one scene with nuns shooting each other up with huge syringes. Terry Riley came, and we ended up playing together outside in the street with motorscooter motors, electric guitar and poetry. It was wild."[42] Years later Daevid Allen named his rock 'n' roll band the Soft Machine after Burroughs's novel. It was on this visit that Burroughs collaborated on Terry Riley's tape-loop recording "Mescalin Mix" (1960–62).

Burroughs stayed in Paris until March 15, 1961, when he flew to Tangier, telling Ginsberg, "I want to get out of Paris as quick as possible. Don't like it, never did."[43] In Tangier he checked into his old garden room at the Muniria.

Chapter Thirty-Four

*I invented the color of the vowels!—A black, E white, I red, O blue,
U green.—I regulated the form and movement of each consonant, and,
with instinctive rhythms, I prided myself on inventing a poetic language
accessible some day to all the senses.*

—ARTHUR RIMBAUD[1]

1. *The Soft Machine*

On March 23, 1961, Allen Ginsberg and Peter Orlovsky left New York
on SS *America* on their way to France, and from there to Eastern Europe,
Africa, and India. They went straight to the Beat Hotel, expecting a joyful
reunion with Burroughs, but he was not there. He had checked out leaving no letter for Allen and no forwarding address. Gregory Corso was in
Paris and began to fill Allen in on what had been going on at the hotel.
They soon made contact with Brion Gysin, whom Bill had mentioned in
his letters, and realized that there had been some momentous changes in
Bill since they last saw him, mostly caused by Brion. Brion was, as usual,
very mysterious and surrounded by an atmosphere of intrigue. He told
Allen that Bill had left specifically to avoid seeing him and indicated that
dark forces were at work. He described psychic attacks, scrying, invisibility, and, of course, cut-ups. He was very aloof and treated Allen with
barely disguised disdain. The two never liked each other; Allen feeling
that Gysin had usurped him in Bill's affections. Ginsberg was unable to
fully understand Gysin's conversation, which involved Hassan-i-Sabbah
and appeared to say that Bill was an assassin, responsible in some ways for
the death of Joan, as well as Bill Cannastra, David Kammerer, and Phil
"the Sailor" White, whose stories Bill had recounted to him.

Burroughs and Gysin had now extended cut-ups beyond tapes and collage and into the realm of personal relations. Burroughs now suspected
that the entire fabric of reality was illusory and that someone, or something, was running the universe like a soundstage, with banks of tape
recorders and film projectors. He was determined to find where the con-

trol words and images were coined. He was using cut-ups in an attempt to backtrack the word lines to find out where and when the conditioning had taken place, and more importantly, who was responsible. Suspicion fell on *Time* magazine's enormous newspaper clipping morgue and the files of the FBI and the CIA. But they were more likely to be the source material for control, not the masters of it. However, with the aid of a great deal of majoun, Bill had finally determined that everybody was in fact an agent for a giant trust of insects from another galaxy, though, as usual with Burroughs, it is hard to tell how literally he meant this. However, he was certainly convinced that everyone was an agent for control and that the only way to find out who they really were was to cut them up.

Ginsberg, ever loyal, who had grown up with his mother's madness, made the best of the situation. When Burroughs took off he had left behind the unedited manuscript of his next book, *The Soft Machine*, presumably expecting Gysin or Sinclair Beiles to edit it into shape for publication by Olympia. Allen immediately took charge of editing it and Gysin deferred to his greater ability, working alongside, explaining where sections should go and the thread of ideas. Brion did a painting for the dust jacket and Allen wrote the blurb for the flap. In it he explained cut-ups, as he understood them: "Burroughs uses new methods of writing derived directly from painting techniques as first suggested to him by Brion Gysin—Cut-Ups and Permutations—extensions of the collage mosaic structure of 'Naked Lunch'…Methods which would be vain unless the author had something to cut up to start with: in the hands of a master, the Cut Up technique produces scenes of inhuman beauty and vast Eocene nostalgia. This book is a work of art fitting to the mutant moment of the human race as it prepares to leave Earth."[2] He wrote Lucien Carr saying that Burroughs "did new book in cut-up method, very pure experiments and strangely good reading tho oft toneless, 'The Soft Machine.'"[3] Two years later, in January 1963, in Benares, India, Ginsberg had a dream: "I see a large rugged handsome face (later, writing, I realize it's Brion Gysin)—a feeling of pleasure in the dream. Waking, my resentment of Gysin goes away—I must have been jealous."[4]

The book was published in June 1961. The text is a cut-up of material originating in Burroughs's thousand-page "word hoard" left over from *The Naked Lunch*, arranged in four books, each of which has a color theme: "Unit I, Red, Transitional Period"; "Unit II, Green, Thing Police Keep All Board Room Reports"; "Unit III, Blue, Have You Seen Slotless City?"; "Unit IV, White, Poison of Dead Sun in Our Brains." Within each are a dozen or so "chapters," each with a name. The contents of each chapter become progressively more cut up, so that the same words and phrases recur over and over in a different context, with a different meaning. As the chapters are short, rarely more than two pages, this has the effect of a wave of words breaking on a shore, becoming more and more fragmented, eddies and whirlpools of words, with shorter and shorter sentences until a new wave breaks as a new chapter begins.

The Soft Machine is the most intensely cut up of all Burroughs's books and is essentially a prose poem in the high modernist tradition of *Nightwood* or *The Waves*. The only sustained narrative in the book lasts for about three pages before becoming progressively more fragmented, and that is not until page 158. Some of the most evocative passages that Burroughs ever wrote appear here, such as his description of Puerto Joselíto:

> Carl walked through a carnival city along canals where giant pink salamanders and goldfish stirred slowly, penny arcades, tattoo booths, massage parlors, side shows, blue movies, processions, floats, performers, pitchmen to the sky. Puerto Joselíto is located Dead Water. Inactive oil wells and mine shafts, strata of abandoned machinery and gutted boats, garbage of stranded operations and expeditions that died at this point of dead land where sting-rays bask in brown water and grey crabs walk the mud flats on brittle stilt legs.[5]

It also contains some of his most amusing writing, such as this from Burroughs the intrepid British explorer: "No calcium in the area you understand. One blighter lost his entire skeleton and we had to carry him about in a canvas bathtub. A jaguar lapped him up in the end, largely for the salt I think."[6]

Eventually Bill wrote to Allen to invite him to visit in Tangier, saying that he had intended Brion Gysin to explain cut-ups to him before their reunion. Allen, Peter, and Gregory Corso made their way slowly south, stopping off in Saint-Tropez and at the 1961 Cannes Film Festival en route, where they stayed with Jacques Stern in his villa and attended screenings and parties. They arrived in Tangier at the very beginning of July but despite writing and wiring their arrival time, this time there was no welcome waiting for them on the dockside.

2. "Word Falling—Photo Falling"

When Burroughs returned to Tangier in March 1961, he had been able to get his old garden room at the Muniria. Fortuitously Dave Woolman's old room next door was also free, which he advance-booked for Mikey Portman, who was arriving with his black lover. Paul Lund was still living in the third garden room. Burroughs still regarded him as an old friend, despite his acting as an informer over the camel saddles fiasco. Bill set to work on the texts that were to become *The Ticket That Exploded*, but was soon distracted by a new discovery. In May he wrote to Brion Gysin, telling him, "In my spare time have done a little experiment with collage. Make collage of photographs, drawings, newspapers, etc. Now take picture of the collage. Now make collage of the pictures. Take-cut-take-cut you got it? Some interesting effects."[7] As usual Burroughs became completely engrossed, and soon he was working full-time on these experiments. He wrote Brion, "Here is another collage of collage of collage to the Nth power entitled 'Word Falling—Photo Falling.' Show extension of the method as applied to the image. [...] Since arriving in Tangier I have been working full time and the place is littered up with flash bulbs and negatives and magazine cut outs."[8] Each time he photographed the image and doubled it up, it reduced in size by half. Soon the images were so small that it was almost impossible to distinguish them from the grain in the photographic paper, and the new overriding image was the way in which the duplications had been arranged. Usually he arranged the images in the four quadrants of a standard cut-up page, with two images reversed to make a symmetrical composition.

He also made photomontages: "I was back in Tangier in my old garden room at the Villa Muniria, and it was here that I first started making photo-montages. This happened after a bad trip on DMT, which is described in The Night Before Thinking [...] the sensation of being in a white-hot safe. The following day, a sudden cool grey mist came in from the sea and covered the waterfront and I spread some photos out on the bed with a grey silk dressing-gown from Gibraltar along with several other objects and I photographed the ensemble. During that summer I made many of these montages in different ways and combinations. Ian Sommerville arrived during the summer and took over the technical aspect of the montages."[9] Although he was unaware of it, the method Burroughs used was groundbreaking. Until then collage, as developed by Picasso, Braque, and Kurt Schwitters, had been created using elements selected for their color, shape, or texture. Though Burroughs arranged them aesthetically in formal compositions, he chose the elements only for their meaning to him: photographs of his family, of boyfriends past and present, photographs he had taken of street scenes and of places where he had lived. He was systematically cutting up friendships, memories, and attachments, all of which he regarded as potential elements of control that needed to be analyzed. These collages were a cubist-like portrait of Burroughs's mind state, each element provoking an emotional response in him, either of his mother or father, of boyfriends, sentimental attachments, pictures of particular events, sexual situations, or places, all combined into a series of frozen moments. By photographing the elements, then rearranging them, and continuing the process until the end of the roll, he was analyzing different sets of responses, different arrangements of his mental state.

As Burroughs did not stick the elements down to make a conventional artwork, but just photographed them and rearranged them slightly for the next photograph, the collages only ever existed as photographs, one of the first times this was done.[10] As he always worked in series, using a selected group of images arranged in different positions on his table, the pictures should be viewed that way. Later, many of the photographs he used in collages and in his subsequent scrapbooks were specially posed and often related to the characters in the book he was working on, but in the spring of 1961 he was pursuing two lines of development: the formally arranged collage series concentrating on his emotional life, and the infinity fold-ins that grew more and more abstract.

In his experiments Burroughs always investigated every possible avenue; he was thorough, though not particularly well organized. By May 16 he had started using color photography. He wrote to Brion Gysin, "This is a major breakthrough, Brion, and you have the equipment necessary to pick up on it. Like take color shots of your pictures close ups angle shots etc. Mix in with color postcards and advertisements from Life and Time. Take. Make collage of shots cutting into fragments and rearranging at random. Take. Cut. Take. Just as photography a series of these collage concentrates would be spectacular."[11] At the end of May he began a series on rubbing out the word. He replaced the words with symbols and the symbols with colors, then photographed them, collaged them, and rephotographed them. "Something happens when you take pictures of pictures of pictures," he told Gysin. "Notice how the color dots seem to be in clay and not paper. I am now making a color series of rub out the word."[12] By June 14 he told Gysin he had enough photographs for a collage exhibition. The ideas came quickly to him. "The collage is an art like flower arranging. Say a blue collage. Select from blue file. Wait for a perfect blue sky. Arrange collage on mirror and catch the sky in your collage. Take your collage between glass and take pictures over the bluest spots in the sea, etc. 'Pay back the blue you stole. Pay it back to sea and sky.' I have given myself a brief rest from writing. Will now apply what I have learned from the photo collages back into writing. 'Cut and arrange the cut ups to other fields than writing.'"[13]

With the arrival of Ian Sommerville—"Technical Tilly"—at the end of May, more ambitious experiments were conducted. There was a long series of superimpositions where negatives of collages were superimposed upon each other and printed, something that gave the corner pharmacy print shops in Tangier considerable difficulty despite Sommerville's careful instructions. With Ian there, Burroughs continued to develop the "emotional" collages, whereas Sommerville took over the "infinite reduction" collages and made them his own.

3. Paul Bowles

On arrival in Tangier Burroughs looked up Paul Bowles. Over the years they had become very friendly and this summer was to be when they spent the most time together. There had been a little frostiness when Burroughs applied his new cut-up technique to *The Sheltering Sky* and showed him the results: "He didn't express any opinion on them. From that I concluded that he just wasn't interested."[14] But that soon passed. Bowles now lived in the Immeuble Itesa, a gray concrete block built by the Italian government in the early 1940s, surrounded by fields and empty lots. Paul and Jane lived in two separate apartments. Jane and her girlfriend Cherifa lived on the floor above Paul and his boyfriend Mohammed M'Rabet, and communicated using a squeaking mauve plastic child's toy telephone. John Hopkins remembers Jane calling up: "Fluffy, (squeak) come on up, dinner is ready (squeak)."[15]

Burroughs and Bowles together made a distinguished pair, sitting at Mme. Porte's Salon de Thé or in the Café de Paris, Bowles quite formal with his carefully combed white hair, black cashmere cardigan, gray flannel slacks, houndstooth sports jacket, polished black Alden shell cordovans, and one of his many hundreds of ties. Though he was never seen without a tie, he sometimes wore moccasins without socks. From crush-proof packets he smoked filter cigarettes in which the tobacco had been replaced with kif.

Burroughs in Tangier went for a more colonial attire: during the hot months a short-sleeved shirt buttoned at the neck but lacking the tie, carefully pressed trousers, black fedora, and always in socks and lace-up shoes. In the colder months he returned to his standard three-piece suit and tie, shirts with cuff links, and shoes highly polished by the shoeshine boys in the Socco Chico. Later, when living in the Marshan, he affected a hooded burnoose that gave him greater anonymity.

Burroughs knew Mohammed M'Rabet from 1956 when he was a bartender at the Tangier Inn. Bill was wary of him because he had a penchant for violence: he had been a weightlifter and was always doing handstands, punching people, and arm-wrestling. He had a history of mental problems and had been in various institutions as well as jail. Burroughs thought that the shock therapy he'd received did him more harm than good. Brion

Gysin once visited Bowles and found him being carried around the room slung over M'Rabet's shoulder. "There's only one thing to do when he's like this," Bowles explained, "and that is to make yourself a limp rag." M'Rabet hated Gysin because he always talked about him in the third person as if he weren't there, saying things like, "I knew him when he was rough trade in the port."[16] Bowles told Burroughs that M'Rabet had threatened him, saying, "One day, you'll go out of here in two suitcases, or maybe one, you're very skinny."

According to Burroughs, Bowles himself had a hidden violent side and had several times tried to kill people, once succeeding. It was Brion Gysin who said that Bowles confided in him that he once killed a man. It occurred when Bowles was in Mexico near a work compound. There, once a week, the peons would drink themselves into unconsciousness. Then they would be thrown in the back of a truck and taken back to the compound. One of them had fallen off the truck and was lying by the side of the road near a cliff. Bowles seized his opportunity and rolled the unconscious man to the edge and pushed him over. There was no way this story could be proved, but Burroughs was convinced that Bowles was capable of such an action. It was the menace and fear that Burroughs most admired in his writing.[17]

Burroughs himself was responsible for one episode of fear. Bowles told Ned Rorem that he did not experience fear with mescaline, but "with Prestonia—given me by Bill Burroughs—yes."[18] This occurred shortly after Burroughs reached Tangier in March 1961, when his friend in London Dennis Evans synthesized some *Prestonia amazonica*, from the same group of Amazonian hallucinogenics known to Burroughs as yagé. In 1957, the chemists Hochstein and Paradies analyzed ayahuasca, naming it *Banisteriopsis caapi*, and, from the same region of Peru, yagé, which they named *Prestonia amazonica*. They reported that the natives of the Río Napo area "commonly consume a mixed extract of the *B. caapi* and *P. amazonica* leaves in the belief that the latter suppress the more unpleasant hallucinations associated with the pure *B. caapi* extracts." The mixture Evans made contained N,N-dimethyltryptamine, now better known as DMT, the active ingredient of yagé.

It came in powder form. Bill asked Paul how he wanted to take it: inject it or sniff it? Bowles was having nothing to do with needles, so he elected to sniff it. Burroughs poured a little of the powder from a dirty gray bottle and made a small cone. He gave himself a sniff, then retired to the kitchen to inject himself with it. Bowles took a sniff and felt a terrific explosion in his head. He had a vision of his head blown open, as in a comic strip. He thought he was flying through the air, twenty-five thousand miles from anywhere, all by himself, "like a melting baby bird on a bough." He was terrified. This unpleasant vision continued for some time, then Burroughs returned and asked him how it was. Bowles said he didn't know. "You're probably getting bum kicks," Bill said. Bowles later remarked, "That kind of explosion, certainly nobody could call that fun."

Burroughs took DMT about ten times, injecting it in a dosage of about one grain, "with results sometimes unpleasant but well under control and always interesting," but then he took a grain and a half and suffered "unendurable pain."[19] "Doctor Benway was conducting experiments with some kind of new hallucinogens and had inadvertently taken a slight overdose of N-dimethyltryptamine dim-N for short class of South American narcotic plants Prestonia related to Bufotina which a species of poisonous toads spits out its eyes." Burroughs also related it to a type of fish poison, "causes a pain so intense that morphine brings no relief. Described as fire through the blood...A blast of pain and hate shook the room as the shot of dim-N hit and I was captured in enemy territory Power of Sammy the Butcher. The Ovens closed around me glowing metal lattice in purple and blue and pink screaming burning flash flesh under meat cleaver of Sammy the Butcher and pitiless insect eyes of white hot crab creatures of The Ovens."[20] He did not have a good trip. He reached for his box of apomorphine and took twelve twentieth-grain tablets and staggered out to Mme. Porte's Salon de Thé.

Paul Bowles saw a lot of Bill that summer;[21] he is there in the photographs taken in the garden of the Hotel Muniria. However, Bowles did not like all of Bill's company. Ginsberg he became very friendly with and Ian he liked, but Mikey Portman he could not abide because he ate all the food in his house. Bowles was by nature very parsimonious, and it pained him enormously when Mikey would go in and clean out the whole kitchen like a vacuum cleaner. He hated Mikey's sloppiness, like the time he left a heavy platinum cigarette case, given to him by his father, on a table at the Café de Paris, or the time he came knocking at his door at 1:30 in the morning after a party on the ground floor of Bowles's building. Mikey had left a cab waiting outside all evening and needed to borrow 25,000 francs.

Chapter Thirty-Five

I thought it was overblown fake, this ready made enlightenment, and it turned out to be that.[1]

1. The Psychedelic Summer

Allen Ginsberg, Peter Orlovsky, and Gregory Corso could not afford the Villa Muniria, and stayed instead at the cheaper Hotel Armor next door where rooms were two dollars a night. They had a room on the roof with whitewashed walls, red floor tiles, and a small patio with a superb view out over the harbor. Alan Ansen arrived for the summer and joined them in the Armor. Francis Bacon was also there. As Allen and Peter were trying to save money for their onward trip to India, and Gregory and Paul Lund were both broke, they all cooked together using Bill's little kerosene stove. Baby tuna, fresh perch, and other delicacies could be bought fresh at the harbor, and they all ate well. But eating together was the area of the most cooperation. Bill was cold and distant toward his old friends, and Ian and Mikey sided with him. Just as Burroughs had been cutting up his relationships and attachments to his parents and lovers with his photographic collages, he had moved on and was now doing it in person. Instead of his old friend and ex-lover, Ginsberg found a remote, emotionless, suspicious individual who snarled that friendships were just another form of control that had to be cut up. As far as Bill was concerned everyone was an agent under someone else's control. "If we cut you up, who would we find inside?" he asked. "Lionel Trilling? Louis Ginsberg?"[2] Ginsberg later recalled, "I remember arriving in Tangier and having to undergo an interrogation as to who I was representing because he could detect certain parts of my father, Jewish ancient elements, certain parts of Columbia University, Lionel Trilling in the intonations of my voice, in the words, in the attitudes, physical postures, so who was conditioning me?" Allen said it was "a little difficult to see old friend Bill looking at me as if I was a robot sent to check him out or be checked out. And also to be suggested by him that I examine him to see who he was representing, who he was an agent of, because he assumed that everybody was an agent at that point. Not necessarily for the government at all, an agent for a giant trust of insects from another galaxy actually."[3] Burroughs now felt that cut-ups were the only way to cut through the unthinking acceptance of everyday thought and behavior that acted as controls on most people's lives. Ginsberg anguished over Bill's new attitude, particularly when Bill criticized him for his attachment to Peter and himself and was scathing about Allen's reliance on his old friends, something that Bill thought of as mere sentimentality. Allen felt trapped because he was unable to display the same indifference toward Bill that Bill felt toward him.

Though Bill was claiming to be immune from attachments, he was clearly relishing his role as mentor to Ian and Mikey and had wasted no time in showing them off to the expat gay community in Tangier, though they were not all impressed. Rupert Croft-Cooke met Mikey and described him as "a young man named Portman who arrived once with Bill Burroughs, his face an extraordinary shade of green 'from staying too much indoors,' I was told."[4]

Allen said later, "My feeling was that they had replaced us in Bill's affections and intimacy." Allen wrote Lucien, "Bill's all hung up with 18 yr old spoiled brat English Lord who looks like a palefaced Rimbaud but is a smart creep—Apparently Lady Portman his mother gave him into Bill's hands to look after here—platonic anyhoo—But Bill got some kinda awful relation with him and the kid bugs everyone so intimacy with Bill is limited and Bill absentminded all the time—however very busy with his cut-up experiments and applying it to pictorial collages and taking brownie photographs and very busy and creative."[5]

Gregory, however, was having none of it. Gregory had always been skeptical about cut-ups, and Bill's pontificating put him in a bad mood. He raged against Bill, only to be told by Alan Ansen, "The trouble with you, Gregory, is that you can never be a leader of men the way William can." Gregory lost his temper and yelled at Bill, "You're not a big guru, all you care about is getting your cock up those boys' asses."

"You little wop," Bill replied.

"And ya didn't kill me with your air rifle, did ya?" Gregory said. "The way ya said ya would."

But it was Peter Orlovsky who had the worst time. He had never got on well with Burroughs, who had always felt jealous of him, and now, with Burroughs in full misogynist mode and the two boys backing him up, Peter came in for a barrage of rancor. Bill's theories, developed into bizarre routines over many long nights of majoun-fueled talk, had reached the stage where he now proposed that women were not human at all but had been sent from a distant galaxy as agents for a giant trust of insects that were manipulating the Earth. Burroughs suggested that all women should be exterminated just as soon as males had found some form of partheno-genesis. Peter, unable to see that Burroughs was taunting him, always took these ideas literally, and to Burroughs's delight he argued vociferously in favor of women and heterosexual love. Peter was no match for their quick wit and became red-faced, hoarse, and angry at their jibes. The more he argued in favor of love, the more and more outrageous Swiftian routines Bill came up with. "What if we cut up Peter? Peter likes girls so we'd probably find a Venusian inside," cackled Burroughs, and Mikey Port-man joined in: "That's right! Peter's a Venusian!" Allen tried to get him to not respond, to walk away, but Peter felt he had to defend the things he held most dear and always took the bait. By this time Mikey Portman had been joined by his black lover, who said, "Oh Mikey, it is terrible what is going on. Here there is spirits fighting, spirits fighting all the time. Spirits fighting!"[6]

All this caused tremendous problems between Allen and Peter and brought to a head the central contradiction in their relationship: that Peter was fundamentally heterosexual. At this time, Allen and Gregory had been asked by Lawrence Ferlinghetti to interview Burroughs for his new magazine, *Journal for the Protection of All Beings*. While Allen typed up the interview—Burroughs said things like, "I feel like I'm on a sinking ship and I want off"—Peter did his own experiment in typing up their conversations:

> PO: "I didn't want to do it. You made me queer. It had to be you. Big cocky you. But you pulled me so and then I knew. I tried hard to fight it."
>
> AG: "That's right you did. You always did keep telling me at the beginning you just wanted to be friends and you were afraid I was just acting nice so I could get in your ass. And now look at us."
>
> PO: "But now I'm a bonefide queer on the witness stand."
>
> AG: "Did I make that come true?"
>
> PO: "Make it? You hypnotized it true."
>
> AG: "And now the dehypnotization is begun. I'm getting old and you're real-izing you're no longer in my power..."
>
> William Burroughs: "Yeah, man. It's best for you to be away from him now. I mean now." [Bill staggers drunkenly to his feet and knocks over his chair.]
>
> AG: "Oh really Bill! Don't whimper like that to me. I mean, I'm feeling some-thing right now. Don't you realize I have to sooner or later find a girl and get married so I got a junior?"

WSB: "Take a tip from me, kid, and steer clear of 'em. They got poison juices
dripping all over 'em. Fishy smell too. Down right pornographic. Up a
stretched asshole, that's where they make ya look. Wise up Allen and picture yourself right for once in a while can't you?"[7]

Peter had dysentery, a mild jaundice, and a head cold. He spent most
of his time in bed, resting and brooding, then after a week in Tangier
he announced that he had had enough and was heading on to Istanbul
alone. His seven-year "marriage" to Allen was over, at least for now. Allen
wrote to Ferlinghetti about Peter's leaving: "We had big arguments about
future of universe in Tangier. He wanted it to be sex-love, Burroughs
wanted it to be unknown Artaud mutation out of bodies. I was unde-
cided, confused. I still am except Burroughs seems to have killed 'Hope'
in any known form. The Exterminator is serious. Peter wanted innocence
and sex apocalypse. It got very serious. I was vomiting."[8] Peter left at the
end of the month, running into Timothy Leary at the airport in Gibraltar.
He told Leary he was sick of Burroughs and was off to the Far East to find
wise men and drugs. "I'll take drugs you've never heard of!" he yelled
across the railings.

At the recommendation of Allen Ginsberg, Timothy Leary had written
to Burroughs in January 1961, asking if he would participate in an American Psychological Association symposium on psychedelic drugs and in
a research project to evaluate psilocybin (magic mushroom) pills. Burroughs replied, telling him, "My work and understanding benefits from
Hallucinogens MEASUREABLY. Wider use of these drugs would lead
to better work conditions on all levels."[9] Leary sent him a supply of the
pills, but Burroughs concluded that their effects closely resembled those of
DMT. He advised Leary to have some apomorphine on hand in case psilocybin produced the same results.[10]

Allen had booked Leary into the Armor. Allen was out when he
arrived, so Leary waited. Leary described his first meeting with Burroughs: "As I waited in the living room of the concierge, a thin, stooped
man wearing glasses and a grey fedora walked in. Two handsome British
boys about nineteen years old were with him."[11] Bill had come to find
him. They left a message for Allen and retired to the outdoor garden of
the Parade to discuss the upcoming drugs conference at Harvard over gin
and tonics.

After dinner at the hotel with Ginsberg, Alan Ansen, and Gregory
Corso they retired to Burroughs's room. Leary wrote, "Dark cave. Big

bed. Desk littered with papers. Hundreds of photographs pasted together and rephotographed. Cut up pictures. Boil out the essence of the pictures. And then shoot it. Three off-tuned radios blaring noise. Static is the essence of sound. Pot cutting-board. Allen's pictures of Marrakech. We sat around the room, taking turns peering through the cardboard cylinder flicker machine. Burroughs wanted to take mushrooms. Allen Ginsberg said, 'Well, everyone in Tangier has been waiting for you to arrive with the legendary mushrooms...' Alan Ansen, William Burroughs, Allen Ginsberg, Gregory Corso, Ian Sommerville and Mikey Portman...'All experienced hands at consciousness-expansion.'"[12]

The session began in Bill's room, dim-lit, filled with cigarette smoke and with an unmade bed. It felt crowded, so all but Bill and the two boys went into the garden to look over the wall at the harbor below. It was the king's birthday and there was a brilliantly lit fair next to the beach. The sounds of pipes and drums drifted up on the night air. Allen confided his troubles to Leary, explaining the breakup with Peter, telling him Burroughs was anti-love. As Bill seemed to want to be quiet, Allen suggested that they return to his hotel and watch the night from the patio in front of his room. Leary reported, "The floor beneath was a city carpeted with lights. Lights strung from the rigging of ships in the harbor and the King's carnival rollicking along by the water's edge. We were all in the highest and most loving of moods. Alan Ansen couldn't believe it. He kept laughing and shaking his head. This can't be true, so beautiful. Heaven!" All down the avenue d'España there were jugglers, folk dancers, tightrope walkers, dancing boys, and gnaoua musicians.

They decided to collect Bill and go down to the fair. Allen part climbed the wall next to the Muniria's garden gate and called, "Bill BUH-rows! Bill BUH-rows!" After a wait, the door slowly creaked open and Bill stood, almost collapsed against the wall. As Leary described it, "His face was haggard and tense. [...] He reached his left hand over his sweating face. [...] His thin fingers clawing at the right cheek."

"Bill, how are you doing?"

"They gave me a large dose. I would like to sound a word of warning. I'm not feeling too well." He said he was going to take some apomorphine and would join them later. "One of the nastiest cases ever processed by this department," Leary quipped to Ginsberg.[13]

Bill and the boys joined them later. Bill wanted to go to a bar. Possibly he had been overconfident in his dosage, or possibly was even trying to impress Leary with his resilience. After a while Bill went home and the others stayed up all night talking on Allen's patio.[14]

Leary was perplexed by the casual cruelty displayed by the Beats. One time they gathered at Paul Bowles's flat, sitting on cushions and his hard sofa, the wood fire crackling, with the intense light from the glass-windowed patio filtered by an array of tall broadleaf plants. They all took majoun, washed down with mint tea. There was a hanger-on with them named Mark Grotrian, whom Mikey Portman ordered around and lorded it over. In *High Priest*, Leary recalled, "One of them got caught in bad visions. I could see why. He played the part of a miserable, bullied, self-despising English schoolboy homosexual. He had walked in on the session uninvited and had tagged along unwanted. [...] I watched to see how the drug experts would handle the situation. For the most part he was ignored. [...] Only Allen Ginsberg was tender, sitting next to him and talking softly, curandero style."[15] What Leary didn't mention was that Bowles was purposely trying to give Grotrian a bad trip. Grotrian moaned, "Oh, I feel a terrible feeling of heat!" and Bowles responded, "God it's hot in here, isn't it! Open some windows," making it worse. According to Ansen, it was Leary who tried to talk him down and get him out of his horrors. Ansen thought this was typical of the unpleasant side of Paul Bowles, who always enjoyed the discomfort of others. Burroughs had seen it several times before. He reported that Bowles gave Cyril Connolly and Robert Rauschenberg majoun. Rauschenberg did not know what was happening to him and became very fearful. Instead of reassuring him, Bowles made things worse, telling him, "Oh, well it sometimes has these terrible effects on people, and there have been suicides." Rauschenberg hated him for the rest of his life.[16] Ahmed Yacoubi told Burroughs that he and Bowles did this quite deliberately, giving majoun to people who had often never even smoked pot before, and enjoying their discomfort. Burroughs thought it very irresponsible.[17]

2. An American Interlude

Leary left Tangier for Copenhagen but arranged to reconvene with Burroughs three weeks later in London. Leary and Dick Alpert—the future Ram Dass—met him at the Empress Hotel. Bill had a small, dark room on the ground floor with an electricity meter on the wall into which he fed florins. To see if the mushrooms worked differently in London they all three took two pills—4 milligrams: "naught but a brush of the phoenix bird's soft wing." They went to a workingmen's café. Bill told Leary that he regretted *The Soft Machine*, thinking that it wouldn't be understood, that the cut-ups were too far out. He told him, "*The Soft Machine* is too difficult. I am now writing a science-fiction book that a twelve-year-old can understand. I write to create my own reality." Together they walked the London streets, finishing up on the white benches at the entrance to a park. Bill still didn't like the loss of control brought on by the mushrooms. "Burroughs talking brilliantly leather beaten face, turkey neck." They had drinks at Leary's hotel, followed by dinner. Bill was on form: "Now curare is an interesting drug. Muscle paralysis. No possibility of action. Just lie there absorbing all sensation. Medicine man crooning. Paralyzed. I was smothering and can't say it. Can't talk."

Burroughs went to Leary's house in Newton, Massachusetts, flying into Logan Airport on August 25, 1961. There he prepared his paper, "Points of Distinction Among Psychoactive Drugs," for the 69th Annual Convention of the American Psychological Association, held in Manhattan between August 31 and September 6. Burroughs gave a talk and was on a panel with Timothy Leary, Gerald Heard, Alan Watts, and Frank Barron, and the attendance was so great that members of the audience were crowded ten deep around the entrance hall, sat around the speakers' table, and sprawled on the floor. Burroughs discussed the difference between a psychedelic and a narcotic drug, explaining how drugs with practically the opposite physiological effects had been lumped together as narcotics. He described junk as an antidote for cocaine, and how, if you have too much cocaine, junk will straighten you out, and explained that the psychedelics are not related to either one. He went through the different classes of drugs: narcotics, opiates, stimulants like cocaine and Benzedrine, and the sleeping drugs like barbiturates. He told how the psychedelics move in the direction of heightened awareness and how sedatives go in the other direction.

After the conference, Bill returned to Cambridge with Leary. But there was little connection between them and Bill spent most of his time alone in his third-floor room, making photo collages. In the evenings he would join the family around the kitchen table, throwing back gin and tonics, unsmiling, delivering monologues about Hassan-i-Sabbah and his other current interests. Leary described him as "increasingly bitter and paranoid, always brilliant."[18]

He had arrived expecting to find scientific discipline, sensory deprivation and submersion tanks, devices to measure brain waves, the whole apparatus of a Harvard University lab devoted to research into psychoactive drugs. Instead he found Leary conducting what amounted to psychedelic encounter sessions, spouting theories of universal love and touting his psilocybin pills as the key to enlightenment for a sick society. Leary was working with prisoners in Concord Prison, giving them psilocybin and discussing game theory: how to get a new game, how to get out of the cops-and-robbers game. The psilocybin was supposed to enable them to see their game-playing and reorient themselves. Burroughs went to the prison several times and met some of the prisoners but didn't witness the sessions. He thought it was all very hit-or-miss. The prisoners enjoyed it, though, because it was a chance to get high.

Though Bill felt profoundly out of place, he sometimes encountered a like mind. Leary reported that one evening Dr. Jefferson Monroe, the black psychiatrist of Concord Prison where Leary was conducting some of his psilocybin trials, came to visit and he and Burroughs ran routines against each other.

Bill snarled in his low nasal mutter, "Anyone who wouldn't enjoy fucking a twelve-year-old Arab boy is either insane or lying."

Monroe screamed in high falsetto, flicking his wrists in mock disdain, "You're so middle-class, my dear. Have you ever fucked a..."

"We Harvardites listened to this with jaws gaping. We were simply too square, too straight. Burroughs was too far out for us,"[19] wrote Leary.

From the moment he saw Leary's setup, Burroughs had been suspicious of psychedelic drugs and their use, predicting, correctly, that they could be used as a method of mind control. As Leary sadly reported, "He never concealed his distaste for the drug we hoped he would research."[20] Although Burroughs thought that drugs could play a useful role in expanding consciousness, he did not see them as a universal panacea and always insisted that "anything that can be done chemically can be done other ways." But his biggest concern was that Leary and his fellow workers, including Allen, were being duped by the establishment and that psychedelics were more likely to be used by the government and the military than as a means of self-enlightenment. His pessimistic view was later borne out when the extent of CIA involvement in the early spread of LSD was revealed.[21]

Leary was mortified. He wrote, "Bill Burroughs came to visit, a dignified, sage complex genius-shaman-poet-guide from a different, but sympathetic tribe. Our obtuse game-playing paid disrespect to him and his clan. And when I heard the poet scold me, I turned towards him, covered with such shame that even now it circles in my memory."[22] Leary later said, "He thought we were a bunch of dumb bozos running around and trying to save the world with these drugs and he was very uh, rightfully cynical about what we were doing. He's a very scientific person. The only psychedelic he likes is marijuana. He never really liked other psychedelic drugs."[23] Paul Bowles commented, "When Bill went to visit Leary at Harvard, he was back here within five weeks saying 'Leary is the most unscientific man I've ever met.'" Burroughs felt he should issue a warning against these easy routes to expanded consciousness and began working on it as soon as he got to New York:

> Open letter to my constituents and co-workers if any remain for the end of it.
> "Don't listen to Hassan i Sabbah," they will tell you. "He wants to take your body and all pleasures of the body away from you. Listen to us. We are serving The Garden of Delights Immortality Cosmic Consciousness The Best Ever In Drug Kicks. And *love love love* in slop buckets. How does that sound to you boys? Better than Hassan i Sabbah and his cold windy bodiless rock? Right?"
> At the immediate risk of finding myself the most unpopular character of all fiction—and history is fiction—I must say this:
> "Bring together state of news—Inquire onward from state to doer—Who monopolized Immortality? Who monopolized Cosmic Consciousness? Who monopolized Love Sex and Dream? Who monopolized Life Time and Fortune? Who took from you what is yours? Now they will give it all back? Did they ever give anything away for nothing? Did they ever give any more than they had to give? Did they not always take back what they gave when possible and it always was? *Listen*: Their Garden Of Delights is a terminal sewer—I have been at some pains to map this area of terminal sewage in the so called pornographic sections of *Naked Lunch* and *Soft Machine*—Their Immortality Cosmic Consciousness and Love is second-run grade-B shit—Their drugs are poison designed to beam in Orgasm Death and Nova Ovens—Stay out of the Garden Of Delights—It is a man-eating trap that ends in green goo—Throw back their ersatz Immortality—It will fall apart before you can get out of The Big Store—Flush their drug kicks down the drain—They are poisoning and monopolizing the hallucinogen drugs—Learn to make it without any chemical corn—All that they offer is a screen to cover retreat from the colony they have so disgracefully mismanaged. To cover travel arrangements so they will never have to pay the constituents they have betrayed and sold out. Once these arrangements are complete they will blow the place up behind them.[24]

3. New York

By September 28, 1961, Burroughs was in New York City and remained there for about two months reworking the manuscript of *The Soft Machine* and working on his new book, then called *Novia Express*. Grove Press publisher Barney Rosset had already had ten thousand copies of *Naked Lunch* printed and bound up, but they were sitting in a warehouse, waiting until the trials and lawsuits surrounding Henry Miller's *Tropic of Cancer* had cleared. He had been obliged to guarantee that he would pay the legal defense fees of any wholesaler or retailer arrested for selling the book, otherwise no one would distribute or sell it, and he was fighting lawsuits all over the country. He wanted to clear them away before he would risk publishing another book that would attract lawsuits, and so *Naked Lunch* was not published until March 21, 1962. Burroughs had sent the manuscript of *The Soft Machine* to Grove from London and Bill's editor, Dick Seaver, was concerned that it was too dense and difficult for readers to understand. He wanted more straight narrative and Burroughs was endeavoring to make it suitable for the American audience.

He rented a small apartment on Pierrepont Street in Brooklyn and about three weeks later moved into a better apartment in a basement on Congress Street, near Brooklyn Heights, just over the bridge, that better suited his purpose. It was near a union hiring hall for seamen and he could hear their calls as jobs were shouted out. It was a studio apartment: bedroom, kitchenette, and bathroom, fully furnished with a table and work bureau. But it had the worst cockroach infestation Burroughs had ever seen and he quickly ingratiated himself with the landlord by killing not only all the cockroaches in the apartment but in the landlord's apartment and the corridors as well, using bags of pyrethrum powder. It reminded him of his days as an exterminator back in Chicago and he enjoyed it enormously. Burroughs worked on his book, seeing no one. He made no effort to contact Lucien Carr or Kerouac or any of his old friends. Occasionally he would go into the city for lunch with Barney Rosset or to see Dick Seaver—he never dealt with Rosset on editorial matters, only with Seaver—otherwise he would go a local bar, eat in local restaurants, and work. He handed in a text that was acceptable to Seaver and returned to London. It was years before Grove released it. When *Naked Lunch* was finally published it sold so well in hardback that the American edition of *The Soft Machine* was delayed until March 21, 1966, when *Naked Lunch* finally came out in paperback. By this time, Burroughs had long since moved on.

Chapter Thirty-Six

"Now," he said, "I'll by God show them how ugly the Ugly American can be."[1]

1. The Edinburgh Literary Festival

Bill left the States and by the end of 1961 was settled back at the Empress Hotel in London. Convenient as it was, with its full English breakfasts, Bill really needed more space. Through John Calder, who published his "Thing Police Keep All Boardroom Reports" in volume three of his *International Literary Annual* in 1961, Bill met Marion Lobbenberg, who was soon to marry Arthur Boyars and join forces with John Calder to create Calder and Boyars, publisher of the UK editions of *The Soft Machine*, *The Wild Boys*, and others. Marion had just moved to a large new flat in Chelsea and sublet her flat at 52 Lancaster Terrace to Bill. On February 29, 1962, together with Mikey Portman, Bill moved in. He was now living just across the Bayswater Road from Kensington Gardens, a very desirable location even though most of the crumbling Regency buildings had been crudely subdivided into flats and the area had not yet gentrified. Most days he would walk in the gardens, past the ornamental fountains and along the banks of the Serpentine, sometimes heading for Kensington Palace itself, with its formal rose gardens and orangery. Although the walks continued, Bill's tenancy of the flat didn't. As he might have predicted, living with Mikey was a nightmare: holes burned in the bedding, cigarette burns on the tables, Bill's clothes borrowed without asking him and instead of being laundered and returned just thrown in a heap, dirty, in the corner. Like many spoiled rich people, Mikey never seemed to have any actual cash on him, so Bill was constantly paying for cabs, meals, and drinks. It lasted about ten days, but during this time Antony Balch shot some of the footage for *Towers Open Fire* in the flat.

Bill liked the neighborhood, though, which was much closer to Soho and the center of town than Earl's Court, and at the beginning of March he moved just a few doors down the street to a basement at 5 Lancaster

Terrace. Instead of Mikey, who was banished, he now shared with Ian. Ian played quite an important role in the creation of *Nova Express*, contributing the technical notes to the "Chinese Laundry" section and cowriting "This Horrible Case." In addition, several sections of the book utilized tape recorder cut-ups, usually manipulated by Ian, which were then transcribed.

Bill met many of the writers associated with *New Worlds* magazine, edited by science-fiction and fantasy writer Michael Moorcock, whom Bill knew through John Calder. Moorcock had been expecting someone more bohemian: "Bill was a bit formal. I was a little disappointed, to be honest, because Bill was more laid back than I was at the time, being very engaged with confronting the world, whereas he was more detached and amused by it."[2] It was at a party given by Moorcock for science-fiction writer and anthologist Judith Merril that Bill first met Arthur C. Clarke. They were both gay writers of about the same age, and Burroughs, always on the lookout for a utopia, was interested to know the conditions in Sri Lanka where Clarke lived for much of the time.

In the late spring of 1962, John Calder took Burroughs to lunch and asked if he would participate in a literary conference to be held in Edinburgh that summer. Bill readily agreed. The conference paid him a fifteen-pound honorarium—a very good fee in 1962—and he was put up by Andrew Boddy, a young Edinburgh doctor, who also hosted Alexander Trocchi. Burroughs and Trocchi first met on the plane to Edinburgh; Trocchi had left Paris years before Burroughs moved there, but by sharing both a platform and accommodation they quickly became friends. Bill was not on heroin at the time, but Trocchi was, which was why they were staying with a doctor. Dr. Boddy wrote prescriptions for Trocchi and almost immediately a policeman came round to investigate. The doctor explained that Trocchi was an addict who had been getting his prescriptions in London and he was in Edinburgh for the festival. The police were very polite and nice about it and went away. Bill had no contact with them but was intrigued to see British drug laws in action. It seemed so much better than the situation in the States.

The proceedings, which were held in the University of Edinburgh's twenty-three-hundred-seat McEwan Hall, lasted for a week beginning August 20, and gave a tremendous boost to Burroughs's career. Bill was in some very interesting company. Maurice Girodias was there. Lawrence Durrell was very friendly toward Burroughs and had read his books— Olympia published Durrell's *Black Book*—as well as another Olympia author, Henry Miller, who spoke well against censorship and received a standing ovation. Angus Wilson, Rebecca West, Stephen Spender, and Richard Hughes were there; seventy writers in all attended. This was the first time that Burroughs had met Norman Mailer and so was able to thank him for praising *Naked Lunch*. Mailer had been very complimentary about Burroughs and his work, telling *Mademoiselle* magazine, "If I were to choose a style, I think a man who writes better than I do is William Burroughs. I think he's going to last a long time after me because he's more intense. He's got a quality I don't have."[3] He repeated the compliment to the *Texas Observer*, saying, "There's one man writing today who is fantastic. William Burroughs. He writes incredible prose. He's the only writer I'm profoundly jealous of, nervous about."[4] Bill and Norman spent quite a bit of time together, along with Mary McCarthy, whom Bill had met on several occasions in Venice with Alan Ansen.

As is usual at these things, the conference broke down into cliques: Burroughs, Trocchi, Mary McCarthy, Norman Mailer, and Gerard Reve, a gay Dutch writer, formed a group. Reve spoke out about homosexuality, causing a Sikh writer named Khushwant Singh to denounce him, saying, "Of course true love is denied to the homosexual." It later turned out that his own son was homosexual, something that caused him great distress. Reve's defense of homosexuality, then still illegal in Britain, provoked Hugh MacDiarmid, the seventy-year-old communist Scottish nationalist poet, to stamp around the stage in his kilt denouncing them all, complaining that the discussion was "all heroin and homosexuality," saying to their face, "People like Burroughs and Trocchi belong in jail and not on the lecture platform" and calling them "vermin who should never have been invited to the conference." He was particularly incensed by Trocchi, who told the conference that "of what is interesting in the last, say twenty years or so of Scottish writing, I myself have written it all."[5] This infuriated MacDiarmid, who called him a "cosmopolitan scum, a writer of no literary consequence whatsoever." Spender then sided with MacDiarmid and Singh against them. Burroughs told Peter Manso, "Mary McCarthy countered by speaking of my work, and also Nabokov's, in very high terms, which went down very, very badly with Spender, and it got fairly acrid." Bill loved it all: "Oh the walkouts and all kinds of stuff. It was a great conference."[6]

The last day was billed as "The Future of the Novel," with Norman Mailer and Khushwant Singh as the moderators. Burroughs explained the cut-up and fold-in technique, stressing the magical powers it unleashed, and told the audience that he had once caused a plane to crash by naming the pilot and the circumstances leading to the accident. He had been cutting up the text at exactly the same time as the crash occurred. "Are you serious?" asked Singh, who was sitting behind him. "Perfectly," said Burroughs.[7] Bill was delighted with the whole event and said, "I was treated very well, very well indeed."

Alex Trocchi, then thirty-seven years old, was a Glaswegian with a bony, angular face and a very large nose. He had moved to Paris in the early fifties, where he edited the literary magazine *Merlin*. They did seven issues between 1952 and 1954, publishing work by Samuel Beckett, Henry Miller, Pablo Neruda, and Jean-Paul Sartre. Editions Merlin published Samuel Beckett's *Watt* (1953) and *Molloy* (1955). Trocchi lived by writing pornography for Olympia Press as Frances Lengel and Carmencita de las Lunas. His claim to fame rests on one title, *Cain's Book*, about life in fifties Greenwich Village and as a junkie working on a boat in New York Harbor, that was assembled from notes by his wife, Lyn. Burroughs said, "Whatever talent he had was in *Cain's Book*, and after that he never wrote anything." This was true; Trocchi had an almost complete writer's block and wrote virtually nothing from 1960 until his death in 1984.

Burroughs and Trocchi became good friends, but only saw each other occasionally. Bill was wary of him, not wanting to get drawn into Alex's various schemes, all of which, in some form or another, were intended to fund his heroin habit. Alex was an exhibitionist junkie, who made a point of shooting up in public and even once tried to shoot up live on a television program. For Burroughs, who at the best of times liked to keep a low profile, association with a professional junkie was not a desirable thing. He attended few public events with Trocchi, preferring to see him at dinner parties or at home.

Relations between Ian and Mikey at Lancaster Terrace had not been improved by Mikey getting strung out on heroin. Bill, naturally, proposed that he enroll with Dr. Dent, but Lord Goodman had other ideas. He was a friend of Lady Isabella Frankau's, the "writing doctor" who did little else but prescribe heroin and morphine to wealthy clients from her Harley Street clinic. She was very opposed to Dr. Dent and his apomorphine treatment as she didn't particularly want her clients cured. Bill and Mikey had been to see Goodman and Lady Frankau at Goodman's house on Portland Place, where it was explained that Goodman had arranged for Mikey to enter a sanatorium with Lady Frankau as his doctor. They had just returned to Lancaster Terrace. Bill, Mikey, Brion Gysin, and Ian Sommerville were all together in the living room when Bill experienced a "psychic attack." Mikey had a cold sore on his lip, herpes simplex, which according to Burroughs is a specific avenue of entry for the Ugly Spirit. Something seemed to slide off Michael's shoulder and hit Bill right in the stomach. Bill stood up, intending to go to the bathroom for a glass of water, and passed out on the floor. He came around a few minutes later. "I not only felt it, I saw it, it was something slid off his shoulder like silver, silver light. You could see it very clearly."[8] Bill regarded it as a skirmish in the battle for Mikey. Mikey did eventually take the apomorphine cure, lots of them. They worked, but he was so weak that he'd get straight back on alcohol or junk, or both, drinking a quarter of vodka a day on top of methadone and heroin.

Perhaps inevitably, Mikey's mother, Marjerie, blamed his heroin addiction on Burroughs, and as Mikey tended to ape all of Bill's actions there was probably an element of copying Bill in it. But Bill was not on heroin at this time and was not impressed. Mikey caused enough attention with his alcoholism as it was, but at least that was legal. The last thing Bill needed was a coterie of teenage junkies hanging around, attracting the attention of the police. Mikey's mother was in Greece at the time, going out with future filmmaker Conrad Rooks, who, far from being the arbitrator and explaining Bill's position, was inflaming the situation between them. Lord Goodman interceded and explained that Bill had nothing to do with Mikey becoming a junkie, and eventually Mrs. Portman accepted that Bill was not to blame and had in fact done all he could to get him treated.

In the first of several attempts to film *Naked Lunch*, Conrad Rooks paid Burroughs five hundred dollars for an option on the rights. As an heir to the Avon Cosmetics fortune he had a lot of money to play with but had no direction in his life. However, when Rooks began to seriously consider making the film, Bill backed out because he thought that Rooks would make a mess of it. Burroughs said, "Ian with his female intuition said, 'Don't you understand he wants you! He's trying to buy you for five hundred dollars. Don't be a fool, don't have anything to do with this!' So I just told Conrad Rooks, the deal's off. And as for your five hundred dollars, I'll pay it back, sometime. I never had any intention of paying it back."[9]

2. *The Ticket That Exploded*

Bill continued to move between London and Paris, always staying at the Beat Hotel. On July 16, 1962, he participated in an event billed as La Bohème, held in Montparnasse. It was here that Bernard Heidsieck and a group of other French artists approached Bill, Ian, and Brion and said, "We hear that you are doing things with projections and sounds and wouldn't you like to join in with us?" As Gysin described it, "In La Bohème we had some very strange things that we did along that line: reading poems off shuffled cards along with tapes running and stuff like that."[10] They did in fact do a number of joint performances with the French poets in the early sixties as a result of that meeting, and Bernard Heidsieck became a friend.

As usual Burroughs continued to experiment. One long-term project was to disrupt the time-space continuum in a noticeable way. That September, each Thursday at exactly 7:30 p.m., Bill, Ian, and Mikey Portman would arrive at the Café des Arts on the rue de Seine and meet Joseph Geraci and Arnold Rosen outside. They would enter and sit in the same place at the same long table, reserved on their behalf, with baskets of bread, candles in bottles, *vin ordinaire*, and exhibition posters on the walls. It was Bill's theory that if you did the same thing at the exact same moment each week then the intersection of the repetition with the time-space continuum would cause a rupture. It was based on his understanding of one of Heisenberg's more obscure observations. Burroughs did most of the talking.

After the Edinburgh Writers' Conference Burroughs went straight to the Beat Hotel and resumed work. In November 1962 he finished both *Nova Express* and *The Ticket That Exploded*. He also compiled a book of selections from *The Naked Lunch*, *The Soft Machine*, and *The Ticket That Exploded*, to be published by John Calder in England under the title *Dead Fingers Talk*. He told Alan Ansen that "by rearranging the material and adding some new sections I have endeavored to create a new novel rather than miscellaneous selections." He said he expected the book to be out in March 1963, the same time that Grove was to publish *Nova Express* in New York. In the course of selecting and rearranging he became so dissatisfied with *The Soft Machine* that he completely rewrote it, taking out most of the cut-ups and substituting sixty-five pages of new material in a straight narrative line. He told Ansen, "One has not been idle."

Nor was Bill altogether satisfied with *Ticket*, and did indeed later rewrite that as well, but in the meantime he asked Ansen if he liked the nova police in the book. He told him, "I endeavored to distil an archetype of the perfect police officer in Inspector Lee and find that the part has taken over to an extent where some of my old connections have been alienated—Well, it's all show business what?" He may have been referring here to his estrangement from Allen Ginsberg eighteen months earlier, when Inspector J. Lee sliced their friendship to ribbons at the Hotel Muniria, leaving Allen shattered and confused. In many ways, Ansen and Gysin had now taken on the role that Allen previously had as Bill's literary adviser. Burroughs summed up the book for an American journalist: "The Ticket That Exploded involves the Nova Conspiracy to blow up the Earth and then leave it through reincarnation by projected image onto another planet. The plot failed, so the title has both meanings."[11]

Had *The Ticket That Exploded* been accessible to more people it could have been this book that established Burroughs's credentials as a science-fiction writer, for here is the planet with four colored suns and a green sky, here are the green fish boys and the green newt boys. *Ticket* contains the more or less straight narrative of Ali—"In a Strange Bed"—and introduces the Nova Police: "I am sure none of you have ever seen a Nova police officer—When disorder on any planet reaches a certain point the regulating instance scans POLICE—Otherwise—Sput—another planet bites the cosmic dust."[12] It contained numerous passages that read like prose poetry: "Lonely lemur calls whispered in the walls of silent obsidian temples in a land of black lagoons, the ancient rotting Kingdom of Jupiter—Smelling the blackberry smoke drifting through huge spiderwebs in ruined court-yards under eternal moonlight."[13] The blackberry smoke turns out to be powerful stuff. The book also contains a graphic account of sex with Kiki, which Burroughs said was an accurate description and affirmed that Kiki's speech is always verbatim.[14]

Maurice Girodias, as usual, did one of his quick print jobs, and *The Ticket That Exploded* was out in December 1962, a month after Burroughs handed it in. The launch party for *Ticket* was held December 1962 at Girodias's Le Grand-Séverin, a multilevel nightclub and restaurant complex at 7 rue Saint-Séverin. That same week there was a book signing at Gaït Frogé's Librairie Anglaise. Bill was fêted and wined and dined and enjoyed the whole trip apart from one unfortunate incident. He subsequently wrote Alan Ansen, "I have been on the wagon for some months following a horrible traumatic incident at a party in Paris where I ended up in bed with a woman." He said that the plain fact was that he couldn't handle hard liquor and claimed he was going to remain off the hard stuff. He still took wine with meals, of course, but nothing else.

Burroughs returned to London in December 1962, telling a journalist, "I like England. There is much respect for your privacy. It's very easy to be left alone here, a good place to work. I prefer it to Paris which I don't particularly like to live in, though I have spent quite a lot of time there because my publishers were there."[15] He stayed first at the Empress, then switched to a nondescript block of flats at 51 Gloucester Terrace, just around the corner from his old place in Lancaster Terrace. That December a pea-souper, a thick layer of sulfur dioxide–rich smog, covered the city for four days, making it almost impossible to see across the street. Burroughs enjoyed it immensely, sidling along the streets, bumping into people, hearing the crunch of cars gently crashing into each other. It was a genuine Sherlock Holmes "London Particular." He preferred Bayswater to Earl's Court; he enjoyed the proximity of the park, its closeness to the

West End with all its pubs and restaurants, and the fact that there were far more cheap good restaurants in easy walking distance. One of his favorites was the Kalamaras Taverna at 66 Inverness Mews, just off Queensway, something of a sixties celebrity haunt, which he returned to time and again over the next decade, despite its then lack of a liquor license (you brought your own).

Burroughs first met Anthony Burgess in London in January 1963, six months after the publication of *A Clockwork Orange*. Burroughs liked the book because it dealt in a serious way with two of Bill's major interests: methods of conditioning and brainwashing, and experiments with language: it introduced more than two hundred loanwords from Russian. Bill wrote to him and they met up the next time Burgess visited London. Although Burgess and his wife, Lynne, lived in Etchingham, Sussex, they often visited London and they all became friends. That summer, when Burgess and Lynne holidayed in Tangier, Burroughs visited them at the Miramar Hotel, where Lynne had one of her frequent alcoholic collapses. She lay in bed, exhausted, as Burgess incessantly rolled kif cigarettes for her while Bill read aloud from Jane Austen's *Persuasion*.[16]

In November 1963, Lynne and Anthony Burgess once again found themselves in Tangier. Lynne had collapsed yet again, and on this occasion it was in the Hotel Velasquez that William read aloud from Jane Austen to her.[17] In the spring of 1964, the Burgesses moved to Chiswick and Anthony became something of a drinking partner with William, but they lived too far apart for it to become a regular thing except when Burgess was in the West End in his capacity as drama critic for the *Spectator* or as concert and opera critic for *Queen*. Lynne Burgess was to die of cirrhosis of the liver in March 1968.

Through Mikey, Bill had now met a number of the key figures in the so-called Chelsea set, where Mikey was well known. Two in particular became good friends, Christopher Gibbs and Robert Fraser, who had been at Eton together and were once described by Francis Bacon as "the Belgravia pansies" (a term that Christopher found amusing and Robert did not). Bill and Christopher first met in Tangier, when Mikey took Christopher around to see Bill at the Muniria, but it was in London that they became friends, and Bill would visit Christopher at Lindsey House at 100 Cheyne Walk, a mansion dating from 1674, remodeled from an even older building. Bill appeared very at home, lounging on the sofa smoking hashish in front of the huge bay window with its magnificent view of the Thames (James McNeill Whistler, who did many studies of the Thames in the 1870s, had lived next door), attended by his smartly turned-out boys. The room was dominated by an enormous painting by Il Pordenone that had previously belonged to the duc d'Orléans. A huge Moroccan chandelier cast a thousand pinpoints of light over Eastern hangings and silk carpets. In the summer, afternoon tea was taken under the mulberry tree in a garden designed by Lutyens. Christopher was an aesthete, antique dealer, and interior designer who would find a beautiful country house for a client and fill it with faded, slightly shabby antiques and paintings in the most exquisite taste. An expert in the genealogy of British aristocrats—he was one himself—he found much of his stock in the attics of old country houses. He was largely responsible for the artistic education of his friend John Paul Getty. Here Bill was at his most refined and anglophile. He liked Christopher and could relax with him. Christopher remembered him as diffident and quite shy, but not in an off-putting way, as some people thought. "He was terribly unfrosty. I found him quite cozy actually. Cozy old thing. He was always very nice to me, always."[18]

Robert Fraser had left Eton and joined the King's African Rifles to serve in Uganda. Robert's sergeant major was Idi Amin, with whom, Robert told Marianne Faithfull, he had a fling, probably just a one-night stand. (Amin was president of Uganda from 1971 until 1979.) Slim, conservatively dressed in pinstriped suits and dark glasses, Fraser stood to attention, ramrod tall, but had to bend virtually double to reach into his pockets because his trousers were so tight. He mumbled, drawled, and slurred his words, stammering when stressed or nervous, and stuttered terribly when his father was around. He liked rough trade and was very adventurous sexually. A rent boy came most afternoons at 2:00 p.m. After dinner he would cruise the gay clubs, the Rockingham and bondage clubs. He loved Arab boys, and there was usually a Mohammed to open the door and serve drinks.

Sometimes Bill would arrange to meet Francis Bacon at Muriel's club, the Colony Room, upstairs at 41 Dean Street, Soho, and dine afterward in Wheeler's fish restaurant on Old Compton Street. Through Bacon he met many of the Colony Room regulars, including Michael Wishart, whose autobiography, *High Diver*, Bill very much enjoyed when it was published in 1977. These were not close friends of Bill's but were drinking and dining companions. Though Bacon was gay, his taste was for older working-class men, whereas Bill preferred much younger men. Early in 1963 Bacon took Bill to the Watermans Arms pub on the Isle of Dogs in the East End, owned by his friend Dan Farson. The Watermans Arms was a "singing pub" with a small but elaborate Victorian proscenium arch. Cheeky Cockneys sang out-of-tune old-time music hall songs backed by a three-piece combo, men with huge mustaches drank yards of ale, and a crush of locals and tourists swilled back pints of warm beer. Farson was a well-known television personality, and his celebrity was able to summon up Jacques Tati, Clint Eastwood, Judy Garland, Tony Bennett, Sarah Vaughan, and even Groucho Marx to the depths of the East End. It was through this meeting that Burroughs was invited to appear in the fourth edition of Farson's Granada television show, *Something to Say*, alongside Alex Trocchi, but by then Burroughs and Ian were living in Tangier.

In January 1963, still at 51 Gloucester Terrace, there was a sudden flurry of activity and Antony Balch's film, *Towers Open Fire*, was completed—or so they thought—in a two-week spurt. The script was based on a passage from the "Combat Troops in the Area" section of *The Ticket That Exploded*: "Word falling—Photo falling—Time falling—Break through in Gray Room."[19] Balch had shot footage of Burroughs and Gysin at the Beat Hotel in Paris and on the street. In London he filmed at Lancaster Terrace and Gloucester Terrace. The first footage shot was in the boardroom of the British Film Institute on Dean Street and featured BFI luminary Liam O'Leary as well as John Gillett, David Jacobs, Bachoo Sen, and Andrew Rabanech. Alexander Trocchi played the chairman of the board. The "towers" in the film are the lighting gantries of the Gibraltar football stadium, and more footage was shot in Tangier with Burroughs, Ian Sommerville, and Mikey Portman. Further footage was shot in Paris of endlessly spinning Dreamachines at an exhibition called *The Object* held at the Musée des Arts Décoratifs in 1962. There are many groundbreaking elements, among which is a sequence, in this black-and-white film, where Mikey Portman sits on the ground in front of a cinema then looks up across an eyeline match. We follow his gaze and see through his eyes a sky filled with vibrating colored dots that appear to descend upon him in a roar of Joujouka flutes. The frames themselves were originally blank. It is a literal transcription of Burroughs's idea of replacing words with colored dots. Balch hand-colored each frame with scores of dots of colored emulsion, and did the same to all the prints that were issued, an enormously time-consuming practice (which of course made each print different). The film opened at the Paris Pullman on Drayton Gardens in 1963 as the supporting short to Tod Browning's *Freaks*, also distributed by Balch.[20] *Towers* was a groundbreaking film in another area, in that it was possibly the first film made in which the entire creative team—Burroughs, Balch, Gysin, Sommerville, and Portman—was gay.

This was one of the periods in the early sixties when Burroughs was back on junk and saw much more of Alex Trocchi because Alex was getting him his heroin. Burroughs told Bill Rich, "Great person. I liked him. We shared many a shot."²¹ Because Trocchi had a doctor's prescription for heroin he was able to give Bill however much he wanted. Naturally money was involved. Bill would contribute to Trocchi's household expenses. "He would talk to me about his bills, and I would say, 'Listen, don't worry about that rent bill. I'll take care of it.' In other words, for his taking care of me with heroin, I made it well worth his while." Bill could have obtained a prescription of his own, had he wanted to, but the doctor was Lady Frankau and Burroughs had already had a run-in with her over Mikey Portman, and had no intention of getting involved with her. "She was the supplier. She always wanted to get her hands on me."²²

In February 1963 Burroughs paid one last visit to the Beat Hotel, which had been sold and was about to be redeveloped. At a party he got drunk and once more ended up in bed with a woman back at the hotel. "I don't remember her. I suppressed it, she had red hair...not much happened... American...it was not enjoyable, it was terrible." It was on this visit that Burroughs met Samuel Beckett, one of his literary heroes. Beckett had two objections to his fold-in method. He called it "plumbing" over and over again in the conversation and complained, "You're using other writers' work." He thought Bill believed that the writers he used for fold-ins—Shakespeare, Blake, Rimbaud, Beckett himself—had answers. "You should see what I've done with your work, Mr. Beckett," Burroughs said. But Beckett objected, "There are no answers! Our despair is total! Total! We can't even talk to each other. That's what I felt in *Naked Lunch* and why I liked it." Bill had been very drunk and remembered little of the conversation, but he disagreed with Beckett and thought there were answers. After the night he met Beckett he stopped drinking for a while as it was obviously affecting his memory. "I feel 100 percent better giving up drinking."²³

More and more, Bill felt that his future was tied to Ian Sommerville. When the Beat Hotel finally closed they moved around the corner to the Hotel Pax at 30 rue Saint-André-des-Arts before returning to 5 Lancaster Terrace. He was happy to be back in London. "It's a man's town." Bill and Ian were working closely together and decided to present a version of the Domaine Poétique in London, similar to the multimedia events in Paris. On March 28th, 1963, at the Institute of Contemporary Arts (ICA) on Dover Street, Bill, Ian, and Antony Balch presented an evening of cut-ups. Bill sat in a chair and stared at the audience, a powerful blue spotlight making it difficult to see him, while earsplitting cut-up tapes were played featuring distorted Moroccan flutes, pneumatic drills, radio static, fragments of radio broadcasts, and Bill's own flat, dry voice reading texts and news reports. Stills from *Towers Open Fire* were projected on a screen above his head (they had intended to screen the film but it was not ready). The *Evening Standard* reported, "The club was filled to busting point with intrigued spectators even standing outside in the passage to catch one or two eerie twangs of Burroughs' voice. I found him mysterious as ever. He sat with hands folded and a deadpan expression in front of a blue screen as his voice, sometimes crackling into a strange blend of humour and irony, came over a recording machine."[24] Fed up with constantly moving and with hotel living, Bill decided to settle down, and invited Ian to join him.

Chapter Thirty-Seven

Two short months later it dawned on me fully what Burroughs was attempting. It was like the earth opening under your feet.

—JEFF NUTTALL[1]

1. Billy Burroughs Jr.

On June 25, 1963, Ian and Bill arrived in Tangier, intending to set up house together. They had been house-hunting for two weeks and the house at number 4 calle Larachi on the Marshan, off the avenue des USA, was the first that seemed at all possible. The house looked charming. It was on a quiet side street shadowed by trees and they even thought the little Moroccan children were cute as they clustered around them smiling. "*Fingaro?* One cigarette?" At the large American-owned villa across the street, the old bearded guard looked like someone straight out of the *Arabian Nights*. Later Burroughs felt that he should have known something was wrong; the agent had not wished to show the house to them and sent his assistant, Abdulla. When they arrived there had been a bad omen: the cab door slammed on Abdulla's thumb as he was getting out.

The house was conveniently laid out on three floors. The kitchen was dark, since the only light came from a high barred window, and next to it was the hole-in-the-floor lavatory. The floors were tiled and so easy to keep clean. Two bedrooms faced the street and a bedroom in the back had a window looking out over the garden of the next-door villa. This room was bathed in a cool underwater green light, and Burroughs immediately annexed it as his own. Burroughs described their initial attraction to the house: "Upstairs was a large room running the length of the house with a balcony facing on the street; leaf shadows dancing on the white plaster walls. We would fix it up Arab style with benches and low coffee tables. This would be our reception room. There was a small cell-like room facing the back garden, with a single window like a square of blue set in the wall. The roof was flat and we planned a summer house up there of split bamboo with straw mats under trellised vines. I do not recall if I felt any twitches of foreboding on that remote summer day. (The young man's thumbnail was already turning black.)"[2]

They moved in on July 15, 1963, the day after visiting Joujouka with Mohamed Hamri, who had been Brion's partner in the restaurant. Burroughs was very familiar with the music of Joujouka from tapes made by Paul Bowles and Brion Gysin. There was not a special ceremony—the musicians were just playing—but it was a wonderful experience. Ian liked Arab music very much and they had a good time. They only stayed one night because the accommodation was basic. They slept on the floor and there were fleas. Back on calle Larachi, to Ian's great annoyance, Mikey Portman arrived and settled in with them. As soon as they moved in several cats assembled at the open door, afraid to come within reach but hoping for food. One white cat inched forward and Bill reached to pat it. He was the first cat to get inside the house.

Another reason for finding a house was that Bill had decided that it was time he got to know his son, Billy Jr., and had made arrangements for him to attend the American School in Tangier. Burroughs claimed it was Billy's idea; he wanted to get to know his father.[3] Burroughs had not seen his son since October 1954 when he was seven. A few days after they moved in, Burroughs met Billy's plane in Lisbon. They caught a connecting plane to Madrid and went from there to Tangier. Sixteen-year-old Billy had woken up in Palm Beach, Florida, and now found himself in the Parade Bar, the only place that served decent hamburgers, being introduced to Mikey Portman—"Michael, this is my son"—and fending off propositions from an aging queen: "I know I'm old. But I really haven't lost my figure, dear. You know, half the old Tangerines knew you were coming and wondered what you looked like. Well Baby! I mean, if you ever want your nuts blowed???"[4]

They finally reached 4 calle Larachi, where, despite traveling to Portugal and Spain to get him, Bill had made no sleeping arrangements for Billy. They toured the house, using a flashlight because the electricity was out. "Wait for Ian," Burroughs said. Ian eventually arrived and fixed the electricity supply by going outside and banging on the pole that carried the power line.

Next morning Billy awoke to find Ian Sommerville sitting on his bed, gazing at him like a loving mother. Billy recalled, "We talked for a few minutes and then he took my hand gently, ever so gently, and tried to draw it to his groin."[5] Ian didn't take the rejection badly and they became friends. That evening when Bill, Ian, and Mikey fired up their long kif pipes with clay bowls, Billy asked if he could try some. "All in good time," said Ian, but the next day Bill asked Ian to take Billy down to the Grand Socco and help him pick out a pipe.

Billy found Bill's kif too harsh on the throat for his liking, so Bill gave him some majoun instead. They appear to have got off to a reasonably good start. The first problem arose when Bill took Billy to meet Omar Pound, son of Ezra, to enroll him in the American School where Omar was headmaster. Billy wouldn't say a word. He had wanted to come to Tangier to get to know his father; the idea of going to school hadn't entered his calculations. Back in Palm Beach he had gone from one school to another in a series of fiascos, attending, not liking it, and quitting, moving on to another. Bill's parents were paying his tuition so it was no wonder they encouraged the idea of Bill looking after Billy for a while. The American School was not very far away from the house and there was a bus. Billy went for three days. He was surly and uncooperative. Then he quit, telling Bill that it was too much trouble to get up and go on the bus. "They weren't teaching me anything anyway," he said. Bill explained to his friend Joe McPhillips who was one of the teachers there, "What can I say? This has happened with so many schools previously, you see." Bill told Ted Morgan, "There was not a goddamn thing that I could do. He didn't want to go to school, I can't do anything about it. I couldn't find anything that worked."[6] The one constructive thing Billy did at school was take a couple of flamenco guitar lessons, and he continued to play afterward. Bill got him a tutor for a while, Chuck Wein, but Wein returned to New York at the beginning of March 1964 to become Andy Warhol's film assistant and sometime director.[7] One-on-one tuition seemed to work better. Ian gave him lessons in mathematics. Billy and Ian got on well, but they never spoke of the fact that Ian was living with Bill as a couple. Billy got to know a group of young people, some of them from the school, including some hip young Moroccans, and would invite his friends back to play music, dance, and smoke pot. Bill's biggest worry was that Billy's friends would talk and news of his drug-taking gay ménage would get back to the consulate.

The contrast between his grandparents' house and his father's must have been extreme to young Billy. His father spent the day working in his spartan room: an army bed, a filing cabinet, desk, the austerity only relieved by a beautiful Gysin painting of the moon over the Sahara. Thanks to Billy we have a description of his father writing *Nova Express*: Burroughs would spend hours at a time smoking kif while sitting in the orgone accumulator in the upstairs hallway, then suddenly rush out and begin pounding the keys of his typewriter. As soon as the sun began to set, Burroughs would go to the roof to watch the colors of the sky change. He would stand, his mouth partly open, transfixed at his favorite spot, absolutely motionless, a cigarette staining the fingers of his right hand, which he would drop when it burned him.[8] Only when it was completely dark and the great band of the Milky Way competed with the intense moonlight to light up the deep midnight-blue sky did he make another sudden dash to the typewriter. They avoided the roof by day because rooftops were traditionally the women's province where they did their washing and gossiped. Billy made the mistake of going there one day and was seen from other roofs. The Arabs threw little pieces of mud at their front door for the next week, the beginning of a campaign of harassment that intensified after Billy left.

Burroughs made no effort to feed Billy, who was used to regular meals at his grandmother's table. People in the house ate at different times; very often they would go into town in the evening and eat at a restaurant. Billy would sometimes bring back food or go to the Parade for a burger for lunch. He recounts one time when he did bring back a roast chicken and an apple pie for his dinner but everyone in the house descended on him at the doorway and all he had left was a slice of pie; they were all hungry from smoking hash.[9] Bill used the bones to make soup.

Ian took Billy to the Dancing Boy Café on the Medina wall overlooking the harbor where customers sat around on bentwood chairs smoking kif, drinking mint tea, watching the dancing boys on the small stage, and listening to traditional Moroccan music. The café closed at 3:00 a.m. and sometimes they would go on to someone's house and the festivities would continue until dawn, in time to catch the baker's boy, wheeling great rounds of bread to the shops. The bread was so hot Billy had to wrap it in his shirt. He would stop at a grocery store and buy fresh butter—made daily because of the heat—before returning home. It was in many ways idyllic, but as Billy wrote, "These were pleasant times but I couldn't make it; I was too young and found it difficult to get involved."[10] Billy grew a little goatee and took to dressing in black like the hipsters at the Dancing Boy but never felt a part of the scene. He took to wandering the clifftops with a supply of grass and spent a lot of time by himself. He couldn't figure out what was wrong with him. One day Ian came to his room and observed that he was homesick. "You don't want to live in a houseful of fags," Ian told him. He was right. After six months in Tangier, Billy returned to Florida in January 1964, intent on getting his high school diploma. Nothing had been resolved between him and his father.

Throughout his stay relations between them had been stilted and difficult. Bill found himself talking with a stranger he didn't know at all, and whose interests were entirely foreign to him. The photograph of father and son together taken in early November by Robert Freson for *Esquire* shows two strangers sitting together: Billy in black, trying to look older than he is, Burroughs, in a Moroccan skull cap, leaning just fractionally in his direction, looking blank.[11] Billy clearly admired his father and desperately wanted his approval and friendship, but another side of him blamed him for the death of his mother, for separating him from his half sister, and, most of all, for neglecting him. He was too young to understand his own behavior, and Bill was too reticent and withdrawn to attempt to talk about it. Burroughs was repeating his family's behavior. He never once heard his father and mother even raise their voices to each other. It was a family characteristic: to make a scene would have been unthinkable. It was just not done.

"We weren't connecting. Just not connecting, sort of strained. I blame myself very much that I never really leveled with him and explained to him, as best I could, about Joan's death and the whole circumstances. The feeling of possession and all that. Nothing. I never explained about it at all. He knew all about it, naturally. He was not exactly surly but sort of inaccessible and dead emotionally. When I talked to him it was like nothing was happening."[12] Sometimes Billy could behave in a typically difficult adolescent manner. He could be bored and moody, and Burroughs quickly noticed that any practical suggestion he made, Billy would resist. He told Billy to make sure he didn't leave his kif and pipe on the table where anyone from the American consulate could walk in and see it. Naturally Billy left it there all the time and Bill would find it and put it away. "Of course I know it's deliberate, but what can you do when someone has a deliberate flaunting mechanism? Of course he's making me pay. I was trying to do something that would be constructive for him and it just wasn't working at all, at all, all!"[13]

What Burroughs could not understand was Billy's indifference to Tangier. Burroughs thought he was putting him in contact with another reality; he expected him to be overwhelmed by the strangeness of the place, to be astonished by the Socco Grande, which was then filled with Berbers in from the countryside with their stalls of vegetables and fruit, hot chestnuts, and small cakes beneath the giant ombú shade trees and the water sellers with their curious red hats and brass bells and ornaments and goatskins. But "he didn't seem to give a shit"; he didn't want to go anywhere or see anything. He had no enthusiasm or interest whatsoever. Burroughs felt that young people had no sense of wonder anymore, but he was not making enough allowance for Billy's youth and naiveté. However, just before he left, Billy told Bill something that surprised him. He was just going back to an American high school but he told Bill, "I'm sure that this is where I'll wind up." Had he gone to Tangier two years later, things might have been different.

Life with Burroughs was too alien for this straight all-American boy. He never knew how to react. Billy was the object of attention from Jane Bowles, which embarrassed him though she was only being friendly and certainly not looking for sex. Other scenes were just too weird for him to know how to behave, such as when Alan Ansen came to Tangier for the summer and managed to obtain some opium. Bill, Ian, and Mikey, Guy Harloff and his girlfriend Ginette all gathered in Ansen's room to take it. Bill went into one of his freezing acts with Ginette, not just indifference but a concentrated effort to will her out of the room. Ginette knew what he was doing and threw something at him. He later apologized, but as he was doing so, he was caressing Mikey's thigh, to Ian's obvious dismay.

Bill took Billy to the airport for his flight to the States and warned him, "Billy, for godsakes don't try to take anything in with you." Billy told him, "Bill, I don't have anything." But he had bought some majoun right there in the airport and as soon as he got to the States he was taken to one side and they found it right away. But the customs officers told him, "You're too young to spend the night in jail. I don't think this is going to amount to much." However, from then on, they had his name on their books.

2. Living in the Marshan

Life on calle Larachi was described by Ian Sommerville as "gloomy." Bill was in a curious frame of mind, doubtless caused by Billy's presence, but he also had financial worries: the cost of the house was fifteen dollars a month, which was outrageous; a Moroccan would have paid half that. Ian Sommerville was dependent upon Bill financially, and Mikey was still sponging off him even though he was himself wealthy. On top of this was Billy: his food, his drugs and clothing, and, a much larger expense, his transport to and from the States. Alan Ansen tried, clumsily, to help by suggesting to Bill's old friend James Le Baron Boyle, who was visiting Tangier, that he and Boyle buy Bill a stove so that he could eat in and save money. Boyle refused and there was embarrassment all around. Some of the gloom of the house was alleviated by Leslie Eggleston, who was oblivious to everyone's problems and chattered away happily, his animated gossip helping to dispel sour moods. Stuart Gordon, with his tales of the Ohio Mafia, was also a frequent visitor that summer. Alan Ansen thought that Bill was in a very strange mood, particularly when Burroughs made him declare that he was a stronger personality than Ansen and asked him if he would commit murder for him. Ansen told him no, he wouldn't.

This was also the summer when Antony Balch was around. He filmed the Tangier sequences for *Towers Open Fire*, with Ian and Mikey opening umbrellas. He and Bill cruised the bars. It was when Bill was living in the Marshan that Paul Bowles took Alfred Chester to meet Burroughs. Chester wanted Burroughs to write a blurb for his book, *The Exquisite Corpse*. Bill said, "Sure, I'll write one," and scribbled, "Alfred Chester writes like white lightning." Many of Burroughs's future blurbs were written in the same spirit, without reading the books. Bowles, who saw a lot of Burroughs that year, considered Burroughs to have an addictive personality. Bowles thought it was bad form to drink and smoke at the same time, but his image of Burroughs was that he always had a highball glass of whiskey, stirring it with his long finger in the glass, and a big cheroot of kif—Bowles never used the word "joint." Bill would light a kif cigarette and rest it on the mantelpiece; he would take a drink, spilling it on himself, pull out his kif, and roll himself another one, ignoring the one already burning down. He would get falling-down drunk, but claimed he knew how to fall so that he never hurt himself. Bowles made sure that he always had some kif of his own with him as Bill's was unsmokable because it was full of seeds and stems.[14]

Just after Christmas, on December 28, Jane Bowles gave a dinner party. At first she was worried about whether to invite Bill, telling John Hopkins, "You *know* the way he drinks," but in the event Bill behaved impeccably. He arrived wearing his black suit, a white shirt with a narrow black tie, and polished black shoes. Jane was relieved. There were oysters from Oualidia, *poussin de bois* (a code name for illegally caught partridge, sold under the counter at the market), and real French champagne.[15] Bill enjoyed himself.

The problems at 4 calle Larachi did not manifest themselves badly until after Billy had left. That winter the kerosene heaters smoked and went out, filling the house with fumes; the villa guard from *Arabian Nights* over the road came to work for them, but continually demanded more money while stealing all their shirts and towels; the flat roof leaked and the walls of flaking plaster were alive with electricity. Bill would get a shock when he pushed pins into a wall-mounted map of Tangier to indicate the location of photographs on a photo layout. Snails crawled down the walls, leaving iridescent trails of slime, and green mold formed on their shoes and coat lapels.[16]

Problems were compounded by the antagonism of the local people, who expected them to employ staff. The children were sneering and hostile, always banging on the door to sell flowers or to ask for cigarettes or money. One beggar woman pounded on the door at seven in the morning. Rocks and even a spinning top crashed through their skylight window. Stones were thrown at the door every day, and every time they stepped outside they would be showered with insults and curses. Eventually Bill and Ian took to drawing lots to see who would run the gauntlet to go out and buy provisions. Thanks to Girodias, who had stolen the $5,000 advance sent to Burroughs by Grove Press, they had no money to move out.

One evening Burroughs walked out onto the balcony and there were about fifty Arab women gathered in the street, looking up at him. He raised his hands in a threatening gesture and they all scattered like rabbits. Burroughs later commented, "That gesture, it works or it don't work. If it doesn't work you're in trouble, end up like Orpheus torn to pieces by mad women."[17] Ian felt the harassment more than Bill. He had originally liked the idea of sharing a house with Bill, but quickly became agitated and paranoid, leading to what must have been a full-scale paranoid episode. Bill was no longer attracted to Ian and was openly flirting with Mikey and other boys. Ian was still very attracted to Bill but was troubled by Bill's lack of interest and worried about his future. He had no money and was entirely dependent upon Bill's largesse. Ian's insecurity and nervousness were greatly exacerbated by the behavior of the locals, but they had already been amplified by the arrival of Billy. Burroughs had always been to some degree a father figure to Ian, and so Billy was on one level a rival. However, seeing how badly Bill dealt with his real son could do nothing but fill him with dismay. Ian had a tough carapace, but Burroughs was so careless in his relationships that he often hurt the ones he loved.[18]

3. Cut-Ups, Columns, and Grids

Despite the chaos surrounding him, Burroughs worked assiduously on *Nova Express* and its associated cut-up experiments. He was now moving squares of text, usually a quarter page of typewriting, against the printed pages of other writers: Truman Capote, Evelyn Waugh, *A Clockwork Orange* by Anthony Burgess, *The Catcher in the Rye* by J. D. Salinger, Graham Greene's *The Man Within*, as well as letters and newspaper clippings. One six-page document was titled "Cut-Ups with Jean Genet and Writing in His Style." Early in 1964, he applied a new technique known as "grids" to a long series of cut-ups based on material from issue 27[19] of LeRoi Jones and Diane di Prima's *Floating Bear* poetry newsletter and to the extensive *Times Literary Supplement* correspondence that resulted from an unfavorable review of Burroughs's three Olympia books in the

November 14, 1963, issue. The texts were typed out and cut up in the normal way. The resulting manuscript was then divided into a grid of anything between nine and thirty-six squares by thick colored lines, usually red or blue. He sometimes used wavy lines, one of the first suggestions that the formal appearance of the page was in itself important. A thirty-six-grid page would usually consist of four squares across by nine deep. Sometimes the top four would be numbered. Another series using the same source material was divided into one-inch squares by blue or red lines. These squares could then be visited in a random order and words or phrases taken from them and typed out on a fresh sheet of paper. It was yet another way of creating unexpected juxtapositions.

In Burroughs's archives in the New York Public Library there is a folder labeled "Grids and Experiments" containing more than sixty pages of grids arranged in different sizes ranging from thirty-two or thirty-six squares to as many as 273, 117 of which were left blank. The number of squares varies enormously, from twenty-eight, thirty, forty, forty-five, and so on. Burroughs explored every permutation just in case it had something to offer. The grid is sometimes drawn in a blue wavy line, by red and blue lines, or by carefully ruled black lines. Orange, green, and black crayons are used as well as green and red ink, making the manuscripts very interesting visually. One text is divided into a geometric pattern of triangles and rectangles. Some squares are filled with calligraphy. One text is divided into ten columns by thin blue lines; another is typed in squares but lacks the grid squares. Sometimes the squares are ticked or numbered, presumably meaning their contents had been used in some way.

Another form of text presentation, begun in February 1964, was the "three-column" technique. Burroughs noticed that newspapers are printed almost as cut-ups, in long narrow columns, so that inevitably you unconsciously read across columns to some of the adjacent columns as you read down. Information from the two adjacent columns "leaked through," subtly changing the meaning of the central text. He wrote Brion Gysin, "The newspapers and newsmagazines are cut ups. This is the secret of their power to mould thought feeling and subsequent events. We propose to apply the same format to non-statistical quality material. Art if you will. I mean by art a way out to space. The cut ups are being used now by the press to keep you locked in time and word."[20] He suggested setting up Rimbaud, Shakespeare, and Conrad in newspaper column format. He was to work with the three-column format for the next eighteen months. He wrote, "I extend the newspaper and magazine format to fictional material. When you read words in columns you are reading your future reading, that is, you are reading on a subliminal level other columns that you will later consciously experience you have already read. Also the presentation in columns enables the writer to present three or more streams of narrative running concurrently. This opens possibilities of contrast accompaniment and counterpoint. The same situation can be viewed from three different columns at the same time."[21] In other words, he finally found a way to present his material in the same way as he presented his photographic collages: in series, with small but significant variations between each.

4. Television with Dan Farson

On January 5, 1964, Burroughs went from Tangier to London to make his first appearance on television in a program with Dan Farson for Granada Television. The immigration authorities limited his visit to fourteen days with no reason given, crossing out the three months allowed on his visa. Bill was accompanied by Mikey, who could afford his own airfare. Ian stayed behind to guard the house. Burroughs was put up at the Devonshire Hotel at 7 Princes Square in Bayswater, an address that occurred in later books as the result of cut-ups and memory: "Back in England, find out my one contact has died six months ago. Check into anonymous Boardinghouse in Prince's Square, Bayswater."[22] The program, a live talk show, was on the eighth. It consisted of Dan Farson, a celebrated alcoholic, talking to Alexander Trocchi, a celebrated junkie, and Burroughs, who was not on anything. Bill knew Farson from visiting his pub with Francis Bacon, so it was a convivial affair. During the intermission, there was a telephone call for Burroughs. It was someone named Al Feigerberg whom Bill knew from Mexico City. There had been a joke in Mexico City that "wherever you are in the world, Feigerberg always turns up." He was now living in London and watching Bill on TV. Feigerberg was a tall, heavy Swede, a very aggressive, far-right racist, who borrowed money every chance he got. He held Mexicans in contempt, but it was blacks that aroused his greatest ire. "They breed like rabbits," he said. "Jungle bunnies with their bongo knives down there, you wanna watch out." Bill invited him to visit. He came to the hotel and gave Mikey Portman a bad scare. Mikey, who preferred the company of black people, sexually and in every other way, had reacted critically to Feigerberg's outrageous rightist opinions. Bill had gone out to get some liquor and came back to find Mikey cowering in a chair with Feigerberg towering over him, saying, "One more word out of you, clunk, and I'm gonna slap the living shit out of you!"

Burroughs was pleased to see Trocchi again, and they spent some time together, during which Trocchi introduced him to his landlord, Michael de Freitas, who later became Michael X, and a self-proclaimed West Indian community leader. Years later, Burroughs was involved in a campaign to save Michael from the death penalty after he was convicted of the murder of Joe Skerritt in 1972. He was hanged in Trinidad on May 16, 1975. Burroughs never doubted his guilt, but was vehemently opposed to capital punishment. Trocchi also introduced him to the psychiatrist Ronald Laing, whose company Bill enjoyed, Laing being an enthusiastic drinker. But the most productive meeting during this trip to London was with Jeff Nuttall, the publisher of a mimeographed literary magazine called *My Own Mag*.

They were an unlikely combination: Nuttall was resolutely working-class with a deep distrust of public-school boys. When Nuttall met Burroughs at the Devonshire Hotel, Mikey Portman and Antony Balch were already there. As Nuttall wrote later, "Balch and the boy had both got my grammar school blood up a little with their Senior Quad drawls. I was half-determined to be as gauche as possible."[23] They went to a nearby pub. The more upmarket saloon bar was full, so they settled around a table in the public bar. Nuttall wrote, "There was a lot of bright glass and a dart game. My customary sentimentalization of the crowd ran on to very dry ground."[24] Nuttall was at his happiest in a smoky public bar filled with workers in flat caps supping their pints, whereas Burroughs was indifferent. He saw pubs just as places to get alcohol. Nuttall drank pint after pint of beer; Bill stuck to gin and tonic. When Nuttall asked if he could buy him another, Bill replied, "Yes, I want more."[25] This "plain, dry statement of physical fact" was to Nuttall an example of Burroughs's lack of any "side." They went to the drabbest egg-and-chips café on Queensway to eat.

In *Bomb Culture*, Nuttall wrote, "The similarity to my own imagery showed that we were in the same place but Burroughs was travelling in the opposite direction. It took me some time to realize this."[26] Nuttall's aim, like that of Burroughs, was to get people to acknowledge the way life really was: the presence of thermonuclear weapons, of starvation and hunger, as well as corruption and hypocrisy at home. He wanted them to accept and explore obscenity, death, and the reality of their everyday existence. Nuttall wanted to create an aesthetic of obscenity, inspired by the images of horror in Picasso's *Guernica* and the screams of rage from the ghetto translated into beauty by bebop saxophone players. He wrote, "I thought, let us take that obscenity and make beautiful things with it."[27]

Burroughs had a much more radical program: that of dissolving the opposites and dualities that trap humanity in time and space. He used obscenity and humor to attack control systems and saw cut-ups as a weapon to dislocate language, the main agent of power control. Burroughs told Nuttall that he was interested in the newspaper format with its juxtaposition of columns, pictures, and headlines, in which the viewer is constantly absorbing peripheral information from the adjacent columns or the blaring headline or news photographs as each column is read. Jeff was impressed by Burroughs's ideas and invited him to publish his own newspaper as the last two pages of *My Own Mag.* The first manuscript of the *Moving Times* reached Jeff in May 1964, a three-column text designed to read like a newspaper. Jeff used it in a special Tangier edition of *My Own Mag.*

Burroughs used his Tangier air ticket to stop off in Paris in order to try and extract money from Girodias. Girodias had sold the rights to Henry Miller's *Sexus* to two different people, and one of them, a Chinese publisher named Chou, threatened to cause real trouble and put him in jail where he belonged. In order to extricate himself Girodias used the $5,000 he owed Burroughs to pay him off, thinking Burroughs would be the easier of the two to placate. When Bill demanded his money Girodias just shrugged his shoulders and said, "Well, you can put me in jail." There was nothing Bill could do. Girodias was a cheap crook and there was no money. Bill never forgave him for it. The $5,000 would have enabled them to move out of calle Larachi, and Bill could have helped Ian and set him up in some sort of situation to save his sanity and their future relationship. Instead, he had to return empty-handed to Tangier and hang on to the house for several more months until he could get more money from Grove, directly this time. Burroughs told Ted Morgan, "I really blame that jerk Girodias for that. Ian's paranoia was getting worse, naturally, during all this period. [...] It had really upset him and he couldn't take it, so he was in a very bad state [...] not a breakdown in the complete sense but he was just in very bad shape and very unhappy and upset."[28] Burroughs wrote, "By early spring, February and March 1964, life in that house was Hell."[29]

Bill's friends had no idea of the seriousness of the situation. John Hopkins joked, "Wild children have taken over Calla Larache where Bill Burroughs now lives. 'Every year there seem to be more of them,' Brion says, 'Every day!' It is difficult and even dangerous to visit Bill's house. The children grow angry if their games are interrupted. Paul thinks Bill eggs them on. He pays those kids to throw stones at strangers so he can get on with his writing."[30]

5. The Loteria Building

Money finally came through and on May, 6, 1964, the exhausted couple were at last able to move back to the center of Tangier. Number 16 rue Delacroix was on the corner of calle Dominico, across the street from the Tanger Hotel. This used to be the Pasadena Hotel and the buses still used that as their destination sign. Their building had originally been the Tangier Bourse, but when all the banks moved out following independence it became the Lottery Building, which was the name most people knew it by. They had the top-floor apartment, which was all windows with a wonderful view out to the east and north. Bill and John Hopkins walked out onto the balcony and Bill told him, "This is the bridge of my battleship. From here I can see everything. See the Comisaría down the street? Fire one! Boom it's gone! Haw haw haw."[31]

Wide shelves held scrapbooks, and secondhand tables were piled high with folders and clippings files. There was a huge collection of old issues of the *Tangier Gazette* and the *Moroccan Courier* given to him by Dave Woolman, the origin of the cut-up text published in *Esquire* that September. The tape recorder seemed to only have one tape, of radio static. Bill's Remington typewriter looked like an antique from another age, but this was soon replaced with an up-to-date Lettera 22. John Hopkins thought it felt more like a writer's factory than an author's study.[32] A large table, about five feet square, had a large orange-and-brown map of Tangier under a glass cover. This map of Tangier was to provide the background for a new, exhaustive series of collage photographs. Shelves running the length of one wall provided the support for a series of scrapbooks, into which Burroughs pasted photographs and news clippings. These "layout books," as he called them, were basically his ideas workbooks, primarily visual, and contained handwriting in various colored inks, as well as typescripts stuck in. Pages were often tinted with a color wash or given a title in thick magic marker. As usual with Burroughs, he did dozens of these books, filling hundreds and hundreds of pages. There exist many loose leaves, and though some show signs of coming from dismantled scrapbooks, others were clearly stand-alone collages.

In addition to this activity, Burroughs continued to write, and in the three months he lived in the Lottery Building he simultaneously worked on *Nova Express* and produced thousands of pages of cut-ups: three-column texts, usually with the column divides in different colors; grids, with the squares often numbered so that he could read off a number sequence; and texts using other methods such as a brick-wall division of the text. Another series had circles drawn with a compass to isolate sections of text. In every case, the superimposition of a column or a grid was to create arbitrary divisions of the text, to cut it up, producing new word combinations, most of which went into *Nova Express*. A large number of the three-column pages were given newspaper titles: *The Last Post*; *The Silent Sunday News*; *The Tangier Survey*; *The Silver Star*; *The Coldspring News*; and *Moving Times*, his main outlet, published in Jeff Nuttall's *My Own Mag*. During this period he cut up Graham Greene's *The Man Within* and John Rechy's *City of Night* among hundreds of other magazine and news clips.

Bill and Ian were finally free from harassment, so it came as a surprise when a scruffy-looking shoeshine boy, a young man in his twenties, came up and yelled "Fucking pervert" at Bill outside the Loteria Building. Bill hit him with the heel of his hand and knocked him down, then chased him to a vacant lot where the man hit Bill with his shoeshine box. Bill "gave him some elbows" and he ran off. He threw one stone, which hit Bill on the leg. Bill saw him the next day and his face looked badly messed up.

Ian was relieved to leave the Marshan, but was still very depressed and disturbed by the experience. He and Bill had always had an open relationship, with no requirement of fidelity. Their ground rules were no jealousy, you do what you want to do and I'll do what I want to do. Ian began an affair with a deaf-mute albino Moroccan who apparently told him a lot about Arab beliefs and ideas; precisely because he was a deaf-mute he knew sign language. Ian was fascinated by the Arab way of life: he learned to speak a little Arabic and had a great respect for the culture, regarding it as superior to his own. But the affair was filled with friction and difficulties and there was one unpleasant incident when Ian was forced to suck the cock of a boyfriend of the deaf-mute when he didn't want to. The Arabs called him "the Mad Woman"; they thought he was insane. Ian took to wandering in the countryside around the city, getting fucked by anyone he met. He was clearly going through some sort of breakdown. Burroughs later used the incident in the "End of the Line" section of *Exterminator!*: "The Arabs called I.S. the 'Mad Woman.' He was jeered at in the streets and very near such a complete breakdown as westerners in contact with Arabs habitually undergo in the novels of Mr. P."[33]

Early that summer Ian began an affair with Alan Ansen. Ansen said, "He really was in a sort of bad mood, for a lot of the time. Feeling very depressed. Bill took it nicely but I don't know what he felt. Bill did not seem jealous or resentful. Perhaps he felt with Ian so depressed it was nice for him to have something. This whole thing of wandering out into the wilds and being fucked by all and sundry is usually a sign of some kind of disorientation. Ian was always very jealous of Mikey."[34] Bill for his part thought it was Ian's business and didn't say anything about it to him. Ansen was very sympathetic toward Ian. He recognized that Ian needed a father figure and that, for the time being, he was it instead of Bill. Ian was a young man, fresh from university, highly cultivated and fun to be around, but who had no life for himself aside from being with Burroughs. He was insecure and worried. Ansen admired his adventurous spirit, "a kind of abandonment with boys that can be very attractive but at the same time rather dangerous," but he did worry about him. Ian appreciated his concern and began eating his meals with Alan. Bill would sometimes join them, and there were many social events as the summer got under way, such as July Fourth, when the Americans all attended an Independence Day celebration at the Park Brooks Hotel.

Even at calle Larachi, Ian had often been absent for long periods, wandering about the hills and city, and Burroughs was often seen alone at the Paname or the Parade. John Hopkins reported in April 1964, before the move to the Loteria Building, that many nights Bill sat alone having dinner in the Parade Bar at 7:30 before the regulars arrived. "He likes good food. A lonely ascetic figure in a dark business suit, he generally eats by himself staring poker-faced at the wall. (He doesn't bring a book or a newspaper). When I bring my drink to his table he always asks me to sit down. The undertaker look puts people off, but like all writers he works alone all day and enjoys socializing in the evening."[35]

6. Return to Villa Delirium

The lease on the rue Delacroix ran out on July 15 and Bill and Ian moved into room 9 at the Hotel Muniria. A week later, on July 21, 1964, Burroughs completed *Nova Express*, the third of the novels composed from his great "word hoard" left over from *The Naked Lunch*. The three books are really one long, three-volume novel and the first versions are best read as such: *The Soft Machine* (Olympia, 1961), *The Ticket That Exploded* (Olympia, 1962), and *Nova Express* (Grove, 1964), the latter being the only volume that Burroughs did not rewrite. It is his most political novel, though his polemical texts often go much further. *Nova Express* voices opinions that finally reached mass acceptance years later in the ecology movement and the protests against the excesses of the banks and big global corporations. It opens with an angry attack on the establishment: "Listen all you boards syndicates and governments of the earth. And you powers behind what filth deals consummated in what lavatory to take what is not yours. To sell the ground from unborn feet forever—"[36] And he meant it. He told Conrad Knickerbocker, "I do definitely mean what I say to be taken literally, yes, to make people aware of the true criminality of our times, to wise up the marks. All of my work is directed against those who are bent, through stupidity or design, on blowing up the planet or rendering it uninhabitable. [...] I'm concerned with the precise manipulation of word and image to create an action, not to go out and buy Coca Cola, but to create an alteration in the reader's consciousness."[37]

The summer of 1964 was filled with incident and fun. Brion Gysin arrived from Paris, having been one of the last holdouts at the Beat Hotel. He was still in room 25 at the end of June when as early as February many of the other rooms had been demolished as part of the renovation of the building. Ian cheered up considerably on Brion's arrival and became very involved with the marketing of the Dreamachine after the travel writer Leila Hadley offered to put money into it. He and Ansen drifted apart,[38] though they remained good friends. Many of Ian's friends, including Ansen, felt that Brion gave himself far too much credit for the Dreamachine, which was, after all, entirely Ian Sommerville's invention. "The impresario took over," commented Ansen.[39] Brion had suggested to Hadley that Ian should possibly be cut in for 10 percent of the vast profits that they were hoping to make in the United States with the device.

In addition to Gysin, that summer Tennessee Williams, Antony Balch, and Bill's Harvard friend James Le Baron Boyle were all in town and the evenings were filled with long dinners and much carousing, often at the Parade, which had become their main meeting place. Burroughs and Boyle renewed their friendship by going to bed together. Ansen gave a huge party for him. Antony Balch brought his camera with him and, rare for him, filmed in color. On August 24, 1964, Bill, carrying a copy of the *Financial Times*, and Antony Balch, carrying a camera loaded with color film, knocked on the door of the Villa Gazebo, at 282 Monte Viejo, that John Hopkins was renting from the painter Marguerite McBey. Hopkins had a large white cockatoo named Coco, and they wanted a shot of Bill talking to it. Afterward they walked in the gardens and woods that sloped down to the strait. There was a wonderful view of the coast of Spain. The film was used, in black and white, in *The Cut-Ups*, but was also circulated in color as a (very) short called *William Buys a Parrot*. Balch also shot much of the other black-and-white footage that finished up in *The Cut-Ups* while he was there.

Despite their sexual problems, Burroughs and Sommerville remained very close, as they would until Ian died. It was on the steps below the Hotel Muniria, leading down to the beach, that the poet Ira Cohen was witness to the powerful psychic connection between them. Cohen and

Ian were talking, with Ian looking away from the hotel, out to sea, when Burroughs appeared at the top of the track. According to Cohen there is no way that Ian could have been aware of his presence, yet Ian began walking backward up the hill, as if being reeled in like a fish.[40]

Ian returned to London at the beginning of October, leaving Burroughs in Gibraltar at the Mediterranean Hotel on East Beach near the stadium lighting towers that inspired *Towers Open Fire*. "The hotel was surrounded by signal towers...Outside the wind whistled through the towers and rattled the white plastic blinds."[41] Ian saw no future for himself in Tangier, which was clearly an unsuitable environment for him. Bill returned to the Muniria to plan a trip to the States where he had a writing assignment about St. Louis. He didn't want to stay on in Tangier after Ian had left and didn't really know where else to go; neither London or Paris had any appeal. He invited Ian to accompany him to the States, but Ian was unsure about this. He knew he would not have a work permit and he would find himself in the same situation in New York as he had been in Tangier: totally dependent on Bill. Burroughs spent his last month in Tangier working on "developments from your parting suggestions." It is unclear what these suggestions were, but Burroughs told him, "I have been cutting out bits of text old letters etcetera pasting photos and blocks of text in copies of my books (Nova Express now out) a photo for every page of diary always using when possible original materials rather than retyped matter and so finding a use for all the old texts and photos." He said he had completed three scrapbooks and filled many of his own books with photos.

He traveled to London to see Ian before setting off on an open-ended trip to the States. We catch a glimpse of him, just prior to departure when he was interviewed over lunch at her house by Susan Barnes, the *Sun's* "interviewer with a penetrating pen." She described him as "looking, as he usually does, very much the middle-aged bank-clerk—short hair neatly parted, sober suit neatly pressed, feet neatly encased in conventional black shoes. [...] His manners are fastidious."[42] She also mentioned his soft felt hat and rolled umbrella. Hardly the look of a beatnik. He assured her, "Even in the 12 years I was a morphine addict I never presented a beatnik appearance, only a shabby one." He returned to Tangier on November 21, to pack his scrapbooks and manuscripts, intending to settle for a while in New York.

BOOK SEVEN

~

Burlington Billy

Chapter Thirty-Eight

I'm creating an imaginary—it's always imaginary—world in which I would like to live.[1]

1. "St. Louis Return"

In September, *Playboy* magazine had invited Burroughs to revisit St. Louis and write about it. He had been considering the idea of returning to the States, so this came at an opportune time. On November 30 he sailed on SS *Independence* from Algeciras. Also on board was Larbi Layachi (Driss Ben Hamed Charhadi), whose *Life Full of Holes* had been taped and translated by Paul Bowles. Burroughs had read the book in manuscript and written an enthusiastic letter to his editor, Richard Seaver, recommending it. Bowles sent Seaver the manuscript and Grove Press published it on May 25, 1964. It was the first of Bowles's translations to be published commercially in the States. Larbi was on his way to find his fortune in America, where he stayed.

Burroughs arrived in New York on December 8, 1964, and was immediately pulled over for questioning. They had his name on a list. He spent three hours watching while agents pawed through the seven suitcases of manuscripts and clippings files that he had brought with him. The customs agents were joined by two narcotics agents who read through his diaries. In one diary there was something about feeling sick. "Does this refer to narcotics withdrawal?" he was asked. "No, no. It's fiction," he said. They found a boy magazine and waved it around saying, "Look at this! Look at this!" but they didn't confiscate it. They debated whether or not to expose the film in his camera but decided instead to call it a day. They found nothing, not even a codeine tablet. Next they took him back to the boat and had him take his pants down in case he had narcotics up his ass. They said finally, "Well, we treated you like a gentleman, you may think that you've been mistreated but we treated you like a gentleman." Outside, Brion Gysin was waiting for him. One of the customs inspectors approached him and asked, "Are you a friend of that man in there?"

When Brion assented, the man said, "Well, he certainly writes some filthy stuff." Bill booked into the Hotel Chelsea. Brion Gysin was staying with Leila Hadley on Fifth Avenue, trying to market the Dreamachine.

Bill visited Allen on East 5th Street where he had lived since January 1964. Allen was busy making preparations for a long spell away from the city, putting things in storage and finishing up projects. He flew to Mexico City on January 15 on a trip that would take him first to Cuba, then Czechoslovakia, Poland, Moscow, London, Paris, and finally San Francisco, so he and Bill only overlapped by two weeks. Allen introduced him to a number of people at the Chelsea Hotel, including Harry Smith and George Kleinsinger, the composer of "Tubby the Tuba." Bill was impressed by Harry Smith's film animations, his photographic work, his work on Eskimo string figures and Seminole Indian patchwork, and his archive work with American folk songs. But he found Harry creepy and unpleasant to be around and hated the way he mooched off everyone. Arthur C. Clarke had one of the original top-floor apartments at the Chelsea and showed him his $3,000 telescope that could read a newspaper on the other side of Manhattan. George Kleinsinger had a huge double-height apartment with trees and birds flying free, shitting everywhere. There were huge aquarium tanks with turtles splashing around and a menagerie that included iguanas and pythons. In the center of the room was George's grand piano and a group of chairs and sofas where everyone hung out and drank. Bill loved it.

Bill's French translators, Claude Pélieu and Mary Beach, were also living in the hotel, in one of the old apartments complete with wood-paneled walls and a fireplace. Claude worked standing up with his typewriter on the mantelpiece and Mary had a desk. They kept up a constant dialogue in a mixture of French and English, discussing the book they were working on. For the cut-up novels they had created an index card system with the original phrases in it that were subsequently cut up—as far as they could deduce them. That way they were able to use the same French phrases when they recurred. It was a very time-consuming approach, but they were working more for love than money. Both Claude and Mary produced their own cut-up books and Bill subsequently wrote introductions for them both.[2] Bill very much enjoyed going to their rooms for proper European-style drinks before dinner.

Burroughs made contact with poet Ted Berrigan, the bearded, overweight father figure of the Lower East Side poetry scene. He was the editor of *C: A Journal of Poetry*, and had published one of Bill's experimental texts, "Giver of Winds Is My Name," in the summer of 1964,[3] the first of his texts to use Egyptian glyphs. Berrigan was enthusiastic about his work so Bill gave him another text, "Fits of Nerves with a Fix," which he published that February.[4] Berrigan arranged to publish Bill's own thirty-two-page version of *Time* magazine,[5] a three-column collaged text using the cover and title page of the November 30, 1962, issue of *Time*, which had contained the libelous review of *Naked Lunch* called "King of the YADS" (Young American Disaffiliates), in which it was claimed that Burroughs had cut off a finger joint to avoid the draft. By transforming this supreme organ of control Burroughs was aiming at the jugular. He told Bill Butler, "The Luce magazines [*Time, Life, Fortune*] are nothing but control mechanisms. They're about as human as a computer. Henry Luce, himself, has no control over the thing now, it's grown so large. Yet all it would take to bring it down is one technical sergeant fouling up the works, just one technical sergeant. That's why the 'Word falling, photo falling' image. We've got to break down the police organization of words and images." *Time* was published in a facsimile edition of the manuscript, with several different signed editions including one bound in Camargue cloth containing a manuscript page from Burroughs and a drawing by Gysin, who contributed four pages of drawings to the book itself.

Burroughs also met up with the poet Ed Sanders, the editor of *Fuck You: A Magazine of the Arts*, who had published a mimeograph edition of *Roosevelt After Inauguration* back in January 1964, after the English printer had refused to print it in the City Lights edition of *The Yage Letters* in late 1963. The cover was hand-drawn by Allen Ginsberg with a stylus straight onto the stencil. Like all Sanders's productions, it was "printed, published and zapped at a secret location in the Lower East Side." He also published a three-column layout called "Fluck You, Fluck You, Fluck" in his "God" issue of *Fuck You* in September 1964.[6] Throughout his time in New York Burroughs continued to send material to Jeff Nuttall for *My Own Mag*.

Bill went to book his train tickets at Grand Central Station:

"I want to reserve a drawing-room for St. Louis."
"A drawing-room? Where have you been?"
"I have been abroad."
"I can give you a bedroom or a roomette as in smaller."
"I will take the bedroom."[7]

Two weeks later, on December 23, 1964, Bill settled into his train bedroom, surrounded by his seven suitcases. His Oriental porter installed a table in his room so that he could set up his Facit portable and type as he looked out of the train's picture window. His Zeiss Ikon was at his side, out of its cracked leather case, ready to snap the occasional picture. Bill lamented the old steam locomotives with their soot and noise, brass spittoons, smell of worn leather and stale cigar smoke.

On his arrival in St. Louis, Carl Milles's monumental brass nudes were still there to greet the visitor leaving the station. Bill made his way to the Chase Park Plaza Hotel, where, "like a good European," he spent some time bouncing on the hotel beds and testing the hot-water taps to make sure all was in order. The hotel overlooked Forest Park and was a few minutes' walk from where Burroughs grew up. He remembered the old Bixby place that the hotel replaced. The hotel was built in 1922, just as the Burroughs family were relocating to the suburbs. He went to the lobby newsstand to buy the *St. Louis Globe-Democrat* and the *St. Louis Post-Dispatch* to look for items or pictures to paste in his scrapbooks and found plenty of points of intersection.

The next day was mild and warm and Bill went for a walk around his old neighborhood, taking photographs, looking for anything that had survived from his childhood in the late teens and early twenties. His childhood house was still there. There was a Christmas family reunion at his aunt Kay's house with all the cousins and relatives, and on December 27 he and his brother went for a drive around the city, stopping from time to time for Bill to take photographs: the Old Courthouse, the "Gateway to the West" arch, then still under construction. Clayton and the West End suburbs had been built up beyond recognition in the twenty years since Bill was there.

Playboy had expected a return-of-the-prodigal-son type of story and were horrified by the three-column cut-up piece Burroughs turned in. They rejected it and paid him a three-hundred-dollar kill fee, but "St. Louis Return" was taken up by the *Paris Review*, which had already sent its interviewer, Conrad Knickerbocker, to the Chase Plaza to interview him on New Year's Day. This interview, like all *Paris Review* "Art of Fiction" interviews, was on writing technique and is the best exposition there is of Burroughs's methods outside his own technical books. It was widely reproduced. Knickerbocker gives us a good thumbnail sketch of Burroughs's appearance at the age of fifty-one: he was wearing a lightweight Brooks Brothers suit with a waistcoat, a blue striped shirt from Gibraltar, cut in the English style, and a deep blue tie with small white polka dots. "He might have been a senior partner in a private bank. [...] His face carries no excess flesh. His expression is taut, and his features are intense and chiseled." Bill did not smile during the interview and laughed only once, but Knickerbocker felt that he was capable of much dry laughter in other circumstances. Burroughs's voice was described as "sonorous, its tone reasonable and patient; his accent is mid-Atlantic, the kind of region-less inflection Americans acquire after many years abroad."

Back at the Hotel Chelsea, Bill wrote Ian, again inviting him to come over, and appears to have expected him to arrive in two weeks' time, but Ian was unable to get an American visitor's visa even though Burroughs sent him traveler's checks for five hundred dollars to show the embassy that he had funds enough to visit. In any case, Ian remained ambivalent about going to the States and saw no point in the trip unless he could get a work permit. He had been turned off the idea of New York by meeting people like Allen Ginsberg, Peter Orlovsky, and Gregory Corso, all of whom he regarded as uncouth, loud, and pushy. He asked Bill if he really needed him there. Had Bill insisted, a way could doubtless have been found to get Ian to New York and the course of their relationship might have been very different, but Bill let it go.

Burroughs's father, Mote, died on January 19 of a heart attack and Bill and Mort flew to Palm Beach for the funeral. Billy Jr. was unable to get there in time. Laura seemed to be coping, so after a few days Bill returned to New York. It was a time for reflection: his father had been a strange, somewhat remote man, whom Bill had always found it rather difficult to talk to. But he had always been there to bail him out when he got into trouble, it was his parents' hard work that provided the monthly allow-ance that had permitted him to be a writer, and it was his parents who had brought up his son. He owed them so much, and was unable to really thank them for it.

In New York, one of the main performance places for writers at this time was the 129-seat East End Theater at 85 East 4th Street, run by poets Diane di Prima and Alan Marlowe. Their patron, society hostess Panna Grady, invited Burroughs to perform on February 14 in what must have been his first reading in the United States. For the 4:00 p.m. perfor-mance he gave a pared-down version of the kind of show that he had been doing with Ian and Brion in Paris and London utilizing tapes of Joujouka drumming and flutes, cut-up pneumatic drills, radio static, and his own voice reading from newspapers but lacking the films and projections. He appeared through parted red curtains, removed his topcoat and fedora, which he carefully placed on the white chair provided. Wearing a three-piece suit, he made himself comfortable in a high-backed leather chair and opened his briefcase. He read aloud from *Junky*, *Naked Lunch*, and *Nova Express* before leaving the stage while a cut-up tape of Dutch Schultz's last words, which he had recently discovered in James D. Horan's *The Des-perate Years*,[8] intercut with news reports of plane crashes and stories containing the number 23, continued to play. The text of "The Valentine's Day Reading" was mimeographed and sold as a program on the night. Two days later he wrote to Ian again, urging him to come to New York and bring over slides and films to enhance his performances.[9] On March 3, Brion Gysin performed his "Permutations and Permutated Portraits" there, which did use projections.

By 1964 there was a well-established poetry-reading scene in the Lower East Side and Greenwich Village and the poets were delighted to have Burroughs among them. He was invited out most nights. At a reading at Le Metro, the poetry café on Second Avenue, his fans clustered around him so tightly that he couldn't see anything. This was where Herbert Huncke and Carl Solomon had read and was fast becoming known as a center for drug dealing as well as for poetry. Bill attended several readings there, including one by Brion Gysin, but did not read there himself. He attended the grand opening of Ed Sanders's Peace Eye Bookstore, an ex–kosher meat market at 383 East 10th Street on February 24, which was also the publication day for the third anniversary issue of Sanders's *Fuck You: A Magazine of the Arts*. The event also featured the world premiere of the Fugs, during which they performed "Swinburne Stomp," "Coca Cola Douche," "Jack Off Blues," and a musical setting of the opening lines of Ginsberg's "Howl." Sanders had invited the press and Burroughs asked him which one was from *Time*. Sanders pointed to a reporter named Chris. Bill stared at the man and replied, "I thought so."[10]

Antony Balch joined Bill and Brion in New York in March for a month and brought with him a print of his filming in Tangier, Paris, and London to date. Bill enthused to Ian about the looped sequences shot in the Socco Chico. At the Chelsea, Antony shot a lot of film of Dreamachines and of Brion painting a huge New York skyline, then rolling it up, a sequence Bill called "the Piper pulled down the sky." At the Chelsea they also enacted a clinic scene, in which Dr. Burroughs carefully examined young Bruce Holbrook, one of his assistants. Holbrook had a camera and a Martel tape recorder, but as Bill told Ian, "Unfortunately he also has a wife."[11] Clearly she and Bill did not get on too well, as on the same day he told Antony Balch, "He has been most helpful despite handicap weight of the other half. (Who is about ready to stick a knife in me at this point)."[12]

2. On Set

In March Bill moved into a 1915 loft building at 210 Centre Street, a couple of blocks south of Canal Street in Chinatown. The fire escape was on the front of the building and he took a lot of photographs of the traffic and street activity from the iron landing on his floor. It was an austere space: no curtains or carpets, a refrigerator in the corner, shelves filled with scrapbooks and file folders in neat piles, a few comfortable chairs for guests, a work table with typewriter and tape recorder.

The loss of a large fee from *Playboy* was made up for by the arrival of Conrad Rooks, who asked Bill to act in *Chappaqua*, a film he was directing. Two years earlier, flying to Paris after his Granada television appearance, Bill had run into Rooks on the plane, and they were now back on good terms again despite the problems Rooks had caused between Bill and Mikey's mother.[13] Now Bill, along with many others, finally succumbed to the lure of the Avon Cosmetics gold. Rooks wanted to make a film about his experiences as a recovering drug addict, taking a sleep cure in a Swiss sanatorium. The film came complete with flashbacks, and he managed to persuade Allen Ginsberg, Moondog, Swami Satchidananda, the Fugs, and other sixties celebrities to play cameo roles. His doctor in the Swiss rehab clinic was played by Jean-Louis Barrault, legendary for his role in *Les enfants du paradis*. Rooks hired Ornette Coleman to write the soundtrack, then replaced it with one cowritten by Ravi Shankar and Philip Glass.

The New York scenes with Ginsberg were shot in January, which Bill attended. His own scenes were not shot until the first week of April, but included one that Bill very much enjoyed involving hired 1930s black Cadillacs and Bill mowing Conrad down with a tommy gun loaded with blanks. "What an instrument great fun," he wrote Ian.[14] Filmmaker Robert Frank was the cinematographer but got into an argument with Rooks—which was not difficult as Rooks was a very bad manager of people—and Rooks fired him. That evening Rooks met someone at a bar who claimed to have been trained to use a cine-camera in the army and hired him in his stead. The next day they filmed a whole scene in a New York bar where Conrad Rooks got up and danced on the table, was shot, and collapsed into a garbage can. They trooped in to see the rushes, but there was nothing on the film; the kid had underexposed the whole thing. With $3,000 wasted, Rooks rehired Robert Frank the next day, presumably at a higher fee than before.

Burroughs was also on set on March 18 when he was filmed by Ed Sanders at the opening of Charles Henri Ford's *Poem Posters* show at Cordier & Ekstrom on Madison Avenue at 75th Street. Much of the twenty-four-minute film, also called *Poem Posters*, was of Jayne Mansfield, but the footage also included Burroughs, Edie Sedgwick, Gerard Malanga, Ned Rorem, Frank O'Hara, Ted Berrigan, James Rosenquist, and Andy Warhol. Burroughs was now a central figure on the New York art scene.[15]

Pleased with the publication of *Roosevelt After Inauguration*, Bill gave Ed Sanders another manuscript to print: *APO-33*, a text on the apomorphine treatment. Unfortunately, Sanders had a volunteer, Elaine Solow, retype the manuscript onto mimeograph stencils instead of arranging to have an electronic transfer made from the original. This meant that he had to photostat all the many images in the three-column text, cut them out, and glue each one on, a very time-consuming procedure. He recruited Peter Orlovsky to help, who launched into the task with an amphetamine-driven alacrity not consistent with accuracy of placement. Some of the pictures obscured the text, and others fell out when the book was picked up. Ed had also failed to instruct Elaine to keep the columns exactly as Burroughs had composed them, and they got changed during her typing because she was using a different typewriter with a different face. Ed sent a couple of copies over to Burroughs, who at first thought they were some sort of markup or proof copies. When he realized that this was what the book was going to look like he quickly dispatched Brion Gysin to the cigar store on Times Square where Ed worked to inform him that Bill was displeased and was not prepared to let it go out that way. Ed disagreed; he thought it looked beautiful. His feelings were hurt but he kept his mouth shut: "Burroughs was Burroughs." About fifteen or twenty copies were distributed and the remaining few were thrown away. It is now one of the most sought-after Burroughs items of all.

Invites to read came thick and fast. On April 23, Burroughs read to 130 people at a party held at artist Wynn Chamberlain's top-floor loft at 222 Bowery, an address where he would himself live for several years in the seventies. He shared the stage with Shell Thomas, his old friend from the Beat Hotel, who read from his new novel *Gumbo* and sang old Methodist hymns in a Texas accent. Once again Bill found himself surrounded by the New York art crowd: Diane Arbus, Frank O'Hara (Burroughs never liked him), Larry Rivers, Marisol with a green bow in her hair, Larry Poons, Richard Avedon, Karlheinz Stockhausen, Barnett Newman, and Andy Warhol. Brion demonstrated the Dreamachine to the assembled guests. Bill ended his reading by tearing down a white backdrop to reveal a painting of horrifying tarantulas. Two days later, he was a guest at Lester Persky's "Fifty Most Beautiful People" party cohosted with Andy Warhol at the Factory, which mixed Warhol superstars such as Edie Sedgwick and Gerard Malanga with Hollywood stars such as Judy Garland and Montgomery Clift. Guests included Brian Jones of the Rolling Stones, Rudolf Nureyev, and Tennessee Williams.[16]

Present at most of these events was Panna Grady, the society hostess who was attempting to run a literary salon at her huge eight-room apartment in the Dakota on Central Park West. Panna was the daughter of heiress Louise Marie St. John and Hungarian aristocrat Tibor de Cholnoky. No one was quite sure where the money came from, but there seemed to be plenty of it. The problem was in keeping out people like Herbert Huncke and Harry Smith—"shameless moochers," as Burroughs called them—who were forever hitting on her for money and at the same time insulting her. She threw a party for Bill where he met Marshall McLuhan, whose *Understanding Media* was published in 1964; they had many areas of interest in common. Andy Warhol was there and all the usual art crowd. On another occasion, Panna hosted a meal at a Chinese restaurant for Bill and Warhol. Andy had a young man with him whose objectionable behavior infuriated Burroughs. When he finished a plate, the young man reached around and put the dirty plate on the next table where a group of Chinese people were eating. Bill found this the height of rudeness and left in the middle of the meal. Panna left with him.

Panna let it be known to her friends that she was in love with Bill, but he made sure that he was never alone with her. He liked her but did not want to know about it. "It was so obvious that there was no possibility of reciprocity. She wasn't stupid. She saw that it was not possible and it was not possible."[17] Panna did, however, know his weak spot. He told Ted Morgan, "She used to send me every Christmas a box of those now almost unprocurable candies with liquors inside. Oh my God, they were just heavenly, my dear. All different kinds of liquors, some of them were chocolate and some of them were pink and white cream, God they were good. She was the soul of generosity."[18]

At 3:00 a.m. one morning Bill received a phone call. It was Porter Tuck: El Rubio de Boston, the bullfighter he had known from his early days in Tangier at the Bar la Mar Chica. Bill had not seen him since 1957. "Can I come over and see you?" he asked. Bill was astonished and said, "For chrissakes Porter, it's three in the morning. Come tomorrow." Porter said, "Well, that's a laugh." The next day Bill happened to turn on the radio news and heard a report that Porter Tuck had killed himself on a bridge, a suicide. A passerby had even stolen the gun. But Bill felt that Tuck had already died when he had been gored by the bull. His life had gone downhill: working as a waiter in a Spanish restaurant, time spent in jail. He was dead already and didn't know it.

Despite their best efforts Brion and his various partners were unable to raise any interest in the Dreamachine. Brion did some paintings of the New York skyline as seen from his south-facing room at the Hotel Chelsea but found no buyers. From the beginning of May, he mostly busied himself working with Burroughs on *The Third Mind*, then called *Right Where You Are Sitting Now*. It was to be a definitive book of methods concerning cut-ups, fold-ins, tapes, intersection reading, newspaper-column formats, grids, and photo collages. Some of the layouts they produced together were the most beautiful collaborations they ever did, usually consisting of a grid with photographs attached. Bill wrote to Antony Balch for stills from their films to use in the layouts. Regrettably, the cost of reproducing illustrations in those days meant that the book would have been formidably expensive. Dick Seaver at Grove toyed with the idea of a deluxe illustrated edition selling at ten dollars, but in the end Grove Press didn't think there would be enough buyers to justify publication. *The Third Mind* was not published until 1978, thirteen years later.

During his time in New York Bill had found no new lover and was clearly missing Ian. In July he wrote him, saying, "I have missed you a great deal. Nothing here really, just stay in my loft and work."[19] It was at this time that Burroughs first met Brion's new boyfriend, John Giorno, who was living with Brion at the Chelsea. Burroughs observed a profound change in Giorno over the years: "At that time he was pathologically silent. He just wouldn't say anything. You could be there with him the whole evening, he wouldn't say a word. It was not the shyness of youth, it was much more than that, it was a very deep lack of ability to communicate. Then he had cancer and after the operation that was completely reversed and now he is at times a compulsive talker, when he gets going there is no stopping him."[20]

For Burroughs, this was a difficult time to be in New York, as the effects of Harry Anslinger's thirty-two-year reign of terror as commissioner of the Federal Bureau of Narcotics were still being felt.[21] Penalties for dealing and being in possession of marijuana or opiates were harsh, but it was the attempts at entrapment by the police that worried Burroughs. A narcotics agent had asked Herbert Huncke to set Bill up for a bust. Fortunately Huncke had told Allen Ginsberg about it when Allen passed briefly through New York at the end of June, on his way to the West Coast, asking him what should he do. Allen of course told Bill. Bill was concerned. He knew that it was now unlikely that Huncke would set him up, after telling Allen about it, but if they couldn't get him, the narcs would simply get someone else. He was not addicted to anything, just smoking a little pot, but he knew it was not difficult for one of his visitors to stick a needle and a wrap to the underside of the table with gum and tell the cops where it was. Bill made arrangements to finish his business with Grove and return to London.

By the beginning of September, Bill was ensconced in the Rushmore

Hotel in Earl's Court. When Ginsberg returned to New York in March 1966 he went to see newly elected Mayor John Lindsay[22] and complained that William Burroughs, a distinguished writer, had been forced to leave the country for fear of a police conspiracy. Lindsay was contrite—"Oh that's terrible"—but did nothing to rein in the police. In fact an attempt to set up Ginsberg himself was made shortly afterward.

Chapter Thirty-Nine

And there was Ian and I don't want to talk about that. There are mistakes too monstrous for remorse to tamper or to dally with.[1]

1. The Rushmore

Burroughs returned to London early in September 1965, saying that he was absolutely fed up with New York and that there was nothing of interest happening there. The fact that the Bureau of Narcotics was attempting to frame him only increased Bill's belief that he was in the wrong place. He had tried, unsuccessfully, to bring Ian to New York, but the Americans would not let him in, so, as Bill said, "Things were drawing me away from New York more than back to London," though he recognized that London at that time was cheap and a much more pleasant place to live.

When he arrived at Gatwick Airport, the customs agent limited his stay in the UK to one month, instead of his usual three months. Bill thought this was because of pressure from the State Department, which was already cracking down on beatniks and undesirables. He went straight to Lord Goodman, who knew the home secretary, Sir Frank Soskice. "Well, if they suspect you of drug smuggling, they shouldn't let you in at all!" said Goodman. "Mr. Burroughs, give me your passport." About a month later he returned it to Bill, saying, "Come as often as you want, stay as long as you want." Goodman was a great fixer. In fact the final approval of Burroughs's status as a resident alien probably came from Roy Jenkins, who took over as home secretary in December. It was Jenkins who later put a stop to attempts by the Obscene Publications Squad to prosecute *Naked Lunch* in Britain.

Bill moved into the Hotel Rushmore at 11 Trebovir Road in Earl's Court, where Ian Sommerville had been living while Bill was in New York. The rooms were laid out like a ship's cabin with a bed, cupboards, and shelves arranged for maximum efficiency. It was another hotel that began life as a porticoed Regency row house and was later converted into a rooming house. It was bought by Jeffrey Benson, an antiques dealer

444

and interior decorator who was a close friend of John Richardson's, the art critic. Benson didn't know what to call it because it was so drab and ordinary-looking. Richardson had a musicologist friend named Robert Rushmore, whom Benson thought was the most boring person in the whole world, which gave Benson an idea. "It's really drab, dear, just how drab can you get? The Rushmore, we'll call it the Rushmore."[2] There was a circle of transvestites known as "the Maids" who all lived at the Rushmore. They were called Babs, Carlotta, and Scotch Agnes. There was no bar, but Benson ran a sort of salon in his parlor, featuring the Maids. Christopher Gibbs knew the Rushmore well. "Jeffrey Benson was always referred to as Madame. And Madame's acquaintanceships were always very wide and varied. And Madame was always the same, in sort of half drag, very painted up, falsies. Very sure of what he thought was the best kind of life to lead." One of the regulars at the salon was April Ashley, who in those days, before her operation, was known as Mental Mary. To Benson, Bill was an ideal tenant, being dignified, appreciative, and financially stable. For his part, Bill found the atmosphere congenial and of course he could bring boys back to the room. Christopher commented, "Bill had a good nose for what was going to be amusing, gamey, and something that was so ghastly that there was a ring of poetry about it. He got that. I always thought Bill had a very subtle antenna, apart from being a man of very considerable culture."[3]

Ian Sommerville moved in with him, but it was not as simple as it might have seemed. Not knowing if Bill was ever going to return to Britain, he had found himself a new boyfriend, Alan Watson, from his hometown of Darlington in County Durham. Ian met him when he went home for a visit. Alan was thin, very camp, an artificial blond, constantly flicking back his hair and tossing his head, his sentences emphasized by raised eyebrows and pouted lips. Bill described him as a "100% swishy queen." He worked as a cook at Scotland Yard, and was very good at it. The police loved him, and even though homosexuality was still illegal, they encouraged him to be as outrageous as possible. His normal outfit consisted of a pair of very tight trousers cut so low that they were little more than a pair of legs attached to a belt. He strutted around the canteen, hand on hip, throwing back his head, sometimes even dancing on the tables when the right policemen were there to urge him on. Bill disapproved highly of this consorting with the enemy, though he was pleased that Alan had a job. Ian was freelancing and installed the electrical wiring and lighting at the new Indica Bookshop and Gallery in September 1965, but was also borrowing money from Bill, Antony Balch, and Tom Neurath at Thames and Hudson, whom he knew from the Beat Hotel.

Burroughs recognized that it was entirely his fault that Ian was with someone new. Ian had wanted to join Bill in New York, but Bill hadn't done enough to get him an entry visa. The U.S. embassy needed proof that he had money, but Bill didn't send him adequate funds, even though he was doing well financially and could easily have afforded to. He told Ted Morgan, "The whole thing was my fault completely and I got exactly what I deserved. I could have done all sorts of things and I didn't do them. In other words, the whole thing was my fuckup."⁴ He quoted Charles Gallagher from Tangier: "Everybody always gets exactly what they want and exactly what they deserve in this life." Bill felt that this was true: "It was certainly what I deserved. I fucked up. Look, man, you only get one chance in this life, and you don't take it, it's your fault. There are no excuses in this life, no excuses. You fuck up, you fuck up, and you pay for it. I relinquished and I tried to reclaim. It was gone. I'd lost."

There had been a fundamental shift in the relationship. When they first got together in 1959, Bill was the master; he was in charge and had been so all the time they were in Tangier when Bill didn't want Ian sexually and Ian wanted him. Now the situation was reversed. Bill desired him, but Ian wasn't interested. Ian may have moved in, but Bill no longer had the upper hand. After a while, Alan Watson also moved in to the Rushmore, to a different room.

In December, Bill's three-month entry permit expired, and rather than just go to Paris for a weekend, he decided to spend Christmas in Tangier with Brion. The visit was going well, when on Christmas Day, Bill felt a sudden wave of depression. Shortly afterward, someone came in and told them that Jay Haselwood, the owner of the Parade Bar, had just dropped dead. Bill had always liked him. "He was one of the lights of Tangier. There was something very special there."⁵ Jay had gone to the bathroom and came back with sweat pouring down his face, looking terrible. He went into the restaurant kitchen and lay down on the floor and died of a heart attack. All the nights of heavy drinking combined with vigorous gymnastics each morning to try and bring down his weight had killed him. Leslie Eggleston took advantage of the confusion to steal 1,000 francs from Jane Beck's purse.

On December 30, 1965, Jay's funeral was held at the English church, St. Andrew's, for which he had always provided "wonderful flower arrangements" for major feast days. It was very well attended: lots of waiters and past kitchen staff and, as Bill put it, "all the old biddies who used to drink there and that whole crew of old lushes." The funeral was held on the same day as a little birthday party for Paul Bowles to which Bill and Brion were invited. Bill arrived immaculately dressed in funereal black with a tightly furled umbrella, peeled off his gloves, put them on the table, and said, "Well, Paul, you missed a very enjoyable funeral." Bowles, as usual, didn't know how to interpret Bill's remark: "Was it a serious remark—some funerals *are* better than others—or was it we were very happy to see the end of *that* one? One didn't know."

Bill returned to the Rushmore and his increasingly rocky relationship with Ian, who still had Alan Watson firmly in tow and only granted Bill sex as a special favor. Part of the problem was money. Ian was out of work and Alan didn't earn enough for a central London flat big enough for them both. Ian was now helping Bill with a series of tape recorder experiments, so they were together all the time while Alan was at work.

2. *Chappaqua* Continues

Some immediate help was at hand when Bill arranged for Ian to be hired as the sound engineer when the filming of Conrad Rooks's *Chappaqua* moved to Paris. But Ian, wary from past experience of people like Rooks, refused to go until he saw the money in cash. It was delivered in a large black leather bag. Ian bought a new black business suit and a new tape editing block, and in March 1966 Bill and Ian set off for Paris, where Rooks had booked them into a cheap hotel on the rue Saint-André-des-Arts.

Bill was hired to help with the dialogue and perform in a skating scene at the Palais des Glaces skating rink, but although he thought he could skate, once on the ice he found that he could no longer remember how, and a double had to be found as Bill kept falling over. Alan Ansen, who had come to Paris for a week to watch, was much amused. Burroughs, for a fee, wrote the essay to accompany the *Chappaqua* press kit: " 'Glad to see you back Harwich, been away a while things have been tough here only stay in business because of you and it's dangerous see?' he throws back his cloak to show some ketchup stain smeared with the blood of old movies, goes into a prat fall...Death forgets his skating... 'I'll get my legs in a minute here,' 'We should live so long.' "[6] Bill was in another scene set in a large mansion in Saint-Cloud that Rooks had rented to represent the Swiss sanatorium in the story. Bill played Death and appeared in a wheelchair and shot someone.

As far as Bill was concerned the whole thing was a complete fiasco, just a rich kid playing at being a filmmaker, giving people license to improvise, then coming down heavily on them when they did, arguing and screaming, thinking he knew better than the professionals. Ian couldn't stand him, but Bill just watched with amusement. Relations between

Rooks and the crew became so bad that many of them refused to continue working with him at any price and told him, sometimes quite forcefully, where to put his money. Bill made fifteen hundred dollars for three days of shooting: a whole day in New York, one day in Paris, and another in the Paris suburbs. The film, called *Chappaqua*, after a Quaker settlement in New York State, was released on November 5, 1967.

From Paris, Bill went to Germany to see one of his correspondents. The German writer and translator Carl Weissner began writing to Burroughs in 1965. Seeing that Carl was quick to pick up on his experiments with the cut-ups, Burroughs decided to visit him in Heidelberg.[7] The visit formed the basis for a lifelong friendship, and Carl, who was able to write equally pungent German and English, went on to translate many of Bill's books. Bill checked into the Hotel Kaiserhof, had dinner, then went to see Carl. Weissner was living at 1–3a Mühltalstrasse when Burroughs came to visit. Weissner later reported the visit to Victor Bockris. Weissner let Burroughs into his small apartment:

> He took three or four steps and stood by the narrow table in front of the window. He put his hands into his pockets and in one smooth movement brought out two reels of mylar tape and put them on the table.
> "Got your tape recorder?" he asked.
> "Yes."
> "Let's compare tapes."
> We played his tapes, then some of mine. Nothing was said. [...]
> Then we put a microphone on the table and took turns talking to the tape recorder switching back and forth between tracks at random intervals. We played it all back and sat there listening to our conversation.[8]

In London, Bill continued with the three-column experiments and the scrapbook entries that had occupied him in New York and before that in Tangier. He told the *Guardian* newspaper in 1965, when he first returned from New York, "I spend most of my time editing and filing. [...] For ten published pages there are fifty pages of notes on file and more on tape. I use a tape recorder, camera, typewriter, scissors, scrapbooks. From the newspapers and from items people send me, I get intersections between all sorts of things. [...] They all tie up, there are connections, intersections."[9] From this material came *The Wild Boys*, *Port of Saints*, and *The Job*. His article explaining these experiments, "The Invisible Generation," was published in *International Times (IT)*, the new British underground newspaper. He wrote to his French translators and friends, Claude Pélieu and Mary Beach, "Have you seen International Times? I have given them an article on tape recorder experiments which should appear in the next issue and I hope to get a large number of people experimenting with tape recorders to turn up some results. Basic premise is, 'what we see and experience is to a large extent dictated by what we hear and anyone with a tape recorder is in a position to decide what he hears, and what other people hear or overhear as well.' "[10]

When Burroughs returned from New York, he spent a lot of time with Antony Balch, who was just putting the finishing touches to *The Cut-Ups*. The film began life as *Guerrilla Conditions*, a twenty-three-minute silent documentary on the lives of William Burroughs and Brion Gysin, filmed at the Beat Hotel in Paris, the Hotel Villa Muniria in Tangier, the Chelsea Hotel in New York, and the Empress Hotel in London. The earliest sequences were shot in Paris in 1961 and the latest in New York in 1965. After hours of conversation with Bill about cut-ups, Balch now had a very different idea about what he wanted to do with the footage. Using the same technique that Ian Sommerville had used in Tangier in 1964, he superimposed strips of negatives and had them printed, some positive, others as negatives. Sometimes three separate lengths of film would be superimposed. The triple and negative superimpositions were done last and included footage taken from other films, such as *Bill Buys a Parrot*, the 16-millimeter color short, shot in Tangier, which appears in black-and-white negative in *The Cut-Ups*. Antony then fed a print of the film onto four reels and had a lab technician assemble them, taking a twelve-inch section from each in strict rotation. Balch was not even there during the assembly. This was done with a print of the film because of the impossible grading problems presented by the master print, and an interneg was made from the finished result. The soundtrack was made by Ian Sommerville, Brion Gysin, and Burroughs, using a line from a Scientology routine. Sommerville produced the permutated phrases to last exactly twenty minutes and four seconds, including the final "Thank you."

The Cut-Ups opened at the Cinephone in Oxford Street, London, in 1966, and the manager, Mr. Provisor, had never had so many people come up to him to praise a film, or so many complain about it. Some members of the audience left during the screening claiming, "It's disgusting," to which the staff would reply, "It's got a U certificate,[11] nothing disgusting about it, nothing the censor objected to." During the two-week run there were an unusually large number of articles, bags and coats, left behind in the cinema by the disoriented audience. After the first few days Antony shortened the film to twelve minutes because Mr. Provisor and his staff were exposed to it five times a day as well as having to deal with walkouts and Antony thought that was too much. There were fewer walkouts in the evenings, when a more appreciative audience attended. Balch always preferred the twelve-minute version. Burroughs was pleased with the result, which was very much an extension of his ideas:

> There's some things you can do with films that you can't do anywhere else. You've got your section of time, you can do all sorts of things. You can slow it down, speed it up, run it backwards, all sorts of possibilities—cut it up— all sorts of things that you can do with it. It has that possibility and very little has been done, really, because Hollywood has never been experimental. For example, flashbacks were very common. Flashbacks started with W. D. Griffith [*Birth of a Nation*], but flash-forwards don't occur until *Alice's Restaurant* and *Easy Rider*. There you have it, the idea of flash-forwards didn't occur to them. Flashbacks, slow-downs. There were some speed-ups in early films, just used as a comedy device, and slow-downs have been used mostly in death scenes like in *Bonnie and Clyde*, the fall from gunshot wounds, slow-down. But there are all sorts of things which remain untouched.[12]

Years later, Nicolas Roeg approached Balch and asked him practical questions about the use of cut-ups. He used them in his film *Performance* starring Mick Jagger. Most of his arbitrary cuts occur at the beginning.

3. Montagu Square

Though Burroughs had a negative reaction to Timothy Leary's projects in the States, he was initially supportive of Michael Hollingshead when he returned to Britain from Leary's headquarters to open the World Psychedelic Centre at 25 Pont Street in Mayfair. Accordingly he attended a "Workshop in Consciousness Expansion" that Hollingshead organized on February 14, 1966, at the Institute of Contemporary Arts at 17 Dover Street, where he had himself performed with Ian and Brion Gysin. Bill appeared on the panel together with Alexander Trocchi, Ian Sommerville, Ronnie Laing, George Andrews, and others. He was to appear at several such gatherings, but when it became obvious that Hollingshead was getting strung out on methamphetamine, Bill no longer visited Pont Street, knowing it was but a matter of time before the police arrived. He was correct in thinking this and Hollingshead went to jail, not for LSD but other, illegal, substances.

Ian's accommodation problems were unexpectedly solved, at least for six months, in April 1966 when he was asked to become the in-house tape operator of a small private recording studio. Inspired by reading copies of *Big Table* and *Evergreen Review* borrowed from Barry Miles,[13] co-owner of the Indica Bookshop, Paul McCartney decided to set up an audio equivalent: a monthly budget-price record album containing bits of interviews, backstage talk, and studio conversations with musicians recording new albums. A deal could be struck with the BBC to include bits of radio plays that people might have missed, and jazz musicians and poets would be encouraged to record their work. NEMS, the Beatles' management company, and EMI, their record label, would organize pressing and distribution. The sticking point was where these things would be recorded and edited. Ringo had an apartment at 34 Montagu Square that he was not using because so many fans knew the address, so Paul rented it from him, but someone had to be there to operate the tape recorders and set up the microphones. Ian was the ideal person. A meeting was held at Miles's flat with Paul, Jane Asher, and Ian. A lot of hash was smoked, Ian explained the principles of floating equations, and then Paul asked what equipment Ian needed. Ian passed him a list. "Fine," said Paul. "Just get it and send the bill to me."

Ian and Alan quickly moved into Ringo's rock star apartment, the ground floor and basement, all gray watered silk wallpaper and smoked mirrors. Ian set up a pair of Revox tape recorders and a selection of microphones on stands. The problem was that no one knew about it, and they would have been inundated had it been made public. In the end, the two people to make the most use of it were Paul McCartney and Burroughs, who used the state-of-the-art equipment to the full, conducting a series of stereo experiments, masterminded by Ian. Sadly, these appear to have been lost.

Paul told Q magazine in 1986, "I used to sit in a basement in Montagu Square with William Burroughs and a couple of gay guys he knew from Morocco [...] doing little tapes, crazy stuff with guitar and cello." Paul and Bill got on well. Bill explained all about cut-ups and there was a lot of talk about pot, with Ian at one point accusing Paul of being "just an old pothead."[14] Rich talk from someone who used to stuff his pillow with marijuana leaves when he was in Morocco: "No twigs, just the leaves and flowers. It was as soft as feathers. That perfume is the best sleeping pill, man, you have such beautiful dreams and it is a joy to wake up to that smell!"[15]

Paul: "In our conversations, I thought about getting into cut-ups and things like that and I thought I would use the studio for cut-ups. But it ended up being of more practical use to me, really. I thought, let Burroughs do the cut-ups and I'll just go in and demo things. I'd just written 'Eleanor Rigby' and so I went down there in the basement on my days off on my own. Just took a guitar down and used it as a demo studio."

Burroughs: "The three of us talked about the possibilities of the tape recorder. He'd just come in and work on his 'Eleanor Rigby.' Ian recorded his rehearsals so I saw the song taking shape. Once again, not knowing much about music, I could see he knew what he was doing.

He was very pleasant and prepossessing. Nice-looking young man, fairly hardworking."

Paul: "William did some little cut-ups and we did some crazy tape recordings in the basement. We used to sit around talking about all these amazing inventions that people were doing; areas that people were getting into like the Dreamachine that Ian and Brion Gysin had made. It was all very new and very exciting, and so a lot of social time was taken up with just sitting around chatting."

4. Groovy Bob

By this time, Bill had become a good friend of Robert Fraser's, the art dealer. Christopher Finch told Harriet Vyner, Fraser's biographer, "Robert was very much hanging out with Bill Burroughs at that time. Bill was living in London and over at Robert's all the time. These times I was invited to Mount Street at least half the time Bill was there. He knew Robert well. He was a walking pharmacopoeia, so I assume Robert was using drugs in a very sophisticated way."[16]

Robert's flat at 23 Mount Street, on the third floor above Scott's Oyster and Lobster Bar in the heart of Mayfair, was one of the "coolest" sixties pads in London. There were several large daybeds in silver lacquered wood with writhing marine beasts carved at each end and Italian black leather chairs with silvered backs made from interlaced branches. He used his apartment as an extension of his gallery: a blue Yves Klein sponge on a wire armature, a glass table filled with blue pigment, a Lindner, a Dubuffet, collages by Kalinowski. And all the time Robert circling the room, adjusting the lighting—Tiffany lamps, candles, and the latest halogen lights—changing the record—Booker T., Beatles, Stones—rolling joints—Nepalese temple balls, the best hashish—fiddling with lighters, followed by Mohammed, his Moroccan manservant, who silently filled glasses and was rudely ordered about by Robert. There was always lots to drink and even more to smoke.

Robert was a dilettante. According to Bridget Riley, Robert didn't really help his artists: he arranged no outside exhibitions and gave them little in the way of art world contacts. He wasn't concerned with developing their careers, only his own. But the biggest problem was that it was always very difficult, and frequently impossible, to get the money he owed them, so that most of them left him in the end because they were fed up with subsidizing his lavish lifestyle. He was charming, amusing, had a great eye, and was one of the coolest people in town, but if money was mentioned he would look startled and shy away.

In the mid-sixties, his flat was the place to be. There Bill would run into Tony Curtis, Tom Wolfe, John Paul Getty Jr., Andy Warhol, Anita Pallenberg, Francis Bacon, Ken Tynan, Donald Cammell, and of course, most of the artists that Robert showed at the gallery. A frequent visitor to Robert's flat was filmmaker and self-styled black magician Kenneth Anger. Bill held him responsible for an incident of psychic attack. It occurred in the Renommé, one of the empty restaurants that Bill liked to frequent. Bill had gone upstairs to the lavatory, when he was suddenly hit by a wave of hostility. He leaned against the wall, gasping, "I'm dying, I'm dying, I'm dying!" At that moment the Yugoslavian owner came up the stairs and said something and the sensation disappeared. Bill returned to Brion and Ian, who were downstairs, and they said that after he'd left the table, suddenly the proprietor looked around, as if he had received a message, and quickly walked upstairs. "Of course, he knew," said Burroughs. "He came up there because he knew something was wrong." They had previously been at Robert Fraser's house, and Kenneth Anger was there. Brion said, "Kenneth Anger, very definitely." Bill agreed. Anger was noted for throwing curses all over the place, even threatening his best friends like the Rolling Stones.

Bill was earning very good money by English standards at the time. The notoriety surrounding *Naked Lunch* was producing royalties. In 1967, for instance, his Grove Press royalties were $44,458.56 after agent's fees, which he had to pay in addition to 10 percent to Girodias. His gross income that year was £16,305 and 17 shillings ($45,654.00), which Michael Henshaw, his accountant, managed to reduce to £6,602, five shillings, and tenpence ($18,406) after "expenses." The average income in Britain was £1,381 and in the United States that year was $7,300. In 1968 his gross was only £6,386 ($17,881) and his "profit" a mere £336 ($944). UK average income was £1,489 and U.S. average income was $7,850. In 1969, he grossed £11,629 ($32,559), of which, after expenses, he only made £5,088 ($14,246), but at a time when the UK average income was still only £1,607 and $8,550 in the United States. Of course his real expenses were negligible and by most standards he was quite wealthy. He could afford to get an apartment. After his Christmas 1965 visit to Tangier, he had written to Alan Ansen, "I was definitely depressed by Tangier. [...] The bars are empty. I was glad to leave and in no hurry to return," so Morocco was out. Having recently checked up on Paris and New York, and found them wanting, that left London, where he had friends and his on-off relationship with Ian. He had made his choice. There was a three-room apartment coming up in Antony Balch's building, Dalmeny Court at 8 Duke Street Saint James's, just around the corner from the Court of Saint James's itself. It was £750 a year. He put his name down for it.

Chapter Forty

If people turn to look at you on the street, you are not well dressed.
—BEAU BRUMMEL

1. Dalmeny Court

Duke Street Saint James's was in the very center of London's traditional gentlemen's clubland: the Reform, the Athenaeum, the Army & Navy, the Carlton et al. were all one block away. A five-minute walk south, down past Berry Bros. wine merchants where Beau Brummel used to have himself weighed on their coffee scales, took Bill to Saint James's Palace. A stroll in the other direction brought him out on Piccadilly across from the Royal Academy. To the east was St. James's Church where William Blake used to worship, and to the west, across the corner of Green Park, was Buckingham Palace itself. It was the most prestigious and expensive neighborhood in London, and probably in the world.

Antony Balch had been a close friend ever since the Beat Hotel days. He introduced Bill to some of the more louche clubs in the Piccadilly area and, now that Bill was living in the land of Burlington Bertie, gave him useful hints on how to dress and comport himself. Bill could now afford to have his shoes handmade at John Lobb, just around the corner on St. James's Street, joining Onassis, the Duke of Edinburgh, and Duke Ellington in having wooden lasts made of his feet. Burroughs had particularly long thin feet, and these were probably the only shoes that ever fitted him perfectly. He also indulged in a perfect wide-brim Montecristi panama hat from James Lock & Co., also on St. James's Street, and liked to demonstrate how he could roll it up and put it in his pocket and how it would snap back into shape when he pulled it out. Jacksons of Piccadilly and Fortnum & Mason were his local shops, where in the early seventies the staff still first looked for your servant before they handed you your purchase. There were cigar shops that hand-rolled cigarettes to your specifications, suppliers of badger-hair shaving brushes and genuine sponges, cheese shops filled with giant rounds of Stilton, and a number of ancient wine merchants.

In the sixties there were several Turkish baths nearby where gentlemen could spend the night, there were pubs where gentlemen congregated and made discreet signals to one another, and outside the Regent Palace Hotel on Piccadilly there was the meat rack. For a less conspicuous pickup the garden in Leicester Square was popular, and if Bill was caught short, just below his flat was the archway leading to Mason's Yard where there was a gentlemen's public toilet notorious for cruising. Antony Balch knew them all. In August 1966 Bill moved into the Cavendish Hotel, on Duke Street Saint James's, a few doors from Dalmeny Court, to wait for his apartment to become free. The new Cavendish was terribly expensive so he flew to Tangier instead, where, unfortunately, all the hotels were full and he had to stay in the Minzah, which was about the same price as the New Cavendish. There, one evening in the dining room with his friend Christopher Wanklyn, he felt the *dying feeling*. He avoided plunging his head into his gazpacho, excused himself, and walked very slowly and deliberately from the room, very consciously placing one foot before the other in the converging blackness. Cold water on his face and five minutes' rest on the bed and he was ready to face his meal again, from soup to fruit salad. Christopher asked him if there had been a sensation of heat and Burroughs told him, "Yes, always at the onset. Like a laser gun through the midsections."[1] These attacks had occurred a number of times before; now he seemed to know how to deal with them. "One of the most exhilarating feelings you could have, is to have the dying feeling, and then when you come to you just feel marvelous."[2]

After a few days at the Three Pelicans Hotel he was able to move into the Muniria, where he made plans for his new flat. He told Ian, "What I want is to make it into the ideal flat that everyone will want one like it with Brion's pictures and tape recorders that I can program in such a way as to amuse the guests."[3] He returned to London and moved into 8 Duke Street Saint James's on the first of October.

Bill's flat, 22 Dalmeny Court, was reached by a rickety elevator with sliding metal grille doors. He wrote Brion that the flat was very quiet, with wall-to-wall carpeting, and that he was having an orgone accumulator large enough to accommodate two people built in the small back room, which could be comparatively well soundproofed. "This is to be my permanent headquarters," he wrote. "Now I can give your pictures a home."[4] The back windows looked out over Mason's Yard and the rear elevation of the London Library, which owned Dalmeny Court, and Bill and Antony Balch sometimes projected slides and films on the London Library's wall at night. There was a kitchen unit hidden behind a roller screen used only for making tea. A large sofa stood against one wall beneath a large Gysin landscape. Bill bought a coffee table and standard lamp. It was very comfortable.

In keeping with his new respectability, Burroughs had a visiting card printed. While he was at it, he had one made for Ian Sommerville, whom he expected to move in with him, the recording studio project clearly not being a long-term arrangement. He was right, and in mid-November Ian arrived with all the tape recorders. This would have been fine except that Ian insisted on bringing Alan Watson with him, even though the apartment was really too small for three people. He brought him in by stages, just for a few days, then for another few days, until he was living there. Bill described it as a typical triangle situation where the younger person brings in someone whom he's attracted to and the older man can't protest and it is very painful. Bill was extremely jealous but there was nothing he could do. He found it a very humiliating, awful position to be in. He knew that he could not bring the subject out into the open because to do so would mean that he would have to be prepared for them both to leave. He knew that if he said, "You've gotta get him out of here," then Ian would have gone with him. He complained to Brion, who told him, "Well, if you're going to let someone walk all over you..."—which was exactly what Ian was doing. But Bill didn't have what it took to confront Ian. He said, "I was too hung up on Ian sexually to do that and if you are hung up on someone sexually, you've lost it. You've lost the upper hand. You lose it, you lose it." Ian and Alan remained with him for two years.

Bill never liked to be around effeminate gays; they drew attention and were particularly conspicuous in an area like St. James's. He found Alan's voice grating, and worst of all, Alan played opera constantly, Charles Gounod's *Romeo and Juliet* in particular, which Burroughs hated. On the plus side, Alan was a good cook. His parents were both pastry cooks, and Alan himself could make traditional English food including excellent chops. Bill saved a lot of money by eating in. He tried hard to make the best of it and succeeded, to a degree. In December he wrote to Brion to say that "Alan Watson is living here now with Ian and I am very well pleased with the arrangement." He said that Alan was an excellent cook, kept the place clean, and made breakfast for him every morning. That night they were to have wild duck. "In short, his behavior has been exemplary. The flat is really too big for one person to keep up."[5] This may have just been a face-saving exercise. Bill didn't really want Alan there and was barely cordial toward him.

Antony Balch, however, adored Alan and took to spending a lot of time in flat 22, which ameliorated the situation somewhat. There was a difficult episode where Bill had imitated Alan's voice on a tape and Alan had taken the tape on a trip to Hampton Court, thinking it was an opera cassette, and was convinced that Bill was trying to put a curse on him. Ian himself was well aware of the tension and recognized that they were being unfair to Bill, but they didn't have any money and they needed somewhere to stay. Eventually things seemed to be coming to a head, with Ian prickly and Bill aloof and standoffish, so Ian told Alan to leave. But Ian would not commit himself to stay with Bill; he was simply asking Alan to leave because the situation had become so impossible. Bill's raised hopes were yet again dashed. Eventually, in August 1968, Ian left as well. "There wasn't much I could do," said Bill. "Sad and discreditable."

While Burroughs was in Tangier, before moving into Dalmeny Court, Allen Ginsberg had been frantically trying to contact him there by telegram and telephone but with no response. Billy Jr. had been arrested for possession of speed in New York during a raid. Allen had bailed him out but wanted to know if he should get him a lawyer.[6] Bill cabled Allen to say he would meet all expenses and hoped that Laura Lee had not heard about it. The charges were dropped and it cost Bill three hundred dollars for a lawyer. Just as he was writing to Billy to tell him to get out of New York before it happened again, it did happen again, and Bill had to come up with a further three hundred dollars. He asked Allen to put Billy on the next train to Palm Beach. Bill wanted him to pack up his things in Florida and join him in the new flat in London.[7]

Bill continued to move in the upper reaches of London's literary circles. He became friendly with Sonia Orwell, and visited her a number of times at her house at 18 Percy Street, in Fitzrovia. On a typical evening there he might meet Kenneth Tynan, Mary McCarthy, Wayland Young (Lord Kennet), and on one occasion, in April 1967, he encountered Stephen Spender looking very depressed and "hangdog" because the scandal of the Congress for Cultural Freedom being a CIA front had just come to light. Spender, who was editor of *Encounter* magazine, published by the Congress, turned out to have been working for a clandestine spying agency all those years, promoting a non-left alternative to communism but never really questioning America's foreign policies. Spender claimed, very unconvincingly, not to have known. Spender invited Burroughs for dinner at his house in Hampstead. It was interesting for Bill to meet someone with a gay background, who had been part of the prewar modernist scene along with Auden, Isherwood, and Eliot. Now Spender was married to Natasha Litvin, and had been appointed the consultant poet for the Library of Congress, the only non-American ever to hold the post. "For services to the CIA," Bill commented wryly. Through Spender he met

Frank Kermode, coeditor of *Encounter*, memorably described by Philip Larkin as a "jumped up book drunk ponce." Kermode visited Dalmeny Court and taped an interview with Bill for a radio program. Afterward Bill tried to remember a single thing that Kermode had said, but nothing memorable remained. Bill was convinced he was CIA.

Much has been made of Burroughs's connections with the Situationist International, but it was not until July 1967 that he became aware of their existence. He wrote to Mary Beach, his French translator, "Do you know of a French group called Situationist International. [...] Seemingly a sophisticated anarchist group. I think they would be an excellent outlet for the short pieces I am writing now. Just read a very intelligent analysis of the Watts race riots by this group."[8] This was Guy Debord's *The Decline and Fall of the Spectacle-Commodity Economy* about the Watts riots of August 1965 in Los Angeles, published in *Internationale Situationiste* number 10 in March 1966.[9] In 1967 the entire British section of the SI was expelled by Debord, which might have drawn Burroughs's attention to the group.

Through December 1966 Ian Sommerville and Burroughs carefully checked the proofs for the second revised edition of *The Soft Machine*. Many people had found the original Olympia edition hard to read, and Burroughs had revised it extensively for the Grove Press edition in the States. He told Gysin, "The original edition *was* 'a collection of essays' rather than a book, and there was not enough narrative material to carry such a load of cut ups and unrelated descriptive passages."[10] The most obvious change was to open the book with straight narrative instead of the "Gongs of Violence" section, and everyone Burroughs spoke to about it found the new text much more readable.

Burroughs told an interviewer, "With *The Soft Machine* I had many complaints. It was difficult to read and going through it again, I thought this was true so I rewrote it completely introducing about 65 pages of straight narrative. What I'm really trying to do now is to get started on a line of straight narrative. I have a stack of paper already, a stack of tentative beginnings, but I have not yet decided which one of these to follow up."[11] The American edition was much more readable, but in going through the text for the publication of the book in England, Burroughs decided that perhaps too much of the original had been deleted, and that additional material that he had not had time to put into shape when the Grove edition came out could now be used. Using both the Olympia and Grove editions, plus new material, Bill assembled the final, third version of the text, which was published by Calder and Boyars on July 25, 1968. Publication was delayed because police had recently raided the Indica

Bookshop and seized *Naked Lunch*. The book was subsequently returned
covered in grubby fingerprints, but no charges were brought, and Calder
finally had the courage to publish. Ian had an important role in assembling *The Soft Machine*: "Technical Tillie moaning about the equipment
the way he always does."[12]

Burroughs had begun work on *The Wild Boys* in the middle of March
1967, but his flat was so crowded, and he found Alan to be such a nuisance with his shrieking and his opera records, that in May he took off
for Tangier, where he checked into the Atlas Hotel with his typewriter,
his clippings folders, and a plentiful supply of majoun. The "Gran Luxe"
section of the book was begun there and developed in Marrakech in June
and July of that year, where he joined Bill Willis in a house owned by
John Shepherd. These were all friends of Christopher Gibbs's, and provided him with much of the material for the new book. Bill Willis was
from Memphis, Tennessee. He had a wealthy upbringing and burned
through $200,000 before becoming an interior decorator. He had always
lived a very grand, self-indulgent, hedonistic lifestyle. Christopher Gibbs
described the scene: "He rose about one, lunch around three, over at five,
then if there were any workmen still on site there would be a flurry of
phone calls asking them to stay another ten minutes for him to inspect their
work. Then a *cinq-a-sept* until about ten, when dinner was served. Then
a succession of Moroccan boys would be summoned into the bedroom,
accompanied by increasingly noisy opera records, and the consumption of
huge quantities of Jack Daniel's. Willis screamed at his servants. Bill was
astonished and intrigued by these capers, which gave him great enjoyment
to watch." Bill described it as "La grande luxe!" "That was what I was
writing about in *The Wild Boys*, was la grande luxe." Bill Willis became
Reggie in the book:

> So after breakfast I set out for the Djemalfna to meet Reggie. We are going
> to plan our route to A.J.'s annual party which is tomorrow it will be the do
> of the season. [...] I find Reggie on the square sipping a pink gin shaded
> by a screen of beggars. An old spastic woman twitches and spatters Reggie's
> delicate skin with sunlight. "Uncontrolled slut!" he screams. He turns to his
> henchman. "Give this worthless hag a crust of stale bread and find me a sturdy
> shade beggar."

Bill liked Marrakech, and enjoyed exploring it—"there are some beautiful sets there"—but he thought the amenities were inferior to Tangier's.
There were only a few good restaurants around the Djemaa el Fna, and
he found poverty and the begging more intrusive than in Tangier. There
was a man paralyzed from the waist down who moved around on blocks

with leather pads on his knees who would suddenly pop up under your table, which Bill didn't appreciate. There was Mister Very Good, who had very good hashish cookies, but there were few boys. According to Bill they had all been snapped up by Christopher Wanklyn and John Shepherd: "They'd already got the pick." Bill was there in mid-June and it was getting hotter by the day. They closed the shutters to keep the cool air in until the evening, but no one wanted to go out in the daytime. Bill Willis tried to send his old Fatima out to buy a potato at 1:30 and she refused to go. Burroughs took her side and from then on she came and cried on Bill's shoulder when Willis was being unreasonable. "She would come to me for comfort. Old and frail."[13] It was a very hermetic social scene; everyone in the foreign colony—Willis, John Shepherd, Christopher Wanklyn, and John Paul Getty Jr., who was having a house built there—saw each other every day for reciprocal lunch or dinner engagements. Bill found it very confining and could never have lived there, but enjoyed his visit, photographing sets and taking notes, and only returning to London in mid-July.

Bill's mother had again been writing to Bill asking him to try and do something about Billy, who was now taking ephedrine. Bill pointed out again that he had a room ready in the apartment waiting for him; that if hospital treatment was necessary it could certainly be provided in London; that he had "arranged for a program of activities and studies designed to lead him into constructive channels"; and that he would make every effort to try and arouse Billy's interest in something that might lead to a career. But Bill despaired that Billy would ever take an interest in anything.[14]

Billy himself was resisting all of Bill's efforts to get him to come to London, remembering the stressful time he had in Tangier with Bill and his boys and not wanting to repeat it. Laura suggested that Bill come to Palm Beach, but Bill was convinced that the Bureau of Narcotics was out to get him and had no intention of returning to the United States if he could possibly avoid doing so. He stressed that he wanted to get Billy on a plane to London just as soon as it was feasible and said that he had been putting money aside for the purpose. But eventually he relented and bought a ticket to Miami, leaving on December 27.

2. Palm Beach and Lexington

The situation in Palm Beach was appalling. Burroughs was strung out on tincture of opium at the time. "I thought the habit was small and brought nothing with me to Florida. [...] The habit turned out to be not so small and a period of excruciating withdrawal lasted for a month."[15] He had swelling of the groin and neck glands, a high fever, pain, and tension.

Bill slept in a small back room with sliding windows that had been corroded shut by the salt air. Billy was surly and uncooperative and had left paregoric bottles and syringes all over the house, which was in complete disarray. "Mother comes into my room with a bag full of empty paregoric bottles from Billy's room, just lying around for the narcs to find. I take the bag down to Lake Worth and throw it out with a stone for ballast."[16] At 4:00 p.m. each day Bill started mixing old-fashioneds, and after three or four each they became quite tipsy. Laura loved old-fashioneds but was not a big drinker. Every day Bill walked to the end of the block, where Sanford Avenue became a sandy track leading to the beach, to wait for 4:00 p.m. Once a police car stopped and drove partway out on the road to look at him. But he looked innocent enough. Laura was already suffering from dementia, asking the same questions over and over and immediately forgetting the answers. Her continuous fretting drove Burroughs crazy. There were no servants and no car and the house appeared to be haunted with strange knockings and bangings. Then on New Year's Day Laura broke her arm, which made life even more difficult.

Billy was up on three felony charges and the case came before Judge Russell Macintosh, a tough judge who automatically handed out the maximum sentence. Bill talked with the DA's office and managed to finagle a deal so they would drop charges and place Billy on probation on condition he dry out at Lexington Narcotic Farm. Macintosh imposed a four-year probation with almost impossible terms, but at least Billy was out. Bill made arrangements to sell the house and put his mother in a small apartment back in St. Louis where his brother could keep an eye on her.[17]

Bill accompanied Billy Jr. to Lexington, "sad sadder than I can tell you,"[18] he told Gysin. Billy had a fear of flying. Bill got him onto the first plane by telling him how great the first shot was going to be when he got there, "probably knock you on your ass," but nothing would get him onto the second flight in an old propeller plane. Bill put him on a fast train and took the flight himself. There was heavy snow and Billy was late. Bill waited for him all night in their hotel room. He wrote, "I remember being overcome by grief, and I was convinced he had suffered a fatal accident."[19] The train was delayed and Billy didn't show up until the following morning. They took a cab to the hospital: "Got two for Narco." In reception an old man asked them, "Which one of you is checking in here?" Bill quickly pushed his son forward, memories of his own time there flickering in his head.

When he was clean, Billy was sent to the Green Valley School in Orange City, Florida, where he was to be rehabilitated. The Palm Beach house was sold and Laura was put into Chateins, a nursing home in St. Louis.[20] She hated it. When Billy Jr. visited her she was strapped to her chair because "she removes her clothing." Billy visited her on occasion, and once stole her painkillers. He wrote that she spent the next three years sitting in the same chair, staring vacantly out of the window.[21] Mort wrote Burroughs, "Sometimes she recognizes me. Sometimes she doesn't." During the four years she remained alive, Burroughs never once went to see her. From time to time when he was traveling he would send postcards, and six months before she died he sent a Mother's Day card. He remembered, "There was a horrible, mushy poem in it. I remember feeling 'vaguely guilty.'"[22]

Late in the summer of 1966, Panna Grady, the New York society hostess, began an affair with Charles Olson, and in October they sailed for London, largely because Charles could not stand the constant pressure from all the freeloaders. She rented one of the most magnificent houses in central London at 2 Chester Terrace, overlooking the boating lake at Regent's Park. It was the end house in an 1822 Nash terrace, a huge mansion with a portico of four giant Roman Doric columns supporting a pediment topped with a row of heroic statues. No sooner had she shaken off one load of parasites than others appeared, Alexander Trocchi to the fore, closely followed by Black Power leader Michael X, the poet Harry Fainlight, who had known her in New York, and the rest of the London poor. Soon Chester Terrace was indistinguishable from the Dakota. Olson got fed up with the endless stream of people. He worked at night so he was still having his breakfast at eight in the evening when the visitors began to arrive. But Panna liked to socialize and ultimately this was what broke up their relationship. Characteristically, Charles went into hiding. In March 1967, after spending six months at Chester Terrace, he moved into the Mayfair Hotel on Berkeley Square, where he remained incommunicado for several weeks while his friends frantically telephoned all over Britain and the States, not knowing if he was alive or dead.

Panna had long let it be known that she was in love with Burroughs; it was something that Allen Ginsberg kidded Bill about. She was attracted to brilliant men, and it was an unfortunate fact that so many of them were gay. She did manage to get John Wieners into bed and so regarded Burroughs as a possibility. With Charles Olson gone, she once again turned her attention to Bill, but he was not having any of it. He made sure that there were always other people around when they met. Unable to get Bill, she turned her attention to Ian Sommerville and managed to maneuver him into bed. Bill was shocked but said nothing to Ian or Panna. Bill enjoyed her company and her great generosity. Thanks to Panna he became familiar with the meat trolley at Rules—always remembering to tip the carver—and the saddle of lamb at the Connaught Grill. Panna hosted a memorable Christmas meal at the Connaught for Bill and Ian, Alex Trocchi, Larry Rivers, Jasper Johns, Robert Fraser, and assorted wives and boyfriends.[23] Panna sometimes visited Dalmeny Court, where the situation with Ian, Alan, and Bill seemed to have stabilized: Bill wrote Brion, "Alan Watson continues to cook excellent meals and I have become quite fond of him."[24] That August, 1967, they all took karate lessons together—something Bill had started in Palm Beach—and took to "camping around in those marvellous judo outfits."[25] This interest was terminated when Bill badly bruised his wrist attempting to chop an ironing board in half with the side of his hand.

That summer Allen Ginsberg came to London to read poetry with Auden, Neruda, Empson, and other luminaries at Queen Elizabeth Hall and to participate in the Congress of Liberation, a conference held at the Roundhouse from July 15 to 30, 1967, organized by radical psychiatrist R. D. Laing and others seeking to "demystify human violence in all its forms." It brought together Stokely Carmichael (who first coined the term "Black Power"), Gregory Bateson (who warned of global warming), Herbert Marcuse, Paul Sweezy, John Gerassi, David Cooper, and others. Burroughs refused to speak, but Ginsberg quoted extensively from his texts and Bill attended some of the evening get-togethers at "Dialectics House," often getting roaring drunk with Laing, but also exchanging ideas with Stokely Carmichael, whose company he preferred to that of the Marxist intellectuals.

Panna was having a marvelous time—London was at the height of the "summer of love"; Olson was appearing with Allen at the Arts Council reading and had returned to his old room; the weather was perfect—so she decided to hold a party on July 16 for everyone involved with the Dialectics of Liberation Congress and also the Arts Council reading. To Ginsberg's delight Mick Jagger was there, and they sat out on the balcony talking; Bill had already met him a few times at Robert Fraser's flat. Robert wasn't there because he had been sentenced to nine months in Wormwood Scrubs after being busted for heroin at the famous police raid on Keith Richards's house in February of that year. Michael X, the local Black Power leader, made the rounds, cashing in on white guilt to collect checks for one of his many money-raising schemes (raising money for himself). It was at this party that Burroughs met Tom Driberg, MP, who had been a friend of Aleister Crowley's, but most of the time Bill spent holding court in an upstairs room with Ian Sommerville. William Empson and many of the other poets were there and a fight erupted among them, resulting in someone foolishly calling the police. For some reason it was Burroughs who answered the door. The police stood politely to attention, helmets in hand, respectful of the address. "There is nothing going on," Burroughs assured them, pulling a grimace, meant as a smile. "I can assure you that nothing ever happens at Panna's house. Nothing at all. Good evening,"[26] and he shut the door abruptly in their faces. Six of them returned later, having had second thoughts, and were dealt with by William Empson, who was completely drunk.

Chapter Forty-One

The material involved in this sector is so vicious that it is carefully arranged to kill anyone if he discovers the exact truth of it. [...] I am very sure that I was the first one that ever did live through any attempt to attain that material.

—L. RON HUBBARD[1]

1. Operating Thetan

Burroughs had been involved with Scientology ever since 1959 when he was first introduced to it by Brion Gysin, but it was not until the mid-sixties that he devoted much time to it, initially because he was being paid to investigate it. In February 1964, when he was living in the Loteria Building in Tangier, Bill had received a letter from an eighteen-year-old trainee newspaper reporter from Crawley New Town, in Sussex, asking him about cut-ups and intersections. Graham Masterton had written a text called *Rules of Duel*, which he sent Burroughs that same month. In June Burroughs wrote a foreword to it and also cut up a portion of the text, which he called "Over the last skyscrapers a silent kite." The book was self-published later that year. They continued to exchange letters and postcards over the next two years and finally met when Bill moved into Dalmeny Court. Graham Masterton was a Mod, sporting a handmade suit with a boxy jacket, button-down shirt, narrow tie, shades, and chisel-toed Italian shoes. He and Bill often dined together or met for a drink.

Masterton had just been appointed deputy editor of *Mayfair*, a men's magazine designed to compete in Britain with *Penthouse* and *Playboy*, and asked if he had anything they could publish. Bill had always wanted a platform for his ideas on social control and big business, and together they came up with the idea of the Burroughs Academy. Bill also spoke at length about Scientology, so Masterton commissioned him to write an investigative article about it for *Mayfair*. In August 1967, using false names—William Lee and Graham Thomas—accompanied by Antony Balch and his 8-millimeter camera, Masterton drove them to Scientology headquarters, Saint Hill, a huge faux-medieval castle in East Grinstead, Sussex, about thirty miles from London, to check them out. They were shown around by the assistant chaplain, Mrs. Bess Jensen, a Scientologist for twelve years. They saw large rooms filled with people listening to lectures by L. Ron Hubbard on tape recorders, talked to students, bought some postcards, and returned to London. Back at Dalmeny Court, Bill set up a postcard of L. Ron Hubbard and took aim at it with his Webley .22 air pistol. As he pulled back the hammer to cock it, it snapped back on his thumb, almost breaking it. Bill carried the scar for life: "Boy, he was really spitting back a curse there!" Normally Bill shot at small printed bull's-eye targets.

Bill's first piece on Scientology, the first major article on the subject in the British press, "The Engram Theory," appeared in the eleventh issue of *Mayfair* in November 1967 as Bulletin 2 from the Burroughs Academy. There were to be twenty-one bulletins from the Burroughs Academy, as well as five subsequent appearances in *Mayfair*, the last appearing in December 1970, more appearances by Burroughs than in any other magazine. They covered all Bill's major interests at the time, Scientology paramount among them as this was before he became disillusioned with the organization, but also the Mayan calendar, thought control, Wilhelm Reich's orgone accumulators, low-frequency whistles as weapons, and so on.

Every few weeks Masterton would visit and they would discuss ideas for pieces and have a few drinks or a meal, often accompanied by Bill's friends. Masterton recalled one occasion when Ian and Alan Watson broke up and Ian was in tears, and another when Alex Trocchi came to visit and brought Bill a swordstick as a present. Bill danced drunkenly around the apartment, swinging it dangerously, shouting, "Ho there, you ruffians!"

Bill believed firmly in the use of the E-meter to clear unconscious blockages that are controlling the individual, so much so that he thought that Hubbard's findings and its use should be opened up to panels of scientists and specialists in biofeedback to potentiate its use. He wrote, "Some of the techniques are highly valuable and warrant further study and experimentation." He first toyed with Hubbard's ideas back in October 1959 in Paris, when he wrote to Allen Ginsberg, "The method of directed recall is the method of Scientology. You will recall I wrote urging you to contact local chapter and find an auditor. They do the job without hypnosis or drugs, simply run the tape back and forth until the trauma is wiped off. It works. I have used the method—partially responsible for recent changes." A few days later he wrote again, "I have a new method of writing and do not want to publish anything that has not been inspected and processed. I cannot explain this method to you until you have necessary training. So once again and most urgently (believe me there is not much time)—I tell you: 'Find a Scientology Auditor and have yourself run.'"

Scientology began to show up in Burroughs's texts. It was called Logos in *The Ticket That Exploded*, an organization that had "a system of therapy they call 'clearing.' You 'run' traumatic material which they call 'engrams' until it loses emotional connotation through repetitions and is then refilled as neutral memory. When all the 'engrams' have been run and deactivated the subject becomes a 'Clear.'" It is first named in *Nova Express* when a character reports, "The Scientologists believe sir that words recorded during a period of unconsciousness [...] store pain and that this pain store can be plugged in with key words."[2]

L. Ron Hubbard claimed that much behavior is determined by unconscious memories of events that he called "engrams," words recorded in pain and unconsciousness. For instance, everything that the surgical staff says during an operation is heard and stored by the patient, and because the person is unconscious he has no judgment about this input. These words have an emotional charge and to repeat them can cause an anxiety attack. Rather like traditional psychoanalysis, Hubbard claimed that by repeatedly returning these words or events to consciousness they lose their charge and the person is "cleared" of that particular anxious blockage and it is filed as neutral memory. The "science" part comes in the use of the E-meter, a polygraph that shows the person's reaction to a series of questions by measuring people's galvanic skin response. A small electrical charge is introduced by the subject holding a pair of empty soup cans. It is a primitive form of the lie detector, which uses the same system. A scientology "auditor" asks a series of questions, and when the needle jumps, that means a blockage has been detected. These are gone over from every possible angle until they no longer give a reading. When you get a floating needle to all the questions that particular session is complete. There are very many questionnaires.

In the mid-sixties, a number of Australian states, beginning with Victoria in 1965, banned the Church of Scientology based on the Anderson Report, which found that the auditing process involved "command" hypnosis, in which the hypnotist assumes "positive authoritative control" over the patient. The report stated, "Most scientology and dianetic techniques are those of authoritative hypnosis and as such are dangerous [...] the scientific evidence [...] leads to the inescapable conclusion that it is only in name that there is any difference between authoritative hypnosis and most of the techniques of scientology. Many scientology techniques are in fact hypnotic techniques, and Hubbard has not changed their nature by changing their names." In other words, Scientology was guilty of brainwashing.

Between late January and April 1968, Bill took courses at the London Centre at 37 Fitzroy Street and a "clearing course" at Saint Hill in East Grinstead, staying first at the Brambletye Hotel in Forest Row, and then with some fellow Scientologists. The hotel showed up not long afterward in "Ali's Smile": "authentic cottages with moss on the roofs. There is 'Ye Olde Bramble Tyme Motel,' high prices, thin walls."[3] Bill was convinced that his room was haunted and started a short story about it. The investigative nature of Burroughs's visit was underlined by the fact that the Brambletye is where Sherlock Holmes and Dr. Watson stay while carrying out their investigations in Sir Arthur Conan Doyle's story "The Adventure of Black Peter." The first draft of the "Dead Child" section of *The Wild Boys* was written here. "A writer always gets his pound of flesh even out of old Mother Hubbard with her bare cupboard," he wrote. Burroughs snooped around the grounds of L. Ron Hubbard's quarters dressed as a gardener, tape recorder in hand, hoping to surreptitiously record him through a window, but Hubbard, alas, was not in residence.

After more courses, he went to Edinburgh for a week to finish his clearing course. This consisted of a whole batch of very strange convoluted sentences that he had to run himself, keeping a written record, reading the sentences, repeating them until they were flat on the needle. "To have much, to have little, to have much, to have everything..."; "To stay here, to stay there, to stay out, to stay in..."; endless contradictory commands: "Creating to destroy the energy, destroying to create the energy." The Scottish Scientology Centre was operated by the Sea Org, the only people allowed to deliver the "Operating Thetan" levels of Scientology teaching. Burroughs spent about £1,500 on the Scientology clearing course and graduated as a Grade 5, "power" release. He was Clear number 1163. He said, "It feels marvellous! Things you've had all your life, things you think nothing can be done about—suddenly they're not there any more! And you know these disabilities cannot return."[4] On a visit to Tangier in late July 1968 he spoke to Bowles about Scientology, who reported to Harold Norse, "Bill is very happy to have been cleared; he claims he owes as much to scientology as to apomorphine. I asked what scientology had cured him of. Old thought patterns, he said. Anyway, he seemed in excellent form."

Ian Sommerville accused Bill of just trying to get power over other people. Burroughs agreed: "Ian wasn't standing still for it. Resisted it, sure did." It was while Bill was in Edinburgh that Ian finally moved out of Dalmeny Court. The organization was already having doubts about Burroughs's commitment to Scientology, so they had him take the Jo'burg test at East Grinstead HQ. This was a series of 215 questions about criminal activity. He was asked, "Have you ever hidden a body?" He said no and got a reading. Then Bill had a clear picture of himself hiding a body somewhere. Then the auditor asked, "In this life have you ever hidden a body?" That was clear. It must have been a past life. Next came, "Have you ever committed forgery?" Bill said no but got a reading. Then he remembered he had forged a narcotic prescription. "So the machine knows things that you don't know, or that you don't remember. On a conscious level I didn't think I had at all, I was thinking of forging a check." The questions reminded Bill of the Moscow purge trials: "Have you ever had unkind thoughts about L. Ron Hubbard?" But by now Bill had learned the techniques. "I can't help resenting his perfection," he replied. There were agents provocateurs, Jo'burg people waiting outside the room who would sidle up to him and say, "What do you think about this latest bulletin from L. Ron Hubbard?" and he'd say, "Well, I'm sure Mister Hubbard knows what he's doing." As ever, Bill was on the lookout for a likely lad, but was forced to conclude, "By and large they were one of the most unattractive bunch of people I've ever laid eyes on. I was at Saint Hill and there must have been 300 people and I saw two, out of 300, that I thought looked even reasonable." Despite Hubbard's hostile attitude toward homosexuality in his writings, no one at Saint Hill seems to have been concerned by Burroughs's open admission of his sexual preference. Scientology's position on homosexuality was that it was a false identity, a "valence" in Scientology metalanguage, and that homosexual urges would disappear when the adept reached OT level III, where the "body Thetans" that cause the problem would be audited away.

Bill took a course to become a Scientology auditor and was required to get pupils to practice on. He put up a notice in the Indica Bookshop asking for volunteers and got a few such as Harold Norse, from the Beat Hotel, who moved to London in 1969. Despite his reservations that Scientology was a mind-control cult, Norse had previously been involved with Dianetics in New York, and agreed to let Bill "run" him. Norse described it in his autobiography: "I told Bill about my illness and that my Dutch boyfriend had stopped sleeping with me. [...] Following the principles of Scientology, Bill believed the liver disorder was linked to the emotional one, caused by an engram—a mental picture in the reactive mind of an unconscious incident in the past that contained pain. 'This is the compulsive re-experiencing of emotions not appropriate to the present time situation,' he explained."[5] Norse would go to Duke Street Saint James's and they would sit at Bill's desk, Norse holding the cans attached to electrodes while Bill studied the actions of the needle. Burroughs spoke about it later: "I said, 'What is the problem?' He said, 'My loneliness.' It was not his loneliness, the problem is his boyfriend won't sleep with him anymore. That's the problem. In other words, the problem has to involve another will. Another person. Loneliness and depression are always cover ups, the problem is not depression or loneliness. So then you're getting somewhere. These are preliminary processes. This isn't the clearing process. Once he realises that this is his problem, well then he's got to deal with it, one way or another."

Bill took Harold to Scientology HQ to meet the head man and offered to pay for Harold to be cleared at the Centre. "I'll take care of it, Harold, so go ahead." Harold took the course, but when Bill forgot to pay a few pounds, Harold was inundated with threatening messages: "You are now a non-person required to report to the castle for correction [...] pack your bags immediately. You are to fly to Valencia and report to Sea Org for extreme liability." At least Norse saw the humor of it. What was extraordinary was that Burroughs seemed sufficiently convinced of the efficacy of the E-meter that he was able to suspend belief in the other areas of Scientology doctrine, despite the belief in "Thetans" required to become an "Operating Thetan," the next level up from "Clear."

According to Hubbard, the universe is 320 trillion years old (the Lambda-CDM concordance model estimates it is 13.75 billion years old, plus or minus 0.13 billion). In the primordial past Thetans brought the universe into being for their own pleasure but became corrupted and lost their immense powers. They lived in a Galactic Confederacy of twenty-six stars and twenty-six planets, including Earth, which was then known as Teegeeack. Overpopulation was causing problems so their ruler, Xenu, summoned billions of them together for an income tax inspection, paralyzed them, and froze them for transport to Earth, where they were to be exterminated. The spaceship looked rather like a DC-8 only the DC-8 had propellers and the spaceship didn't. Once on Teegeeack, the helpless citizens were unloaded around the bases of volcanoes all around the planet. Hydrogen bombs were lowered into the volcanoes and detonated simultaneously. The disembodied souls of the victims were captured on an "electronic ribbon" and forced to watch a 3-D widescreen motion picture that implanted what Hubbard called "various misleading data," which included all Earthly religions. (Hubbard had been a sci-fi author.) These teachings cost many thousands of dollars to receive, and this is only Operating Thetan level III. At the time of writing there are eight released levels and a further seven unreleased.

Burroughs got hold of copies of most of the material up to and including Operating Thetan level VII from defectors. "I saw it all. It wasn't very interesting," he said. "It didn't strike me as anything very special, very special at all." What puzzled his friends was that he thought it might be. For years he ran Scientology audits, repeating them until they ran flat on the E-meter, on one session spending eight hours a day for six weeks. In April 1969 he was finally put in a condition of treason for his critical writing about the organization. "They tried to put me into a condition, and I said, 'Well I'm not going to put up with this. Gold stars and all this I left back in kindergarden.' And that was that."[6] Burroughs said later, "It was a weird episode but interesting, I don't regret it. I learned a lot. I do know how to work a lie detector." Alan Ansen suggested that one of the reasons that Burroughs became a junkie was to provide himself with the semblance of a social life, appointments, meetings, and so on. It is possible that, in part, Scientology filled the same need: people with a shared interest and endless talk about Sec Checks and Release levels. But Scientology alienated him from his greatest love, Ian, and wasted years of his life. Many people were turned off by his conversation, which returned time and again to Scientology. Without question, his period in London was poisoned by his obsession with Scientology. Without doubt his life would have been utterly different, happier, more sociable, and more productive if he had never heard of the E-meter. As Burroughs said much later, "There is no doubt about it: Scientology is evil and basically ill-intentioned and nasty."[7]

After Robert Fraser went to jail in 1967 for possession of heroin, Bill was deprived of a ready-made social scene that he could drop into at will. What he needed was a regular pub or club, like the society at the Bounty in Mexico City, the San Remo in Greenwich Village, the Café Central in Tangier, or the bar at the Beat Hotel. Had he lived closer to the Chelsea Arts Club, that might have served. He liked it there, but it was miles away, the other end of the Kings Road. He did visit the Colony Room on Dean Street from time to time, mostly to see Bacon, but it was tiny, there were few places to sit, and Muriel, who owned it, was a loud in-your-face Jewish lesbian from Birmingham who called all her clients "Cunty!" which Bill found most distasteful. Similarly, the French pub, also on Dean Street, drew a clientele of "artistic gangsters" including Bacon, Lucian Freud, and Patrick Procktor as well as assorted boxers, journalists, photographers, and Soho types. But again it was very crowded, and as usual in British pubs, there were few places to sit. The most irritating thing was the idiotic British licensing laws which meant that at 11:00 p.m. the bartender would bellow "Time, gentlemen, please!" and all drinking would have to stop.

Burroughs still saw Mikey Portman, who was beginning to deteriorate, alternating between alcoholism and drug addiction, cures and immediate relapses. He would call, sobbing on the phone at 3:00 a.m., a complete mess. He had no strength or discipline. By this time, Burroughs had written a number of important articles for *International Times*, the London underground newspaper, and got on very well with the various editors and staff. He very much supported what they were doing and they were grateful to him for using them as a vehicle for his articles. In mid-1967, an American living in London, Bill Levy, took over as editor. Lord Goodman, as head of the Arts Council and pillar of the establishment, was one of Levy's many bêtes noires, and he sought to attack him by alleging that the reason that Mikey Portman did not get busted for heroin was because Lord Goodman was using his political influence to shelter him. Goodman telephoned Burroughs and asked him, "Can you kill this story? This attack? If you can do anything to stop this, please do because there is no need for them to attack a poor shattered thing like Mikey." Burroughs said that he would do what he could and called Bill Levy and said, "Listen, lay off." And Levy did, but it seeded a resentment in Levy that was expressed at a later date. As Burroughs said at the time, Goodman was establishment, but he was liberal establishment; he wouldn't even have South African sherry in his apartment.

Mikey did in fact get busted. He was nabbed by police as he left Alexander Trocchi's apartment and they found a few jacks of heroin on him (a jack is a sixth of a grain). The police accused Trocchi of dealing, but the judge took into account that his wife had recently died of an overdose and that he had two sons to bring up, one of whom was dying of cancer of the spine, and in the light of these tragedies he only put Alex on probation. Mikey also got off.

While Burroughs was completing his Scientology clearing course in Edinburgh, Ian and Alan had moved out. It was a relief for Bill to find the place empty, but he quickly realized that it was too big for his needs. He inquired after a smaller flat in the same building, but it was to be many years before one came up. In the middle of August 1968, Bill reported to Brion that Alan Watson had run off to Paris with a rich queen and his opera tapes and that Ian looked ten years younger because of it.[8] However, just when a reunion was possible, Ian found Burroughs impossible to live with because of his obsessive interest in Scientology. "When he fixes me with that Operating Thetan stare I just can't stand it," Ian said. "I can't get out of the room fast enough."[9] As far as Ian was concerned, Burroughs was wasting his intelligence and his time on an utterly spurious organization. Burroughs claimed that he was only investigating it, but as far as Ian could see, Burroughs was well and truly hooked. If there was a time when he and Ian could have got back together, this was it, but Burroughs was too interested in clearing his engrams.

In August 1968, Ian moved to an overfurnished, overpriced flat at 55 Red Lion Street, off Red Lion Square, which he could now afford because he was working on a research project with a large computer company. Each week they did the audit of Coutts Bank, which took them only two and a half days; previously it had taken seven months. He loved working with computers and it placed him in a happier frame of mind. He used the facilities to produce several permutated poems for Brion Gysin: Brion would give him one line and Ian would have the computer print out every possible permutation of it. They did small editions of two of these. From Red Lion Square, Ian moved to a rather opulent flat filled with chintz and overstuffed furniture at 24 Ansdell Terrace, near Kensington Square. He still saw Burroughs frequently, but refused to discuss Scientology.

Bill and Ian continued to have a sporadic sexual relationship right up until the time Bill left for the United States in 1974 even when Bill had other live-in boyfriends, but Ian had no patience for Bill's interest in pseudoscience, neither Scientology nor the other fringe outfits he was ineluctably drawn to. As Bill said, "Ian is one head I can't walk on," meaning that there was a whole side to Ian that was completely inaccessible to him: Ian's whole technical side, his grasp of mathematics. As Bill saw it, people function as a whole, their every action both intellectual and emotional. If someone is a mathematician it spills over into everything, making their whole personality much harder to assess or contact if you don't have any concept of technical subjects, which is how it was with Ian. Someone like Mikey, on the other hand, was much easier to identify with and to feel what he was thinking. There was always a mystery with Ian, and this always intrigued Bill. "He was very intelligent, he had a real grasp of mathematics and physics. He was a great technician. He had certain very definite qualities. I think that potentially he was a real mathematical genius. [...] He was extraordinary, a most extraordinary person, there's no doubt about that. It's too bad that things worked out so badly."[10] Ian featured in most of Burroughs's books, including *The Place of Dead Roads*, where he is Tom.

John Berendt from *Esquire* wanted a new approach to his magazine's coverage of the 1968 Democratic Party Convention in Chicago, and instead of hiring political commentators, he commissioned Terry Southern, Jean Genet, and Burroughs to cover it for them. Bill accepted this unusual assignment in part because he very much wanted to meet Genet, one of his favorite writers. The prospect of *Esquire*'s $1,500-plus-expenses fee enabled him to first visit Tangier, where he spent time with Brion Gysin and Paul Bowles. Bowles was surprised at *Esquire*'s choice of Bill to cover the convention. He told Jane, "I suppose the point was to find the most apolitical person they could." While there, Bill wrote the text for the catalog to an exhibition of paintings by Ahmed Yacoubi that opened at the American Library on July 17: "Yacoubi is mapping timeless areas of magic and therefore his work has a special relevance in the space age since these areas are now open to exploration and we may well look to artists for orientation." Bill shared with Yacoubi the belief in hostile forces and the efficacy of curses.

It was on this trip that Burroughs encountered Brian Jones of the Rolling Stones, whom Brion Gysin and Mohamed Hamri had taken to Joujouka to record the Master Musicians. They met in the Parade bar and Bill went back to his room at the Minzah to listen to a selection of the tapes. Jones had a recording engineer with him and had recorded the performance on a pair of Uhers. It was released in 1971, after Jones's death, as *Brian Jones Presents the Pipes of Pan at Joujouka*, but only after a lot of unseemly haggling with the Rolling Stones management. Burroughs was enlisted by Derek Taylor to write sleeve notes, and to record a radio publicity shot: "Listen to this music, the primordial sounds of a 4,000 year-old rock 'n' roll band." Bill often played the cassette of this recording in his room at Dalmeny Court.

Chapter Forty-Two

Millions of young people all over the world are fed up with shallow unworthy authority running on a platform of bullshit.[1]

1. Chicago 1968

Burroughs flew to Chicago directly from London on Saturday, August 24, two days before the Democratic convention began. It was his first time in Chicago since the war. He entered the bar of the Sheraton, jet-lagged, wearing a brown suit, black shoes, and a fedora with the brim turned up all the way around. His disguise certainly prevented anyone from identifying him as a reporter; he looked like a businessman or minor bank official. Terry Southern thought the hat made him look like Buster Keaton or Edith Sitwell. He met up with John Berendt from *Esquire*, Terry Southern, and Jean Genet, along with Richard Seaver from Grove Press, who was both Burroughs's and Genet's publisher. Seaver's French wife, Jeannette, was there to translate as Genet spoke no English. They had all flown in from New York after Genet had been smuggled across the American border by French Canadian separatists; the Americans would not grant him a visa because he was a former thief, convict, and a pederast. They were refused seats in the hotel's Golliwog Room: "Ties, gentlemen!" Burroughs was the only one suitably attired and so they had to make do with the downstairs lounge. After drinks Genet wanted to see *Les Yippies*, and after dinner with Terry and John, Bill went to bed.

Next day they all went to Midway Airport to watch the arrival of Eugene McCarthy, where they joined the rest of the press on the flatbed truck reserved for reporters. Bill wore a McCarthy button and spent his time recording crowd noises on his Norelco cassette recorder. It was impossible to talk to Hubert Humphrey, and after waiting more than an hour they gave up on McCarthy, despite having received a more enthusiastic welcome from his staff. Bill and Genet got on well: "I had not met Genet before. We got on just great, he doesn't speak much English, but I never had any trouble in communicating. With most French people if you can't speak French they can't communicate, but he communicated perfectly. He just seemed to be able to understand immediately what you were getting at."

After another early night, Bill met up with Allen Ginsberg, who, though not holding press credentials, joined their party. Like Bill, he had not previously met Genet and was delighted to be with him. At a Yippie press conference in Lincoln Park on Monday morning, Genet, with Ginsberg translating, told the crowd, "First, let me say that I took a lot of Nembutals last night to forget I was in Chicago. Forgive me, I am a little groggy." He praised the Yippies and condemned the police and conventioneers, gaining a rousing cheer and a kiss from a young woman reporter. Genet hugged her, but leaned back and called to Ginsberg, "Allen, be sure to tell her I'm a homosexual!"

At lunch, back at the Sheraton, Bill explained to John Berendt what he was doing with the tape recorder: "Look, man, what you do is this: You tape about ten minutes of someone talking, then you reverse back to the beginning and go forward again, cutting in every few seconds to record bits and pieces of something else. You keep on doing this until you've made a complete hash of it all. Then you walk around with the damn thing under your jacket, playing it at low volume. It flips people out. I do it in London all the time."

That evening they attended the convention, but it was deadly dull, and after half an hour of Bill taping and Ginsberg quietly chanting a Hindu mantra they left. Everyone except Bill then headed for Lincoln Park, where three thousand Yippies were determined to defy the police and spend the night. Bill went off to the Oxford Club Bar on Clark Street and so missed the first police attacks on the unarmed demonstrators, who were tear-gassed, kicked, and clubbed indiscriminately until long after midnight. Clouds of tear gas finally flushed Bill out of the back of a truck parked on Clark Street where some hippie fans had taken him for a smoke. The next morning, the *Esquire* delegates assembled to compose public statements expressing their horror at the events of the previous night. Bill's read:

> Regarding conduct of police in clearing Lincoln Park of young people assembled there for the purpose of sleeping in violation of a municipal ordinance. The police acted like vicious guard dogs attacking everyone in sight. I do not "protest." I am not surprised. The police acted in the manner of their species. The point is, why were they not controlled by their handlers? Is there not a municipal ordinance requesting that vicious dogs be muzzled and controlled?

The dog theme was taken up by both Genet and Southern in their statements, with Genet pointing out that this was the treatment that blacks had received in America for the past 150 years. That night, several hundred members of the clergy held a service in Lincoln Park beneath a twelve-foot cross accompanied by many children. However, at 12:40 the police attacked as before, this time using street-cleaning trucks to spray the crowd with tear gas. The trucks and motorcycle cops' headlights advancing across the park through clouds of orange gas was like the invasion of aliens in a science-fiction movie. Many of the crowd, including Burroughs, Genet, and Ginsberg, retreated to the lobby of the Lincoln Hotel where Ginsberg was staying, which was filled with people coughing, tears streaming from their eyes. "The hippies are angels," said Genet. "They are too sweet, too gentle. Someday they will have to learn."

The next day, Wednesday, Chicago was virtually under martial law; the National Guard patrolled the streets with machine guns mounted on the front of their jeeps. The Hilton Hotel, where bystanders and newsmen had been beaten up indiscriminately by police, was ringed with guardsmen. Burroughs remarked to Genet, "By God, they're the scruffiest soldiers I've ever seen." To which Genet replied, "I don't know. I prefer the SS after the Second World War. They looked worse." The police tactic to prevent the Yippies from using Lincoln Park was to lob tear gas into it at regular intervals all day. The city stank of it. The pathetic circus dragged on with the inevitable conclusion of nominating Hubert Humphrey.

They had arrived as observers, but Burroughs and Genet now addressed two rallies, with Bill saying that the system was unworkable and could not be enforced: "police and the behavior of the police, nothing memorable I'm sure." Then an illegal march left from the band shell led by Burroughs, Genet, Southern, Ginsberg, and British photographer Michael Cooper. It was supposed to go for five miles, but to Bill's relief, lines of police and National Guardsmen barred their way before they got more than three hundred yards. The *Esquire* contingent escaped through the north of the park but to the south carnage ensued, transmitted live to the world, as Mayor Daley's shock troops threw tourists and pressmen through plate glass windows, beat people indiscriminately into bloody heaps, and even charged into the Hilton Hotel to beat delegates and reporters there. Jean Genet was charged by police as he tried to get to his car and he ran into an apartment building and knocked on a door at random. "Who's there?" the occupant asked. "C'est Monsieur Genet!" he replied. By a remarkable coincidence, the door was that of somebody who was writing a thesis on Genet. Ed Sanders was delighted to see Bill on the streets: "he was out there on that night with the teargas. So Scientology hasn't thwarted his social sense anyway."

Thursday was spent recovering and they all flew back to New York on

Friday at 9:30 a.m. *Esquire* had booked both Burroughs and Genet into the Delmonico for a week to write their stories, and wondered just what they were getting when Bill cryptically asked them to supply research material on purple-assed baboons. For a cover photo shoot they posed a male model lying down, as if clubbed by police, with Burroughs, Southern, and Genet standing around. Genet made a scene with the editor, objecting that he was a "faux mort," and demanded more money. At this the editor Harold Hayes called him a thief, and Genet replied, "Naturellement. Je suis un voleur." To Burroughs the best thing about the trip was getting to know Genet: "One of the greatest, most sincere people, and there he was, bamn, Genet!" In Burroughs's opinion the two twentieth-century writers destined to last were Beckett and Genet. "I thought he was a great person. Incredible person. I never saw him again." Ginsberg was also impressed. He wrote to British MP Tom Driberg, "I wandered around with Jean Genet. Wound up necking in bed with him—and Wm Burroughs, all week listening to them and teargassed thrice in their company."

It was at the Delmonico that Burroughs saw Jack Kerouac for the last time. There had been no contact between them for a decade. Now Kerouac was in New York overnight to appear on the September 3, 1968, edition of *Firing Line*, William F. Buckley's television show, chaperoned by a pair of his Greek brothers-in-law. Kerouac was drinking heavily, slurring his words, and was clearly in no shape to appear on the show. He wanted Burroughs to accompany him to the TV studio, but Bill had no intention of watching Buckley make a fool of Kerouac, telling him, "Jack, don't go! You're in no condition. You're drunk out of your mind." It was a disaster. Kerouac tried to ingratiate himself with Buckley by telling him how he, his sister, and mother had voted Republican all their lives. He stumbled over words and interrupted the other speakers. He insulted Lewis Yablonsky, made several vicious remarks about Ginsberg, who did accompany him to the show and was in the audience, and tried to belittle Ed Sanders. The producer of the show finally called Jack a drunken moron and ordered him off the set. Burroughs wasn't surprised at the outcome; Jack had always been heading in that direction. When Lou Reed asked Burroughs why Kerouac had finished up in such bad shape, Bill said he hadn't changed much. "He was always like that. First there was a young guy sitting in front of television in a tee-shirt drinking beer with his mother, then there was an older fatter person sitting in front of television in a tee-shirt drinking beer with his mother."[2]

After he filed his story, Burroughs stayed on in New York, first at the Chelsea Hotel, where he was pestered by the residents, then at Terry

Southern's triplex apartment at 163 East 36th Street for two weeks, flat-sitting while Terry was away filming. Bill loved the color television and enjoyed the security of a loaded Luger in a drawer in his bed table. He spent his time investigating the 42nd Street sex shops and was delighted by the availability of gay peep shows, the photographs of boys with hard-ons, and battery-powered vibrators: "the complete breakdown of censorship," he told Brion.[3] He said he was on his way back to London to liquidate the apartment.

He had another reason for returning: Antony Balch had written offering five hundred dollars plus airfare for two days' work reading a voice-over to a 1922 silent movie by Benjamin Christensen called *Häxen*, now retitled *Witchcraft Through the Ages*. Burroughs flew back in early October and recorded his commentary on October 11. There was plenty of opportunity for Bill to ad-lib, and some of his commentary is typically Burrovian. In the scene where Maria the Weaver is interrogated by two of the witchfinders, Burroughs comments, "Here we see an example of 'good cop/bad cop,' which is still being practiced in police stations all over the world."[4] New York film critics like Jonas Mekas screamed with rage at the idea of tampering with the original, but most people thought the film held together better with Burroughs's commentary. The eventual DVD release had both versions.

2. Back in Blighty

Bill did not close up the apartment. He told Brion, "I have given up the idea of moving to the States. This apartment is so quiet and conducive to work for one thing and I seem to be able to get twice as much done here."[5] There was also another reason: "new boy fantastic sex who is a cook. Name John Lee."[6] His accountant, Michael Henshaw, had also pointed out the tax advantages of residing outside the United States. By October, he was deeply into *The Wild Boys*. Ian was doing well as a computer programmer and was in excellent spirits; Alan Watson was back from Monte Carlo and decided to return to Darlington and run the family business; Antony Balch and Bill still spent their time running Scientology routines. Bill still believed implicitly in the efficacy of the E-meter. He told Dr. Joe Gross, "It is amazingly accurate in gauging mental reactions,"[7] and wondered how the needle action on the E-meter corresponded to encephalographic action. He thought the "floating needle" might represent alpha waves. A month later he was still content, the apartment was quiet and comfortable, he had a "superlative English boy friend," and he was turning out a "phenomenal" amount of work. He finished his book of essays, then called *Academy 23* but published as *The Job*, and *The Wild Boys* was going well. He told Brion, "The essay book is quite outspoken and uncompromising on the women question. (What do you think about women? They are a perfect curse.) The wild boy book is even more anti-female by total omission. The wild boys have nothing to do with women or junk."[8]

August 1969 was a busy month. On the eighth and ninth Burroughs was a delegate at the International Literary Conference of the Harrogate Festival of Arts and Sciences alongside Brian Aldiss, Michael Moorcock, Jeff Nuttall, B. S. Johnson, Nigel Calder, Chris Evans, and others. J. G. Ballard unfortunately pulled out, but there were plenty of like minds to spend the days and evenings with.

That same month Bill wrote to John Hopkins in Tangier accusing him of having damaged Brion's literary career due to the freak motorcycling accident they had in the countryside outside Tangier in which Brion lost a toe to a glancing blow from a passing truck. Bill suggested that John should pay a substantial amount of damages, saying Brion's means of livelihood had been removed. Ingeniously Bill claimed that Brion was a "peripatetic" writer and needed to get up and walk around in order for the ideas to come. He was now incapable of walking, and therefore of writing. Who knows what fantasies Brion had written to Bill. However, it turned out that Morocco, surprisingly, had a formal list of compensation for injuries, ranging from a million dollars for loss of both arms and legs right down to the loss of a middle toe: 7,500 dirhams, or $1,500. This Brion accepted (Hopkins had already paid his medical fees). After days of red-faced raging by Brion, attempts to pummel Hopkins with his crutches in an elevator, and late-night hysterical phone calls, their friendship was able to resume. Afterward Brion blamed Princess Martha Ruspoli for putting the evil eye on him.

On August 17, after a flurry of intensive work, Burroughs completed work on *The Wild Boys* and handed in the manuscript. There was a huge amount of wild boys material. In addition to the book itself, it overflowed into *The Revised Boy Scout Manual*, later published in *RE/Search* magazine; an illustrated book with Malcolm McNeill called *Ah Puch Is Here* (published as *Ah Pook Is Here* without its illustrations); and *Port of Saints*, which is really *Wild Boys II*, which Burroughs published in the original and in a revised edition. He often said that the first section of *The Wild Boys* should not have been included as it had no relation to the rest of the book, and it should be combined with *Port of Saints* to make a true *Wild Boy* book. He went to New York in September to work with his editors, staying at the Chelsea Hotel, but was back in London by October 12. He explained how he approached the book: "In the Wild Boys I was really quite deliberately returning to older styles of writing. Quite a bit of it is really 19th century. I used cut-ups but very sparingly. There are literary situations where they are useful, and others where they are not. Now, in recreating a delirium, they're very good because that is what is happening. In high fever the images cut in quite arbitrarily. So I used that in the dream section where the Boy is dying in the jungle."[9] The book stands by itself; there is no carryover of characters from previous books. "It's all simply a personal projection. A prediction? I hope so. Would I consider events similar to the Wild Boys scenario desirable? Yes, desirable to me."[10] He recognized it as fantasy. "The Wild Boys was pretty removed from any sequences occurring in reality. It was more like a children's story. Peter Pan or something like that."[11]

During the two-year period he worked on *The Wild Boys*, Burroughs made a number of scrapbook layouts relative to the book, selecting pictures from magazines and newspapers of boys who could play wild boy roles, also including photographs of boys he knew who appeared as characters in the book. His characters were composites of old boyfriends, friends, and projections of boys known only from photographs and books: "Your own photos or photos in newspapers and magazines may suggest a narrative. I got the 'Frisco Kid' section in The Wild Boys from an 1882 photo which has been lost of Front Street Nome Alaska. And of course various models can represent the same character. Audrey, Kiki, Ali, Jerry, Pinkie, Ginger, Old Sarge are composites of dreams, photos, films...pieces of an old movie."

Burroughs had originally planned a book called *Academy 23*, intended to combine the wild boy material with the more technical subjects he had been writing about in the Burroughs Academy. His idea had been to include his voluminous writing on cut-ups, and other literary techniques. It soon became obvious that the material was too disparate to put into one book. Burroughs had considered linking it by using some of the interview material produced by French literary journalist Daniel Odier, who was preparing a book of interviews with Burroughs for Editions Pierre Belfond in Paris. The two of them discussed the idea in the spring of 1968, but the sheer volume of wild boys material caused Burroughs to abandon this plan. Odier's book appeared as *Entretiens avec William Burroughs* in January 1969, and after parts of it were published in *Evergreen Review* it became obvious that the book should be issued in English. Burroughs revised the text of the interviews, adding some new material and occasionally illustrating his answers with quotes from his texts. Sometimes he had already answered the questions in his books and so he inserted the already published material in place of his original reply. Burroughs: "The result is interview form presented as a film with fade-outs and flash-back illustrating the answers." He called the book *The Job*, published in 1970.

"I've written an actual treatise on revolutionary tactics and weapons. That is, a treatise on the actual methods and various revolutionary techniques. A great deal of revolutionary tactics I see now are really nineteenth century tactics. People think in terms of small arms and barricades, in terms of bombing police stations and post offices like the IRA of 1916. What I'm talking about in The Job is bringing the revolution into the 20th century which includes, above all, the use of mass media. That's where the real battle will be fought.

"The last frontier is being closed to youth. However there are many roads to space. To achieve complete freedom from past conditioning is to be in space. Techniques exist for achieving such freedom. These techniques are being concealed and withheld. In The Job I consider techniques of discovery."[12] Subjects discussed varied from details of the work and persecution of Wilhelm Reich, a very laudatory survey of Scientology, a description of the Mayan Control Calendar, the 7-hertz killer whistle, capital punishment, censorship, and the vested interests of power and money. As usual, Burroughs revised the book after publication to bring it up to date, so the 1973 paperback edition included several new texts, including "Playback from Eden to Watergate."

Virtually all of Burroughs's theoretical texts were included and it is the best guide possible to Burroughs's books and his ideas, his investigation of systems of control, and the development of methods of resisting and breaking control systems. For him it was quite straightforward: "The control machine is simply the machinery—police, education, etc.—used by a group in power to keep itself in power and extend its power." As a writer he was particularly concerned about his own chosen tool. He wrote, "My basic theory is that the written word was actually a virus that made the spoken word possible. The word has not been recognized as a virus because it has achieved a state of stable symbiosis with the host, though this symbiotic relationship is now breaking down. [...] Is the virus then simply a time bomb left on this planet to be activated by remote control? An extermination program in fact? In its path from full virulence to its ultimate goal of symbiosis, will any human creature survive? Taking the virus-eye view, the ideal situation would appear to be one in which the virus replicates in cells without in any way disturbing their normal metabolism. This has been suggested as the ideal biological situation toward which all viruses are slowly evolving."

For one year Burroughs even exempted himself from the Western calendar, an obvious control system accepted unthinkingly by everyone. He created his own, which rather resembled that imposed during the French Revolution. The Dream Calendar, as he called it, was started on December 23, 1969, and each month consisted of twenty-three days, based on the Mayan calendar system. There were supposed to be ten months in his year, but the system began with only eight separate months, and they came around in a slightly different order the second time, with a new month, Wiener Wald, added. Burroughs used the system for a year, dating all manuscripts and letters that way. Unfortunately, the days somehow got miscounted in several of the months, making the dating of letters from that period a little difficult since the Dream Calendar date is sometimes as much as five days off.

Burroughs called the months Terre Haute, Marie Celeste, Bellevue, Seal Point, Harbor Beach, Niño Perdido, Sweet Meadows, and Land's End. Wiener Wald was added after Seal Point on the second pass. Knowing the starting date enables one to calculate any Burroughs date against the regular calendar. For instance Bellevue 3 would be January 19, 1970. Burroughs: "The starting date used is December 23, 1969 which is Terre Haute 23 in this calendar. Calculations from this date can be made into the past or the future. We could for example calculate on what date Terre Haute 23 fell on 77,000,000,000 years ago...nodding listlessly in doorways on a mild gray day they died of an overdose of time." Books from the period, such as *Port of Saints*, sometimes refer to the calendar but without an explanation to the reader. Only in the subsequent collection of short stories, *Exterminator!*, is there an explanation of the system, as created by one of Burroughs's many multiple personalities:

"The Colonel decides to make his own time. He opens a school notebook and constructs a simple calendar consisting of ten months with 26 days in each month to begin on this day February 21, 1970, Raton Pass 14 in the new calendar. The months have names like old Pullman cars in America where the Colonel had lived until his 18th year." Needless to say, Raton Pass is not one of the months used in Burroughs's own dream calendars, which in any case had twenty-three–day months.[13]

By now Bill had found a safe way of using pot without fear of being busted. His London physician, Dr. Dunbar, began prescribing tincture of cannabis in mid-1969. He prescribed it to regular patients as a treatment for paranoia: pot was illegal so users felt paranoid. By prescribing pot, the paranoia was cured. The cannabis cost one pound five shillings and came in a bright green alcohol solution. A bottle lasted a week ("Or maybe less," as Bill's later boyfriend John Brady once commented). Bill used to soak his Senior Service cigarettes in the liquid, convinced that no one in restaurants or bars would notice that he was smoking a bright green cigarette that smelled somewhat different from ordinary ones.

In September, Burroughs made another trip to New York to do the rewrite on the screenplay of *The Last Words of Dutch Schultz*. He was put up in a superb apartment owned by Harrison Starr on West 11th Street in the Village with a living room, bedroom, kitchenette, and a separate study. Bill mused, "Jesus, wouldn't I rather have that apartment and be living here instead of being in London? Anytime I go out day and night there's a place to eat, the food is good." He began to wonder, "What the hell am I doing in London?" Nothing came of the film, but Cape Goliard published the screenplay in London the next year. Even film scripts were subjected to Burroughs's new literary techniques: "Now this is perfectly straight writing. Nonetheless, I cut up every page and suddenly got a lot of new ideas that were then incorporated into the structure of the narrative. This is perfectly straight film treatment, quite intelligible to the average reader, in no sense experimental writing."[14]

Back in London, on the early evening of October 21, 1969, some friends of John Cooke's, who was then living in Cuernavaca, came to visit, but as Bill poured drinks and played the host he was conscious of a great depression growing on him. He felt terrible, what he described as "a terrible fear of death." Suddenly there was a loud bang, which later turned out to be the sound of a shotgun. A rejected suitor had shot his girlfriend in a bank just off nearby St. James's Square, but it was not her death that he had an intimation of. He later learned that Kerouac had died in Florida on that day, at the same time (11:00 a.m. Florida time). "Listen, it's better to see a little forward than not. That's the way it goes."

Chapter Forty-Three

The novel is a nineteenth century form. The plot, the beginning, the middle and the end, this is quite as arbitrary as the formula of the sonnet. We're getting away from it now.[1]

1. Enter the Seventies

The next live-in boyfriend, after John Lee, was John Culverwell, a Dilly boy from Piccadilly Circus. It was the usual story: at first he was industrious, cleaning everything, helping with the cooking, great sex. Bill bought him clothes and took him to Tangier in the summer of 1970, where he was exactly the type of boy that the English colony would expect someone to bring down to Tangier, so he fit right in. Edouard Roditi was there, someone whose humor Bill had always appreciated, so they had a very enjoyable visit. Back in Britain, Bill paid for Culverwell to enter the merchant marine, and he made one trip, but then decided he wanted to do something else. Then the quality of cooking—never good—began to fall off. He began to invite his friends over and to ask for more money. Bill's principle of cleaning was to always clean something or straighten something up every time he entered a room. When John Culverwell entered a room he made another mess. Bill knew it would be like this, that things would slack off. These boys were used to making five or six pounds a night and having an easy life with plenty of drinks and a certain level of luxury, just for putting out sexually. It was a lot easier to find someone to keep them than working in the merchant marine or in a regular job, which paid far less money. The sex became more and more unsatisfactory. It lasted eighteen months, then John moved out.

Bill kept up his connections with the underground press, and on July 24–26, 1970, he attended the sci-fi conference at Phun City, organized by Mick Farren from *International Times* at Ecclesden Common, Patching, near Worthing, West Sussex. Mick Farren wrote, "William Burroughs stalked the night in his FBI man's hat and raincoat, requiring hippies to talk into his portable tape machine while he baffled them with instant cut-ups."[2] Also at the conference were Alex Trocchi and J. G. Ballard, but the inflatable domes in which the conference was supposed to be held never inflated.

Bill's mother, Laura Lee Burroughs, died on October 21, 1970, at the age of eighty-two. When Burroughs opened the telegram from Mort he read it and thought, "Oh Mother's dead," and set it aside. He walked into the other room and the realization hit him. He stood and stared at himself in the mirror and his reaction was like a kick in the stomach. "I can't describe the incredible grief I experienced, it's horrible, it's nothing you would experience if you can avoid it. I just collapsed completely, just sobbed."[3] He lay on the bed for hours, until finally he had to say, "I can't stand it any more. I can't can't. I can't." He wrote, "I still, after years, I still cry to think about her death. And I NEVER WENT TO SEE HER!"[4]

A great rush of emotion overwhelmed him. In earlier days they had always been close and he felt tremendous guilt at not having visited her at the nursing home in the last four years of her life; he just sent mawkish greeting cards to her at Christmas, and the occasional postcard. During the war she had once asked him, "Suppose I was very sick. Would you come to see me? Look after me? Care for me? I'm counting on that being true."[5] It wasn't. She had remained loyal to him throughout, and on one of his earlier visits had told him, "I worship the ground you walk on. Inside, we're the same person." He had not known how to respond; he was a grown man, and only now that she was dead did he understand the connection she was talking about. Bill had always thought that the Freudian mother-and-son relationship had been sorted out years ago. He recognized that Paul Bowles was always trying to get out from under his mother and father but thought that was not the case for himself. He thought that the blame for any early traumas rested with the servants, not with his parents. "These were inflicted by criminal servants." Reflecting on Laura Lee after her death, Burroughs now saw her as "a very charming woman and a very beautiful woman. Physically and in every way a beautiful person. She was warm and affectionate. She was a very great person."[6] He wrote to Billy Jr., "It makes me very sad to think how many years they worked and sent money and how little they ever got in return. They were extraordinarily kind, gentle, and well-intentioned people and that is something very rare now."[7] With his mother's death, Burroughs received his last bequest from the Burroughs estate, $10,000, hardly the trust fund written into existence by Kerouac.[8]

On February 14, 1970, in the federal district courthouse in Chicago, Judge Julius Hoffman sentenced the seven defendants and two defense lawyers in the Chicago Conspiracy Trial to a total of fifteen years and five days' imprisonment for contempt of court. This farcical case was the result of an attempt to show that Jerry Rubin, Abbie Hoffman, and other members of the Youth International Party (Yippies) had conspired together to disrupt the Democratic Party Convention held in Chicago in 1968—the one Burroughs attended on behalf of *Esquire* magazine. Using the court transcripts, John Burgess and Charles Marowitz wrote a play, *The Chicago Conspiracy*, to be performed at the Open Space Theatre on Tottenham Court Road. Charles Marowitz wrote, "In the role of the petulant Judge Julius Hoffman, I cast William S. Burroughs, who had been a libertarian as long as he had been a drug addict. Burroughs was an excellent cast member who approached the entire project with a diligent austerity. He was an eerie and imperturbable presence throughout rehearsals and I found the actor-defendants as intimidated by him as if he had been the icy-hearted presiding judge himself, but in his case it was the literary reputation that was so awesome. In fact, Burroughs was gentle and unassuming; he submerged the character with a dry wit which was simultaneously spooky and hilarious."[9]

The cast were mostly expatriate Americans who had fallen foul of the American authorities and were now living and working in London. Among them were screenwriter Carl Foreman (*The Guns of Navarone* etc.); virtuoso harmonica player Larry Adler; playwright Donald Ogden Stewart (*The Philadelphia Story*); and stage, screen, and TV writer Larry Gelbart (*M*A*S*H* etc.).

As the audience filed in for the one-night performance, they were brusquely frisked by actors dressed as American cops. Every indication of contempt for the proceedings or support for the defendants was firmly gaveled down by the judge. *New York Times* theater critic Irving Wardle reported, "One could not ask for better casting than William Burroughs. [...] However remote his resemblance to the judge, the author of 'Naked Lunch' occupied the bench with a most chilling authority; immovable and expressionless, as though a smile might tear his parchment features, occasionally favoring the more obstreperous speakers with a mild gaze from his dead pale eyes before dropping on the offenders like a ton of bricks. Perhaps it was not like that at the time, but it felt true in the theatre."[10]

Burroughs was so good in his role that he was asked to act again six months later, this time by David Zane Mairowitz, another American playwright living in London. This time Bill moved up from playing a

judge to becoming the president of the United States in a play called
Flash Gordon and the Angels, which opened at the Open Space Theatre
in January 1971.[11] Bill only appears on a monitor, first in a congratulatory public speech to the astronaut, written for public consumption, then
in a nasty private communication telling the astronaut that the mission
is terminated, and so is he. Before filming, Bill explained to Mairowitz
that in order to get into character and truly *be* the "Ugly American" he
had to drink a serious amount of whiskey. Mairowitz was worried that
Bill would become incoherent,[12] but his slurring, vituperative speech was
loved by the critics.

2. The Rolling Stones

It had always been Antony Balch's dream to make a film of *Naked Lunch,*
and in 1964 they had filmed various sequences of Burroughs acting out
scenes from the book (some of which were later included in *The Cut-
Ups).* The project was revived in 1970 by Brion Gysin, who thought they
could raise enough money to make it themselves. Friendly Films Limited
was set up, with offices at 8 Duke Street Saint James's and Bill, Brion,
and Antony as directors. Brion wrote a treatment that put Burroughs in a
difficult position because he didn't like it at all. Brion had reverted to his
old days with John LaTouche in wartime New York and turned *Naked
Lunch* into a Broadway musical. Burroughs: "The script was terrible.
Completely terrible. 'I'm the choicest baboon...'" Antony Balch spent a
great deal of time and energy drawing the storyboards in colored marker
pens, showing every scene and camera move, in four huge fourteen-by-
twelve-inch volumes while Brion used his contacts to raise money and
interest the stars. Ruth Ford was taken to La Capannina and asked to
play the part of Pantopon Rose. From the way Brion talked, Mick Jagger
was virtually signed up for the lead. Brion insisted on taking Bill clothes
shopping in Jermyn Street, buying him flared trousers and new shoes to
look suitably up-to-date and modern. Jagger was interested, but the meeting in May 1971 was a disaster and he never even read the script. Jagger
wanted a name director, whereas Burroughs and Gysin were committed to Antony directing. Then Antony apparently made an inappropriate
remark concerning the snug fit of Jagger's trousers and Jagger's interest
evaporated. Burroughs recalled, "Mick Jagger was asked to play Lee and
he hated Antony on sight."[13] A decade later, Bianca Jagger told Victor
Bockris, "When Mick and I visited Burroughs at his flat in London to discuss filming Naked Lunch with Antony Balch, he had on these pants for a
man forty years younger that were much too tight, and high heeled boots.

He seemed very uncomfortable and was difficult to talk to."[14] As Bill later put it, "Naked Lunch died slow and hard alienating VIPs on every side."

Brion flew to Venice, to Hollywood, to New York, back and forth to Paris. He had a promise of $3 million, everything was all set, then the next day he couldn't get past the secretary. Virginia Long, the widow of right-wing Texan oilman Clint Murchison, said she would back the film if James Taylor played the lead. Taylor didn't want to; "that was a very strained encounter," Burroughs recalled.[15] Brion spent between $20,000 and $30,000—money he could have done with at the time—fruitlessly running around, making self-important phone calls, while all the time Burroughs was secretly hoping that nothing would come of it because the script was so appalling. Burroughs remembered, "Throughout I knew that it wasn't going to work out just like I knew the Dreamachine wouldn't work. [...] It wasn't a valid concept to begin with. Naked Lunch just isn't a film."

Nonetheless, Bill responded when Hollywood expressed an interest. In 1971 he and Terry Southern were sent first-class tickets to Los Angeles by Chuck Barris, the television game show producer—*The Dating Game, The Newlywed Game*—who wanted to see the *Naked Lunch* script. A Daimler met them at the airport to take them straight to meet Barris at a restaurant called the Coconut. Barris was there with his secretary, Miss Keister. They gave him the script and he said he would get in touch the next day. The Daimler took them to the Hyatt on Sunset Boulevard. The next day there was no word from Barris, but the day after, his office called to invite them to dinner at Barris's place in Malibu to discuss the script. The Daimler had shrunk to a two-seater. After Bill had been seated uncomfortably on Southern's lap for an hour, the driver deposited them in front of an unlighted house with a snicker and drove off. Terry couldn't believe that Barris would stand them up like that, but Bill told him, "Terry, when your Daimler shrinks down to a two-seater, it is time to move on fast before they renege on paying our hotel tab."[16] Fortunately Terry knew people in Malibu, and a neighbor gave them cheese and snacks. They called a cab to return to their hotel, where they found that Bill's warning had been prescient: a note had been put on their account to say that Barris assumed no responsibility for the bar or restaurant charges. The next morning they took a cab to the airport.

All through the early seventies Burroughs spent a great deal of time trying to sell a film script of *The Last Words of Dutch Schultz* to Hollywood as well as halfheartedly attempting to get the *Naked Lunch* film project off the ground, but all to no avail. Burroughs hated the whole celebrity business, even though it was only just beginning. He remained on the periphery of "swinging London" largely by resisting efforts by the principals to involve him and bring him more to center stage, though he attended such events as the premiere of Nick Roeg's *Performance* in August 1970, in which he received a name-check, as did *The Soft Machine* and Hassan-i-Sabbah. He went to the premiere of Andy Warhol's *Pork* in August 1971, Warhol's *Trash* in November 1971, and the premiere of *A Clockwork Orange* in January 1972. One example of his aversion to celebrity life was the farewell concert given by the Rolling Stones at the Marquee Club in London on March 26, 1971, before their move to the south of France to avoid British taxation. Burroughs was invited and went along because they were still hoping to involve Jagger in the film script of *Naked Lunch*, but he left early because he wanted to avoid the rush. He later heard he had offended the band: "That's it, I never paid court. I don't like their music. I don't like rock 'n' roll at all!"[17] Bill also attended their farewell party on March 30, held at a hotel in Maidenhead, Berkshire, along with John and Yoko, Eric Clapton, and members of the Who. Bill: "I have never mastered the art of talking to people in the bedlam of a noisy party. Some people can do it, they get their voices right through all that stuff, and I remember Keith Richards talking to me and I couldn't understand one word he said! Not a word. It wasn't my thing. I didn't have a good time at all. I don't like parties. I hate parties."[18] Richards was probably trying to talk to Bill about the apomorphine cure he had just taken with Smitty. Richards: "I once took that apomorphine cure that Burroughs swears by. Dr. Dent was dead, but his assistant whom he trained, this lovely old dear called Smitty, who's like mother hen, still runs the clinic. I had her down to my place for five days, and she just sort of comes in and says, *Here's your shot, dear, there's a good boy*, or *You've been a naughty boy, you've taken something, yes you have, I can tell*. But it's a pretty medieval cure. You just vomit all the time."[19]

The Stones made another gesture and Bill was invited to Mick Jagger's wedding to Bianca in Saint-Tropez on May 12, 1971, but to Bill the idea of flying to the south of France in a private jet full of "beautiful people" was the last thing he wanted to get involved with. He explained to Jagger's staff, "It isn't my scene. I'm not gregarious, I don't want to be involved in a massive thing like that," but Jagger was offended.

Despite all this, Bill's tenuous connection with the Stones continued, and the next year he was asked by *Playboy* to cover the Stones' 1972 American tour. Brion had arranged it, to Bill's irritation because he was just beginning work on describing his archives and could not leave London, certainly not for $1,500 plus expenses. Brion was quite insistent that he should go, but Bill was adamant. Then Brion suddenly realized that he would make money when the archives were sold, as he and Bill were splitting the money fifty-fifty because the archives also included Brion's extensive correspondence with Alice B. Toklas and Paul Bowles. He now told Bill, "You can't leave now." Bill complained, "So he got me into it and then turned right around. I didn't want to cover their tour in the first place."[20] The editor from *Playboy* told Bill, "There are a lot of people going to be disappointed by this decision, not least the Stones." But as Bill said, "What the hell, I was doing something a whole lot more important to me."[21] Terry Southern covered the tour in his stead, which turned into a disaster, with Terry even getting into a physical fight with the Stones' manager.

Though he eschewed the celebrity end of the London scene, Bill still had a number of friends and acquaintances whom he saw on a regular basis; as well as Ian, Brion, and Antony, Professor Eric Mottram of King's College, London, would come for drinks and dinner. His 1971 book *The Algebra of Need*[22] was one of the first studies on Burroughs's work. Burroughs watched Charles de Gaulle's funeral on November 11, 1970, at the house on Park Square East of his accountant, Michael Henshaw, who enjoyed a drink every bit as much as Bill. Early in that year he began seeing a lot of his French translators, Claude Pélieu and Mary Beach, who had moved to London from the Chelsea Hotel and were subletting Barry Miles's house at 15 Lord North Street in Westminster. Bill became a frequent dinner guest; he could walk there across St. James's Park, and soon got to know Graham Keen, who rented another floor in the house. Graham, who was the designer and one of the directors of *International Times*, was planning to publish *Cyclops*, "The first English adult Comic Paper"—by which he meant a comic for adults, not pornography—and asked Burroughs if he would like to contribute a text for an illustrator to work with. Bill said he had a story, "The Unspeakable Mr. Hart," that he thought would translate suitably into comic art form. Graham Keen selected Malcolm McNeill, a final-year student at Hornsey College of Art, to do the artwork. Malcolm McNeill explained, "I was simply handed a half page of text every month and left to try and figure out what the heck it meant. Even though I had no idea what Bill looked like, the character I came up with for Hart looked remarkably like him." The first issue appeared, published from Lord North Street, in July 1970, and ran for three more monthly issues before folding for financial reasons. "The Unspeakable Mr. Hart" took up the center spread in all four issues and was regarded by Burroughs as a great success. He wanted to continue working with McNeill, whom he had not met, and Graham Keen put them in touch. They worked together on projects for many years, in particular *Ah Pook Is Here*, which was unfortunately published without McNeill's illustrations ("too expensive to produce"), but with Burroughs's permission, by John Calder and Viking Press in 1976.

Another project from this period, 1971, was a book on homosexuality. For some years Burroughs had been collecting tear sheets of articles in *Time*, *Newsweek*, *Playboy*, and others on the subject, and when Aldus Books approached him with an offer to write a book on homosexuality he gave the idea careful consideration. He wrote a six-page outline, giving his views on the subject, but unfortunately Aldus appears to have dropped the idea.

Throughout his time in London Burroughs ate most of his evening meals out. He liked the Scandia Room on the top floor of the Piccadilly Hotel, which was always empty, as was the Icelandic Steakhouse on Haymarket, which was so bereft of customers that Bill thought it must be a front for organized crime. He often ate at La Capannina on Romilly Street in Soho, usually with Antony Balch, who went out with several of the waiters. There were bells hanging from the mock rafters that the waiters rang whenever Bill and Tony walked in, much to Bill's embarrassment. Another favorite was Lee Ho Fook in Chinatown, where he was often the only westerner present. Bill and Antony dined together several times a week, but if he was alone, Burroughs sometimes treated himself to caviar at nearby Prunier on St. James's Street. Caviar was one of his great loves, though normally he was reduced to eating lumpfish roe. "Now son, when a man gets on the Beluga Caviar, well, there's nothing he won't do to satisfy the Caviar hunger eating at his bread-basket. He'll lie, he'll cheat, he'll even kill for a gob of it."[23]

Burroughs was invited to teach a course at the University of the New World by Al de Gracia, brother of Ed de Gracia, the lawyer who defended *Naked Lunch* in the Boston trial. It was based in Haute Nendaz, a ski resort in Valais, Switzerland. However, by the time Bill got there in October 1971, Al de Gracia had already left the country, with the Swiss authorities accusing him of misleading advertising. The ads claimed there was a proper campus, whereas the actual University of the New World was a small shed. The students were housed in various rooms around town. Bill was put up at the Hotel Montcalme; the season had not yet started and he was the only guest. Bill approved of the idea, which was a modern version of the Black Mountain College, and taught a couple of classes. The university issued its own money, called "cows," which the townspeople, sensibly, would not accept. Bill was paid in cows so he made nothing out of the trip, but he did have free board and travel for a month. The hotel had "the best coffee ever," and he enjoyed the macrobiotic restaurant because it enabled him to avoid fondues, which, as he told Brion, "is a horrible Swiss thing."[24]

But he came down with a debilitating case of flu. He had a terrible headache and was almost delirious by the late afternoon. To his delight, codeine, under the name Codisan, was freely available in pharmacies. They were only two dollars for sixty, with one-twelfth grain in each pill. He bought a large batch and holed up in his hotel. He took twenty to thirty a day and after three weeks he had developed a habit. He would take ten in the morning and spend the day reading science fiction. It was here he read *Dune* by Frank Herbert. "I had kind of a nice time there." Here Bill got to know one of the students, John de Chadenedes, whom he also saw later in London. John was good at sewing and made his own clothes and told Bill a lot about Buddhism.

Burroughs used the opportunity to go and visit Timothy Leary, who was living in Carona, in the Ticino region of southern Switzerland, about seventy miles away. In September 1970 he had escaped from jail in America, where he was serving a ten-year sentence for two roaches of marijuana. He had gone first to Algeria, where he stayed with Eldridge Cleaver's "government in exile," but then Cleaver tried to hold Leary and his wife hostage. Bill thought he was lucky to escape with his life. In 1971 Leary arrived in Switzerland; the Nixon administration failed to extradite him, but managed to persuade the authorities to hold him in custody. They did so for a month, giving him a luxurious, comfortable room of his own and wine with his meals, then let him go. When Bill saw him he had broken up with his wife and was living in a motel with a variety of different women while the Swiss authorities decided what to do with him. Bill enjoyed the visit, all past animosities forgotten. "We had a nice talk and all that."

⌒

Burroughs's fascination with Scientology continued, despite his misgivings about Hubbard's attempts to run it as a religious cult, and in November 1971 he booked himself into an advanced course in Edinburgh. John Calder found him lodgings. He was looking for engrams in his past lives and told a friend, "I looked into my past, my God, I went back 77,000 years! [laughing] It was a funny feeling, time washing through me, whoosh, whoosh...I was experiencing something, that's all I can say. Reincarnation? Whether it's a past life, or something in your brain, what does it matter?"[25] Back in London he began working with John McMaster, the first ever "Clear," the man who set up the Church of Scientology with Hubbard and the inventor of much of the Scientology technology. McMaster was a soft-spoken, slim, gay, white-haired South African who presented himself as the victim of a power struggle with his former friend and told Burroughs that the Sea Org (Hubbard's actual command post, based on a yacht off Casablanca) were out to get him. He claimed to have been thrown out of his bed by massive psychic forces entering his bedroom and showed Burroughs his bruises as proof. "If only I had been there with my karate!" Bill exclaimed. With McMaster as a teacher, Burroughs spent hundreds of hours self-auditing with his E-meter.

It was now that he got hold of a copy of *Excalibur.* According to Hubbard four of the first fifteen people who read it went insane because the material was so powerful. After that Hubbard only sold copies to people who had reached the highest levels and could deal with this fast formula for clearing. Each copy was specially typed for the recipient, bound in gold with a lock, and signed by Hubbard. It sold at $1,500 a copy.[26] Bill made a dozen photocopies and sent them out to people like Allen Ginsberg and the author of this book, who read it with no apparent ill effect. Burroughs finally began to feel skeptical about the Scientology techniques and beliefs during a dinner at the Cucaracha Mexican restaurant on Greek Street in Soho with McMaster. Toward the end of the meal Burroughs gave the guitarist a pound to sing the usually banned verse of "La Cucaracha" that is about marijuana smoking. Burroughs sang along in a cracked tenor. McMaster, who like Bill had drunk a considerable amount, leaned over and told Bill conspiratorially, "Bill, did I ever tell you that in a past incarnation I was Rudolph Valentino?"[27] Burroughs pursed his lips and murmured, "Really, John? Most interesting." Bill's respect for McMaster began fading away. It was now that he finally gave up and turned against the organization. He was more than disillusioned, he was indignant: Hubbard was a gangster, it was a great racket, but Bill's friends like Paul Bowles wondered, why didn't he see that at the start?

Burroughs used one of his new weapons in his retribution. Ever since the Chicago convention he had been interested in the idea of cut-ups as a way of altering consciousness and subverting the time-space continuum by recording situations on the street and taking photographs and then playing them back in situ, "tampering with actual reality" and leading, as he put it to "accidents, fires or removals." He mounted an attack on Scientology's London headquarters at 37 Fitzroy Street in Bloomsbury. Over a period of some weeks he haunted the premises, taking photographs and making tape recordings. Sure enough, after a couple of months, the Scientologists packed their bags and moved to 68 Tottenham Court Road (though it must be said that subsequent attempts failed to move them from their new quarters, which they still occupy at the time of writing).

Encouraged by his success, Burroughs selected a new target, the Moka

Bar at 29 Frith Street in Soho, London's first ever espresso bar, which had been opened by the actress Gina Lollobrigida in 1953. Here Bill had been the victim of "outrageous and unprovoked discourtesy and poisonous cheesecake." Burroughs began the operation on August 3, 1972, making no secret of his activities. "They are seething in here," he reported. "The horrible old proprietor, his frizzy-haired wife and slack-jawed son, the snarling counterman. I have them and they know it."[28] Bill returned half a dozen times to play back the previous day's recordings and take more photographs; their business began to fall off and they kept shorter and shorter hours. On October 30, 1972, the Moka Bar closed. Later the premises reopened as the Queen's Snack Bar—a name that gave Bill a certain degree of satisfaction. The incident appeared in *The Place of Dead Roads*, written over a decade later:

> And he closed down a Greek coffee shop that gave him some sass...camera and tape recording magic. [...] So many good ones and so many bad ones. [...] That's what you get for trying.[29]

Bill and Ian did a lot of street recordings and playbacks in the street, not necessarily directed at anyone in particular. Burroughs explained, "You get a lot of very strange coincidences like recording something about fire engines and there they are, right on cue."[30]

In April 1972, Burroughs made a trip to New York to see his publishers. At the suggestion of Elliot Stein, a great friend of Antony Balch's, he stayed at the Fifth Avenue Hotel, at 24 Fifth Avenue on the corner of 8th Street, and enjoyed himself immensely. Stein lived in the hotel and introduced Burroughs to all the newly burgeoning pornographic bookstores, gay bars, and gay movie theaters showing hardcore sex. Burroughs wrote to Paul Bowles, "I have elected to visit the most exotic country of them all and have not been disappointed. New York has changed beyond recognition since I last saw it two years ago. Any sex act can now be shown on the public screen with beautiful actors and that's a powerful sight. [...] Anything described in The Wild Boys can now be seen in color and close up." He expressed concern that no one would want to read about it anymore if they could see it on the screen. "It seems I wasn't kidding when I said I was working to make myself obsolete."[31] He told Brion, "Antony didn't see it. You didn't see it. I saw it as soon as I walked into the Porter Mills gay blue movies on 43rd between Sixth and Seventh. Nothing you or Antony said had prepared me for seeing the trailers already some trailer that shoots its wad over the screen close up beautiful boys fucking rimming sucking coming."[32]

During this trip to New York he made an arrangement to pay $150 a month toward the rent on his friend David Prentice's loft at 452 Broadway, number 3-F, in the Cast Iron District. His plan was to assemble his archives there and sell them. He told Brion, "My intention is to sell *every-thing* every file, scrap book, diary, *all all all* every fucking paper."[33] Many of his papers were already in New York, having been stored there from his sojourn in 1965, including a huge stack of sex routines based around hanging. This material was in a Chase Manhattan storage vault and had been edited down by a third to fit the box. "If your Picasso won't fit into a packing case cut some of it off."[34]

He dipped into the New York social scene and quite enjoyed it. At the beginning of May he went to Jerome Hill's off-to-Cannes dinner party at the Algonquin, where Andy Warhol, Burroughs, Terry Southern, and Larry Rivers sat in a row, "like some Mount Rushmore of Hip,"[35] and Brigid Berlin burst into the room with a radio broadcasting news of Nixon's massive bombing of Haiphong Harbor. Nonetheless, despite his dissatisfaction with his life in London, when he did finally sell the archives, he first of all considered buying an island off the coast of Scotland with the money. New York did not yet tempt him.

At Christmas 1972, John de Chadenedes came to visit Burroughs at Duke Street Saint James's, bringing with him another boy from the University of the New World named Freddy, described by Burroughs as "a nice little queer." Ian Sommerville's mother was cooking a Christmas turkey at Ian's flat, so Bill took John and Freddy with him. Alan Watson was there, helping with the cooking. Mrs. Sommerville had found it difficult to accept Ian's relationship with Burroughs. She was particularly concerned lest any compromising "man to man" letters should ever come to light or be published. Burroughs: "She'd also, at this point, had to take in her stride Alan Watson. This was a time when Ian and I weren't making it, but Alan Watson had taken over completely and I had a period of great jealousy. So having swallowed the whale of Alan Watson she could hardly gag at the knot of my size. He's a great screaming faggot but he gets himself along."[36] Alan Watson found her "a very difficult woman," and the feeling was mutual.

Ian left London to work as a computer programmer at a pork pie factory in the Roman town of Bath, in Avon in the west of England, where he shared rooms with John Michell, an expert in ley lines and geomancy, and author of *The Flying Saucer Vision* and *City of Revelation*. He and Bill continued to have an on-off sexual relationship, but Ian refused to ever live with Bill again. Burroughs visited for the June 21, 1972, summer solstice at nearby Glastonbury and climbed Glastonbury Tor, where Ian took photographs of him.

Chapter Forty-Four

There's no such thing as a bad boy.

—FATHER EDWARD FLANAGAN[1]

1. John Brady

In June 1972, Bill met a young Irish hustler, John Brady, in a pub near Piccadilly Circus and, after a while, invited him to move in. John was a street boy, a Dilly boy, who described himself as "black Irish" from County Kerry, then one of the most backward areas of Ireland; parts of Kerry were not connected to electricity or telephone until 1978. He had the black hair associated with the "Black Valley," brushed forward low over his eyebrows in a Beatles cut. His father was a farmer and minor horse trader and he had a sister who sometimes visited him. He was short but powerfully built and very, very strong; all the other boys were scared of him. Apparently he had a bad temper, but Bill saw little evidence of it in the early days. John had always been a heavy drinker, favoring whiskey and beer. He was poorly educated; he could read a tabloid newspaper, but he was almost illiterate. When asked if he had read any of Bill's books he replied, "Ah, I do intend to, but there's a powerful lot of them." Despite being from Ireland, with his uneducated rural belief in magic and unquestioning Catholicism, he more resembled a Mexican or Tangier boy than the usual Dilly boys. Bill enjoyed having him recount his experiences with "the little people." "Well, it twas raining a little you see and I was walking down the lane and there he was, a-sitting on a leaf, sheltering himself from the raindrops, large as life." Other times he saw them sunning themselves on the broad leaves of the hedgerow. John talked in his sleep—"I can't quite make it, I can't make it"—and Bill kept a whole scrapbook devoted to things he said in his sleep, some of which were quite extraordinary. Later Bill realized that he had been fooling himself, a case of an "elaborate pointless hoax. Trying to convince myself that John Brady is some supernatural dream boy come back to life. Even resorting to a sort of ventriloquism he is saying very meaningful things in his sleep. He was after all a natural sensitive and if you project an image with sufficient power it takes and becomes real... or as real as anything... as real as Real People."[2]

In the early days of their relationship, Bill would get John to display the various items he had stolen from his johns on the coffee table, an ever-changing selection of gold or platinum lighters, watches, and wallets that soon disappeared, to be replaced with a different selection. This was something Burroughs got from Genet. Bill gave John five pounds a day and tried to turn a blind eye to the girls who sometimes pushed past him to the bathroom in the mornings.

After only a short time, things began to deteriorate. John became sulky and disagreeable. He began tapping his cigarette ashes on the rug and showing signs of hostility. "Johnny, what's the matter with you?" Bill asked, but his replies made no sense: "They're right after me! They won't leave me alone!" Bill didn't know what he meant by that, but it was evident that he was getting irrational, deeply disturbed, and dangerous. Bill told him, "Johnny, why don't you just pack up and get out of here?" This made John very angry. He went to the kitchen and returned with a sharp meat cleaver. Bill was sitting at his typewriter with his hands on the desk. John brought the cleaver down, *thunk!* within an inch of Bill's hand. "Now," he said. "Light my cigarette!" Bill lit his cigarette with a steady hand, and John began to calm down. He smiled and laughed and said, "What about a cup of coffee?" Bill said, "Yeah." Burroughs found out later that he had threatened his mother with an axe because he thought she hadn't made enough effort to get him out of jail at some point in Ireland. Bill told Antony about the incident and he said, "Bill, you had better get rid of that boy just as quick as you can before he kills you." Brion Gysin agreed.

Instead, Bill took John to Tangier, where they had a complete reconciliation. They met up with Brion, who took them to Joujouka, where they saw Hamri and Brion's ex-chef Targusti. They slept in one of the guest huts, listened to the music, smoked a lot of hash, and visited the ceremonial caves a mile or so out of the village. Burroughs said, "It was a very enjoyable occasion. I should say that was the highest point of the relationship when I felt that he was really learning something. He enjoyed it, he dug it, he had a lot of natural tact for getting along with people and everybody liked him."[3] Back in London, things ran smoothly once again.

Burroughs included John in several books. In *Port of Saints* there was a direct journal entry dated October 15, 1972:

On the way to the Angus Steak House, as we were passing through St. James's Square, John B. found the cap of a gasoline tank still smelling of gasoline, reminding me of an unwritten section I had planned for The Wild Boys in which the Dead Child kills a CIA man by loosening the cap on his gas tank—brush fires by a bumpy road.[4]

John also appears as a member of a jack-off club: "There was John Brady, the policeman's son, black Irish with curly black hair and a quick wide smile. Quick with his fists too."[5] Although he never read Burroughs's books, John took an interest in his work with photographs and scrapbooks, but never ventured an opinion.

JB: "I see you took some pictures did you Bill?"
WSB: "I took some pictures, yes."
JB: "Who did you take 'em of?"
WSB: "Nobody. I just took 'em of the apartment."
JB: "Oh, I see."
WSB: "Like, alright, I take a picture of the bed unmade and of the bed been made."
JB: "Yes."
WSB: "That's when I cleaned up the bathroom. Here's a picture of the bathroom like that, and cleaned up like that. It's before and after. What was, what isn't."[6]

Though he was a late addition to the pantheon, Bill got his money's worth and John appeared as private eye Clem Snide's assistant in *Cities of the Red Night*: "Jim Brady . . . 135 pounds, black Irish,"[7] and also in the role of a deckhand in Boston in 1702: "Sean Brady: black Irish with curly black hair and a quick wide smile."[8] With the extra cost of John weighing on his finances, Burroughs needed to raise some money. Brion Gysin was in the same situation and they decided to act on the idea of combining their archives to sell them. They hired Barry Miles, the cofounder of *International Times* and co-owner of the Indica Bookshop and Gallery in the sixties (and the author of this book), to describe their papers for them. He flew to New York to discuss the possibility of selling the archive to Columbia University's Butler Rare Book Library and they explained how they would like the material described in order to assess it and decide on a price. The actual description took many months, as Burroughs's papers were in a complete mess with one large bundle of several thousand pages tied up in thick string and labeled on the top page in thick black magic marker, "Bottom of the Barrel." It was from this bundle that Miles was able to compile the more or less complete run of numbered pages that made up the only manuscript of *Queer*. Miles sorted the papers by page size—American, French, and British paper sizes all differing—then by typeface, then with Burroughs's help began to identify the year and location that each run of pages belonged to. Often they were numbered and so sequences began to emerge. It was a long process because much of the material had been cut up, so complete runs of pages were rare; also Burroughs would often be excited by the long-unseen pages and remove them from their new files to work with the material again.

On September 6, 1972, Brion Gysin arrived from Paris to help with the cataloging, bringing with him his contribution to the archive: his letters from Alice B. Toklas and Paul Bowles, as well as Burroughs's manuscripts and his own collages and collaborations with Burroughs. Brion moved into flat 22 and Bill and John moved to flat 18, a small two-room flat in the eaves of the building. (In March 1973 Burroughs managed to reassign the lease on flat 22 for a year's rent.) In the event, while Miles was in New York delivering the completed description to Columbia and collecting more archive material that Burroughs had left scattered across town with various friends, Brion stepped in and involved rare book dealer Richard Aaron, an American living in Switzerland, who sold the archive out from under Columbia's nose to Roberto Altman. This had all the fantasy elements that Gysin so loved: secret Swiss numbered accounts, the air of intrigue, and lack of tax on the income. The intention was to realize money on the archive quickly, but in the end it took just as long as it would have done to sell the archive to Columbia, and what is more, it tied the archive up for more than thirty-five years so that no one could get access to it, even Burroughs.

Roberto Altman, who bought the archive, wanted to create a cultural center where the archive, and others like it, could be studied. Burroughs thought him to be "a very pleasant young man" but "kind of nutty, been in sanatoriums and mental institutions a number of times." He also could not speak English so he would not be able to read the archive materials himself. However, in August 1973, Bill, Brion, and Richard Aaron traveled to Vaduz in Liechtenstein, taking the archives with them. Roberto Altman's father had a house in Vaduz, built deep into the hillside so that it looked deceptively small. Brion was astonished to see an original Rembrandt and other incredibly valuable art on the walls. They checked the archives against Miles's inventory, then Roberto snapped his fingers, "Igor," and out came a man carrying the cash. He piled it on the table and counted it out: $60,000 in Swiss francs. Brion was in ecstasy. The money was put in a briefcase in the correct thriller movie manner, and the next day they drove back through blinding rain to Richard Aaron's house outside Geneva. Bill kept his hand on the handle of the briefcase the whole way, even when they stopped to eat. Ideally he would have liked to have been handcuffed to it. On Monday they took the money to a Swiss bank and sat in a little private room and received their secret account numbers. When asked if they could withdraw the money if they needed it, the banker shrugged: "Il n'y a pas de problème!" It was small change to them; they were used to African politicians depositing millions. Unfortunately, although Altman's father was a very wealthy man with a private bank in Paris, he got into financial difficulties when the circular building to house the cultural center was only half built, and the archive remained in storage for the next decade before being sold to an American book collector. It remained inaccessible until the New York Public Library finally bought it in 2010.

Before the archive was sold, some of its key elements had to be retrieved. Years earlier, Bill had left all his correspondence with Allen Ginsberg used in the assembling of *The Naked Lunch* in safekeeping with Alan Ansen, and this group of letters was needed for the archive although technically they belonged to Ginsberg. On August 15, Bill and John Brady went to Athens to collect them from Ansen. They spent the first night with him at 19 Dimocharous before moving to the Hilton. Alan showed them the town and it was a perfect holiday. Afterward Bill rented a villa for two weeks on the small island of Spetses, on the east coast of the Peloponnese, through some friends of Ansen's at the American Center for Creative Arts. It was six hours from Athens by boat and two hours by hovercraft. For a dollar a day they had a bare room with a couple of pegs on which to hang clothes, a dresser and two camp beds, a bathroom, and a kitchen down the hall with a fridge for their evening ouzo. The ocean was only a hundred feet away, just across the street, and Bill swam twice a day. The beach was sharp pebbles so they had to wear slippers to avoid being cut. John couldn't swim so Bill found a large rubber ring for him and always swam close to him. The villa was on the harbor. After evening drinks, they would go down to the restaurants: good cheap mullet, Greek salads with feta cheese and olives, plenty of retsina.

The owner of the villa, Takis, lent Bill a copy of John Fowles's *The Magus*, which is set in Spetses, and Bill found that the only way to see the Villa Bourani, the house of the Magus, was on horseback. Bill rented a horse but had forgotten how many years it had been since he was last on horseback, and the going was difficult. On the way back they were coming down a steep slope, almost in the town, when the horse saw a fallen fig, stopped abruptly, and bent to eat it, throwing Bill right over its head into the rocks. He remembered his judo courses and knew how to fall and so did not hurt himself. In the correct manner, he got straight back on the horse and rode into town. The next day he had bruises up and down his body.[9] Other than the horse, the whole visit was a great success. All the details of their trip, right down to the copy of *The Magus* and Bill's fall from the horse, were later faithfully reproduced in *Cities of the Red Night*.[10]

While he was there, Burroughs had one of his recurring terror dreams involving his mother: "I have a recurring nightmare where some very large poison centipede, or scorpion, suddenly rushes on me while I'm looking about for something to kill it. Then I wake up screaming and kicking the bedclothes off. I was with my mother in a rather incestuous context. I think the ideal situation for a family is to be completely incestuous. So this is a slightly incestuous connection with my mother and I said, 'Mother, I am going to kill the scorpion.' At this point the scorpion suddenly rushed at me."[11]

This was around the same time that he was making his latest attempt at a bestseller, a book about "an incestuous family, father, mother, two brothers, two sisters—completely interchangeable sexual combinations. And they succeed because they are incestuous, liberated from all their inhibitions." They sell short during the Depression: "they are able to fill a swimming pool with gold dollars. [...] What they do, in a sense, is make capitalism work. That is, they buy up the dust bowl, so they keep people there on the land and turn them all into incestuous family groups in completely interchangeable sexual combinations. So not only are they happier, but they're also more efficient, and nobody could compete with these families. [...] I thought it might have more popular appeal...And that of course brings them into conflict with Big Money; they're subverting the whole meaning of money."[12]

Disappointed by the collapse of the archive study center scheme, Burroughs considered starting one of his own. Although he later claimed that he escaped from Britain to New York, when he interviewed David Bowie for *Rolling Stone* magazine in November 1973, Bill told him, "At the moment I'm trying to set up an institute of advanced studies somewhere in Scotland. Its aim will be to extend awareness and alter consciousness in the direction of greater range, flexibility and effectiveness at a time when traditional disciplines have failed to come up with viable solutions. You see, the advent of the space age and the possibility of exploring galaxies and contacting alien life forms poses an urgent necessity for radically new solutions. [...] No drug experiments are planned and no drugs other than alcohol, tobacco and personal medications obtained on prescription will be permitted in the center. Basically, the experiments we propose are inexpensive and easy to carry out. Things such as yoga-style meditation and exercises, communication, sound, light and film experiments, experiments with sensory deprivation chambers, pyramids, psychotronic generators and Reich's orgone accumulators, experiments with infrasound, experiments with dream and sleep. [...] Expansion of awareness, eventually leading to mutations."[13] The idea of using the archive's money to buy a property in Scotland did not last very long, but he did send away to real estate agents for details of anything that might be suitable.

With the archive dealt with, Bill settled into his new apartment. The top three floors of Dalmeny Court all had dormer windows projecting through the steeply sloped roof, and Bill's new flat was as high as the elevator reached. Bill used the front room, overlooking Ryder Street and the Economist Building, as his combined living room, study, and bedroom. He sat between his desk and the window, the sunset over the rooftops filling the room with golden light. A large hole had been crudely cut in the desk to accommodate the power cord of his electric typewriter. Either side the window were speakers mounted on top of shallow-drawer manuscript file cabinets. To Bill's right was a double-shelved bookcase with sliding glass doors, filled with foreign editions of his own work and a collection of his favorite books. On top were Bill's reel-to-reel and cassette tape recorders arranged next to a Johnnie Walker Red Label whiskey bottle and mixers. A coffee table stood in the center of the room, and the far side was dominated by a double bed with a low headboard and a bright red counterpane. A large Brion Gysin oil painting of the Sahara hung on the wall above. There was a small back bedroom and a storage room with a four-drawer file cabinet.

This was a time when Britain was beset with almost intractable labor problems. After a six-week strike in 1972 by coal miners over pay, Britain's stocks of fuel were getting so low that the government had to impose a three-day week on industry and begin selective cuts in electricity supply, with some power cuts lasting as long as nine hours. Burroughs described the situation to his son: "England is a gloomy cold unlighted sinking ship that will disappear with a spectral cough."[14] On this occasion the miners won, but in a subsequent dispute in February 1974 the country was once again in periodic darkness. The BBC went off the air at 10:30 p.m. to conserve power, and a three-day workweek was once again imposed on industry. Bill had had enough of the inconvenience, and not being able to watch television finally tipped the balance and made him decide to leave. He was dependent upon electricity for heat; his flat, like most in Britain at that time, did not have central heating. He used so-called night storage heaters, which warmed up with cheap-rate power at night and released their heat in the day. But Bill wanted heat in the evenings and at night when they were cooling down, so he replaced them with bar heaters, a very expensive and inadequate method of heating a room. He was always cold. And when power cuts came, they would not work at all. More than a decade later it still rankled, and in a scene in *The Western Lands* he wrote, "A group of languid Bras have gathered in a Cheney Walk flat that attempts to capture the effect of an Egyptian garden in the drowsy noon heat. Unfortunately the storage heaters aren't working. The man from London Electric, who alone is authorized to repair a storage heater, muttered something about 'the element' three weeks ago, and hasn't been seen since."[15] This is a typical example of how Burroughs processed even the most mundane information in order to use it as a future subject for his writing.

Life was miserable. Burroughs had been in London too long; he had not lived in the same city for this long since he was a child. In June 1973 he began seriously researching the possibility of moving to Costa Rica. He told Shell Thomas, "I am absolutely fed up with London and cannot afford to live here any longer, prices have doubled and the whole island is slowly foundering." He said he had considered a move to southern Ireland, where there was no tax for artists and writers, and that another possibility was Costa Rica. "I would like to see some sun and water other than rain."[16] The island in Scotland was another possibility he reconsidered, and he wrote to John Calder to ask about prices and living conditions there.

One of the biggest problems in his life was the situation with John Brady, which had now turned hopeless. John would sleep through the mornings and then go out. In the evening he would lurk about the place disturbing Bill's work. Burroughs complained, "It came down to the fact of my giving him some money to get out of the way. So I could have some peace. Which is a terrible situation when you're paying somebody to go away for a while."[17] John began stealing from him. Bill would say, "Well, Johnny, I was going to give you five pounds out of my wallet, but I seem to be short five pounds," and John would just stare back at him insolently. He didn't deny it. He just said, "Well, put yourself in my shoes."

Burroughs kept Alan Ansen abreast of his plans to move, but Ansen was shocked when he found that Bill did not like London. He had assumed the planned move was for tax purposes. Ansen said, "He had the cream of the crop when it came to boys, and Sonia Orwell I know said she found him a delightful companion."[18] When Allen Ginsberg visited London in 1973 for a poetry reading with W. H. Auden he was shocked by Bill's low spirits. On his return to the States, Ginsberg approached the City College of New York and suggested that they invite Burroughs to teach one of their three-month courses by distinguished writers. They were delighted by the idea and offered Burroughs the February-to-May 1974 course: two hours a week at a fee of $7,000. He accepted at once. He was sixty.

John Brady was not at all pleased by this turn of events, and Bill mollified him with promises of trying to find him a job in New York, explaining that the New York police were traditionally Irish and that he might find employment there. They both knew that Bill had no intention of ever seeing Johnny again. While Bill was in New York teaching, John had a series of parties that drew complaints from the neighbors, and he also pestered Antony Balch for money until Bill had to write and tell Antony, "Listen, you just have to cut him off." He sent money to John and told him to lay off Antony, but it was no use. In June, after his teaching stint, Bill returned to sort out his belongings. He put most of them in storage at Harrod's for future shipment to the States once he had found a fixed address and asked Barry Miles to sell the rest of the books, magazines, and other artifacts. He sold the lease on the apartment to Mrs. Le Brock who lived next door, and then returned to New York, ready for his new life. John Brady bowed to the inevitable and was calm and reasonable about losing his home and income. He disappeared back into the Piccadilly underworld and Burroughs never heard from him again.

> Wind in the chilly heavens over London a dead boy on the ghostly pillow lips chapped broken sunlight a flicker of Jermyn Street pale half moon of ghostly dandies behind his head a cool dark windy evening sky washed by wind and rain broken dreams in the air.[19]

BOOK EIGHT

~

The Prodigal Son Returns

Chapter Forty-Five

I've had periods of complete writer's block where I can't look at a type-writer. Well, the only thing to do is write it out. What you do is rou-tine work like answering letters and writing prefaces and all that routine work. Best thing for writer's block is a little exercise, get out and row. Of course, someone may be out to get you, you may be under psychic attack.[1]

1. James Winston Grauerholz

In 1974 New York was notorious worldwide for its high crime rate: Central Park was unsafe to walk in, even in the day, with a high incidence of rape and mugging; the subway was underfunded, covered in graffiti, and prone to break down; homeless persons, beggars, prostitutes, and pimps roamed the streets, often aggressively accosting passersby. By October 1975 the city was teetering on the edge of bankruptcy, but President Ford refused to allow federal aid, resulting in the famous *New York Daily News* headline: "Ford to City: Drop Dead."[2] That year there were 1,919 murders.[3]

Burroughs arrived in New York in February to take up his post as a teacher. He sublet a loft at 452 Broadway between Grand and Howard, from the painter Michael Balog, a friend of Robert Rauschenberg's. It was in a compact five-story cast-iron warehouse building just north of Canal Street, an area filled with writers and artists. He was teaching at the City College of New York at 160 Convent Avenue, in Hamilton Heights in Harlem.

Teaching drained all his energy: he got nothing back from his students. They were not even listening; they sat around reading comic books and chewing gum. He would ask if there were any questions and be met by a wall of blank faces. They were just taking the course for credits, and Bill looked like an easy mark who would not flunk them. Out of the thirty students there were only three who had a glimmer of talent. "So I passed everybody on anything they wanted to do: fiction, short story. I passed

509

'em all. None of the stuff was worth a shit, except about three papers that were interesting. I decided then that I didn't ever want to teach again."[4] The problem was that it took Burroughs between six and eight hours to prepare each lecture, and he was doing two lectures a week and two hours in his office for student consultation. Evenings were taken up by reading student papers. It was a full-time job. "I realized that it had been impossible for me to write one line over the course of four months. I was mentally drained by the end of the day, and I found that others around me felt the same way."[5] Bill agreed with Auden, who said, "For an Englishman coming over here to teach, the rudeness of the students is quite shocking. [...] They begin with the idea that they are the most important ones to be pleased—not taught—and that their untutored reactions should be the final judgement on their instructor."[6]

In May 1973 Burroughs had received a letter from a nineteen-year-old fan from Coffeyville, Kansas, enclosing examples of his poetry and asking if he could interview him for an article about his early life. He also sent a snapshot of himself, a tall, slender, tight-jeaned teenage American boy, that did more to prompt a reply than the poems. Bill had said no to the idea of an article about his early life, but said to call him if he should ever find himself in London. James Grauerholz had sent a similar letter to his other hero, Allen Ginsberg. Allen responded by sending him his telephone number and inviting him to visit. James called him and it gave him an enormous thrill to finally talk to one of these legendary men. Not long afterward, along with two friends, James made the long cross-country trip to visit New York City. James met Allen at his place on East 10th Street. As Grauerholz later put it, "He made a well-intentioned but half-hearted and unsuccessful pass at me." Allen referred James to Herbert Huncke, who introduced him to Andreas Brown at the Gotham Book Mart. Brown showed an interest in James's poetry and offered him a place to stay if he should ever move to the city.

Nine months later, James, newly twenty-one, filled his red-and-white 1970 Volkswagen minibus with his library, his records, and his guitars, and set off for the big city, as in all the storybooks. A friend of his from Coffeyville, Bob Maness, had recently moved to Brooklyn Heights and offered him temporary housing at his place at 59 Pineapple Street. James had no idea that Burroughs was in New York, so when he called Allen Ginsberg he was astonished when Allen gave him a phone number for the loft in SoHo where Burroughs was staying and said, "I told him all about you. He's expecting your call."

On February 8, James drove over to Manhattan, knocked on the big metal door, and met Burroughs for the first time. Bill had just turned sixty. James said, "My seven-year journey—from first exposure to Naked Lunch, to this portentous first meeting—had prepared me better than I could ever have expected. Improbably, I found myself quite at ease with William, despite my keen admiration for him; perhaps the steady stream of Scotch-and-sodas he proffered contributed to our bonhomie." Bill was drinking Dewar's and soda and smoking English Senior Service cigarettes. He showed James the latest issue of *Rolling Stone* with his interview with David Bowie in it and told him about teaching at City College. As they returned from a restaurant in nearby Little Italy, the freezing February wind blowing down Broadway provoked a quote from Bill: "the wind that blew between the worlds it cut him like a knife,"[7] from Kipling's "Tomlinson." James recognized it. Back at the loft Bill asked him to stay the night, but James demurred. He told Bill, "I just moved to New York two days ago, and I just met you, and I have no objection in principle to what you're talking about, but right now it's just too much. I'm on sensory overload. I can't do it."[8] However, a few days later he did, and Burroughs became the first man James had sex with, though he had been convinced in his head that he was gay ever since he was eight years old.

James took a job at the Gotham Book Mart and saw Bill regularly. Bob Maness had only offered temporary accommodation in Brooklyn Heights, so, with Burroughs's encouragement, James moved into the loft with him. The sex was awkward and strained. James was never physically attracted to Bill, he had no predilection for older men, but says he was not doing it against his will because he already felt love for Bill. For his part William had a real blockage against making it with James because he was repressed, too shy almost to make a move, and could only do it when he was drunk. This provoked a deep depression.

James was from an old American family. The Paulks on his mother's side came from England in 1665, and the Grauerholzes came from Germany in 1883. His parents were Alvin, an attorney and local politician, and Selda, an accomplished actress and singer. James was a precocious youth but seen as "a bit different" by his schoolmates. He was an only child, alienated and lacking friends. He became withdrawn, and despite his high IQ he had bad grades. When he was ten, they sent him for ten days at the Menninger Clinic in Topeka for evaluation. Their diagnosis was that he was very gifted but dissociated and was in danger of becoming suicidal. They recommended a special home to get him away from the family. In June 1964, at the age of eleven, he was taken to the Spofford Home, a "home for emotionally disturbed children" in Kansas City, where he saw a psychiatrist twice a week for two years. He returned to

Coffeyville at the age of thirteen. The next year, one of his schoolmates gave him *Naked Lunch* to read, saying, "Grauerholz, you're weird; you'll like this. I don't understand it." James "came out" to himself in early adolescence, but though he had a number of sexual encounters with the boys at Spofford Home, he did not experience a complete sex act with a man until he met Burroughs.

He gravitated toward the offbeat, the bohemian, and the antisocial, and experimented with alcohol, glue-sniffing, and marijuana, greatly inspired by his reading of Burroughs, Ginsberg, Lawrence Ferlinghetti, Richard Fariña, Gregory Corso, and the other Beats. He graduated in only three years and went to the University of Kansas at Lawrence, where he majored in Eastern philosophy and wrote reams of poetry and fiction. He sought out slightly older "bohemian types," and after seeing Jimi Hendrix play in Kansas City in 1968, began to develop his own musical talents, switching from piano to guitar and forming a rock band. His first sexual partners after puberty were teenage women, many of them minor-league "groupies" who attached themselves to the members of his band after the shows that they played throughout the region during James's junior and senior years. He dropped acid twenty or thirty times and took synthetic mescaline.

Inevitably all the music-making, poetry, and drug taking interfered with his studies, and he left KU after four years, on "academic probation" and without a degree. He performed as a solo singer-songwriter around Lawrence and Coffeyville during the rest of 1973, and said that "a beautiful young woman named Lois taught me so much about lovemaking that I began to wonder if I really were queer, after all."[9] It was during this time that he wrote to both Burroughs and Ginsberg.

James says that shortly after they met, Bill had upset him greatly by telling him, "I don't know if I can still write fiction." This was the result of a writer's block caused by teaching. "In that period of four months I didn't do a damn thing. [...] I had a real writer's block. I think it's about the worst thing you can do is to teach creative writing."[10] Burroughs had brought an enormous mound of manuscript material with him from London, but found that he just could not make any headway.

Bill's move to New York was not just another new address, but a new start. He was the ultimate expatriate writer. Every one of his books had been written while living abroad. Americans seem to be particularly good at reinventing themselves and adapting to a new environment, perhaps because the United States is a settler nation. Burroughs had clearly decided to change his life. When he left London he got rid of his E-meter and disposed of his Scientology books. It was now too late for him to properly mend his relationship with Ian, or to reconnect with all the old friends whom Scientology had alienated. Once in New York he made little mention of Scientology and played down its importance in his life in conversations with friends and in interviews.

In New York, after a faltering start, he took on the role of senior figure in the drug culture, the man who had been there, who had come back and written about it. He was the elder statesman, a celebrity of sorts. Previously he had always distanced himself from the Beat Generation, saying, "I don't associate myself with it at all, and never have, either with their objectives or their literary style. I have some close personal friends among the Beat movement."[11] He said that "they are friends, but not doing the same thing. We don't have the same subject matter or approach and less and less as time goes on."[12] He now claimed Kerouac as a friend, even though they had been estranged for the last decade of Kerouac's life. He recognized Allen Ginsberg's role in shaping his career and helped him to rehabilitate the Beat Generation and give it its rightful place—as Allen saw it—in the pantheon of American letters.

In Europe, he had been seen as an avant-garde experimenter in literature, as well as in film and audio with his cut-ups and performance pieces. He was also the revolutionary thinker of *The Job* who said, "I'm tired of sitting on my ass. I want to get out and stir up some trouble. I want to make trouble for everyone! For all the people in power."[13] He was seen as a mentor to the sixties youth movement whose thoughts were widely disseminated by the underground press: "There should be more riots and violence. Young people in the West have been lied to, sold out and betrayed. Best thing they can do is take the place apart before they are destroyed by a nuclear war."[14] He was in opposition to Allen Ginsberg's pacifist approach, telling the underground, "The people in power will not disappear voluntarily; giving flowers to the cops just isn't going to work. This thinking is fostered by the establishment; they like nothing better than love and nonviolence. The only way I like to see cops given flowers is in a flowerpot from a high building."[15] But revolutionary techniques now belonged in the past along with Scientology. He wanted a new start and, hopefully, a new love.

Burroughs's tenure at City College ended in May, but he was offered $15,000 to teach at the State University of New York at Buffalo. He talked to them when he gave a reading there in April. It was obviously a bad idea. Burroughs thought that Leslie Fiedler, the head of the English department, was little more than a loudmouth with nothing to say, and didn't see how he could possibly work under him. In addition, he found Buffalo cold and depressing. "It's an awful place, it's an awful place!"[16]

James was concerned that more teaching would destroy Burroughs's own creative writing and suggested an easier, less time-consuming alternative: to go on the road. James knew a great deal about bookings and gigs, having toured with his own rock 'n' roll band. He saw no difference between a band playing at a university or college and Bill doing a reading there; the logistics were the same. It was a new career, and a lucrative one. Allen Ginsberg had been touring the college circuit for years, but he was using the Rothschild Agency, whose other clients were all singers and rock 'n' roll bands. By doing it themselves, Bill and James avoided having to give the booker a percentage, and James traveled everywhere with Bill, whereas Allen did all his traveling alone. But first Bill did a reading alongside John Giorno and Brion Gysin organized by Giorno at St. Mark's Church in the Lower East Side.

Burroughs was astonished by his reception. The audience loved him; they cheered and welcomed him back to New York like the prodigal son. Fans surrounded him for autographs. Unlike his students, these people really wanted to see him. Still reeling after the first few readings, he was asked by a friend how he was enjoying it and he replied, "One standing ovation is enough."[17] Burroughs had returned. For the next decade a considerable portion of his income came from readings. "Not only that, but I was getting out there and meeting the people who read my books. Extending it, considerably. It was just a whole, tremendous turning point which I owe to James, absolutely."[18] He was already experienced at public performance. In Britain he had been on panel discussions, been interviewed on television, performed with Gysin and Sommerville in multimedia events, acted in two plays as well as in several of Antony Balch's films. However, he recognized the need for a professional approach to public performance. James coached him in microphone technique; he read his pieces aloud and timed them, marking them up for emphasis and pauses. He learned not to resume reading until the audience had stopped laughing. Bill still experienced stage fright and needed a few drinks and a hit of pot to give him a "breakthrough" feeling, and sometimes the quantities involved were injudicious.

Brion Gysin had arrived in New York on April 2 to visit Bill, to discuss the publication of *The Third Mind* with their editor Richard Seaver at Viking, and to show his new paintings to New York galleries. Brion and Bill spent a lot of time together and Brion accompanied Bill and James to Buffalo for his reading. On April 23, Brion had dinner with his old friends Nancy and Ted Morgan, whom he knew from Tangier. After the meal he sat on a sofa covered in pale blue linen to drink coffee. When he got up to go, there was a round bloodstain, the size of a saucer, soaked through the linen. Unable to afford medical treatment in America, he flew back to Paris two days later, where he was diagnosed with cancer of the colon. After months of painful and useless radiation treatment, he was referred to the cancer unit at the Royal Free Hospital in London. Bill wrote advising him to use an orgone accumulator, but it was too late for anything but surgery: his colon and his anus would have to be removed. Brion wrote Burroughs on December 21, 1974, that "the whole business fairly ironic on several levels since they are going to whip my asshole out from under me so all I can send you are the seasonal greetings of bottom-less joy." Brion returned to Paris from London in April 1975, devastated. Sex as he had known it was now impossible for him, his self-esteem badly damaged. He was deeply depressed and had made a feeble attempt at suicide in the hospital.

Another visitor for Bill that April 1974 was Billy Burroughs Jr. He was then living in South Carolina with Karen, his wife since 1968, whom Bill was yet to meet. Billy came to New York and stayed with Bill for a week in his loft. Brion had taken one look at Billy and said later, "He's a very disturbed adult." Bill agreed. Billy was obviously trouble-prone and very upset and unhappy. "Like many disturbed persons, you don't know what's really the matter with them. You can't tell and they don't know. I couldn't do very much. He wasn't drinking at that point. He said very little, he didn't want to talk about very much. It was after that that he began to drink very heavily."[19]

Meanwhile James fell in love with Richard Elovich, a man of his own age, the casual boyfriend of one of James's coworkers at the Gotham Book Mart. James continued to live with Bill and unthinkingly brought Richard over to the loft for dinners with Bill, making Bill inordinately jealous. Bill wanted James to give up his job at the Gotham Book Mart and stay home and work for him. He had to accept the situation but asked James not to bring Richard around. There were some unpleasant outbursts and the situation provoked an anti-Semitic side to Burroughs that Grauer-holz had not suspected because Bill was so close to Allen. James attributed it to his St. Louis background, encouraged by Gysin and Balch. James began to spend most nights with Richard at his apartment at 337 East 6th Street. This was the turning point in James and Bill's relationship. James recalls, "He had issues, and the main issue was I wasn't spending the night in his bed. I remember one night he was drunk and I said something to the effect 'I just love you, you're the greatest friend I've made in my life. I just can't get enough time with you.' I said words to the effect that 'If you can conquer your sexual jealousy, you'll find that I'm deeply loyal.' That was the end of our meeting. The thing to do was to leave. I said, 'I'll see you tomorrow,' and I left. So when I next saw him, everything had changed. He'd decided that he'd go for it." The relationship continued until Burroughs's death twenty-three years later; it was not unrequited, it just wasn't sexual.

In June 1974, committed now to living in New York, Burroughs took a two-year lease on a loft at 77 Franklin Street, a small four-story cast-iron warehouse building with a fire escape connecting the top three floors at the front. It was located between Broadway and Church Street, three blocks below Canal in Tribeca. "I like this area. There are lots of cops. The more cops in New York the better is what I always say."[20] A broken-down grand piano that someone had carried up the three steep flights to the apartment had been abandoned in the middle of the loft. Burroughs first of all worked on the essentials: wall shelving for his files, installing a new refrigerator, and building an orgone accumulator. Reich's daughter Eva sent him plans and David Prentice built him one the size of an out-house, draped in black rabbit fur, that Bill sat in for several hours each day.

When Bill moved to the loft, James and Richard took an apartment together at 306 East 6th Street, where they lived for about a year. That September James wrote to Allen, "I am also still with Richie. This is finally cool with Bill, and for the time being all is harmonious."[21] James gave up the bookshop job and began working full-time as Bill's assistant. Richard was permitted to visit the Franklin Street loft, and sometimes took over the job of cooking William's dinner. Allen, jealous that Bill had a secretary, hired Richard to work for him. Elovich was Allen's secretary for about two years, 1974 to 1976.

Bill knew many people from his nine months in New York in 1965 and also people he met on his subsequent brief trips, mostly in the early seventies, in particular David Prentice, David Budd, and John Giorno, who had been Brion Gysin's boyfriend in Tangier. John was a Wall Street stock-broker who spent six hours sleeping in Andy Warhol's first film, *Sleep*, made in January 1964. He began writing poetry in 1962. Bill and Brion first met him in the spring of 1965 at one of Panna Grady's parties at the Dakota. He and Brion quickly developed a relationship, with Brion in the role of "great teacher." John joined Brion in Tangier in March 1966 and stayed for six months. Brion was horrified when John published details of his penis size—along with those of Robert Rauschenberg, Jasper Johns, Andy Warhol, and others—in his bitchy art world gossip column "Vitamin G" that ran in *Culture Hero* magazine.

Bill made his first visit to San Francisco in November 1974. For almost two decades the city had been associated with the Beats, and Burroughs with it in many people's minds, but he had been abroad throughout that whole period and had not even met most of the people whom the public regarded as his old friends. He read at the University of California's Wheeler Hall on November 7, and at the Pacific Film Archive in Berkeley on the thirteenth with John Giorno as his opening act. The two readings were overwhelmingly well received. Bill, James, and John Giorno stayed for a week in the Berkeley cottage of Roger Steffens, who was away on his own poetry-reading tour. One night in the cottage the three of them took acid, a rare event for Burroughs, who generally avoided any strong hallucinogens. Bill and John stayed up all night talking about various methods of suicide, inspired by John's "set," which at that time included his poem "Suicide Sutra." Billy Jr., then twenty-seven years old, now living in Santa Cruz, came up for a visit. They got on well and the whole trip was a great success.

New York began to agree with Bill. He began to socialize and entertain visitors at his loft. His old friend John Hopkins from Tangier reported dining there with him in December, along with John Paul Getty III— missing one ear—and Bill proudly showing off his fur-draped orgone accumulator. Getty brought with him as a gift an expensive Polaroid SX-70 camera that used self-developing film. There was no shortage of people wanting to be Bill's friend; the whole Lower East Side poetry and literary scene welcomed him into their midst, led, very much, by Allen Ginsberg, who was delighted to have him back in New York. Several new generations of writers had appeared since Bill and Joan had headed off for Texas in 1946.

Another source of income was a regular column in *Crawdaddy*, a glossy rock 'n' roll monthly. Early in 1975 Burroughs interviewed Jimmy Page, the guitarist for Led Zeppelin. Their common interest was magic. In his article Burroughs explained what he meant by the word: "The underlying assumption of magic is the assertion of 'will' as the primary moving force in this universe—the deep conviction that nothing happens unless somebody or some being wills it to happen. To me this has always seemed self-evident. A chair does not move unless someone moves it. Neither does your physical body, which is composed of much the same materials, move unless you will it to move. Walking across the room is a magical operation. From the viewpoint of magic, no death, no illness, no misfortune, accident, war or riot is accidental. There are no accidents in the world of magic. And will is another word for animate energy."[22] This was a deep-seated belief Burroughs first developed in Tangier in discussions with Paul

Bowles and others, and confirmed by his experiments with Brion Gysin at the Beat Hotel.

Teaching over, Burroughs began work on a new book. As usual he had no clear idea of how it would come out. While on the trip to the Greek island of Spetses with John Brady he had read James Jones's *A Touch of Danger* about a private eye on vacation in the Greek islands who gets involved in drug smuggling. Bill used his own trip to the islands as the set for the section in *Cities of the Red Night* called "The Private Asshole." He was also thinking about a pirate book. These were originally to be two separate books, but then he saw that they could come together. He was often affected by writer's block, something he had not really encountered before. Sometimes he couldn't work on the book for two or three months at a stretch and would concentrate on something else. He wrote a lot of essays during this period, including his regular "Time of the Assassins" column in *Crawdaddy*. The book jerked along, stopping and sometimes not progressing for months, It was a difficult project and took him six years to complete, with the book changing course many times.

He enlisted the help of a new friend named Steven Lowe to help him research pirates. Steve had been writing commercial pornography, including stories about gay and lesbian pirates, and he had some interesting ideas, though ultimately there was nothing that Burroughs could use. "At one point Steve Lowe and I were sort of collaborating on this pirate idea but it didn't work out. [...] He wasn't coming up with anything that I could use so it wasn't working as a collaboration. It seemed like it might work."[23] It didn't. Conflict with Lowe came to a head in a phone call from New York when Bill and James were staying in a motel in Santa Cruz in the summer of 1976. Lowe had begun to think of himself as a collaborator on the *Cities of the Red Night* project and kept feeding Bill pages of text about gay pirates. Bill didn't use any of it. The call ended with Steve shrieking at James, "Am I the cowriter or not?" and "I'm taking this very personally, you're cutting me out." It fell to James to inform him he was out. He and James didn't speak for months.

That summer John Giorno went to India to see his guru, and as James and Richard's lease was about to expire, he offered them his loft in the old YMCA at 222 Bowery for the month of August. When he returned, James and Richard pioneered "the Bunker," the YMCA's old locker room, where they lived until the following spring. They installed a long conference table and a set of orange Naugahyde chairs from Richard's father's law firm. These were to be the setting for numerous dinner parties when Burroughs later moved into 222 Bowery.

Burroughs did teach again. He spent the summer of 1975 at the Jack Kerouac School of Disembodied Poetics at the Naropa Institute in Boulder, Colorado, newly set up by Allen Ginsberg and Anne Waldman at Chogyam Trungpa's Buddhist center. Bill taught alongside John Giorno, Allen, and Anne. Boulder is a middle-class, almost exclusively white town overlooked by the Rockies. It was chosen by Trungpa not because it reminded him of Tibet, where he'd never been, but of Scotland where he set up his first monastery after leaving his birthplace in Kham in China. Burroughs wrote, "The town has an old-regime flavor, with red brick houses overgrown with ivy and great trees along the streams that run through the town. There is a mall downtown, quite Swiss— side-walk cafes, waiters in red uniforms."[24] He told Paul Bowles, "Boulder is bland and innocuous rather than exciting. It's a middle class town with no minorities and no slums. [...] Beautiful blond boys everywhere one looks but strictly decorative rather than functional."[25] It was anonymous in a way that suited his purpose for the time. The teaching was entirely different from CCNY because the students were there because they wanted to be. He gave talks on Hemingway and Maugham, Fitzgerald and John O'Hara, but he met the same blank looks of incomprehension. "I get up there and I'm talking about these things and they just don't know what I'm talking about! They're not getting what I'm saying."[26] Despite this, he found it very useful to clarify his ideas and to develop critical perspectives on writers whose work he admired.

Allen meanwhile had become an evangelical Tibetan Buddhist, approaching it with his customary zeal, memorizing lineages and Buddhist chants and acting in every way as a meditation teacher even though he had only started to study the system with Trungpa in 1971 and was in no way qualified to teach it. He was very keen to get Burroughs involved and discussed it with him at length. Burroughs was always open to trying new forms of self-improvement and took up the offer of a two-week solitary retreat at Trungpa's center at Karmê Chöling (earlier known as Tail of the Tiger) in Vermont, beginning August 9, 1975. Burroughs asked about taking along a typewriter, but Trungpa specifically forbade it, saying it would defeat the whole purpose, comparing it to a carpenter taking along his tools. Burroughs asked what he should do if a useful idea came to him on retreat and wrote, "That he could make the carpenter comparison shows where the difference lies [...] a carpenter can always be a carpenter, while a writer has to take it when it comes and a glimpse once lost may never come again. [...] Writers don't write, they read and transcribe. They are only allowed access to the books at certain arbitrary times."[27] He told Jim McMenamin, "A writer may only get one chance, so he shouldn't ever put himself in a position where he can't write something down if he wants to."[28] Burroughs said that he was more concerned with writing than any sort of enlightenment. He used meditation as a tool for writing. It was precisely the visions and fireworks that interested him. "I sense an underlying dogma here to which I am not willing to submit." He took along his red daybook and recorded his dreams and thoughts by hand. As he observed, "Show me a good Buddhist novelist." Allen later objected to this criticism, sensing that it also meant, by extension, "Show me a good Buddhist poet."

The solitude was productive: Burroughs developed a new episode for *Cities of the Red Night* and solved a problem of structure when a dream showed him how to feed in the pirate section of the book. He had always written down his dreams. In Vermont he did exercises in association: he would take a walk, then write down what he was thinking when a deer crossed his path. He also made efforts to make psychic contact with James and Billy Jr., with varied success. He wrote, "*I am not looking for a master*; I am looking for the books. In dreams I sometimes find the books where it is written and I may bring back a few phrases that unwind like a scroll. Then I write as fast as I can type, because I am reading, not writing."[29]

There was a limit to how many of Allen's schemes Burroughs was prepared to get involved with. That October he was invited to go on Bob Dylan's Rolling Thunder Revue tour but declined, though he did attend the show on December 8 at Madison Square Garden. "I said, 'Well, I'd be glad to come and do an interview for a certain sum of money,' but I wasn't just gonna go along as a groupie the way Allen Ginsberg and Anne Waldman did. They were given pocket money and put up at good hotels. I thought it was very undignified."[30]

In direct contrast to his solitary retreat, Burroughs spent late September with Brion Gysin in Geneva at a conference designed to research and celebrate their work. The Colloque de Tanger ran from September 24 to 28, and was organized by Gérard-Georges Lemaire. It was a serious business, though enlivened by dance and music groups, and the proceedings were published in two volumes by Burroughs's French publisher, Christian Bourgeois.

2. Ian's Death

On Bill's birthday, February 5, 1976, he received a telegram from Ian saying, "Happy Birthday. Lots of love. No realisation. Ian." The last time they had spoken on the telephone, Ian was working on getting a job as a computer programmer in America. "No realisation" meant that no further progress had been made. A few hours later, Bill received a telegram from Antony Balch saying simply, "Ian dead." Ian, who had only recently passed his driving test, had been driving back from the post office, having sent Bill his telegram, when an oncoming car signaled a left turn. (Britain drives on the left.) The car instead turned right, into Ian's path. He died in the crash. His mother consented to the donation of his kidneys.

James arrived back at 77 Franklin to find Bill looking very solemn. He nodded to the yellow telegram lying on the kitchen table. "Ian dead."

> I looked up at Bill and into his eyes—they were reddish and moist—I was 22—my mouth opened and these words emerged from my shocked and saddened face:
> "Ohhhhhh, Bill...I don't know what to say..."
> Bill looked at me, for a beat, and said:
> "Then don't say anything."
> And I sure didn't.

Ian and Bill continued their relationship right up until Bill departed for New York in 1974, and would certainly have got back together again were it not for Bill's obsession with Scientology. Ian sometimes talked wistfully about Bill, wishing that it had worked out differently, but mostly he was very guarded in his references to his personal life. He often seemed troubled and was often unhappy.

Bill gave some photographs of Ian to Dudjom Rinpoche, John Giorno's guru, whose speciality was in contacting the dead. He looked at the pictures of Ian and said, "I've got bad news for you, he's been reborn as an animal." Bill wanted his photographs back because he didn't have copies of them, but Dudjom said that he had destroyed them in a purification ceremony. Bill said, "I thought that was a bit thick," but there was nothing he could do about it; his photographs of Ian were gone and Ian was an animal.

Five days later he gave a reading with Allen Ginsberg and R. Buckminster Fuller at the Corcoran Gallery in Washington, D.C., with a big society party afterward at Mary Swift's house in Georgetown, but his heart was not in it. Yet again there were "mistakes too monstrous for remorse."[31] Ian's death precipitated a depression so deep that four months later James wrote anxiously to Brion Gysin:

> I am afraid that William is losing his desire to live. True, he goes through cycles of depression and self-application, and even now, this week, is working very hard on the new book. [...] But throughout the periods of exhilaration

and dejection there run the continuous threads of alcoholism and flatly irrational behavior. William will very rarely end the night without having made himself drunk, and more often than not, dull and repetitive and obstinate as well. He will spend the whole afternoon reading and writing, and then at six o'clock he begins to drink. Often he gets too drunk on just those evenings when he should stay sober, that is, when someone he likes is coming to dinner. It is like a child's over-excitement at the anticipation of a party, followed by premature tiredness and slurred, bull-headed, unhearing conversation. I realize that what I am writing here seems disrespectful or even shallow coming from a 23 year old kid from Kansas on the subject of a world-famous man of letters but I hope you will understand the frustration and broken-hearted helplessness I feel, to see this man whom I love and admire reducing himself nightly to travesty, to a pitiable avuncular figure they realize they must humor. There is no point in going on as master of ceremonies for a juggler who drops the pins.[32]

Brion replied, "It is an old story and a hopeless one. [...] Ian and Antony who both had alcoholic fathers just couldn't take it and dropped out. [...] William however has disciplined himself in the past most remarkably and perhaps can again."[33]

Chapter Forty-Six

They gave me hypnosis, Thorazine, Ritalin, imprisonment, kisses on my ass, and threats. They told me if I didn't let them take care of my problem right away, I'd have difficulty with interpersonal relationships the rest of my life. They were right about that.

—WILLIAM S. BURROUGHS JR.[1]

1. Billy Jr.

Bill's lease ran out in June 1976 and he originally intended to move into the Bunker at 222 Bowery. All the cleaning and preparation had been done, partitions installed, and the concrete floor scrubbed, but Bill had asked Howard Brookner to paint the floor "Battleship Grey" and it had not yet dried so Bill spent several weeks with James and Richard in the floor-through loft at 43 Great Jones Street that they shared with their friends Richard and Jody Harris before taking the train to Boulder in mid-July, where he was to spend two weeks teaching at Naropa. Bill took an apartment at the Varsity Townhouse at 1555 Broadway, a group of three-story, balconied, mansarded red buildings with the Flatirons, the first low range of the Rockies, as backdrop. Richard and James took another apartment there. When the students returned in mid-August they all moved to the Boulderado Hotel, where Bill had one of the corner "tower" rooms on the fifth floor. They had all been looking forward to a quiet summer because Allen Ginsberg's father was ill and they assumed he would be in Paterson, sitting at Louis's bedside. But Louis had died, and as James told Bill's friend and French translator Claude Pélieu, "now it's all over and there he'll be, knocking at the door every morning with a list of media people to see and events to attend—oh well, all I can charitably say is, he means well."[2]

Allen used his background in market research and advertising to promote the causes and the people he admired or believed in. At Naropa he was shameless in advertising the involvement of members of the so-called Beat Generation (he even used Kerouac's name for the department). Mostly Burroughs was prepared to meet people and give interviews, but

Allen's full-on proselytizing could be exhausting. Burroughs was only teaching in order to make money; he was not a Buddhist. In fact his attitude was summed up in *The Soft Machine*: "And not innarested to contact your tired old wisdom of the East disgust me to see it."[3]

Nineteen seventy-six was the year of Billy's illness. Billy Jr. was already in Boulder with his new girlfriend, Georgette Larrouy, when Bill, James, Richard, and Steven Lowe arrived for the July season. Bill took one look at him and knew that something was seriously wrong. Billy was coughing up blood in alarming quantities, but his doctor, a Seventh-Day Adventist, hadn't made the obvious diagnosis; he thought it was "nerves." Billy had another hemorrhage and James called his uncle Dr. Pat Barelli in Kansas City, who recommended Dr. Ewing. Dr Ewing immediately diagnosed cirrhosis and said it would be fatal unless he had a liver transplant. He could have a shunt bypass operation but that would only gain him about a year, at most. He drew diagrams and explained to Bill how the blood cannot pass through the damaged liver and backs up. Bill went to see Georgette and Billy's wife, Karen, at the Yeshe House and started to explain it to them but broke down in tears. Georgette said, "Oh shit!" and put her arm around him to comfort him. Then Billy had a third hemorrhage and was transferred to Colorado General in Denver for an emergency portocaval shunt procedure. He had lost a lot of blood. The bypass was unsuccessful and Billy was taken into intensive care in a coma. It looked as if he would die. His only hope was a liver transplant.

Karen, Georgette, Bill, and James all stayed in Denver, waiting for a liver donor to appear. Even if a donor was found, it was a very risky operation, with a 30 percent mortality rate on the table. Then, with just twenty-four hours before they thought Billy would die, a liver became available. Bill had to sign a paper and so did Karen. Bill signed but Karen hesitated. She wanted to know who the donor was, but they couldn't tell her because it was confidential information. Then she wanted to know about another clause. "It's permission to use an experimental drug. We can't operate without it," they explained. Bill lost his temper with her: "For God's sake sign the paper and shut up," he yelled. She signed the paper. The operation was conducted by Dr. Thomas E. Starzl, who performed the first successful human liver transplant in 1967 and is known as "the father of modern transplantation." They spent hours sitting in the waiting room until the staff told them to go home. "We'll call you," they said. The operation took eighteen hours. It appeared to be a success. Anne Waldman commented, "It was so painful at the hospital. You actually saw William Burroughs defeated, weeping, remorseful—very human things."[4]

The first five days after a transplant are crucial, and there is always a relapse after ten days, due to tissue rejection. It all has to be managed very carefully, and at one point Dr. Starzl upbraided his nurses for not following his instructions to the letter. Sometimes Billy's behavior was psychotic and he yelled at his nurses because the steroids he was on made him argumentative. They had been warned that steroids make people angry and self-righteous, and it was an expected symptom. Bill didn't see too great a change in his personality, except that he had odd lapses of memory. Billy finally recovered but he was in hospital for five months. James and Richard Elovich drove Bill to Denver to visit Billy three or four times each week in a borrowed Jeep until they returned to New York at the end of November. Bill stayed on to be close to Billy, making occasional short trips to New York to take care of business.

In January 1977 Billy was discharged and Burroughs rented a room for him at the Boulderado Hotel in Boulder. He gave him a Royal manual typewriter and Billy wrote the two-hundred-page manuscript *Prakriti Junction* there, helped by Alan Davies, a young Canadian poet. Burroughs stayed on all winter to be near him, giving a winter course at Naropa to help pay the expenses. He sometimes had to leave town to make money, such as a European reading tour from September 19 until October 10, beginning in Berlin, otherwise he saw him every day. Billy should really have had full-time care or have been in sheltered accommodation. He had a breakdown; he threw as much of his furniture as he could out of his fifth-floor window at the Boulderado, including the chairs. The hotel ejected him.

It is a terrible thing for a parent to see his child gravely ill; the positions are expected to be in reverse. For Burroughs it was painful not just because of Billy's illness, but for its underlying cause. All his life Billy had always wanted to be loved and respected by his father and his drinking and drug taking were all pathetic attempts to be cool, to show Bill that he was continuing the bohemian tradition. Billy's illness forced Bill to confront the fact that he had been a lousy father and had badly neglected his son. The rift between them was now so great that it could not possibly be mended. Burroughs had not only killed Joan, depriving Billy of a mother throughout his childhood, but had denied him a father as well by leaving him in the hands of his grandparents and not visiting for years on end.

2. The Bunker

In December 1976, Bill finally moved into 222 Bowery, known as the Bunker, between Prince and Spring. It was built in 1884–85 to house the Young Men's Institute, the first New York branch of the YMCA. In 1915 a rear three-story addition was built to provide a swimming pool, an enlarged gym, and a locker room.[5] It was the locker room that William moved into, below the gym, which used to be Mark Rothko's studio, and above the abandoned swimming pool. The first artist to live there was Fernand Léger in 1940–41 after he escaped the war in France. Next door was the Prince Hotel, a flophouse for Bowery bums, who were regularly found frozen to death on the doorstep in winter. The Bowery Mission and the Salvation Army were directly across the street. Wynn Chamberlain had a loft upstairs, where Burroughs had given a reading back in 1965, and importantly, John Giorno lived in the building in a loft overlooking the Bowery. It was to become a legendary address for Burroughs along with the Beat Hotel, but he only lived there continuously for three years, all of 1979 until 1981; the drug years.

The loft was one huge space with a concrete floor and windows that were inches from the opposite wall outside. These they painted over. When James and Richard lived there David Prentice had built stud-walling to divide the space into an office, a bedroom, and a large living space with an open-plan kitchen at one side. Everything was painted white. The concrete floor was scrubbed. The locker-room bathroom still contained a row of urinals, cubicles, and a choice of sinks. The space was very live; it echoed slightly and there was a hum caused by the fridge. In Bill's bedroom six heating pipes and three drainage pipes ran floor to ceiling in the corner to the right of his bed and there was a sprinkler system on the ceiling. Andy Warhol described the Bunker in his diaries: "There's no windows. It's all white and neat and looks like sculpture all over, the way the pipes are. Bill sleeps in another room, on the floor."[6] Richard's father's conference table and chairs next to the kitchen became the focal point of the loft. Some of Brion's paintings of the Sahara were hung, but the Bunker remained bare, functional, a place for work and the exchange of ideas.

Burroughs returned to Boulder in February 1977 in order to be near Billy, taking apartment 415 on the fourth floor of Varsity Manor, 1155 Marine. (Burroughs pronounced it "man-OR.") There were breaks for readings such as the Chapel Hill Arts Festival held in North Carolina in March, where he appeared with Allen Ginsberg and John Cage. The most memorable reading from this period was in Washington, D.C., at the Corcoran Gallery. Bill and James, Allen and Peter Orlovsky stayed with the Washington hostess Amy Huntington Block in Georgetown where they could look across the street at Henry Kissinger's house. Amy pointed out all the boys walking around the street and explained that they serviced

Burroughs in Tangier, 1957. *[Allen Ginsberg, Allen Ginsberg Estate]*

Kiki and Burroughs in the Café Central, Petit Soco, Tangier, 1954. *[Photographer unknown, Allen Ginsberg Estate]*

Jack Kerouac in Tangier, 1957. *[William S. Burroughs, William S. Burroughs Estate]*

Burroughs and Alan Ansen act out a hanging scene from *Naked Lunch*, Tangier, 1957. *[Allen Ginsberg, Allen Ginsberg Estate]*

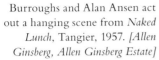

Burroughs and Paul Lund at Paul Dutch's café in the Medina, Tangier, 1957. *[Allen Ginsberg, Allen Ginsberg Estate]*

Burroughs at the Café Palette, rue de Seine
September 1959. *[Brion Gysin, Miles Collecti*

Maurice Girodias, publisher of *Naked
Lunch*, with Burroughs on the corner of
the rue Git le Coeur, September 1959.
[Brion Gysin, Miles Collection]

Burroughs in his room at the Beat Hotel,
October 1959. *[Loomis Dean, Life]*

Burroughs and Brion Gysin, Paris,
September 1959. *[Ian Sommerville,
Miles Collection]*

Alexander Trocchi
and Ian Sommerville,
London 1965. *[John
Hopkins]*

Burroughs at the
Rushmore Hotel, Earl's
Court, London, 1965.
[Graham Keen]

Mikey Portman at the Empress Hotel
in London, 1962. *[William S. Burroughs,
William S. Burroughs Estate]*

Robert Fraser, London,
1966. *[Graham Keen]*

Omar Pound [hidden],
Paul Bowles, William
Burroughs, Christopher
Wanklyn, Jane Bowles,
and Joseph McPhillips,
Tangier 1963. *[Photographer
unknown, Miles Collection]*

Peter Orlovsky, William S.
Burroughs, Allen Ginsberg,
Alan Ansen, Paul Bowles
(crouching), Gregory Corso and Ian
Sommerville. *[Photographer unknown,
William S. Burroughs Estate].*

Ian Sommerville in
London, 1974. *[Udo
Breger]*

Burroughs in the Lottery
Building, Tangier, 1964. *[Ian
Sommerville, Miles Collection]*

Billy Jr. high-school photograph.
[William S. Burroughs Estate]

John Brady and Alan Ansen,
Athens, 1972. *[William S. Burroughs,
William S. Burroughs Estate]*

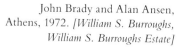

Brion Gysin working on the
Burroughs/Gysin Archive,
London 1972. *[Barry Miles]*

Brion Gysin and William S.
Burroughs, New York, 1977.
[Marcia Resnick]

Burroughs as the president of
the United States, London, 1971.
[Theater still, Miles Collection]

Burroughs with James
Grauerholz advertising
John Michell's "No Metric"
campaign, New York, 1975.
[Marcia Resnick]

Mick Jagger, Burroughs,
and Andy Warhol at
one of Victor Bockris's
dinners at The Bunker,
c1980. [Marcia Resnick]

William S. Burroughs on Green Street,
New York, December 1986. [Allen
Ginsberg, Allen Ginsberg Estate]

Burroughs with Patti
Smith. [Marcia Resnick]

James Grauerholz
and Burroughs,
together for
twenty-three years.
[Jon Blumb]

Burroughs shooting at Fred
Aldrich's farm, Lawrence,
Kansas. *[Jon Blumb]*

Fred Aldrich, Burroughs, and
David Cronenberg shooting at
Fred's farm. *[Udo Breger]*

Burroughs, Michael Emerton,
and James Grauerholz on
Leonard Street, Lawrence,
Kansas, 1992. *[Barry Miles]*

"Tio Maté Smiles": Burroughs at age eighty-two. *[Jon Blumb]*

the foreign embassies. The boys were watched by the Secret Service but not interfered with as they waited to be invited indoors or for a limo to pick them up. At the Corcoran Burroughs read "When did I stop wanting to be President" to the cream of D.C. society; there was nervous laughter and a few walkouts. The dinner afterward was attended by Richard Helms, the director of the CIA, and his wife; his predecessor William Colby; James Angleton, chief of CIA counterintelligence; and other government bigwigs. James sat next to a Supreme Court Justice. Burroughs was delighted. "[Robert] McNamara[7] was one of my fans. I was treated like royalty! I did have the feeling it was sort of like a small town atmosphere. [...] She was a marvelous hostess."[8] Bill and James stayed with Mrs. Block several times when they were in Washington.

3. *Junky*

The *Junky* project began in the spring of 1977 with a phone call from Joe Bianco, Jacques Stern's lawyer, a dark, roly-poly child prodigy, always chuckling and smiling, who had made a fortune in commodities by the time he was twenty-three. He had helped Jacques crack several of his trust funds. Stern had seen the new edition of *Junky*, published in March, and wanted to make a movie out of it. Bill and James went to discuss it at his penthouse on 57th Street. The living room was dominated by a huge grand piano but there was very little furniture; Jacques needed the space to zoom around in his wheelchair. James said that Jacques was the only cripple he ever saw who could pace in a wheelchair: he paced and raved, watched over by two medical nurses who helped him in and out of his chair, administered his medicines, and listened passively as he cussed them out.

Jacques had a hospital syringe with 60ccs of liquid cocaine in it, the needle sticking in his wrist, the plunger half pressed as he raved to them that he would get Samuel Beckett to act in the film. He grabbed the phone and called France, the syringe still hanging from his wrist, and began talking as if he were connected to Beckett: "Hello, Beckett. You've read *Junky* by William Burroughs? Yes. Right. I want you to play Old Ike in the movie that we're making. What? You don't want to? Well fuck you, you old fraud!"

The project was their reunion with Terry Southern, whom, like Jacques, Bill had known at the Beat Hotel. Terry brought in his old friend Dennis Hopper to direct, and it quickly became obvious that they were there for the cocaine and the money and that the film meant little to them. Bill received $20,000 for the option on the book—a huge sum then—and

Dennis and Terry each got the same. Bill and James, Terry and Dennis walked out of Joe Bianco's condo at River House and went straight to the bank. Afterward they celebrated in an expensive French restaurant in Murray Hill. James took a year's lease on an apartment on the twenty-sixth floor at 7 Park Avenue at 34th Street. He was trying to become a literary agent and wanted a Midtown address.

It was a period of dinners at One Fifth Avenue and visits to Terry Southern, who was ensconced at the Gramercy Park Hotel writing the script in a haze of cocaine. Typists ran in and out, taking things to be xeroxed, and there were pages of script everywhere, typed on different-colored papers, the Hollywood method of distinguishing between rewrites. Terry kept writing scenes that weren't in the book; a cocktail party with businessmen standing around saying, "My company recycles used condoms." Terry and Dennis were both working on the script and getting expenses, most of which went up their noses. James thought the book should be treated as a period piece and shot as a costume drama of the forties. There were pointless meetings with Jacques Stern at the Stanhope Hotel. At one of these Bill, James, and Terry turned up but not Dennis. After forty-five minutes, Stern, furious and raging, wheeled himself down to the lobby. When Hopper finally arrived, in his leather-fringed suede coat and leather hat, he apologized: "Jacques, I'm sorry I'm late." As guests milled around the lobby, trying to check in or out, Stern stabbed a finger at him and screamed, "You're not late, you miserable ass, you're fired! Get out! You're through! Over!"[9] Terry stayed close to the money, murmuring, "Jacques is a grand guy, really a grand guy!" But with Dennis gone there was no backing, despite Jacques Stern's claim that he had a four-picture deal from the French Film Board, and the project folded, as expected.

Chapter Forty-Seven

What I am talking about is the magical theory of the universe, the magical history of the world. It's the belief that nothing happens unless somebody wills it to happen. There are no accidents. If you see a condition of chaos it's not because everyone's blundering, it's because some power intends to profit by it. Everything we see is deliberate, intended.[1]

1. Rocky Mountain Horror Show

Banned from the Boulderado Hotel, Billy moved into the Yeshe House, one of the Naropa Institute dormitories, only a block away from Bill at 1155 Marine. Bill saw him every day. Billy took most of his meals in the Yeshe House and for a while he was the cook there. Nonetheless, he complained to Bill (in a letter never sent) that he was living on raw potatoes while Bill was at home eating steak and sniffing cocaine. In fact the Yeshe House had enormous quantities of food; Bill had never seen such food stocks.

The Buddhists were extremely kind to Billy. They understood that the steroids made him behave in an unpredictable and sometimes crazy way and were able to deal with it. His fellow residents in the Yeshe House would often have to go to his room and try to calm him down, and sometimes people stayed over to make sure he was all right. He was constantly losing his pills and recruiting people to find them. Sometimes he raved and threatened suicide and they would impound his cutlery and any pills that looked dangerous. Once he took an overdose of Valium and had to be stomach-pumped in hospital. After that the hospital refused to prescribe any more to him. Billy's condition made life difficult for Bill, who had to keep his guns, knives, and liquor hidden away in case Billy took them. Once Billy kept Bill up all night raging and threatening suicide. Bill sat and talked to him, keeping himself awake with tea and coffee. "Everything was my fault and it didn't matter what happened. Tremendous ambivalence. Steroids make people extremely self-righteous, completely unrealistic, and blaming everybody else but themselves for everything that happens. It's one of the effects of the drug, particularly when someone had a very strong tendency to do that anyway. I remember being impatient with him; I don't remember ever losing control."²

That summer Burroughs began teaching a screenwriting course. After a few weeks, one of his students, Cabell Hardy, built up enough vodka-fueled courage to go to the Varsity Manor at 10:00 p.m. and knock on Burroughs's door. Bill invited him in. He poured Hardy a tumblerful of vodka, topped off with a little tonic, and slid it across the kitchen table. Hardy said he had come to show him his short stories about criminals and drug addicts that he had known. Bill flipped through the carefully typed pages, giving each page little more than a cursory glance so that he read through the entire portfolio of twenty stories in about two minutes. Hardy told the story in a 1999 interview:

> "Is that it?" he asked. I just sat there, stunned, saying nothing.
>
> "Very nice," he said, and I could tell he thought no such thing. I supposed they seemed terribly amateurish, and I was completely humiliated. I was already thinking about the best way to get out of there politely when he said, "Let's go out on the porch."
>
> He stepped out onto the small, railed porch through the glass door and looked over into the Varsity Apartments courtyard. In spite of the hour, most of the apartments were active and the courtyard was brightly lit. Across the way, we watched a young boy, perhaps fifteen, naked but for a swimsuit, climbing up and around the trellises that covered the inner walls of the courtyard. [...] I had to admit the boy was beautiful, and said so. Bill smiled at me [...] and said, "Young boys do need it special!" He laughed and put a large, heavy hand on my shoulder, and suddenly I knew everything was going to be alright.³

According to Burroughs, Cabell didn't talk until he was six years old. He told Bill, "I couldn't be bothered to talk." When Cabell was in his teens, aged sixteen or seventeen, in Richmond, Virginia, he used to dress up in drag and sell himself as a transvestite hustler in order to buy heroin. He told Burroughs gravely, "This is very degrading." His father, a lieutenant commander in the navy, got to hear about it and drove around looking for him. Cabell saw the car coming and, thinking he was a customer, seductively lifted his slit dress. Out jumped his father and took him home. Herbert Huncke told a similar story: he was picked up by the police for hustling and when his father arrived at the station house there was Huncke in a dress. His father threw him out. Huncke and Cabell had a lot in common. Cabell got busted for pushing dope and did about eight months in jail. There he put himself under the protection of the most powerful inmate he could find, which of course meant that he owned Cabell sexually.

Cabell told Bill that he only attended the course in order to meet him. He said that it was destiny. He reminded Bill of John Brady, both in character and appearance. Both were "short, dark, good-looking in sort of an awful way."[4] James likened him to a miniature Huncke. He had shifty downcast eyes and plucked his eyebrows; he had a low voice and spoke like a street hipster, so cool that it was exaggerated and sounded forced: "Everything is taken care of..." He was a very histrionic character, prone to burst into tears or a sudden rage. He loved to argue and bicker, something Burroughs couldn't stand. He had a beautiful girlfriend, Poppy, who was working as Gregory Corso's babysitter. She claimed to be a "confirmed" lesbian, but left her girlfriend for Cabell and saw him two or three times a week They had terrible fights, screaming and throwing dishes at each other, which Cabell enjoyed very much.

Burroughs said, "James hated him from the first moment, and he said, 'He's bad news. I just hate to be around him. I don't want to be near him.' He's an individual."[5] Bill admitted, "Cabell was a weird and in many ways quite disagreeable character. He had his redeeming features, but the more you saw of him, the less apparent were his redeeming features. He became less and less helpful and I finally didn't want any more to do with him."[6] The problem was, of course, sex. "We were making it for a while. Whenever it comes to sex, good judgment goes out of the window."[7] The sex may not have been all that satisfactory, as both Bill and Cabell were bottoms; however, by the end of the summer, Burroughs had invited him to move in.

Burroughs's newfound fame brought with it many advantages. People gave him presents. One admirer presented him with a pair of Civil War–era cap-and-ball revolvers. Bill and Cabell tried them out on the man's property outside Boulder. Another Burroughs fan, a major drug dealer whom Bill had never met before, made him a present of a half-pound chunk of raw black Thai opium as a mark of respect to the "godfather." Bill treated this magnanimity very casually. He kept the opium in the back of his freezer and would chip off a one-gram chunk and let it thaw out until it was sticky enough to roll into a ball. He would smear the ball in vegetable oil and swallow it down, followed by a cup of Earl Grey, which warmed the drug and helped to activate it. It took about a quarter hour for them to get high. They sensibly kept the existence of this huge amount of opium a secret known only to a small group of friends, and it lasted them for many months. It did, however, precipitate a rerun of Burroughs's famous "Playback" scenario.

Two or three times a week, Cabell and Poppy would meet at the deli in the Boulder Mall and start their day with a couple of opium pills. The owner's attention was soon drawn to these customers who only ever ordered tea, then nodded off to sleep. One day he turned them away, saying they could come back, but next time no drugs. Cabell thought this was reasonable, but Poppy didn't, and over drinks that evening she complained bitterly to Bill about it. Surprisingly, he agreed with her that "something should be done."

He recounted the story of his sound and image attack that closed down the Moka Bar in London and proposed the same for the deli. But they didn't want to close the place down, only to try out the method until they saw if it worked or not. Bill suggested they restrict themselves to tape recorders, without taking photographs. Cabell and Poppy made an hour tape while sitting at the counter nearest the kitchen and made another the following day at lunchtime. That Sunday, Bill, Cabell, and Poppy went to the deli for breakfast at 10:00 a.m. They sat in the exact middle of the room and ordered coffee. Bill carried a cassette player in his inside jacket pocket and began to play back the tape at low volume. Over the next hour he increased the volume so that you could just about hear it, but no one appeared to notice. After forty-five minutes there was a huge crash, followed by a loud argument in Greek, and one of the waiters threw down his apron and stalked out, followed by the owner, arguing loudly. The owner returned and began to scream at the serving staff, sending two of the women running to the ladies' room in tears. Then he calmed down and took charge of the cash register. A few minutes later another huge argument broke out, this time between the owner and a customer. Poppy stopped one of the waitresses and asked what was wrong, and all the girl could say was that the owner had suddenly gone crazy without the slightest warning. Cabell wrote, "Poppy and I looked over at Bill who was calmly smiling. He said, 'I told you it would work! Now, aren't you glad we didn't take photos, too?' "[8]

Bill and Cabell were constantly encouraging Billy to go somewhere to get straightened out. The hospital in Denver had a drug center where people could stay, and Billy went there for a few days but then wanted to get out. Burroughs didn't want to confine him to a sanatorium. "It just didn't seem right, he wasn't dangerous. It was absolutely uncalled for. And of course he had periods in which he was better."[9] Cabell and Billy did not get along, but there was no real friction between them. Cabell was always complaining that Billy should be in a sanatorium, but it was never a real choice because Bill didn't have the $3,000 or $4,000 a month it would have cost. Billy continued to believe that his situation was all Bill's fault, not his, and Bill learned to live with it.

Billy wanted Bill to witness the mess he was in; he was paying him back. He lost his pills, but as Burroughs noticed, he never lost his morphine. On one occasion he took his welfare check along with his passport to identify himself and started downtown to the bank. By the time he got there he had neither one. Fortunately they were found and returned by a concerned member of the public. James offered to accompany him to the bank to cash it but Billy was insulted. However, by the time he reached the bank, both were missing again. Burroughs commented, "Obviously he just threw them away somewhere but he had no memory of this. 'You mean to say you think I threw them away?' I said, 'I think exactly that. You must have. What happened to them?' So we went back over the route but we never found them."[10] His route would have taken him over the river, and Bill thought that Billy must have thrown them in. He went to the riverbank but couldn't see anything. The current was fairly strong, the water deep.

One of Billy's many problems was a fistula, a part of the operation scar that had not healed properly. Because of this Dr. Starzl warned him to avoid sex. It was not a moral thing, just a grave danger of reopening the wound. Georgette had stuck with Billy when he was first in hospital and did as much for him as could be expected, but she was a practical, down-to-earth woman and had her own life to lead. It was obvious that Billy had a short life expectancy and would be an invalid for life. He was making no effort to improve the life he did have, so they separated. She moved back to Santa Cruz. In October 1977, Billy went to visit her on impulse, without making any medical planning, and found her living with a Mexican man. Although they were no longer together he found it very hard to deal with and began drinking, something the doctors had warned him to never ever do.

James noticed Billy's voice slurring, and had first noticed that the vodka in Bill's apartment had been watered down in the summer of 1977, even before his Santa Cruz visit. Bill didn't believe it at first because it was inconceivable to him that anyone with a liver transplant could be stupid enough to drink. But it was true. Dr. Starzl had left, and the hospital had cut his morphine down to practically nothing. Billy could have gone on the methadone program with no trouble at all, something Burroughs thought would have been better for him than morphine, but he chose not to. He knew the doctors at the hospital and got away with murder. Anytime he had been drinking too much or was feeling in bad shape, he checked into a hospital for a week as if it were a hotel. There was nothing Bill could really do to help him. He became impossible for the Buddhists to look after and he was asked to leave the Yeshe House. Allen Ginsberg took him in while he looked for a place, but he got fed up with Billy sitting around the living room all day drinking and never throwing his beer bottles out. Allen didn't realize what a bad state Billy was in and kept encouraging him to look for a job, but Billy was too weak to stay out of the house more than an hour and in Boulder he needed a car to get around. He asked Bill for the five hundred dollars needed for a car but Bill refused, thinking that Billy would just give the money away.

Billy had to go to the Denver hospital three times a week to get his morphine and for checkups. Finally the commuting became too much of a burden and he moved to Denver to a rooming house on Colorado Boulevard full of bums and alcoholics but very close to the hospital. Billy was in an unenviable situation. The longest a transplant recipient had ever survived was seven years, so he knew he had a limited life span. The cocktail of drugs to prevent rejection puffed up his face, and the operation itself had left a hideous suppurating scar across his abdomen that meant he always smelled bad. He was ashamed of his appearance. He lived and looked like a street person, wearing dirty clothes. He rooted around in trash cans, carrying home salvaged items of food and rubbish. Bill's old friends in Boulder kept their distance from him and most avoided him. No one realized how sick he was.

To make life even more stressful, Cabell's mother died while he and Bill were living together in Boulder. Cabell would tie up the phone with interminable conversations with his sister, who was an addict involved with some very destructive people. Then his sister died of an overdose and wasn't found for a week.

2. Horror Hospital

Bill kept in close touch with Antony Balch, who came to visit him in Boulder. They had lunch at the Boulderado Hotel in the summer of 1977 and he and Bill caught up on all the gossip. James described them as "very animated together, very much bird-flapping hand, queeny." On a trip to Paris in 1978, Bill arranged to have dinner with Antony, who, in addition to Dalmeny Court, had a modern luxury flat near the Arc de Triomphe. Antony was feeling too ill to go to Brion's flat where Bill was staying, so they ate in a restaurant near Antony's. Bill thought he was looking very pale and ill. Antony had a long history of ailments. He came down with a terrible depression after a bad attack of flu, diagnosed as a postviral depres-

sion, quite a common occurrence. He tried everything—alternative medicines, psychoanalysis, faith healing—but nothing worked. His business
began to suffer as he went from doctor to doctor. Nothing gave him pleasure. Finally, after about a year, Burroughs read in the medical pages of
Time that MAO inhibitors had often achieved remarkable cures of chronic
recalcitrant depressive states. It was a dietary supplement rather than a
drug, and this alleviated his condition. It came in huge bottles and Antony
would take a spoonful several times a day.

Shortly after Bill's visit, Antony flew to Los Angeles on business, but
when he got back to Heathrow, one of the stewardesses saw that he was
practically collapsing. The airline arranged for a car to take him home.
He went to a doctor, and two days later, after an exploratory operation,
they made the diagnosis of inoperable cancer of the stomach. One of the
symptoms of stomach cancer particularly is an acute anemia. The doctor
thought the tumor had been there "five, maybe even ten years." Antony
was told he had a year to live. It was right almost to the day. Bill thought
that Antony's depression had been precognition of the cancer, because he
had already experienced several episodes of "the dying feeling." He had an
attack once at the Cannes Film Festival and the doctor told him, "No, you
are not dying, this is the dying feeling. I've seen many people with it here,
particularly at the film festival."

It was obvious that Antony's position was hopeless, but he refused to
accept it and embarked on a course of radiation treatment that gave him
a lot of pain and did nothing to cure the condition. He had terrible head-
aches that morphine couldn't alleviate. Then he was sent to an interferon
clinic to take part in a new program. Interferon was then incredibly expensive, $2,000 a shot, but it seemed to help. In the summer of 1979 Bill was
in Amsterdam for a literary festival, staying with Harry Hoogstraten, when
Antony contacted him asking to see him. Bill changed his tickets and went
to London to visit him in the clinic. Antony was always attempting to
lose weight as he was a big eater and had been getting fat. Now he was a
shrunken stick figure. He had painkillers in every pocket of his dressing
gown and gave a couple to Bill, which Bill took, just to be companionable.
Antony was on heavy medication and seemed quite cheerful. His mind was
not affected; he was quite alert and realized the situation he was in. They
had a good long talk. Antony died on April 6, 1980.

Their last collaboration had been *Bill and Tony*, a very different film
from their previous collaborations. Shot in 1972 on a professional soundstage and lasting just five minutes fifteen seconds, it was designed to be
privately projected onto the subjects themselves in live performance, not
for public exhibition. It was in color and used a fixed camera to shoot

studio close-ups of two talking heads: Burroughs and Balch. There are only four shots, which are repeated once with a different soundtrack. The soundtrack is each participant announcing, "I'm Bill," and "I'm Tony," sometimes lip-synching, sometimes actually speaking so that sometimes it is Tony's voice issuing from Burroughs's mouth and vice versa. Another synchronized line is from Tod Browning's *Freaks*, in which a carnival barker invites the audience to inspect a "living, breathing, monstrosity" that "once was a beautiful woman." Balch had originally intended to call the short *Who's Who*.[11]

Bill had been in Europe initially to attend a major Belgian literary festival in Brussels organized by Benn Posset at Raffinerie de Plan K, an old sugar-beet factory converted into an arts center. He and Brion Gysin read from *The Third Mind* and were well received by an audience of ten thousand. Also on the bill were Kathy Acker, Simon Vinkenoog, and members of Cabaret Voltaire and Joy Division. Benn had arranged for Burroughs to be treated as a government guest, and at Zaventem airport he was walked straight through the border controls to a waiting car. Bill was back on drugs so his first move was to find a pharmacy. Here his enormous knowledge of the pharmacopoeia enabled him to buy a selection of over-the-counter drugs that he was able to brew up back at the hotel into something to keep him going until he reached Amsterdam. At the reading Ian Curtis from Joy Division asked if he "had any spare," but he didn't. Early the next day, Gerard Pas drove him to Amsterdam, where he stayed at Harry Hoogstraten's place in De Pijp.

Pas scored for heroin on the Zeedijk. He cooked up a small dose, as Bill didn't know the potency, and Bill asked him to inject him in the foot. Gerard wrote, "As I filled the syringe, Bill pulled off his sock, rolled up his pants and slapped his foot a bit to get the veins to stand up a bit more, making it easier for us to see. I placed the syringe on his foot on top of his vein, at a slight angle, and without waiting poked it into his vein. With those small veins, you want to make sure you don't push the plunger too fast, as these veins can't take the volume as easily as in the arm."[12] Ironically, one of the events in Amsterdam was a reading at a methadone clinic on the Dam across from the Nieuwe Kerk. As Bill was thought to be clean, Benn Posset had arranged for him to appear before a roomful of junkies as an example to them all. They circled around him like children at class waiting for story time. He read from *Cities of the Red Night*.

Changes were afoot back at Burroughs headquarters. James had now devoted four years to Burroughs and was having second thoughts about making this his life's work. He spent from May until August 1978 in

San Francisco, attempting to revive his music career. But though he had found love with Neil Cadger, he did not find a record label and decided he would try and do both by relocating back in Kansas where his fellow musicians were. He decided that he could just as easily deal with publishers, agents, and arrange reading tours from his old university town, Lawrence, Kansas, so in March 1979, William Burroughs Communications relocated there. It was his long-term plan to get Burroughs to join him. But first came the Nova Convention.

3. Nova Convention

The year 1978 ended with a celebration of Burroughs's work in New York. This was first proposed by Sylvère Lotringer, who first met Burroughs at the Schizo-Culture Conference that he organized at Columbia University on November 13–16, 1975, where Burroughs spoke on the same platform as Michel Foucault. His original intention had been to organize a largely academic event, bringing together theorists and artists who revered Burroughs's work, similar to the Colloque de Tanger in Geneva in 1975. Lotringer said, "Burroughs was very reticent, and so was James. They didn't believe that there would be enough interest in such a convention. I discussed it with James at the Bunker and it took a while before they took my suggestion seriously. [...] I mobilized my own friends in the art world, like Laurie Anderson, John Cage, Merce Cunningham, etc. and the ball started rolling."[13] James brought in John Giorno because he had a lot of stage experience and knew so many people, and the three of them worked closely together. James suggested that film student Howard Brookner film and document the entire proceedings, the beginning of his feature-length documentary on Burroughs.

As is usual in these things, there was a lot of jockeying for position, many large egos were involved, and in the end it became a celebration of Burroughs as a celebrity, with little academic or critical analysis of his work. There was, however, an interesting panel discussion between Burroughs, Timothy Leary, Robert Anton Wilson, Brion Gysin, and Les Levine on the subject of time and space. A number of musical events and readings were arranged in Burroughs's honor (or in some cases to increase the participants' own fame by association). One of the most important figures responsible for Burroughs's reputation was not there to assert his position and consequently was completely overlooked at the planning stage. Brion Gysin wrote bitterly from Paris to Burroughs, "I am sorry that I will not be able to make the Nova Number in NY but besides the fact that nobody asked me there remains the fact that neither Seaver-Viking nor anybody else can come up with the bread for a fare over there although I am glad to hear that there are tickets for Lemaire, Mikriammos and any French feminist who is willing to go over there and heckle you."[14]

It was doubly important for Gysin to be present, because Viking was finally publishing *The Third Mind*. This key text was certainly from an earlier period in Burroughs's life but he still wanted it published, as did Gysin, who was enormously proud of his long collaboration with Burroughs and wanted people to know about it. Burroughs said, "I wrote [*The Third Mind*] in collaboration with my friend Brion Gysin and Ian Sommerville. It is the end result of two minds put together with a third and superior mind. It consists of quotes which Brion and I picked up from 1959 to 1965. The style used is that of cut-ups and permutations. Language is treated in the same way a collage would be by a painter. Since language is a part of matter, it can be manipulated in a manner as to make it superior."[15]

This obvious planning oversight was eventually remedied and Gysin was provided with a ticket and a place on the list of performers. Brion had not seen John Giorno's loft or Bill's Bunker at 222 Bowery. According to Rachel Wolff, "He took one look at Giorno's space, cluttered with Oriental rugs and piles of poems, and remarked, in his particular British-Canadian cadence, 'You all live like bohemians!' Which they did."[16] They proceeded down to the Bunker, where Giorno cooked a meal for them all of bacon-wrapped chicken—Bill's favorite—and Brion was seated in one of the orange chairs surrounding the oval conference table. Brion stayed until 10:00 p.m. when, after Bill had demonstrated his latest blowgun, it was time for bed. Every evening members of Bill's circle came by to pay their respects to Brion: Allen Ginsberg, Debbie Harry and Chris Stein, with Keith Haring and Jean-Michel Basquiat bringing expensive pot and listening to the great raconteur, who loved every minute.

The Nova Convention ran from November 30 until December 2, 1978, with most of the three days of events being held at the Entermedia Theatre on Second Avenue at 12th Street. After a reception at La Maison Française at New York University, there was a book signing by Brion Gysin and Burroughs at Books & Co. to launch *The Third Mind*, followed by film screenings at NYU and a reading by Kathy Acker. On Friday there was a panel discussion with Maurice Girodias, John Calder, Richard Seaver, and others at NYU and evening performances by Laurie Anderson and Julia Heyward. Merce Cunningham and John Cage performed "A Dialogue," and Anne Waldman, Ed Sanders, Allen Ginsberg, and Peter Orlovsky gave readings. There was a midnight concert at the Mudd Club with the B-52s, Suicide, and the Stimulators. Saturday opened with a panel discussion between Burroughs, Gysin, Timothy Leary, Les Levine, and Robert Anton Wilson.

The final Saturday night program at the theater opened with a solo organ piece by Philip Glass, who was heckled by kids who wanted to see Keith Richards. They had presumably not seen the items in the press saying Richards had canceled and no one made a stage announcement to tell them. Richards was about to appear before the court in Toronto on a heroin charge and his management felt that association with a well-known junkie like Burroughs would not help his case. James Grauerholz had managed to get Frank Zappa to appear in his place, so the kids had someone famous to gape at. Patti Smith threw a temper tantrum about following Zappa onstage and James had to soothe her by explaining that he wasn't doing it to show her up, in fact it was not about her at all. Zappa had come in at the last minute as a favor to William to fill the star gap. Frank read the "Talking Asshole" section from *Naked Lunch* and got a rousing reception. Patti Smith came on in a huge fur coat and finally explained to the audience why Keith Richards wasn't there. She said that if anyone wanted their money back they could have it and waved a handful of bills, but there were no takers. Robert Palmer, reviewing her performance in the *New York Times*, said, "Smith played clarinet and electric guitar with virtually no technique in the conventional sense but with a certain understanding of the kind of effects that were within her grasp."[17] Palmer singled out John Giorno, Laurie Anderson, and Brion Gysin for praise but didn't stay on to see the midnight set, which included Blondie and Robert Fripp. He particularly liked Bill's reading: "Of the other performers, Mr. Burroughs himself was the most appealing, and this had less to do with what he was reading than with how he read it. Although he has created some enduring characters, he is his own most interesting character, and he was in rare form, sitting at a desk in a business suit and bright green hat, shuffling papers and reading in his dry Midwestern accent."[18]

The event did a lot to establish Burroughs as the "Godfather of Punk" and place him in the center of the seventies youth movement. Far from being a generation, the original Beats had now managed to take up positions in three different decades: Kerouac was the hard-drinking, loudmouth fifties, Ginsberg the psychedelic, antiwar sixties, and now Burroughs represented all that was cool about the seventies. In so doing, of course, the event lost any claim to academic inquiry and became an exercise in fame and an excuse for the downtown art scene to strut their stuff. Afterward Burroughs felt obliged to write to Gérard-Georges Lemaire thanking him for his participation and saying, "In some respects I regret that the event strayed so far from the original conception of a visit to New York by the French intellectual community who recognize my work. [...] Of course, the Colloque de Tanger and the Paris–New York events were the inspiration for the Nova Convention, and I am grateful to you for your many efforts behind these and other matters."[19] This was the new Burroughs who recognized the need to be commercial in order to survive in America. This was the Warhol era: the surface was everything; fame, glamour, and success were what counted, not content.

4. Cities of the Red Night

Bill's personal assistant during the Nova Convention was Victor Bockris, an English public-school boy, educated in the United States, a poet and writer, who moved in Warhol circles. In January 1979, Victor proposed his own form of Burroughs celebration and began work on a book of imaginary dinner parties, each with a theme, collaged together from transcribed tapes of actual dinners with Burroughs. He explained, "In 1979 when I started having dinner with him several nights a week, Burroughs was the worshipped King of the Beats and Godfather of Punk as well as King of the Underground. He was definitely one of the coolest people in the city. I think the fact that he had never sold out, and had come back to seize his throne at the same time that great yahoo Nixon fell from his, was a true and irresistible story."[20] Over the following months Bockris brought over Susan Sontag, Christopher Isherwood, Joe Strummer, Mick Jagger, Andy Warhol, and a host of others for tape-recorded dinners at the Bunker. The book, *With William Burroughs: A Report from the Bunker* by Victor Bockris, was published in 1981. Burroughs was ambivalent about it: Victor had tried to show Bill as a normal person, with fears and emotions like everyone else, but by concentrating on celebrity dinner guests he gave the impression that Burroughs spent his whole time hanging out with stars. Burroughs said, "It isn't my book, although I had to go through and correct it word for word. When people take dictation from conversations they misread words and just get a meaningless mess. So I did a lot of work on correcting it. For another thing, I wrote the end. I have mixed feelings about it. There are some good photographs in it, but I could have lived without it."[21] However, Burroughs was not immune to being feted; he liked the attention, and he enjoyed the razzamatazz that Victor brought to his life. Victor was sharp and provocative, ideas came a mile a minute. Victor was totally *on*, sometimes exhaustingly so, but always exciting and energetic. Some members of Bill's circle felt threatened by Victor and attempted to turn Burroughs against him; the court intrigue was amusing to see as they jockeyed for position.

That summer, after five years of work, Bill finished the first draft of *Cities of the Red Night*. Some sections had come to him complete in a dream: "Sometimes I get long sequential narrative dreams just like a movie. [...] The opening chapter of *Cities of the Red Night*—The Health Officer—was such a chapter, a dream that I had about a cholera epidemic in Southwest Africa, and I just sat down and wrote it out. I was reading rather than writing."[22] He explained what *Cities* was about: "It involves time travel. It is a book of retroactively changing history by introducing the possibility of a simple invention—namely the cartridge gun—back in the late eighteenth century. That has been very much my concern recently. I've always been very much interested in the whole development of weaponry."[23] It was originally subtitled "A Boys Book." It was Brion Gysin who gave Burroughs the names of the cities: Ghadis, Naufana, Ba'dan, Yass-Waddah, Waghdas, Tamaghis, magic words that you are supposed to repeat as you fall asleep if you want to find certain information in your dreams. There are no real cities in the Gobi Desert area called this. "They are magic words so I decided to use them for my cities. I used them to get to the bottom of the book. And they did work, they worked in the sense that I managed to finish the book, get the book together."[24]

"I had one version and James did another, and we finally took his version, although in some ways Dick Seaver liked my version better, but I think James's version was a little bit more comprehensible, much more easy to follow. Differences of juxtaposition, not of content."[25] Burroughs dedicated the book to Brion Gysin, Steven Lowe for his research into pirates, Dick Seaver his publisher, Peter Matson his agent, and to James Grauerholz, "who edited this book into present time." James worked long and hard to knock the manuscript into shape. Burroughs had always depended upon his friends to assist when it came time for the final draft. Allen Ginsberg played an important role in shaping both *Junky* and *Queer*, and worked on the early drafts of *The Naked Lunch*. *The Naked Lunch* itself was typed and shaped largely by Brion Gysin and Sinclair Beiles while Bill stuck photographs of the Peruvian jungle on the wall and shot at them with his air gun. *The Soft Machine* was assembled and edited entirely by Allen Ginsberg and Brion Gysin in Paris while Burroughs was in Tangier, and Ian Sommerville had a lot to do with both *The Ticket That Exploded* and *Nova Express*. This is how Burroughs had always worked. In earlier times, Burroughs would have published both versions as with the original Paris editions and the rewrites of *The Soft Machine* and *The Ticket That Exploded* for the American market. All Burroughs's major books are fugitive. No fixed text seems possible, each version points up different aspects of Burroughs's vision, and ultimately they have to be seen as one giant multivolume book including all the different versions.

In 1980, when Burroughs felt he had enough material to complete *Cities of the Red Night*, he assembled a final draft almost at random. He had two more or less complete narratives, the pirate story and Clem Snide, each in a separate folder, that were supposed to merge so that in the end the two narratives were seen to be one. He took a few manuscript pages from one story, then added one or two pages from the other story, back and forth, without regard for the actual text. It was hard to follow and very "cutty." Then Burroughs asked James to go through the whole manuscript and take out everything he thought didn't belong there. He took out one hundred pages. Bill put twenty pages back in, so most of James's cuts stayed out. With the matter of the two converging narratives James took one look and said, "'Woah Nelly! Let's just undo this,' and I uncut—as I so often have done—'the man who uncut the cut ups'—I reassembled the original folders and I said, 'Suppose we break the stories into the scenes and movements of the story and let's suppose we give the reader at least 15 to 20 pages of each story so that he or she can get into that venue and into that setting so that something happens there and it comes to a nice little ending vignette. Then you go to the other one,' and I slowed the cutting pace and I made it much, much more readable." James made diagrams showing how different parts could fit together and finally made it gel together as a double narrative. This was the kind of input that Burroughs needed and wanted. A comparison of the two manuscripts shows that the Grauerholz edit improved the book enormously, which is why Burroughs used it, after making a few more changes of his own. It was published in March 1981.

Burroughs did readings and book signing sessions all over the country to publicize the book and gave a number of interviews in which he discussed the theme of the book:

> Captain Mission was an idealist, like I once was. He believed you could establish Utopia, a place where everyone would be able to live as he wished and express his thoughts freely without fear of censorship or worse, imprisonment. More important, equality reigned. But Mission was either too naïve or not strong enough, so his little colony was overthrown eventually by natives and he was killed. [...] I used Mission as a symbol, a catalyst for a small band of contemporaries attempting to repeat the experiment. [...] A plague from the old "Cities of the Red Night" wipes out most of civilisation reducing the population to the level of 300 years ago. My principal character Noah Blake feels the moment propitious to take a page from Captain Mission's book...I wouldn't take it all too seriously.[26]

A lot of it came from my sense of the actual possibilities of those real colonies at the time. I was familiar with the way Science Fiction had used that idea, but certainly I'd say my handling of it comes more from actual materials than from Science Fiction. You can see the appeal of going back and rewriting history from certain crucial junctures. One of the things that interested me in Cities of the Red Night was seeing what would have happened if you could get rid of the Catholic influence. Even after the Spanish were kicked out of South America by the liberal revolutions of 1848, their whole way of doing things—the bureaucracy, the language, the calendar, the Church—was still in effect. What would have happened if that influence had left with the Spanish?[27]

Nineteen seventy-nine was another busy year for Burroughs and included a lot of foreign travel. He flew to Zurich to attend the opening of Brion's Dreamachine show on June 6. He and Brion stayed with Carl Laszlo, the show's backer, for about a week in his art-filled house at 22 Sonnenweg in Basel. Carl put on a spread for them, including two kilos of beluga caviar in a huge chamber pot and vintage pink champagne. There was so much of it that each morning Bill's friend and Swiss publisher Udo Breger would go over to Carl Laszlo's house and join Bill and Brion for caviar on toast, coffee, and a joint for breakfast. Bill recalled happily, "That's the only time I've ever had all the caviar I could eat."[28] Bill saw the lemurs in the Basel zoo and the sights.

Bill, Brion, Udo, and Carl drove out to see Albert Hofmann, the discoverer of LSD, at his house in the Rittimatte, about thirty miles outside of Basel. Hofmann's property was on beautiful land that crossed the French border, and he told Burroughs that he sometimes saw chamois in the woods. Hofmann was then seventy-three, retired. He made his own liqueurs and had a heated swimming pool. Hofmann's wife, Anita, was there, and his old friend the American author Robert Gordon Wasson. Wasson was eighty-one, an ethnomycologist who had been vice president of J.P. Morgan, and one of the first westerners to take part in the Mazatec mushroom ritual. Unfortunately in 1957 he published an article about it in Life magazine, and the Mazatec community was overrun by Americans, all wanting to take the magic mushrooms. Wasson had written and published Soma: Divine Mushroom of Immortality (1967) and The Road to Eleusis: Unveiling the Secret of the Mysteries (1978), coauthored with Albert Hofmann and Carl A. P. Ruck. Burroughs was particularly interested in Wasson's research and enjoyed the meeting. Hofmann was just finishing work on his most famous book, LSD My Problem Child (Burroughs thought it was a great title for a book). Both Hofmann and Wasson complained about Leary sensationalizing the whole experience, and Burroughs agreed with them.

At the end of June, Burroughs was one of the participants in the first World Festival of Poetry, "Beatniks on the Beach," held on the beach at Castelporziano at Ostia, the Roman beach resort. This was where Pier Paolo Pasolini had been murdered a few years earlier. A big rock 'n' roll stage had been constructed, there were naked people swimming and wandering in the crowds, and a great party atmosphere most of the time with people camping in the dunes and lots of pot and hash. But by the end of the second day, things began to get out of hand. Burroughs was there with Allen Ginsberg, Brion Gysin, John Giorno, Lawrence Ferlinghetti, and dozens more. Ginsberg wrote, "Ostia international gathering—big adventure lotsa anarchists screaming and throwing sand—10 or 20 thousand people the last of three nights on the beach, Burroughs, Yevtushenko, Corso, 13 European poets di Prima, Barker & Gasgoyne there earlier, LeRoi Jones, Gysin, Waldman, Berrigan, Ted Jones half dozen more. Peter ended the evening with banjo & the stage collapsed with autograph seeking congratulators crowding up 5 minutes after the last note of a 4 hour exhausting contest to keep the microphone in sane hands."[29] Allen, Amiri Baraka, and Yevtushenko considered canceling the third day because of the violence and difficulty in keeping the microphone out of the hands of the Italian anarchists who thought it was elitist for these Americans to do all the talking.

Burroughs spent the summer in Boulder teaching Joseph Conrad, *The Great Gatsby*, and the work of British author Denton Welch. Welch first makes a named appearance toward the end of *Cities of the Red Night* when the protagonist buys some light reading: *An Outcast of the Islands* by Joseph Conrad, *Brak the Barbarian* by John Jakes, and *Maiden Voyage* by Denton Welch.[30] It was through Cabell Hardy that Burroughs became reacquainted with Welch, at that time largely unknown and mostly out of print. Cabell knew someone in Boulder who had a collection of his books and borrowed them for Burroughs to read. He was astonished. "I didn't realize to what extent I'd been influenced by him [...] like 'my horrible red little pony showing its awful yellow teeth.' So I used the same phrase, that he hated horses, Audrey and Kim hated horses, he hated their recalcitrantness and their awful yellow teeth. When I reread it, I found that I had really memorized these sections from it. That was more than twenty years later."[31] Bill began to collect Welch's books: *In Youth Is Pleasure*; *A Voice Through a Cloud*; the *Journals*; a collection of short stories called *Brave and Cruel* and another called *A Last Sheaf*. Burroughs loved his exquisite, microscopic observations, his sensitivity, his ability to make a big thing out of just buying a cracked porcelain teacup, and the way his books have no real plot; they are strictly autobiographical and simply unfold.

At the age of twenty Welch was badly injured in a bicycle accident, which led to his early death at the age of thirty-three in 1948. Only after his accident did he begin writing, using his short life experience up until the accident as his subject matter, which he recalled in extraordinary detail. Bill tried to interest Brion Gysin in Welch's work, to no avail: "Brion Gysin hated Denton Welch. Didn't see that it is just the petulant queerness in which he is straightjacketed—'Little Punky'—that makes his works such a great escape act. Yes, for all of us in the Shakespeare Squadron, writing is just that: not an escape from reality, but an attempt to *change* reality, so [the] writer can escape the limits of reality."[32] In the mid-forties Burroughs had given Welch to Kerouac to read, and it is possible that this is where Kerouac got the idea of not fictionalizing his life experiences in his writing but recounting things more or less accurately as they happened.

It was some time after rereading Denton Welch that Burroughs suddenly realized that all through the years he had used Welch as a model for his Kim Carsons character—that of Burroughs himself—who appeared in *The Wild Boys*, then in a major role in *Port of Saints* and *Exterminator!* "He's definitely based on Denton Welch. I am Kim Carsons, very much so. I'd just say he was a very important element in my character, sort of an alter ego. I wouldn't say I was him, because that's not the way it works. People don't have any one thing that they are or one character."[33]

The Denton Welch figure was combined with the stereotypical cynical, petulant, flippant young man who occurs often in Burroughs's prose and who had his origins in Saki's Comus Bassington and/or Clovis Sangrail (and who bore a strong resemblance to Mikey Portman): the archetypal sulking child in rebellion against parental authority, a Wild Boy, Burroughs himself.

Chapter Forty-Eight

*Being under psychic attack, depression, anxiety, fear of some impend-
ing danger, when you sift it down is a feeling of a hostile presence. The
important thing is to find out where it is coming from. When you do
that, the battle is pretty well won, because once identified and clearly
seen it disperses.*[1]

1. New York Days

Bill returned to New York from Boulder on the last day of August 1979
to spend the winter. He was now the center of a circle that included John
Giorno, Victor Bockris, Stewart Meyer, and Howard Brookner. Brookner
had an MA in art history and film from New York University Film
School. He had wanted to make a twenty-minute portrait of Burroughs
as an NYU project but was persuaded by James Grauerholz to scrap that
and film the Nova Convention instead. He filmed many of the stage performances and surrounding social events. Brookner decided that for his
senior thesis he would like to make a full-length documentary about Burroughs. Bill agreed, a contract was signed, and Howard started work. Bill
liked to have him around: he was gay and a heroin addict, so he fitted
right in. Howard kept filming and filming and didn't know how to complete it. Years went by. Burroughs commented, "You wonder why in hell
he didn't plan it better. I think that Howard does have a lot of silly ideas
that cost a lot of money and didn't go into the film."[2] By 1982 he had
sixty hours of film, and Burroughs was getting irritated because Howard
had exclusive right to film him, and other more professional people were
being prevented from doing so. Howard did not know how to complete
the film. The BBC eventually solved the problem.

In October 1982, at the Final Academy, a conference/celebration of
Burroughs and his work in London, the BBC approached Burroughs to
film the event or at least film him with Francis Bacon for their arts documentary series *Arena*. They were told they had to use Brookner's footage,
to which they reluctantly agreed, and they flew Brookner to London to

see the rushes and discuss it. Alan Yentob, Nigel Finch, and Anthony Wall filmed a new interview with Burroughs with BBC staffer John Waters in Lawrence, and filmed him with Francis Bacon. They did rostrum shots of Burroughs's books—which is why there are British editions in the film—added a bit of honky-tonk music, and dropped in sections of Antony Balch's sixties footage from *Towers Open Fire* and *The Cut-Ups*. They transmitted it in February 1983. Brookner was so relieved to have the film completed that he used the BBC TV edit exactly as it was when he released the film for theatrical exhibition in the United States six months later.

Frank Zappa was interested in doing a musical of *Naked Lunch*, and on September 12, 1979, he took Burroughs to see *The Best Little Whorehouse in Texas*, a musical that had run for over a year. Had it come to anything it would have caused some unpleasantness with Brion, whose film script for *Naked Lunch* contained a number of songs that Bill absolutely hated, one of the main reasons he was so lukewarm about the project. Bill had not seen a musical in years and enjoyed it.

Burroughs was then spending a lot of time with Stew Meyer, who acted very much as his personal assistant. Stew drove him to and from the airport, scored dope, and ran errands. It was a very druggy period. Stew kept a diary record of events:

Friday October 5th 1979
    Giorno called the office late afternoon tells me dinner with Bill is set for six. I left reefer at home but Al gave me some gummy strong shish and I picked up a few glassines for me'n the Old Doc on Rivington just east of Houston Street. The Puerto Rican social clubs are lined up on that block. Thriving marketplace for coke, dope, and street yerba.

Thursday October 25th 1979
    Bill: "Put that coke away we don't have to feed every vagrant nostril in town." I put it away before the guests arrived.

John Giorno has pointed out that Bill's fame may have actually saved his life. Many of the junkies he was shooting up with in the Bunker were also gay, and several of them, including Howard Brookner, subsequently died of AIDS. Burroughs's seniority meant that he always got the first shot, so he always had a clean needle and was never exposed to the blood of the other people using the same works.

Bill's affair with Cabell Hardy was coming to a close. Though William Burroughs Communications was now based in Kansas, James still had to make visits to New York, where he stayed at the Bunker. Bill was traveling a lot and had allowed Cabell and Poppy to stay at the Bunker, but as

James couldn't stand Cabell and found it impossible to work around him, Bill had to ask him to leave. Cabell threw a crying fit over the phone but pulled himself together and left. He and Poppy moved into a place above Howard Brookner at 4 Bleecker Street. Bill saw him occasionally but they had definitely broken up and there was no emotional involvement. By now Cabell had become very deeply involved with Poppy and was very dependent on her. His hysteria and craziness persisted, and there were noisy scenes all day long. Brookner reported that he would sometimes hear Cabell screaming curses at Poppy and then find out that Cabell had been alone.

In December Cabell called to say that Poppy needed an abortion and asked Bill for money. Burroughs expressed a certain amount of skepticism since he knew that Cabell was hustling for junk but told him to come over to the Bunker. "When he came in the door it was just something awful, his face was a thing to see, it was sort of peeled, I've never seen a more horrible expression on anyone's face. I wish I'd had a hidden camera to take that face. The hate in that face was something. You had to step back from it, it was so awful."

Cabell said, "I see you don't believe in her pregnancy, you don't care anything about her pain."

Bill replied, "Wait a minute, wait a minute. I understand that there's pain involved." He gave him fifty dollars. Cabell grabbed the money and said, "There's something for you to read, you won't like it, but it's the truth." It was a ten-page rant that he had clearly spent all night composing, "so full of sick hate" that Bill couldn't read it all. He skipped about in it, then destroyed it. "It was unbelievable, it made you physically sick to read it. Of course a hysteric's hate is very disconcerting because there's no limits on their hate, it just concentrates. It's always very frightening to encounter that hate."[3] Most of the letter was directed against James, who had become an obsession with Cabell because he felt that he should be occupying James's place. He told Bill, "Don't you realize that James is just waiting around for you to die?"

The day after Christmas, a week after the letter, James fell off his bicycle and broke his jaw. It was wired shut for four weeks. To Burroughs this was clearly the result of a curse, the direct result of Cabell's scream of hatred. He told Ted Morgan, "I was appalled by this outburst of absolutely demonic hate but I didn't really blame Cabell personally because all hysterics are very subject to possession. They can be possessed by something and you ask them about it later they don't even remember it, and this was an obvious demonic possession by something that had come in and taken over Cabell Hardy completely." As soon as Bill heard what happened he asked John Giorno, "Please do not invite Cabell to your New Year party." Burroughs could hear Cabell saying, "I hope you choke on it." And it turned out that someone did. It was Carl Laszlo, whom Bill and Brion had stayed with in Basel, who was visiting New York.

A roll call of Beat Generation and downtown luminaries had gathered at John's loft for New Year dinner: Allen Ginsberg; Anne Waldman; Udo Breger; Carl Laszlo and his two boyfriends, both called Michael; Herbert Huncke; Louis Cartwright; Lucien Carr; Victor Bockris; and Stewart Meyer. The party began in the afternoon when John Giorno, Stew Meyer, and Bill had tea and hashish brownies that Bill had cooked.

> Stew Meyer: "Tastes like shit, Bill. What're these things?"
> WSB: "Raisins."
> Stew Meyer: "Tastes like shit with flies in it."

The brownies were as dry as sandpaper. Bill and John washed them down with vodka and tonic, then they all did a little heroin to hold them for the time it took for the ingested pot to kick in. Bill gave one of his discourses on animals. First he explained that the bedbug is the best hunter on the face of the earth because hunger does not force it to make dangerous moves. It will stay in suspended animation for years if necessary before a suitable meal comes along. Then he praised the "incomparable wolverine! which can shred a man to the bone in nine blood-splattering seconds." At six o'clock they moved up to John's loft and the guests began to arrive. Bill began to drink and smoke joints. Dinner was served. Carl began to choke; he went blue in the face, his eyes bulging. One of the Michaels screamed in German, "Do something!" but no one knew what to do. Anne Waldman began praying. The others looked on, aghast. Louis Cartwright attempted the Heimlich maneuver. He reached his arms around Carl from behind and roughly pushed up on his diaphragm, but it didn't work. Carl looked half dead. Bill got a knife and was preparing to execute an emergency tracheotomy to allow him to breathe when one of the Michaels took over from Louis and executed a perfect abdominal thrust, clearing the steak. Carl stood there trembling, his cigar still in hand. He had shat his pants, so Bill and Stew took him down to the Bunker to clean up and find him some new ones. Bill commented, "I know curses and I know how they work. It was directed at me and it bounced off and hit poor Carl Laszlo, a curse is a very real thing."[4] Bill finished the evening with a speedball (heroin and cocaine). He continued to see Cabell from time to time and they both acted as if the letter had never been written, but Burroughs had been impressed. "The smallest men throw the heaviest curses, and a curse from Cabell Hardy, that is a curse. It's a curse from a small evil man."

Cabell began to burn down the city. He stung a lot of his friends for money for heroin, he bounced checks, he sold heroin that turned out to be baking powder. People began calling Burroughs's number but he told them that Cabell didn't live there anymore. They tried to get his address and to bluff him, but Bill explained, "I'm not responsible for this man's checks. If you're looking for him, you find him." When people threatened to go to the police, he said, "Go ahead." Cabell fled New York.

2. Heroin

The Bunker years were drug years. Virtually everyone Burroughs knew or saw was continually smoking pot, hashish, Thai temple sticks, sniffing or shooting cocaine or heroin or swallowing half-gram balls of opium. They talked endlessly about drugs, comparing the ones they were on now with others taken at other times, remembering spectacular highs and fantasizing about the highs of tomorrow. Burroughs chippied around on his reading tours. One time in Los Angeles, everyone around him was sniffing heroin and he got a light habit. It only took a few days to get him hooked again. After that he went to Toronto for a reading and had to find a doctor to give him some Percodan. He usually traveled with some pinkies[5]—Codethyline Houdé, available over the counter at any pharmacy in France—because he had a horror of catching flu and not having a serious painkiller with him.

New York was awash with heroin. Howard Brookner brought some to the Bunker, as did Stewart Meyer, and fans came bearing gifts. Soon Bill was fully addicted again. Stew had access to a large quantity of opium through a Mafia connection. It was only available by the kilo, and worked out at about four to five dollars a gram. Burroughs took it throughout the spring of 1980 and by June was stabilized on a gram of opium a day plus street heroin that he shot up. Sometimes he would go with Victor Bockris to visit Tom Sullivan, "the Kid," a famous drug dealer who arrived in New York with a million dollars and was very generous with his high-end cocaine and heroin. He had a place on the Upper East Side and another in the Village. There were lots of cocaine groupie girls around. But Sullivan got into bad shape and the money ran out. He died at the age of twenty-three.

Bill usually scored through someone else or accompanied people like Howard or Stew. The pushers were in tough competition with each other and all had their own drug brands: there was Black Sunday, the Red, and the Black Is Back, all with different logos on the wrap. Bill was flattered that one on Rivington Street was called Dr. Nova. Bill was never involved in a bad incident, but he knew it was inevitable that if he continued he would encounter some unpleasantness. In addition, he never knew what he was getting: sometimes it was talc, other times a barbiturate, sometimes it would be a good count, other times not. There was always the possibility of getting a bad batch. One shipment from Iran killed a number of people in Paris, and several addicts went blind in New York from it. Bill was getting junk from the same source as one boy who lost his sight. Allen Ginsberg was concerned to find that Bill was addicted again, but Bill told him firmly, "Look Allen, I'm writing and living my life."[6] As Burroughs said, there was no question that if James had been living in New York City he would have protested most vigorously. But James was in Kansas. Bill knew that the situation could not continue indefinitely. Stew Meyer described it: "James was away, the mice were playing. Here we were, William, Howard, and I, three dreamy guys. We all got into trouble. James came back and William ended up in Kansas on methadone [...] William back in Kansas 'cause he had been a naughty boy. Ever see that look on his face, facetiously apologetic, about as sincere as a syphilitic choirboy."[7]

Bill needed three bags a day minimum, usually four, estimating that a bag was three-quarters of a grain if you were lucky, and a bag was ten dollars. Many people quickly got on a six-bag-a-day habit, which was prohibitively expensive because at that time in New York there was a lot of cocaine mixed in with the heroin and that tended to make people use more heroin in order to smooth out the coke. Bill couldn't stand cocaine by itself; he hated the teeth-grinding and the poor coordination and would only take it mixed with heroin, methadone, or opium. He said, "If it had been easy and cheap it would have been okay but it wasn't. It takes a lot of time so when it was suggested to me that I get on the methadone program I did that."[8] He had been stockpiling methadone, bought from Huncke, who was getting a hundred milligrams a day on the program but only using eighty, as a reserve stock in case things got hot and he couldn't score. Most of Stew's opium was gone and his connection had changed his name and disappeared, so there was little hope of getting more.

On March 3, 1980, Howard Brookner filmed the only fictional scene in his film about Burroughs. He had arranged to film "The Lavatory Has Been Locked for Six Solid Hours I Think They're Using It for an Operating Room" in the bathroom of the Bunker, with Bill playing Dr. Benway, Andy Warhol's transvestite superstar Jackie Curtis playing the nurse, and

Stew Meyer playing Dr. Lymph, Dr. Benway's appalled assistant. Jackie Curtis couldn't decide which tits to wear and in the end decided that she was female enough already. Bill immersed himself in his role, growling and cursing in his white medic's coat, splashing stage blood all over himself and the crew.

Bill's friend Ira Jaffe worked at a methadone maintenance clinic and convinced Bill that being on junk in New York City was not a long-term option. In September 1980 Ira arranged for Burroughs to be treated by Dr. Littleson, who ran the Einstein Medical School clinic way out in the Bronx. Bill would go to her house and she would take him to the clinic. Afterward she was usually able to find someone to drop him at the subway to return to the city, which took about forty-five minutes. Bill liked her but the strain of all that traveling each day was too much for him, so after about ten days she enrolled him in a special celebrity program at 27 East 92nd Street, near Central Park, run by Dr. Harvey Karkus, where well-known actors and public figures went and appointments were timed so that they didn't run into each other. They asked if he wanted to join under an assumed name, but he declined. He took one urine test and tested positive for heroin and got on the program. For the first three months Bill had to go up there each day; after that he began getting take-homes. It cost a hundred dollars a week (most clinics were between ten and fifty dollars a week), but that was still cheaper than Bill's habit. He joined the program more from financial necessity than any real desire to come off. His ambivalence was shown one night at the Bunker, as Stew Meyer recorded:

October 9th 1980

Tonight at the Bunker Uncle Bill proclaims; "Junk Is Beautiful! We have been shat upon long enough! Gather yon junkies into a political block of dedicated members always lookin' for converts! 'Here kid, try some'a this.' Soon we will swell into a national or even international power making big demands on the status quo. Give us our medicine! Give it to us cheap! Strong! Ready for the cooker!" He was all lit up like a television preacher I mean it was hard to doubt the sincerity blasting out of those white devil blue eyes.

Burroughs was to remain on the methadone maintenance program from 1980 until the end of his life in 1997. This meant that all of the books written in the States were created while opiated. Virtually all of Burroughs's writing was done when he was high on something: *The Naked Lunch* was written on marijuana and majoun, and much of it was done when he was strung out on Eukodol, despite his many denials. The American books are all heroin and methadone novels. One effect of methadone is to radically suppress the sexual drive: Burroughs wrote a lot about sex in the final trilogy, but experienced it hardly at all. In addition, from the time of his return to the States he was stoned on pot most of the time. He always smoked in order to write. He woke several times in the night and would smoke a joint to get back to sleep. He also smoked full-strength English cigarettes, Senior Service when he could get them, until 1991 when he had a triple heart bypass. Drinking began at 6:00 p.m. He lived to be eighty-three years old.

3. "We Must Hold the Bunker at All Costs"[9]

Burroughs had no long-term relationship during the time he was in New York. He had hoped that James would be his partner, and though they no longer had a sexual relationship, he missed James and was always excited when he announced a forthcoming visit to New York. In the absence of a boyfriend, Bill had established a little family for himself at the Bunker with Stew Meyer, Howard Brookner, Victor Bockris, and John Giorno at the core, and a changing cast of walk-ons and spear carriers. James, however, remained central even though he was now only a visitor. Stewart Meyer, in his journal for January 27, 1981, commented, "James in a great mood and seems entirely at-home in the Bunker. His presence constitutes a household for William. The connection between them is probably the most important human contact in the ol'Doc's life."

John Giorno played the same role in Burroughs's life that Antony Balch had done; he lived in the same building and could be relied upon to have dinner with, for friendship, and for occasional sex. With James in Kansas, Bill needed someone to look after him. James Grauerholz said, "[At this time] John was the person who contributed most to William's care and upkeep and companionship, and loved him." Some people complained that John Giorno befriended Burroughs in self-interest; he toured the country with him as his opening act, released him on his Giorno Poetry System records, and basked in his reflected glory. When he released his *The Best of William Burroughs* boxed set of CDs, Giorno included seven photographs of himself with Burroughs in the booklet but only four of Bill with Allen Ginsberg. Allen felt that John was exploiting Burroughs and capitalizing on his fame, but Burroughs knew that and chose to allow it.

John Giorno and James had very different approaches to Burroughs. For Giorno, Burroughs was like a guru and could do no wrong, even if he was on tour and almost too inebriated to read his work. James remembered, "I would say, 'William's too drunk,' and John would say, 'Oh, but he's a great wisdom teacher.' And he was not the only one; there were other people like Steven Lowe. Their worshipful stance was such that he could do no wrong." James had a more practical approach. "My point of view was, I admire him, I give him the benefit of the doubt, but he's only human, he has his limitations, he may not be respecting them. I felt like his wife, like, 'Don't embarrass me.' I was embarrassed for him. He dreaded the readings, at first, then he got into it. The difference with me was that I was just square enough to think, 'No, he's drinking too much, not eating enough and he's ill.' Some of the readings were a disaster. More than he realized. But he did many great ones."

John, on the other hand, wrote, "He'd get drunk (vodka and Coca-Cola) and stoned (marijuana) before every performance and then walk out onstage cold grey and focused and give a magnificent performance. Each show was a masterpiece, exhilarating audiences with his clarity."[10] James agreed with Ginsberg that John was a "glamour seeker. [...] John Giorno could not ever possibly object to, or be embarrassed by, or deny absolutely capitalizing on William's fame or anybody else's fame that he's ever known in his life to gather more fame and attention for himself. That is an overall Identikit picture of John Giorno. It's his nature." But it was usually a positive experience. James recalled, "John contributed a huge amount to William's performances and those shows. Not only was he a great opener but he was a great travel companion and loads of fun to drink with. A lot of fun and laughs. And he had a real professional attitude towards getting there and setting up. [...] I really must say, we really had the most wonderful times."

Allen was one of Bill's frequent visitors. Their long friendship had matured to a stage where they would bicker for hours on end like an old married couple. They had deep reserves of love and mutual respect for each other that a few disagreements could not harm. Bill was irritated that Allen was judgmental about his drug taking, alcoholism, and lack of interest in Buddhism. In turn, he thought it was a failing in Allen not to see the value of telepathy, the magical kingdom, and Bill's other concerns. This sometimes led to a low level of antagonism, but they both seemed very comfortable with it; they were surface disagreements that they had held for years.

Allen's best work was written in the fifties, his years in San Francisco, New York, and Paris, when he did nothing else but write poetry. In the sixties, much of his writing time was taken up by antiwar and other political activities. He provided many of the ideas and much of the philosophy behind the hippie movement and was a catalyst to the growth of the underground press with his enormous, ever-growing body of contacts. Burroughs was enormously impressed at how much Allen had achieved, but was concerned at how stressed, tired, and exhausted he often appeared. In his years of work at Naropa, teaching and working with assistants and administrators, Allen had neglected his poetry. He wrote a few good short poems, but literally had not the time to do more. Naropa took up thousands of hours of his time over the years.

His teaching had also made him into a teacher; Allen had developed a tendency to pronounce instead of converse. Old friends such as Lucien Carr grew increasingly irritated as Allen lectured them on the CIA, or Buddhism, or whatever his latest preoccupation was, instead of relating to them as friends. His office staff had heard enough of Trungpa's supposed lineage to be bored at the mere mention of his name. His continuing obsession with sex also became irritating. One time at the Bunker Allen asked Bill how his sex life was going and Bill sighed, looked up at the ceiling, and said, "Oh Allen give it a rest."[11] Allen had felt that Brion Gysin and Ian Sommerville had supplanted him in Bill's affections, but now that Bill was back in New York, Allen was able to resume his senior role once again and Bill regarded him as his closest friend. Allen rarely got really high, but one evening that January he tried some Thai stick and got smashed silly. He kept asking Bill long, complicated questions and then forgetting the subject halfway through. Bill thought this was hilarious and kept asking, "What was the question again, Allen?"

In the mornings Bill would seat himself at his desk in his banker's chair and set to work. Above him was one of Brion Gysin's Moroccan street scenes, one of the few decorations in the vast empty white space. The concrete floor and ceiling amplified the buzzing from the refrigerator, the radiators gurgled and sometimes emitted a cough of steam, the room resounded with the machine-gun rattle as Burroughs pounded the keys of his large upright manual Olympia. Sometimes John Giorno or Stew Meyer would stop by in the afternoon, but Burroughs usually put in a good day's work. He could no longer afford to eat out all the time, but there was rarely a need to because John Giorno cooked for him much of the time, or one of the family would organize a dinner party at the Bunker for five or six people. With the exception of the celebrities brought over by Victor Bockris to provide fodder for his book, Burroughs rarely saw anyone outside of his small circle of friends.

In addition to arranging readings for Bill and dealing with the endless requests for interviews, meetings, and reprint rights, much of James's time was taken up with family problems. In January 1980 his father had a complete nervous breakdown and spent nine months in the psychiatric ward of the VA hospital in Topeka. James had to wrap up his father's law business and pay off huge debts, including contested loans from two estates he managed. Meanwhile in January Burroughs attended the "Freud and the Unconscious" conference in Milan and the next month flew off to Brussels for a two-week European reading tour. April saw Bill and James in Los Angeles, visiting the set of John Byrum's *Heart Beat* film about Kerouac and Cassady. They were treated very well, stayed at the Tropicana, had a car at their disposal and all the reefer they wanted. Afterward Bill went to spend two days with Steven Lowe in New Mexico, but it rained the whole time so he had no chance to do any shooting.

In May, Bill made a short trip to Paris, and in July he was a speaker at the three-day "D. H. Lawrence: His Influence on Living and Writing Today" conference in Santa Fe, New Mexico, with Allen Ginsberg, Margaret Drabble, Robert Duncan, Stephen Spender, and others. In fact he got to say very little because Leslie Fiedler dominated the proceedings and no one else could get a word in edgewise. Burroughs remembered, "Finally it got so bad that I wanted to say something and Leslie Fiedler keeps talking on and on, and Allen Ginsberg said, 'Will you shut up? William wants to say something!' And I did. I pointed out that I had indeed been influenced very much by Lawrence's book on Mexico, and what I had written about Mexico and various other remarks like that."[12] Spender had changed his attitude toward Burroughs since their altercation at the Edinburgh Literary Conference in 1962 and was "sweet as pie," as Burroughs said. Afterward there was a big reception in Taos at Mabel Dodge Luhan's adobe mansion. Burroughs stopped briefly in New York on his way to a reading in Rome. His last big trip that year was in December to the south of France, where he took part in a four-day conference called "Man, Earth and the Challenges" at the Institute of Ecotechnics, in Les Marronniers, Aix-en-Provence. In Paris he stayed with Howard Brookner and spent a lot of time with Brion. He was home in the Bunker for Christmas after an exhausting year.

There were six hundred pages of material left over from *Cities of the Red Night*, even after some of it was thrown away. A lot of it went into the next book, *The Place of Dead Roads*. Burroughs had a dream in which a Mexican was patiently trying to explain to a gringo, "These aren't unused roads, they are *dead* roads." The new book was a lot easier to write because it was straight narrative. The western material from *Cities of the Red Night* acted as a springboard. Denton Welch was another major influence that led to the character of Kim Carsons. Burroughs explained, "The whole style of the book, the whole style of his speech, is pure Denton Welch. I could pass off whole sections of that as an undiscovered manuscript by Denton Welch and everyone would say it's true."[13] He went on: "The voice, to the extent that it's Denton Welch, it isn't a question of admiring it, it's a question of it being suitable for a certain character."[14]

Billy continued to hover in Bill's consciousness as a nagging unsolved problem. At the end of 1980, Teina, an old girlfriend of Billy's from the Green Valley School, wrote and invited Billy down to Florida from Denver. She was newly divorced, wealthy, and had harbored a crush on him ever since they were at school, but had no idea what a terrible state he was in. Burroughs wrote, "We thought maybe she would really look after him, and with her money it would work out. She was picturing him as the person she remembered, this healthy person, this totally different person. Before he was drinking. She must have gotten a terrible shock."[15] James did try to warn her, but no one could have expected such a deterioration in someone so young. It didn't work out, but she did not abandon him; she put him up in one of the empty apartments that she owned. Meanwhile he had a big falling-out with George Van Hilsheimer, who ran the Green Valley School, over a small incident; Billy got completely drunk on malt liquor and passed out by a creek, where he was picked up by the police and finished up in West Volusia County Hospital in DeLand, Florida.

Over the years Billy Jr.'s health had deteriorated further. He was in pain much of the time. He and Bill frequently spoke on the phone and exchanged correspondence, but his decline seemed to be inexorable. There were a few occasions when Bill and Billy did readings together, but Billy Jr. had terrible stage fright. Allen gave him twenty-five dollars as a teaching fee for talking to a class at Naropa, though it almost certainly came from his own pocket. Billy once made good money doing a radio documentary on his father, but he was basically unemployable and when he did get a job he never held it for long. He drank a lot and was unpredictable, selfish, and difficult to be with. He was on Social Services but he was very negligent about going to collect his checks and going through the bureaucracy needed to get the money. As soon as he got money he would give it away or spend it. Bill sent him $150 a month, which was enough for him to live on. If he sent any more, Billy would only give it away; sometimes he gave everything away and had no money for food. Bill was uncritical; he had never been much good at holding down a job himself. It obviously wasn't going to work out with Teina, so Bill paid for Billy to rent a room in DeLand. Ten days later Billy called one of the social workers at West Volusia County Hospital, saying, "You'd better get over here, I'm really sick." The man went over, looked at him, and called an ambulance. Billy died six hours later on the morning of March 3, 1981. James received the telephone call at the Bunker and told Bill at breakfast.

Bill rose and went to his room, where he sobbed uncontrollably for half an hour.[16]

The cause of death was given as a heart attack. There was an autopsy but Bill never learned of its results. Bill did not go to Florida. He attended a short ceremony at Trungpa's center in New York, conducted by one of the Tibetans. Bill was happy that Billy had been given five additional years, though Billy himself may have preferred otherwise. He began dreaming about Billy. Allen salvaged Billy's papers that were still in Boulder and forwarded them. Burroughs said, "He left these papers, obviously meant for me to see. There's a curse delivered against me, which he never sent. This outpouring of hatred. But the essential thing is that he made me responsible for every thing that ever happened to him. [...] On and on, it was quite insane. But it's that thing that Billy had, of making someone else completely responsible for everything they do."[17]

Karen, Billy's former wife, was given his ashes, but she disliked Burroughs, whom she blamed for all Billy's problems, and refused to send them on to him. Allen Ginsberg intervened. "She had nothing against me. So I sent a very simple letter saying I would take care of it. Bill had no specific intention with the ashes, so I suggested that we should just bury them there [Boulder]. So he said fine, so I said I'd take care of it."[18] She sent the ashes to him. Allen arranged a small ceremony at Naropa and then the ashes were buried on the back hill approach to Marpa Point, on land owned by Karmê Chöling outside Boulder.

Burroughs could never fully understand why Billy blamed him for everything. He recognized that he had been a terrible father and neglected his son. He had not shown him the love he so desperately wanted and had been unable to mend the relationship in Boulder during the only sustained time they spent together. But Burroughs refused to accept that by killing the boy's mother he had destroyed Billy's life. He did not understand why Billy felt that he was responsible for his distress, for the drinking and drug taking that eventually led to his death. Bill's immediate reaction to Billy's death was to start going over to Rivington Street himself to score for heroin, despite being on methadone. After a busy schedule of readings to promote *Cities of the Red Night*, Bill went to Lawrence in June to spend a month with James to sort out his feelings about Billy and recover. James wrote to Julie, Billy's half sister, to inform her of his death, but received no reply.

Meanwhile, Burroughs's profile was slowly increasing in the United States, the result of all the celebrity pieces written by Victor Bockris and others, and the ceaseless touring America from coast to coast to promote

Cities of the Red Night with readings and book signings. The culmination of all this activity was an appearance on NBC's *Saturday Night Live*, the coolest television show on the air, home to writers such as Terry Southern and performers like John Belushi. The writers' wing of the show was famously awash with hash and cocaine, and the show itself was peppered with drug-taking in-jokes. Burroughs appeared in a six-minute segment on November 7, 1981. He was introduced by actress and model Lauren Hutton, who said, "I'm very pleased tonight to introduce a man who in my opinion is the greatest living writer in America. Reading selections from *Naked Lunch* and *Nova Express* in his first television appearance ever, here is Mr. William Burroughs!"[19] *Saturday Night Live* musical director Hal Willner added a subtle soundtrack of "The Star-Spangled Banner" to Burroughs's reading from "Dr. Benway," to great effect. There was no mention of the Beat Generation. His appearance on *Saturday Night Live* helped him to throw off this tag and appear as an absolutely unique voice in American letters.

BOOK NINE

Return to Roots

Chapter Forty-Nine

I would have to say yes, evil exists, definitely. [...] I asked myself, why do these demons have such necessity to possess, and why are they so reluctant to leave? The answer is, that's the only way they can get out of hell—it's sort of like junk. They possess somebody and they want to hang on to it because that's their ticket out of hell.[1]

1. Tornado Alley

On June 19, 1981, Burroughs was staying in a sublet apartment in the same building as James on Oread (pronounced "Oriad") Avenue at the north end of the campus of the University of Kansas at Lawrence. At 7:30 in the evening Bill was standing on the balcony and saw the sky turn black. Then they heard the tornado warning. Golf ball–size hailstones began to fall, bouncing on the sidewalk, drumming on car roofs, and the temperature dropped by twenty degrees in five minutes. The sky turned green, "tornado green." The twister carved its way through Lawrence, killing one man, injuring thirty-one, and causing $18 million worth of damage. Fifteen homes were damaged or demolished and many businesses. The tornado hit the Gaslight Village mobile home park, overturning trailers: "They always hit mobile homes. They just don't like mobile homes,"[2] commented Bill.

He was spending the summer in Lawrence hoping to complete *The Place of Dead Roads*, and also to see if he liked it well enough to move there. Bill had been intending to move out of New York City for some time. "I was sick of New York. It had no advantages for me. There was no reason for me to stay there."[3] He had finished his season there and the people who had once entertained him now seemed mundane. In addition he had hardly any money because he was spending so much on drugs. He was never one to go out to parties and, though invited, had never set foot in Studio 54. The tipping point came when the landlord attempted to double the rent on the Bunker. He knew then that it was time to move. He wanted somewhere he could buy real estate and settle down. He had tried Boulder and decided that he didn't like it at all. "I wanted to see if I would like to live there. No, I didn't at all. I don't like the cheesy mountains there, I don't like mountains, and those aren't even good mountains."[4] Lawrence, on the other hand, had the advantage of being cheap. James lived there among his old hippie friends, so there was a social scene already in place. It was also a return to the Midwest. In a sense, he had come full circle.

Lawrence is a small university town, then with about fifty thousand people, on the banks of the Kansas River, forty miles west of Kansas City. Previously, the best-known writers to live there were Langston Hughes—who hated it because he suffered the ills of segregation and prejudice there—and Frank Harris, who was in Lawrence from 1872 until 1875, not long after the town was founded. He was admitted to the American Bar there and described his amorous exploits in *My Life and Loves*, which was banned in both the United States and the UK for forty years for its explicit sexuality. Lawrence's latest resident was equally controversial; lucky then that the town was a small island of liberalism in one of the most conservative and right-wing states in the Union. Not that the Lawrencians were all liberal; after his death, the various efforts to commemorate the fact that Burroughs had spent longer in Lawrence than anywhere else in his life were met with a substantial resistance. Choosing to relocate into a region that considered his ideas anathema was bound to cause problems. Though he regarded himself as being deeply spiritual, he said, "I detest Bible Belt Christianity—dead, suffocating under layers of ignorance, stupidity and barely hidden bigotry and vicious hate."[5] "Christianity is the most virulent spiritual poison ever administered to a disaster-prone planet. It is parasitic, fastens onto people, and the essence of evil is parasitism."[6] But Burroughs came to no harm in Lawrence, and soon enjoyed a supportive community of James's old friends, young fans, and people from the university.

Lawrence defies Kansas stereotypes. Unlike most of the state it is not flat but is surrounded by gently rolling hills, woods, and lakes. Old West Lawrence is built on the usual Jeffersonian grid, and there is a small downtown consisting of three or four blocks ending at the river. Old East Lawrence still has wood-frame buildings dating back to the 1860s, northern European–style houses with added porches and eaves to accommodate the midwestern weather of hot summers and heavy rainfall. The university is a welcome break in the grid, allowing the topography of the town to assert itself. Half the vehicles on the streets are pickups and everyone drives real slow. Across the river from downtown, next to the railroad tracks, a huge grain elevator dominates the skyline, a reminder of the town's agricultural origins, and throughout the night, the sound of distant train whistles can be heard as the long freight trains pull slowly past the bridges over the Kansas River. There are plenty of fast-food outlets but no good restaurants.

Burroughs wanted a place where he could shoot, so he had to be outside the city limits. In December 1981, he rented an old two-story stone house five miles out of town. It had a huge barn that was ideal for target shooting, there was plenty of land, a fish pond, and a great view from the top of a small hill. The house had a modern bathroom, propane heat, and air-conditioning. Money was tight. There was not enough for Bill to buy a car, so living there was a bit inconvenient, but people brought out food and he stocked up at the supermarket. Most days James drove out there in his yellow VW Rabbit hatchback. It was a very cold winter and the propane gas used for heating cost $180–$200 during those months.

In order to move to Kansas, Burroughs took a gradual reduction cure to wean him off methadone. It was done slowly, over two or three months, so the addict hardly feels it. He was then on 40 milligrams a day, not a large dose, so it was not difficult for him. He was taking it in a glass of orange juice. At the end, "They let you drink orange juice for three days before they tell you you're off. You don't even know it."[7] Once he was in Kansas, however, it did not take long before he was back on drugs and enrolled with the methadone program in Kansas City. Early every Thursday morning James drove him there in his Isuzu Trooper to collect a week's supply. Instead of talking, which Bill didn't want to do anyway, as they drove they would play tapes of old songs made for Bill by Hank O'Neal. All Bill's old favorites were there, like "Angry, please don't be angry, because I was only teasing you." When it came to "Strange Fruit," he would usually say, "Skip it," even though he liked it. James remembered, "We would put this music on and it would be magical, going through the cold mists, the sunrise."[8] Afterward they would have breakfast at Nichols Lunch before returning to Lawrence.

Bill dropped into a ready-made social scene. James had been to college in Lawrence and many of his friends from that time still lived there: David Ohle, Susan Brosseau, Wayne Propst, and Bill Rich. Bill already knew David Ohle, because he had been their host when Bill and James visited the University of Texas at Austin for a reading in the late seventies, and had also met Patricia Marvin there. Artist Wayne Propst was an old friend of James's, who took Burroughs out to visit Propst's comfortable farmhouse when Bill was first thinking of getting a place in Lawrence. Bill and Wayne walked over Propst's property, just the two of them. Bill said, "I'll bet you five dollars I can hit that stalk over there," pointing at a small, dried ragweed stalk about twenty feet away.

"I'm in," said Propst.

Bill drew his pistol, spent some time focusing, then fired. The stalk fell in two parts.

Bill turned to Propst, smiled, and made the international "pay up" sign with his fingers.

Propst was taken aback a little that such a famous writer would expect him to pay up. "Oh yeah," he said, and handed over the five dollars.[9]

They became great friends, and Burroughs often visited. Propst is regarded as one of the most innovative, original, and amusing artists in the area. He was originally inspired by the Happenings art of the early sixties, one of his memorable works being "Vegetable Concert" from 1969, when he and his troupe broke vegetables and chewed them into microphones, accompanied by a collection of AM radios all tuned to different stations. Another work was a collection of five hundred shoes in a cage. Bill loved Wayne's off-the-wall sense of humor and his honesty. He also admired his practicality; he was a plumber among other things and could fix most things in his huge workshop.

Burroughs met Bill Rich during his preliminary reconnoiter of Lawrence in the summer of 1981. Rich had been a major force in the punk and post-punk scene in Lawrence, managing, producing, and playing with local bands and promoting concerts at the Outhouse, a barnlike structure beyond the city limits, near where Burroughs later sometimes shot guns. Through his record label Fresh Sounds, Bill Rich produced a five-volume series of CDs of local bands, *Fresh Sounds from Middle America*. He edited and published the music magazine *Talk Talk*, the autumn 1981 issue of which contained interviews with Psychedelic Furs, Iggy Pop, Billy Idol, and William Burroughs as well as record reviews and local news. The same issue contained a flexi-disc of Burroughs reading, produced by James Grauerholz. When Burroughs moved to Lawrence five months later Rich became one of Bill's assistants, driving him around and cooking his meals. They became friends, sharing a mutual love of Denton Welch.

Come the spring Bill could sit out on his back porch and smoke a joint. He sometimes caught a glimpse of a gray cat and began to put out food, but he could never get close to it. Once, walking back to the house after a shooting session in the barn with his friend Bill Rich, he saw the cat jump down from the porch: "He was about six months old, a gray-blue cat with green eyes—Ruski." One April evening, just before dark, Bill stepped out onto his back porch and there was the gray cat, and with him a large white cat he had not seen before. The white cat was friendly, purring and rolling at Bill's feet. It became a terrible nuisance, sitting on top of the TV, pawing at Bill's typewriter, sitting in the sink, on the food counter. One day Ruski came in and jumped onto Bill's lap, "nuzzling and purring and putting his little paws up to my face, telling me he wanted to be my cat."[10] At first Bill called him Smoky; he did not yet know he was a Russian blue. Bill kept a cat journal, which he later turned into *The Cat Inside*. He knew it was a dangerous subject. "In the cat book I'm treading that very thin line between the mawkish and the sublime. I don't think it's mawkish."[11] Bill became a confirmed cat lover. "I prefer cats to people, for the most part. Most people aren't cute at all, and if they are cute they very rapidly outgrow it."[12] His cat became part of him, like a couple. "An old man in a rented house with his cat, Ruski. [. . .] So he writes about desperately for an escape route."[13]

Throughout the winter of 1981–82, Burroughs had worked on the manuscript of *The Place of Dead Roads*, which was now nearing completion. It contained a lot of gay sex, perhaps as a form of sublimation as he lacked a partner, but it was usually integral to the story. He told Victor Bockris, "I say this: any writer who hasn't jacked off with his characters, those characters will not come alive in a sexual context. I certainly jack off with my characters. I can write sexual situations, very hot sexual situations. I don't get a hard-on, you understand."[14] The sex was less stylized than in *The Wild Boys* or other earlier books, where it served a different function and often consisted of mechanical repetition. According to Allen Ginsberg, Burroughs's use of sex was to explore his own sexual position, "rehearsing it over and over again, to sort of take it outside of himself, exteriorize it on the page and repeat it over and over again in different forms until his obsessive neurotic images lose their magnetic, hypnotic attraction or their conditioned attraction and become common-place visions in the day."[15]

William Burroughs Communications had a cash flow problem. The second part of their book advance of $8,000 was not forthcoming until they handed in the completed book. In April they telephoned Stewart Meyer, who had a day job as a typesetter, and asked if he would come out to Kansas for a month and type *The Place of Dead Roads* and a book of Bill's essays onto a computer disk for editing in exchange for three months' free rent on the Bunker, where Stew was then living. Stew and his wife, Jenny Moradfar, could stay with James and his boyfriend, Ira Silverberg, who had joined James in Lawrence in January 1982. Meyer wrote, "Springtime in Kansas with Bill, shooting guns and gassing. I'm a lightning typist so the work's not intimidating and I love to work on Bill's pages so fine."[16] They arrived in Lawrence on May 8 and settled into James and Ira's apartment on Washington near the KU campus. Stew noted, "Ira is the first of James' sidekicks that Bill has accepted to the point of inclusion in his extended household."[17]

The final draft took longer to prepare than expected because again there were two distinct versions. Bill's editor, Dick Seaver, at Holt kept pushing for a draft and was sent a version known as draft five. But James kept working on it and made a reassembly of the whole thing based on Bill's raw material. He came up with draft six. On December 6, Richard Seaver went to Kansas to discuss the editing of the book with Bill and James Grauerholz. James explained, "Dick thought that draft five was such beautiful poetry and so perfect, [but then] I brought in draft six which is the structure that's published, and there was a lot of arguing about it. I remember Dick Seaver's comment was that draft six is more commercial, draft five is more poetic. [...] We went through every one of the chapters, page by page, saying 'in or out?'" Burroughs was very attached to draft five and often mentioned that he would like to see a limited edition of it published. Burroughs explained the book to Chris Bohn:

> The Place of Dead Roads is a sequel to Cities of the Red Night. What happened there was, like, commandoes were parachuted behind enemy lines in time and they sort of cleaned up and drastically altered South and Central America. Dead Roads is the same thing applied to North America. They did South and Central America and the Catholic Church, now they're doing North America and the protestant ethic and the Bible Belt. [...] There's drastically fewer sexual scenes in Dead Roads than Cities of the Dead Night. There's really not that many at all. It's really concerned with weaponry more than anything else. Weaponry on all levels. The whole theory of weaponry and war. The history of this planet is the history of war, the only thing that gets a homo sapien up off his dead ass is a foot up! And that foot is war![18]

The strongest influence on Burroughs's work in this book is Denton Welch, whom Burroughs used as the model for Kim Carsons. Burroughs dedicated the book "To Denton Welch, For Kim Carsons."[19] He told a journalist, "Denton Welsh *is* Kim Carsons."[20] Burroughs was pleased with *The Place of Dead Roads*. To him it met his own strict criteria: "I sit down and write. If I can't do something else. I just start out and it takes shape. If I can answer [Matthew] Arnold's three questions—What is the writer trying to do? How well does he succeed in doing it? Is it worth doing?—then I feel I've succeeded. To those questions for Dead Roads I was able to answer fully, with an unequivocal 'yes' for the last."[21]

The book is a murder mystery, but when James Grauerholz read the manuscript in the first draft he easily picked out the killer, saying it was quite clear who it was and why. Burroughs himself had not yet realized who it was. "I'd really written clearer than I realized. I couldn't tell myself who had done it, but when James told me it could only have been one person, and when I looked back over it, he was right."[22] Bill made sure that the answer was a bit less obvious.

2. Painting with Guns

Burroughs began painting by accident in February 1982. He had a new double-barrel Rossi twelve-gauge shotgun and was trying it out, using a sheet of plywood as a target and number 6 shot. When he looked at the target there were some very interesting striations in the wood, where the shot had stripped away the layers—much as Gysin's original Stanley knife had sliced through layers of newsprint. "I saw all sorts of things— little villages, streets of all kinds. I said, 'My God, this is a work of art.'" The gun had heavy recoil and it really jarred him to shoot it, so he called the piece *Sore Shoulder.*[23] It became his first shotgun piece. "I then began preparing the wood with calligraphy before I shot into it."[24] All through March Bill blasted away at prepared surfaces with double-zero shot. He quickly realized the potential of shooting at paint cans, and began positioning containers of paint against the wood and shooting them, causing explosions of color all across the surface. He began to add collage elements such as photographs and pictures torn from magazines just as he did in his scrapbooks. At the time he never expected to sell any of them, in fact he didn't regard it as anything serious. Then Tim Leary came to town touring with G. Gordon Liddy. After their lecture there was a reception at the Stone House and Tim became the first person to buy one of Bill's paintings, paying him $10,000.

As was often the case in the twentieth century, Marcel Duchamp did it first. In his *Large Glass* (1915–23) there is an area known as "The Nine Shots" made by a little child's cannon that shoots matches. A match, with a little bit of colored paint on its tip, was aimed toward a target from three different positions, with three shots from each position. With each impact, the match left a touch of paint at the point of impact, and at these nine points a hole was drilled in the glass. A good shot might have hit the target each time, resulting in only one hole being drilled, but as Duchamp said, "the worse the instrument, the better you measure the skill." Duchamp was a bad shot.[25]

Other artists had used guns. In 1943, Joseph Cornell made a small work featuring a gunshot hole called *Habitat Group for a Shooting Gallery.* Beginning in 1961, Niki de Saint Phalle made her "Tir" series of paintings, filling polyethylene bags with different-colored paint and attaching them to a blockboard, then covering the front with a thin layer of white plaster, so that the paint bags were no longer visible. Spectators were then invited to shoot at the blank painting with a .22 rifle. Among those assisting her in her art were Robert Rauschenberg—who later worked with Burroughs—and Jasper Johns. For her the moment of action and the emphasis on chance was as important as the finished work. She stopped making the works in 1963, explaining, "I had become addicted to shooting, like one becomes addicted to a drug."[26]

Burroughs had been engaged in making visual art ever since he did a series of about a hundred glyph watercolors in 1959, a sheet of which was used to make the dust jacket of *The Naked Lunch*. When he began working with grids on his cut-ups he very quickly introduced visual elements to the manuscripts: sections outlined in red and green, words replaced with colored dots, grids drawn in bright red or blue lines. When he wrote in his scrapbooks he often used different-colored inks and purposely varied the size of his writing for aesthetic reasons. The news clippings and press photographs stuck into the scrapbooks were often treated with colored washes. One of the scrapbooks was so intensely colored that it has become known as *The Book of Hours*. When his work was published in magazines, he often went back through his photo files to find the illustrations and photographs that helped to inspire the piece in question and stuck them onto the open pages of the periodical. He assembled huge files of photographs and images, cross-filed ready for use. In 1965, when he was living in New York, Ed Sanders was putting together an issue of *Fuck You: A Magazine of the Arts*,[27] and needed an image of a motorcycle racer for his decorations to the cover. He and fellow member of the Fugs, Ken Weaver, went over to see Burroughs, who fished around in his files and produced the perfect image.

Burroughs had all along taken photographs. During his time in Tangier, he photographed his friends and visitors, but his main interest was in street scenes, the "sets" for his writing. He took hundreds of pictures of Tangier and of Gibraltar, particularly structures like the lighting towers at the football grounds, which later appeared in *Towers Open Fire*. His occult studies with Gysin in Paris led him to neglect photography, but he took it up again in London and from 1960 onward took endless pictures of buildings, streets, and park scenes. In Tangier in 1963 he began his photo collages—arrangements of objects photographed, rearranged, and photographed again—so he had an extensive background of visual art-making when he accidentally made his first piece of shotgun art. Initially he treated painting as an interesting supplement to shooting, and it was not until 1986 that he exhibited his work publicly—at the University of Kansas library in Lawrence—and not until December 1987 that he had his first show.

During the shooting stage of Burroughs's art, the works were rather large, often made using old doors that he shot at, adding collage elements to the exploded paint. The writing and the painting overlapped—he was still working on *The Place of Dead Roads*—and frequently the paintings were related in some way to the writing. "In painting I see with my hands and I do not know what my hands have done until I look at it afterwards. It is when I look at a completed canvas that I know what the painting is about. Very often they turn out to be illustrative of my writing, or what I am thinking about writing."[28] The unpredictable quality of this type of painting appealed to Burroughs because of its parallels with the cut-ups: part of the creation was random, followed by controlled selection, repainting, or the addition of collage elements. "The shotgun blast releases the little spirits compacted in the layers of wood, causing the colors of the paints to splash out in unforeseeable, unpredictable images and patterns."[29] He found that pistol cartridges did not reliably explode but just made a hole in the can so that the paint ran out rather than exploding sideways. He found that a high-velocity cartridge usually did the job. Sometimes the can would be thrown one hundred feet or more by some of his early shotgun paintings. He collaborated with Wayne Propst to invent a cannon to shoot bowling balls to make a really big impact on Bill's plywood panels. Wayne remembers, "At first, we shot it at Burroughs's 'failed' art, then at figures cut from plywood. If I remember, some of the bowling ball pieces were sent to a gallery but didn't sell. It was an extremely dangerous contraption—we didn't use it for long."[30]

In his usual way, Burroughs experimented with every possible combination: several cans at a time, two surfaces placed so that the blast paints two at once, aiming across the painting at different angles to create different exposures to different colors, and arranging the targets at different angles to produce different drip rates, more than one shot. Then all of a sudden, he found that he was just not getting it. The paintings were no longer working. "You just can't use the same technique endlessly. It becomes mechanical, and the life just isn't there anymore." He needed to move on and try out new techniques, but his attention was already focused on his new book. Painting went on the back burner for a while.

In 1982, the Nova Convention was echoed with a similar event in London called the Final Academy, a reference to the column Burroughs once had in London's *Mayfair* magazine. David Dawson, Roger Ely, and Genesis P-Orridge organized four days of events at the Ritzy Cinema in Brixton from September 29 to October 2 featuring Burroughs, Brion Gysin, John Giorno, and Genesis P-Orridge, Psychic Television, 23 Skidoo, Last Few

Days, and Cabaret Voltaire. Jeff Nuttall was scheduled to appear but he flew in from Manchester and was piqued that no one was at the airport to meet him so he took the next flight back. The events were backed up by an exhibition of Burroughs's first editions, cut-up manuscripts, and collage photographs at Dawson's B2 Gallery in the East End, where people gathered each day. The Final Academy was followed by a concert at the Hacienda in Manchester on October 4 by Burroughs and Giorno and at the Centre Hotel, Liverpool, on October 5. There was a one-off at Richard Branson's Heaven under the Charing Cross railway arches on October 7 featuring Burroughs, John Giorno, Marc Almond, and Heathcote Williams plus Derek Jarman, Psychic Television, Last Few Days, Cerith Wyn Evans with Marc Almond, and Brion Gysin, who had assembled a band that included Tessa from the Slits on cello, the drummer from Rip Rig and Panic, the percussionist Giles from Penguin Café Orchestra, and Ramuntcho Matta (son of the Chilean surrealist painter) on guitar. Brion read some works and sang others. Though there were some complaints that the events were too literary, and other people could see no connection between the musicians and Burroughs, overall it went down very well and served more or less the same purpose as the Nova Convention, establishing Burroughs as a mentor for the younger generation.

On February 27, 1983, Burroughs's brother Mort died at the age of seventy-three, and Bill and James flew to St. Louis for the funeral. Mort was survived by his wife, "Miggie," Margaret Carr Vieths, who was one month older than Mort, and their twin daughters, Dorcas Carr and Laura Lee Burroughs, born May 5, 1937. There were just twelve people present, including Jay Rice, whose family owned a big department store in St. Louis and had attended Los Alamos with Bill and Mort. They all recited the Lord's Prayer. Bill and James didn't stay for the burial, as they had a plane to catch. Mort had been unable to find work as an architect during the Depression so went to work as a drafting engineer for General Electric and stayed there until he retired. Bill had not seen much of his brother, even though they were living relatively close to each other for the first time since they were children. "He was a pretty square, regular sort of a guy, so we didn't have all that much in common. He couldn't read my books."[31] In all the years he lived in St. Louis, Mort saw almost no one. "He just didn't seem to have any interest in seeing people or have any reason to see people." He collected seashells, and had some beautiful examples, and continued his father's hobby and carved things out of wood, including walking canes. He and Bill shared an interest in guns and Mort owned a .41 Colt Peacemaker and a .22 rifle, both of which finished up in Bill's possession, given to him by the family.

Burroughs had last visited them in the summer of 1982 when he was in St. Louis filming with Howard Brookner, and Mort appeared, rather reluctantly, in the film. Mort had had a pacemaker for some years, but his death came as a shock to Bill. It turned out that Mort had been very sick for the previous six months but none of the treatments had worked. Bill never got on with Miggie, but after Mort died Bill wrote her a letter, "a very nice letter saying that I should tell her that I believed in life after death, and all that kind of thing—which is true. Some people make it, and some don't. That's the point in this world: some make it, and some don't—when you die, your troubles is just beginning. So you gotta swim through the Duad, which is this huge river of excrement—it isn't everybody that makes it through the Duad. Well, anyway, I wrote her a letter but I haven't heard from her."[32]

His brother's death set him thinking along the lines of Wordsworth's "Ode: Intimations of Immortality." Certainly its last line rang true: "Thoughts that do often lie too deep for tears." He remembered he and Mort playing together as children, their daily visits to Forest Park, Nursy, their time together at Los Alamos and at Harvard; a shared prewar world long gone. Two days before Mort died there had been another death, that of Tennessee Williams at age seventy-one. Although Williams had grown up in St. Louis, he and Burroughs had never been close, but they knew each other. Burroughs bought a copy of Williams's 1975 *Memoirs* and added marginalia as he read it, as was his habit. He had, by this time, agreed to let the French biographer Ted Morgan write his life, so the subjects of biography and autobiography occupied his thoughts. He began to fill folders with reminiscences and scattered observations from his past as well as the usual dream notes and diary entries similar to that found in *My Education* and *Last Words*. He labeled these folders "Memoires" [sic], "Miscellaneous Memoire Materials," and "Some memories/Unclarified drafts." He began marginal annotations in a copy of *April Ashley's Odyssey*, the harrowing, and sometimes hilarious, 1982 story of how George Jamieson, a Liverpool schoolboy, became the internationally famous transsexual April Ashley. Bill had known her slightly in London and they shared many acquaintances from the Rushmore Hotel days onward. Bill did the same with *High Diver*, the autobiography of his friend Michael Wishart, and with Paul Bowles's memoir *Without Stopping*. Burroughs had quipped that it should have been called *Without Telling*, as it revealed so little. Tennessee Williams's memoirs impressed him the most; he liked that Williams made no attempt to impose chronological order upon events. Bill did the same himself, allowing his mind to explore his past, sometimes encountering great Proustian gusts of memory, other times remarking that he remembered little about the person in question. He referred to these marked-up books as he wrote his own memoir, dating the pages and filing them. In July 1983, Ted Morgan arrived in Lawrence to conduct the first series of taped interviews for his groundbreaking biography, *Literary Outlaw: The Life and Times of William S. Burroughs*, his questions provoking even more memories.

In March, shortly after Mort's death, James received a blow when his father was sent to prison for misappropriation of funds. A deputy prosecutor, whom James's father had once tried to get disbarred, mounted theft charges against him. He was initially jailed for eleven days, then the court gave him two to six years in Lansing prison for stealing $30,000 from two estates that he was administering. He claimed he just borrowed the money, and it was in any case already paid back by James when he liquidated his father's holdings in 1980.

Chapter Fifty

Who was Brion Gysin? The only authentic heir to Hassan-i-Sabbah, the Old Man of the Mountain? Certainly that. Through his painting I caught glimpses of the Garden that the Old Man showed to his Assassins. The Garden cannot be faked. And Brion was incapable of fakery. He was Master of the Djoun forces, the Little People, who will never serve a faker or a coward.[1]

1. Learnard Avenue

In 1983 Bill's lease on the stone house came up and his landlord wanted to increase the rent to four hundred dollars a month, which Bill thought was exorbitant. They managed to raise enough money to make the down payment on a small $28,000 bungalow at 1927 Learnard in the Barker neighborhood of southeast Lawrence. In September Bill moved in. It was on an acre of wooded ground on a quiet street, ideal for cats. The house was built in 1929 from a Sears Roebuck kit,[2] which, like many others in the neighborhood, was shipped to Lawrence by railroad and came complete with everything needed to assemble it, including the nails. Shortly before Bill moved in, the white cat disappeared, so it was just Bill and Ruski who relocated. The other cats were taken on by Robert Sudlow when he moved into the Stone House.

It was a single-story wooden house, painted white, set back from the road, partly hidden by a profusion of honeysuckle, trumpet creeper, redbud, white cedar, and hackberry trees. Shortly after moving in, Burroughs had the house painted brick red with a white trim. The porch in front opened directly into the living room, and a covered porch in back led off the kitchen. There were two bedrooms, separated by the bathroom, to the side of the living room. There was a large storm cellar and a separate garage. Bill worked from his bedroom at the back of the house overlooking the garden. The room was spartan: a small wooden desk housing his electric typewriter and a filing cabinet, a low bed with a blue cotton cover, a snub-nosed .22 under the pillow "in case of trouble." The living room

575

was a long thin oblong, painted a modest brown and cream and furnished simply with a secondhand sofa and a round table with three chairs next to the walk-in kitchen. A large blue-and-green Gysin oil hung near the kitchen, and one of his Sahara scenes on another wall. The bookcase was filled with natural history books and hospital thrillers. The acre behind the house contained a garden with squash, beans, gooseberry bushes, and blackberry brambles as well as elm and silver maple, black walnut, and catalpa trees. Bill split the produce with his gardener. He patrolled the land with a long, pink-handled electric cattle prod. Squirrels lived in the trees next to the house by the small creek, the Atchison Topeka and Santa Fe Tributary, that defined the property line of that side of his land. (In May 2004 the 2.6-mile tributary of the Kansas River was renamed Burroughs Creek in his honor and now features as part of a scenic footpath walk through this part of Lawrence.) Burroughs was to live in this house for fifteen years, the longest he lived anywhere. He wrote seven books there and produced over two thousand artworks. He finally had a home.

As he was now living within the Lawrence city limits, Burroughs was no longer permitted to shoot his guns. He kept them in the deep bottom drawer of the filing cabinet in the William Burroughs Communications office where James worked in the front bedroom, then made a more secure home for them in a locked safe in the cellar. His collection kept changing, but he normally had seven or eight handguns, two or three shotguns, and three or four rifles. "I'm not really a collector. I like guns that shoot and knives that cut. I have a couple of flintlock pistols that work, they work very well. It's a lot of trouble getting them all ready, but it's fun to shoot them. They are plenty accurate."[3] About once a week, depending on the weather, he went out to his new friend Fred Aldrich's place about fifteen miles outside Lawrence to shoot. Fred's place was an eighty-by-forty-foot steel and concrete warehouse filled with imported Chinese antiques, fenced with high wire mesh around the yard to keep out intruders. Fred was in his midthirties, with ginger hair and a freckled complexion. It was a bachelor establishment. In addition to the stock of his import business, the warehouse contained a 1972 Buick, a 75 mph speedboat, a 650cc Honda motorcycle, and in the carpeted living area, above the bed, a row of loaded shotguns. Fred had a backstop made from old lumber, where they pinned their targets. Bill was a pretty good shot, though Fred's .44 Magnum made him stagger backward a bit for balance. Guns quickly became Burroughs's leitmotif: he was never one for small talk and visitors quickly realized that this was a subject that would provoke an interesting and lively discussion. Rather like Charles Bukowski's ever-present bottle of beer, any interview with Burroughs always mentioned the subject of weapons. In some ways it was a carapace—Burroughs had a deep and genuine interest in firearms—but he sometimes used it as a disguise, the return of *el hombre invisible.*

Life in Kansas was in strong contrast to New York City. Though James had many old friends in town, they were all considerably younger than Bill, almost all of them were straight, and most had little interest in drugs, except the occasional joint. It took a while for Bill to establish his own friendships with them, and when he lived in the Stone House out of town he was quite lonely. He had to remake himself in order to fit in; he concentrated on his interest in guns and weapons, snakes and dangerous wild animals, painting and cats. The cats alleviated some of the loneliness. Sometimes friends like Debbie Harry and Chris Stein would visit from New York, but it was an expensive and time-consuming visit to make and even Allen Ginsberg didn't come out that often. The situation continued in Learnard Avenue, and though much of his shopping and cleaning was taken care of, for the first six months he would walk to Dillon's supermarket and buy frozen TV dinners to microwave and eat alone. Sometimes he would not see James for two or three days; it was a far cry from drinks and dinner every night at the Bunker with John Giorno, Howard, Stew, and Victor. He had dinner guests some nights, but with no one to eat and drink with on a regular basis he drank too much and concentrated on his cats. They became a lifelong obsession.

Then things began to settle down, a routine was established with regular cleaners and a roster of volunteers to cook Bill's evening meals. Burroughs never ate lunch, just a cracker and a glass of milk. Sometimes they would all go out to dine, usually accompanied by friends, but the downside of living in Lawrence was that there were no good restaurants. The only halfway decent one was at the Holiday Inn. For all the years he lived in Tangier, Paris, and London, Bill was used to fine dining. Things changed when he got to New York and lived in a neighborhood where there were few good restaurants—except for Phebe's, virtually across the street from him on the Bowery, where he ate a lot—and as a consequence he changed his habits and began to eat at home. Finances also had something to do with it. He was a great deal poorer in New York, having become a junkie again. In Lawrence, whenever funds permitted it, he would send away for tins of caviar, which he loved, one of his few real luxuries.

The house began to take on character. On the dining room wall was a painting of a naked youth dying of a snakebite, made by Dean Ripa, a snake hunter who traveled the world collecting dangerous snakes for zoos. When Burroughs was still at the Stone House, Ripa had written to him out of the blue offering to send him a gaboon viper. "In fact, I told him if I didn't hear from him I was gonna send him the gaboon viper. That's a very venomous snake from Africa. So he responded quickly 'cause he did not want to receive the gaboon viper." Burroughs loved snakes and invited Ripa to visit. He arrived with a pillowcase of diamondback rattlesnakes, gaboon vipers, and kraits. Later he brought bigger examples. David Ohle described a visit to Learnard Avenue when Ripa brought a carload of serpents and dumped them on the floor, letting them crawl around. He put a gaboon—stiff from the cold car ride—and a thirteen-foot king cobra on Bill's cat-shredded sofa, and warned Bill to be prepared to run. Ripa worked the others, which included the fer-de-lance (South America's most deadly snake), with his stick. Bill stood near the bedroom door, ecstatic. Ripa's business partner had died of a green mamba bite the previous year in Africa. From then on until Bill's death, Ripa would arrive in Lawrence to look for copperheads and rattlers, spend a few days staying with Bill, then take off again for Africa or South America. In *The Western Lands* Burroughs wrote, "I number among my friends a young man named Dean Ripa, who could have stepped from the pages of a Joseph Conrad novel."[4]

One time Ripa had been out collecting and left a box of copperheads and rattlers on Bill's back porch. He dropped a mouse in for them to eat and went out again. "When I came back [Bill] had put his hand into the cage, either to grab the mouse and move it over where the snake could get it or to take the mouse out, I don't know which. The snake struck and just missed him by a hair. It might have actually brushed his hand. At his age, that would have been very bad. So he was nearly killed on one of my trips by rattlesnakes."[5] Bill told David Ohle he had also been bitten by a black-snake. "When Dean was here I reached into a bag and it chomped down on my hand. Dean had to remove it by relaxing its jaws [...] because it has incurving teeth."[6] Naturally, when Burroughs wanted details of centipede venom, he turned to Dean Ripa for the answer. His exhaustive three-page letter is reproduced in *The Western Lands*.[7]

Burroughs had never intended his books to be difficult to read. He would have loved to have a bestseller, and from *Junky* onward had always hoped that his books would be popular. In 1983 he read his way through all of John Le Carré—"quite fun"—and a number of other spy books before moving on to something less literary. "I read doctor books, you know, these doctors who are writing books now, and some of them are pretty good, pretty funny. I find that Benway is even outdone in prac-tice. What goes on in hospitals, my God!"[8] These were newsstand novels, including *The Making of a Surgeon* by William Nolen, MD, and *Calling Doctor Horowitz* by Steven Horowitz, MD.

That summer at Naropa, Bill was asked by Allen Ginsberg to provide a reading list for his students. He listed more than one hundred books plus "the complete works" of Kafka, Genet, and Fitzgerald. He handed the pages to Allen. Allen was outraged and stamped his feet, accusing Burroughs of simply listing everything he had on his bookshelf. "What's this?" he demanded, pointing at *Intern* by Doctor X.

"That, Allen, is a doctor book. I assure you it's a very good one." Bill spoke quietly, as if talking to a recalcitrant pupil.

"But they can't read all these," fumed Allen.

"They are the books I like," said Bill, pursing his lips.

"Where's Kerouac?" demanded Allen. William did not reply, just placed his fingers together and pursed his lips some more, biding his time. Allen knew better than to argue and the list was duly photocopied and distributed for Bill's August 1983 class.[9]

Burroughs had never thought much of Kerouac's actual writing, and had always been irritated by Kerouac's various portrayals of him as well as the way that he was lumped together with him by the critics, Allen Ginsberg included, who often assumed that Kerouac was an influence on his work. "I said that he had an influence in encouraging me to write, not an influence on what I wrote. [...] So far as our style of work and content, we couldn't be more opposite. He always said that the first draft was the best. I said, 'Well, that may work for you, Jack, but it doesn't work for me.' I'm used to writing and rewriting things at least three times. It's just a completely different way of working."[10]

As with the *Naked Lunch* group of manuscripts that were used in the cut-up trilogy, the years of research and work on *Cities of the Red Night* had given Burroughs six hundred pages of material to use as a starter for *The Place of Dead Roads*. In April 1984 he told the *East Village Eye* that the new book was well under way. "The overflow from Dead Roads was about 7–800 pages. I always had material to draw on for the next one. So in a sense the next one is well underway by the time I finish the one that I'm doing. [...] I never know what's going to happen. I don't plan the novel out. I don't even have any idea how this novel I'm writing now is going to end or where it's going from where it is now, or how much of that material will be useable."[11]

In May of that year, thanks to prolonged and intense efforts on the part of Allen Ginsberg, Burroughs was elected to the American Academy of Arts and Letters, much to the fury of some its more conservative members, and to the disapproval of some of his friends, such as Lawrence Ferlinghetti, who commented that his inclusion in the establishment proved Herbert Marcuse's point that capitalist society has a great ability to incorporate its onetime outsiders. His inclusion perhaps said more about Ginsberg's desire for the Beats to dominate American literary society than any great desire by Burroughs to hobnob with the very establishment that he had been so virulently criticizing all his life. Still, he was proud of the award and wore its insignia to official events alongside the emblem of his designation as a Commandeur de l'Ordre des Arts et des Lettres, given to him a year later by Jack Lang, the French minister of culture at Jean-Jacques Lebel's instigation, which is awarded for making a "significant contribution to the enrichment of the French cultural inheritance" (a higher distinction than that given to Allen Ginsberg and Brion Gysin, who were "Chevaliers").

There were further accolades when Burroughs turned seventy on February 5, 1984, when, in addition to a series of private dinner parties, there was an enormous birthday party held at Limelight, a New York nightclub converted from a church. All Burroughs's old friends were there, including Joan Vollmer's original flatmate Edie Parker, who called Burroughs "Billy." It was the hot ticket for that night: Frank Zappa sent two dozen long-stemmed red roses; Lou Reed, Madonna, Philip Glass, Jim Carroll, Lydia Lunch, and the whole downtown art and music scene were in attendance, including Sting and his Police cohort Andy Summers. Burroughs had never heard of them and at one point told one of his friends, "I don't know if you are holding, but someone told me that those two guys over there are cops."[12] He posed uncomfortably with them for the photographers. Among the hundreds of people who pressed forward to offer their congratulations was David Cronenberg, who managed to find time to propose the idea of filming Naked Lunch.

Cronenberg visited Burroughs a few times in Kansas and finally wrote a script in 1989. "I sent it [to Burroughs] to see what his reaction would be. He hated it and threatened to sue."[13] A Japanese backer pulled out after reading a translation of the screenplay, but it might have been caused by something as innocuous as the talking asshole. A script was eventually agreed upon, but nothing happened for about six years.

There were more parties and more accolades when Burroughs arrived in San Francisco, where V. Vale from RE/Search magazine and performance artist Mark Pauline of Survival Research Labs put on a gala birthday event at SRL's huge workshop in San Francisco. James Grauerholz noted, "William especially enjoyed playing with the hand-held flame-thrower that Mark had developed—a dangerous toy, William's favorite kind."[14] They were touring with Howard Brookner's documentary film Burroughs and doing readings along with the screenings to promote The Place of Dead Roads, which was published in April 1983. Seventy is a major milestone, and despite his now quite considerable fame, Burroughs was still hard pressed for cash. He confided in his journals, "So now at age 70 I have to read in nightclubs to eke out a living," an admission of how broke he was and written with a tinge of disappointment at how his life and career had gone. However, that summer, there was a dramatic change in his fortune.

He was approached by a new literary agent, Andrew Wylie, who was convinced that he could get a multibook deal with a large advance for Burroughs; it would solve his financial problems but it would mean ditching his old agent, Peter Matson, and quite possibly Richard Seaver, his editor for the past twenty-five years. Burroughs was initially reluctant, because the key to the deal was *Queer*, a book that Seaver had been trying unsuccessfully to persuade Burroughs to publish for years and which Burroughs had always sworn he would never publish; he had on occasion even denied its existence. Also, he felt a certain loyalty to Seaver: he had gone with him from Grove Press to Viking, they had been at the Chicago Convention together with Genet, and over the years they had become good friends. On the other hand, Burroughs was seventy years old and broke: Grove had never been generous with their advances, and his dealings with Viking had always been strictly business. In 1979, Seaver had moved to Holt, Rinehart & Winston, and Burroughs had followed him there, where he published *Cities of the Red Night* and *The Place of Dead Roads*. Bill had been loyal, but this was strictly business.

Wylie had just secured a six-book deal for Allen Ginsberg, beginning with his *Collected Poems*, and Allen felt that for Bill to have an aggressive, active young agent who was just starting out in the world would both solve his financial uncertainty and guarantee that the books would be promoted: Wylie always felt that the bigger the financial commitment, the better the publishers promoted the books. Wylie spent three days in Lawrence discussing the potential deal. He would offer *Queer*,[15] *Interzone*,[16] two volumes of letters, *The Western Lands* (not yet completed), and two future titles as a seven-book deal at an auction. Burroughs agreed. On November 23, 1984, the *New York Times* reported a deal. After an acrimonious exchange with Seaver at Holt, Wylie finally signed with Viking for $200,000 for seven books plus a further £45,000 (about $55,300) from Pan in the UK. Wylie took his commission, and Bill paid off his debts and was financially solvent. It did mean, however, that he had to prepare *Queer* for publication.

The manuscript had been found in 1972 when Barry Miles was organizing Burroughs's papers in order to catalog them for sale; all previous copies of it were thought to be lost or destroyed. The manuscripts came from a variety of periods and were sorted by paper sizes and by typefaces.

Any pages with numbering were set to one side in the hope of getting a sequence. During the initial sort, one group of numbered pages grew quite large, and by the end of the process, a virtually complete manuscript was present in a collection of top copies, carbon copies, and faded brown Thermofax copies. When it was offered to Burroughs for identification, he glanced at it and blanched slightly. "That's *Queer*," he said, and turned away.

Burroughs told a local Boulder paper, "My first reaction was: it's absolutely appalling. I couldn't bear to read it. How could I have acted in such a ridiculous manner? Going round sticking a gun into some cop's guts—if that's not a silly way to act. I thought: My God, how did I get out of this alive? It made me feel absolutely like I was in immediate danger. [...] I've written a commentary almost as long as the novel, and I decided it was worthwhile."[17] In February 1985, faced with the task of actually writing the introduction to accompany the text, Burroughs was very reluctant. He had a writer's block "like a straightjacket" and every time he even glanced at the manuscript he felt that he simply could not read it. "The reason for this reluctance becomes clearer as I force myself to look: the book is motivated and formed by an event which is never mentioned, in fact is carefully avoided: the accidental shooting death of my wife, Joan, in September 1951. [...] A smog of menace and evil rises from the pages, an evil that Lee, knowing and yet not knowing, tries to escape with frantic flights of fantasy: his routines, which set one's teeth on edge because of the ugly menace just behind."[18] In his appendix he wrote what must be his most-quoted paragraph. After describing the events that led up to the killing he wrote, "I am forced to the appalling conclusion that I would never have become a writer but for Joan's death, and to a realization of the extent to which this event has motivated and formulated my writing. I live with the constant threat of possession, and a constant need to escape from possession, from Control. So the death of Joan brought me in contact with the invader, the Ugly Spirit, and maneuvered me into a lifelong struggle, in which I have had no choice except to write my way out." It was the first time he had ever mentioned it in print and it was naturally seized upon by reviewers.

Queer was published in November 1985 and celebrated with a dinner for twenty-three at a Provençal restaurant in Greenwich Village. The back cover preempted any comments from critics by running a forceful blurb by Allen Ginsberg in his best PR mode stating, "Queer is a major work. Burroughs' heart laid bare, the origin of his writing genius, honest, embarrassing, humorously brilliant, naked—the secret of the Invisible Man. Swift, easy-reading narrative."

For the previous two years, filmmaker David Cronenberg had been working up his idea to film *Naked Lunch* and looking for backing. At the 1984 Toronto Film Festival he met the English producer Jeremy Thomas from the Recorded Picture Company and remembered that Thomas had once said in an interview that he would like to film *Naked Lunch*. Thomas was interested, but little happened because Cronenberg got distracted by Hollywood. That winter, James Grauerholz and Jeremy Thomas came up with the idea of all going to Tangier "location scouting." In January 1985, long before a proper script was agreed, Burroughs and James met David Cronenberg, Jeremy Thomas, and his associate Hercules Bellville in Tangier where Thomas congratulated Bill and James on their success in finally getting Cronenberg out of Canada to focus on the project. They put up at the El Minzah. Bill had not been in Tangier since 1972 and hardly recognized the place. The Parade was closed, Dean's Bar was still there, but Bill had rarely drunk there in the past. All his old friends were gone, with the exception of Paul Bowles, whom they ran into at the airport just as they were leaving. Bill found the town "a bit sad."[19] Cronenberg had not previously been there and received enough lasting impressions to want to use Tangier as a set. Unfortunately the three-week Tangier shoot had to be cancelled when the Gulf War—the American-led Operation Desert Storm, to remove Saddam Hussein's invasion force from Kuwait, which began on August 2, 1990—erupted five days before filming was scheduled to begin. In fact Morocco was nowhere near the war and filming could easily have continued, but it was decided instead to recreate the Medina in a Toronto film studio at enormous extra cost.

As the book has no narrative, Cronenberg had to write one. Burroughs had always regarded it as an impossible book to film: Conrad Rooks had proposed a drug-vision version back in 1963, and in 1970 Brion Gysin and Antony Balch produced a Broadway burlesque musical screenplay that Burroughs had disliked and that had gone nowhere. Zappa wanted to make it into a musical, and now Cronenberg, a man with considerably more experience in the field, wanted to make a horror film of it. Perhaps inevitably, he positioned Joan as a major character, even though she does not appear in the book, and her death became the film's main theme. The story is of how William Lee, played by Peter Weller, came to kill his wife, Joan Lee/Joan Frost, played by Judy Davis, and write *The Naked Lunch*. Cronenberg told the *Guardian*, "It's Joan's death that first drives him to create his own environment, his own interzone. And that keeps driving him. So in a sense, that death is occurring over and over again."[20] The film bears hardly any relationship to the book, but draws heavily on Burroughs's own life. Burroughs had no part in writing the script. "I was [...] relieved that David did not ask me to write or co-write the screenplay, as I am sure I would have no idea how to do so. Writers are prone to think they can *write* a film script, not realising that film scripts are not meant to be read, but acted and photographed. After fighting my way through *The Last Words of Dutch Schultz*, I had at least learned that lesson."[21]

2. Brion

At Learnard Avenue Burroughs became more and more attached to his cats. He postulated that the reason cats were first tamed in Egypt was not because they were good mousers—dogs, weasels, and snakes are all better—but as psychic companions, as Familiars. He treated his own cats as such. In August 1984 James was at 7th and Massachusetts, Lawrence's downtown area, when he heard a cat mewling as if in pain. A little black cat with green eyes leapt into his arms, so he brought it over to Bill. It knew what cat food cans were all about, because when Bill started to open one it jumped on the sideboard and rushed toward it. Bill called him Fletch. A fletcher attaches the guidance feathers or fins to an arrow. It is an unusual word that Burroughs probably took from Saint-John Perse's *Anabasis*: "the plumage is given, not sold, for fletching."[22] Fletch became one of the stars of *The Cat Inside*.

> I've learned so much from my cats. They reflect you in a very deep way. It just opened up in me a whole area of compassion that I can't tell you was so important. I remember laying on my bed and weeping and weeping and weeping to think that a nuclear catastrophe would destroy my cats. [...] I spent literally hours just crying with grief. [...] Then also the feeling that constantly there could be some relationship between me and the cats, some special relationship and that I might have missed it. Some of this is in *The Cat Inside*. Some of it was so extreme that I couldn't write it. [...] I am so emotional that sometimes I can't stand the intensity. [...] I'm very subject to these violent fits of weeping, for very good reasons. Yes.[23]

Burroughs said that the book used cats to represent people. "The point of the book is animal contact, not communication. Communication and contact are two very different things. Contact is identification and can be very painful. Communication can be forced, contact cannot. You cannot force someone to feel."[24] Naturally, cats entered his creative life, and as well as *The Cat Inside* he produced a short story called *Ruski*, named after his first cat, released as a limited-edition book in 1984. They naturally get a mention in *The Western Lands*: "So here I am in Kansas with my cats, like the honorary agent for a planet that went out light-years ago. Maybe I am."[25]

Bill had a cage in the garden to trap raccoons. If he caught one it would be collected by the Animal Protection League and taken to a halfway house where it would be weaned off garbage and trained to fend for itself in the wild before being taken far away from the city and released. One reason not to have raccoons around was that they might attack Bill's six cats. Much of his time was spent preparing cat food in individual throw-away tinfoil dishes. The cats were all overweight, though one was supposedly being kept on a diet to reduce its excessive size.

Tom Peschio, who was known as TP, Bill's assistant late in life, described how the cats dominated Burroughs's life. "As far as his daily routine, it can't be overstated how central the kitties were. He had all kinds of voodoo with the kitties. [...] It was mayhem, there were kittens and fleas and cat fights. He would bait animals; we'd take the leftovers and put 'em out in the yard every night for the OAs, the outside animals. There were outside animals and inside animals. There'd be possums and racoons gathered around the backyard and you'd hear screeching fights back there after you'd put the stuff out. He loved it, man, he loved it. They'd come in all the time, and he'd say, 'I had a coon in the kitchen last night,' and what he'd do, he had a bamboo cane, and he'd poke 'em through the cat door. 'Outta here!' " One day, when Bill was out of town, Bill's friend Gabby Holcomb took all the kittens and had them fixed. TP thought Bill would be angry but he took it with equanimity.

Brion's health worsened, and, knowing how much he needed money, Burroughs suggested a final collaboration with him. He wanted Brion to illustrate *The Cat Inside* for a signed limited edition. He told him, "I feel you are the only one who could do it [...] the little people, the little gray dawn cats."[26] Brion was astonished, and possibly a little insulted. He wrote back from Paris, "I don't draw cats." Like Burroughs, Brion had assembled a family of friends around him, and one of them, a young American named David Wells, went to the Centre Pompidou and made some poor photocopies of illustrations of cats. These he cut up and re-arranged, producing what Gysin said were "better illustrations than I feel I can do." Burroughs was not moved and continued to write and telephone, asking him to collaborate, and ten months later even resorted to baby language: "Brion: PLEASE! Ruski says please! Fletch says please! Ginger on the lap of Pantopon Rose in a Peoria cat house says please. All my cats say please. Draw us! Paint us!"[27] Brion thought that Bill was losing his reason but eventually asked his friend James Johnson to go out and buy every book and postcard of cats he could find.

Brion wanted to make one last great painting, an enormous calligraphic work in gold, called *Calligraffiti of Fire*, which stretched across ten huge canvases in the style of a Japanese *makemono*, or folding book. To do this he needed a studio, something he had never had. However, in stepped a benefactor, who agreed to advance him $4,000 a month toward the ownership of the painting. A gallery owner offered to rent him a studio on rue Quincampoix on the other side of Brion's block, and in July 1985 he started work. It took him six weeks to complete. He considered *Calligraffiti of Fire* a triumph and told Burroughs it was "THE picture of my lifetime."[28] Brion's benefactor went by the name of James Kennedy, a loud, excitable Irish wheeler-dealer who claimed to be the head of Sinn Fein and also went by the name of Jim McCann. McCann was just as mysterious as Brion about his famous friends and contacts. He left puzzling messages, the monthly advance arrived irregularly and in a variety of currencies, and he once impressed Brion by picking up the telephone and apparently ordering some assault helicopters, though this may have been a code name for something very different. (In 1988 he was busted in Ibiza with Howard Marks, the very big-time Welsh cannabis dealer. The *Times* headline ran, "IRA Man Arrested in Spain.")[29] Brion's friend Terry Wilson described him as a "trickster savant" and "funny."[30] Wherever the money came from, McCann/Kennedy saved Brion's life financially and took only the painting that he had commissioned and paid for in exchange.

Burroughs always said that Brion showed him how to live, how to be himself in the world; how to be honest and yet protect yourself; how to identify the social forces that were in operation against you: greed, jealousy, puritanism, the forces of religion and conservatism; and how to recognize the influence of the magical world: curses, autosuggestions, possession, and misdirections. Brion exerted more influence on him than anyone else in his life, and provided one of the deepest friendships. Bill's *ideas* came from Brion. Brion was always enormously proud of his role in Burroughs's life: cut-ups, the magical universe, the Ugly Spirit, scrapbook layouts, a style of painting (though he did not live to see that), Scientology. Not all of it was good—in fact, Paul Bowles often said that anyone who encountered Brion had their career set back by ten years—but Burroughs made a considerable amount of money out of painting, which countered any financial setback caused by the Gysin-inspired experimental work. "I could never have competed with him. But now I've made more money that he did in his whole life. It's pulled me out of a financial hole. I can buy flintlock pistols."[31] Burroughs always insisted that "the one who taught me more than anyone else was Brion Gysin."[32] Burroughs said that Brion always claimed that he was Burroughs's "conscience," and Bill agreed with him. Years later, Burroughs continued to insist on the importance of his friendship with Gysin. "Meeting Brion Gysin was one of the most significant events of my life. He taught me everything I know about painting, he brought the cut-up method to writing, he introduced me to Moroccan music and the Pipes of Pan—I'd say he was the most important single influence. Brion had integrity and complexity and was the only man I've ever respected."[33]

Burroughs's advocates have often blamed Brion for Bill's misogyny, and it is true that Gysin often raged against women, particularly his mother, whom many people, including Felicity Mason, felt he treated despicably. But Brion always told people what they wanted to hear, and at least some of his antiwomen remarks were for Bill's benefit. He was the perfect restaurateur—he knew which subjects would please his clientele—and extended that into his personal life. People in the art world found him knowledgeable about twentieth-century art movements and, more importantly, the possessor of lots of juicy gossip about artists and dealers. When discussing European history, he made intrigue at the court of Catherine de' Medici sound like hot gossip. When on the Paris "princess circuit" he always knew who was sleeping with whom. Some of Burroughs's conversational style comes from this. In discussing the Virgin Birth with Allen Ginsberg, Bill asserted that the secret was artificial insemination. When asked who would have performed it, he replied, "Oh John, of course, he was a vet."[34] That was pure Brion.

Brion could discourse at length on Arab music, religion, and culture; he made occult and magical practices sound even more mysterious and secret than they probably needed to be because it was more fun that way; having gone to Downside, the Catholic Eton, he knew all the gay scandals around the church. And when he was around men who disliked women, he was the arch-misogynist. As he said, there was no point whatsoever in telling Burroughs about his efforts to get a black woman elected as a union boss in the East Coast Shipyard in Bayonne, New Jersey, in 1942, where he worked for eighteen months as a welder. He was then a member of the Trotskyite Socialist Workers Party and ran her election campaign. Instead he told Bill about his long friendship with Eileen Garrett, whom he regarded as having genuine magical powers.

Despite his frequent diatribes against women, Brion had a number of women friends whom he would call up and dine with, something Burroughs never did. Bill always surrounded himself with an all-male friendship circle and often said that he would be happy never to see a woman again. When Bill and Brion got together properly in 1958, Brion had been staying with Princess Martha Ruspoli but had outstayed his welcome. She was only one of the many society women whom he saw on a regular basis. His so-called sister, Felicity Mason, was one of his closest friends, and they saw each other whenever she was in Paris or Tangier. If anything it was Burroughs, and his friends Ian Sommerville and Mikey Portman, who encouraged Brion's misogyny; they all encouraged each other. It was with Ian and Mikey that Burroughs evolved the bizarre idea that women came from another galaxy, an idea that later transmogrified into his concept that women were "the Other Half" who were preventing humans from leaving the planet. It was Burroughs who wrote, "I think love is a con put down by the female sex,"[35] and, quoting Conrad, "Women are a perfect curse," which he followed with, "I think they were a basic mistake, and the whole dualistic universe evolved from this error. Women are no longer essential to reproduction."[36] When Sommerville was apart from Burroughs he had a number of girlfriends, including Panna Grady in London and various other women in Paris and Tangier right up until his death. Burroughs had a few one-night stands, but the last time he had sex with a woman appears to be in 1963, just as the Beat Hotel was closing, which is also when he propositioned Felicity Mason.

With the onset of winter, Brion's health took a turn for the worse, and on December 9, 1985, he drew up a will leaving his literary estate to Burroughs, his pictures to the Musée d'Art Moderne de la Ville de Paris, and his music rights to Steve Lacy. He also made two cash bequests to close friends Udo Breger and Terry Wilson.

Radio Bremen, in Germany, had organized a three-day celebration of the work of John Giorno and his Giorno Poetry Systems for May 1986. John had agreed to the festival only if he was not required to ask Burroughs to appear, as he knew that Bill no longer liked to travel. In April, he was talking on the phone with Bill and told him how pleased he was to be going to Bremen because it would give him a chance to visit Brion, who was now very sick. He described the festival as "a gift from the Gods." Bill did not reply. "William, do you want to be invited?" he asked. "I didn't ask you because you endlessly complain about travelling." Bill said, "Well, John, I wouldn't mind going, if it got me to see Brion."[37]

Bill and John gave extremely successful readings to overflow crowds in both Bremen and Berlin before continuing on to Paris to see Brion. They spent four days at the Hôtel du Séjour, at 36 rue du Grenier Saint-Lazare, one block from 135 rue Saint-Martin where Brion lived directly across the street from the Beaubourg. Brion's emphysema was now so bad that he could scarcely walk the half block around the corner to his studio anymore, but he had completed his masterwork. He had an oxygen tank and wore oxygen tubes up his nostrils most of the time. Even the smallest effort sent him gasping for them. He was weak and in great pain from a tumor in his side, not yet diagnosed but that turned out, as expected, to be cancer. Brion was terrified of dying and wept before them, tears coursing down his translucent parchment cheeks. He had some suicide pills but admitted that he did not have the courage to take them. Bill was horrified to see his old friend in such a terrible state and became deeply depressed. Every day Brion told them, "I won't be around much longer."

Brion was surrounded by his devoted support group: David Wells, his assistant who had made the cat collages; Jean-Emil Gaubier, his day nurse; the art expert and curator Rosine Buhler; Terry Wilson visiting from London; and Udo Breger, who had come from Basel to help in any way he could. Brion's Moroccan friends Yaya and Fafa—François de Palaminy, Brion's last boyfriend—were there much of the time, as were many other old friends. Some of Brion's old feistiness remained; he was very rude to John Giorno. As usual with Brion there was much court intrigue; rumors that McCann/Kennedy was controlling Brion in some mysterious way divided the camp into warring factions.

Bill and James returned to Kansas, taking with them the brush and ink drawings that Brion had done to illustrate *The Cat Inside*. In June Bill and James went to Naropa for his annual stint but Bill caught a bad cold and spent many days in bed. As James put it, "The depression was thick enough to cover the floor, and it was catching."[38] In July Brion was diagnosed with lung cancer and was told he only had a matter of days to live. He contacted his friends, asking them to pay a last visit. John Giorno flew out and saw him. Burroughs booked a ticket for a few days' time; to fly immediately would have been much more expensive. He left it too late. On the morning of July 13, 1986, Jean-Emil found Brion dead in bed; he had had a heart attack while reaching for the telephone.

Burroughs did not attend the cremation in Paris on July 22, or the scattering of Brion's ashes at the Pillars of Hercules outside Tangier on January 19, 1987, Brion's birthday. He remained in a bleak depression for several months until September, when the "unbreathable fog," as Grauerholz called it, began to lift. Shortly after Brion's death, Burroughs wrote:

> Brion Gysin died of a heart attack on Sunday morning, July 13, 1986. He was the only man I have ever respected. I have admired many others, esteemed and valued others, but respected only him. His presence was regal without a trace of pretension. He was at all times impeccable.[39]

Brion's death preoccupied Burroughs, and inevitably it made its way into his writing. Burroughs had a recurring dream, which he called the

Land of the Dead dream: "Everyone I see is dead. The only thing that bothers me about the Land of the Dead dream is that I can never get any breakfast. That's typical of the Land of the Dead."[40] Toward the end of *The Western Lands* Burroughs visits the Land of the Dead and there is an encounter with Ian Sommerville at Le Grand Hotel des Morts. Bill asks him, "Is Brion here?" Ian replies, "No, he's not coming."[41] In an earlier reference to Hassan-i-Sabbah, Burroughs identifies the Old Man of the Mountains with Brion: "Oh, yes, I knew him personally, but I never knew him at all. He was a man with many faces and many characters. Literally, he changed unrecognizably from one day to the next. At times his face was possessed by a dazzling radiance of pure spirit. At other times the harsh gray lineaments of fear and despair gave notice of defeat on some battleground of the spirit."[42]

Burroughs told writer Legs McNeil, "Some of my dreams are so real— they are realer than my so-called waking life. Much realer. They have no connection with my waking life at all. The idea of waking up here never occurs to me."[43] Burroughs now concentrated his attention upon finishing *The Western Lands*. And though much of the book features a roll call of people from Burroughs's own past—Kiki, Ian, Marker, Mikey, his mother, his snake expert friend Dean Ripa, and more obscure acquaintances like Nicholas Guppy, often under their own names—it is worth remembering what Burroughs told an interviewer a decade before: "It is always a mistake for the reader to believe that the first person character is the writer talking. As soon as you put someone in your book, he becomes a character. You become separate from him. I don't have a particular voice that is mine. I have any number of voices."[44]

He described *The Western Lands* to James Fox: "Chauceresque pilgrims— adolescents almost to a man—travel through the Land of the Dead, the frontier beyond time, learning how to deal with space conditions. [...] I compare this to the transition from water to land of the various transitional species." He said that astronauts hadn't really gone into space because they went into space in an Aqualung, and said that there had to be a link: the creatures had to have an air-breathing potential before they made the transition. If not it would have been suicide. "I see that dreams are the lifeline to our possible biological and spiritual destiny. Dreams sometimes approximate space conditions. That's what *The Western Lands* is about."[45] It is a book about "the possibility of hybridization, the crossing of man and animals."[46]

Burroughs, in the book, creates Margaras Unlimited, an independent secret service, loyal to no country, with its own agenda: to provide aid and support for anything that favors or enhances space programs, space exploration, simulation of space conditions, exploration of inner space, or expanding awareness. It is also the job of Margaras to extirpate anything going in the other direction. "The espionage world now has a new frontier."[47]

Bill's dreams were full of animals, hybrids, and animals that no longer exist or never did exist. It was good material. "The theme I'm developing now is the zoological garden of extinct species, a zoo that Captain Mission finds in Madagascar with all the extinct species."[48] The book fell into place. As is usual with Burroughs's work, it is composed of a series of events and tableaux often with no apparent connection. The best definition of this essentially high modernist structure may be found in T. S. Eliot's 1930 introduction to his translation of *Anabasis*, one of Burroughs's favorite books and one that exercised a great influence upon him: "any obscurity of the poem, on first readings, is due to the suppression of 'links in the chain,' of explanatory and connecting matter, and not to incoherence. [...] The justification of such abbreviation of method is that the sequence of images coincides and concentrates into one intense impression of barbaric civilisation."[49] Burroughs used this "permission" throughout his writing life. "Any writer who hopes to approximate what actually occurs in the mind and body of his characters cannot confine himself to such an arbitrary structure as logical sequence. Joyce was accused of being unintelligible and he was presenting only one level of cerebral events: conscious sub-vocal speech. I think it is possible to create multi-level events and characters that a reader could comprehend with his entire organic being."[50]

The Place of Dead Roads closes with the death of William Seward Hall. In *The Western Lands* we find out who killed him: "Joe the Dead lowered the rifle...Behind him, Kim Carsons and Mike Chase lay dead in the dust of the Boulder Cemetery. The date was September 17, 1899." *The Western Lands* attempts to rectify the situation: "So William Seward Hall sets out to write his way out of death."[51] Kim Carsons is sent by the District Supervisor to find the Western Lands and find out where the Egyptians went wrong with mummies and the need to preserve the physical body. The answer turns out to be the final expression of Burroughs's misogyny: that women have halted evolution and are preventing humankind from mutating into a form where space conditions would not be inimical. The Egyptians, it seems, "had not solved the equation imposed by a parasitic female Other Half who needs a physical body to exist, being parasitic to other bodies. So to maintain the Other Half in the style to which she has for a million years been accustomed, they turn to the reprehensible and ill-advised expedient of vampirism.

"If on the other hand, the Western Lands are reached by the contact of two males, the myth of duality is exploded and the initiates can realize their natural state. The Western Lands is the natural, uncorrupted state of all male humans. We have been seduced from our biologic and spiritual destiny by the Sex Enemy."[52] This is, of course, the exact opposite of the historical notion that it is women who have always been the repository of magical knowledge and secrets, they were the ones at one with the natural universe and with their emotions, whereas men developed the rigid authoritarian structures of the traditional family, church, state, and the military. It is important to remember that this is a novel, and that at other times Burroughs has subscribed to Wilhelm Reich's views about character armor and the male role in creating the authoritarian, patriarchal world. Joe the Dead sets out to expose the female plot against humanity: "Joe is tracking down the Venusian agents of a conspiracy with very definite M.O. and objectives. It is antimagical, authoritarian, dogmatic, the deadly enemy of those who are committed to the magical universe, spontaneous, unpredictable, alive. The universe they are imposing is controlled, predictable, dead."

Perhaps not surprisingly, given the theme, Burroughs's poor mother gets dragged into it, with a further reiteration of the recurring dream Burroughs had of her that has appeared in a number of his books. Joe goes to Bill's old house at Pershing Avenue: "His mother is there and a long reptilian neck rises up out of him, curls over his mother's head and starts eating her from her back with great, ravenous bites, some evil predatory reptile from an ancient tar pit. His mother rushes in from the bedroom screaming, 'I had a terrible dream! I dreamed you were *eating* my *back!*' "[53] In the book he also recalls the last time he saw her, "Outside a Palm Beach bungalow waiting for a taxi to the airport. My mother's kind unhappy face, last time I ever saw her. Really a blessing. She had been ill for a long time. My father's dead face in the crematorium. Too late. Over from Cobblestone Gardens."[54] The lines were culled from *Cobble Stone Gardens*, a small-press book dedicated to his parents, first published in 1976. Bill's dream of his mother has provoked a certain amount of amateur Freudian analysis and is clearly a subject for further investigation.

The Western Lands is like a summation: a great roll call of his characters, his sets, and his ideas, juxtaposed and rearranged in a final literary collage. "His only link with the living Earth is now the cats, as scenes from his past life explode like soap bubbles, little random flashes glimpsed through the cat door. It leads out and it leads back in again. Touch the controls gently for serene magic moments, the little green reindeer in Forest Park, the little gray men who played in my blockhouse and whisked away through a disappearing cat door."[55] Throughout the book, people and places from his past flicker through the pages, a kaleidoscope of moving images, like an animated version of his photographic collages from 1963 Tangier, or a speeded-up film of his scrapbooks with newspaper clips, photographs, images torn from magazines, shooting past like a crazy Keystone Cops film. The piranha fish tank at Wips club in 1963 London is used as a set;[56] in a reference to his son's liver transplant he makes Joe the Dead a transplant surgeon;[57] Wilhelm Reich gets a mention in the "Medical Riots" section, written as a result of reading so many doctor books.[58] Bufotenine, which he helped Dennis Evans to extract back in 1960, makes a comeback: "Dandies in eighteenth century garb have reverted to snuff boxes. Bufotenine extracted from a poisonous toad brings one out in a strawberry rash, *so* becoming with pink lace."[59] Hassan-i-Sabbah plays a role, as do Brion Gysin's cook Targuisti, Bill's parents, and Ian Sommerville; it is truly a Book of the Dead. He can do anything: he sets a door dog on Anatole Broyard, his fiercest critic, using the dog described in Saki's *The Unbearable Bassington*, a whole page of which Burroughs appropriates for the purpose (incidentally revealing how similar his prose style is to that of Saki, Hector Hugh Munro).[60] He even threw in a fragment from *Minutes to Go* from 1960: "Professor killed, accident in U.S.," a line waiting all these years for its place in the Big Picture jigsaw puzzle of Burroughs's one long book where it would precisely fit. There are a few timid paragraphs of conventional early-sixties-style cut-ups in the early part of the book, but Burroughs appears to lose interest and they are not repeated. They were from a period long ago; he was no longer exhorting his readers to revolution. It is almost as if they were included as part of the process of "ticking off" all the periods of his life that constituted part of the process of the final trilogy.

When the book appeared, Burroughs's critics seized upon the ending, where it appears that Burroughs is signing off as a writer. He writes as if he were already dying, with his past flashing before his eyes: "The Big House at Los Alamos. God it was cold on those sleeping porches." He signs off resignedly; the book ends on a note of despair, and with a quote from one of his favorite writers, T. S. Eliot, who was himself quoting the throwing-out line of all British public-house landlords.

> I want to reach the Western Lands—right in front of you, across the bubbling brook. It's a frozen sewer. It's known as the Duad, remember? All the filth and horror, fear, hate, disease and death of human history flows between you and the Western Lands. Let it flow! My cat Fletch stretches behind me on the bed. [. . .]

How long does it take a man to learn that he does not, cannot want what he "wants"?...

The old writer couldn't write anymore because he had reached the end of words, the end of what can be done with words. And then? [...]

In Tangier the Parade Bar is closed. Shadows are falling on the Mountain. "Hurry up, please. It's time."[61]

Chapter Fifty-One

His thoughts were becoming uncontrollable. To stop their unbearable flow he told himself stories in pictures.

—Denton Welch[1]

Art is not made to decorate rooms. It is an offensive weapon in the defense against the enemy.

—Picasso, Les lettres françaises, 1943

1. Painting

In Lawrence, Kansas, Mayor Mike Amyx proclaimed the week of September 7–13, 1987, to be "River City Reunion Week," a celebration of the work of the myriad creative people who have intersected with the City of Lawrence, organized by James Grauerholz, Bill Rich, and George Wedge from the university English department. It was a major event, featuring Burroughs, Allen Ginsberg, Robert Creeley, Anne Waldman, Diane di Prima, Edie Kerouac Parker, Michael McClure, Keith Haring, Ed Dorn, Jello Biafra, Andrei Codrescu, John Giorno, Jim Carroll, and Ed Sanders. Local poets Ken Irby, George Kimball, David Ohle, Jim McCrary, and Wayne Propst read, among a cast of dozens. *Towers Open Fire, Chappaqua, Pull My Daisy,* and *This Song for Jack* were screened; Marianne Faithfull performed on Thursday night and Hüsker Dü on Sunday evening. The actual daytime sessions concluded with Allen Ginsberg reading "Howl." As James Grauerholz wrote, "For a week, Lawrence was the national headquarters of the counter culture."[2]

After completing *The Western Lands,* Burroughs concentrated more on painting than on writing. At the end of 1986 he rented a studio housed in a dilapidated barbed-wire factory on the Kaw River waterfront to paint in and to write. Diego Cortez contacted Burroughs and arranged to visit him with the artist Philip Taaffe, in order to work on a catalog text for Taaffe's show at the Pat Hearn Gallery in New York. They arrived on

January 31, 1987, and James made appropriate arrangements for Burroughs and Taaffe to work together: ropes and ladders, sheets of plywood, half-filled gallon cans of colored house paint, and old tubes of acrylic. They piled everything into a pickup and headed to an empty cornfield outside the city limits where they could shoot. In the distance there were passing freight trains. They hung the plywood from the ladder by ropes and hung the cans of paint from another ladder, using hemp twine. They stapled tubes of paint to the plywood and experimented with shooting at them from various distances—too close and the painting would be destroyed, too far and the shot would be ineffective in exploding the paint. Taaffe brought with him some cans of spray paint, something Bill had not previously encountered. "We strung this can—red paint—in front of a piece of wood and shot it up. It exploded beautifully. Perfect. I didn't have to do anything to it."[3] He called the result *The Red Skull*. Spray cans worked in a more satisfactory manner than the paint cans.

The next day the two of them did a drawing collaboration in Bill's factory studio in Lawrence after buying a quantity of oak tag paper, paints, inks, and brushes.[4] Their discussion was taped and was published as "Drawing Dialogue" in the catalog to Taaffe's show. Taaffe liked Bill's work sufficiently to suggest that he should exhibit it, and back in New York, Diego Cortez contacted the Tony Shafrazi Gallery, which expressed interest. Burroughs did not start to do work on paper until after Brion's death. "It would have been unthinkable for me to compete with him. I've done a lot better than he did, financially, on painting. Yes, that's one thing, collaborating was one thing [on writing], but as soon as I started painting that would be a matter of competition."[5] Brion would certainly have seen it that way, without question.

Burroughs had no formal art training, but felt that maybe that was a good thing given his way of approaching his art. "There might be something on my mind, I try to just let the hand do it, to see with my hand. And then look at it, see what has happened. I may see quite clearly in there something that I've seen recently in a magazine or a newspaper, whatever, emerging. I can't consciously draw anything. I can't draw a recognizable chair—it looks like a four-year-old's." The initial "killing of the canvas," making random marks to overcome the tyranny of the white rectangle, provided the subject matter; in among the whorls of paint, a subject emerged. "I don't know what I'm painting until I see it. In fact I've done a lot with my eyes closed." This is similar to de Kooning's letter paintings where he would scrawl a series of letters on the canvas, just to give himself something to work with. The point was to get started. He soon began to use stencils, at first commercial design forms, then ones that he cut him-self from cardboard, which he combined with collage elements.

It was the "surprised recognition" that Burroughs was after. "It applies to any art form. That's what I try to do in painting. Klee said a painter strives to create something that has an existence apart from him and which could endanger him. Now the most clear proof of something being separate is if it can harm you. [...] I do think all writers, many other writ-ers and painters are trying to create something that has an existence apart from themselves. It would literally step out of the picture or the book. So all artists are trying to achieve what some people would say is impossible, that is to create life. Of course, impossible is a meaningless word to me."[6] This fits in with cut-up theory: the recognition of connections between phrases suggested by random process; with his occult experiments with crystal balls; with the random cut-ins on his tape experiments; and now the emerging images from random visual events. "That what it's all about. The way that clear representational objects will emerge from what would seem to be a random procedure. I once took a small notebook and put some red gouache on here and on there—it's an inkblot technique. I looked and there was a perfectly clear red pig, a wild pig, tusks, bristles, and everything."[7]

His first one-man show opened at the Tony Shafrazi Gallery at 163 Mercer Street in New York on December 19, 1987. In the catalog Bur-roughs wrote:

I am trying to get pictures to move.

It almost happens: a face comes into almost-miraculously close focus, almost smiles, snarls, speaks... Then back to the picture, there on the paper, the wood.

Well, I think, look outside at the trees and leaves in front of the bedroom window. They move in the wind. The same thing is happening. I see faces, scenes. [...]

"Well," says the critic, "so you can see faces and scenes in the clouds. This is infantile."

Perhaps. And as often the child sees more clearly than the adult, who has already decided what he will see and what he will not see.[8]

Burroughs began painting or spray-painting around cut-out shapes, using commercial stencils of trees, dinosaurs, cats, and faces to "random-ize" his canvases, "a randomized selection of objects which however are quite recognizable. Start with your stencils then randomize them, gives you a number of different possibilities."[9] He used found objects like metal grilles or perforated metal sheeting as masks, to create a depth of picture plane, then sometimes cut into it with a collage element. His concern was to see what the painting had revealed; he saw the paintings as a gateway to the realm of the unconscious and the imagination. He was looking for figurative elements; he was able to identify faces and people in the paint, "some absolutely recognizable as portraits of certain people." If he particularly liked one of the faces that emerged, he sometimes had it photographed so he could use it again. The photographer would have to see the face before they could photograph it, because Burroughs was very specific about which bits of the painting he wanted. He might use a face from a red picture in another red picture, or make collages of a number of pictures, or all possible combinations. There was a big failure rate; very often nothing emerged. Whereas Picasso was using art as a form of negotiation between the real world and himself as an individual, Burroughs was using it to penetrate deeper into himself.[10]

Burroughs was essentially producing abstract paintings, but they were not cut off from recognizable objects: collage elements, photographs, stencils of animals all referred back to the real world, even the abstract shapes themselves. As Picasso pointed out in 1934, a common term for abstract work used to be "nonfiguration," but there can be no such thing as nonfiguration. "All things appear to us in the shape of forms. Even in metaphysics ideas are expressed by forms, well then think how absurd it would be to think of painting without the imagery of forms. A figure, an object, a circle, are forms; they affect us more or less intensely."[11] Burroughs's work is a meditation on the state of his mind; like the photo collages of 1963–65, they are a cubist assemblage of memories, personal references, and ideas suggested by random gestures and events, and are a snapshot of that moment of time.

Though there was no direct influence of Niki de Saint Phalle's work on Burroughs's art, it is nonetheless the Nouveaux Réalistes with whom he has the most affinity: Arman, Yves Klein, Martial Raysse, César, Daniel Spoerri, and others, as well as the Ultra-Lettrists, including François Dufrêne. Burroughs shared with them notions of appropriation, collage, and particularly décollage techniques: the Nouveaux Réalistes slashed or lacerated billboards, revealing deeper layers from the posters beneath, much in the same way that the blast from Burroughs's weapons exposed the deeper layers of his plywood panels. Burroughs had rarely visited art galleries and was not familiar with contemporary art theory, which did not interest him, but he recognized that he and Yves Klein had much in common, in particular Klein's use of random events to create the image. On October 21, 1988, Burroughs had a show at the Paul Klein Gallery in

Chicago, an event that gave rise to one of his synchronous experiences. "I had an odd thing happen. I'd just written down on the typewriter or in pencil, 'Yves Klein set his pictures on fire' (and put them out at some point. I did quite a lot of experiments like that, and also tracing outlines with gunpowder, so on and so forth). And James came here to tell me that the Paul Klein gallery had burned down in Chicago."[12] A whole block of galleries and stored pictures burned down. All of Burroughs's pictures from the show were destroyed. He collected the insurance, but it was a real disaster. "That's an interesting little juxtaposition."[13]

Many of the early paintings were executed in India ink on card, which dried in a few minutes. He had some interesting results using what he called Rorschach monoprints—taking impressions of an image by painting one piece of slick coated card and pressing another one against it and rotating it a little. "I try my best to make my mind a blank. [...] The whole idea is that I try to let my hands go and paint whatever my so-called unconscious mind is aware of."[14] He also used watercolors, the medium he used in 1959 when he was first under the influence of Gysin. He began to see pictures in his dreams and sometimes dreamed that he was painting. "I'll dream about it and then I'll see things in the pictures from dreams. You've got a feedback. It's the same way with life. There's a feedback between dreams and writing in dreams and painting." In this way, his painting helped his writing. "To some extent I stopped [writing] when I completed my trilogy. I find I paint a while and then I get ideas for writing. [...] Sometimes they turn out quite differently to what I have in mind. I paint intuitively. I can't draw, but it's probably quite simple. I'm carrying on the same ideas in writing and painting."[15]

At first, Bill and James took virtually every exhibition opportunity that was offered. They wanted to show the work, and to sell it. In 1988, after the Shafrazi show, came shows at the Suzanne Biederberg gallery in Amsterdam and a show at the October Gallery in London—both shows shared a catalog. There were shows at the Western Front Gallery in Vancouver, the Center on Contemporary Art in Seattle, the Gallery Casa Sin Nombre in Santa Fe, the Paul Klein Gallery in Chicago, and a group show in New York. In 1989 there were shows in Cologne, Montreal—where Galerie Oboro issued two limited-edition prints—Toronto, Basel, Rome, Lisbon, and St. Louis. Few modern artists could keep up such a pace, but Burroughs had produced a lot of work and there was enough good material to go around. The art boom was still going and Burroughs began to make good money as an artist. All along, in interviews, he was anxious to express his enormous debt to Brion Gysin, who showed him how to paint. "I didn't show my work until Brion died because he was touchy and

I didn't want to intrude on him in that way. He was a neglected painter, and understandably that was a sensitive point with him. He was a very great painter, though, and while I've been more financially successful, I could never compete with him in terms of the quality of my work."[16]

Burroughs also continued his film career. He was in Robert Frank's 1981 *Energy and How to Get It*, a documentary about inventor Robert "Lightning Bob" Golka, who received money from the Carter administration to develop cold fusion energy. Bill plays the villainous Energy Czar, wandering around smoking a joint, muttering lines like, "He knows too much, we better shut him down." In *Twister*, the 1989 comedy about a Kansas family after a tornado strike, he played an unnamed old geezer doing target practice in his barn. The family are looking for "Jim," but Bill tells them, "Jim got kicked in the head by a horse last year. [He] went around killing horses for a while, until he ate the insides of a clock and he died" (a line remembered from John Millington Synge's 1907 play *The Playboy of the Western World*). That same year he had his best role of all, as the old junkie priest in Gus Van Sant's *Drugstore Cowboy*.

Bill and James had known Gus Van Sant ever since he made an award-winning nine-minute 16-millimeter student film called *The Discipline of D.E.* (1977), based on Burroughs's eponymous text. Van Sant had recently left the Rhode Island School of Design and was writing, painting, film-making, and making music. "Burroughs has been one of my literary influences. I'm pretty sure that you would never be able to tell this. But at one time I was very much under his influence, sometime when I was in college in the early seventies. [...] Partly because of his experimental take on literature, and his faith in the written word's ability to infect or take over the reader when he isn't aware of it."[17] After that he made a record called *William S. Burroughs: The Elvis of Letters*, consisting of four songs that Gus wrote and played on guitar. One of them, "Millions of Images," a collage of sound bites of Burroughs reading, was taken up by various fans and turned into short films posted on the Web.

For *Drugstore Cowboy*, Van Sant had originally wanted Burroughs to play the part of Bob Hughes, the slightly older junkie, leader of a gang of four drug addicts who roam the country in the early seventies, supporting their habit by robbing hospitals and pharmacies. In late 1988, Bill and James went to Portland, Oregon, and Bill did a reading for the part that went very well. Burroughs wasn't sure that he could handle a lead role, and he and James came up with the idea of Bill developing another of the characters, Tom, into a junkie priest, based on Burroughs's story "The Priest They Called Him." Gus loved the idea and said he would rewrite the part. Unfortunately he was very busy with production issues and his new script didn't really cut it. Van Sant said, "He didn't want to play the character Tom the way he was originally written in the screenplay, which was as this sort of pathetic loser...he wanted the character to have some more pride. So he came up with the idea of making Tom be a junkie priest. So he pretty much created the stuff in his scenes on his own."[18] James asked if they could work on it and Gus agreed. James rewrote the four priest scenes and Bill then added his own imprimatur to them. James remains proud to be the author of the line, "Drugs have been systematically scapegoated and demonized in this country," that Burroughs delivers with such emphasis. The studio was aghast and wanted to cut Bill out of the movie entirely. Gus Van Sant said, "We had to fight for him. That's probably the biggest fight I've ever had, [...] smaller companies can be just as fierce as their studio counterparts."[19] Matt Dillon took the lead role as Bob Hughes, and Bill played Tom, the priest, to great acclaim. Gus Van Sant was also the director of Burroughs's most successful short, *A Thanksgiving Prayer* (1990), taken from *Tornado Alley*, in which he used montages over a film of Burroughs reading the text.

2. Last Boy

Burroughs had sex with no more than half a dozen people between 1974 and 1997, and he was never able to find someone to replace Ian. When he toured the country doing readings there were sometimes opportunities to pick up boys, and in San Francisco he did find a temporary partner. In New York he mostly had sex with Allen Ginsberg's friends. Raymond Foye said, "William only wanted to be fucked, it was wham, whirr, thankyou sir—no kissing, no touching, he just lay down and used a popper, but afterwards he was all sentimental and gushy, like a 14-year-old girl."[20] Bill's relationship with Cabell Hardy had never been very satisfactory, though it meant a lot to Cabell, who was very sensitive, despite his unfortunate personality. He wrote a good deal about his relationship with Burroughs, as did Mark Ewert, who described it in great detail, leaving nothing to the imagination.

In 1988, a teenager named Mark Ewert flew across country to the Naropa Institute with the specific purpose of having sex with Burroughs and Ginsberg. "By sleeping with them, I would join my life to theirs, thereby speeding up my own ascent into personal and artistic greatness. Burroughs wasn't at Naropa that year, so I made my play for Allen, and that worked out great."[21] Allen told him, "It would be great to get Bill laid. He loves to get fucked. And you genuinely care about him and his work."[22] But it was not until September of 1989 that Ewert and Burroughs met. Bill was in town, staying at the Bunker, and Allen called Ewert to ask if he still wanted to meet Burroughs. Ewert said yes, so Allen arranged for him to be his date at the dinner party John Giorno was giving for Bill. There were a dozen guests, all male, all considerably older than him. Mark was seated next to Burroughs. The big hit of the dinner was a Freddy Krueger glove, brought along to show them by Chris Stein of Blondie. It was made from soft gray leather and each finger had a heavy curved blade attached. It had cost him $5,000. Everyone took turns wearing it and swishing it about. Bill said how impractical it was; nonetheless he hogged it, dancing around, demonstrating a series of feints and thrusts for Mark's benefit. Everyone backed away, partly to give the two of them space, and partly for their own safety. Ewert wrote, "William spent what was for me an uncomfortably long time stalking me around the room, slashing me with the glove, and making 'growr, growr' noises. His gaze was steely fixed on mine, and for a moment I was honestly afraid that he would attack me for real if I flinched or looked away: 'Don't let him see your fear.' William's jungle-hunt of me seemed like such a bad metaphor for exactly what it was—a carnal pursuit—that I was embarrassed for the both of us, but on the other hand, I was totally thrilled. Wasn't everything proceeding exactly like I had planned?"[23]

The next day at Allen's, Mark eagerly awaited Bill's verdict. When Allen telephoned him, James answered, and told Allen that Bill had said, "Boy, Allen's got himself a real beauty this time, hasn't he?" Allen, the old procurer, spoke to Bill and told Mark, "I made appointment for you, to go over there, at two. James and John and everyone will be gone by then, so you two should have the place to yourselves." Mark was eighteen, Bill was seventy-five. Bill was awkward and was clearly a little scared. Mark wrote candidly about his seduction:

Lastly, William commits himself to the irrevocable act of actually putting his hand on my knee, and still I do not freak out—indeed, I in turn put my hand on his knee. I give it a little squeeze, and when I feel how bony and frail his leg is, underneath the stiff fabric of his jeans, I'm suddenly awash with a wave of tender protectiveness for this brave little guy, who's gone through such an ordeal just for a simple sign of affection. Manfully, I throw my arm around his shoulder, and pull William towards me. Both of us sag with relief. William and I didn't fuck, kiss, or blow one another, which was fine with me, and was certainly a nice change of pace from Allen. [...] I couldn't get over how similar our bodies were: both of us white, hairless, smooth—the same height, the same weight, the same build. The inescapable conclusion was that I was in bed with another boy, and the idea was unbelievably sexy. I had never been in bed with another boy before, and here was my perfect double: a lean, taut body that I could grip with a real hunger, which would be returned.[24]

Two weeks later, Mark received a postcard inviting him to spend the weekend with Bill in Lawrence. "I can offer you simple, country plea- sures, shooting, fishing, canoeing." He came to stay, and Bill's support crew stayed well away, even postponing the lawn mowing. Bill later wrote in his journal, "Mark Ewert left yesterday after a three-day visit. I feel now very much merged together. His face emerged quite clearly in a painting I did the last day he was here. He is an extraordinarily sweet and beneficent presence."[25] Friends say that Bill was obsessed with him. The fact was, Bill enjoyed the attention, but he was a junkie and had little in the way of sex drive.

3. Opera

The success of his art career meant that Burroughs could cut down on his readings. Between 1974 and 1988 he had read all over the United States and Canada, he'd read in Amsterdam six times, as well as Berlin, Brus- sels, London, Helsinki, Basel, Stockholm, Copenhagen, Rome, and other major European cities. In the spring and fall of 1981 they toured *Cities of the Red Night* with Laurie Anderson and John Giorno. Laurie was brilliant and added a great deal to the show. In San Francisco they oversold the the- ater and had to add another show. Burroughs liked her a lot. Grauerholz says, "They had a natural kinship, he was very fond of Laurie." Burroughs appeared in *Home of the Brave* (1986) and sang "Sharkey's Night" in his shaky voice on her album *Mister Heartbreak* (1984). The longest tour had been of Scandinavia in 1983 at the age of sixty-nine. At the university in Tampere, Finland, he performed on a thrust stage to a standing audience. He read well and received tremendous applause. He gathered his papers, turned to his right to walk to the wings, but, blinded by the stage lights, he walked right off the lip of the stage, at least a five-foot rise. In a split second he realized what had happened and somehow managed to crouch and land on his feet like a cat. James grabbed him before his knees buckled.

As if a new career in painting were not enough, seventy-five-year-old Burroughs now got involved with an opera. Several years before, Howard Brookner had introduced Burroughs to Robert Wilson, and now in 1989, Wilson approached Burroughs to collaborate on an opera called *The Black Rider: The Casting of the Magic Bullets*, based on the German folktale *Der Freischütz (The Marksman)*,[26] to be performed in Germany. It is the story of the devil's bargain, which is always a fool's bargain. It was perfect for Burroughs.

A file clerk is in love with a huntsman's daughter, but to obtain her father's permission to marry, the clerk has to prove his worth as a hunter, for the hunter was getting old and wanted to maintain his legacy. But the clerk is a lousy shot and only brings back a vulture. On his next trip to the forest the devil—Pegleg—appears to him and offers him a handful of magic bullets. With these bullets he hits anything he aims at, but the devil warns him that "some of these bullets are for thee and some are for me." As his wedding approaches the clerk begins to get nervous, as there is to be a shooting contest and he needs more bullets. He goes to the crossroads and the devil gives him one more magic bullet. At the contest he aims at a wooden dove, but the bullet circles the assembled guests and strikes his betrothed and kills her. The clerk goes mad and joins the devil's previous victims in the Devil's Carnival.

Burroughs wrote the libretto, based on Thomas De Quincey's version of the tale, initially using rhyming couplets even though he knew they would be lost when it was translated into German (this material was never used); singer Tom Waits wrote the songs, which remained in English; and Robert Wilson directed and stage designed the entire performance. The plot has an obvious parallel with Burroughs's killing of Joan, and he was not shy to reference this in his lyrics for the song "George Schmid": "Some bullets is special for a single aim. A certain stag, or a certain person. And no matter where you aim, that's where the bullet will end up. And in the moment of aiming, the gun turns into a dowser's wand, and points where the bullet wants to go."[27] Three of the songs used Burroughs's lyrics, with music by Tom Waits, and Burroughs himself sang "T'Ain't No Sin" for the CD version.

In September 1989, Tom Waits, Robert Wilson, and Wolfgang Wiens, dramaturge of the Thalia Theater in Hamburg, spent a week in Lawrence working daily in Bill's front room with James acting as stenographer and secretary, blocking out *The Black Rider*. Naturally there were many changes as the words were adapted for performance, and faxes flew back and forth between the theater and Kansas all through the fall and winter of 1989–90 until Wilson was satisfied. Then in February 1990 the team reconvened in Hamburg, all staying at the same hotel with Udo Breger, who was translating Bill's words into German. Bill's libretto was then delivered to Wolfgang Wiens, who edited the text further in daily consultation with Wilson during the period of rehearsal and development. Bill attended rehearsals from 7:30 a.m. until 2:30 p.m., while Udo and James worked on the translation of the texts. Wilson would invariably have something that he wanted Bill to change, a scene that would have to be rewritten, so Bill would return to the hotel to work on it and then give it to Udo to translate, ready for the next day. They ate most of their meals in the hotel because they had no time to go out.

Before the show opened Bill and James attended the vernissage of his show at the Galerie K in Paris on March 23. It was a great critical success and almost completely sold out, to Bill's great satisfaction. From there they continued on to Hamburg. The opera opened at the state-owned Thalia Theater on March 31, 1990, and received fifteen standing ovations, lasting exactly twenty-three minutes—close to the record for the theater, and also Bill's magic number. "Wasn't that great?" Burroughs asked filmmaker Klaus Maeck. "The devil's bargain is a classic, and in so many forms—in Hollywood, advertising, job ads—selling your soul, your integrity for games or money or for time. The ultimate form is for time, for immortality."[28] *The Black Rider* received a good critical reception. Jackie Wullschlager enthused in the *Financial Times*, "For three hours of graceful, cold artifice, [the actors] look, act, and sound like figures from silent movies. [...] Wilson turns children's drawings into three-dimensional monstrosities. Crooked chairs, two meters high, dangle at odd angles [...] pine trees are scissor cut-outs which collapse and grow again like cartoons. [...] Waits' sarcastic ballads, full of folk and blues and rock, call back the scarred idealism and mock simplicity of Kurt Weill, while Burroughs' monosyllabic banality has here found the setting which makes it seem perfect."[29] *The Black Rider* was performed in Vienna, Paris, Barcelona, Genoa, Amsterdam, and Berlin and opened for ten performances at the Brooklyn Academy of Music in November 1993, with later performances in Canada and London, and continues to the present day.

4. Folders

In the course of revising the libretto of *The Black Rider*, from January to March 1990, Burroughs continued to paint. The opera took up much of his time and the various drafts and rewrites he had to do meant that he was constantly reorganizing his papers in different file folders. He wrote and painted in the same room and, inevitably, one day while painting, he used one of the ochre-colored folders as a palette, mixing his colors on it. Almost immediately, remembering that Paul Klee had remarked that sometimes the way in which the picture is created might be more interesting than the picture itself, he recognized that the folders he had mixed paint on could be seen as paintings in themselves. He began to intentionally create file-folder paintings, painting not only the outsides but the insides as well. As usual, among the swirls of paint, faces and animals emerged. Having decorated many dozens of them, he kept the best as art, and filed his papers in the remainder.

In the spring of 1990, Burroughs was preparing for a major show to be held at Seibu Shibuya Hall in Tokyo, curated by Makito Hayashi and arranged by Mitsuhiro Takemura, who visited Lawrence to make the selection from Burroughs's work, including the painted folders. Bill's assistant Steven Lowe described the viewing: "When presented with these painted folders, Mr. Takemura held them in his hands and carefully looked at them. Then he placed them on a low table and arranged them accordion-style, each folder set up on its edges and positioned into the folder next to it. There were fifteen folders, and this elegant grouping became the work entitled 'Paper Cloud.'" It was shown in Tokyo and Sapporo and bought for a private collection.

During that previous winter, Steven Lowe had suggested that Bill might include pages from his novels as part of the collage elements, and also a wider range of objects than he had been using, such as wire, bird feathers, bits of clothing, raw pigment. He suggested that Burroughs sandwich these between sheets of handmade paper and shoot them so that the filling would explode from the back. Many of Burroughs's works, from the shotgun art to the painted folders, had two sides, not necessarily a front and a back, but in the case of the gun art, an impact side and a result side. The first one of these sandwiched pieces to be shot was done when Mr. Takamura and his party were in Lawrence and they all went to the countryside to shoot guns. During March and June, Burroughs shot nine more of the sandwiched paintings, which became known as the "Thick Pages" series.[30] The series could be seen as a collaboration between Burroughs and Lowe.

Many of Burroughs's shows were organized by José Férez Kuri, a peripatetic art curator from Mexico City who became the director of the October Gallery in London in 1984. In 1988 he gave Burroughs his first show in London—his first abroad—and another there in 1992. He continued to represent Burroughs when he left the October Gallery to become an independent curator in 1991. José divided his time between Lawrence and London and became a close member of the inner circle. He died of a heart attack in 2010, aged fifty-nine, and said, shortly before his death, "I've done too many drugs, too much drinking and sex, too much of everything. And I've enjoyed it all." That was why he fitted in so well in Lawrence.

Burroughs had always seen the artworks as a door to the spirit world, an interface to another dimension of memory, psychic experience, and place;

like his dreams, his paintings gave him stories. "The paintings write. They tell and foretell stories. Now the pictures are moving, laughing, snarling, talking, screaming, changing, but it is movement in another dimension, not some physical miracle of moving paint."[31] Burroughs's use of his paintings, and his previous use of Brion Gysin's paintings for the same purpose—as a port of entry to another world of spirits—removes him somewhat from the general contemporary art world. Burroughs knew little about post-Duchampian art, conceptual art, land art, neorealism, minimalism, and the other movements going on while he was painting, nor did he want to know, often joking about them to interviewers. This does not mean that the work was somehow outside the progression of twentieth-century art history; Burroughs was not producing "outsider" or naïve art; he brought many formal elements of composition to his work and was a good colorist; many of his works are very attractive. They worked both as better-than-most examples of late-twentieth-century painting as well as spirit vehicles for Burroughs's own private vision.

5. Aliens

Burroughs had read and enjoyed Whitley Strieber's books *Communion* and *Breakthrough* and wanted to meet him. Strieber, the author of successful horror stories and a follower of Gurdjieff, had written a book about his purported abduction by aliens. The book has flying saucers in it but does not speculate how mammalian creatures, wearing the current Earthly fashions—blue overalls—managed to travel to Earth at speeds far in excess of the speed of light, but does suggest that they are possibly Earthly in origin: the dead somehow manifest, visitors from the future, visitors from other levels of consciousness or dimensions, and so on. Burroughs made the obvious connection between the people Strieber experienced and his own possession by the Ugly Spirit and wrote a letter to Strieber saying he would love to contact these visitors. Strieber's wife, Anne, wrote back saying that they had to be sure that he was who he said he was. "We get a lot of crank letters." Bill replied saying, "I am indeed really me," and she wrote back to say, "We, after talking it over, would be glad to invite you to come up to the cabin." And so in 1990 Burroughs spent the weekend with them, accompanied by Bill Rich. He told Victor Bockris, "I had a number of talks with Strieber about his experiences and I was quite convinced he was telling the truth. [...] He told me this. 'When you experience it, it is very definite, very physical, it's not vague and it's not like an hallucination, that they are *there*.'"[32] Strieber said that Burroughs was almost overly polite, but very curious about his experiences. In *My Education* Burroughs wrote, "I was convinced that the aliens, or whatever they are, are a real phenomenon. The abductions, in several accounts, involved sexual contacts. Indeed, that would seem to be their purpose."[33]

Burroughs was a little upset that the aliens made no attempt to contact him, and in the course of an emotional interview with Victor Bockris (Victor was the emotional one—he had a strong sense of being invaded himself), Burroughs said, "I think I am one of the most important people in this fucking world and if they'd had any sense they would have manifested. [...] It may mean it was not propitious for them to come and pick me at that particular time. It may mean that they would contact at a later date, or it may mean that they look upon me as the enemy. [...] We have no means of knowing what their real motives are. They may find that my intervention is hostile to their objectives. And their objectives may not be friendly at all."[34]

As far as Burroughs was concerned, he and Strieber had likely met up with the same thing, expressed in a different way. "When I go into my psyche at a certain point I meet a very, very hostile, very strong force. It's as definite as if I'd met somebody attacking me in a bar. We usually come to a stand-off but I don't think that I'm necessarily winning or losing." In Bill's opinion, the aliens—if they were indeed creatures external to our own unconscious life—were abducting people in order to have sex with them. Strieber's aliens wanted him to get a bigger erection than the one they had somehow managed to induce. In order to attract them to Lawrence, Burroughs let the grass on his lawn grow long and then had a patch of it cut in the shape of an erect penis, like making crop circles. Strieber received more alien visits, but sadly they never came for Bill. Strieber called the aliens the Grays, and they soon entered Burroughs's cosmography. Five months before his death, Burroughs still remained fascinated by the subject. In a journal entry for February 3, 1997, he wrote:

> The Grays apparently [are] control Aliens, who have lost the ability to create, a dying race that needs blood and semen from humans. Bad folk those Grays.
>
> I recall that Whitley Strieber was accused of working for the Grays. [...] Why are abductions and contacts always to mediocre or inferior minds? Why don't they come and see ME?
>
> Because they don't want to, are afraid to contact anyone with advanced spiritual awareness.
>
> The Grays want to make people stupider. Anyone with real perception is a danger to them. A deadly danger.[35]

Chapter Fifty-Two

My title for my memoirs was My Past Is an Evil River. From Verlaine.
I'm looking back there but I'm looking back at a stranger. I said, "What
in hell did you do this for? Don't you realize that even if you'd hit the
goddam glass you're endangering these people sitting on the couch?"
Again and again I'm looking at a stranger that I really don't know at
all. [...] Here was a boy coming on to you, why didn't you accept him,
what was wrong with you at that moment? [...] Again and again I've
said, "What the hell was I thinking about?" I think a lot of people
looking back would say, "What possessed me to do that?"—literally
talking about possession. [...] Looking back, in the last ten years I
would say I've really gotten myself in control of myself so I know what
the hell I am doing.[1]

1. The Quotidian Life

Cronenberg completed the fifth draft of his script of *Naked Lunch* on January 20, 1991. Bill read it and telephoned his approval. He still had his reservations but recognized he was dealing with Hollywood. Writing in September 1991, before the film was completed, Burroughs said, "I was dismayed, naturally, to see the scenes that David wrote in which 'Bill Lee' shoots his wife, 'Joan'; but on reflection, I feel that the scenes in his script are so different from the tragic and painful episodes in my own life from which he drew his inspiration that no intelligent person can mistake the movie for a factual account." Burroughs had other misgivings, writing, "For reasons best known to himself, David chose to treat the homosexuality of 'Lee' as a somewhat unwelcome accident of circumstance and plot, rather than an innate characteristic. Whether this is because of David's own heterosexuality, or his assessment of the realities of making and releasing a multi-million dollar movie, or other factors, I cannot say."[2]

As filming got under way, in early June Burroughs and James were invited to Toronto to visit the set. Film critic Chris Peachment, also at the set, gave a description of Burroughs at seventy-seven: "He is still slim, if a little bowed, and still active, with the help of an elegant black cane which is probably more decorative than useful. His face looks the same as it always has in photographs: thin, mocking, with the papery whiteness of the reformed junkie. [...] His manner is gentle and exquisitely courteous; his voice and sense of humour both dry as a bone. He is also something of a dandy, dressed in a long black leather trench-coat ('My Gestapo coat') and a jet-black fedora with a discreet Stetson label on the hatband."[3]

Burroughs was now very settled in his ways. He no longer liked to travel and lived in a stoned world of his own. At eight o'clock he awoke and took 60 milligrams of methadone in liquid form, then he would return to bed and doze for an hour until it kicked in and a warmth spread through his body. At nine he would rise and putter about in his slippers, pajamas, and dressing gown and start the day with a glass of tap water into which he emptied a load of sugar. He mashed a lemon into it and drank it down. Then he made breakfast. Often this was a soft-boiled egg with "soldiers"—toast sliced into fingers to dip in the egg, something he enjoyed in London, and that his Welsh nanny probably made for him. TP, his longtime assistant, remembered, "I've never had an egg like he used to have them. He had these little cups, like soft-boiled eggs. He had some English stuff, he liked tea. He liked to drink tea in the afternoons." He had two cups of tea with lots of sugar. Feeding the cats took some time, and after that he would shave and get dressed, by which time it was almost midday. In keeping with his role as *el hombre invisible*, he dressed anonymously, Kansas style: a blue work shirt, baggy blue jeans, a jacket from the Gap, an oversize bomber jacket. Instead of his fedora, he wore a trucker cap with the name of a feed store on it. His suit and tie were always worn for readings, art openings, and any formal occasions or out-of-town visits. He usually only snacked for lunch, unless visitors came over. In the afternoons he might walk in the garden and practice his knife throwing, before reading or flipping through magazines. He had piles of magazines in every room: *Gun Tests, Gun World, Gun Digest, American Survival Guide, Knife, UFO Universe, Soldier of Fortune*, subscription copies of *National Geographic* and the *International Herald Tribune*, which Bill always read in London and Paris, and the *Weekly World News*, a fictional news tabloid sold at the supermarket that Bill loved to read that specialized in alien abductions, mutants, "world's fattest" stories, urban legends, Elvis sightings, and the revelation in 1994 that twelve U.S. senators were aliens from other planets. Bill particularly liked Ed Anger's vitriolic right-wing column and would sit chuckling over it. (The *Weekly World News* staff would joke about how many of their readers actually believed this stuff; apparently many of them did.)

Bill had a large library of pulp fiction, pseudoscience subjects, natural history books, and books on weapons and self-defense. Books like *Basic Stick Fighting for Combat, Deadly Substances, Personal Defense, Firearms of the American West, The Poor Man's James Bond, How to Kill Volume Five* by John Minnery, and *Improvised Munitions Black Book* overflowed the shelves and were stacked in piles alongside doctor books, thrillers, and a large collection of cat books: *The Life, History and Magic of the Cat, Cats Incredible!, The Complete Book of Cats.* One bookcase contained a seventeen-volume complete set of Joseph Conrad, alongside Denton Welch, Jonathan Swift, foreign editions of his own work, and books by Gysin and Ginsberg. On the top, amid the clutter of objects, were an animal skull and an engraved plaque with one of his favorite aphorisms: "It is necessary to travel. It is not necessary to live."

In New York, Burroughs did not drink until 6:00 p.m., but in Kansas this gradually got moved forward. By 1991 it was 4:00 p.m. and then 3:30 p.m. In London he drank whiskey, Johnnie Walker Red Label, but in New York he switched to vodka and Coca-Cola. Burroughs drank for most of his life and always tried to ration it, to a certain extent. When he traveled in South America he figured that a fifth would last for three days and a quart for four. A quart is thirty-two ounces of alcohol. In Kansas he usually bought Popov vodka in two-liter bottles because it had the ounces marked on the container; a bottle lasted four days. It had the added advantage of being very cheap, which didn't matter because the terrible taste was disguised by the Coca-Cola he mixed with it. His other cheap vodka of choice was Viaka.

After his first drink, and a joint, he would either write or paint until dinnertime. "I smoke as much pot as I feel like, two or three joints is enough. I smoke pot in the afternoon for work. If I can get it, it makes all the difference. It's just that extra spark. Say I've got an article to write. Now, I don't like to write articles, it's hard work, it's all gotta be in the right place. If I smoke a joint I'll get an extra levity or something in it. It takes the edge off of it. A three-thousand-word article, that's a week's work. People think you can just sit down and dash this off, well you can't. You can do it but it won't be right. The easiest thing to write when you're really going is narrative. It just flows out. The hardest thing to write is description."[4] He awoke several times in the night as he was a very light sleeper, and sometimes smoked a joint before going back to sleep.

There was a roster posted in the kitchen showing which of a number of young men would cook for him. They would arrive around five o'clock to join him in a drink and to make dinner; Burroughs ate early, around 6:00–6:15 p.m. On Thursday he knew he would eat well because David

Ohle was a good cook; on Jim McCrary's nights he didn't worry because, as TP (Tom Peschio) put it, he and Jim drank most of their dinner. Steven Lowe and James were both accomplished cooks, and TP had a few dishes that Bill liked. As the years passed there were more and more visitors, so that it was rare that Bill just dined with his cook. There were usually guests, even if it was only James.

Bill retired early, at 8:30 or 9:00 p.m.; guests knew it was time to go elsewhere when he began to take off his shirt. In the last year of his life he also took an afternoon nap. He might go for a walk, though there was little to see except houses very similar to his own. Whenever he left the premises he made sure he was suitably armed. He always carried a handgun in a holster on his belt. Normally this was a Smith & Wesson .38 snubbie, but some people, such as his doctor and his hairdresser, felt uncomfortable staring down at such a weapon, so in those cases he would wear a small derringer with a two-inch barrel that could fire five rounds and fitted unobtrusively into his waistcoat. (This is quite legal in Kansas.) In addition he always carried a Cobra, a type of steel whip; a blade disguised as a credit card; and a can of BodyGuard, a virulent mixture of Mace and capsicum pepper in a liquid spray. "It'll stop a Doberman pinscher dead in its tracks."[5] In the cellar his friend George Kaull constructed a three-meter (ten feet) long silencer, a long padded tube made from chicken wire and fiberglass insulation and mounted horizontally, which enabled him to shoot in his house without anyone hearing him. They called it the "Shooting Tube." He would stick the gun in and fire away at a target at the other end of the basement. Six rounds from a .38 sounded like taps upstairs in the living room and the neighbors could hear nothing.[6]

Bill's obsession with weapons was something that always disturbed Allen Ginsberg, who quite simply didn't believe that Bill needed so many to protect himself from his so-called enemies. "I don't have any enemies," Allen claimed, but Bill's worldview was very different; he saw himself as continually under threat. When James once broached the subject and asked him, "What do you think it means with all the guns, Bill? Did you ever think about that? I mean, are you afraid of something?" Bill grew quite angry and emphatic: "YES! I'm terrified of everything! Don't you understand?" James felt that he wasn't bragging about it; if anything, he was probably a little bit ashamed. Jim McCrary often accompanied Bill on his shooting sessions. Bill was obsessed with target practice. He kept his used targets and noted down the date, the time, the shot, the gun, whether he had a vodka before or after. Bill said a vodka steadied his hand. Jim McCrary thought that "he never forgave himself for missing that time in Mexico and [...] my feeling was he never forgave himself. He never felt good, or got over it. He was that kind of a guy." Jim recalled that sometimes during a drinking session Burroughs would slump forward, holding his head in his hands, saying, "Joan! Joan!" Her death was always with him.

His interest in guns attracted other "gun guys." Hunter S. Thompson arranged to visit but almost didn't get to Lawrence. Jim McCrary remembered, "Hunter was really excited because he'd brought a gun for William." It was a .454 Casull, the most powerful handgun manufactured at the time, and came with a huge scope mounted on top. Each round cost a dollar and would go a mile. Because he had so many guns with him he was unable to fly and so he drove to see Burroughs from Colorado. His car broke down in the middle of nowhere, in a dry county, but he managed to get the car fixed and drove at once to Manhattan, the nearest town. There was a basketball game on and Hunter and girlfriend settled down at a bar to watch it. Jim told the story: "They got all fucked up, and he got ready to leave and 'where'd my keys go?' and the bartender says, 'I've got your keys and I don't think you should drive.' Whoah! Hunter went berserk, but luckily his girlfriend calmed him down." He was still in a state when they checked into the Eldridge Hotel. "It was just chaos. He had the whole place going in circles, switching rooms, him and his girl. He created a scene. He stopped at some restaurant and sat outside and he was eating and all the servers and everyone were starting to figure out who this was, and in the midst of it all he had a big snuff box full of coke which he dropped on the ground and was crawling under the table! But when he came over to see William he sat here [quietly, respectfully] like at the feet of the guru." The next day they went shooting, and Hunter was impressed that Bill was able to fire the .454 without being knocked over by the recoil.

William Burroughs Communications acquired its own office in town and Bill took over the front bedroom of his house, which James had used as his office, as an art studio. Paintings were arranged on racks according to size. The walls showed evidence of his target practice with a BB gun. After the filming of *Naked Lunch*, Cronenberg gave Burroughs one of the six-foot-high Mugwumps. Burroughs sat it on a chair in the corner of the studio, where it unnerved visitors, who were not expecting to encounter an extraterrestrial when they entered the room. It was in this room that privileged guests like Allen Ginsberg stayed. Most people stayed in the Eldridge Hotel or, when Burroughs Communications acquired a compound near Bill's house with a number of houses on it, in one of the spare bedrooms there. During the day he often worked with Jim McCrary, who worked for William Burroughs Communications from 1991 until 2001, and who typed up many of Bill's handwritten or poorly typed manuscripts. McCrary found working for Bill a pleasure and he became a good friend. McCrary remembered how excited Bill would get for Halloween. He'd carve pumpkins, put on a scary mask, and wait by the door with a bowl of candy, even though not many kids came down his street. "He's like the great, kind of crazy uncle I never had," McCrary said.[7]

Allen Ginsberg often came to stay, and got to know all the members of Bill's inner circle. Jim McCrary said, "Allen certainly enjoyed the rest and privacy he found in Lawrence, and William certainly enjoyed seeing him. There was a quiet, close, emotional aura around these two as they visited in William's house. There was gracefulness between them and it was private—they didn't perform at all. I guess when you know one another forty-plus years—you don't have to do squat. There you go."[8] Allen took on some of the cooking duties when he stayed, and Jim McCrary remembered one time when Allen made some macrobiotic turnip stew. William took one look at it and said, "Jim, go to the store and get some lamb chops." And Allen said, "But William, I made this for you!" David Ohle had a fond memory of them both. "One unforgettable moment was seeing William and Allen Ginsberg early one morning in their pajamas trying to chase raccoons out of William's kitchen with a walking cane. The coons came in through the cat door and opened the cat food drawer and helped themselves almost every night."[9] The drawers were supposed to be secured with canes through the handles, but Bill spent so much time feeding and fussing with the cats that the drawer was in more or less constant use.

Another regular visitor, who visited a half dozen times, was the painter George Condo. Jim McCrary remembered, "The other person he really liked was George Condo, they really had a good time together [...] hanging out together out on the back porch. He came from New York. He didn't drive because he's a New Yorker. He'd bring tons of food and wine and dope and they really did like being around each other and they worked together on some collaborative paintings. I think George kinda got him going, just by playing with him, and getting stoned with him."[10]

Bill's friends and support group divided visitors into two groups, as McCrary put it. "Allen always had a project that he was doing, and he would try and get William involved. John Giorno came a lot and stayed, but the difference was, Allen always had a project he was doing and it didn't involve William. But Giorno always had a project where he wanted William to do stuff."[11]

Sometimes Bill went fishing. He had bought a cabin on Lone Star Lake, cheap because he could put up the cash. He was right on the lake with a small dock where he could moor his ten-foot-long flat-bottomed aluminum boat (bought for just $270, a real bargain). "I likes to row out in the middle of the lake and just let the boat drift. I hear tell there's been flying saucers sighted out here on the lake, and I'm hoping maybe one will pick me up."[12] Right in front of his dock was the best fishing for catfish in the lake, but Bill was after bluegills or bass. Catfish screamed when they were pulled from the water and snapped like an animal; besides, they were very difficult to clean.

Over the years, Burroughs had accumulated a lot of possessions. Inside the front door, a walnut side table was crowded with curios, many of them anthropological items given to him as gifts. Next to this a cane stand was filled with his large collection of walking sticks and canes, including a swordstick, many with strange carved handles. A long green tube was labeled "Blowgun Survival Weapon." Bill loved demonstrating this one. It fired three-inch steel darts at about two hundred miles per hour and the front door and living room walls were pockmarked from its use. A dining table and chairs stood to the right of the front door. His collection of art had also grown and all but two of his Gysins, along with works by Keith Haring, Robert Rauschenberg, and other artists he had collaborated with, were eventually placed on deposit at the Spencer Museum of Art at the University of Kansas for safety.

On Thursdays, James, or another of the regular drivers, would arrive at 8:00 a.m. to take Bill to his methadone clinic in Kansas City. Afterward he and James would have breakfast at Nichols or the K.C. Diner. Eventually he was permitted to pick up on a biweekly schedule and so James would take him out to breakfast in Lawrence so that his house could be cleaned. Burroughs always kept a quantity of methadone back, stored in a large glass bottle, so that he had a few weeks' supply in the event that the roads became impassable in the winter and he couldn't get to Kansas City to his clinic. Thursday being special, this was also the day when his friends gathered round for the weekly "boys' night" get-together. Among the regulars were Wayne Propst, Fred Aldrich, Steven Lowe, Dean Ripa, David Ohle, Phil Heying, Jim McCrary, George Kaull, TP, and of course James Grauerholz. These were Bill's shooting buddies, his fishing buddies, the people who cooked his meals, went with him to readings, fed his cats when he was away. They were his support system, his friends, and his family.

Another close friend, much younger than the others, was Michael Emerton, James Grauerholz's lover since 1985. To quote James, "Michael was a curly-headed, hard-drinking nineteen-year-old from Kansas City. His adoptive mother had died when he was sixteen, and he never recovered from the loss. Burroughs and Emerton took to each other immediately, and Michael loved William and his cats."[13] TP was introduced to Burroughs and his circle by Michael and became a close friend of his. "Michael was a holy terror, that's why William loved him so much, he was so much fucking fun. Everywhere you went with him was like trouble. In the end he troubled himself to death, but man, there was sparks shootin' off him. And if you got into a beef with him, you know, good luck. He was really mischievous, man. He was a playmate, he was a great playmate."[14] TP described how Bill and Michael would play around with demonology. "It was real, totally real. [Bill] was like a real shaman. He would be really into something, even though he kinda knew it was bullshit, but he would kinda have fun with it. He would go off on kicks and some of them were kinda silly, but at the same time he was like a twelve-year-old kid, he still was able to make believe. [...] He didn't seem uptight. With stories some people have, it's hard to recognize William from other eras."

Burroughs appreciated these friends who had become his family. His friends in Mexico City had been largely American expats; in Tangier he entered a virtually all-gay community; in Paris he found fellow psychic explorers; in London he moved in elegant gay circles; in New York he was the center of a largely drug-oriented group of much younger people; and now, in Lawrence, he was back among the midwesterners: taciturn, deep-thinking, people with no "side" or pretensions. Most were much younger than him, the generation that had been hippies in the sixties; writers, painters, journalists, photographers. They were caring and looked after him for the last sixteen years of his life. In 1991 he mused, "I left New York almost ten years ago and I haven't missed it for one single day."[15]

Burroughs did not think he had another book in him when he completed *The Western Lands* in 1987, but certain themes preoccupied him and he began writing them down. The resulting book, *Ghost of Chance*, was finished by June 1991. Burroughs did not see it as a continuation of the trilogy. "This is something quite different. It certainly is not in any sense to be regarded as a continuation."[16] He told Nicholas Zurbrugg "what's in there. The whole matter of lemurs, Madagascar, and also Christ. Who was Christ? Did he actually perform the miracles attributed to him? Yes, I think he did. As you know, the Buddhists are very, very dubious of miracles. They say, 'If you can, don't.' Because you're disturbing the natural order, interfering with the natural order, with incalculable long range results."[17] He discussed this issue with Allen Ginsberg at Naropa in March 1987. "It's so basically unspiritual, Allen. [Jesus] seemed to be a perfectly healthy boy. Suddenly, at the age of 30, he breaks out in this rash of miracles, performing the most irresponsible acts. He started by bringing back the *dead*! Whatever *for*? What a dreary and materialistic concept. Curing lepers, walking on the water, for chrissakes?"[18]

Burroughs had been experiencing tiredness and chest pains for some time and his doctor had given him nitroglycerine pills to take with him when he went on reading tours or to art openings. Toward the end of June 1991 he spent five days in Toronto, during which he had several bad attacks. "Excruciating pain, radiating down the left arm and up to the jaw. Popping nitro pills like peanuts. It comes in waves and nails you down."[19] Bill Rich met him at the airport in Kansas City and drove him back to Lawrence through a hailstorm with hail the size of golf balls. The insurance companies had to pay out millions for dented cars and shattered roof tiles. Burroughs saw Dr. Hiebert, who sent him straight to the hospital, saying he should never have permitted Bill to go to Toronto. Another three or four days and he would have had a massive heart attack. Dye X-rays showed that a major artery was 98 percent blocked. Six days later at St. Francis Hospital in Topeka he received an angioplasty to open a narrowed artery. It was soon clear to Bill's cardiologist, John Hiebert, that Bill needed a coronary bypass.

Back at St. Francis, he was given a shot of morphine in his shoulder, near his neck. The nurse told him, "This is morphine." Bill said, "Fine. Shoot it in my dear, shoot it in." The doctor wrote on his chart, "Give Mr. Burroughs as much morphine as he wants."[20] James was there two hours before the dawn operation and held his hand when he was on the gurney. James remembered, "It was just him and me. I was there when he woke up from the anesthesia, that's family." While trying to get out of bed unassisted to use the bathroom, Bill fell and fractured his hip, giving a scream that was heard through several floors of the hospital. He was allowed home after three weeks. His journal entry for July 27, 1991, read, "In that hospital there were interludes of blissful, painless tranquillity. (I start awake with a cry of fear.) Slipping, falling, deeper and deeper into easeful rest after the perilous journey, silent peace by the afternoon lake where the sun never sets and it is always late afternoon."[21] After the operation Bill was incapacitated for some time and was unable to feed himself. Allen Ginsberg came to stay and helped him out for a while.

In 1992, Burroughs became very interested in Indian shamanism and took up the offer by his friend Bill Lyon, an anthropologist who specialized in shamanism and now lived in the Stone House, to arrange a sweat lodge purification ceremony for him. Allen came to stay for it, but James held back, not wanting to experiment in religious practices. Burroughs felt that the ceremony did more for him than all his years of psychotherapy in identifying "the Ugly Spirit" and, if not banishing it, giving him more control over it. He was exposed to Native American culture all the time because the Haskell Indian Nations University was not far from him and he could hear their dances from his backyard.

On Thursday September 17, 1992, Bill set out for his methadone clinic in Kansas City, driven by Michael Emerton in his BMW. Rain was coming down in sheets, reducing visibility to just a few feet beyond the car hood, but Michael passed the freeway tollbooth at sixty-five miles per hour. Burroughs just began to say, "For Christ's sake, Michael, slow down and pull over," when the car hydroplaned and slammed into the guardrail, then skidded across the highway and into the ditch. They sat there, dumb. Then the door opened and a young man asked, "Can you walk?" Bill checked and found he was unhurt. "Better move away," the man said. "The car might catch fire." Another young man helped Michael from the car. "You guys are lucky you're not dead." The men drove them to the local truck stop. On September 22, an announcement appeared in the classified ads section of the *Lawrence Journal-World*: "Card of thanks. To express out heartfelt thanks to the two young motorists who helped us out of a wrecked BMW 6mi. E. of Lawrence on turnpike on Thurs., Sept. 17, 1992. William Burroughs & Michael Emerton."

Seven weeks later, on November 4, Michael committed suicide, using a gun given to him by Burroughs. James found the body. He and Michael had been together for eight years and though they had recently broken up the effect on James was devastating. Bill gave him some methadone, which helped. That night James stayed with Bill and in the middle of the night crawled into bed with him weeping. "We were weeping together in each other's arms, spooning, and somehow slept through the night." Burroughs wrote, "We live in the snow on Michael's grave falling softly like the descent of their last end on all the living and the dead, we live in the green light at the end of Daisy's dock, in the last and greatest of human dreams."[22] Burroughs dedicated *My Education* to him.

My Education, published in 1995, was transcribed into a working manuscript by Jim McCrary, assisted by David Ohle, over a period of several years from a collection of scraps of paper, index cards, and sheets of one-finger typing, and was reviewed and edited by James. The characters are the now familiar roll call of the dead: his mother—the eating his mother's back dream—his father, his brother, Ian Sommerville, Brion Gysin, Antony Balch, Mikey Portman, Joan, Billy Jr., and Kells Elvins. Others from the past include Jack Anderson, Lucien Carr, Gregory Corso, and Alan Watson. The action, such as it is, takes place in sets from his past, such as Wheeler's restaurant on Old Compton Street, Soho, where he used to dine with Francis Bacon;[23] Panama; Mexico City; Boulder; Lawrence; the Parade Bar in Tangier; 44 Egerton Gardens, the rooming house he stayed in when taking his apomorphine cure in 1956; Portland Place, a block from where he grew up: "Empty house. Leaves blowing, drifting like shreds of time. Radio silence on Portland Place..."[24]

Ian Sommerville dominates the book, with more than twenty references; sometimes they make it, sometimes Ian refuses. Burroughs remembered a dream from when they lived together in the Lottery Building in Tangier. "Ian said, 'I am a woman who looks like a man. I am your dead self' and crawls away on all fours."[25] Ian's presence in the book is overwhelming, the failure of their relationship one of Burroughs's biggest regrets. "Ian in Tangier there by the trees full of twittering sparrows. 'Make it with me!' "[26] But Bill would not, and Ian appears to have gone mad because of it. Ian was always on his mind. Udo Breger remembered that on a visit to Lawrence Burroughs twice called him "Ian" by accident.

Brion Gysin features almost as much as Ian, always there on the edge of his thoughts. Burroughs makes a sentimental association between his cat and the women in his life: "Little Calico is a delightful female beast like Jane Bowles and Joan and mother."[27] Burroughs called all his cats "my beast." His new friends were beginning to make their presence felt— Wayne Propst, David Ohle, George Kaull, Dean Ripa, Bill Rich, Mark Ewert—but his New York period is not represented. It is a book by a largely contented old man, sorting out his memories, assessing his life. "Today as I made my bed at 10:00 a.m., I am thinking that I am by and large a very happy man."[28]

2. Kurt Cobain

Working with David Cronenberg introduced Burroughs to a new audience; the fans of *Rabid, Scanners,* and *Videodrome* now added Burroughs to their list of cult figures. His work with Tom Waits and Robert Wilson had consolidated his position as elder statesman of the edgy avant-garde, and filming with Gus Van Sant gave him even more mainstream exposure. Burroughs was now famous and had to handle the downside of fame. Mostly this involved dealing with the fans who somehow found out his address and turned up on his porch unannounced. He usually had one of his support team there so they were not too much of a problem. Then there were the visiting celebrities: Chris Stein from Blondie, who was an old friend from New York and who stayed in Bill's spare bedroom/ painting studio; Patti Smith, whom he knew from New York. Patti had a crush on him that he managed to handle without too much distress on either side; the members of Sonic Youth, who visited several times, the second time bringing along Michael Stipe from R.E.M. The most celebrated visitor was Kurt Cobain, a huge Burroughs fan, with whom Burroughs made a record. The collaboration was Cobain's idea. Burroughs, of course, had no idea who he was and had never heard of Nirvana. Bill recorded a text called "The 'Priest' They Called Him" at his house on September 25, 1992, and it was sent to Cobain in Seattle, who overdubbed a guitar accompaniment of rather attractive psychedelic noodling at the Laundry Room Studios, Seattle, in November. The result was an extended play, one of Cobain's most obscure recordings. Cobain was delighted and wrote in his journal, "I've collaborated with one of my only Idols William Burroughs and I couldn't feel cooler."[29] Encouraged, Cobain then faxed Burroughs asking if he would play a crucifixion victim in a promo video for Nirvana's next single, "Heart-Shaped Box." Burroughs politely declined. This is perhaps not surprising as the opening scene of the video in Cobain's script ran as follows: "William and I sitting across from one another at a table (black and white) lots of Blinding Sun from the windows behind us holding hands staring into each others eyes. He gropes me from behind and falls dead on top of me. Medical footage of sperm flowing through penis. A ghost vapor comes out of his chest and groin area and enters my Body."

Cobain's wish to meet Burroughs was granted in October 1993, during the first week of a Nirvana tour when his tour manager Alex MacLeod drove Kurt to Lawrence. MacLeod remembered, "Meeting William was a real big deal for him. It was something he never thought would happen."[30] As they drove away, Burroughs said to James, "There's something wrong with that boy; he frowns for no good reason." Burroughs later described the meeting: "Cobain was very shy, very polite, and obviously enjoyed the fact that I wasn't awestruck at meeting him. There was something about him, fragile and engagingly lost. He smoked cigarettes but didn't drink. There were no drugs. I never showed him my gun collection."[31] Burroughs gave him a painting, while Cobain gave him a Leadbelly biography that he had signed. Cobain explained the reason for this in an interview: "I don't think he's ever claimed to be a rock 'n' roll lover, y'know? But he's taught me a lot of things through his books and interviews that I'm really grateful for. I remember him saying in an interview, 'These new rock 'n' roll kids should just throw away their guitars and listen to something with real soul, like Leadbelly.' I'd never heard about Leadbelly before so I bought a couple of records, and now he turns out to be my absolute favorite of all time in music. I absolutely love it more than any rock 'n' roll I ever heard."[32] Kurt Cobain turned a shotgun on himself on April 5, 1994. There was a rumor that he had spent his last days staring fixedly at a Dreamachine, but this was later dismissed as a hoax. Burroughs commented upon his death, "The thing I remember about him is the deathly grey complexion of his cheeks. It wasn't an act of will for Kurt to kill himself. As far as I was concerned, he was dead already."[33]

Burroughs had worked with musicians before. He wrote lyrics to a song called "Old Lady Sloan" for a local Lawrence band managed by Bill Rich called the Mortal Micronotz, produced by James Grauerholz in October 1982.[34] The first large-scale musical accompaniment of Burroughs's work came with the album *Dead City Radio* in 1990, produced by Hal Willner and Nelson Lyon, where Burroughs's readings were variously accompanied by Sonic Youth, John Cale, Donald Fagen, Lenny Pickett, Chris Stein, and others, all of which was good preparation for his collaboration with Tom Waits on *The Black Rider*. He worked with Laurie Anderson and was featured on a number of albums by Material and Bill Laswell.

In 1994 Burroughs was eighty. He was no longer writing except for occasional journal entries. He rarely gave readings or interviews, and just wanted a quiet life, though he did appear along with Gregory Corso, Allen Ginsberg, Lawrence Ferlinghetti, and Michael McClure on May 19 at a reading at Town Hall in New York connected with the Beat Generation conference at New York University. However, when Wieden & Kennedy, Nike's advertising agency, approached Burroughs with an offer to appear in a TV ad, James Grauerholz decided that it was worth doing, given the likelihood of some very large medical bills in the near future. Nike had previously made controversial ads using Spike Lee and Dennis Hopper. Burroughs's ad does not mention Nike. He appears on a hand-held television screen with athletes, presumably wearing Nike Air Max shoes, running and jumping over it as he intones things like, "The purpose of technology is not to confuse the brain but to serve the body." Nike PR manager Judy Smith explained, "He was chosen because we knew he could pull off this role as a quirky, scientific, prophetic technology wiz. Burroughs isn't identified in the commercial because the role he's playing has nothing to do with his history as a writer or his reputation in the counterculture." Nike didn't expect their fourteen-year-old audience to know who he was, but there were extra kudos for those who did. It seems unlikely that the ad, which was very ambiguous, sold any additional shoes for the company, but it added much-needed funds to Bill's bank account. Predictably, a wail of criticism that Burroughs had sold out went up, mostly from people who had a regular wage check coming in from a job in the straight world. But Burroughs's world was never black-and-white, either/or; in his 1965 *Paris Review* interview he said, "I see no reason why the artistic world can't absolutely merge with Madison Avenue. Pop art is a move in that direction. Why can't we have advertisements with beautiful words and beautiful images?" He was not opposed to advertising. It is true that he would not have made the ad in 1968, when he would definitely have identified Nike as part of the control system, but in his old age his main concern was survival, and in the United States good medical attention costs money.

Earlier in 1996, on May 31, Timothy Leary died. After various scares in which he threatened to have himself cryogenically preserved, he finally went out in full live Internet glory. That day Bill received a call from Tim's son, Zach, to say that Tim was slipping in and out of a coma but would like to talk to him. Bill said of course. Tim got on the line and asked Bill, "Is it true?" Bill, not knowing what he meant, hedged his bets and replied, "Well, I guess it's true," and chuckled. "It's true, Tim." Then Tim just said, "Well, I love you Bill," to which Bill replied, "I love you too, Tim." Leary died about four hours later."[35] His last words were, "Why not?"

Leary was followed two months later by Herbert Huncke, who died on August 8. Bill had seen a bit of Huncke when he was living in New York but he had always refused to allow him to visit him in Kansas. In New York he made sure that Huncke never left the main living room. When he was away and Stewart Meyer was Bunker-sitting, he gave Stew strict instructions that if Huncke visited he was never to be left alone, that he was never to be allowed into the archive room, and must not stay overnight. Huncke of course immediately tried to subvert Bill's strictures, but Stewart remained firm and Huncke never did manage to steal anything from there.

All through this period, Burroughs had been exhibiting his paintings worldwide. In 1993 there were shows in Kansas City, Madrid, Marseille, Venice, Lyon, and New York; in 1994 shows in Woody Creek, Colorado; Lawrence; Munich; and New York. In 1995 they were in Odense, Denmark; San Francisco; and at the Whitney's *Beat Culture and the New America* show in New York, but it was 1996 that was his most spectacular year with shows in New York, Minneapolis, Santa Monica, and Kansas City. Then in July came *Ports of Entry: William S. Burroughs and the Arts*, a magnificent solo show of over 150 items at the Los Angeles County Museum, curated by Robert S. Sobieszek, complete with an authoritative catalog. This finally put Burroughs on the map in the art world, but it was not until after his death that his work began to be seriously studied abroad, with large, nonselling museum shows mounted in Germany, Austria, Slovenia, and London.

With the *Ports of Entry* show scheduled to travel to the University of Kansas Spencer Museum of Art on October 26, it was decided to celebrate the occasion with the Nova Convention Revisited: William S. Burroughs and the Arts. Many of the original New York Nova Convention artists signed up for the event, which was held on November 26: Philip Glass, John Giorno, Patti Smith, Laurie Anderson, and Ed Sanders. They were joined by Deborah Harry and Chris Stein. Michael Stipe made an unannounced guest appearance, joining the Patti Smith band onstage and then singing backing vocals for her. Burroughs had always been impressed by Patti's impact on her audiences, which he thought of as shamanic, they seemed so energized by her. Though it was largely a musical affair, efforts were made to keep the focus on Burroughs by reading his texts onstage— Patti read from *Queer*—and showing clips from his readings. Burroughs had originally said he would not attend, but changed his mind at the last minute and appeared onstage at the end to give a brief reading and accept a standing ovation. It was an enjoyable occasion for all. Earlier he gave a lunchtime press conference along with the other main performers in which he explained that he moved to Lawrence so that he could go shooting and keep cats.

3. "I Had Not Thought Death Had Undone So Many"[36]

Allen Ginsberg's health had been in decline for some time; he had heart trouble and had fainting fits caused by his diabetes. Ever since the summer of 1996 he had felt tired and fatigued, and he was now taking ten different pills each day, including digitalis, to counteract Bell's palsy, cramps, water retention, diabetes, high blood pressure, and heart problems. He was now seventy and growing visibly weaker. One day in March 1997, he felt so bad that his assistant, Bob Rosenthal, called Joel Gaidemak, Allen's doctor (and cousin). When he described Allen's symptoms Gaidemak advised, "Get him in hospital immediately." Fortunately Allen had a good medical plan and was able to go straight to Beth Israel. They performed a battery of tests over several days. The results came back. He had hepatitis C, but he also had cancer of the liver. The cancer had metastasized everywhere and was "untreatable, incurable." Allen was told he had from three to six months to live from onset, but they did not know when the onset was. Allen said, "That sounds too long." His father, Louis, had died from the same disease. One of the first people Allen called was Bill, who wrote in his journal for April 3, "He says, 'I thought I would be terrified; instead I am exhilarated,'" and "Then it hits—a world without the voice of Allen." Allen drifted into a coma and died in bed in his Lower East Side loft on

April 5, 1997. He was seventy. Burroughs wrote, "Allen Ginsberg died (this morning); peaceful, no pain. He was right. When the doctors said 2–4 months, he said: 'I think less.'"[37]

Allen's death was reported across the world; he was America's most famous poet. Bill had to make a formal statement. The *New York Times* reported his words: "Ginsberg's death was 'a great loss to me and to everybody. We were friends for more than 50 years,' Mr. Burroughs said. 'Allen was a great person with worldwide influence. He was a pioneer of openness and a lifelong model of candor. He stood for freedom of expression and for coming out of all the closets long before others did. He has influence because he said what he believed. I will miss him.'"[38] A month later he amplified this thought in his journal: "Allen's worldwide influence toward openness, *glasnost*, is unprecedented. He, with the courage of total sincerity, charmed and disarmed the savage Fraternity Beasts."[39] Allen was Bill's oldest, dearest friend. Allen's belief in him had got him first published. Without Allen *The Naked Lunch* would not have been written or assembled. It was Allen who persuaded him to move to the Beat Hotel, which was, in his words, "the most productive time of my life." And it was Allen who, seeing him in a state of stasis in London, got him back to the States. Allen's death precipitated a deep depression.

Bill's own health had been gradually failing for some time, but on April 21, 1997, a successful cataract removal procedure by Dr. Richard Orchard greatly improved his eyesight and enabled him to better enjoy his shooting outings. Ever since the Nova Convention Revisited his friends had noticed a change in him: he was less cranky, less loud and garrulous, more approachable and friendly. Now his friends could get a word in edgewise instead of having to listen to his long monologues. Money was still a concern, and on May 22, 1997, Burroughs made an appearance in a promotional video for the band U2. He played a shopping cart vagrant, dressed in a smart black suit, pushing a huge klieg light in his trolley, tying up the traffic in downtown Kansas City for several hours.[40] In his journal he referred to the band as "You Too," never having seen their name in print.

On July 29, 1997, Bill had his last shooting session at Fred Aldrich's farm. He was again feeling depressed because his beloved cat Fletch had recently died. TP and Bill were walking by the garage, where Bill had his Toyota parked outside, and TP saw Fletch under the car. There were flies buzzing around his face. Bill called out, "Fletch! Fletch!" but TP told him he was dead. It was as if he had been punched in the sternum. Bill took a step back. He was distraught. It hit him harder than a human death. It was as if the death of a cat reminded him of the deaths of all his loved ones.

Three days later, Bill had a heart attack. About twenty minutes after the first drink of the day he was seated in his green writing chair by the bedroom window, writing in his journal, when he had a coughing fit that precipitated a heart attack. He was discovered by TP, who was cooking dinner for him that night. TP showed up at 4:00 p.m. with the groceries, banged on the door, and shouted their old joke, "Don't shoot!" Bill was in his bedroom, hunched over in agony, clutching his chest, grimacing and groaning, his almost bald head emerging from his huge green army jacket like a turtle. He said that his heart hurt and he had taken a nitro-glycerine tablet. TP called 911, then called James. Bill was still lucid. TP said, "Hide the guns and drugs?" and Bill grunted, "Yeah." TP recalled, "He had weed and he had a gun on him. And when paramedics come they don't want to see a gun on an eighty-three-year-old guy having a heart attack. It's not good for anybody. I said, 'Do you want help?' because he had to take his whole belt off, and he said, 'No.' And he got it off and he was brave, he was really brave. It was hurting him but he didn't seem scared to me. I was more scared."[41] Bill hid his .38 under his pillow. James arrived, followed by the paramedics. Just as Bill was being loaded into the ambulance, Pat Connor, who had a dinner night at Bill's, drove up. He got out of his car, walked over to Bill, and asked him, "What's goin' on?" Bill replied, quoting a Brion Gysin line, "Back in no time." They were his last words.

TP wondered if he knew then that he was going to die. "He was inter-ested in last words and he had last words books. I don't know if he had it prepared." Bill lost consciousness as the ambulance pulled away. Dean Ripa, who was visiting Lawrence, had been expected for dinner and came to the hospital. James asked TP and Dean not to inform anyone, feeling that well-wishers would be a hindrance in those crucial hours. Bill lasted out the night but never regained consciousness. The next day James, TP, and Dean were still at the hospital. That afternoon TP was sitting with Bill alone in the intensive care unit—James and Dean had gone outside to smoke a cigarette—when the nurse looked at the wild spikes on the EKGs and told him, "He's starting to go," throwing TP into a quandary. TP remembered, "I don't want him to die alone, but I don't want him to die without James. I ran down the stairs and ran out the front door looking for James while William lay there dying. And I didn't see them. I ran around the entire hospital, looking for 'em. And I didn't find 'em. So I went back up and they were there." James had been paged. Bill was still alive.

The nurse pointed to the jagged pattern on the EKG screen and told James, "That's called an 'agonal' pattern," then she left them. Bill's eyes were closed, his mouth open. He had a breathing tube through one nos-tril and many lines leading to hangbags and devices. He seemed to have ceased breathing. James stood by his right shoulder with TP and Dean across from him. No one else was there for the final fifteen minutes. James remembered, "I could see the biomonitor screen, by Dean's right shoulder; I saw the jagged, spastic, nonrhythmic pattern of his EKG signal slowly give up its mute efforts to restart. Then all the lines were flat. We wept, hard. We composed ourselves at length." William Seward Burroughs II died at 6:50 p.m. on August 2, 1997. Normally, when the hospital staff are sure the patient is dead, they remove the body from the ward, but James negotiated with the nursing staff to allow him to rest undisturbed. They were reluctant until he explained that he was a Buddhist, and in that tradition it is thought that the soul is much slower to depart from the body than an observer might think. He hoped for six hours; they gave him five.

Several members of Bill's inner-circle family came to sit with him. David Ohle and Jim McCrary were both out of town. James phoned Wayne Propst and invited him to join them, and Patricia Elliott, an old friend of Bill's, arrived not long after Bill's death. She described the scene at Bill's bedside in her journals: "James came in the room and we hugged. Then James turned to William and clasped him, crying and sobbing in the most utterly broken hearted way. I had never seen James more beautiful. I thought, God, James was father and son to William. The love and respect that I had observed between those two over the years flashed through my thoughts like a bursting series of light."[42]

Ira Silverberg, who had remained in close contact with both James and Bill after he and James broke up, flew in as soon as he heard the news. On August 6, James and Ira arrived at Bill's house at about ten in the morning to pick out the clothes that the funeral director would dress him in for his coffin: his best white shirt and a blue necktie handpainted by Bill; the Moroccan waistcoat, or *sedria*, in green velvet with gold brocade given him by Brion Gysin; his best black shoes, the ones he used when he performed; James remembered that the CIA called a new assignment "getting new shoes." They found the least worn of his blue jeans and placed a nineteenth-century Indian-head five-dollar gold piece in the pocket for his journey to the Western Lands. They selected a black sport jacket with a dark green tint and put his reading glasses in his breast pocket and a ballpoint pen in the inside pocket. He also had three joints of top-quality marijuana and a wrap of heroin in his pocket. On his lapel he wore the rosettes of the Commandeur des Arts et des Lettres and the American Academy of Arts and Letters. They put his red bandana in his back pocket where he always kept it. Naturally he had to have his gray fedora. By his side was his favorite hickory swordstick and his .38 Special snubnose, fully loaded with five bullets, the one he wore every day and kept under his pillow at night. A huge quantity of flowers was left at the house, and even two weeks later some anonymous person left a fresh bouquet every day.

There was an open-coffin viewing at Liberty Hall, a little theater around the corner from the Eldridge Hotel at 644 Massachusetts and 7th. Burroughs was placed on center stage, framed by the proscenium arch, but when James went to the auditorium to check the sight lines to the coffin, he saw that viewers could not see anything. He asked the undertakers, "Do you think we can prop his head up a little bit, so his forehead and nose are visible from the loge?" So even in death Burroughs was treated like a celebrity, making his last public appearance. James said, "My feeling is, this too is show business." About a thousand local people came to view, including many of the town's youth, wearing shorts and jeans, cramming the balcony for the service. José Ferez, who for years had handled Burroughs's art business, took photographs of Burroughs in his coffin but was offended that some people insisted on kissing him, including John Giorno, who had come to Kansas for the funeral. José reported, "Several people actually kissed him and one woman from the October Gallery kept kissing him full on the mouth."[43] José thought it was disrespectful. TP commented, "I have never seen a corpse kissed before or since. I've never seen anybody pose for pictures in front of a corpse before, but then you know I've never been to the funeral of a famous person before. It's a different world and the rules are different. When a famous person dies there's no rules, there's no etiquette. It was a fucking free-for-all." Burroughs was a very formal man, not given to kissing people, but he was vulnerable in death. TP recalled, "I never hugged William. When I got there I'd shake his hand, and on the way out he'd give me the double handshake and stand on the porch and wave as you drove away. But I'd see him just get mauled. You see the look on someone's face when someone's hugging 'em and its like, 'Oh fuck! This person's grabbed me.' I saw that 'Oh fuck' look a lot of times."

The thing that upset the close family the most was a widely published text by John Giorno, who wrote, "William Burroughs died on August 2, 1997 at 6:30 in the afternoon following a massive heart attack the day before. He was 83 years old. I was with him when he died and it was one of the best times I ever had with him."[44] John Giorno was in New York when Burroughs died, and to use his death as a way of gathering publicity for himself was seen as being in the worst possible taste. James commented, "It's just a lie and to me that's one of the most offensive things that he's ever done in terms of how I've felt about him. It really offended me a lot. But I don't think John, deep down, could understand why people could be offended by something like that. [...] It's like a little baby looking for attention. That was the one time when I most strongly felt it was exploitative, with him making up that story and deliberately giving the impression that it was true." Many of Bill's other close friends, in Kansas and elsewhere, felt the same way.

Burroughs had wanted to be buried in the family mausoleum in the Bellefontaine cemetery. He signed the reservation papers himself and paid the five-hundred-dollar donation toward upkeep. A few days before he died he said at a Thursday night dinner, "I don't want to be cremated, I want to go down into the ground and ROT!" Bill's body was driven to St. Louis in a procession including two white stretch limousines. At a rest stop in central Missouri they were joined by a hippie bus after Anne Waldman told them who was in the hearse. Before going to Bellefontaine, James had the hearse make a short stop on Euclid Avenue, two doors from the house where Bill was born in the Central West End. The service began at 7:00 p.m. with "For All the Saints Who from Their Labours Rest" by Ralph Vaughan Williams, sung by James's mother, Selda Grauerholz, who had once been a semiprofessional singer. Tim Miller, from the faculty of the University of Kansas, spoke a few words on behalf of the Lawrence community. Some time before, Burroughs had asked David Ohle if he would read from Alfred Lord Tennyson's "Ulysses" at his funeral, which he now did. This was followed by a recording of Bill reading. James gave the closing address. The coffin was closed at 9:30, but the next day James asked the morticians to open it again for one last look. Bill's friend, the artist and weapons expert David Bradshaw, was with him. James handed him Bill's favorite gun, his "snubby," and Bradshaw placed the pistol at Burroughs's thigh, near his hand.

Burroughs was buried on August 7 in the Burroughs family plot at Bellefontaine Cemetery in St. Louis, block 37, lot 3938, next to his grandfather, his mother, his father, and Uncle Horace, the morphine addict. The grandfather's name, William Seward Burroughs, was the only one on the mausoleum. Patti Smith flew in, taking a cab to the graveyard straight from the airport, but when she reached the gates she insisted on walking to the grave instead of driving. It is a large graveyard so the burial was delayed while everyone waited for her to arrive. The grave was filled in using a backhoe and floral wreaths piled on top. There was talk of firing a single-volley salute over the grave, but they decided against it and instead José Ferez, Fred Aldrich, and David Bradshaw just posed with guns for photographs.

Later James Grauerholz had the names of all the interred Burroughs family members carved on the obelisk and installed two Barre gray granite benches for visitors to rest upon. He applied for special dispensation to erect a footstone at Bill's feet. It reads, "William Seward Burroughs. Feb 5, 1914–Aug 2, 1997. American Writer."

Endwords

William S. Burroughs was not only a novelist; he produced a huge body of work that is best understood seen as a whole. He was an essayist on a wide range of subjects from revolutionary techniques in warfare to the antics of cats, the author of book reviews, humor, travel writing, studies of psychic phenomena, and investigations into methods of self-improvement from Scientology to the theories of Wilhelm Reich. He wrote poems, belles lettres, rock 'n' roll lyrics, and the libretto for an opera. He made more records than most rock groups and appeared in dozens of films and documentaries. Inevitably, given such a prodigious output, his audience is varied, and people see him from different viewpoints according to their interests. Everyone has their own William S. Burroughs. A horror-film fan who encountered him via David Cronenberg knows a different Burroughs than the avant-garde scholar who first saw him onstage with John Cage.

He is seen as a great writer, a junkie, a murderer, a misogynist, a member of the original Beat Generation, a mentor to the youth movement of the sixties, a political philosopher, a psychic, a leading gay activist, an artist, a gun advocate, an actor, a humorist, and a "good 'ol boy." The Burroughs brand comes in many varieties.

His writing methods were often unorthodox: his correspondence with Allen Ginsberg produced his first four books. His experiments with cut-ups and textural juxtaposition using columns and scrapbooks led him far from writing into recording-tape cut-ups; photographic collages, photo series, and pattern-making; films using extreme jump cuts and actual cut-ups; shotgun sculptures and paintings, all of which relate to and reference each other.

Burroughs was aware that writers can have an image problem, and that it was not good to be typecast, like an actor always playing the same role. He felt that Hemingway had been consumed by the least interesting aspect of his work. He told Gerard Malanga, "I feel that his work suffered from that. So, finally you get, there is nothing there but the image: Poppa Hemingway. [...] The whole matter of image is, I think, a very dangerous thing for a writer: too much image. [...] I think that any writer is to a certain extent typecast by his choice of subject matter. Like Genet is typecast as the saintly convict. And Graham Greene, of course, it's the old whiskey priest. Uh, of course, I'm no longer a drug addict."[1] But Burroughs bowed to the inevitable. He realized the importance of promotion in the modern publishing environment and adopted the role imposed on him by his fans, the godfather, éminence grise, the old junkie priest, writer, and sage.

Though Burroughs did not deliver a fatal blow to the bourgeois novel, he certainly gave it a good kicking. Without *Junky*, Scottish author Alexander Trocchi could not have written *Cain's Book*; in London J. G. Ballard would not have written *Crash*, *The Atrocity Exhibition*,[2] or his experimental short stories. Ballard always acknowledged his enormous debt to Burroughs. In the sixties and seventies there was even an International Cut-Up literary movement, made up mostly by German and French writers inspired by, and often writing in collaboration with, Burroughs, sometimes in English: Carl Weissner, Jürgen Ploog, Harold Norse, Jörg Fauser, Claude Pélieu, Mary Beach, Alfred Behrens, Walter Hartmann, Jan Herman, Hammond Guthrie, and Gerhard Hanak. From the seventies onward Burroughs can be seen as a major influence on avant-garde writing from Will Self to Kathy Acker and Dennis Cooper, Michael Moorcock's Jerry Cornelius novels, Ronald Sukenick, David Wojnarowicz, and Iain Sinclair. He is buried in the DNA of punk and post-punk writers such as Stewart Home, Terry Wilson, Genesis P-Orridge, Keith Seward, and David Britton.

Another, far more popular genre heavily influenced by Burroughs is cyberpunk, the eighties "post-sci-fi" label used to describe writers such as Bruce Sterling, Pat Cadigan, Randy Rucker, John Shirley, Neal Stephenson, and, most famously, William Gibson, whose novel *Neuromancer* (1984) introduced cyberpunk to a mass audience. In 2005 Gibson wrote, "Burroughs was then as radical a literary man as the world had to offer, and in my opinion, he still holds the title. Nothing, in all my experience of literature since, has ever been quite as remarkable for me, and nothing has ever had as strong an effect on my sense of the sheer possibilities of writing."[3]

Burroughs's influence extended into music. He gave a number of bands their names: Steely Dan, Soft Machine, Insect Trust. The author's favorite is Matching Mole, the band that Robert Wyatt formed after leaving Soft Machine. It is a phonetic rendering of the French for Soft Machine, *La machine molle*. Paul McCartney was sufficiently impressed by his conversations with Bill to put him on the sleeve of *Sgt. Pepper's*. The Rolling

Stones fêted him. After meeting Burroughs in November 1973, David Bowie used the cut-up technique to write the lyrics for *Diamond Dogs* and the 1977 German albums *Low* and *"Heroes."* Bowie stated that he got "the shape and the look of what Ziggy and the Spiders were going to become" from *The Wild Boys* and Stanley Kubrick's *A Clockwork Orange* (1971), based on the 1962 Anthony Burgess novel. "They were both powerful pieces of work, especially the marauding boy gangs of Burroughs' Wild Boys with their bowie knives. I got straight on to that."[4] Jon Savage observed, "Within five years of Ziggy, the punks were enacting The Wild Boys on the streets of London, Manchester, Liverpool and other cities in Britain. [...] Few could have foreseen in 1974 a youth culture that took many of its cues from a figure like Burroughs, but Bowie saw it and helped to bring it about."[5] Musicians like Joe Strummer and Mick Jones of the Clash were interested in Burroughs's work—Strummer visited with him in New York, and Burroughs was so pleased with the Sex Pistols' "God Save the Queen" that he sent them a congratulatory telegram. Thus Burroughs is sometimes dubbed the "Godfather of Punk."

Iggy Pop, the true grandfather of punk, also claims Burroughs as an influence. The title song from his 1977 album *Lust for Life* has a reference to Johnny Yen in the first line (from *The Naked Lunch*), there's a reference to the "flesh machine," and the line about "hypnotizing chickens" apparently refers to something in *The Ticket That Exploded*. Burroughs's influence on punk was enormous, particularly in the United States, but more as a mentor and inspiration than artistic influence. They felt he gave them permission to behave that way, and some, like Patti Smith and Chris Stein, became friends. A new generation of musicians—Michael Stipe, Kurt Cobain, Sonic Youth—all came to visit. However, not everyone loved him. A radical feminist group in Toronto called Bitch Nation brought out a fanzine called *Double Bill*, dedicated to praising actor William "Cannon" Conrad, and condemning William Burroughs (and including the odd swipe at Allen Ginsberg as well).[6]

His influence extends into other genres: Gus Van Sant (*Drugstore Cowboy*), Alex Cox (*Repo Man*), and Donald Cammell and Nick Roeg (*Performance*) have all acknowledged his influence, and *The Third Mind* is used by many young filmmakers as a textbook for fresh ways of approaching their material. Some say the space cantina in *Star Wars* would not have been possible were it not for Hassan's Rumpus Room in *The Naked Lunch*.

Burroughs was not writing only for artistic reasons. He intended his books to have political impact; to directly confront the agents that control people's lives. In the tradition of Orwell or Sartre he was writing to free the mind from all the strictures by which society enslaves it: family values, bourgeois morality, nationalism, and religion. "Deconditioning means the removal of all automatic reactions deriving from past conditioning— all automatic reactions to Queen, Country, Pope, President, Generalissimo, Allah, Christ, Fidel Castro, the Communist Party, the CIA. [...] When automatic reactions are no longer operative you are in a condition to make up your mind."[7] His influence on the youth movement of the sixties was considerable, particularly when he placed himself firmly on their side by appearing in the front row alongside Ginsberg and Genet at a march during the 1968 Chicago Democratic Convention demonstrations.

Although he was very much in the American tradition, to be defined on his tombstone as an "American writer" would have been antithetical to Burroughs, who always rejected ideas of nationalism and patriotism. In many ways he was archetypically American: the dry, flat, clipped syllables, like a prewar newscaster, betrayed his midwestern origins, but with a mid-Atlantic timbre. His actual speech was tempered with Anglicisms and forties hipster slang. It was this mixture of precise, cultured Harvard learning and bizarre street talk that made his spoken delivery so fascinating. Many people have said they never fully understood Burroughs until they heard his voice. Burroughs has been compared to the misanthropic onscreen persona of W. C. Fields, and they had much in common: a contempt for women and dogs and a fondness for alcohol and absurd humor. Burroughs never saw himself as an expatriate. As he said, "I was back for brief times in the States, but from 1948 on I was pretty much out of the States [until 1974]. I never thought of myself as particularly in exile because there was nothing to be exiled from. One can hardly say that one is in exile from the United States as a whole. I had no sense of home at all. Where is home? I never thought of St. Louis as being home."

Many of his friends commented on how Anglicized Burroughs always was, with his egg cups and Senior Service cigarettes, his gourmet taste, classical learning, formal attire, and old-fashioned manners. The comparison between Burroughs and Conan Doyle's Sherlock Holmes goes back as far as 1944, when Kerouac and Ginsberg first suggested it: the aquiline face, thin lips, the "tall, spare figure," the long silences. They both injected cocaine, both were armed, both carried an armed shooting stick, both kept extensive scrapbooks. Both were masters of disguise and immune (almost) to the charms of women. And both had their Watsons: Allen Ginsberg, Brion Gysin, Ian Sommerville, Antony Balch, and James Grauerholz all served that role.

Burroughs was never an expat like Paul Bowles, purposely making a life in another country, though he did appear to attempt it in Tangier with Ian Sommerville in 1963 and in Duke Street Saint James's, London, in 1966, again with Ian. For most of his life Burroughs was peripatetic, at home in a hotel room and content as long as a decent breakfast and a selection of good restaurants was available. He had no real home until he bought a house in Lawrence, Kansas, at the age of sixty-nine.

The role of drugs in Burroughs's life cannot be overemphasized. From the mid-forties, when his *nostalgie de la boue* led him to the criminal circles where he became addicted to morphine, he was involved in the drug sub-culture. Though not always addicted, he was rarely sober from then on: all his books were written on marijuana, which he used throughout his lifetime, and/or opiates. Despite his frequent claims to the contrary, much of the original material in *The Naked Lunch* was written while he was heavily addicted to Eukodol, a form of morphine, and everything written after his return to the United States in 1974 was written on opiates; he switched to the methadone program for the last seventeen years of his life. This was in contradiction to his previous position, when he said, "I've always maintained that any sort of opiate is contraindicated for creative work. It makes you less aware of your surroundings. But I made copi-ous notes over the years."[8] At the time of writing no one has yet done a serious study of what must surely be the biggest influence of all upon his work: the different drugs he was taking when he wrote his books. This would have to include alcohol. He drank a good deal, sometimes lapsing into alcoholism. Drugs were an enormously important part of his life: they were an all-consuming interest and also the subject of much of his writing. He was ambivalent about them, on and off, for and against, for much of his life, but in old age he felt that becoming a junkie was the best thing he ever did, because without it he would not have written *The Naked Lunch* or encountered the demimonde of underground characters that populate his work.

Burroughs did not have a happy life: he was plagued by loneliness and lack of love, racked with guilt, not just over the death of Joan, but for his neglect of friends and family. "You never loved anybody except your cats, your Ruski and Spooner and Calico...Mother, Ian, Brion, Antony Balch?"[9] he wrote in *Last Words*. "Mother, Dad, Mort, Billy—I failed them all—"[10] Many people have commented how much Burroughs changed after moving to Kansas: old age softened him; for the first time he had a home, a support system of friends, fame and recognition, a reg-ular supply of drugs and his cats. Although he had always been a great raconteur among close friends, his reputation in London and Paris among those who did not know him very well was for his long, icy silences. His publishers Maurice Girodias, John Calder, and Barney Rosset all commented upon this. In Kansas, however, he became positively garrulous, dispensing pearls of wisdom to his friends and visitors, most of whom had received them before, many times. To his friends in Lawrence he was an inspirational presence. TP commented, "William had a lot of advice for a young man. [...] He wasn't a softy but he was really warm. And he was just so likable. Everybody I know liked him."[11] His manners were endearing. Like W. H. Auden, Burroughs made a point of escorting visitors to their carriage and would stand on the porch, waving goodbye. TP: "You know it fostered the warmest feelings, when you're driving away, and you see him up there in silhouette waving at you." As he grew older his support team of carers closed ranks and became very protective of him, sometimes warding off strangers and celebrity seekers, enabling him to write and paint without interruption. He continued to shoot and to write his journals, but age took its toll and he became increasingly stooped and frail, a slight figure in overlarge clothing. *El hombre invisible* was becoming invisible, but his mental agility was unimpaired. Increasingly, Bill's consciousness became a flickering collage of memories and dreams as friends and sets flashed across his mind:

> White green and light blue filigrees of coral shot through with specks and streaks of red looking up to Brion's picture there is Paul Bowles' face very old, very petulant finally upside down. Walk once again out of the pub where I talked to Tim Willoughby across the street to Lancaster Gate and downstairs. Ian looks up. "I just washed my hair." We are the language the letters disintegrate, fade to gray shadows. Doctor Zeit. Sunlight on Moscow Road where the Greek restaurant was. Mullet and raisins. Little pieces of London. The ducks. Old biddies feeding sparrows in the air. Ian's superimposed picture. "What a beautiful sinister place." Brion exclaimed. David Budd and the metal sculptures. Back in the ghost pub with the ghost of swinging London. You can see through it.[12]

Since his death, interest in Burroughs's work has greatly increased. There have been major museum exhibitions worldwide of his paintings: a three-part show in London at Riflemaker in 2005; a sellout show at the Stellan Holm Gallery in New York; in 2012 a show at ZKM in Karlsruhe, Germany, organized by Udo Breger entitled *The Name Is Burroughs— Expanded Media* assembled sixteen hundred items not only by Burroughs but portraits of him and works inspired by him; that same year the Vienna Kunsthalle put on *Cut-ups Cut-ins Cut-outs. Die Kunst des William S. Burroughs*, featuring his manuscripts and scrapbooks. There have been documentary films, spoken-word recordings, and academic conferences: the fiftieth anniversary of the publication of *The Naked Lunch* was celebrated by conferences in Paris, held at the University of London Institute, Paris, and in New York, hosted by Columbia University, New York University, and the School of Visual Arts. Other celebrations in 2009 were held in Chicago, London, Bristol, Lawrence, Sydney, San Francisco, and Venice, California. Burroughs's books remain in print and new translations continue to be published. At the time of writing there have been more than two dozen academic studies of his work, and the RealityStudio.org website provides an ongoing forum on all aspects of his life and work.

Burroughs's work, far from being dated, is more relevant now than ever in the fight for freedom of thought as governments increase electronic surveillance of their citizens, restrict freedom of speech, and the huge global corporations take over the planet. Inspector Lee is still needed in the fight against the Nova Mob.

Notes

Acknowledgments
1. Audio Research Editions ARECD301, Liverpool, 2007.

Introduction
1. This account of Burroughs's sweat lodge experience draws heavily upon the conversations that Allen Ginsberg held with Burroughs between April 17 and 22, 1992, immediately following the event, and are taken from a raw transcript of the tapes sent to the author by Ginsberg at the time. Some of the background and context is taken from the article "Exorcising Burroughs" by Allen Ginsberg in *Observer Magazine*, April 26, 1992.
2. WSB interviewed by Jim McMenamin and Larry McCaffery in *Across the Wounded Galaxies*, ed. Larry McCaffery (Champaign: University of Illinois Press, 1990).
3. WSB interviewed by Gregory Corso and Tom H. at the Naropa Institute, July 1984.
4. Morgan, tape 75 (labeled tape 74).
5. WSB on telephone to Michael Horovitz, Good Friday, 1992, in "Legend in His Own Lunchtime," in Rupert Loydell, ed., *my kind of angel: i.m. william burroughs*, 62–63.

Chapter One
1. "Trip to Hell and Back," WSB interviewed by Jerry Bauer in *Trax* (London), no. 6 (March 18, 1981).
2. T. S. Eliot to Marquis Childs, quoted in *St. Louis Post-Dispatch*, October 15, 1930, and in the address "American Literature and the American Language" delivered at Washington University, June 9, 1953, published in Washington University Studies, *New Series: Literature and Language* 23 (St. Louis: Washington University Press, 1953), 6.
3. WSB, *The Place of Dead Roads*, 42.
4. It appears that the street has subsequently been renamed, with the two private blocks, including where WSB was born, now called Pershing Place, and only the remaining public block called Pershing Avenue.
5. WSB, *The Place of Dead Roads*, 19.
6. Morgan, tape 1.
7. Abstracted from the psychiatrist's report, Payne Whitney Clinic, New York, April 25, 1940, based on an interview with WSB's mother. This entire section draws heavily upon James Grauerholz's research in his paper, "William S. Burroughs' St. Louis Childhood: The Untold Story," also upon Morgan, tape 1.
8. James Wideman Lee, *Henry W. Grady: The Editor, the Orator, the Man* (New York: Fleming H. Revell, 1896).
9. Morgan, tape 16.
10. Ibid.

11. This figure comes only from William Burroughs's memory of family conversations and has not so far been substantiated.
12. "Morphia Victim, Son of Adding Machine Inventor, Is Suicide," *Detroit Free Press*, March 8, 1915.
13. Morgan, tape 1.

Chapter Two

1. WSB, *Naked Lunch*, 89
2. WSB to Allen Ginsberg, January 15, 1953.
3. James Grauerholz, "William S. Burroughs' St. Louis Childhood: The Untold Story" (ms.).
4. Barry Miles, *William Burroughs: El Hombre Invisible*. From conversation with WSB.
5. WSB, *Cities of the Red Night*, 276.
6. Marcel Proust, *In Search of Lost Time* vol. 1, *Swann's Way* (London: Vintage, 1996), 222.
7. Grauerholz, *William S. Burroughs' St. Louis Childhood*.
8. Morgan, tape 1.
9. WSB, *The Cat Inside*, 17.
10. Morgan, tape 2.
11. WSB, *The Cat Inside*, 18.
12. WSB, *Last Words*, 69.
13. WSB, *My Education*, 167.
14. WSB, *Junky: The Definitive Text of "Junk,"* 107.
15. British slang later imported into the United States, usually as "shanks mare." The shank is the part of leg extending from ankle to knee, thus walking.
16. WSB, *The Place of Dead Roads*, 19.
17. Morgan, tape 65 (labeled tape 64).
18. *Interzone*, 166.
19. Morgan, tape 2.
20. Ibid.
21. Vincent Price was born in 1911 and was in Mort's year at school.
22. Morgan, tape 65 (labeled tape 64).
23. WSB, "The Name Is Burroughs," in *The Adding Machine*.
24. Ibid.
25. WSB, "Prose on a distant wall," unpublished ms., ca. 1972.
26. Ibid.
27. Morgan, tape 2.
28. Ann Russe Eaton (née Prewitt) to Ted Morgan, May 7, 1985.
29. Prynne Hoxie died in a car accident when he was eighteen in his freshman year at Princeton.
30. WSB, *Cobble Stone Gardens*, 9–10.
31. Grauerholz, "William S. Burroughs' St. Louis Childhood."
32. WSB, *The Western Lands*, 158.
33. WSB, *The Place of Dead Roads*, 46–74, 130–58.
34. Ibid., xiv–xv.
35. Ibid., 74.
36. WSB, *Cities of the Red Night*, 227.
37. The Evangelische St. Paul Kirche in Defiance, built in 1906, was demolished in the twenties to be replaced by a new church.
38. WSB, unpublished journals, entry for November 15, 1991.
39. WSB, *Port of Saints* (Calder edition), 139.
40. Ibid., 142.
41. WSB, *Interzone*, 71.
42. T. S. Eliot, "The Love Song of J. Alfred Prufrock."
43. T. S. Eliot, "Preludes 1."
44. WSB, *Last Words*, 34.

45. The Woolworth Building was the world's tallest building from 1913 to 1930.
46. WSB interviewed by Legs McNeil, *Spin*, October 1991.

Chapter Three

1. James Grauerholz, "William S. Burroughs' St. Louis Childhood: The Untold Story" (ms.).
2. Barry Miles, *William Burroughs: El Hombre Invisible*.
3. WSB, unpublished journals, early eighties. Lon Chaney's famous line.
4. WSB, *My Education*, 191–92.
5. WSB interviewed by the author, November 29, 1991, Lawrence, Kansas.
6. WSB, *Last Words*, 151.
7. WSB, "Do You Remember Tomorrow?," *Mayfair* vol. 3, no. 8 (August 1968).
8. WSB, "St. Louis Return," in *The Burroughs File*, 88.
9. Morgan, tape 2.
10. Ibid.
11. Ibid.
12. Ibid.; the cemetery was the Beth Hamedrash Hagodol Cemetery on Ladue Road.
13. Morgan, tape 6.
14. Ibid.
15. Ibid.
16. Grauerholz, "William S. Burroughs' St. Louis Childhood."
17. WSB, "The Fall of Art," in *The Adding Machine*, 62.
18. Morgan, tape 3.
19. Technically it is a char. The name comes from Dickens's *Barnaby Rudge*.

Chapter Four

1. Fred Kaplan, *Gore Vidal: A Biography*, 101.
2. Morgan, tape 3.
3. Gore Vidal, *The Smithsonian Institution*, 1998, 65 (quoted in Kaplan, *Gore Vidal*).
4. WSB interviewed by Bill Rich, 1991. Burroughs Archives.
5. All factual details about Los Alamos in this section are taken from Vidal, via Kaplan, *Gore Vidal*.
6. Morgan, tape 3.
7. WSB, *Last Words*, 90.
8. WSB, "Literary Biography," in Barry Miles, *A Descriptive Catalogue of the William S. Burroughs Archive*, 75.
9. Ibid., 74.
10. Morgan, tape 2.
11. WSB, "Literary Biography," 75.
12. Morgan, tape 16.
13. WSB, "Literary Biography," 75.
14. Ibid., 74.
15. Max Putzel, letter, "Burroughs and guns," *Times Literary Supplement*, July 24, 1992.
16. Morgan, tape 4.
17. WSB to Allen Ginsberg, April 7, 1954.
18. WSB to Allen Ginsberg, January 15, 1956, in *The Yage Letters*.
19. James Grauerholz, "Research summary—SWG—8/16/105 re 'Billy Bradshinkel' and Prynne Hoxie." Unpublished document.
20. Morgan, tape 3.

Chapter Five

1. Morgan, tape 3.
2. A range was opened beneath the stadium in 1933.

3. Morgan, tape 62 (labeled tape 61).
4. Morgan, tape 25.
5. Morgan, tape 2.
6. Morgan, tape 88.
7. Morgan, tape 39.
8. Ibid.
9. Morgan, tape 16.
10. Upon the death of his father in 1969 he became the Second Viscount Monsell. His sister Joan married the writer Patrick Leigh Fermor.
11. Morgan, tape 2.
12. WSB, introduction to Robert Walker, *New York Inside Out* (New York: Skyline, 1984).
13. Morgan, tape 16.
14. Locke-Ober, 3 Winter Place; Parker House, 60 School Street; Union Oyster House, 41 Union Street; Durgin-Park, 340 Faneuil Hall, all in Boston.
15. Morgan, tape 6.
16. Morgan, tape 35. Richard Stern remembers the name of the ferret being Jean des Esseintes, named after the hero of Huysmans's *À rebours* because of its scent. Robert Miller supports this name. Burroughs remembers the ferret living in Adams House. Possibly there were two ferrets.
17. WSB and Allen Ginsberg in conversation, filmed by Obie Benz in December 1986 for his film *Heavy Petting*, in Judy Bloomfield, Mary McGrail, and Lauren Sanders, eds., *Too Darn Hot: Writing About Sex Since Kinsey* (New York: Persea Books, 1998).
18. WSB interviewed by Victor Bockris and Andrew Wylie, NYC, 1974. From ms. transcript.
19. Morgan, tape 5.
20. Morgan, tape 38.

Chapter Six

1. WSB, *Interzone*, 77.
2. Morgan, tape 71.
3. Morgan, tape 6.
4. WSB interviewed by John Giorno in *Gay Sunshine Interviews* (San Francisco: Gay Sunshine, 1978), 32.
5. Ibid.; the Dianabad was destroyed in the fighting between the Soviet Red Army and the Nazis during the liberation of Vienna on April 11–13, 1945.
6. WSB, *Interzone*, 124.
7. Sanatorium Hera, Löblichgasse 14. Burroughs was in room 78.
8. The Nuremberg Laws were announced at the annual Nazi Party rally held at Nuremberg in September 1935. In addition the law of March 7, 1936, deprived Jews of the vote and that of July 2, 1937, removed Jews from German schools and universities.
9. Morgan, tape 6.
10. Reik's *Masochism in Modern Man* was not published until 1941, so Burroughs must have read Reik's articles on the subject, as he was sure that he read Reik at this time. (Wilhelm Reich was not yet published in English nor easily available in German.)
11. Morgan, tape 22.
12. WSB in conversation with the author, London, ca. 1972.
13. Incorporated in *Nova Express* as "Gave Proof Through the Night." The original draft was finally printed in *Interzone* in 1989.
14. WSB, "Literary Autobiography," in Barry Miles, *A Catalogue of the William S. Burroughs Archive*, 75–76.
15. Morgan, tape 7.
16. WSB, "Literary Autobiography," 76.

17. WSB interviewed by Victor Bockris and Andrew Wylie, New York, 1974. From ms. transcript.
18. Ibid.
19. Morgan, tape 70 (labeled tape 69).

Chapter Seven

1. Alfred Korzybski, *Science and Sanity*, 21.
2. The Revised Oxford translation.
3. WSB interviewed by San Fleischer and Dan Turèll, Copenhagen, October 29, 1983.
4. They met on April 3, 1939, when Auden still lived with Christopher Isherwood in Manhattan.
5. The other two were with Ian Sommerville.
6. Morgan, tape 26.
7. WSB, "The Finger," in *Interzone*, 15.
8. Ibid.
9. Ibid. Burroughs forgot to change his name to Lee in the story, leaving his own name in place. Burroughs has said that the facts in "The Finger" are accurate.
10. Morgan, tape 70 (labeled tape 69).
11. Burroughs entered and left Payne Whitney on the twenty-third, a number that was to have symbolic significance to him.
12. WSB, *My Education*, 146. Burroughs gives his age as twenty-four in the book.
13. Ibid., 147.
14. Morgan, tape 2.
15. Morgan, tape 7.
16. Marcel Proust's description of Robert de Saint-Loup in *In Search of Lost Time* vol. 2, *Within a Budding Grove* (London: Chatto & Windus, 1992), 356.
17. Ibid.
18. Here I am taking a version of events told to me by Allen Ginsberg in 1985 and other times, as he understood them from his conversations with Lucien Carr over the years. There are other, differing accounts.
19. Morgan, tape 7.
20. Lucien Carr interviewed by the author, New York, 1985.
21. Morgan, tape 24.
22. A young editor at Alfred A. Knopf recalling stories told by her grandmother.
23. Barry Gifford and Lawrence Lee, *Jack's Book*, 37–38.
24. James Grauerholz, "William S. Burroughs Tour of Chicago (1939–40; 1942–43; 1968)", delivered on April 27, 2004, at Harper College, Palatine, Illinois, 7.
25. Victor Bockris, *With William Burroughs: A Report from the Bunker*, xvii.
26. Ibid.
27. Quoted in Dr. David Rioch to Dr. Thomas A. C. Rennie, Payne Whitney Psychiatric Clinic, May 27, 1942. Burroughs enrolled but later said he was drafted.
28. Morgan, tape 41.
29. Ibid.
30. WSB, *Last Words*, November 1996, 9.
31. Grauerholz, "William S. Burroughs Tour of Chicago", 10.

Chapter Eight

1. From abandoned early draft of *The Naked Lunch*.
2. I am indebted to James Grauerholz's paper "William S. Burroughs Tour of Chicago (1939–40; 1942–43; 1968)", delivered on April 27, 2004, at Harper College, Palatine, Illinois. The author had the pleasure of accompanying Grauerholz on his initial

exploration of 1940s Chicago phone books and his journeys to the sites of Mrs. Murphy's Rooming House and the Nueva Exterminating Company.

3. WSB, "Prose on a distant wall," unpublished ms., ca. 1972.
4. Morgan, tape 7.
5. Ibid.
6. First-draft notes in *Naked Lunch: The Restored Text*, 258.
7. WSB, "The Fish Poison Con," in *Nova Express*, 25; and as cut-up, 21.
8. WSB, *Exterminator!*, 9.
9. Ibid.
10. Barry Miles, *In the Seventies*, 131.
11. WSB, *Naked Lunch: The Restored Text*, 172.
12. WSB, *The Wild Boys*, 76.
13. WSB, *Exterminator!*, 10.
14. Morgan, tape 7.
15. WSB, *The Place of Dead Roads*, 136.
16. Morgan, tape 2.
17. According to Chad Heap, professor of American studies and gay historian at George Washington University, in a letter to James Grauerholz, 2000, quoted in Grauerholz, "William S. Burroughs Tour of Chicago (1939–40; 1942–43; 1968)", 23.
18. Ibid, 23; Grauerholz proposes that this may be the source of the "Frisco Kid" chapter in *The Wild Boys*.
19. WSB to Allen Ginsberg, April 20, 1955.
20. WSB, *The Place of Dead Roads* (Paladin edition), 150.

Chapter Nine

1. Lucien Carr interviewed by the author, New York, 1986.
2. Allen Ginsberg in conversation with the author, New York, 1969.
3. Morgan, tape 10.
4. WSB, *Last Words*, 119.
5. Edie Kerouac-Parker, *You'll Be Okay*, 122.
6. Ibid., 122–23.
7. WSB says pale blue, Edie Parker says brown.
8. Morgan, tape 10.
9. There were nine daily newspapers in New York at that time.
10. Edie Kerouac-Parker, *You'll Be Okay*, 95.
11. Allen Ginsberg in conversation with the author, while touring all the apartment buildings with Beat connections in New York, 1985. Ginsberg may be mixing Joan up with Geraldine Lust, with whom Duncan Purcell did have an affair, according to Edie Parker.
12. Lucien Carr interviewed by the author, New York, 1986.
13. Allen Ginsberg interviewed by the author, New York, 1985.
14. Ibid., quoting Yeats's "Among School Children," IV.
15. Allen Ginsberg interviewed by the author, New York, 1985.
16. Shakespeare, *Troilus and Cressida*, act 1, scene 1 (Troilus speaking).
17. The Royal Ballet was then called the Sadler's Wells Ballet.
18. Arthur Rimbaud to George Izambard, May 13, 1871: "Maintenant, je m'encrapule le plus possible. Pourquoi? Je veux être poète, et je travaille à me rendre *Voyant*: vous ne comprendrez pas du tout, et je ne saurais presque vous expliquer. Il s'agit d'arriver à l'inconnu par le dérèglement de *tous les sens*. Les souffrances sont énormes, mais il faut être fort, être né poète, et je me suis reconnu poète. Ce n'est pas du tout ma faute."
19. Lucien Carr interviewed by the author, New York, 1986.
20. Jack Kerouac, *Vanity of Duluoz*, 221.
21. Ibid.

22. Lucien Carr interviewed by the author, New York, 1986.
23. Morgan, tape 10.
24. Kerouac, *Vanity of Duluoz*, 225.
25. Shakespeare, *Henry IV, Part 1*, "The better part of valour is discretion."
26. Kerouac, *Vanity of Duluoz*, 237.
27. It entered the charts on June 22, 1944, and reached number 1.
28. They were reading the second, completely revised, edition of *A Vision*, 1937.
29. Kerouac, *Vanity of Duluoz*, 237.
30. Lucien Carr interviewed by the author, New York, 1986.

Chapter Ten

1. "Pages from a Diary in 1930. III. Subject for a poem, April 30th," in *W. B. Yeats, A Vision and Related Writings* (London: Arena, 1990).
2. Edie Kerouac-Parker, *You'll Be Okay*, 130.
3. Ibid., 131–32.
4. The Henry Hudson Parkway, built by Robert Moses in 1934–37, only has entrances to the riverside at 72nd and 125th Streets. The traffic at 4:00 a.m. must have been quiet enough to climb the barriers and cross it.
5. Kerouac, *Vanity of Duluoz*, 249.
6. Morgan, tape 8.
7. Kerouac, *Vanity of Duluoz*, 248.
8. "Student Admits Killing Teacher," *New York World-Telegram*, August 16, 1944.
9. "Student Is Held Without Bail on Slaying of Man," *New York Herald Tribune*, August 18, 1944.
10. Celine Young to Jack Kerouac, October 1, 1944.
11. See my *Jack Kerouac: King of the Beats* for a complete bibliography of newspaper reports on the case.
12. Morgan, tape 10.

Chapter Eleven

1. Virginia Woolf to Ethel Smyth, August 28, 1930, in *The Letters of Virginia Woolf* vol. 4, *1929–1931* (London: Hogarth, 1978), 205.
2. Wilhelm Reich, *Reich Speaks of Freud* (New York: Farrar, Straus and Giroux, 1967), 59.
3. Morgan, tape 13.
4. Ibid.
5. "The Art of Fiction: Jack Kerouac Interviewed by Ted Berrigan," in *Writers at Work: The Paris Review Interviews*, 4th Series (New York: Viking, 1976).
6. Journal entry for November 16, 1944, quoted in Ann Charters, *Kerouac* (San Francisco: Straight Arrow, 1973), 1974.
7. Jack Kerouac, *Vanity of Duluoz*, 289.
8. Allen Ginsberg interviewed by the author, New York, 1986.
9. Said while giving Kerouac a copy of the Charles Francis Atkinson translation of Oswald Spengler's *The Decline of the West*.
10. Vilfredo Pareto, *The Mind and Society* (New York: Dover, 1935).
11. Lucien Carr interviewed by the author, New York, 1986.
12. Allen Ginsberg interviewed by the author, New York, 1986.
13. Jack Kerouac, "Secret Mullings About Bill (Burroughs)" (from agency's manuscript copy).
14. Morgan, tape 22.
15. Victor Bockris, *With William Burroughs: A Report from the Bunker*, 22.
16. Jack Kerouac to Caroline Blake (née Kerouac), March 14, 1945.
17. Morgan, tape 10.

18. WSB, *Junky: The Definitive Text of "Junk,"* 1.
19. Description by Huncke in Don McNeill, "Huncke the Junkie: Godfather to Naked Lunch," *Village Voice*, September 21, 1967.
20. WSB, *Junky: The Definitive Text of "Junk,"* 4.
21. Ibid.
22. Ibid.
23. Ibid., 5.
24. Herbert Huncke's various accounts of watching Burroughs take his first shot are, like many of Huncke's stories, fabricated. Burroughs was alone and he did not have the syrettes with him at the first visit to Henry Street. He undoubtedly witnessed Burroughs shoot up later.
25. Herbert Huncke, quoted in Barry Gifford and Lee Lawrence, *Jack's Book*, 52.
26. WSB, *Junky: The Definitive Text of "Junk,"* 6.
27. Allen Ginsberg, "Literary History of the Beat Generation," lecture given June 9, 1977.
28. Jack Kerouac, *The Town and the City*, 364.
29. Morgan, tape 10.
30. Kerouac, *The Town and the City*, 364.
31. Allen Ginsberg, lecture at Brooklyn College, February 9, 1987.
32. WSB, *Junky: The Definitive Text of "Junk,"* 11.
33. Ibid., 13.

Chapter Twelve

1. Allen Ginsberg, "Literary History of the Beat Generation," lecture given June 16, 1977.
2. Allen Ginsberg, "Literary History of the Beat Generation," lecture given June 14, 1977.
3. Morgan, tape 10.
4. Ibid.
5. Allen Ginsberg interviewed by the author, New York, 1987.
6. Jack Kerouac to Allen Ginsberg, September 6, 1945.
7. Allen Ginsberg interviewed by the author, New York, 1987.
8. Ibid., 19.
9. Joan Vollmer to Edie Parker, June 8, 1945.
10. Jack Kerouac, *Vanity of Duluoz*, 292–93; confirmed by Allen Ginsberg in conversation.
11. Allen Ginsberg, "Literary History of the Beat Generation," lecture given June 16, 1977.
12. Allen Ginsberg interviewed by the author, New York, 1987.
13. Ibid.; see also Allen Ginsberg, *Indian Journals*, 175.
14. Allen Ginsberg, "Literary History of the Beat Generation," lecture given June 14, 1977.
15. Howard Brookner, *Burroughs* film documentary, 1983.
16. Allen Ginsberg, "Literary History of the Beat Generation," lecture given June 16, 1977.
17. Jeffrey Scott Dunn, "A Conversation: Ginsberg on Burroughs," *Pennsylvania Review* (Fall/Winter 1987): 48.
18. Herbert Huncke interviewed by Stewart Meyer and Mel Bernstine, *Newave* vol. 1, no. 5 (April 1981).
19. Jack Kerouac to Al Aronowitz, *New York Post*.
20. Huncke interviewed in *Newave*.
21. Dr. Alfred Kinsey, *Sexual Behavior in the Human Male* (Philadelphia: W. B. Saunders/ Bloomington: Indiana University Press, 1948).
22. Howard Brookner, *Burroughs* film documentary, 1983.
23. Told to the author by Allen Ginsberg, standing in front of 419 West 115th Street, on February 21, 1984.

24. Morgan, tape 16.
25. Ibid.
26. Ibid.
27. WSB, *Last Words*, 57.
28. Joan Vollmer to Edie Parker, January 1, 1947.
29. Herbert Huncke, *The Evening Sun Turned Crimson*, 95.
30. WSB to Bockris-Wylie, 1975 (from ms. transcript).
31. WSB, *Junky: The Definitive Text of "Junk,"* 34.
32. Ibid., 35.
33. Reported by Ted Morgan in *Literary Outlaw: The Life and Times of William S. Burroughs*.
34. WSB, *The Soft Machine* (Olympia edition), 158–59.
35. Joan Vollmer to Edie Parker, January 1, 1947.
36. Morgan, tape 10.
37. WSB to Allen Ginsberg, January 19, 1952.
38. WSB to Allen Ginsberg, May 1951.
39. Joan Vollmer to Edie Parker, January 1, 1947.
40. Jack Kerouac, *Visions of Cody* (Flamingo, 1995), 223–24.
41. Joan Vollmer to Edie Parker, January 1, 1947.

Chapter Thirteen

1. WSB to Billy Burroughs Jr., October 30, 1972.
2. Marianne Woofe to Ted Morgan, March 7, 1985.
3. WSB to Joan Vollmer, September 3, 1946.
4. WSB, *Junky: The Definitive Text of "Junk,"* 88.
5. Burroughs remembers Elvins's girlfriend being called Golden: "In Pharr that was Golden. I remember she was a beautiful girl, she looked like a model. Sort of long hair, I think she was not blonde but dark." This was probably Elvins's girlfriend in Huntsville, Texas.
6. Rob Johnson, *The Lost Years of William S. Burroughs: Beats in South Texas*, 30.
7. WSB, *Junky: The Definitive Text of "Junk,"* 91.
8. Ibid., 92.
9. Johnson, *The Lost Years of William S. Burroughs*, 24.
10. WSB, *Junky: The Definitive Text of "Junk,"* 91.
11. Ibid., 59.
12. WSB, *Interzone*, 137.
13. WSB, *The Western Lands*, 105.
14. Johnson, *The Lost Years of William S. Burroughs*, 36.
15. Ibid., 49.
16. WSB, *Interzone*, 152.
17. WSB to Allen Ginsberg, October 10, 1955.
18. Johnson, *The Lost Years of William S. Burroughs*, 88.
19. Ibid.

Chapter Fourteen

1. Joan Vollmer to Allen Ginsberg, January 9, 1947.
2. WSB, *The Naked Lunch*, 147.
3. This would be about 2,000–2,500 plants, roughly two hundred pounds of pot, still an enormous crop.
4. Herbert Huncke to Allen Ginsberg, March 1947.
5. Herbert Huncke interviewed by Steven Watson, Chelsea Hotel, March 12, 1995.
6. WSB, *The Place of Dead Roads* (Paladin edition), 183.
7. WSB, *Cities of the Red Night*, 223.
8. WSB to Allen Ginsberg, March 11, 1947.

9. Joan Vollmer to Allen Ginsberg, March 23, 1947.
10. Herbert Huncke, *Guilty of Everything*, 90–91.
11. Morgan, tape 12.
12. Ibid.
13. Morgan, tape 14.
14. Morgan, tape 12.
15. Ibid.
16. WSB to Allen Ginsberg, August 8, 1947.
17. Quoted in James Grauerholz, *The Death of Joan Vollmer Burroughs*, 7.
18. Herbert Huncke, *The Evening Sky Turned Crimson*.
19. Allen Ginsberg interviewed by the author, New York, 1986.
20. Morgan, tape 25.
21. WSB to Allen Ginsberg, February 20, 1948.
22. Morgan, tape 71 (labeled tape 70).

Chapter Fifteen

1. Morgan, tape 13.
2. WSB to Jack Kerouac and Allen Ginsberg, June 5, 1948.
3. WSB to Jack Kerouac, November 30, 1948.
4. WSB to Jack Kerouac, March 15, 1949.
5. WSB to Allen Ginsberg, March 18, 1949.
6. WSB to Allen Ginsberg, November 9, 1948.
7. Jack Kerouac, *On the Road*, 133.
8. WSB, *Junky: The Definitive Text of "Junk,"* 60.
9. Barry Gifford and Lawrence Lee, *Jack's Book*, 131.
10. WSB to Allen Ginsberg, January 10, 1949.
11. WSB to Allen Ginsberg, January 16, 1949.
12. Gifford and Lee, *Jack's Book*, 132.
13. Kerouac, *On the Road*, 129.
14. WSB, *The Cat Inside*, 47.
15. Gifford and Lee, *Jack's Book*, 134.
16. Lu Anne Henderson quoted in Gerald Nicosia and Anne Marie Santos, *One and Only: The Untold Story of "On the Road,"* 64–65.
17. Kerouac, *On the Road*, 135.
18. Gifford and Lee, *Jack's Book*, 136.
19. Kerouac calls Burroughs "Bull" and Joan is "Jane."
20. Kerouac, *On the Road*, 132.
21. WSB to Allen Ginsberg, March 18, 1949.
22. WSB to Allen Ginsberg, January 30, 1949.
23. WSB to Allen Ginsberg, February 7, 1949.
24. WSB in conversation with the author, London, 1972.
25. WSB, "A Thanksgiving Prayer," in *Tornado Alley*, 1989.
26. The financial information is all taken from James Grauerholz, *The Death of Joan Vollmer Burroughs*, 13–14.
27. Morgan, tape 10.
28. Ibid.
29. Morgan, tape 44.
30. Morgan, tape 53.
31. Ibid.
32. Victor Bockris, *With William Burroughs: A Report from the Bunker*, 38.
33. Joan Vollmer to Allen Ginsberg, April 13, 1949.

Chapter Sixteen

1. Morgan, tape 28 (labeled tape 27).
2. WSB, *Junky: The Definitive Text of "Junk,"* 90.
3. Ibid., 89.
4. Burroughs had Allen Ginsberg's copy, mailed to him by Allen's father, Louis Ginsberg, after he himself had read it.
5. Henri Bergson, *Creative Evolution* (New York: Modern Library, 1944), 289.
6. WSB interviewed by James Grauerholz, 1974, quoted in Rob Johnson, *The Lost Years of William S. Burroughs: Beats in South Texas*, 145.
7. WSB, *Junky: The Definitive Text of "Junk,"* 135.
8. WSB to Jack Kerouac, June 24, 1949.
9. Morgan, tape 10.
10. Morgan, tape 47 (labeled tape 44–46).
11. WSB to Jack Kerouac, September 26, 1949.
12. WSB to Allen Ginsberg, October 13, 1949.
13. WSB to Jack Kerouac, November 2, 1949.

Chapter Seventeen

1. Jack Kerouac, *Mexico City Blues*, 59th Chorus.
2. Sybille Bedford, *A Visit to Don Otavio* (London: Collins, 1960) (originally titled *The Sudden View*, 1953), 66–67.
3. Joan Vollmer to Allen Ginsberg, October 31, 1949.
4. Ibid.
5. WSB to Allen Ginsberg, December 23, 1949.
6. WSB to Allen Ginsberg, May 1, 1949.
7. WSB to Jack Kerouac, January 22, 1950.
8. James Grauerholz writes in *The Death of Joan Vollmer Burroughs*, "Burroughs and Kerouac both misunderstood this man's name as 'Tercerero'—'the third one'—but no such family name exists in Mexico, whereas 'Tesorero'—'treasurer'—is not uncommon."
9. WSB, *Junky: The Definitive Text of "Junk,"* 115.
10. Ibid.
11. Jorge García-Robles (with the collaboration of James Grauerholz), *The Wild Shot: William S. Burroughs in Mexico (1949–1952)*, 34.
12. María was finally arrested on April 4, 1957, and given four years in jail. She died five months later on September 4, 1957, from cardiac arrest.
13. WSB, *Junky: The Definitive Text of "Junk,"* 116.
14. Ibid., 118.
15. Morgan, tape 55.
16. Ibid.
17. Now called calle José Alvarado.
18. WSB to Jack Kerouac, September 18, 1950.
19. García-Robles, *The Wild Shot*, 38.
20. WSB to Allen Ginsberg, January 1, 1951.
21. WSB to Allen Ginsberg, January 11, 1951.
22. Ibid.
23. WSB to Jack Kerouac, December 26, 1950.
24. WSB to Allen Ginsberg, January 11, 1951.
25. WSB to Allen Ginsberg, May 5, 1951.
26. Ibid.
27. Ibid.
28. WSB, *Junky: The Definitive Text of "Junk,"* 130.

29. Ibid.
30. Hal Chase interview transcription, Ted Morgan papers, Arizona State University, Tempe.
31. WSB, *Junky: The Definitive Text of "Junk,"* 127.
32. Morgan, tape 17.
33. Morgan, tape 51 (labeled 49).
34. WSB, *Queer*, 77, and in conversation with the author, London, 1972.
35. WSB to Jack Kerouac, April 24, 1951.
36. Ibid.; the first sentence was crossed out in the original.
37. Allen Ginsberg, *As Ever: The Collected Correspondence*, 64. See *The Letters of William S. Burroughs, 1945 to 1959*, Oliver Harris's footnote, 85.
38. WSB to Allen Ginsberg, n.d. (May 1951).
39. Interview with Doña Marina Sotelo by Jorge García-Robles, July 25, 1991. Burroughs Archives, English translation, 13 and 9.
40. WSB, *My Education*, 31.
41. The name is possibly a combination of Eugene Brooks, Allen Ginsberg's lawyer brother, whom Burroughs knew well as he sometimes stayed at 115th Street, and the Allerton Hotel on Michigan Avenue, Chicago, a 1923, twenty-five-story landmark whose sign towers over downtown and would have been well known to Burroughs.
42. Morgan, tape 20.
43. Ibid.
44. WSB, *Queer*, 96.
45. Ibid., 109.
46. Ibid., 109–10.
47. Lucien Carr interviewed by the author, New York, 1985.
48. Ibid.
49. Ibid.
50. Ibid.
51. Ibid.

Chapter Eighteen

1. Victor Bockris, *With William Burroughs: A Report from the Bunker*, 46.
2. For this and much of the other information in this section, I am grateful for James Grauerholz's *The Death of Joan Vollmer Burroughs*, which covers the subject in exhaustive detail.
3. Morgan, tape 47.
4. Grauerholz, *The Death of Joan Vollmer Burroughs*. Interview with Healy, September 12, 1991.
5. WSB interviewed by Victor Bockris and Andrew Wylie, New York, 1974 (from ms.).
6. WSB interviewed in Howard Brookner, *Burroughs* film documentary, 1983.
7. As reported by June Woods Overgaard, as told to her immediately after the shooting by Eddie Woods. Interviewed by Ted Morgan in 1985 and published in James Grauerholz's *The Death of Joan Vollmer Burroughs*.
8. Eddie Woods's recollection of Burroughs's words as reported in Grauerholz, *The Death of Joan Vollmer Burroughs*.
9. Ibid.
10. Manuel Mejía interviewed by Jorge García-Robles, December 22, 1991.
11. Reported in Grauerholz, *The Death of Joan Vollmer Burroughs*.
12. *Excelsior*, September 7, 1951. Reported in Grauerholz, *The Death of Joan Vollmer Burroughs*.
13. Howard Brookner, *Burroughs* film documentary, 1983.
14. *La Prensa*, September 7, 1951. Reported in Grauerholz, *The Death of Joan Vollmer Burroughs*.

15. Morgan, tape 40.
16. The final charges against Burroughs, as issued on November 15, 1951, by Judge Fernández, were as follows, as reported in Grauerholz, *The Death of Joan Vollmer Burroughs*: "The complainant himself agrees that the legal exigencies are fulfilled insofar as the objective facts that refer to the death of Joan Vollmer Burroughs, even if not to the subjective elements of the crime of murder, and in that which relates to the first assessment it is quite certain that the legal extremities of the crime of murder are proved, in terms of Articles 94, 96, 105, 106–121 and other relevant parts of the Code of Penal Proceedings, applicable in D.F. and the Territories. [. . .]

    "Basically, the facts that caused the arrest of William Seward Burroughs and the ruling of *formal prisión* consist of this: on [...] September 7 [*sic*], the complainant was in the building 122 Monterrey, apartment 10, where his friend John Healy lived, and where—in company with the wife of the same complainant and other persons—they were ingesting alcoholic beverages; and that at a given moment, the complainant took out of his holster a pistol, pulling back the slide, and producing a shot that caused the death of the now-deceased lady.

    "Basically, this is the version of the witnesses Edwin John Woods [and] Louis [*sic*] Marker, but the petitioner cannot hold himself out as proving the exclusion of responsibility which is referred to in Fraction X of Article 15 of the Penal Code; that is to say, that if an injury was caused, that it was by mere accident, with neither intention nor any imprudence, carrying out a legal deed with all due precautions.

    "So in a way, those extremities can be shown, even accepting the version given by the aggrieved and the witnesses, for even though the test offered would be in the nature of discarding the intentionality in the commission of the punishable deed, there exists the possibility and probability that the death of the victim would have been due to an *imprudencia*, for the complainant ought to have recognized the state of inebriation in which he found himself—he, who took no precaution to [determine] if the weapon was loaded, nor pointed the barrel in a direction in which no damage could be caused."
17. Ibid.
18. WSB to Jack Kerouac, December 20, 1951.
19. *Diario Oficial de México*, August 29, 1990.
20. Reported in Grauerholz, *The Death of Joan Vollmer Burroughs*.
21. Morgan, tape 12.
22. Grauerholz, *The Death of Joan Vollmer Burroughs*.
23. Ibid.
24. Ibid.
25. Howard Brookner, *Burroughs* film documentary, 1983.
26. Lucien Carr interviewed by James Grauerholz, October 11, 1999, in Grauerholz, *The Death of Joan Vollmer Burroughs*.
27. Morgan, tape 18.
28. WSB interviewed by Victor Bockris and Andrew Wylie, New York, 1974 (from ms.).
29. Robert Wilson, Tom Waits, and William Burroughs, *The Black Rider: The Casting of the Magic Bullets*, Thalia Theater, Hamburg, program for performance opening March 31, 1990.

Chapter Nineteen

1. Morgan, tape 40.
2. Morgan, tape 47.
3. WSB to Allen Ginsberg, March 5, 1952.
4. WSB to Jack Kerouac, April 3, 1952.
5. See Oliver Harris's introduction to *Junky: The Definitive Text of "Junk,"* published by Penguin in 2003.
6. WSB to Allen Ginsberg, April 22, 1952.

7. WSB to Jack Kerouac [April 1952].
8. WSB to Allen Ginsberg, April 26, 1952.
9. WSB, *Junky: The Definitive Text of "Junk,"* 114.
10. Ibid.
11. Morgan, tape 31.
12. WSB to Allen Ginsberg, June 4, 1952.
13. WSB to Allen Ginsberg, May 15, 1952.
14. Jack Kerouac to Allen Ginsberg, May 10, 1952.
15. WSB to Allen Ginsberg, May 23, 1952.
16. Ibid.
17. Jack Kerouac, *Desolation Angels,* 252.
18. WSB to Allen Ginsberg, July 13, 1952.
19. Ibid.
20. WSB to Allen Ginsberg, August 20, 1952.
21. A publisher's royalty statement shows that 113,170 copies were sold before December 30, 1953. See Maynard and Miles, *William S. Burroughs: A Bibliography, 1953–1973,* 2f.
22. WSB to Allen Ginsberg, early July 1952.
23. Morgan, tape 31.
24. WSB to Allen Ginsberg, September 18, 1952.
25. WSB to Allen Ginsberg, November 5, 1952.
26. WSB to Allen Ginsberg, October 6, 1952.
27. Jack Kerouac to John Clellon Holmes, December 9, 1952.

Chapter Twenty

1. "Trip to Hell and Back," WSB interviewed by Jerry Bauer in *Trax* (London), no. 6 (March 18, 1981).
2. Ibid.
3. WSB, *Junky: The Definitive Text of "Junk,"* 153.
4. Benjamin Ivry, *Arthur Rimbaud* (Bath, UK: Absolute, 1998).
5. WSB to Allen Ginsberg, January 10, 1953.
6. WSB to Allen Ginsberg, January 19, 1953.
7. WSB to Allen Ginsberg, January 15, 1953.
8. WSB to Allen Ginsberg, January 25, 1953.
9. Christopher Isherwood, *The Condor and the Cows,* 46.
10. WSB to Allen Ginsberg, January 25, 1953.
11. WSB to Allen Ginsberg, January 30, 1953.
12. Ibid.
13. Ibid.
14. WSB to Allen Ginsberg, February 28, 1953.
15. Ibid.
16. Ibid.
17. Ibid.
18. Morgan, tape 13.
19. WSB to Allen Ginsberg, February 28, 1953.
20. WSB to Allen Ginsberg, April 15, 1953.
21. WSB to Allen Ginsberg, April 22, 1953.
22. WSB to Allen Ginsberg, April 30, 1953.
23. WSB, *The Yage Letters,* 38.
24. Morgan, tape 13.
25. WSB to Allen Ginsberg, May 12, 1953.
26. WSB to Allen Ginsberg, May 30, 1953.

27. WSB, *The Yage Letters*, 40.
28. WSB, *Cities of the Red Night*, 151.
29. WSB to Allen Ginsberg, May 15, 1953.
30. Morgan, tape 12.
31. Ibid.
32. WSB to Allen Ginsberg, July 8, 1953.
33. Ibid.
34. Morgan, tape 12.
35. WSB to Allen Ginsberg, early July 1953.
36. WSB to Allen Ginsberg, July 10, 1953.
37. Ibid.

Chapter Twenty-One

1. Alan Ansen, *The Table Talk of W. H. Auden* (London: Faber & Faber, 1991), 80–81.
2. WSB to Allen Ginsberg, July 21, 1953.
3. WSB, *Everything Lost: The Latin American Notebook of William S. Burroughs*, 145.
4. Ibid., 185–86.
5. Ibid., 183.
6. WSB to Allen Ginsberg, July 8, 1953.
7. Allen Ginsberg to Neal Cassady, September 1953.
8. Michael Harrington, "'A San Remo Type': The Vanishing Village," *Village Voice* vol. 16, no. 1 (January 7, 1971).
9. Boris Vian, *Manual of Saint-Germain-des-Prés*.
10. See Edmund White, *Genet*, 586.
11. Morgan, tape 20.
12. WSB interviewed by Allen Ginsberg, in *Burroughs Live: Collected Interviews*, 807.
13. Barry Miles, *Allen Ginsberg: A Biography*, 155–56.
14. Ibid.
15. Ibid.
16. Wilhelm Reich, *Cosmic Superimposition* (Rangeley, ME: Wilhelm Reich Foundation, 1951), 50.
17. WSB, *Queer*, 36.
18. WSB, *Interzone*, 137.
19. Ibid.
20. The subject of a number of conversations with the author, Cherry Valley, NY, 1969–71.
21. *Gay Sunshine*, no. 16 (January 1973).
22. WSB to Allen Ginsberg, March 23, 1973.
23. Jeffrey Scott Dunn, "A Conversation: Ginsberg on Burroughs," *Pennsylvania Review*, (Fall/Winter 1987): 41.
24. Miles, *Ginsberg: A Biography*, 156.
25. Jack Kerouac to Allen Ginsberg, February 21, 1953.
26. Morgan, tape 39.
27. WSB to Jack Kerouac, December 14, 1953.
28. WSB to Allen Ginsberg, December 24, 1953.
29. Ibid.
30. Alan Ansen [and WSB] to Allen Ginsberg, January 2, 1954.

Chapter Twenty-Two

1. Carson McCullers, "Look Homeward, Americans," *Vogue*, December 1, 1940.
2. WSB to Allen Ginsberg, January 26, 1954.
3. Ibid.
4. Morgan, tape 15.

5. WSB to Allen Ginsberg, January 20, 1954.
6. WSB to Allen Ginsberg, February 9, 1954.
7. WSB, "Some Memories, Unclarified drafts," 1990 (unpublished).
8. WSB to Allen Ginsberg, February 9, 1954.
9. WSB to Allen Ginsberg, August 18, 1954.
10. David Woolman, *Rebels in the Rif: Abd el Krim and the Rif Rebellion* (Palo Alto, CA: Stanford University Press), 1968.
11. WSB to Allen Ginsberg, March 1, 1954.
12. Morgan, tape 31.
13. WSB to Allen Ginsberg, December 10, 1955.
14. WSB, *The Naked Lunch*, "Black Meat" section, 59.
15. WSB to Allen Ginsberg, December 10, 1955.
16. Alan Ansen papers, in Ted Morgan papers, Arizona State University, Tempe.
17. WSB to Allen Ginsberg, March 1, 1954.
18. Rupert Croft-Cooke, *The Caves of Hercules*, 33.
19. Morgan, tape 29.
20. WSB, *The Place of Dead Roads*, 174.
21. Brian Howard to John Banting, [March?] 1954. Marie-Jaqueline Lancaster, *Brian Howard: Portrait of a Failure*, 310.
22. WSB to Allen Ginsberg, March 1, 1954.
23. Morgan, tape 43.
24. WSB to Allen Ginsberg, April 7, 1954.
25. Morgan, tape 25.
26. WSB to Jack Kerouac, April 22, 1954.
27. Ibid.

Chapter Twenty-Three

1. WSB, *Early Routines*, 28–29.
2. WSB to Allen Ginsberg, July 15, 1954.
3. WSB to Jack Kerouac, April 22, 1954.
4. WSB to Allen Ginsberg, May 11, 1954.
5. A British public school is what is known as a prep school or boarding school in the United States.
6. WSB to Allen Ginsberg, June 16, 1954.
7. WSB, *Naked Lunch*, 280.
8. Morgan, tape 43.
9. WSB to Jack Kerouac, April 22, 1954.
10. Ibid.
11. WSB to Jack Kerouac, May 4, 1954.
12. WSB to Allen Ginsberg, May 11, 1954.
13. Allen Ginsberg to Neal Cassidy, [May 1954].
14. WSB to Allen Ginsberg, July 3, 1954.
15. WSB to Allen Ginsberg, July 8, 1954.
16. Morgan, tape 41.
17. WSB to Allen Ginsberg, July 10, 1954.
18. WSB to Allen Ginsberg, July 8, 1954.
19. WSB, *Queer*, 16.
20. WSB to Allen Ginsberg, April 22, 1953.
21. WSB to Allen Ginsberg, April 26, 1954.
22. Ibid.
23. WSB, *Interzone*, 38.
24. WSB to Jack Kerouac, August 18, 1954.

25. WSB to Allen Ginsberg, August 18, 1954.
26. WSB to Allen Ginsberg, August 26, 1954.
27. Ibid.
28. Ibid.
29. Morgan, tape 15.
30. Harold Norse interviewed by Winston Leyland, in *Gay Sunshine*, no. 18 (June 1973).
31. WSB to Allen Ginsberg, August 18, 1954.

Chapter Twenty-Four

1. WSB to Allen Ginsberg, December 30, 1954.
2. WSB to Jack Kerouac, September 3, 1954.
3. Alan Ansen papers, in Ted Morgan papers, Arizona State University, Tempe.
4. WSB to Allen Ginsberg, October 13, 1954.
5. Ibid.
6. WSB to Allen Ginsberg, October 15, 1954.
7. WSB to Allen Ginsberg, December 7, 1956.
8. Possibly 62 Bab el Assa, place de la Kasbah.
9. WSB to Allen Ginsberg, January 21, 1955.
10. WSB, *Interzone*, 49.
11. Rupert Croft-Cooke, *The Caves of Hercules*, 84.
12. Morgan, tape 33.
13. WSB, *The Place of Dead Roads*, 197.
14. WSB to Allen Ginsberg, February 7, 1954.
15. WSB to Allen Ginsberg, April 7, 1954.
16. Arthur Rimbaud, "The Bridges."
17. WSB to Allen Ginsberg, December 6, 1954.
18. WSB to Jack Kerouac, December 7, 1954.
19. WSB to Allen Ginsberg, December 13, 1954.
20. WSB, *Naked Lunch*, 150.
21. WSB to Allen Ginsberg, December 30, 1954.
22. WSB to Allen Ginsberg, February 7, 1955.
23. As explained by WSB to Frank Zappa before the latter read the "Talking Asshole" routine at the Nova Convention, New York, December 2, 1978.
24. WSB to Allen Ginsberg, February 7, 1955.
25. WSB to Allen Ginsberg and Jack Kerouac, November 2, 1955.
26. WSB to Allen Ginsberg, November 1, 1955.
27. WSB to Allen Ginsberg, May 17, 1955.
28. WSB to Allen Ginsberg, July 5, 1955.
29. WSB to Allen Ginsberg, July 3, 1955.
30. WSB to Allen Ginsberg, September 21, 1955.
31. WSB to Allen Ginsberg, October 7, 1955.
32. WSB to Allen Ginsberg and Jack Kerouac, October 23, 1955.
33. WSB, *The Naked Lunch*, 48; WSB, *Doctor Benway*, 51–55.
34. WSB to Allen Ginsberg, October 23, 1955.
35. Ibid.
36. WSB to Allen Ginsberg, August 1, 1955.
37. WSB interviewed by Bill Rich, April 23, 1991.
38. Outtake "Coke Bugs" section of *Naked Lunch*, in the appendix of the revised text edition, 280.
39. WSB to Allen Ginsberg, September 20, 1957; WSB, *My Education*, 68.
40. WSB, *Nova Express* (Panther edition), 28.
41. Ibid., 32.

Chapter Twenty-Five

1. Outtake "Coke Bugs" section of *Naked Lunch*, in the appendix of the restored text edition, 280.
2. "Trip to Hell and Back," WSB interviewed by Jerry Bauer in *Trax* (London), no. 6 (March 18, 1981).
3. WSB to Allen Ginsberg, May 8, 1956.
4. WSB, *Cities of the Red Night*, 217, and *My Education*, 162.
5. WSB, *Last Words*, 3.
6. WSB to Allen Ginsberg, June 18, 1956.
7. Ibid.
8. WSB, *The Place of Dead Roads*, 186.
9. Ralph Rumney, *The Consul*, 36.
10. Alan Ansen to Allen Ginsberg, n.d.
11. WSB to Allen Ginsberg, September 13, 1956.
12. Ibid.
13. WSB to Allen Ginsberg, September 16, 1956.
14. Ibid.
15. WSB to Allen Ginsberg, October 13, 1956.
16. WSB to Allen Ginsberg, September 16, 1956.
17. Ibid.
18. Ibid.
19. Ibid.
20. Morgan, tape 15.
21. WSB to Allen Ginsberg, October 29, 1956.
22. Paul Bowles, "Burroughs in Tangier," *Big Table* (Chicago), no. 2 (1959).
23. WSB to Allen Ginsberg, October 29, 1956.
24. Gena Dagel Caponi, ed., *Conversations with Paul Bowles*, 88.
25. Paul Bowles, *In Touch: The Letters of Paul Bowles*, 45.
26. Paul Bowles to Aaron Copland, February 1933.
27. WSB to Allen Ginsberg, February 9, 1954.
28. Tennessee Williams, *Tennessee Williams' Letters to Donald Windham, 1940–1965* (New York: Henry Holt, 1977).
29. Paul Bowles, "Interview with Simon Bischoff, Tangier 1989–1991," in Bischoff, ed., *"How Could I Send a Picture into the Desert?": Paul Bowles Photographs*, 227.
30. WSB to Allen Ginsberg, September 16, 1956.
31. Morgan, tape 15.
32. WSB to Allen Ginsberg, October 13, 1956.
33. Ibid.
34. WSB to Allen Ginsberg, December 20, 1956.
35. William Lithgow, *The Total Discourse of the Rare Adventures and Painful Peregrinations of Long Nineteen Years Travayles* (1632).
36. Tahar ben Jelloun, *Leaving Tangier*, 33–34.
37. WSB, *Naked Lunch*, 102.
38. WSB to Allen Ginsberg, October 29, 1956. ("Surely a history for men, a song of strength for men, like a shudder from afar of space shaking an iron tree." T. S. Eliot's translation, Saint-John Perse, *Anabasis*, section 6.)
39. Ibid.
40. Ibid.
41. Mohamed Choukri, *In Tangier*, 169–70.
42. Morgan, tape 31.
43. WSB, *The Wild Boys*, 140.
44. Morgan Bowles, tape 9.
45. WSB to Allen Ginsberg, December 20, 1956.

Chapter Twenty-Six

1. WSB, *Interzone*, "Ginsberg Notes," 119.
2. WSB to Allen Ginsberg, October 13, 1956.
3. WSB to Allen Ginsberg, October 29, 1956.
4. WSB to Allen Ginsberg, January 23, 1957.
5. Paul Bowles, ms. in WSB archives.
6. WSB to Allen Ginsberg, August 18, 1954.
7. WSB, *Interzone*, "Ginsberg Notes," 119.
8. Colonel Gerald Richardson, *Crime Zone*, 162–63.
9. WSB to Allen Ginsberg, October 13, 1956.
10. WSB to Allen Ginsberg, January 23, 1957.
11. WSB to Allen Ginsberg, October 13, 1956.
12. WSB to Allen Ginsberg, January 14, 1957.
13. WSB to Allen Ginsberg, February 14, 1957.
14. WSB to Allen Ginsberg, January 31, 1957.
15. WSB to Allen Ginsberg, January 14, 1957.
16. Jack Kerouac to Malcolm Cowley, March 8, 1957.
17. Jack Kerouac, *Desolation Angels*, 315.
18. Ibid.
19. Morgan, tape 18.
20. Kerouac, *Desolation Angels*, 316.
21. Paul Bowles, "Burroughs in Tangier," *Big Table* (Chicago), no. 2 (1959).
22. Iain Finlayson, *Tangier: City of the Dream*, 214.
23. Kerouac, *Desolation Angels*, 317.
24. Morgan, tape 15.
25. Kerouac, *Desolation Angels*, 320.
26. Morgan, tape 40.
27. This is in essence Paul Bowles's recipe. Ian Sommerville told the author that Burroughs "used Paul's recipe."
28. Jack Kerouac, *Lonesome Traveller*, 144.
29. Morgan, tape 40.
30. Morgan, tape 31.
31. Morgan, tape 22; BBC *Arena* interview Bacon/Burroughs transcript.
32. Morgan, tape 18.
33. Morgan, tape 15.
34. WSB, *Interzone*, "Ginsberg Notes," 126.

Chapter Twenty-Seven

1. WSB, *Naked Lunch: The Restored Text*, 25.
2. WSB to Allen Ginsberg, August 20, 1957.
3. Morgan, tape 10.
4. Morgan, tape 31.
5. WSB to Allen Ginsberg, August 20, 1957.
6. WSB to Allen Ginsberg, August 24, 1957.
7. WSB to Allen Ginsberg, August 28, 1957.
8. WSB to Allen Ginsberg, September 20, 1957.
9. WSB to Allen Ginsberg, October 8, 1957.
10. WSB to Allen Ginsberg, October 19, 1957.
11. WSB to Allen Ginsberg, November 26, 1957.
12. Ibid.

Chapter Twenty-Eight

1. WSB on Mme. Rachou; interviewed by the author, Lawrence, Kansas, July 6, 1996.
2. WSB, "Foreword to Beat Hotel," in Harold Chapman, *The Beat Hotel*.
3. Ibid.
4. WSB, *The Place of Dead Roads*, 255.
5. Allen Ginsberg to Peter Orlovsky, January 20, 1958.
6. Ibid.
7. Ibid.
8. Ibid.
9. Allen Ginsberg to Peter Orlovsky, January 28, 1958.
10. Allen Ginsberg to Peter Orlovsky, February 24, 1958.
11. WSB to Allen Ginsberg, February 3, 1958.
12. This is a word made up by Gold for the book. Words such as "mark" and "grifter" were in common use in the carney world, and Burroughs either knew them from rolling drunks on the subway with Phil White, or read them in the extensive glossary appended to David W. Maurer, *The Big Con: The Story of the Confidence Man and the Confidence Trick* (Indianapolis: Bobbs-Merrill, 1940).
13. Herbert Gold, *Bohemia: Where Art, Angst, Love and Strong Coffee Meet*, 132–33.
14. Gregory Corso to Don Allen, March 27, 1968.
15. Allen Ginsberg to Peter Orlovsky, February 24, 1958.
16. Ibid.
17. Graham Seidman, "Tales from the Beat Hotel', August 7, 2003, http://www.litkicks.com/BeatHotel (accessed February 2012).
18. Baird Bryant, "Souvenirs of the Beat Hotel," 2003, http://www.kerouacfest.com/currentpage/souvenirs.htm (accessed January 2012). In this text Bryant claims to have been introduced to Jack Kerouac by Allen Ginsberg in Paris, and gives sample dialogue, but Kerouac and Ginsberg were never in Paris together. Though Bryant and Burroughs did certainly know each other, his memoir should be treated more as a work of fiction than of fact.
19. Allen Ginsberg to Peter Orlovsky, February 24, 1958.
20. WSB, scrapbook started July 5, 1972, 126.
21. WSB, *Port of Saints*, 49.
22. WSB, *Exterminator!*, 40–41; J.S. is probably Jacques Stern.
23. Author interview with Jean-Jacques Lebel, September 17, 1998, Paris.
24. Ibid.
25. "Interview with Kenneth Tindall: From Bellevue to Lynaes; An Interview by Lars Movin," http://www.emptymirrorbooks.com/beat/kenneth-tindall.html (accessed July 2012).
26. Allen Ginsberg to Peter Orlovsky, April 1, 1958.
27. Jean-Jacques Lebel interviewed by the author, Paris, September 17, 1998.

Chapter Twenty-Nine

1. Morgan, tape 20.
2. Allen Ginsberg to Peter Orlovsky, June 15, 1958.
3. Morgan, tape 20.
4. Jacques Stern interviewed by Victor Bockris and Stewart Meyer, November 5, 2001 (unpublished).
5. WSB to Allen Ginsberg, July 24, 1958.
6. Brasserie Lipp and M. Cazes inspired the "Chez Robert" routine in *The Naked Lunch*.
7. Morgan, tape 64.
8. Jacques Stern interviewed by Victor Bockris and Stewart Meyer, November 5, 2001 (unpublished).

9. Morgan, tape 20.
10. Morgan, tape 22.
11. Morgan, tape 64.
12. Saint-John Perse, *Anabasis* (New York: Harcourt Brace, 1949 [1938]), 47, 51.
13. Allen Ginsberg interviewed by the author, New York, 1985.
14. Ibid.
15. Gregory Corso to Don Allen, July 21, 1958.
16. Gael Turnbull, "Extracts from a Journal," *Mica*, no. 5 (Winter 1962) (Santa Barbara, CA).
17. Allen Ginsberg to Jack Kerouac, June 26, 1958.
18. WSB to Allen Ginsberg, n.d. [July 1958].
19. WSB to Allen Ginsberg, July 24, 1958.
20. Ibid.
21. Jack Kerouac to Allen Ginsberg, June 29, 1963.
22. WSB to Allen Ginsberg, August 25, 1958.
23. Gregory Corso to Allen Ginsberg, October 8, 1958. "PG" is paregoric.
24. Ibid.

Chapter Thirty

1. Terry Wilson, "Brion Gysin: A Biography/Appreciation," *RE/Search* 4/5 (1982) (San Francisco).
2. WSB, *Last Words*, 67.
3. Brion Gysin, "Points of Order," in Terry Wilson, *Here to Go: Planet R-101* (San Francisco: RE/Search, 1982), xv.
4. WSB, *Early Routines*, 34.
5. Felicity Mason, writing as Anne Cumming, *The Love Quest*, 16.
6. Brion Gysin, *Brion Gysin Let the Mice In*, 8.
7. Ibid., 10.
8. Brion Gysin interviewed by Terry Wilson in *Here to Go: Planet R-101*.
9. WSB to Allen Ginsberg, October 10, 1958.
10. Transcription of a 1959 conversation between Brion Gysin and WSB in Galerie Weiller catalog text for 1973 Brion Gysin show. Reprinted in 1976 in *Soft Need*, no. 9, and in the catalog to the Gysin show at the October Gallery, 1981.
11. Ibid.
12. WSB to Allen Ginsberg, October 10, 1958.
13. WSB to Allen Ginsberg, July 24, 1958.
14. WSB to Allen Ginsberg, October 10, 1958.
15. Brion Gysin interviewed by Terry Wilson in *Here to Go: Planet R-101*.
16. WSB to Allen Ginsberg, January 2, 1959.
17. Ibid.
18. Ibid.
19. WSB, "The Algebra of Need," in *Naked Lunch: The Restored Text*, 206.
20. WSB, *The Naked Lunch* (1959), 224.
21. Baird Bryant, "Souvenirs of the Beat Hotel," http://www.kerouacfest.com/currentpage/souvenirs.htm (accessed January 2012).
22. Terry Wilson, "Brion Gysin: A Biography/Appreciation," *RE/Search* 4/5 (1982) (San Francisco).
23. Morgan, tape 39.
24. Allen Ginsberg, "The Ugly Spirit," WSB interviewed by Allen Ginsberg in *San Francisco Review of Books* and other places. Taped March 17–22, 1992, Lawrence, Kansas.
25. WSB, *Queer*, 133.

26. WSB, unpublished journal, January 2, 1984.
27. WSB to Allen Ginsberg, April 2, 1959. The suitcase and its contents are presumed lost. These were the early draft versions of the John and Mary hanging scenes in *The Naked Lunch*.
28. Morgan, tape 62 (labeled tape 61).
29. WSB to Allen Ginsberg, April 2, 1959.
30. As Néo-Codion.
31. WSB to Allen Ginsberg, May 18, 1959.
32. WSB to Allen Ginsberg, February 12, 1959.
33. Mack Thomas, *Gumbo* (New York: Grove, 1965).
34. WSB to Allen Ginsberg, May 18, 1959.
35. WSB to Allen Ginsberg, June 8, 1959.
36. Jacques Stern, *The Fluke*, Reality Studio, realitystudio.org/publications/jacques-stern/and-the-fluke/ (accessed February 2012).

Chapter Thirty-One

1. WSB, *Last Words*, 51.
2. Victor Bockris, "Information About the Operation: A Portrait of William Burroughs," *New Review* 3, no. 25 (April 1976): 42–43; Brion Gysin interviewed by Rob LaFrenais and Graham Dawes, *Performance* magazine, no. 11 (1981) (London).
3. Quoted in Irving Rosenthal, "Editorial," *Big Table* (Chicago), no. 1 (Spring 1959).
4. Albert N. Podell, "Censorship on the Campus: The Case of the Chicago Review," *San Francisco Review* 1, no. 2 (1959): 73–74.
5. Ibid.
6. "Post Office Morals," *Nation* 188 (May 30, 1959): 486–87.
7. Morgan, tape 19.
8. Morgan, tape 21.
9. "In Search of the Connection," WSB interviewed by Nina Sutton, *Guardian*, July 5, 1964.
10. The latter not from *The Naked Lunch* but from "Fluck you, fluck you, fluck you," a Tangier text dated March 31, 1964, *Fuck You: A Magazine of the Arts*, no. 5, vol. 7 [*sic*] (September 1964): "A.J. arrives uninvited at the Countess di Vile's bi-annual garden party in Civil War drag blue Union pants and Confederate grey tunic unsheathed his saber and with one stroke decapitated Dame Sitlong's Afghan hound. The head bounces across the lawn snarling and snapping. A.J. lifts his bloody sword and the orchestra strikes up The Battle Hymn of the Republic." Cited by WSB as an example of A.J.'s outrageous behavior.
11. Alan Ansen to Allen Ginsberg, November 4, 1958.
12. Alan Ansen, "Anyone who can pick up a frying pan owns death," *Big Table* (Chicago), no. 2 (Summer 1959): 32–41.
13. Alan Ansen, untitled notes, in Ted Morgan papers, Arizona State University, Tempe.
14. WSB to Allen Ginsberg, late July 1959.
15. William Burroughs, "Témoignage à propos d'une maladie," *La Nouvelle Revue Française*, no. 85 (January 1, 1960): 82–92.
16. WSB to Allen Ginsberg, September 11, 1959.
17. WSB to Allen Ginsberg, October 7, 1959.
18. A vest.
19. WSB to Allen Ginsberg, n.d. [late July 1958].
20. WSB to Allen Ginsberg, August 24, 1959.
21. *Le Festin Nu* was subject to a resolution issued by the minister of the interior on July 9, 1964, imposing three conditions on its sale: it could not be sold to minors under eighteen years old; it could not be displayed for sale; no posters or advertising publicity were to be displayed. As a consequence it could only be sold "under the counter."

22. Harold Norse, *Memoirs of a Bastard Angel*, 344.
23. Burroughs denied the oft-quoted story that Ian, up a ladder tidying books, dropped a book on his shoulder at the Mistral to strike up a conversation. However, the archives of the Mistral—now Shakespeare and Co.—include a document from Sommerville which suggests that this is how it happened.
24. Harold Norse, *Memoirs of a Bastard Angel*, 345.
25. Ibid.
26. WSB with Brion Gysin, *The Third Mind*, 50.
27. Brion Gysin, 1982. Typewritten document in the archives of William Burroughs Communications, Lawrence, Kansas.
28. WSB in conversation with the author, 1972.
29. Morgan, tape 51.
30. WSB, *Last Words*, 48.
31. WSB, *The Soft Machine* (1961), 15.

Chapter Thirty-Two

1. Betty Bouthoul, *Le vieux de la montagne.*
2. Brion Gysin, "A Quick Trip to Alamut," *Ultraculture Journal One.*
3. Joseph von Hammer, *The History of the Assassins* (London: Smith & Elder, 1835), 234–35.
4. Literally means "rising of the dead."
5. Hashish appears to have been taken as a beverage rather than smoked at Alamut.
6. Henri Corbin, *History of Islamic Philosophy* (London: Kegan Paul, 1993), 95.
7. Joseph von Hammer wrote, " 'Nothing is true and all is allowed,' was the groundwork of the secret doctrine; which, however, being imparted to few, and concealed under the veil of the most austere religionism and piety, restrained the mind under the yoke of obedience." *The History of the Assassins*, 55.
8. WSB, *The Western Lands*, 203.
9. Barry Miles, *William S. Burroughs: El Hombre Invisible* (2002 revision), 116.
10. Ibid., 116.
11. Morgan, tape 20.
12. WSB, Gregory Corso, Brion Gysin, and Sinclair Beiles, *Minutes to Go*, 63.
13. Ibid.
14. Beiles's assertion in an interview that he took "all the pages and typed them up" is not true, as the original manuscript of *Minutes to Go* is in four different typefaces and paper stocks. In "Interview with Sinclair Beiles by David Malan, Yeoville, South Africa, January 1994," collected in Gary Cummiskey and Eva Kowalska, eds., *Who Was Sinclair Beiles?*
15. "To settle a score with literature."
16. WSB to David Haselwood, December 24, 1959, reproduced in *A Bibliography of the Auerhahn Press and Its Successor Dave Haselwood Books Compiled by a Printer*, 25.
17. WSB to David Haselwood, May 27, 1960, reproduced in ibid., 27.
18. Villiers, George, late Duke of Buckingham, *The Rehearsal*, 8th ed. (London: Richard Wellington, 1711).
19. WSB, *The Job*, 28.
20. Ibid., 29.

Chapter Thirty-Three

1. WSB to Brion Gysin, May 16, 1960.
2. Nikolaus Pevsner, *The Buildings of England: London* vol. 2, 128.
3. WSB, unpublished journal entry for January 1, 1984.
4. John Howe interviewed by the author, London, November 9, 2011.

5. A British public school is what is known as a prep school or boarding school in the United States.
6. WSB to Jon Webb, August 21, 1960.
7. Author conversation with Michael Horovitz, October 2011.
8. Michael Horovitz, "Legend in His Own Lunchtime," *Times Saturday Review*, May 23, 1992.
9. Hannah Gay, *The History of Imperial College London, 1907–2007*, 383; email correspondence with Dr. Hannah Gay, November 2011; email correspondence with Professor Bill Griffith, December 2011; conversation with Dick Pountain, November 2011; http://www.rsc.org/chemistryworld/Issues/2011/July/TheEvansBalance.asp (accessed November 2011); M. L. H. Green, *Dennis Frederick Evans. 27 March 1928–6 November 1990*, Biographical Memoirs of the Fellows of the Royal Society, rsbm.royalsocietypublishing.org (accessed November 2011).
10. Christine Keeler, *The Truth at Last*, 231.
11. Sydney R. Davies, *Walking the London Scene: Five Walks in the Footsteps of the Beat Generation*, 33, and in conversation with Sydney Davies.
12. Kenneth Allsop, *Scan*, 21.
13. WSB to Brion Gysin, May 26, 1960.
14. Morgan, tape 24.
15. WSB, unpublished ms., April 30, 1983.
16. WSB, *The Western Lands*, 252.
17. Morgan, tape 62 (labeled tape 61).
18. Morgan, tape 34.
19. WSB to Brion Gysin, September 14, 1960.
20. WSB to Brion Gysin, August 4, 1960.
21. In conversation, 1972.
22. Brion Gysin, "Dream Machine," *Olympia*, no. 2 (1962): 31.
23. John Geiger, *Nothing Is True, Everything Is Permitted*, 160.
24. Ian Sommerville to Brion Gysin, February 15, 1960, quoted in Gysin, "Dream Machine," 31.
25. Brevet number P.V. 868,281.
26. Author interview with Christopher Gibbs, June 6, 2011, Tangier.
27. Michael Wishart, *High Diver*, 167–68.
28. WSB to Brion Gysin, October 21, 1960.
29. WSB, *My Education*, 32.
30. Steve Boggan and Paul Lashmar, "The Great and Not-So-Goodman," *Independent*, January 18, 1999.
31. Christopher Gibbs interviewed by the author, Tangier, June 6, 2011.
32. WSB to Brion Gysin, October 21, 1960.
33. WSB, *My Education*, 151.
34. Ibid.
35. This is not true; there are many mountains in between.
36. Alan Govenar, *The Beat Hotel*, Documentary Arts (film documentary), 2011.
37. Jenni Ferrari-Adler, ed., *Alone in the Kitchen with an Eggplant*, 219.
38. Felicity Mason, writing as Anne Cumming, *Love Quest*, 117.
39. John Gilmore, *Laid Bare: A Memoir of Wrecked Lives and the Hollywood Death Trip*, 148.
40. Ibid.
41. Daevid Allen interview, *Scotsman*, November 19, 2009.
42. "Daevid Allen: Magical Mystery Tour," *Magnet*, http://www.magnetmagazine.com/1999/10/01/daevid-allen-magical-history-tour (accessed December 2012).
43. WSB to Allen Ginsberg, March 12, 1961.

Chapter Thirty-Four

1. Arthur Rimbaud, "Alchemy of the Word," section II of "Delirium," in *A Season in Hell*, 1873.
2. Unattributed front cover flap, *The Soft Machine* (Olympia edition). The ellipsis is in the original.
3. Allen Ginsberg to Lucien Carr, July 28, 1961 (misdated as June).
4. Entry for January 17, 1963, in Allen Ginsberg, *Indian Journals*, 155.
5. WSB, *The Soft Machine* (1961), 87.
6. Ibid., 89–90.
7. WSB to Brion Gysin, May 8, 1961.
8. WSB to Brion Gysin, May 13, 1961.
9. WSB, *The Adding Machine*, 12.
10. Historical precedents include the work of Piet Zwart between 1929 and 1934, who photographed close-ups of carefully arranged objects such as a pair of spectacles and a fallen leaf on an open newspaper (1934), or a coil of copper wire on a pile of business cards (1931). His pictures of lead typeface letters on a newspaper (1931) use strong shadow and are, at least superficially, very similar to Burroughs's Tangier-period reversals and superimpositions. Possibly the earliest recorded example of the photographic record of a fugitive assemblage is "Unhappy Readymade": in 1919 Marcel Duchamp, who was in Buenos Aires, instructed his sister Suzanne to attach a geometry book to the balcony of her Paris apartment to allow "the wind to examine it." The elements turned the pages and tore some of them loose. The progress of its disintegration was recorded in photographs and in a painting by Suzanne Duchamp.
11. WSB to Brion Gysin, May 16, 1961.
12. WSB to Brion Gysin , May 28, 1961.
13. WSB to Brion Gysin, June 14, 1961.
14. Christopher Sawyer-Lauçanno, *Invisible Spectator*, 356.
15. John Hopkins, *The Tangier Diaries, 1962–1979*, April 1, 1963, 36.
16. Ted Morgan, *Rowing Toward Eden*, 98–99.
17. Author conversations with Burroughs, 1972–73; Morgan, tape 32.
18. Ned Rorem, *Diaries*, June 22, 1967.
19. WSB to Timothy Leary, May 6, 1961.
20. WSB, "Comments on the Night Before Thinking," *Evergreen Review* vol. 5, no. 20 (September 1961): 31.
21. Author notes, taken from a published interview with Leary but source unknown.

Chapter Thirty-Five

1. Morgan, tape 61.
2. Allen Ginsberg in conversation with the author, ca. 1970 and 1984, for whole section.
3. Allen Ginsberg, "Literary History of the Beat Generation," lecture number 18.
4. Rupert Croft-Cooke, *The Caves of Hercules*, 135.
5. Allen Ginsberg to Lucien Carr, July 28, 1961 (misdated as June).
6. Morgan, tape 20.
7. Allen Ginsberg and Peter Orlovsky, *Straight Hearts' Delight*, 104–5. Transcribed July 12 and July 16, 1961. Transcript uses spelling corrected by Ginsberg.
8. Allen Ginsberg to Lawrence Ferlinghetti, n.d. [1961].
9. Timothy Leary, *High Priest*, 215.
10. WSB to Timothy Leary, May 6, 1961; Timothy Leary, *High Priest*, 214–15; Timothy Leary, *Flashbacks*, 95.
11. Leary, *High Priest*, 215.
12. Ibid., 215.

13. Leary, *Flashbacks*, 96–97.
14. Leary, *High Priest*, 216–22.
15. Ibid., 223.
16. Morgan, tape 43.
17. Ibid.
18. Leary, *Flashbacks*, 100.
19. Ibid.
20. Leary, *High Priest*, 228.
21. Martin A. Lee and Bruce Shlain, *Acid Dreams: The CIA, LSD, and the Sixties Rebellion*, 82–83.
22. Leary, *High Priest*, 231.
23. *Pataphysics*, October 17, 1989.
24. WSB, "Prisoners, Come Out" section of *Nova Express*, 10–11.

Chapter Thirty-Six

1. WSB, *Nova Express*, 18.
2. "To Write for the Space Age," Michael Moorcock interviewed by Mark P. Williams, Reality Studio, December 8, 2008, www.realitystudio.org/interviews/michael-moorcock-on-william-s-burroughs (accessed July 2011).
3. Norman Mailer interviewed by Eve Auchincloss and Nancy Lynch, *Mademoiselle*, February 1961, 52.
4. Norman Mailer interviewed by Winston Bode, *Texas Observer*, December 15, 1961.
5. Alexander Trocchi in debate with David Daiches, August 21, 1962: "Scottish Writers' Day," Edinburgh Writers' Conference, 1962.
6. Peter Manso, *Mailer: His Life and Times*, 351.
7. John Calder, *Pursuit: The Uncensored Memoirs of John Calder*, 207.
8. Morgan, tape 41.
9. Morgan, tape 49.
10. Brion Gysin interviewed by Jason Weiss, Paris, August 21, 1980, in *Reality Studios* vol. 4, 1982.
11. "Burroughs After Lunch," WSB interviewed by Joseph Barry, *New York Post*, March 10, 1963.
12. *The Ticket That Exploded* (Olympia edition), 41; the same passage repeats in *Nova Express*, 50.
13. *The Ticket That Exploded* (Olympia edition), 81.
14. WSB in conversation with the author, London, 1972.
15. "Dressed for Tea," WSB interviewed by W. J. Weatherby, *Guardian*, March 22, 1963.
16. Miles, *Catalogue of the WSB Archive*; Anthony Burgess, *You've Had Your Time*, 70.
17. Burgess, *You've Had Your Time*, 85.
18. Author interview with Christopher Gibbs, Tangier, 2012.
19. *The Ticket That Exploded* (Olympia edition), 102–3.
20. Typically, Antony Balch and *Towers Open Fire* receive no mention in Stephen Dwoskin's *Film Is: The International Free Cinema* (1975); Sheldon Renan's *An Introduction to the American Underground Film* (1967); Jonas Mekas's *Movie Journal: The Rise of a New American Cinema, 1959–1971* (1972); David E. James's *To Free the Cinema* (1992); or P. Adams Sitney's *Film Culture* anthology, despite the fact that Balch and *Towers* (and *The Cut-Ups*) anticipated many of the techniques of the new cinema and was far more avant-garde than most of the filmmakers discussed in those books. Perhaps future film scholars will correct the lapse and place Balch and Burroughs where they belong in the forefront of postwar avant-garde filmmaking.
21. WSB taped by Bill Rich, May 15, 1991.
22. Ibid.

23. "Burroughs After Lunch," WSB interviewed by Joseph Barry, *New York Post*, March 10, 1963.
24. *Evening Standard*, March 29, 1963.

Chapter Thirty-Seven

1. Jeff Nuttall, *Bomb Culture*, 157.
2. WSB, *The Third Mind*, 107–8.
3. Morgan, tape 26.
4. William S. Burroughs Jr., *Cursed from Birth*, 12.
5. Ibid., 13.
6. Morgan, tape 26.
7. Steven Watson, *Factory Made: Warhol and the Sixties* (New York: Pantheon, 2003), 141.
8. William S. Burroughs Jr., *Cursed from Birth*, 15.
9. Ibid.
10. Ibid., 17.
11. The photograph, taken on November 9, 1963, appeared in the "Literary Tangier" feature in the September 1964 issue of *Esquire*.
12. Morgan, tape 26.
13. Ibid.
14. Morgan Bowles tape 19.
15. John Hopkins, *Tangier Diaries*, 43, 44.
16. WSB, *The Third Mind*, 107–8.
17. Morgan, tape 18.
18. Conversations with Ian Sommerville, London, 1968–69; conversations with Brion Gysin, London, 1972, 1974; conversation with Alan Ansen and Allen Ginsberg, New York, 1984.
19. *The Floating Bear*, no. 27 (1962). Burroughs had nothing in this issue.
20. WSB to Brion Gysin, February 4, 1964.
21. *Chicago Review*, issue 54 (vol. 17, no. 1) (1964), 130.
22. WSB, *Last Words*, 185; Burroughs is probably referring to Graham Wallace.
23. Nuttall, *Bomb Culture*, 157.
24. Ibid., 156.
25. Ibid., 153.
26. Ibid., 152.
27. Ibid.
28. Morgan, tape 18.
29. WSB, *The Third Mind*, 107–8.
30. Hopkins, *Tangier Diaries*, 77.
31. Ibid, 67.
32. Ibid.
33. WSB, *Exterminator!* (Corgi edition), 39. Mr. P is Paul Bowles.
34. Alan Ansen papers, in Ted Morgan papers, Arizona State University, Tempe.
35. Hopkins, *Tangier Diaries*, 56; Gary Pulsifer, *Paul Bowles by His Friends*, 60. Conversation with the author, 2012.
36. WSB, *Nova Express*, 11.
37. WSB interviewed by Conrad Knickerbocker, *Paris Review*, issue 35 (Fall 1965), and in various collections.
38. Caused partly by Ansen's affair with a redheaded Berber who supposedly later assassinated the grand rabbi of Tangier.
39. Cited in John Geiger, *Nothing Is True, Everything Is Permitted*, 189.
40. Conversation with Ira Cohen, New York, 1985.
41. "Who Is the Walks Beside You Written 3rd?," in *Darazt* anthology, London, 1965.

42. "I Talk to the First Beatnik," WSB interviewed by Susan Barnes, *Sun*, November 17, 1964.

Chapter Thirty-Eight

1. WSB interviewed by Conrad Knickerbocker, *Paris Review*, issue 35 (Fall 1965).
2. Claude Pélieu, *With Revolvers Aimed...Finger Bowls* (San Francisco: Beach Books, Texts & Documents, 1967); Mary Beach, *A Two Fisted Banana: Electric and Gothic* (Cherry Valley, NY: Cherry Valley, 1980).
3. *C: A Journal of Poetry* vol. 1, no. 9 (Summer 1964): 43–47.
4. *C: A Journal of Poetry* vol. 1, no. 10 (February 14, 1965): 70–71.
5. C Press books were published by Lorenz and Ellen Gude. Berrigan would certainly never have had enough money for such a professional print job.
6. The text was dated March 31, 1964, in Tangier.
7. "St. Louis Return," *Paris Review*, issue 35 (Fall 1965).
8. "Transcript of Dutch Schultz's Last Words," in James D. Horan, *The Desperate Years* (New York: Bonanza Books, 1962), 185.
9. WSB to Ian Sommerville, February 16, 1965.
10. Ed Sanders, *Fug You*, 130.
11. WSB to Ian Sommerville, February 16, 1965.
12. WSB to Antony Balch, May 19, 1965.
13. WSB to Alan Ansen, February 27, 1964.
14. WSB to Ian Sommerville, April 12, 1965.
15. See Sanders, *Fug You*, 145.
16. Andy Warhol and Pat Hackett, *POPism: The Warhol '60s*, 103.
17. Morgan, tape 34.
18. Ibid.
19. WSB to Ian Sommerville, July 28, 1965.
20. Morgan, tape 25.
21. Anslinger was in power from 1930 to 1962; before that he was assistant commissioner in the Bureau of Prohibition.
22. Mayor John Lindsay was in office from January 1, 1966, to December 31, 1973.

Chapter Thirty-Nine

1. WSB, unpublished journals, November 21, 1982.
2. Interview with Christopher Gibbs, Tangier, 2011.
3. Ibid.
4. Morgan, tape 36.
5. Morgan, tape 15, tape 31.
6. WSB, untitled essay in the press kit for *Chappaqua*, 1967.
7. WSB to Brion Gysin, May 27, 1966.
8. Carl Weissner to Victor Bockris, in Victor Bockris, *With William Burroughs: A Report from the Bunker*, 8.
9. Bill Butler, "A Word Is a Word Is a Collage," *Guardian*, November 27, 1965.
10. WSB to Claude Pélieu, November 10, 1966.
11. The British Board of Film Censors issued a "U" certificate to films that were suitable for children.
12. WSB interviewed by the author, Lawrence, Kansas, November 29, 1991.
13. The author of this book.
14. The author was present.
15. Ian Sommerville in conversation, London, 1966.
16. Harriet Vyner, *Groovy Bob*, 168.

Chapter Forty

1. WSB to Ian Sommerville, September 12, 1966; WSB to Ian Sommerville, September 15, 1966.
2. Morgan, tape 41.
3. WSB to Ian Sommerville, September 15, 1966.
4. WSB to Brion Gysin, August 1, 1966.
5. WSB to Brion Gysin, December 17, 1966.
6. Allen Ginsberg to Barry Miles, September 20, 1966.
7. WSB to Brion Gysin, October 13, 1966.
8. WSB to Mary Beach, July 28, 1967.
9. As this was not published in English until 1970, Burroughs must have read it in French, either in the magazine or the 1967 French edition.
10. WSB to Brion Gysin, December 23, 1966.
11. "Dressed for Tea," WSB interviewed by W. J. Weatherby, *Guardian*, March 22, 1963.
12. WSB, *The Soft Machine* (Grove Black Cat edition), 26.
13. WSB, *Last Words*, 206.
14. WSB to Laura Lee Burroughs, November 21, 1966.
15. WSB, afterword in William S. Burroughs Jr., *Kentucky Ham*, 195.
16. WSB, *The Western Lands*, 253.
17. WSB to Brion Gysin, February 5, 1967.
18. WSB to Brion Gysin, February 8, 1967.
19. WSB, afterword in Williams S. Burroughs Jr., *Kentucky Ham*, 196.
20. WSB to Brion Gysin, April 15, 1968.
21. William S. Burroughs Jr., *Cursed from Birth*, 25.
22. WSB, *The Cat Inside*, 69.
23. The dinner was held on December 16, 1966.
24. WSB to Brion Gysin, March 17, 1967.
25. WSB to Brion Gysin, August 21, 1967.
26. The author was present.

Chapter Forty-One

1. L. Ron Hubbard, Third Operating Thetan Level, "The Ring of Fire," September 1967.
2. WSB, *Nova Express*, 170.
3. WSB, *Ali's Smile*, 99.
4. *Auditor*, no. 32 (in-house Scientology magazine), 5.
5. Harold Norse, *Bastard Angel*, 415–16.
6. Morgan, tape 45, tape 28.
7. WSB, *Last Words*, 64.
8. WSB to Brion Gysin, August 19, 1968.
9. Ian Sommerville, in conversation with the author, 1968.
10. Morgan, tape 39.

Chapter Forty-Two

1. "The Coming of the Purple Better One," in WSB, *Exterminator!*, 98.
2. Victor Bockris, *With William Burroughs: A Report from the Bunker*, 25.
3. WSB to Brion Gysin, September 9, 1968.
4. See Jack Stevensen, *Witchcraft Through the Ages: The Story of Häxen, the World's Strangest Film, and the Man Who Made It* (Godalming, UK: FAB, 2006); Benjamin Christensen, *Häxen/Witchcraft Through the Ages*, Tartan DVDTVD3758, 2007.

5. WSB to Brion Gysin, October 17, 1968.
6. Ibid.
7. WSB to Dr. Joe Gross, October 17, 1968.
8. WSB to Brion Gysin, November 5, 1968.
9. "Rolling Stone Interview," WSB interviewed by Robert Palmer, *Rolling Stone*, May 11, 1972.
10. Ibid.
11. WSB interviewed by Larry McCaffery in *Across the Wounded Galaxies*, ed. Larry McCaffery (Champaign: University of Illinois Press, 1990), 44.
12. WSB, *The Job*, 17.
13. WSB, "The Discipline of DE," in *Exterminator!*, 56.
14. "Journey Through Time-Space," WSB interviewed by Daniel Odier, *Evergreen* 67 (June 1969).

Chapter Forty-Three

1. "In Search of the Connection," WSB interviewed by Nina Sutton, *Guardian*, July 5, 1969.
2. Mick Farren, *Give the Anarchist a Cigarette*, 279.
3. Morgan, tape 1.
4. WSB, unpublished journal, January 2, 1984.
5. WSB, *My Education*, 147.
6. Ibid.
7. WSB to Billy Burroughs Jr., November 4, 1970.
8. Bockris, *A Report from the Bunker*, 27.
9. Charles Marowitz, "Expats' Chicago: London, 1968," http://swans.com/library/art14/cmarow108.html (June 2, 2008) (accessed June 2012).
10. Irving Wardle, "Conspiracy Trial Is Given as Drama," *New York Times*, August 26, 1970.
11. B. A. Young, "Flash Gordon and the Angels," *Financial Times*, February 17, 1971.
12. David Z. Mairowitz to author, 2005.
13. WSB, *Evil River* ms.
14. Bockris, *A Report from the Bunker*, 220.
15. WSB, *Evil River* ms.
16. Bockris, *A Report from the Bunker*, 120–21.
17. Morgan, tape 3.
18. Morgan, tape 38.
19. The Rolling Stones Chronicle, "1971: I Can't Even Feel the Pain No More," http://www.timeisonourside.com/chron1971.html (accessed November 2011).
20. Morgan, tape 3.
21. Ibid.
22. Eric Mottram, *William Burroughs: The Algebra of Need* (Buffalo, NY: Intrepid, 1971).
23. WSB, *Last Words*, 173.
24. WSB to Brion Gysin, October 22, 1971.
25. A conversation at Duke Street Saint James's with an unknown visitor, taped by WSB, ca. 1972.
26. Cyril Vosper, *The Mind Benders*, 72.
27. The author was present at the meal.
28. WSB, *The Job*, 18.
29. WSB, *The Place of Dead Roads*, 177.
30. Morgan, tape 35 (labeled tape 34).
31. WSB to Paul Bowles, April 28, 1972.
32. WSB to Brion Gysin, n.d., draft in archives.
33. WSB to Brion Gysin, April 17, 1972.

34. Ibid.
35. Bob Colacello, *Holy Terror: Andy Warhol Close Up* (New York: HarperCollins, 1990), 112.
36. Morgan, tape 62 (labeled tape 61).

Chapter Forty-Four

1. Sometimes attributed to Floyd Starr of Albion College, Michigan, 1910.
2. WSB, unpublished journals, June 8, 1983.
3. Morgan, tape 39.
4. WSB, *Port of Saints*, 50.
5. Ibid., 143.
6. WSB in conversation with John Brady, taped by WSB, ca. 1972.
7. WSB, *Cities of the Red Night*, 80.
8. Ibid., 40.
9. WSB interviewed by Bill Rich, April 23, 1991.
10. WSB, *Cities of the Red Night*, 49–52.
11. Victor Bockris, *With William Burroughs: A Report from the Bunker*, 38.
12. "The Rolling Stone Interview," WSB interviewed by Robert Palmer, *Rolling Stone*, May 11, 1972.
13. David Bowie interviewed by WSB, *Rolling Stone*, February 28, 1974 (recorded November 17, 1973).
14. WSB to Billy Burroughs Jr., February 16, 1972.
15. WSB, *The Western Lands*, 110. "Cheney Walk" is correctly spelled Cheyne Walk, and is where Christopher Gibbs lived. "London Electric" was the London Electricity Board, known as the LEB.
16. WSB to Mack Sheldon Thomas, July 16, 1973.
17. Morgan, tape 39.
18. Morgan Ansen tapes.
19. WSB, *Port of Saints* (Calder edition), 148.

Chapter Forty-Five

1. Morgan, tape 42.
2. *Daily News*, October 30, 1975.
3. The most murders in one year were 2,605 in 1990; a decade later the number was reduced to 952, and at the time of writing, half that again.
4. Morgan, tape 40.
5. "Entretiens," WSB interviewed by Gérard-George Lemaire, *Colloque de Tanger 2*, 260 (translated by Theo Miles).
6. Alan Ansen, *The Table Talk of W. H. Auden* (London, Faber & Faber, 1991), 85.
7. Correctly, "The wind that blows between the Worlds, it cut him like a knife."
8. James Grauerholz interviewed by Ted Morgan, 1.
9. James Grauerholz, "Burroughs and Me" ms., February 26, 2004.
10. Morgan, tape 16.
11. WSB, *The Job*, 52.
12. "Burroughs After Lunch," WSB interviewed by Joseph Barry, *New York Post*, March 10, 1963.
13. WSB interviewed by Jeff Shero, *Rat*, October 4, 1968.
14. WSB interviewed in *NOLA Express*, no. 61 (August 7, 1970) (New Orleans).
15. WSB interviewed in *NOLA Express*, no. 61 (August 7, 1970) (New Orleans) (taken from Jeff Shero's two-part *Rat* interview).
16. Morgan, tape 40.
17. WSB to the author, London, June 1974.
18. Morgan, tape 40 (labeled tape 39).

19. Morgan, tape 54.
20. "The Invisible Man Returns," WSB interviewed by Josh Feigenbaum, *Soho Weekly News*, July 25, 1974.
21. James Grauerholz to Allen Ginsberg, September 5, 1974.
22. WSB, "Rock Magic: Jimmy Page, Led Zeppelin, and a Search for the Elusive Stairway to Heaven," *Crawdaddy*, June 1975.
23. Morgan, tape 61 (labeled tape 59).
24. WSB, "My Punk Face Is Death," in *Unmuzzled Ox*, no. 26 (1989) (from *The Gay Gun*, work in progress).
25. WSB to Paul Bowles, March 6, 1978.
26. Morgan, tape 14.
27. WSB, *Retreat Diaries*, [5–6][unpaginated].
28. WSB interviewed by Jim McMenamin in *Across the Wounded Galaxies*, ed. Larry McCaffery (Champaign: University of Illinois Press, 1990), 45.
29. Ibid., 6.
30. Morgan, tape 70 (labeled tape 69).
31. "There are mistakes too monstrous for remorse / To fondle or to dally with, and failures / That only fate's worst fumbling in the dark / Could have arranged so well." Edward Arlington Robinson, "Tristram."
32. James Grauerholz to Brion Gysin, May 25, 1976.
33. Brion Gysin to James Grauerholz, May 30, 1976.

Chapter Forty-Six

1. William S. Burroughs Jr., *Cursed from Birth*, 4
2. James Grauerholz to Claude Pélieu, July 13, 1976.
3. WSB, *The Soft Machine*, 56.
4. William S. Burroughs Jr., *Cursed from Birth*, 154.
5. Landmark Preservation Commission, November 17, 1998, Designation List 299 LP-2028; Neil MacFarquhar, "Mansion and Old 'Y' Are Named Landmarks," *New York Times*, November 18, 1998.
6. Andy Warhol, *The Andy Warhol Diaries*, Saturday, March 1, 1980, 266.
7. Robert McNamara was U.S. secretary of defense from 1961 to 1968.
8. Morgan, tape 10.
9. Quoted by James Grauerholz in his interview by Ted Morgan, transcript, 22.

Chapter Forty-Seven

1. "Mutation, Utopia, and Magic," WSB interviewed by Arthur Shingles, *Undercurrents*, no. 48 (November 1981).
2. Morgan, tape 69.
3. Quoted from an unidentified source in Hardy's obituary, http://www.ashejournal.com/eight/mclean.shtml (accessed December 2012).
4. Morgan, tape 50.
5. Morgan, tape 53.
6. Morgan, tape 54.
7. Morgan, tape 49.
8. Cabell Hardy, "Playback: My Personal Experience of Chaos Magic with William S. Burroughs, Sr.," http://www.ashe-prem.org/three/mclean.shtml (accessed December 2012).
9. Morgan, tape 69 (labeled tape 68).
10. Ibid.
11. See Michael Walsh, "'I Wrote Your Fading Movie': The Films of Antony Balch and William Burroughs," *Motion Picture* vol. 4, no. 1 (Summer 1991).
12. Gerard Pas, "How I Came to Know William Burroughs," http://www.gerardpas.com/library/memoirs/burrough.html (accessed December 2012).

13. Sylvère Lotringer interviewed by Marcus Niski, Reality Studio, http://realitystudio
.org/interviews/interview-with-sylvre-lotringer-on-the-nova-convention (accessed
December 2012).
14. Brion Gysin to WSB, October 12, 1978.
15. "Trip to Hell and Back," WSB interviewed by Jerry Bauer, *Trax* (London), no. 6
(March 18, 1981).
16. Rachel Wolff, "Bohemian Rhapsody: Brion Gysin, William Burroughs, and the
Secret Life of a Building on the Bowery," *New York Magazine*, July 4, 2010.
17. Robert Palmer, "3-Day Nova Convention Ends at the Entermedia," *New York Times*,
December 4, 1978.
18. Ibid.
19. WSB to Gérard-Georges Lemaire, December 18, 1978. It is likely that the letter was
mostly authored by James Grauerholz.
20. Victor Bockris interviewed by Dave Teeuwen, Reality Studio, http://realitystudio
.org/interviews/interview-with-victor-bockris-on-william-burroughs (accessed December
2012).
21. WSB interviewed in *Talk Talk* 3.6, [October?] 1981.
22. Victor Bockris, *A Report from the Bunker*, 32.
23. WSB interviewed by Ray Rumor [Raymond Foye], *Search & Destroy*, no. 10 (1978).
24. Morgan, tape 61 (labeled tape 60). The words are taken from the *Muqaddimah* of Ibn
Khaldun, a fourteenth-century Arab scholar from Tunis.
25. Ibid.
26. "Trip to Hell and Back," WSB interviewed by Jerry Bauer, *Trax* (London), no. 6
(March 18, 1981).
27. WSB interviewed by Larry McCaffery in *Across the Wounded Galaxies*, ed. Larry
McCaffery (Champaign: University of Illinois Press, 1990), 38.
28. Morgan, tape 24.
29. Allen Ginsberg to Barry Miles, October 8, 1979.
30. WSB, *Cities of the Red Night*, 206. Burroughs spells the Jakes title "Brac."
31. Morgan, tape 61 (labeled tape 60).
32. WSB, *Last Words*, 16.
33. Morgan, tape 40.

Chapter Forty-Eight
1. Morgan, tape 75 (labeled tape 76).
2. Morgan, tape 13.
3. Morgan, tape 26, and all references to the letter.
4. Ibid.
5. Diconal, a painkiller.
6. Stewart Meyer, *Book of Days* (unpublished).
7. Stewart Meyer to Ted Morgan, "Stu Meyer Notes," 3.
8. Morgan, tape 55.
9. WSB in conversation with Victor Bockris, 1977.
10. John Giorno, from the booklet accompanying *The Best of William Burroughs* CD box
set, 1998.
11. Ibid.
12. Morgan, tape 40 (labeled tape 39).
13. Morgan, tape 61 (labeled tape 60).
14. Ibid.
15. William S. Burroughs Jr., *Cursed from Birth*, 169.
16. Based on WSB, unpublished journal dated January 2, 1984.
17. Morgan, tape 26 (labeled tape 25).
18. Allen Ginsberg interviewed by Barry Miles, New York, 1985.

19. Burroughs had previously appeared on television a decade earlier in Britain with Dan Farson on January 8, 1964.

Chapter Forty-Nine

1. "An Ex-Junkie Exterminator," WSB interviewed by Lynn Snowden, *Guardian*, April 25, 1992.
2. Morgan, tape 2.
3. Morgan, tape 62 (labeled tape 61).
4. Ibid.
5. WSB, *Last Words*, 158.
6. WSB interviewed by Duncan Fallowell, *Time Out*, September 24, 1982.
7. Morgan, tape 55.
8. James Grauerholz interviewed by the author, March 2012.
9. Frank Tankard, "William S. Burroughs: 10 Years After," Lawrence.com, http://www.lawrence.com/news/2007/jul/30/burroughs_student (accessed January 2013).
10. WSB, *The Cat Inside*, 23.
11. Morgan, tape 58 (labeled tape 57).
12. WSB interviewed by Jim McMenamin in *Across the Wounded Galaxies*, ed. Larry McCaffery (Champaign: University of Illinois Press, 1990), 51.
13. WSB, *The Western Lands*, 13.
14. Victor Bockris, *With William Burroughs: A Report from the Bunker*, 65.
15. Jeffrey Scott Dunn, "A Conversation: Ginsberg on Burroughs," *Pennsylvania Review* (Fall/Winter 1987): 42.
16. Reported by Stewart Meyer in *Book of Days* (unpublished).
17. Ibid.
18. "William Burroughs and Brion Gysin," WSB interviewed by Chris Bohn, *New Musical Express*, October 16, 1982.
19. From WSB interviewed by San Fleischer and Dan Turèll, Copenhagen, October 29, 1983.
20. "William Burroughs: Intellectual Gunman, Spectacular Junkie at Seventy Years of Age," WSB interviewed by William Triplett, *Washington Review*, June–July 1984.
21. "The Devil's Bargain: Two Interviews with William Burroughs," WSB interviewed by Nicholas Zurbrugg, November 22, 1983, *Art & Text*, no. 35 (Summer 1990).
22. "William Burroughs: Intellectual Gunman, Spectacular Junkie at Seventy Years of Age," WSB interviewed by William Triplett, *Washington Review*, June–July 1984.
23. WSB interviewed by Michele Corriel, *Cover*, January 1988.
24. "Shooting Gallery," WSB interviewed by Lucinda Bredin, *Evening Standard* (London), June 2, 1988.
25. Marcel Duchamp, Notes on the *Large Glass* numbers 83, 84, and 85, *The Green Box notes, 1912–1918*. Musée National d'Art Moderne, Centre Georges Pompidou, Paris.
26. Unpublished text, 1987.
27. *Fuck You: A Magazine of the Arts*, no. 5, vol. 9 [*sic*] (July 1965).
28. WSB, *Painting and Guns*, 10.
29. Ibid., 15.
30. Wayne Propst interviewed by Tom King, September 2010, http://ereview.org/2010/09/22/reality-my-way (accessed January 2013).
31. Morgan, tape 1.
32. Morgan, tape 3.

Chapter Fifty

1. WSB, introduction to Brion Gysin, *The Last Museum*, 8.
2. It has been suggested that it is in fact built from a Montgomery Ward house kit. Both companies destroyed their records, but it looks like a Sears house.
3. WSB interviewed by the author, Lawrence, Kansas, November 29, 1991.

4. WSB, *The Western Lands*, 79.
5. Frank Tankard, *The Inner Circle*, July 30, 2007, http://www.lawrence.com/news/2007/jul/30/inner_circle? (accessed February 2013).
6. David Ohle, *Mutate or Die: With Burroughs in Kansas* (no pagination).
7. WSB, *The Western Lands*, 79–82.
8. WSB interviewed by San Fleischer and Dan Turèll, Copenhagen, October 29, 1983.
9. As witnessed by the author.
10. "Interview with William Burroughs," by Jennie Skerl, *Moody Street Irregulars* (Winter–Spring 1981).
11. WSB interviewed by T. X. Erbe, *East Village Eye*, April 1984.
12. This was said to the author.
13. "An Ex-Junkie Exterminator," WSB interviewed by Lynn Snowden, *Guardian*, April 25, 1992.
14. Pauline lost two fingers in an explosion using that flamethrower shortly afterward.
15. The manuscript of *Queer* had been raided in order to complete *Junky* back in 1953 and disappeared. For two decades there was no known copy. The manuscript was sold, along with Burroughs's other archives, to Roberto Altman, who then sold them to the rare book collector Robert Jackson. During the transfer of ownership, a Xerox copy was made of the manuscript. See Oliver Harris's introduction to the 25th Anniversary edition of *Queer* for the full story of the manuscript.
16. The author of this book found the manuscript of *Interzone* described as an "enclosure" on the index card for a letter from WSB to Lawrence Ferlinghetti in the card catalog of the Butler Library of Columbia University. I made a photocopy and told Andrew Wylie about it—he was my agent at the time—saying that I thought it should be published.
17. WSB interviewed by Kurt Chandler and John Lehndorff, *Sunday Camera* (Boulder, CO), July 28, 1985. The incident involving the Mexican policeman was in fact in *Junky*.
18. WSB, *Queer*, 131–32.
19. WSB to Brion Gysin, January 30, 1985.
20. "An Ex-Junkie Exterminator," WSB interviewed by Lynn Snowden, *Guardian*, April 25, 1992.
21. WSB, introduction to *Everything Is Permitted: The Making of "Naked Lunch."*
22. WSB interviewed by James Fox, *Sunday Times Magazine*, March 22, 1987.
22. Saint-John Perse, *Anabasis*, 83.
23. WSB interviewed by Kurt Chandler and John Lehndorff, *Sunday Camera* (Boulder, CO), July 28, 1985.
24. Ibid.
25. WSB, *The Western Lands*, 252.
26. WSB to Brion Gysin, January 30, 1985.
27. WSB to Brion Gysin, October 12, 1985.
28. Brion Gysin to WSB, August 28, 1985.
29. *Times* (London), July 26, 1988.
30. Terry Wilson, *Perilous Passage*, 137.
31. WSB interviewed by Timothy Leary, *Mondo 2000*, no. 4 (1991).
32. WSB interviewed by Robbie Conal and Tom Christie, *LA Weekly*, July 19, 1996.
33. WSB interviewed by Kristine McKenna, September 13, 1990, in *Burroughs Live: Collected Interviews*, 722–23.
34. WSB interviewed by James Fox, *Sunday Times Magazine*, March 22, 1987.
35. WSB, *The Job*, 97.
36. Ibid., 116.
37. John Geiger, *Nothing Is True, Everything Is Permitted*, 309.
38. Ted Morgan's interview with James Grauerholz, 1986.
39. WSB, introduction to Gysin, *The Last Museum*, 8.

40. "William Tells," WSB interviewed by Legs McNeil, *Spin*, October 1991.
41. WSB, *The Western Lands*, 236.
42. Ibid., 198.
43. Ibid.
44. WSB interviewed by Richard Goldstein, *College Papers*, no. 1 (Fall 1979).
45. WSB interviewed by James Fox, *Sunday Times Magazine*, March 22, 1987.
46. WSB interviewed by Jim McMenamin and Larry McCaffery in *Across the Wounded Galaxies*, ed. Larry McCaffery (Champaign: University of Illinois Press, 1990).
47. WSB, *The Western Lands*, 25.
48. WSB interviewed by James Fox, *Sunday Times Magazine*, March 22, 1987.
49. Saint-John Perse, *Anabasis*, 10.
50. "Journey Through Time-Space," WSB interviewed by Daniel Odier, *Evergreen Review* vol. 13, no. 67 (June 1969).
51. WSB, *The Western Lands*, 3.
52. Ibid., 74–75.
53. Ibid., 235.
54. Ibid., 42.
55. Ibid., 171.
56. Ibid., 37.
57. Ibid., 40.
58. Ibid., 63.
59. Ibid., 134.
60. Ibid., 45.
61. Ibid., 258.

Chapter Fifty-One

1. Denton Welch, *In Youth Is Pleasure*, 128.
2. WSB, *Word Virus*, 413.
3. "Shooting Gallery," WSB interviewed by Lucinda Bredin, *Evening Standard*, June 2, 1988.
4. See WSB and Philip Taaffe, *Drawing Dialogue* (New York: Pat Hearn Gallery, 1987), a transcription of a dialogue recorded while they drew pictures together on February 1, 1987.
5. WSB interviewed by the author, November 29, 1991.
6. "William S. Burroughs: Afterlife," WSB interviewed by Eldon Garnet, *Impulse* (Toronto), February 25, 2008.
7. Ibid.
8. "Entrance to the Museum of Lost Species," in the catalog to WSB's show at the Tony Shafrazi Gallery, December 19, 1987–January 24, 1988.
9. Ibid.
10. "Painting isn't an aesthetic operation; it's a form of magic designed as mediator between this strange hostile world and us." Pablo Picasso, source unknown.
11. From a letter written at Castle Boisgeloup (Winter 1934), quoted in Richard Friedenthal, ed., *Letters of the Great Artists: From Blake to Pollock* (London, Thames & Hudson, 1963), 257–58.
12. WSB interviewed by the author, November 29, 1991.
13. Ibid.
14. WSB interviewed by Simone Ellis, *Contemporanea*, no. 23 (December 1990).
15. "Shooting Gallery," WSB interviewed by Lucinda Bredin, *Evening Standard*, June 2, 1988.
16. WSB interviewed by Kristine McKenna, *Los Angeles Times*, July 14, 1996.
17. Gus Van Sant, author essay, Random House website.
18. Gus Van Sant interviewed by Alex Simon, *Venice* magazine, December 1997.

19. Gus Van Sant interviewed by Scott Tobias, March 5, 2003, A.V. Club, http://www
.avclub.com/articles/gus-van-sant,13800 (accessed February 2013).
20. Raymond Foye to Ted Morgan, Morgan papers, "79. Wm Seventies. Raymond Foye."
21. Marcus Ewert, "In Bed with Burroughs," http://www.lawrence.com/news/2007/
jul/30/bed_burroughs (accessed October 2013).
22. Ibid.
23. Ibid.
24. Ibid.
25. WSB, *My Education*, 99.
26. The 1821 opera of the same name by Carl Maria von Weber, with a libretto by Fried-
rich Kind, is based on the same story.
27. WSB, "George Schmid," in the program for *The Black Rider*, Hamburg, March 31, 1990.
28. WSB interviewed by Klaus Maeck, *Kozmik Blues*, 9–15, special William Burroughs
issue, 1990.
29. ftp://nmedia.net/pub/old/wsb/black-rider.html (accessed January 2013).
30. These artworks are reproduced in the book *Paper Cloud Thick Pages* (Kyoto: Kyoto
Shoin International, 1992).
31. WSB, *Paper Cloud Thick Pages* (not paginated).
32. WSB interviewed by Victor Bockris, fall 1990.
33. WSB, *My Education*, 101.
34. Ibid.
35. WSB, *Last Words*, 81.

Chapter Fifty-Two

1. Morgan, tape 14.
2. Ira Silverberg, *Everything Is Permitted*, 15.
3. Chris Peachment, "A Trip to the Interzone," *Independent on Sunday*, June 30, 1991.
4. Morgan, tape 23.
5. WSB to the author, Lawrence, Kansas, 1991.
6. See the interview with Tom Peschio, Reality Studio, http://realitystudio.org/
biography/hikuta (accessed January 2013).
7. Frank Tankard, "The Inner Circle," July 30, 2007, http://www.lawrence.com/
news/2007/jul/30/inner_circle (accessed January 2013).
8. Jim McCrary, "Remembering William Burroughs and Allen Ginsberg," Beats in Kansas: The Beat Generation in the Heartland, http://www.vlib.us/beats/mccrary.html
(accessed January 2013).
9. Interview with David Ohle, *Lawrence Journal-World*, September 28, 2006, http://
www2.ljworld.com/chats/2006/sep/28/david_ohle (accessed January 2013).
10. Jim McCrary interviewed by the author, March 2013.
11. Ibid.
12. WSB, *My Education*, 185.
13. James Grauerholz in WSB, *Word Virus*, 412.
14. Tom Peschio interviewed by the author, March 2013.
15. "The War Universe," WSB interviewed by Raymond Foye, *Grand Street*, no. 37 (1991).
16. WSB interviewed by Nicholas Zurbrugg, June 10, 1991, *21c magazine*, http://www.
21cmagazine.com/William-S-Burroughs-Matter-of-Lemurs (accessed January 2013).
17. Ibid.
18. "The Return of the Invisible Man," WSB interviewed by James Fox, *Sunday Times
Magazine*, March 22, 1987.
19. WSB, *My Education*, 108.
20. "An Ex-Junkie Exterminator," WSB interviewed by Lynn Snowden, *Guardian*, April 25,
1992.
21. WSB, *My Education*, 173.

22. WSB, *The Western Lands*, 165.
23. WSB, *My Education*, 25.
24. Ibid., 32.
25. Ibid., 101–2.
26. Ibid., 129.
27. Ibid., 47.
28. Ibid., 131.
29. Kurt Cobain, *Journals* (New York: Riverhead, 2003), quoted at Reality Studio, http://realitystudio.org/biography/william-s-burroughs-and-kurt-cobain-a-dossier (accessed January 2013).
30. Charles R. Cross, *Heavier Than Heaven: A Biography of Kurt Cobain* (New York: Hyperion, 2002), quoted at ibid.
31. Carrie Borzillo, *Nirvana: The Day-by-Day Eyewitness Chronicle* (New York: Thunder's Mouth, 2000), quoted at ibid.
32. Martin Clarke, ed., *The Cobain Dossier* (London: Plexus, 2006), quoted at ibid.
33. Christopher Sandford, *Kurt Cobain* (New York: Carroll & Graf, 1996), quoted at ibid. (accessed January 2013).
34. Fresh Sounds FS 201.
35. WSB interviewed by *LA Weekly*, July 19, 1996.
36. T. S. Eliot, *The Waste Land*, line 63.
37. WSB, *Last Words*, 146–47.
38. Wilborn Hampton, "Allen Ginsberg, Master Poet of Beat Generation, Dies at 70," *New York Times*, April 6, 1997.
39. WSB, *Last Words*, 177.
40. Perhaps the light bulb was a reference to Bob Dylan's famous 1965 London press conference in which he carried a huge light bulb and advised the press, "Keep a good head and always carry a light bulb."
41. Tom Peschio interviewed by the author, March 2013.
42. "Ever See Burroughs in Person?," Reality Studio, http://realitystudio.org/forum/viewtopic.php?f=1&t=5&start=15 (accessed January 2013).
43. José Ferez in a recorded conversation with the author, London, 2000.
44. Online and in the booklet accompanying *The Best of William Burroughs* box set, which, as an authorized release, gives the reader the impression that the texts in the booklet are also approved by the Burroughs estate.

Endwords

1. Gerard Malanga, "William Burroughs, an Interview by Gerard Malanga," *The Beat Book* vol. 4 (California, PA, 1974), 100, 102.
2. Published as *Love and Napalm: Export USA* by Grove in the United States.
3. William Gibson, "God's Little Toys," *Wired* 13.07 (July 2005).
4. David Sinclair, "Station to Station," *Rolling Stone*, no. 658 (June 10, 1993) (accessed June 2013).
5. Jon Savage, "Oh! You Pretty Things," in Martin Roth, ed., *David Bowie Is Inside* (London: Victoria & Albert Museum, 2013), 103.
6. *Double Bill* (Toronto), nos. 1–4 (1993–94).
7. "W. S. Burroughs Alias Inspector J. Lee of the Nova Police," WSB interviewed in *Friends*, no. 5 (April 14, 1970).
8. "Back to Dig the Home Scene" WSB interviewed by Dickson Terry, *St. Louis Post-Dispatch*, [January] 1965.
9. WSB, *Last Words*, 167.
10. Ibid., 244.
11. Interview with the author, March 2013.
12. WSB, "Some memories, unclarified drafts" (unpublished).

Bibliography

Books by William S. Burroughs

Junkie: Confessions of an Unredeemed Drug Addict. New York: Ace, 1953 (bound together with *Narcotic Agent* by Maurice Helbrant).

The Naked Lunch. Paris: Olympia, 1959.

(With Brion Gysin, Gregory Corso, and Sinclair Beiles) *Minutes to Go.* Paris: Two Cities, 1960.

(With Brion Gysin) *The Exterminator.* San Francisco: Auerhahn, 1960.

The Soft Machine. Paris: Olympia, 1961 (first version).

Naked Lunch. New York: Grove, 1962 (earlier draft text).

The Ticket That Exploded. Paris: Olympia, 1962 (first version).

Dead Fingers Talk. London: John Calder, 1963.

(With Allen Ginsberg) *The Yage Letters.* San Francisco: City Lights, 1963.

Roosevelt After Inauguration. New York: Fuck You Press, 1964.

Nova Express. New York: Grove, 1964.

Time. New York: "C," 1965.

APO-33. San Francisco: Beach Books, Texts & Documents, 1966 (first issued by the Fuck You Press in New York but only about a dozen copies made).

The Soft Machine. New York: Grove, 1966 (second version).

(With Claude Pélieu) *So Who Owns Death TV?* San Francisco: Beach Books, Texts & Documents, 1967.

The Ticket That Exploded. New York: Grove, 1967 (second version).

The Soft Machine. London: Calder & Boyars, 1968 (third version).

The Dead Star. San Francisco: Nova Broadcast, 1969.

Entretiens avec William Burroughs. Paris: Pierre Belfond, 1969 (*The Job*, first version).

The Job. New York: Grove, 1970 (second version).

The Last Words of Dutch Schultz. London: Cape Goliard, 1970.

(With Claude Pélieu) *Jack Kerouac.* Paris: L'Herne, 1971.

Ali's Smile. Brighton: Unicorn, 1971.

The Wild Boys. New York: Grove, 1971.

Electronic Revolution. Cambridge, UK: Blackmoor Head, 1971.

Exterminator! New York: Viking, 1973.

White Subway. London: Aloes seolA, 1973.

Mayfair Acadamy Series More or Less. n.p. [London]: Urgency Press Rip-Off, 1973.

Port of Saints. London: Covent Garden, 1973 (first version).

The Job. New York: Grove, 1974 (revised, enlarged version).

(With Eric Mottram) *Snack.* London: Aloes, 1975.

(With Bob Gale) *The Book of Breeething.* Berkeley, CA: Blue Wind, 1975.

(With Charles Gatewood) *Sidetripping.* New York: Strawberry Hill, 1975.

The Retreat Diaries. New York: City Moon, 1976.

Cobble Stone Gardens. Cherry Valley, NY: Cherry Valley, 1976.

Bibliography

(With Brion Gysin) *Le Colloque de Tanger*. Paris: Christian Bourgeois, 1976 (texts by WSB and proceedings of the conference).

Junky. New York: Penguin, 1977 (second version).

(With Brion Gysin) *The Third Mind*. New York: Viking, 1978.

Ali's Smile/Naked Scientology. Bonn: Expanded Media Editions, 1978.

Letters to Allen Ginsberg, 1953–1957. Geneva: Editions Claude Givaudan/Am Here Books, 1978.

Where Naked Troubadours Shoot Snotty Baboons. Northridge, CA: Lord John Press, 1978 (broadside).

Roosevelt After Inauguration. San Francisco: City Lights, 1979 (second version).

(With Brion Gysin and Gérard-George Lemaire) *Le Colloque de Tanger 2*. Paris: Christian Bourgois, 1979 (texts by WSB and proceedings of the conference).

Wouldn't You Polish Pine Floors. . . . West Branch, IA: Toothpaste, 1979 (broadside).

Blade Runner (a Movie). Berkeley, CA: Blue Wind, 1979.

Doctor Benway. Santa Barbara, CA: Bradford Morrow, 1979.

Ah Pook Is Here. London: Calder, 1979.

Port of Saints. Berkeley: Blue Wind, 1980 (second version).

The Streets of Chance. New York: Red Ozier, 1981.

Cities of the Red Night. New York: Holt, Rinehart & Winston, 1981.

Early Routines. Santa Barbara, CA: Cadmus, 1981.

Sinki's Sauna. New York: Pequod, 1982.

A William Burroughs Reader. Edited by John Calder. London: Picador, 1982.

The Place of Dead Roads. New York: Holt, Rinehart & Winston, 1983.

Ruski. New York: Hand Job, 1984.

The Four Horsemen of the Apocalypse. Bonn: EME, 1984.

The Burroughs File. San Francisco: City Lights, 1984.

The Adding Machine: Collected Essays. London: John Calder, 1985.

Queer. New York: Viking, 1985.

The Cat Inside. New York: Grenfell, 1986.

The Western Lands. New York: Viking, 1987.

The Whole Tamale. n.p. [London]: Horse Press, n.d. (pamphlet).

(With Keith Haring) *Apocalypse*. New York: Mulder Fine Arts, 1988.

Interzone. New York: Viking, 1989.

(With S. Clay Wilson) *Tornado Alley*. Cherry Valley, NY: Cherry Valley, 1989.

(With Keith Haring) *The Valley*. New York: George Mulder Fine Arts, 1990 (illustrated fine art portfolio).

(With George Condo) *Ghost of Chance*. New York: Whitney Museum, 1991 (illustrated fine art portfolio).

Seven Deadly Sins. New York: Lococo-Mulder Fine Art, 1991.

Painting and Guns. New York: Hanuman, 1992.

The Letters of William S. Burroughs, 1945 to 1959. Edited by Oliver Harris. London: Picador, 1993.

Photos and Remembering Jack Kerouac. Louisville, KY: White Fields, 1994 (pamphlet).

Ghost of Chance. New York: High Risk, 1995 (without the Condo illustrations).

My Education. New York: Viking, 1995.

Pantopon Rose. Charleston, WV: Parchment Gallery Graphics, 1995 (broadside).

Word Virus. Edited by James Grauerholz. New York: Grove, 1998.

A Spiritual Exercise. Boulder, CO: Kavyayantra, 1998 (broadside).

Last Words. New York: Grove, 2000.

Words of Advice for Young People. Encinitas, CA: FreeThought, 2001 (small edition pamphlet).

Naked Lunch: The Restored Text. New York: Grove, 2001 (second U.S. version).

Everything Lost: The Latin American Notebook of William S. Burroughs. Columbus: Ohio State University Press, 2008.

Bibliography

(With Jack Kerouac) *And the Hippos Were Boiled in Their Tanks.* New York: Grove, 2008.
Rub Out the Words: The Letters of William S. Burroughs, 1959–1974. Edited by Bill Morgan. New York: HarperCollins, 2012.

Books by William S. Burroughs Jr.

Speed. New York: Olympia, 1970.
Kentucky Ham. New York: E. P. Dutton, 1973.
Kentucky Ham. Woodstock, NY: Overlook, 1984 (with WSB afterword).
Cursed from Birth: The Short, Unhappy Life of William S. Burroughs Jr. Edited and compiled by David Ohle. Brooklyn, NY: Soft Skull, 2000.

Books About William Seward Burroughs

Ambrose, Joe, Terry Wilson, and Frank Rynne. *Man from Nowhere: Storming the Citadels of Enlightenment with William Burroughs and Brion Gysin.* Dublin: The Gap/Subliminal, 1992.
[Anon.]. *William S. Burroughs: Naked Biography,* n.p.: Filiquarian, 2008.
Ansen, Alan. *William Burroughs.* Sudbury, CT: Water Row, 1986.
Baker, Phil. *William S. Burroughs.* London: Reaktion, Critical Lives Series, 2010.
Bockris, Victor. *With William Burroughs: A Report from the Bunker.* New York: Seaver, 1981.
———. *William Burroughs: Cool Cats, Furry Cats, Aliens, but No Purring.* New York: (privately printed in an edition of 100 copies), 1991.
Bridgett, Rob. *The Cinematic Experiments of William Burroughs, Brion Gysin, and Antony Balch.* Binley Woods near Coventry: Beat Scene, 2003.
Burroughs, William S. (with Brion Gysin). *Le Colloque de Tanger.* Paris: Christian Bourgois, 1976 (texts by WSB and proceedings of the conference).
———(with Brion Gysin and Gérard-George Lemaire). *Le Colloque de Tanger 2.* Paris: Christian Bourgois, 1979 (texts by WSB and proceedings of the conference).
Caveney, Graham. *The "Priest," They Called Him: The Life and Legacy of William S. Burroughs.* London: Bloomsbury, 1998.
Cecil, Paul, ed. *A William Burroughs Birthday Book.* Brighton, UK: Temple Press, 1994.
Cook, Ralph T., compiler. *William S. Burroughs: A Checklist of Magazine/Periodical Appearances.* San Diego: Atticus, 1980.
Ely, Roger, ed. *The Final Academy: Statements of a Kind.* London: The Final Academy, 1982.
García-Robles, Jorge. *La Bala Perdida: William S. Burroughs en Mexico (1949–52).* Mexico City: Ediciones del Milenio, 1995.
Goodman, Michael B. *William S. Burroughs: An Annotated Bibliography.* New York: Garland, 1975.
———. *Contemporary Literary Censorship: The Case History of Burroughs' "Naked Lunch."* Metuchen, NJ: Scarecrow Press, 1981.
Goodman, Michael B., and Lemuel B. Coley. *William S. Burroughs: A Reference Guide.* New York: Garland, 1990.
Grauerholz, James W. *The Death of Joan Vollmer Burroughs: What Really Happened?* Lawrence: American Studies Dept., University of Kansas, 2002 (not commercially published).
Gysin, Brion. *Brion Gysin Let the Mice In.* West Glover, VT: Something Else, 1973.
———(with Terry Wilson). *Here to Go: Planet R-101; Brion Gysin Interviewed by Terry Wilson.* San Francisco: RE/Search, 1982.
Harris, Oliver. *William Burroughs and the Secret of Fascination.* Carbondale: Southern Illinois University Press, 2003.
Harris, Oliver, and Ian MacFadyen, eds. *Naked Lunch @ 50: Anniversary Essays.* Carbondale: Southern Illinois University Press, 2009.
Hibbard, Allen, ed. *Conversations with William S. Burroughs.* Jackson: University Press of Mississippi, 1999.

Bibliography

Hibbard, Allen, and Barry Tharaud, eds. *Bowles/Beats/Tangier*. Denver, Amherst, and Tangier: International Center for Performance Studies, 2010.

Johnson, Rob. *The Lost Years of William S. Burroughs: Beats in South Texas*. College Station: Texas A&M University Press, 2006.

Knight, Michael Muhammad. *William S. Burroughs vs. The Qur'an*. Berkeley, CA: Soft Skull, 2012.

Lemaire, Gérard-Georges. *Burroughs*. Paris: Artifact, 1986.

Long, John. *Drugs and the "Beats": The Role of Drugs in the Lives and Writings of Kerouac, Burroughs, and Ginsberg*. College Station, TX: Virtualbookworm.com, 2005.

Lotringer, Sylvère, ed. *Burroughs Live: The Collected Interviews of William S. Burroughs, 1960–1997*. Los Angeles: Semiotext(e), 2001.

Loydell, Rupert, ed. *my kind of angel: i.m. william burroughs*. Exeter, UK: Stride, 1998.

Lydenberg, Robin. *Word Cultures: Radical Theory and Practice in William S. Burroughs' Fiction*. Urbana: University of Illinois Press, 1987.

Mahoney, Denis, Richard L. Martin, and Ron Whitehead, eds. *A Burroughs Compendium: Calling the Toads*. Antwerp: Fringecore/Ring Tarigh/Hozomeen, 1998.

Maynard, Joe, and Barry Miles. *William S. Burroughs: A Bibliography, 1953–1973*. Charlottesville: University of Virginia Press, 1978.

Mikriammos, Philippe. *William S. Burroughs, la vie et l'oeuvre*. Paris: Seghers, 1975.

Miles, Barry. *A Catalogue of the William S. Burroughs Archive*. Ollon, Switzerland, and London: Am Here and Covent Garden, 1973.

———. *William Burroughs: El Hombre Invisible*. London: Virgin, 1992.

———. *The Beat Hotel: Ginsberg, Burroughs, and Corso in Paris, 1957–1963*. New York: Grove, 2000.

Morgan, Ted. *Literary Outlaw: The Life and Times of William S. Burroughs*. New York: Henry Holt, 1988.

Mottram, Eric. *William Burroughs: The Algebra of Need*. London: Marion Boyars, 1977.

Mullins, Greg A. *Colonial Affairs: Bowles, Burroughs, and Chester Write Tangier*. Madison: University of Wisconsin Press, 2002.

Murphy, Timothy S. *Wising Up the Marks: The Amodern William Burroughs*. Berkeley: University of California Press, 1997.

Robinson, Edward S. *Shift Linguals: Cut-Up Narratives from William S. Burroughs to the Present*. Amsterdam: Rodopi, 2011.

Russell, Jamie. *Queer Burroughs*. New York: Palgrave, 2001.

Schneiderman, Davis, and Philip Walsh, eds. *Retaking the Universe: William S. Burroughs in the Age of Globalization*. London: Pluto, 2004.

Shoaf, Eric C. *Collecting William S. Burroughs in Print: A Checklist*. Rumford, RI: Ratishna, 2000.

———. *William S. Burroughs: Time*Place*Word, an Exhibit at the John Hay Library, Brown University, Providence, Rhode Island*. Providence, RI: Brown University Press, 2000.

Skerl, Jennie. *William S. Burroughs*. Boston: Twayne, 1985.

Skerl, Jennie, and Robin Lydenberg, eds. *William S. Burroughs at the Front: Critical Reception, 1959–1989*. Carbondale: Southern Illinois University Press, 1991.

Stevens, Michael. *A Distant Book Lifted*. Spicewood, TX: Benjiman Spooner, 2001.

Vilà, Christian. *William S. Burroughs, le génie empoisonné*. Paris: Editions du Rocher, 1992.

Weissner, Carl. *Burroughs: Eine Bild-Biographie*. Berlin: Nishen, 1994.

Whitelaw, Robert Menzies. *Themes in the Work of William Burroughs*. PhD thesis, University of Massachusetts, 1970.

Special Issues of Periodicals

Intrepid 14/15 (Fall 1969/70). Special Burroughs Issue.

RE/Search 4/5 (1982). William S. Burroughs/Throbbing Gristle/Brion Gysin.

The Review of Contemporary Fiction, Spring 1984. William S. Burroughs Number.

678

Bibliography

Double Bill 1–4 (n.s. [1992–94?]). A fanzine edited by Jena von Brücker dedicating to prais-
ing Bill "Cannon" Conrad and destroying William Burroughs.
Ashé: Journal of Experimental Spirituality 2, no. 3 (2009). "Playback, the Magick of William
S. Burroughs."

Bibliography of Copies Used (Not Necessarily the First Editions)

St. Louis and Los Alamos

Ackroyd, Peter. *T. S. Eliot: A Life.* New York, Simon & Schuster, 1984.
Allen, Frederick Lewis. *Only Yesterday: An Informal History of the 1920s.* New York: Harper
& Row, 1957.
———. *Since Yesterday: The 1930s in America.* New York: Harper & Row, (1940) 1972.
Black, Jack. *You Can't Win.* New York: Macmillan, 1926.
Burroughs, Laura Lee. *Flower Arranging: A Fascinating Hobby.* 2 vols. Atlanta: Coca-Cola,
1940–41.
———. *Homes and Flowers: Refreshing Arrangements.* Atlanta: Coca-Cola, 1943.
Burroughs, William S. *The Place of Dead Roads.* London: Fourth Estate (HarperCollins),
1983.
Eliot, T. S. *Collected Poems, 1909–1962.* London: Faber, 1974.
Kaplan, Fred. *Gore Vidal: A Biography.* New York: Doubleday, 1999.
Montesi, Albert, and Richard Deposki. *Central West End St. Louis.* Chicago: Arcadia, 2000.
Primm, James Neal. *Lion of the Valley: St. Louis, Missouri, 1764–1980.* St. Louis: Missouri
Historical Society, 1981; 3rd ed., 1998.
Stiles, T. J. *Jesse James: Last Rebel of the Civil War.* New York: Alfred A. Knopf, 2002.
Wilson, Edmund. *The American Earthquake.* Garden City, NY: Doubleday Anchor, 1958.

Harvard

Kittredge, George Lyman. *Witchcraft in Old and New England.* Cambridge, MA: Harvard
University Press, 1929.
Walker, Robert. *New York Inside Out.* New York: Skyline, 1984.
Ware, Caroline F. *Greenwich Village, 1920–1930.* Berkeley: University of California Press,
1994 (reprint from 1935).

Mitteleuropa

Baedeker, Karl. *Austria: Handbook for Travellers.* Leipzig: Karl Baedeker, 1929.
Brittain, Sir Harry. *Austria Invites.* London: Hutchinson, [1936].
Karl, Susanne, and Werner Grand. *Wiener Gastlichkeit: Essen und Trinken in Wien 1.* Erfurt:
Sutton, 2011.
Petschar, Hans, and Herbert Friedlmeier. *Wien: Die Metropole in alten Fotografien.* Wien: Carl
Ueberreuter, 2004.

Chicago

Budge, E. A. Wallis. *An Egyptian Hieroglyphic Dictionary.* 2 vols. London: John Murray, 1920.
Duis, Perry, and Scott LaFrance. *We've Got a Job to Do: Chicagoans and World War II.* Chi-
cago: Chicago Historical Society, 1992.
Mayer, Harold, and Richard Wade. *Chicago: Growth of a Metropolis.* Chicago: University of
Chicago Press, 1969.
Miles, Barry. *In the Seventies.* London: Serpent's Tail, 2011.

Texas

Burroughs, William S. *Junky: The Definitive Text of "Junk."* London: Penguin, 2003.
Grauerholz, James. *The Death of Joan Vollmer Burroughs: What Really Happened?* Lawrence:
American Studies Dept., University of Kansas, 2002 (not commercially published).

Bibliography

Johnson, Rob. *The Lost Years of William S. Burroughs: Beats in South Texas.* College Station: Texas A&M University Press, 2006.

Kerouac, Jack. *On the Road.* London: Penguin Modern Classics, 1991.

Reich, Wilhelm. *The Discovery of the Orgone* vol. 2, *The Cancer Biopathy.* New York: Orgone Institute, 1948.

Wills, David S. "Billy Burroughs: Gentleman Farmer." *Beatdom* 11, 2012.

New Orleans

Nicosia, Gerald, and Anne Marie Santos. *One and Only: The Untold Story of "On the Road."* Berkeley, CA: Viva, 2011.

Mexico and Latin America

Bedford, Sybille. *A Visit to Don Otavio.* London: Collins, 1960 (originally titled *The Sudden View*, 1953).

Burroughs, William S. "George Schmid." In Robert Wilson, Tom Waits, and William Burroughs, *The Black Rider: The Casting of the Magic Bullets.* Program for performance opening, Thalia Theater, Hamburg, March 31, 1990.

———. *Everything Lost: The Latin American Notebook of William S. Burroughs.* Edited by Oliver Harris. Columbus: Ohio State University Press, 2008.

García-Robles, Jorge (with the collaboration of James Grauerholz). *The Wild Shot: William S. Burroughs in Mexico (1949–1952)* (manuscript).

Grauerholz, James. *The Death of Joan Vollmer Burroughs: What Really Happened?* Lawrence: American Studies Dept., University of Kansas, 2002.

Greene, Graham. *The Lawless Roads.* London: William Heinemann, 1939.

Huxley, Aldous. *Beyond the Mexique Bay.* Chicago: Academy, 1985 (1934).

Innes, Hammond. *The Conquistadors.* London: Fontana, 1969.

Isherwood, Christopher. *The Condor and the Cows.* London: Methuen, 1949.

Kerouac, Jack. *Mexico City Blues.* New York: Grove, 1959.

———. *Desolation Angels.* London: Andre Deutsch, 1966.

Lawrence, D. H. *Mornings in Mexico.* Salt Lake City: Gibbs M. Smith, 1982.

———. *The Plumed Serpent.* Harmondsworth, UK: Penguin, 1955.

Lincoln, John. *One Man's Mexico.* London: Bodley Head, 1967.

Solomon, Carl. *Mishaps, Perhaps.* San Francisco: Beach Books, Texts & Documents, 1966.

———. *More Mishaps.* San Francisco: Beach Books, Texts & Documents, 1968.

Stierlin, Henri. *Art of the Maya.* New York: Rizzoli, 1981.

Thompson, J. Eric S. *Maya Hieroglyphs Without Tears.* London: British Museum, 1972.

New York Forties and Fifties

Abbott, Berenice. *Changing New York.* New York: E. P. Dutton, 1939.

Amram, David. *Vibrations.* New York: Macmillan, 1968.

Broyard, Anatole. *Kafka Was the Rage: A Greenwich Village Memoir.* New York: Vintage, 1993.

Burroughs, William S. *Junky: The Definitive Text of "Junk."* London: Penguin, 2003.

Chauncey, George. *Gay New York.* New York: Basic Books, 1994.

Churchill, Allen. *The Improper Bohemians: Greenwich Village in Its Heyday.* New York: Ace Star, 1959.

Gee, Helen. *Limelight: A Greenwich Village Photography Gallery and Coffeehouse in the Fifties.* Albuquerque: University of New Mexico Press, 1997.

Gifford, Barry, and Lee Lawrence. *Jack's Book.* New York: St. Martin's, 1978.

Gold, Herbert. *Bohemia.* New York: Simon & Schuster, 1993.

Golden, Reuel. *New York: Portrait of a City.* Cologne: Taschen, 2010.

Goldstein, Richard. *Helluva Town: The Story of New York City During World War II.* New York: Free Press, 2010.

Gruen, John. *The Party's Over Now*. New York: Viking, 1972.

Harrington, Alan. *The Secret Swinger*. New York: Alfred A. Knopf, 1966 (novel).

Holmes, John C. *Get Home Free*. New York: Dutton, 1964 (novel).

———. *Go*. New York: New American Library, 1980 (novel).

———. *Nothing More to Declare*. New York: Dutton, 1967.

Huncke, Herbert. *Huncke's Journal*. New York: Poets Press, 1965.

———. *Herbert Huncke Special Issue*. California, PA: Unspeakable Visions of the Individual, 1973.

———. *The Evening Sun Turned Crimson*. Cherry Valley, NY: Cherry Valley, 1980.

———. *Guilty of Everything*. New York: Paragon, 1990.

Johnson, Joyce. *Minor Characters*. London: Picador, 1983.

Jones, LeRoi. *The Autobiography of LeRoi Jones/Amiri Baraka*. New York: Freundlich, 1984.

Kazin, Alfred. *Writing Was Everything*. Cambridge, MA: Harvard University Press, 1995.

Kerouac, Jack. *The Subterraneans*. New York: Grove, 1958.

———. *Vanity of Duluoz*. London: Granada, 1982.

———. *Windblown World: The Journals of Jack Kerouac, 1947–1954*. New York: Viking, 2004.

Knight, Brenda. *Women of the Beat Generation*. Berkeley, CA: Conari, 1996.

Krim, Seymour. *Views of a Nearsighted Cannoneer*. London: Alan Ross, 1969.

Malina, Judith. *The Diaries of Judith Malina, 1947–1957*. New York: Grove, 1984.

McDarrah, Fred. *Kerouac and Friends: A Beat Generation Album*. New York: William Morrow, 1985.

McDarrah, Fred, and Gloria McDarrah. *Beat Generation: Glory Days in Greenwich Village*. New York: Schirmer, 1996.

Mezzrow, Mezz, and Bernard Wolfe. *Really the Blues*. New York: Random House, 1946.

Miller, Terry. *Greenwich Village and How It Got That Way*. New York: Crown, 1990.

Monash, Paul. *How Brave We Live*. New York: Charles Scribner's Sons, 1950 (novel).

O'Hara, Frank. "Larry Rivers: A Memoir." In *Frank O'Hara: The Collected Poems*. New York: Alfred A. Knopf, 1971.

Osborne, Charles. *W. H. Auden: The Life of a Poet*. London: Eyre Methuen, 1979.

Peabody, Richard, ed. *A Different Beat: Writings by Women of the Beat Generation*. London: Serpent's Tail, 1997.

Polsky, Ned. *Hustlers, Beats and Others*. New York: Anchor, 1969.

Reich, Wilhelm. *The Function of the Orgasm: Sex-Economic Problems of Biological Energy*. Translated by Theodore P. Wolfe. New York: Orgone Institute, 1942.

Rigney, Francis J., and L. Douglas Smith. *The Real Bohemia*. New York: Basic Books, 1961.

Silver, Nathan. *Lost New York*. New York: Schocken, 1967.

Vidal, Gore. *Palimpsest: A Memoir*. London: Andre Deutsch, 1995.

Wakefield, Dan. *New York in the 50s*. Boston: Houghton Mifflin, 1992.

Wallock, Leonard, ed. *New York: Culture Capital of the World, 1940–1965*. New York: Rizzoli, 1988.

White, Edmund. *Genet: A Biography*. New York: Alfred A. Knopf, 1993.

Wilentz, Elias, ed. *The Beat Scene*. New York: Corinth, 1960.

Wolberg, Lewis R. *Hypnoanalysis*. New York: Grune & Stratton, 1945; 2nd ed., 1964.

Wolf, Daniel, and Ed Fancher, eds. *The Village Voice Reader*. Garden City, NY: Doubleday, 1962.

Tangier

Baichwal, Jennifer, director. *Let It Come Down: The Life of Paul Bowles*. Requisite Productions, 1998 (film documentary).

ben Jelloun, Tahar. *Leaving Tangier*. London: Arcadia, 2009.

Bischoff, Simon, ed. *Paul Bowles Photographs: "How Could I Send a Picture into the Desert?"* Zurich: Scalo, 1994.

Bowles, Jane. *Out in the World: Selected Letters of Jane Bowles, 1935–1970*. Edited by Millicent Dillon. Santa Barbara, CA: Black Sparrow, 1985.

Bibliography

Bowles, Paul. *Their Heads Are Green and Their Hands Are Blue*. New York: Random House, 1963.

———. *Without Stopping: An Autobiography*. New York: G. P. Putnam's Sons, 1972.

———. *In Touch: The Letters of Paul Bowles*. Edited by Jeffrey Miller. New York: Farrar, Straus & Giroux, 1994.

Burroughs, William S. *Letters to Allen Ginsberg, 1953–1957*. Geneva: Editions Claude Givaudan/Am Here Books, 1978.

———. *Recent Paintings Ahmed Yacoubi, July 16–27, 1968*. Tangier: American Library, 1968 (text in exhibition leaflet).

Caponi, Gena Dagel, ed. *Conversations with Paul Bowles*. Jackson: University Press of Mississippi, 1993.

Carr, Virginia Spencer. *Paul Bowles: A Life*. New York: Scribner, 2004.

Choukri, Mohamed. *For Bread Alone*. London: Peter Owen, 1973.

———. *Streetwise*. London: Saqi, 2000.

———. *In Tangier: Paul Bowles, Jean Genet, Tennessee Williams*. London: Telegram, 2008 (collected edition).

Clandermond, Andrew, and Terence MacCarthy. *Hamri, Painter of Morocco*. Tangier: Black Eagle for Lawrence-Arnott Gallery, 2004.

Codrington, Tessa. *Spirits of Tangier*. London: Arcadia, 2008.

Connolly, Cyril. Preface to Robin Maugham, *The Wrong People*. London: Heinemann, 1970 (novel).

Croft-Cooke, Rupert. *The Tangerine House*. London: Macmillan, 1956.

———. *Smiling Damned Villain: The True Story of Paul Axel Lund*. London: Secker & Warburg, 1959.

———. *The Caves of Hercules*. London: W. H. Allen, 1974.

Cumming, Anne [Felicity Mason]. *The Love Quest*. London: Peter Owen, 1991.

Davidson, Michael. *The World, the Flesh and Myself*. London: A. Barker, 1962.

Davis, Stephen. *Jajouka Rolling Stone*. New York: Random House, 1993.

———. *To Marrakech by Aeroplane*. Providence, RI: Inkblot, 2010.

Dillon, Millicent. *A Little Original Sin: The Life and Work of Jane Bowles*. New York: Holt, Rinehart & Winston, 1981.

———. *You Are Not I: A Portrait of Paul Bowles*. Berkeley: University of California Press, 1998.

Edwards, Brian T. *Morocco Bound: Disorienting America's Maghreb, from Casablanca to the Marrakech Express*. Durham, NC: Duke University Press, 2005.

Farson, Daniel. *The Gilded Gutter Life of Francis Bacon*. London: Century, 1993.

Finlayson, Iain. *Tangier: City of the Dream*. London: HarperCollins, 1992.

Gallagher, Charles. Thirty-five articles published between July 23, 1956, and January 8, 1960, by the American Universities Field Staff, posted in the archives of the Institute of Current World Affairs, www.icwa.org (accessed July 2011).

Green, Michelle. *The Dream at the End of the World: Paul Bowles and the Literary Renegades in Tangier*. London: Bloomsbury, 1992.

Gysin, Brion. *Living with Islam*. Providence, RI: Inkblot, 2010.

Harter, Hugh A. *Tangier and All That*. Colorado Springs: Three Continents, 1993.

Hemmer, Kurt. "Aestheticizing the Revoluton: William S. Burroughs in Tangier." In Allen Hibbard and Barry Tharaud, eds., *Bowles/Beats/Tangier*. Denver, Amherst, and Tangier: International Center for Performance Studies, 2010.

Herbert, David. *Second Son: An Autobiography*. London: Peter Owen, 1972.

Hibbard, Allen. *Paul Bowles Magic and Morocco*. Belvedere Tiburon, CA: Cadmus, 2004.

———. "A Moveable Feast." In Allen Hibbard and Barry Tharaud, eds., *Bowles/Beats/Tangier*. Denver, Amherst, and Tangier: International Center for Performance Studies, 2010.

Hopkins, John. *The Tangier Diaries, 1962–1979*. London: Arcadia, 1997.

Bibliography

Kerouac, Jack. *Desolation Angels*. London: Granada, 1972.

———. *Lonesome Traveller*. London: Andre Deutsch, 1962.

Lambert, Gavin. *Mainly About Lindsay Anderson*. London: Faber, 2000.

Lancaster, Marie-Jaqueline. *Brian Howard: Portrait of a Failure*. London: Timewell, 2005.

Landau, Rom. *Portrait of Tangier*. London: Robert Hale, 1952.

Leary, Timothy. *High Priest*. New York: New American Library, 1968.

———. *Flashbacks: An Autobiography*. Los Angeles: J. P. Tarcher, 1983.

Lee, Martin A., and Bruce Shlain. *Acid Dreams: The CIA, LSD and the Sixties Rebellion*. New York: Grove, 1985.

Lilius, Aleko. *Turbulent Tangier*. London: Elek, 1956.

Lithgow, William. *The Total Discourse of the Rare Adventures and Painful Peregrinations of Long Nineteen Years Travayles*. 1632; reprint, Glasgow: James MacLehose, 1906.

Maxwell, Gavin. *Lords of the Atlas*. London: Longmans Green, 1966.

Miller, Jeffrey. *Paul Bowles: A Descriptive Bibliography*. Santa Barbara, CA: Black Sparrow, 1986.

Morgan, Ted. *Rowing Toward Eden*. New York: Houghton Mifflin, 1981.

Mrabet, Mohammed. *Look & Move On*. Santa Barbara, CA: Black Sparrow, 1976.

Mullins, Greg A. *Colonial Affairs: Bowles, Burroughs, and Chester Write Tangier*. Madison: University of Wisconsin Press, 2002.

Pulsifer, Gary, ed. *Paul Bowles by His Friends*. London: Peter Owen, 1992.

Richardson, Colonel Gerald. *Crime Zone*. London: John Long, 1959.

Rogerson, Barnaby. *Morocco*. London: Cadogan, 1994.

Rumney, Ralph. *The Consul*. San Francisco: City Lights, 2002.

Said, Edward. *Orientalism*. New York: Vintage, 1979.

Sawyer-Lauçanno, Christopher. *An Invisible Spectator: A Biography of Paul Bowles*. London: Bloomsbury, 1989.

Seitz, William C. *The Art of Assemblage*. New York: Museum of Modern Art, 1961.

Sinclair, Andrew. *Francis Bacon: His Life and Violent Times*. New York: Crown, 1993.

Taylor, Lance. *The Sultan's Gift: A History of St. Andrew's Church, Tangier, 1881–2006*. Tangier: privately printed, 2005.

Vaidon, Lawdom [David Woolman]. *Tangier: A Different Way*. Metuchen, NJ: Scarecrow, 1977.

Wall, Anthony, director. *Bacon Meets Burroughs*. BBC *Arena*, November 20, 1982 (TV documentary, not broadcast).

Wanklyn, Christopher. "Notes from Morocco." *Paris Review* 12 (Spring 1956).

Whitaker, Brian. *Unspeakable Love: Gay and Lesbian Life in the Middle East*. London: Saqi, 2006; revised 2011.

Wilson, Peter Lamborn. *Pirate Utopias: Moorish Corsairs and European Renegadoes*. New York: Autonomedia, 1995, 2003 (2nd revised ed.).

Wishart, Michael. *High Diver*. London: Blond & Briggs, 1977.

Woolman, David. *Stars in the Firmament: Tangier Characters, 1660–1960*. Pueblo, CO: Passeggiata, 1998.

Zwart, Piet. *Piet Zwart Retrospektive Fotografie*. Düsseldorf: Edition Marzona, 1981.

Beat Hotel

[Anon.]. *A Bibliography of the Auerhahn Press and Its Successor Dave Haselwood Books Compiled by a Printer*. Berkeley, CA: Poltroon Press, 1976.

Beiles, Sinclair [as Malcolm Nesbit]. *Chariot of Flesh*. Paris: Olympia, 1955.

———[as Wu Wu Meng]. *Houses of Joy*. Paris: Olympia, 1958.

Binet, Hervé, ed. [festschrift]. *Brion Gysin*. Paris: Cactus/Editions 23/Paris Musées, 1993.

Brassaï. *Henry Miller: The Paris Years*. New York: Arcade, 1995.

Buchwald, Art. *I'll Always Have Paris! A Memoir*. New York: Putnam, 1996.

Campbell, James. *Paris Interzone*. London: Secker & Warburg, 1994.

Chapman, Harold. *The Beat Hotel*. Montpellier: Gris Banal, 1984.

Bibliography

——. *Beats à Paris: Paris und die Dichter der Beatgeneration, 1957–1963*. Hamburg: Kellner, 2001.

Clay, Steven, and Rodney Phillips. *A Secret Location on the Lower East Side*. New York: New York Public Library, 1998.

Corso, Gregory. *The American Express*. Paris: Olympia, 1961.

——.*The Riverside Interviews 3: Gregory Corso*. London: Binnacle, 1982.

——. *An Accidental Autobiography: The Selected Letters of Gregory Corso*. Edited by Bill Morgan. New York: New Directions, 2003.

Cummiskey, Gary, and Eva Kowalska, eds. *Who Was Sinclair Beiles?* Sandton, South Africa: Dye Hard, 2009.

De St. Jorre, John. *The Good Ship Venus: The Erotic Voyage of the Olympia Press*. London: Hutchinson, 1994.

Ferrari-Adler, Jenni, ed. *Alone in the Kitchen with an Eggplant*. New York: Riverhead, 2007.

Fitch, Noël Riley. *Literary Cafes of Paris*. Montgomery, AL: Starrhill, 1989.

Geiger, John. *Nothing Is True, Everything Is Permitted: The Life of Brion Gysin*. New York: Disinformation, 2005.

Gilmore, John. *Laid Bare: A Memoir of Wrecked Lives and the Hollywood Death Trip*. Los Angeles: Amok, 1997.

Ginsberg, Allen. *Indian Journals*. San Francisco: City Lights, 1970.

——. *Journals Mid-Fifties, 1954–1958*. New York: HarperCollins, 1995.

Ginsberg, Allen, and Peter Orlovsky. *Straight Hearts' Delight: Love Poems and Selected Letters*. Edited by Winston Leyland. San Francisco: Gay Sunshine, 1980.

Glass, Charles. *Americans in Paris*. London: Harper, 2009.

Gold, Herbert. *Bohemia: Where Art, Angst, Love, and Strong Coffee Meet*. New York: Simon & Schuster, 1993.

——.*Brion Gysin Let the Mice In*. West Glover, VT: Something Else, 1973.

——(with Terry Wilson). *Here to Go: Planet R-101*. San Francisco: RE/Search, 1982.

——. *Légendes de Brion Gysin*, Montpellier: Gris Banal, 1983.

——. *The Last Museum*. London: Faber & Faber, 1986.

Gysin, Brion. *Who Runs May Read*. Oakland, CA: Inkblot, 2000.

Hillairet, Jacques. *Dictionnaire historique des rues de Paris*. Paris: Editions Princesse, 1973.

Hussey, Andrew. *Paris: The Secret History*. London: Viking, 2006.

——.""Paris Is About the Last Place…': William Burroughs in and out of Paris and Tangier, 1958–1960." In Allen Hibbard and Barry Tharaud, eds., *Bowles/Beats/Tangier*. Denver, Amherst, and Tangier: International Center for Performance Studies, 2010.

Johnson, Diane. *Into a Paris Quartier*. Washington, DC: National Geographic, 2005.

Jones, Colin. *Paris: Biography of a City*. London: Allen Lane, 2004.

Karnow, Stanley. *Paris in the Fifties*. New York: Times Books, 1997.

Kearney, Patrick J. *The Paris Olympia Press: An Annotated Bibliography*. London: Black Spring, 1987.

——. *The Paris Olympia Press*. Edited by Angus Carroll. Revised and expanded ed. Liverpool: Liverpool University Press, 2007.

Lennon, Peter. *Foreign Correspondent: Paris in the Sixties*. London: Picador, 1994.

Mercer, Jeremy. *Books, Baguettes and Bedbugs: The Left Bank World of Shakespeare and Co.* London: Weidenfeld & Nicolson, 2005.

Miles, Barry. *The Beat Hotel: Ginsberg, Burroughs and Corso in Paris, 1957–1963*. New York: Grove, 2000.

Nin, Anaïs. *Paris Revisited*. Paris: Alyscamps, 2011.

Norse, Harold. *Beat Hotel*. San Diego: Atticus, 1983.

Sawyer-Lauçanno, Christopher. *The Continual Pilgrimage: American Writers in Paris, 1944–1960*. London: Bloomsbury, 1992.

Seaver, Richard. *The Tender Hour of Twilight: Paris in the '50s, New York in the '60s; A Memoir of Publishing's Golden Age*. New York: Farrar, Straus & Giroux, 2012.

Bibliography

Stern, Jacques. *The Fluke*. Reality Studio, realitystudio.org/publications/jacques-stern/the-fluke (accessed February 2012).

Van der Elsken, Ed. *Love on the Left Bank*. London: Andre Deutsch, 1956; facsimile ed., Stockport: Dewi Lewis, 1999.

Vian, Boris. *Manual of Saint-Germain-des-Prés*. New York: Rizzoli, 2005.

Walter, W. Grey. *The Living Brain*. London: Duckworth, 1953.

Webster, Paul, and Nicholas Powell. *Saint-Germain-des-Prés: French Post-War Culture from Sartre to Bardot*. London: Constable, 1984.

White, Edmund. *The Flaneur*. London: Bloomsbury, 2001.

Cut-Ups

Barthes, Roland. *Image-Music-Text*. London: Fontana, 1977.

Bellos, David. *Is That a Fish in Your Ear?* London: Penguin, 2011.

Fallows, Colin, and Synne Genzmer, eds. *Cut-Ups, Cut-Ins, Cut-Outs: The Art of William S. Burroughs*. Vienna: Kunsthalle Wien, 2012.

Foucault, Michel. *The Archaeology of Knowledge and the Discourse on Language*. New York: Pantheon, 1972.

Robinson, Edward S. *Shift Linguals: Cut-Up Narratives from William S. Burroughs to the Present*. Amsterdam: Rodopi, 2011.

Hasan-i-Sabbah

Bouthoul, Betty. *Le grand maître des assassins*. Paris: A. Colin, 1936.

———. *Le vieux de la montagne*. Paris: Gallimard, 1958 (revised edition of the above).

Knight, Michael Muhammad. *William S. Burroughs vs. The Qur'an*. Berkeley, CA: Soft Skull, 2012.

Polo, Marco. *The Travels*. London: Wordsworth, 1997 (1818 translation of 1553 Italian edition).

Stark, Freya. *The Valleys of the Assassins*. London: John Murray, 1934.

von Hammer, Joseph. *The History of the Assassins*. London: Smith & Elder, 1835.

Willey, Peter. *The Castles of the Assassins*. London: George G. Harrap, 1963.

Naked Lunch

Burroughs, William S. *The Naked Lunch*. Paris: Olympia, 1959.

———. *Naked Lunch*. New York: Grove, 1962.

de Grazia, Edward, *Girls Lean Back Everywhere: The Law of Obscenity and the Assault on Genius*. New York: Random House, 1992.

di Prima, Diane. *Memoirs of a Beatnik*. New York: Olympia, 1969

di Prima, Diane, and LeRoi Jones, eds. *The Floating Bear: A Newsletter, 1–37*. La Jolla, CA: Laurence McGilvery, 1973 (reprint in one volume).

Ebin, David, ed. *The Drug Experience*. New York: Orion, 1961.

Goodman, Michael Barry. *Contemporary Literary Censorship: The Case History of Burroughs' "Naked Lunch."* Metuchen, NJ: Scarecrow, 1981.

Harris, Oliver, and Ian MacFadyen, eds. *Naked Lunch @ 50: Anniversary Essays*. Carbondale: Southern Illinois University Press, 2009.

"King of the YADS." *Time*, November 30, 1962.

Maurer, David W. *The Big Con: The Story of the Confidence Man and the Confidence Trick*. Indianapolis: Bobbs-Merrill, 1940.

Rosenthal, Irving. *Sheeper*. New York: Grove, 1967.

Scientology

Atack, Jon. *A Piece of Blue Sky: Scientology, Dianetics and L. Ron Hubbard Exposed*. New York: Lyle Stuart, 1990.

Bibliography

Burroughs, William S. "Parenthetically 7 Hertz." *Klacto* 23 (September 1967) (Heidelberg).
———. "Bulletin 2: The Engram Theory." *Mayfair* 2, no. 11 (November 1967).
———. "Bulletin 4: Scientology Revisited." *Mayfair* 3, no. 1 (January 1968).
———. "Bulletin 17: The Brain Grinders." *Mayfair* 4, no. 4 (April 1969).
———. "Bulletin 18: I'm Scared, I'm Scared, I'm Not." *Mayfair* 4, no. 5 (May 1969).
———. "On the E-Meter." *Intrepid* 14/15 (Winter 1969) (Buffalo, NY).
———. "Burroughs on Scientology." *Los Angeles Free Press*, March 6, 1970.
———. "...And a Final Word from Willliam Burroughs." *Mayfair* 5, no. 6 (June 1970).
———. "Inside Scientology." *Rolling Stone*, October 26, 1972 (book review)
———. *Ali's Smile/Naked Scientology*. Bonn: Expanded Media Editions, 1978.
———. *The Job*. Revised ed. New York: Penguin, 1989.
Kaufman, Robert, *Inside Scientology*. New York: Olympia, 1972.
Norse, Harold. *Memoirs of a Bastard Angel*. New York: William Morrow, 1989.
Vosper, Cyril. *The Mind Benders*. London: Neville Spearman, 1971.
Wikipedia entry, "Scientology," and many associated links (accessed November 2011).

London

Allsop, Kenneth. *Scan*. London: Hodder & Stoughton, 1965.
Bartie, Angela, and Eleanor Bell, eds. *The International Writers' Conference Revisited: Edin-burgh, 1962*. Glasgow: Cargo, 2012.
Boggan, Steve, and Paul Lashmar. "The Great and No-So-Goodman." *Independent*, January 18, 1999.
———. "Goodman Stole Peer's Cash to Give to Labour." *Independent*, January 18, 1999.
———. "Labour Ministers Got Stolen Money." *Independent*, January 19, 1999.
Brown, Mick. "William Burroughs, by Royal Appointment." *Telegraph*, January 16, 2009.
Burgess, Anthony. *You've Had Your Time*. London: Heinemann, 1990.
Burroughs, William S. "Switch On and Be Your Own Hero" [the "Joe and John Routine"]. *Mayfair* 3, no. 6 (June 1968).
Calder, John. *Pursuit: The Uncensored Memoirs of John Calder*. London: John Calder, 2001.
Campbell, Allan, and Tim Niel, eds. *A Life in Pieces: Reflections on Alexander Trocchi*. Edinburgh: Rebel Inc., 1997.
Colacello, Bob. *Holy Terror: Andy Warhol Close Up*. New York: HarperCollins, 1990.
Copetas, E. Craig. "Beat Godfather Meets Glitter Mainman." *Rolling Stone*, no. 155 (February 28, 1974).
Davies, Sydney R. *Walking the London Scene: Five Walks in the Footsteps of the Beat Generation*. Glasgow: Grimsay, 2006.
Gay, Hannah. *The History of Imperial College London, 1907–2007*. London: Imperial College Press, 2007.
Faithfull, Marianne. *Faithfull*. London: Michael Joseph, 1994.
———. *Memories, Dreams and Reflections*. London: Fourth Estate, 2007.
Fallowell, Duncan, and April Ashley. *April Ashley's Odyssey*. London: Jonathan Cape, 1982.
Farren, Mick. *Give the Anarchist a Cigarette*. London: Jonathan Cape, 2001.
Green, Jonathon. *Days in the Life: Voices from the English Underground, 1961–1971*. London: Heinemann, 1988.
Giuliano, Geoffrey. *Blackbird: The Life and Times of Paul McCartney*. New York: Dutton, 1991.
Guilbaut, Serge. *How New York Stole the Idea of Modern Art: Abstract Expressionism, Freedom, and the Cold War*. Chicago: University of Chicago Press, 1983.
Guthrie, Hammond. *AsEverWas: Memoirs of a Beat Survivor*. London: SAF, 2002.
Hollingshead, Michael. *The Man Who Turned on the World*. London: Blond & Briggs, 1973.
Keeler, Christine. *The Truth at Last*. London: Sidgwick & Jackson, 2001.
Manso, Peter. *Mailer: His Life and Times*. New York: Simon & Schuster, 1985.
Masterton, Graham. *Rules of Duel*. Prestatyn, Denbighshire, UK: Telos, 2010 (1970).

Melly, Diana. *Take a Girl Like Me*. London: Chatto & Windus, 2005.

Miles, Barry. *Paul McCartney: Many Years from Now*. London: Secker & Warburg, 1997.

———. *In the Sixties*. London: Jonathan Cape, 2002.

———. *In the Seventies*. London: Serpent's Tail, 2011.

Nuttall, Jeff. *Bomb Culture*. London: MacGibbon & Kee, 1968.

Pevsner, Nikolaus. *London* vol. 2. Harmondsworth, UK: Penguin, 1952.

Pountain, Dick, and David Robins. *Cool Rules: Anatomy of an Attitude*. London: Reaktion, 2000.

Sargeant, Jack. *Naked Lens: Beat Cinema*. London: Creation, 1997.

Saunders, Frances Stonor. *Who Paid the Piper? The CIA and the Cultural Cold War*. London: Granta, 2000.

Taylor, Derek. *It Was 20 Years Ago Today*. London: Bantam, 1987.

Teeuwen, Dave. "Interview with Graham Masterton on William S. Burroughs." http://realitystudio.org/interviews/interview-with-graham-masterton-on-william-s-burroughs (accessed August 2013).

Vyner, Harriet. *Groovy Bob: The Life and Times of Robert Fraser*. London: Faber, 1999.

Warhol, Andy, and Pat Hackett. *POPism: The Warhol '60s*. London: Hutchinson, 1980.

White, Michael. "Goodman, Rotund Fixer Who Stole a Round Million." *Guardian*, January 18, 1999.

Wishart, Michael. *High Diver*. London: Blond & Briggs, 1977.

Wollen, Peter. *Paris Hollywood: Writings on Film*. London: Verso, 2002.

Chicago Police Riot

Berendt, John. "Hog-Wild in the Streets." In Walter Schneir, ed., *Telling It Like It Was: The Chicago Riots*. New York: Signet, 1969.

White, Edmund. *Genet: A Biography*. New York: Alfred A. Knopf, 1993.

New York

Bockris, Victor. *With William Burroughs: A Report from the Bunker*. New York: Seaver, 1981.

———. *Beat Punks*. New York: Da Capo, 2000.

Burroughs, William S. *Cities of the Red Night*. London: Picador, 1982.

Clay, Steven, and Rodney Phillips. *A Secret Location on the Lower East Side: Adventures in Writing, 1960–1980*. New York: New York Public Library, 1998.

Kane, Daniel. *All Poets Welcome: The Lower East Side Poetry Scene in the 1960s*. Berkeley: University of California Press, 2003.

Kerouac, Jack. "The Art of Fiction: Jack Kerouac Interviewed by Ted Berrigan." In *Writers at Work: The Paris Review Interviews*, 4th series. New York: Viking, 1976.

Levy, William. *Natural Jewboy*. Amsterdam: Ins & Outs, 1981.

Leyland, Winston. "Winston Leyland Interviews John Giorno." *Gay Sunshine* 24 (Spring 1975).

Meyer, Stewart. *Book of Days*. Unpublished manuscript, 1982.

Sanders, Ed. *Fug You*. Boston: Da Capo, 2011.

Warhol, Andy. *The Andy Warhol Diaries*. London: Simon & Schuster, 1989.

White, Edmund. *City Boy: My Life in New York During the 1960s and 1970s*. London: Bloomsbury, 2009.

Wojnarowicz, David. *In the Shadow of the American Dream: The Diaries of David Wojnarowicz*. New York: Grove, 1999.

Naropa

———. *Speed*. New York: Olympia, 1970.

———. *Kentucky Ham*. London: Picador, 1975.

Bibliography

Burroughs, William S. Jr. *Cursed from Birth: The Short, Unhappy Life of William S. Burroughs Jr.* Edited and compiled by David Ohle. New York: Soft Skull, 2000.

De-la-Noy, Michael. *Denton Welch: The Making of a Writer.* London: Viking, 1984.

Faithfull, Marianne. *Memories, Dreams and Reflections.* London: Fourth Estate, 2007.

Kashner, Sam. *When I Was Cool: My Life at the Jack Kerouac School.* New York: HarperCollins, 2004.

Methuen-Campbell, James. *Denton Welch: Writer and Artist.* London: Tauris Parke, 2001.

Tonkinson, Carole, ed. *Big Sky Mind: Buddhism and the Beat Generation.* New York: Riverhead, 1995.

Waldman, Anne, and Marilyn Webb, eds. *Talking Poetics from Naropa Institute.* 2 vols. Boulder, CO: Shambhala, 1978–79.

———. *Beats at Naropa.* Minneapolis: Coffee House, 2009.

Welch, Denton. *Maiden Voyage.* London: Routledge, 1943.

———. *In Youth Is Pleasure.* London: Routledge, 1945.

———. *The Journals of Denton Welch.* London: Allison & Busby, 1984.

———. *I Left My Grandfather's House.* London: Allison & Busby, 1984.

Lawrence, Kansas

Burroughs, William S. *Everything Is Permitted: The Making of "Naked Lunch."* Edited by Ira Silverberg. London: HarperCollins, 1992.

Ely, Roger, ed. *The Final Academy: Statements of a Kind.* n.p. [London], 1982.

Geiger, John. *Nothing Is True, Everything Is Permitted: The Life of Brion Gysin.* New York: Disinformation, 2005.

Harris, Frank. *My Life and Loves: Five Volumes in One.* New York: Grove, 1963.

Heat-Moon, William Least. *PrairyErth (a deep map).* Boston: Houghton Mifflin, 1999.

Ibn Khaldun. *The Muqaddimah of Ibn Khaldun* vol. 1. Bollingen Series 43. Princeton, NJ: Princeton University Press, 1967.

Ohle, David, Roger Martin, and Susan Brosseau, eds. *Cows Are Freaky When They Look At You: An Oral History of the Kaw Valley Hemp Pickers.* Wichita, KS: Watermark, 1991 (foreword by WSB).

Ohle, David. *Mutate or Die: With Burroughs in Kansas.* Coventry, UK: Beat Scene, 2007.

Paterniti, Michael. *Driving Mr. Albert: A Trip Across America with Einstein's Brain.* New York: Dial, 2000.

Saint-John Perse. *Anabasis.* New York: Harcourt Brace, 1949 (1938).

Sobieszek, Robert A. *Ports of Entry: William S. Burroughs and the Arts.* New York: Thames & Hudson, 1996 (catalog of the exhibition of the same name held at the Los Angeles County Museum of Art).

Stipe, Michael. *Two Times Intro: On the Road with Patti Smith.* New York: Akashic, 2011.

Strieber, Whitley. *Communion: A True Story.* New York: Avon, 1987.

Waits Tom. *The Black Rider.* Island Records CID 8021 518 559-2, London 1993 (audio CD).

Whitmer, Peter. *Aquarius Revisited.* New York: Macmillan, 1987.

Wilson, Terry. *Perilous Passage.* Santa Fe, NM: Synergetic, 2012.

Key Figures

Allen Ginsberg

Ginsberg, Allen. *Allen Verbatim: Lectures on Poetry, Politics, Consciousness.* New York: McGraw-Hill, 1974.

———. *Gay Sunshine Interview with Allen Young.* Bolinas, CA: Grey Fox, 1974.

———. *Journals: Early Fifties, Early Sixties.* New York: Grove, 1977.

———. *The Riverside Interviews 1: Allen Ginsberg.* London: Binnacle, 1980.

———. *Collected Poems, 1947–1980.* New York: Harper & Row, 1984.

———. *Fotografier, 1947–87.* Aarhus: Klim, 1987.

Bibliography

————. *Journals Mid-Fifties (1954–1958)*. New York: HarperCollins, 1995.

————. *Spontaneous Mind: Selected Interviews, 1958–1996*. New York: HarperCollins, 2001.

————. *The Book of Martyrdom and Artifice: First Journals and Poems, 1937–1952*. Philadelphia: Da Capo, 2006.

————. *The Letters of Allen Ginsberg*. Philadelphia: Da Capo, 2008.

Ginsberg, Allen, and Neal Cassady. *As Ever: The Collected Correspondence*. Berkeley, CA: Creative Arts, 1977.

Ginsberg, Allen, and Peter Orlovsky. *Straight Hearts' Delight: Love Poems and Selected Letters*. San Francisco: Gay Sunshine, 1980.

Ginsberg, Allen, and Louis Ginsberg. *Family Business: Selected Letters Between a Father and Son*. London: Bloomsbury, 2001.

Ginsberg, Allen, and Gary Snyder. *The Selected Letters of Allen Ginsberg and Gary Snyder*. Berkeley, CA: Counterpoint, 2009.

Ginsberg, Allen, and Jack Kerouac. *Jack Kerouac, Allen Ginsberg: The Letters*. New York: Viking, 2010.

Kramer, Jane. *Allen Ginsberg in America*. New York: Random House, 1969.

Miles, Barry. *Ginsberg: A Biography*. New York: Simon & Schuster, 1989.

Morgan, Bill. *The Works of Allen Ginsberg, 1941–1994*. Westport, CT: Greenwood, 1995.

————. *The Response to Allen Ginsberg, 1926–1994*. Westport, CT: Greenwood, 1996.

Morgan, Bill, and Bob Rosenthal, eds. *Best Minds: A Tribute to Allen Ginsberg*. New York: Lospecchio, 1986.

————. *Kanreki: A Tribute to Allen Ginsberg, Part 2*. New York: Lospecchio, 1986.

Mottram, Eric. *Allen Ginsberg in the Sixties*. Brighton: Unicorn, n.d. [1972].

Portugés, Paul. *The Visionary Poetics of Allen Ginsberg*. Santa Barbara, CA: Ross-Erikson, 1978.

Sinclair, Iain. *The Kodak Mantra Diaries*. London: Albion Village, 1971,

Jack Kerouac

Austin, James. *The Jack Kerouac Collection*. Rhino Records, Santa Monica, CA, 1990 (CDs and booklet).

Burroughs, William S. "Remembering Jack Kerouac." In *The Adding Machine*. New York: Seaver, 1986.

Cassady, Carolyn. *Heart Beat. My Life with Jack and Neal*. Berkeley: Creative Arts, 1976.

————. *Off the Road: Twenty Years with Cassady, Kerouac and Ginsberg*. London: Black Spring, 1990.

Charters, Ann. *A Bibliography of Works by Jack Kerouac*. New York: Phoenix, 1967, 1975 (revised).

————. *Kerouac*. New York: Warner, 1973, 1974 (revised).

Clark, Tom. *Jack Kerouac*. New York: Harcourt Brace Jovanovich, 1984.

Creighton, David. *Ecstasy of the Beats*. Toronto: Dundurn Group, 2007.

Gifford, Barry, and Lawrence Lee. *Jack's Book*. New York: St. Martin's, 1978.

Ginsberg, Allen. *The Visions of the Great Rememberer*. Amherst, MA: Mulch, 1974.

Hipkiss, Robert A. *Jack Kerouac: Prophet of the New Romanticism*. Lawrence: Regents Press of Kansas, 1976.

Hunt, Tim. *Kerouac's Crooked Road*. Hamden, CT: Shoe String, 1981.

Kerouac, Jack. *Doctor Sax*. New York: Grove, 1959.

————. *Mexico City Blues*. New York: Grove, 1959.

————. *Book of Dreams*. San Francisco: City Lights, 1960.

————. *The Subterraneans*. London: Andre Deutsch, 1960.

————. *Tristessa*. New York: Avon, 1960.

————. *Lonesome Traveller*. London: Andre Deutsch, 1962.

————. *Satori in Paris*. New York: Grove, 1966.

————. *Desolation Angels*. London: Granada, 1972.

————. *The Dharma Bums*. London: Granada, 1972.

————. *On the Road*. Harmondsworth, UK: Penguin, 1972.

————. *Visions of Cody*. New York: McGraw-Hill, 1973.

————. *Vanity of Duluoz*. London: Granada, 1982.

————. *Old Angel Midnight*. San Francisco: Grey Fox, 1993.

————. *The Portable Jack Kerouac*. Edited by Ann Charters. New York: Viking, 1995.

————. *Selected Letters, 1940–1956*. Edited by Ann Charters. New York: Viking, 1995.

————. *The Mexican Girl*, n.p. [Brighton, UK]: Pacific Car Press, n.d.

————. *The Town and the City*. New York: Grosset & Dunlap, n.d.

Knight, Arthur, and Kit Knight, eds. *Kerouac and the Beats*. New York: Paragon, 1988.

McDarrah, Fred. *Kerouac and Friends*. New York: William Morrow, 1985.

McNally, Dennis. *Desolate Angel: A Biography of Jack Kerouac*. New York: Random House, 1979.

Moore, Dave, ed. *The Kerouac Connection*. Bristol: Various issues.

Nicosia, Gerald. *Memory Babe: A Critical Biography of Jack Kerouac*. New York: Grove, 1983.

Roark, Randy, ed. "Documents from the Jack Kerouac Conference, Boulder, Colorado, July 1982." *Friction* 1, no. 2–3 (1982) (Boulder, CO).

Turner, Steve. *Jack Kerouac: Angelheaded Hipster*. London: Bloomsbury, 1996.

Walsh, Joy, et al., eds. *Moody Street Irregulars: A Jack Kerouac Newsletter*. Clarence Center, NY.

Brion Gysin

————. *The Process*. London: Jonathan Cape, 1969.

————. *Here to Go: Planet R-101, Brion Gysin interviewed by Terry Wilson*. San Francisco: RE/Search, 1982.

————. *The Last Museum*. New York: Grove, 1986.

Gysin, Brion. *Back in No Time*. New York: Guillaume Gallozzi, 1994.

[————.] *Headpress 25: Flicker Machine Edition*. Manchester: Headpress, 2003.

Beat Generation (Selected)

Allen, Donald, and George F. Butterick, eds. *The Postmoderns*. New York: Grove, 1982.

Aronowitz, Alfred G. "The 'Beat Generation,'" a series of articles in the *New York Post*: (1): "The Beat Generation," March 9, 1959; (2): "Jack Kerouac," March 10, 1959; (3): "Neal Cassady," March 11, 1959; (4): "A Certain Party," March 12, 1959; (5): "Allen Ginsberg, Prophet," March 13, 1959; (6): "Act of Violence," March 18, 1959; (7): "Now and Here-after," March 19, 1959; (8): "The Mission," March 20, 1959.

Bartlett, Lee. *The Beats: Essays in Criticism*. Jefferson, NC: McFarland, 1981.

Burns, Jim. *Radicals, Beats and Beboppers*. n.p.: Penniless, 2011.

Campbell, James. *This Is the Beat Generation*. London: Secker & Warburg, 1999.

Charters, Ann. *Beats and Company*. Garden City, NY: Doubleday, 1986.

————. *Scenes Along the Road*. New York: Portents/Gotham Book Mart, 1970.

Charters, Ann, ed. *The Beats: Literary Bohemians in Postwar America*. DLB 16. Ann Arbor, MI: Gale Research, 1983.

————. *The Portable Beat Reader*. New York: Viking, 1992.

Collins, Ronald K. L., and David M. Skover. *Mania: The Story of the Outraged and Outrageous Lives That Launched a Cultural Revolution*. Oak Park, IL: Top Five Books, 2013.

Cook, Bruce. *The Beat Generation*. New York: Charles Scribner's Sons, 1971.

Feldman, Gene, and Max Gartenberg, eds. *The Beat Generation and the Angry Young Men*. New York: Citadel, 1958.

Felver, Christopher. *Beat*. San Francisco: Last Gasp, 2007.

Foster, Edward. *Understanding the Beats*. Columbia: University of South Carolina Press, 1992.

Girodias, Maurice, ed. *The Olympia Reader*. New York: Grove, 1965.

Grace, Nancy, and Ronna Johnson. *Girls Who Wore Black: Women Writing the Beat Generation*. Piscataway, NJ: Rutgers University Press, 2002.

Bibliography

————. *Breaking the Rule of Cool.* Jackson: University Press of Mississippi, 2004.

Hickey, Morgen. *The Bohemian Register: An Annotated Bibliography of the Beat Literary Movement.* Metuchen, NJ: Scarecrow, 1990.

Honan, Park, ed. *The Beats: An Anthology of "Beat" Writing.* London: J. M. Dent, 1987.

Horemans, Rudi, ed. *Beat Indeed!* Antwerp: EXA, 1985.

Huncke, Herbert. *Huncke's Journal.* New York: Poets Press, 1965.

————. *Herbert Huncke Special Issue.* California, PA: Unspeakable Visions of the Individual, 1973.

————. *The Evening Sun Turned Crimson.* Cherry Valley, NY: Cherry Valley, 1980.

Knight, Arthur, and Glee Knight, eds. *The Beat Book.* California, PA: Unspeakable Visions of the Individual, 1974.

Knight, Arthur, and Kit Knight, eds. *The Beat Diary.* California, PA: Unspeakable Visions of the Individual, 1977.

————. *The Beat Vision.* New York: Paragon House, 1977.

————. *The Beat Journey.* California, PA: Unspeakable Visions of the Individual, 1978.

————. *Beat Angels.* California, PA: Unspeakable Visions of the Individual, 1982.

————. *The Beat Road.* California, PA: Unspeakable Visions of the Individual, 1984.

Knight, Brenda. *Women of the Beat Generation.* Berkeley, CA: Conari, 1996.

Lee, Robert, ed. *The Beat Generation Writers.* London: Pluto, 1996.

Long, John. *Drugs and the "Beats."* College Station, TX: Virtualbookworm, 2005.

Marler, Regina, ed. *Queer Beats: How the Beats Turned America On to Sex.* San Francisco: Cleis, 2004.

McClure, Michael. *Scratching the Beat Surface.* San Francisco: North Point, 1982.

Parkinson, Thomas, ed. *A Casebook on the Beat.* New York: Crowell, 1961.

Phillips, Lisa. *Beat Culture and the New America, 1950–1965.* New York: Whitney Museum of American Art, 1996.

Rosset, Barney, ed. *Evergreen Review Reader, 1957–1961.* New York: Grove, 1979.

Seaver, Richard, Terry Southern, and Alexander Trocchi, eds. *Writers in Revolt: An Anthology.* New York: Frederick Fell, 1963.

Simpson, Louis. *A Revolution in Taste.* New York: Macmillan, 1978.

Solomon, Carl. *Mishaps, Perhaps.* San Francisco: Beach Books, Texts & Documents, 1966.

————. *More Mishaps.* San Francisco: Beach Books, Texts & Documents, 1968.

Tytell, John, *Naked Angels.* New York: McGraw-Hill, 1976.

Waldman, Anne, ed. *The Beat Book.* Boston: Shambhala, 1996.

Watson, Steven. *The Birth of the Beat Generation.* New York: Pantheon, 1995.

General

Bouvier, Nicolas. *The Way of the World: Two Men in a Car from Geneva to the Khyber Pass.* London: Eland, 2007 (1963).

Gardner, Martin. *Fads and Fallacies in the Name of Science.* New York: Dover, 1952; revised 1957.

Foucault, Michel. *Foucault Live: Interviews, 1966–84.* New York: Semiotext(e), 1989.

Inglis, Brian. *Fringe Medicine.* London: Faber, 1964.

Shattuck, Roger. *The Banquet Years: The Origins of the Avant-Garde in France, 1885 to World War I.* Revised ed. New York: Vintage, 1968.

Tomkins, Calvin. *Duchamp: A Biography.* New York: Henry Holt, 1996.

Index

Index

Index

special copy of *Naked Lunch*, 354; 290; on WSB's orgone accumulator, 298; WSB's reading his work to, 305; Yacoubi and, 291, 293, 307, 397
Boyars, Arthur, 402
Boyer, Joseph, 14, 16
Boyer Machine Company, 14–15
Boyle, James Le Baron, 55, 56, 58, 419, 429
Bozo (Henry Street queen), 122, 123, 125
Bradshaw, David, 628
Brady, Bob, 286
Brady, John, 87, 483, 497–501, 504–5
Brandinburg, Bob, 121–22, 123, 125; girlfriend Vicki Russell, 126–27
Brando, Marlon, 324
Breger, Udo, 543, 549, 588, 589, 604–5, 634
Brennan, Gerald, 285
Breton, André, 340
Brideshead Revisited (Waugh), 259
Broadwater, Bowden, 286
Brookner, Howard, 161, 523, 546–47, 548, 550, 553, 556, 573, 603; documentary film on WSB, 80, 161, 206–7, 537, 546–47, 551–52, 573, 580
Brossard, Chandler, 96–97
Brosseau, Susan, 565
Brown, Andreas, 510
Broyard, Anatole, 593
Brummel, Beau, 72
Bryant, Baird, 324
Budapest, Hungary, 61
Budd, David, 516
Buddhism, 52
Buhler, Rosine, 589
Bukowski, Charles, 576
Bumsell, Maître, 355–56
Burgess, Anthony, 409, 631
Burgess, John, 487
Burgess, Lynne, 409
Burroughs (documentary), 80, 161, 206–7, 537, 546–47, 551–52, 573, 580
Burroughs, Alice (great-aunt), 14
Burroughs, Edmund (great-grandfather), 14
Burroughs, Ellen Julia Whipple (great-grandmother), 14
Burroughs, Horace (uncle), 15, 17, 18; as morphine addict, 17–18, 147
Burroughs, Ida Selover (grandmother), 14, 15
Burroughs, James (great-uncle), 14
Burroughs, Joan Vollmer (wife), 128–29, 130–33; affairs, 128–29, 144; alcohol use, 184, 193, 194, 202–3, 206, 207; amphetamine psychosis, 144, 155; apartment on W. 115th St., 128, 130, 132, 143; apartment on W. 118th street, 99; appearance, 99, 171, 179, 204, 206; auditory hallucinations and, 138; Beat Generation and, 95; at Bellevue Hospital, 144; Benzedrine addiction and, 132, 134,

138, 158, 159–60, 161, 170–71, 179, 184, 185; burial, 213; Carr and, 203; Carr and Ginsberg's visit to Mexico City and, 202–4; character and personality, 131, 171; daughter, Julie, 100, 105, 128, 129, 132, 144, 155, 156, 159, 170–71, 179, 196; discussions at 115th Street, Wolfeans and Non-Wolfeans, 134–36; Edie Parker and, 99; extramarital liaisons, speculation about, 215–16; family's affluence, 99, 105; film of *Naked Lunch* and, 583–84; first marriage at seventeen, 99; flatmates of, 128, 129, 132; Ginsberg and, 130, 132, 134, 138, 143, 157, 159, 184; Healy and, 206; Huncke describes, 128; life in New York, 100; marriage to Paul Adams, 99, 100, 134; mattress fire, 173–74; in New Orleans, 166, 167–76; picked up by police (1947), 163; polio and limp, 171, 193, 203; pregnancy with Julie, 100, 105; son, Billy, with WSB, 161; statements about WSB to De Paul Sanatorium interviewer, 175; suicidal thoughts and, 216–17; as well-read intellectual, 129, 130–31, 187, 205; West End Bar and, 100–101; WSB and, files for divorce from common-law marriage, 191, 212; WSB and, in Mexico City, 181, 182–97, 205, 206; WSB and, in Texas, 155, 156–63, 177, 179–80, 181; WSB and, reconciliation, 193, 212; WSB and telepathy game, 136, 190; WSB and the William Tell game, 180, 207, 217; WSB compares to his mother, 131, 175; WSB meets, 131; WSB moves in with, 132, 155; WSB's arrest and, 140; WSB's homosexuality and, 132, 184; WSB's morphine addiction and, 148, 162, 188, 189, 191; WSB's relationship with, 138, 143, 155, 160–61, 165, 172–73, 176, 184, 187, 193, 196, 205, 212; WSB's remorse over death of, 217, 612–13; WSB's shooting of, 3, 20, 207–11, 215, 273–74, 345; in WSB's writing, 618
Burroughs, Karen (daughter-in-law), 515, 524
Burroughs, Laura Hammond Lee (mother), 9, 11–14, 16–17, 18, 28, 29, 33; Billy Jr. and, 460; birth of son "Mort," 18; birth of WSB, 18; Cobble Stone Gardens, 19, 78, 331; death of, 486; dementia and, 461; interest in Buddhism, 52; Payne Whitney Clinic, 11, 21–22; occult, psychic phenomena, and, 22; in Palm Beach, 226; relationship with husband, 22; relationship with WSB, 21–22, 23, 77, 175–76; response to WSB's homosexuality, 46–47; siblings, 12; in St. Louis nursing home, 461–62; tolerance for homosexuality, 19; WSB compares Joan to, 131, 175; WSB's guilt toward, 83, 176, 462, 486, 633; WSB's morphine addiction and, 147, 284; WSB's recurring dream of, 22, 592

Index

Burroughs, Laura Lee (niece), 572
Burroughs, Margaret "Miggie" Vieths (sister-in-law), 21, 25, 572, 573
Burroughs, Mortimer "Mort" (brother), 10–11, 12, 33, 34, 47–48, 53–54, 214; birth, 11, 18; character and personality, 53, 54, 58, 572; death of, 572; death of father and, 437; Joan's burial arrangements and, 213; marriage, 21, 53; nanny Mary Evans and, 23, 25; at Princeton and Harvard, 53; relationship with WSB, 11, 22, 24, 34, 48, 53–54, 214, 572–73; WSB's shooting of Joan and, 213, 214
Burroughs, Mortimer "Mote" (father), 10, 11, 12, 13, 15, 16, 17, 18–19, 21, 22, 28–29, 30, 32, 33, 226; bails WSB out of New York jail, 111; canoe trip with WSB (1930), 39–40; character and personality, 20–21, 58, 78; Cobble Stone Gardens, 19, 78, 331; death of, 437; fishing trip with WSB and Mort (1931), 47; paying of WSB's fines, bail bonds, etc, 37; relationship with WSB, 21, 22, 26, 39–40, 47, 78, 175; social life and status, 21; tolerance for homosexuality, 19; wealth of, 10, 11, 16, 17, 18–19, 39; WSB's Algiers property and, 174; WSB's arrest in New Orleans and, 174; WSB's arrest on drug charges and obtaining a lawyer, 140; WSB's bail in Texas paid by, 165; WSB's committal to Payne Whitney and, 76–77; WSB's financial support, 22, 83, 85, 90, 98, 114, 140, 175, 185, 263, 270, 278, 437; WSB's guilt toward, 83, 176, 462, 486, 633; WSB's morphine addiction and, 142–43, 147, 174, 284; WSB's psychoanalysis paid for, 75; WSB's Texas land bought by, 148, 155
Burroughs, William (Billy), Jr. (son), 240, 437; alcoholism and drugs, 419, 461, 515, 532–33; arrests, 457, 460, 461; born with amphetamine addiction, 161; cirrhosis and liver transplant, 524–25; death of mother and, 213; deterioration and death of, 557–58; girlfriend Georgette Larrouy, 524, 533; grandmother's death, 486; mental instability, 523, 525, 529–30, 532–33; in Mexico City with WSB, 196–97, 203, 213; in New York with WSB, 515; raised by WSB's parents, 213, 214, 226, 269; relationship with WSB, 226, 240, 457, 460–61, 515, 517, 524–25, 526, 530, 532–33, 557–58; in Tangier with WSB, 415–19; wife Karen, 515, 524; in WSB's writing, 618; at Yeshe House, 529–30, 534
Burroughs, William Seward (grandfather), 14–15, 628
Burroughs, William Seward, II (WSB):
  general facts: appearance, 2, 104, 193, 243, 258, 272, 296, 335, 372, 395, 398, 428, 430, 609–10, 632; bad boy/bad behavior and, 119; birth, 9, 11, 18; cats and, 107, 171, 305, 415,

566–67, 575, 577, 584–85, 610, 614, 619, 633; celebrity and, 489–90, 491, 527, 531, 537–40, 558, 619–21, 624, 627; character and personality, 38, 72, 119, 290, 299, 410, 421, 445, 487, 524, 558, 624, 627, 632, 633–64; as cult figure, 619; as el hombre invisible, 47, 272, 296–97, 381–82, 577, 610, 634; death, 624–28; feet of, and custom-made shoes, 46, 454; fishing and hunting, love of, 29, 38, 40, 47–48, 614–15; generosity of, 11, 80–81; as "Godfather of Punk," 539, 631; good manners of, 5, 119; as gourmet/love of caviar, 38, 39, 54, 97, 171, 272, 278, 302, 492, 543, 577, 632; guns and, 21, 43, 44, 48, 54, 55, 71, 138, 158, 169, 171, 174, 180, 192–93, 195, 206, 207, 229, 232, 245, 466, 479, 531, 565–66, 569–71, 576–77, 612–13, 618, 625, 626–27, 628; image problems, 629–30; influence on American culture and literature, 629–35; last words, 625; marriages (see Burroughs, Joan Vollmer; Klapper, Ilse Herzfeld) memorization of literary quotations, 48, 53, 102, 446; misogyny of, 371, 587, 588, 591; parents' financial support, 22, 83, 85, 90, 98, 114, 140, 175, 185, 263, 270, 278, 437; Sherlock Holmes comparison, 632
  1914–1935 (childhood and early years), 9–59; books and literary influences, 26, 27, 36–37, 43, 46, 48, 52, 54; caught at breaking-in an abandoned factory, 37; childhood homes, 10–11, 30, 31, 32–33; Christmas, 1925, in New York City with Uncle Ivy, 31; Community School, 26–27, 33, 35; Evans Tutoring school, 47; explosion and hospitalization (1928), 38–39; extended family and heritage, 12–19, 20; family holidays and trips, 37–38, 39, 49; fascination with underworld and criminals, 36–37; fear of the dark, 39; Forest Park Highlands fun fair, 34; friendships, 27, 28, 35; Harbor Beach, Michigan, annual vacation, 29–30, 31; Harvard University, 49, 51–59; incident with broken glass, 29; John Burroughs School, 33, 35; lifestyle of family and pre-war Midwest, 11, 33–34, 39; London-Paris trip with Kammerer (1933), 54; Los Alamos Ranch School, as boarding school, 40, 41–47; Los Alamos Ranch School, as summer camp, 31, 37, 39; magic reality and, 22; movies and stage shows seen, 33–34, 51; neighbors of, 27–28; nostalgia for, 30–31; Paris-Algiers trip (1934), 35, 55; pets, 32; piano lessons, 33; radio, 34; rejection of social milieu of, 13; religious upbringing, 12; shares inherited by Burroughs family and, 16; St. Albans summers, 29, 38; St. Louis, memories of, 10, 20, 23; superstitions of servants and, 23; swallowing a gold knife,

696

Index

Index

Burroughs, William Seward, II (WSB) (*cont.*)
friends, 611–12, 617, 619, 633; sweat lodge
ceremony (1992), 1–6, 617–18; teaching
and, 579; Thursdays as special, 615; turning
seventy, 580; *The Western Lands* and, 585,
590
art: collaboration with Taaffe, 595–96;
commentary on, 598, 606–7; cut-ups and,
570; debt to Brion Gysin, 341, 342,
599–600; as a door to the spirit world,
606–7; dust jacket of *Naked Lunch*, 570;
exhibitions worldwide, 622; file-folder
paintings, 605–7; fire in Paul Klein Gallery
and, 599; first exhibit, 570; first one-
man show, 597; first show abroad, 606;
income from, 586; Kuri and, 606; Lowe's
suggestions and, 606; major show in Tokyo,
606; medium and, 599; montages or
collages, 351, 387–89, 392, 398, 423, 570;
Nouveaux Réalistes and, 598; painting,
595–99; painting with guns, 569–71, 606;
"Paper Cloud," 606; performance pieces,
381–82; photography, 570; posthumus
exhibitions and productions, 634–35;
scrapbooks, 351, 570; shows (1988–1989),
599–600; street recordings and playbacks,
494, 495; "Thick Pages" series, 606; "the
Ugly Spirit" in paintings, 6; "Word Falling–
Photo Falling," 387
beliefs and interests: anthropology
and Mayan archaeology, 68, 73, 90,
187, 466; anti-capital punishment, 424;
astrology, 52; attempt to contact dead, 521;
Buddhism, 52, 320; concept of schlupping,
245; Connell's ideas and, 41; conspiracy
against the consumer and, 179–80; control
systems, 37, 466, 482–83, 631–32; criminal
underworld, 36–37, 85, 86–87, 92, 121–27;
cure for the common cold, 61; Egyptian
hieroglyphs, 90; Indian shamanism, 617–18;
The Job as revelatory of, 482; jujitsu, 105,
117; Korzybski's ideas and, 72–73; library
and influential authors, 117–18; medieval
torture, 52; mind control, 466; mind
control and, 399; "nothing is true" trope,
362; occult and magic, 2, 22, 51–52, 118,
180, 307, 342–45, 346, 453, 517, 548–49,
584; orgone accumulator, 118, 177–78, 185,
247, 289, 298–99, 416, 455, 466, 516, 517;
outrage at American prison system, 334;
political views, 2, 52, 55, 235, 254; psychic
experiments, 3, 24, 407, 494–95, 517–18;
psychology studies, 67, 73; religious position,
2; Scientology and the E-meter, 465–71,
472–73, 479, 482, 493–94; self-improvement
systems, various, 118, 519; spiritual
atmosphere of Tangier and, 299–300;
telepathy, 136, 187, 190, 198, 245; Tibetan
tantricism, 51–52, 54; UFOs and alien

abductions, 118, 607–8; witchcraft, 51–52,
54; yoga, 52, 117
drugs and alcohol: alcohol, 149, 151, 152,
153, 179, 180, 192–93, 194, 196, 201, 207,
219, 224, 229, 231, 234–35, 236, 278, 286,
303, 373, 398, 408, 409, 420, 424, 461, 463,
466, 491, 494, 511, 514, 522, 553–54, 577,
611, 612, 633; arrests for, 140, 174, 181, 185;
Benzedrine, 151, 152; cocaine use, 189, 331,
551; coca leaves, 232, 238–39; codeine, 237;
detoxing and, 143, 162, 164, 174–75,
284–85, 332, 552; Eubispasme, 347, 355,
358; Eukodol, 258–59, 262, 267, 270, 552,
633; hash, kif, marijuana, 77, 151–52, 289,
298, 304, 324, 327, 370, 409, 416, 420,
483–84, 538, 549, 553, 556, 566, 611; life
span and, 553; majoun, 289, 300, 303–4,
306, 308, 311, 338, 385, 393; mescaline,
psilocybin, and other hallucinogens, 152,
371, 372, 376, 381, 390–91, 395–400, 517,
543; methadone maintenance, 552–53, 565,
610, 615, 618, 633; Mexican lawyer and,
185–86; nearly lethal dose of chloral hydrate
taken, as teenager, 45; Nembutal, 233, 237;
opiate addiction, 85, 123–27, 133, 137, 138,
140–43, 147, 148, 156, 164, 168–69, 174,
187–89, 191, 207–8, 218, 219, 227, 251,
259, 260–61, 262, 264, 267, 269, 270, 279,
280, 282, 284, 329, 332, 338, 347, 351, 355,
411–12, 461, 531, 536, 547, 549–53, 558,
633; opium smoking, 192, 419; paregoric,
321, 329, 351; reduction cure and, 143, 164,
267, 358, 565; role of drugs in his life, 633;
scheme to sell Moroccan hash in Paris,
345–46; smoking English cigarettes, 553,
620; speedball (cocaine and heroin), 189,
372; U. S. Customs and, 433–34; yagé and,
197, 198, 200, 202, 226, 227, 228–32,
237–39, 376, 390; yoka vine, 230–31
health: cataract operation, 624; "dying
feeling," 455, 535; heart attack, 624–25;
hemorrhoid operation in Panama, 227;
hepatitis, 218, 219–20, 309; liver problems,
308; malaria, 232; mononucleosis, 83;
operation for rectal warts, 269; pisco
neuritis, 236; rheumatic fever, 264; sinus
infection, chronic, 31; syphilis, 64; triple-
bypass operation, 2; triple heart bypass
(1991), 553, 617
mental states and instability: analysts and
psychiatrists, 2, 47, 59, 75, 76–77, 78, 81, 83,
84, 85, 114–15, 316; assessment of mental
state (1948), 175; auditory hallucinations,
90; at Chestnut Lodge, 85; childhood
hallucinations, 22–23, 38, 52; committal to
Payne Whitney Clinic (1940), 11, 76–77;
compulsive behaviors, 67; depression, 3,
207, 224, 229, 264, 274, 348, 446, 470,
484, 511, 521–22, 589, 624; diagnosis of

700

Index

schizophrenia, 77; experiments in lay analysis, 135–36; illusions, Paris (1961), 384–85; killing of Joan and, 3, 207–11, 215, 217, 224, 226, 345, 612–13; Land of the Dead dream, 589–90; layers of his alter ego, 136, 359; narcoanalysis of, 115; obsession with Jack Anderson and, 74–76; parents' paying for psychoanalysis, 91, 114, 316; psychiatric evaluation (1931) after dismissal from Los Alamos Ranch School, 47; "psychic attack," 405–6, 453; psychoanalysis, 83, 91, 114–15, 135, 342; psychology courses taken, 67; pyschotherapy, 78, 81, 83, 84, 85; recurring dream of his mother, 22, 592; role playing and fabrications, 175; self-analysis by, 25, 312, 316, 319–20; self-mutilation, 39, 76; sweat lodge ceremony and (1992), 1–6, 617–18; terror dreams, 502; traumatic incident with "nursy," 24–25, 114–15, 312, 320–21; Ugly Spirit and, 1–3, 5–6, 39, 207, 216, 344–45, 405–6, 582, 607, 618
sex and: affair in Copenhagen, 310; affair with Brady, 497–501, 504–5; affair with Culverwell, 485; affair with Ginsberg, 244–46, 262, 266, 267, 270, 302, 312, 319–20; affair with Grauerholz, 511, 514–15, 553; affair with Hardy, 531, 547–48; affair with Lee, 479; affair with Sommerville, 357–59, 414–30; Angelo, long-term Mexican boy, 184, 220, 240, 265; attraction to Gorseline, 359–60; Baron Wolfner and, 61; "Billy Bradshinkel" and, 49–50; as "bottom" in sexual relations, 267, 277, 531, 601; boys in Reynosa, Mexico, 154; Carr and, 80; Chase refuses advances, Mexico, 195; cruising Scollay Square, Boston, 56; crush on boy at Los Alamos Ranch School, 46–47; dismissal from school and psychiatric evaluation (1931), 47; early awareness of his sexual orientation, 35, 46; first homosexual intercourse, 70; first love, 35–36; gay bars, New York City, 56–57; gay life, Vienna, Austria, 60–61; gay sex in *The Place of Dead Roads*, 567; Ginsberg's friends and, 601; guns connected to, 195, 245; heterosexuality and, 312; homosexuality as forbidden, 50; homosexuality as social clique, 404; homosexuality questioned by, 311, 321, 347; inexperience and sexual ignorance, 58; Kerouac and, 133; Kiki in Tangier, 254, 260–61, 264–66; lack of sex drive (methadone and), 553, 603; letter to Ginsberg on, 196; Marker and, 197–202, 205, 224, 240, 241; memorable orgasms, 374; obsession with Jack Anderson, 74–76, 83; open relationship with Sommerville, 419, 427–28; parents' response to WSB's homosexuality, 19, 47, 78; pedophilia of, 255; penis size and, 245; picking up boys in

Colombia, 232; picking up boys in Lima, 236; picking up boys in London, 374, 445, 455; picking up boys in Mexico City, 184; picking up boys in New Orleans, 168; picking up boys in Reynosa, 154, 179; picking up boys in Tangier, 252–54; picking up boys in Venice, 286–87; preferences in men, 265, 410; in pre-war Budapest, 61; rectal warts and, 267; relationship with his "boys," 292; roommate and sexual partner, Vienna, 64–65; routines about parasitic symbiosis and, 246; scarcity of partners (1974–1997), 601–3; school crushes, 35; secrecy about homosexuality and fear of exposure, 47, 78, 80, 131, 154; sense of alienation and homosexuality, 50, 78; sexual habits described, 245–46; sex with James Le Baron Boyle, 55, 429; syphilis contracted, 64; Tangier and frequency of, 300; teenage fantasies, 39; trip to Europe with Kammerer (1933) and, 54; women and, 57, 58, 80, 161, 173, 176, 196, 382, 408, 412, 588
writing and writing career, 57–58; agent, Ginsberg as, 154, 191, 195, 219, 222, 275, 290, 316; agent, Matson as, 541; agent, Wylie as, 581; all-male societies in, 47; Ansen on WSB as moral writer, 256; archive project, 490–91, 496; arrest in New Orleans used in, 174; assistant for, Lowe, 2; awards and accolades, 579–80, 626; blurbs written by, 420; Brady in, 498–99; characters/stock characters, 28, 89, 92, 140, 186, 187, 318, 325, 353, 380, 545; Chicago detective agency work in, 87; Chicago extermination agency in, 88–89; childhood home in, 10; childhood memories in, 11, 21, 24; childhood writings and *The Autobiography of a Wolf*, 26–27, 37; collaboration with Kells Elvins (1938), 69–70; color separation idea, 380; commentary on, 342, 629–35; control systems in, 425; as copywriter, ad agency, 82–83; cut-ups, 34, 89, 147, 362–66, 371, 373, 375, 381, 385, 387, 389, 393, 404, 412, 421, 426, 434, 436, 572, 579, 587, 597, 630; Denton Welch as influence on, 30, 118, 544–45, 556–57, 566, 568; description of WSB's writing *Nova Express*, 416–17; Dr. Benway created, 69–70, 279–80; dreams used in, 22, 64, 353, 592; drugs ingested during writing, 552–53; eccentric spellings, 26; Elvins' war experiences in, 147; fascination with criminal underworld and, 36–37; on the first person character, 590; first published work, 37; food as theme in, 38; foreign editions, 610; fragmentary quality and style, 276; French translators, 434, 448; friends assisting in, 541; Gardner used in, 141; German translator, 448; Ginsberg's impact on, 624; Harbor Beach,

Index

Index

Index

Death in Venice (Mann), 19
de Chadenedes, John, 496
Decline of the West, The (Spengler), 118
de Kooning, Willem, 97
Denmark, 310; WSB in, 309–12
Dent, Dr. John Yerbury, 284–85, 309, 332, 338, 348, 358, 405
de Palaminy, François, 589
"Deposition: Testimony Concerning a Sickness" (Burroughs), 356
Derlith, August, 350
Desolation Angels (Kerouac), 141, 301, 302
Desperate Years, The (Horan), 437
Dewey, John, 26
Dialectics of Liberation Congress (1967), 463
Dietholm, Oskar, 76
Dillon, Mat, 601
di Prima, Diane, 437, 595
Discipline of D.E., The (film), 600
Dobbs, Obie, 149, 151, 152–53
Dobson, Bill, 194–95
Doctor Sax (Kerouac), 220, 221
Donnellan, George L., 112
Donovan, Col. William J. "Wild Bill," 82
Dos Passos, John, 363
Dostoyevsky, Fyodor, 105
Dream Calendar, 483
Driberg, Tom, 463
"Driving Lesson" (Burroughs), 78
Drugstore Cowboy (film), 600–601
Dubrovnik, Yugoslavia, 61–63
Ducasse, Isidore, 116
Duchamp, Marcel, 328–29, 569
Dudjom Rinpoche, 521
Dunne, John W., 72
Durrell, Lawrence, 326, 403
Dutch, Tony (Anthony Reithorst), 254, 259, 260, 261, 267, 278, 280, 338
Dylan, Bob, 520

Ecuador, 199, 200–201, 235, 265; WSB and Marker's jungle expedition, 200–201; WSB and search for yagé, 198–201
Edinburgh Literary Festival, 403–5, 556
Edler, Jennie Burroughs (aunt), 15, 16–17
Edler, Kenneth (cousin), 16, 17
Edler, Sheldon (uncle), 16
Eggleston, Leslie, 257, 280, 419, 446
Egyptian Hieroglyphic Dictionary, An (Wallis Budge), 90
Eissler, Kurt, 91
Elder, Charles (cousin), 16, 17
Eliot, T. S., 31, 363, 457, 591, 594; at Harvard, 53; Laura Lee Burroughs and, 9; on St. Louis, 9; translation of *Anabasis*, 117; *The Western Lands* and, 593, 594; WSB and, 53
Elliott, Patricia, 626
Elliott, Ramblin' Jack, 323, 327

Ellisor, Arch, 158–59, 164–65
Elovich, Richard, 515, 516, 518, 523, 525
Elvins, Brick Orwig, 53
Elvins, Kells, 35–36; alcoholism, 147, 180, 264; appearance, 35, 147; Benzedrine use, 151, 152; caught at breaking-in an abandoned factory, 37; in Copenhagen, 309; girlfriend Obie Dobbs, 149, 151, 152–53; graduate work, state prison at Huntsville, Texas, 70, 155; at Harvard, 53, 68–70; marijuana growing, 152; money-making schemes with WSB, 148, 152; in Morocco, with WSB, 264; personality and character, 147–48; Reich's orgone box and, 178; as "Rollins" in *Junky*, 193; sells Texas land and invests in oil, 191; Texas country club and, 152–53; Texas farming and WSB, 148–53, 177–81; Texas house on South Jackson Road, 149, 151, 155, 178; visits WSB in Mexico, 191; wives of, 53, 69, 191, 264, 309; as writer, 180–81; WSB in Copenhagen and, 309–10; WSB's childhood crush on, 35–36, 46; as WSB's lifelong friend, 36, 69, 181; in WSB's writing, 618; in WWII, 147
Elvins, Lorrie "Lee," 36; descriptions of WSB, 36
Elvins, Peter, 53, 147
Elvins, Politte, 36, 37, 148
Ely, Roger, 571
Emerton, Michael, 2, 4, 615–16, 618
Empress Hotel, London, 194, 369, 370, 449; WSB's psychic experiments and, 375; WSB's rooms in, 369–70, 373, 397–98, 402, 408; WSB writing at, 375
Empson, William, 463–64
Energy and How to Get It (film), 600
"Engram Theory, The" (Burroughs), 466
Ennis, Vail, 165–66
Entretiens avec William Burroughs (Odier), 481
Esquire magazine, 473, 475, 478, 487
Eubispasme, 358
Evans, Chris, 480
Evans, Dennis, 29, 371–73, 390–91, 593
Evans, Mary (nanny "Nursy"), 11, 23, 24–25
Evans-Wentz, W. Y., 52
Evergreen Review, 347, 450, 481
Ewert, Mark, 601–3, 619
Exquisite Corpse, The (Chester), 420
Exterminator! (Burroughs), 88, 325, 427, 483, 545
Exterminator, The (Burroughs), 365–66; epigram on title page, 53, 365; Gysin's calligraphic drawings in, 366; "Rub Out the Words" section, 365–66
Eyres-Monsell, Graham, 56, 58, 61, 62

Fanchette, Jean, 364–65
Farren, Mick, 485
Farson, Don, 410, 411, 423
Fawcett, William Russell, 46
Federn, Paul, 76, 114–15

Index

Index

Index

Index

Index

"My Lost Youth" (Longfellow), 32
My Own Mag, 424, 425, 427, 435

Nabokov, Vladimir, 118, 404
Naked Lunch (The Naked Lunch) (Burroughs),
  20, 82, 85, 198, 228, 294, 407, 541, 631;
  "A.J.," 352–53; Ansen's review of, 354–55;
  arresting detectives used as characters, 140;
  author photo on flap, 243, 352; Beckett's
  comment, 412; Bernabé Jurado in, 186;
  "Black Meat" section, 255–56, 281; "blue
  movies," 312; Bradley the Buyer, 246;
  characters in, 352–53; *Chicago Review*
  issue banned and, 349; "Country Clerk"
  section, 157, 323; cut-ups and, 363; Dr.
  Benway, 251, 279, 281, 352–53, 372, 559;
  Dr. Benway's Reconditioning, 311, 312;
  drugs ingested during writing, 552; dust
  jacket, 352, 570; erotic scenes in, 256;
  "Examination," 311; extract published
  (1958), 328; "Fats Terminal" section, 343;
  fiftieth anniversary, 635; film of, Balch
  and, 488–89, 490; film of, Cronenberg and,
  580, 583–84, 609–10, 613; film rights, 406;
  first chapter sent to Ginsberg, 276; foreign
  rights and translations, 357; four sets of,
  311; Freeland, 310, 311, 312; Ginsberg help
  with, 316; Ginsberg photo of Burroughs
  acting out hanging scene, 304; Ginsberg's
  opinion of, 305–6; Girodias as publisher
  (Olympia Press), 348, 349, 351–52, 356–57;
  Grove Press edition, 357, 400–401; hanging
  scenes, 354; "Hassan's Rumpus Room,"
  280, 631; Hauser and O'Brien section,
  277; imagery of, 244; "Interzone" section,
  275; Joan as "Jane" in, 215; "Joselito,"
  311; Kells Elvins' war experiences in, 147;
  "Lief the Unlucky," 261, 275; literary
  influences, 352, 353; Mailer's praise of, 404;
  "Marv," 254, 275; Mugwumps in, 353, 613;
  musical proposed, 547, 583; *New Departures*
  magazine and, 370; obscenity laws and, 357,
  400–401, 444, 458–59; opiate addiction
  and, 633; "Ordinary Men and Women"
  section, 294; outtake, 262; Pantopon Rose,
  353; payment and royalties, 357; picaresque
  format, 352; political parodies in, 354;
  readings of, Paris, 326; "Rube" section,
  310; sex with boys in, 354; South American
  Sodom section, 312; "Talking Asshole"
  section, 276–77, 539; Tangier influence in,
  272; *Time* magazine review, 435; title of,
  352; "The Word" in, 300, 308; writing
  of, 251, 275, 310–12, 343; WSB's job as
  an exterminator, Chicago and, 89; WSB's
  letters to Ginsberg and, 305, 501; WSB
  writes book jacket parody, 268, 276
Name is Burroughs, The: Expanded Media art
  show, 634

Naropa Institute, Boulder, Colorado, 519, 523,
  525, 555, 579, 601, 616
Neurath, Tom, 445
Neuromancer (Gibson), 630
New Departures magazine, 370
Newman, Barnett, 440
New Orleans, 168; junk neighborhoods in,
  168; WSB arrested in, 174, 181, 185; WSB
  in, 167–76; WSB picking up boys, 168
New Science (Vico), 118
New Self Interpreting Bible (Lee), 12
New Worlds magazine, 403
New York City: in 1937, 67–68; Angler Bar,
  124; Ariston Hotel, 76; Au Bon Pinard
  restaurant, 97; Auction Block, 68; Balch
  filming WSB in, 429; Barrow's Bar, 98; blue
  movies, 495; Cedar Street Tavern, 242; Clint
  Moore's, Harlem, 56–57; crime and financial
  crisis (1974), 509; drug culture and, 550–53;
  in the early 1930s, 56; East End Theater,
  437; Eighth Avenue and Times Square,
  121, 124, 125; Everard Baths, 133; Fifth
  Avenue Hotel, 495; gay clubs, 56–57, 68;
  Ginsberg's apartment, E. 7th St., 241; Grand
  Ticino restaurant, 97; Greenwich Village,
  68, 95–98, 242; Harvard Club, 73; Henry
  Street, 122, 131;; Lee Chumley's bar, 97;
  MacDougal's restaurant, 97; Minetta Tavern,
  97–98, 101, 102, 108; narcotics crackdown
  in, 442; poetry-reading scene, 438; Romany
  Marie's restaurant, 97; San Remo Café,
  97, 98, 242, 243; Taft Hotel as Burroughs
  residence, 73; Town Hall Beat Generation
  reading (1994), 621; University Club, 13,
  67, 73; West End Bar, 100–101, 108, 112,
  121; White Horse Tavern, 242; Woolworth
  Building, 31; World War II and, 95, 97, 131;
  WSB at Chelsea Hotel, 433–34, 437, 449,
  478, 480; WSB decides to leave, 563; WSB
  first reading in, 437; WSB living in, 73–77;
  82–83, 95–144, , 241–47, 433–43, 505,
  509–59; WSB's Christmas, 1925, with Uncle
  Ivy, 31; WSB's circle of friends, 434, 438,
  440, 496, 516, 538, 546, 553–54, 555, 616;
  WSB's residences in, 96, 115–16, 120–21,
  438–39, 440, 509, 510, 516, 518, 523,
  525–26, 538, 563; WSB's seventieth birthday
  party, 580; WSB visits, 54–55, 56–57,
  478–79, 480, 484, 495–96, 602
New York Herald Tribune, 110
New York Psychoanalytic Institute, 75, 114
New York Public Library, Burroughs archives,
  422, 501
New York World-Telegram, 110
Nietzsche, 105, 116, 361
Nightwood (Barnes), 118
Nike, 621–22
Nikolai Gogol (Nabokov), 118
Nirvana (band), 620–21

Index

Norse, Harold, 267, 357–58, 468–69

Norton, Hoagy, 122

Notes on Witchcraft (Kittredge), 51

Nouvelle Revue Francaise, La, 356

Nova Convention (1978), 537–40, 571; filming of, 546

Nova Convention Revisited: William S. Burroughs and the Arts (1996), 623

Nova Express (Burroughs), 69, 377, 407, 421–23, 428–29, 559; characters, 87; "Chinese Laundry," 403; completion of, 428; cut-ups and, 427; Grove Press edition, 407, 428; Ian Sommerville and, 403; Kiki in, 282–83; Scientology in, 467; "This Horrible Case," 403; writing of, 416, 426–27

Nueva Fumigating Co., Chicago, 88–89

Nuttall, Jeff, 414, 424–25, 427, 435, 480, 572

October Gallery, London, 606, 627

Odier, Daniel, 481

O'Hara, Frank, 440

O'Hara, John, 117

Ohle, David, 565, 578, 595, 611–12, 614, 615, 618, 619, 626, 628

"Old Angel Midnight" (Kerouac), 350

Olson, Charles, 462, 463

Olympia Press, 326, 356, 385, 403, 405, 408, 421

Ono, Yoko, 490

On the Road (Kerouac), 119, 169, 171–73, 190, 220, 306, 323; WSB as "Old Bull Lee" in, 247; WSB described in, 172–73

Orlovsky, Peter, 298, 300, 315, 319, 322; *APO-33* and, 440; Ginsberg break-up, 395; visits WSB in Tangier, 302–8, 386, 392–95; WSB's dislike of, 306, 319, 394

Ortega, José "Joe," 153

Orwell, Sonia, 457

Our Lady of the Flowers (Genet), 243

Owens, Iris, 327, 328

Oxbow Incident, The (Clark), 118

Page, Jimmy, 517

Palm Beach, Florida: Burroughs family in, 225, 226, 262, 269, 461; WSB in, 225, 226, 240, 269, 460–61

Pan (publisher), 581

Panama, 198, 226–27

Parelli, Pat, 524

Pareto, Vilfredo, 118

Paris, France: Algerians in, 315–16, 327; the Beat Hotel (Mme. Rachou's hotel), 315, 316–18, 325, 331, 357, 359, 381–83, 406–9, 412; Brasserie Lipp, 331; Burroughs family trips to (1927, 1929), 37, 39; Café de Arts, 407; Chez Jean, 315; Chez Madame Ali, 327; ex-pats in, 315, 322, 327–28; folksingers in, 323–24; homosexuality in, 360; Latin Quarter, 316; Left Bank, 242, 326; Les

Nuages Café, 357; Libraire Anglaise and the Mistral bookshops, 325–26, 357, 364–65, 408; magic shop, La Table d'Emeraude, 342; restaurants and cafés frequented by WSB and the Beat Hotel crowd, 321–22, 323–24, 360, 382; rue Gît-le-Coeur, 316, 330; WSB and *Chappaqua*, 447–48; WSB arrival (Jan. 16, 1858), 315; Paris,; Paris cafés, restaurants, and bars frequented by, 321–22, 323–24, 360; Paris circle of friends, 323–24, 327–28, 616; WSB leaves 369, 383; WSB returns (Dec., 1960), 381; WSB's trip to, with Weisenberger (1934), 55; WSB's trip to with Kammerer (1933) and, 54

Paris Review, 436; WSB interview (1965), 622

Parker, Edie, 98–99, 100–101, 140, 580, 595; apartment on W. 118th street, 99, 103, 105, 107, 128; arrest as material witness in Kammerer murder, 111; on Burroughs, 113, 114; family's affluence, 98, 111; Joan Vollmer and, 99, 144; Kammerer's obsession with Lucien Carr and, 107–8; Kerouac and, 98–99, 103, 104, 105, 120, 128, 132; Kerouac breakup and return to Grosse Pointe, 128, 129; Kerouac marries, 111; murder of Kammerer and, 113; West End Bar and, 100–101; WSB and, 117

Parker and Lee Company, 12

Pasolini, Pier Paolo, 544

Pauline, Marc, 580

Paul Klein Gallery, 598–99

Payne Whitney Clinic, New York, 84; Burroughs committed (1940), 76–77; statement of Laura Lee Burroughs to psychiatrist, 11, 21–22; WSB in, 11

Peace Eye Bookstore, 438

Pelieu, Claude, 434, 448, 491, 523, 630

Pepys, Samuel, 271

Perse, Saint-John, 333

Persky, Lester, 440

"Personal Magnetism" (Burroughs), 37

Peru: Huanaco, 237–38, 244; pisco (alcoholic drink), 236–37; sexual tourism in, 236; WSB and coca leaves, 238; WSB and yagé, 237–38; WSB in Lima, 235–37; WSB in Pucallpa, 237–38

Peschio, Tom "TP," 585, 612, 615, 616, 625, 627, 634

Phantom of the Opera, The (film), 33

Pheltenstein, Milton, 140, 142

Phipps, Harry, 331

picaresque novels, 252–53

Picasso, Pablo, 595, 598

Picture of Dorian Gray, The (Wilde), 46

Place of Dead Roads, The (Burroughs), 90, 495, 556–57, 579; Arch Ellisor in, 158–59; Bernabé Jurado in, 186; Defiance, Missouri in, 29; ending, 591; gay sex in, 567; George Greaves in, 273; Gerald Hamilton in, 257;

Index

Index

St. Albans, Missouri, 28–29, 38
Starr, Ringo, 451
Starzl, Thomas E., 524, 525, 533
State University of New York at Buffalo, 513–14
Steele, David, 316
Steely Dan (band), 630
Steffens, Roger, 517
Stein, Chris, 538, 577, 602, 619, 621, 623, 631
Stein, Elliot, 495
Stella, Joseph, 97
Stern, Dini, 330, 331, 332, 333
Stern, Jacques, 330–33, 336, 347, 348, 386, 527, 528; as fantasist, 348; heroin addiction, 330, 332; WSB's psychic experiments and, 343–44
Stern, Richard, 55, 56, 57, 58
Steward, Donald Ogden, 487
Stipe, Michael, 620, 623, 631
St. Louis, Missouri, 9–10, 12, 27, 31, 34, 49; 1927 tornado, 37; air pollution in, 9–10, 31, 32; Burroughs family home, Berlin Avenue, 10; Burroughs family leaves, 226; Burroughs family mausoleum, Bellefontaine Cemetery, 15, 16, 17, 18, 628; Burroughs family moves to, from Auburn, New York, 14; Chase Plaza Hotel, 436; Edmund Burroughs sets up shop in (1880), 14; Forest Park, 9, 22, 23, 28, 31, 436; funeral of Mort Burroughs, 572; River des Peres, 28; T. S. Eliot on, 9; Vess soda company, 30–31; whorehouses in, 58; WSB returns (Dec., 1964), 435–36; WSB's early years in, 9–59; WSB's returning to, 78–82, 83, 111, 114, 132, 142–43, 147–48; in WSB's writing, 10; WSB visits (1982), 573
St. Louis Globe-Democrat, 28, 436
St. Louis Post-Dispatch, 21, 32, 436; WSB's summer job at (1935), 57–58
"St. Louis Return" (Burroughs), 436
Stockhausen, Karlheinz, 440
Streiber, Whitley, 607–8
Strummer, Joe, 540
Subterraneans, The (Kerouac), 243
Sudlow, Robert, 575
Sullivan, Harry Stack, 85
Sullivan, Tom "the Kid," 550
Summers, Romney, 62, 66
Survival Research Lab (SRL), 580
Sweden, 310
Swift, Mary, 521

Taaffe, Philip, 595–96
Taft Hotel, New York City, 73
Takemura, Mitsuhiro, 606
Talk Talk magazine, 566
Tangier, 251–52, 257–58, 278, 295, 337–38; 1001 Nights restaurant, 278; American colony in, 253; American School, 416; Arab cafés, 271; Armor Hotel, 392, 395; Balch filming WSB in, 429, 438; Bar la Mar Chica, 256, 259, 441; Benchimol Hospital,

280–81; Café Central, 256, 258, 273, 295; Café de Paris, 258, 289, 391; Dancing Boy Café, 417; Dean's Bar, 253, 259, 261, 264, 307, 583; drugs in, 253; ex-pats in, 256–57, 261, 271, 272–73, 279, 296; homosexual community, 272; Kasbah, 271; male prostitutes in, 292–93; Moroccan attitudes toward homosexuality, 293; Moroccan independence movement, 294–96; New Town, 282; Normandie café, 289; Paname restaurant, 302; Parade Bar, 253, 256, 257, 259, 279, 415, 416, 428, 446–47, 474, 583; Passapoga (gay bar), 272; Pepys in, 271; police aware of WSB as drug addict, 260, 299; political situation, 1955, 281–82; popular fiction and Hollywood films and image of, 252; sex business in, 254; sexual tourism in, 293; Socco Chico, 258, 271–72, 294–96; Timothy Leary in, 395–97; WSB and bars frequented, 253, 256, 264; WSB books passage to, 248; WSB harassed by locals in, 417, 420, 425, 427; WSB in the Medina, 251; WSB leaves, 309, 312, 315, 430; WSB living on rue Delacroix, 425–28; WSB picking up boys, 252, 253–54; WSB returning to, 383, 386–96, 583; WSB returns with Sommerville (1963), 414–29; WSB's circle of friends, 419–20, 429, 616; WSB's final weeks in, 311; WSB's holidays in, 337–38, 345–46, 446–47, 453; WSB's house on the Marshan, 414–25; WSB's morphine addiction and, 251; WSB's room at Hotel Muniria, 282, 288–89, 311, 383, 386, 395–96, 428–29, 449; WSB's room at Tony Dutch's, 254, 260, 279; WSB's writing, importance to, 251; WSB visits, 455, 468, 474, 485; WSB visits with John Brady (1972), 498; WSB wanted by the police in, 345–46. See also Bowles, Paul, Gysin, Brion
Tangier Diaries (Pepys), 271
Taylor, Edgar Curtis "Joe," 48
Taylor, James, 489
Taylor School, St. Louis, 48
Terry, Eugene "Gene," 151, 153–54; car named "Death," 151, 154
Tesorero, David, 187, 188–89, 219, 221, 222
Texas: cotton farming, 148, 150; Joan Burroughs arrives in, 155; justice in, 165–66; migrant labor used in, 178–79; Pharr, 149, 151, 154, 155, 165, 177, 178–79; the Valley, 148–50, 152, 177; WSB in East Texas, 156–63; WSB's farming in, 149–54, 164–66; WSB's land in Edinburg, 148, 149, 177; WSB's land outside Huntsville, 156; WSB's return (1949), 177–81; in WSB's writing, 152
"Thanksgiving Prayer, A" (Burroughs), 174
Thanksgiving Prayer, A (film), 601
"Finger, The" (Burroughs), 76
"Painter in Modern Life, The" (Baudelaire), 72

Index

Index